SEA SPLASHERS: Fins, Flippers, and Tails * 89

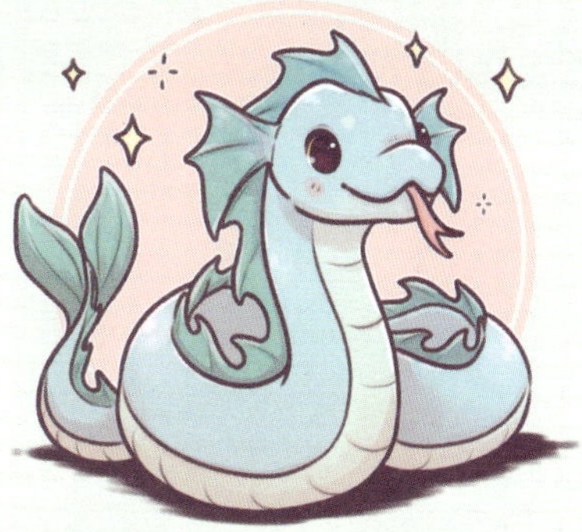

NIGHT DWELLERS: Horns, Fangs, and Claws * 115

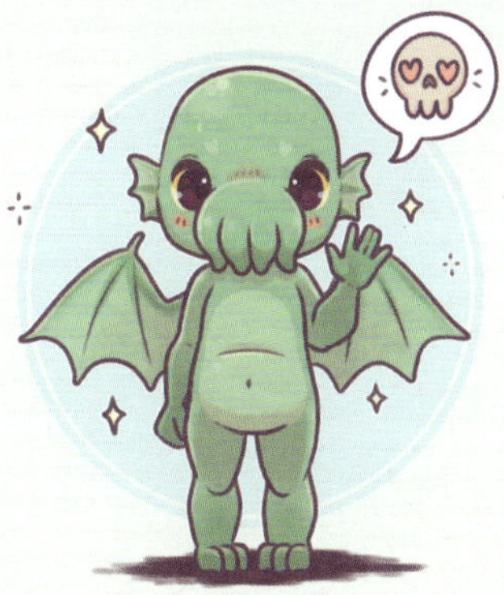

BONUS: Mythical Combos * 143

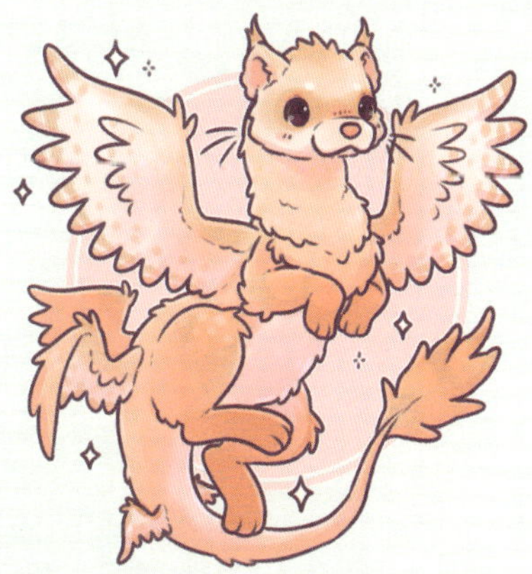

HIYA!

My name is Naomi, but you might have seen me around online as @naomi_lord or @naomilordart. I'm a self-taught artist from the United Kingdom and I have always loved to draw. Around 2017, I began to take my art more seriously and started to draw mostly chibi (Japanese for "small but in a cute way") versions of characters, animals, and creatures. Since then, I've continued to develop my work and explore my own style, which I define as anime-mixed-with-chibi.

Over the years I have posted a lot of my art online and have gained a following of lovely supporters. They have been huge motivators for me to keep drawing and developing my work. Hopefully this book will do the same for any aspiring artists out there. If you want to learn how to draw some adorable versions of fantasy creatures, you've come to the right place!

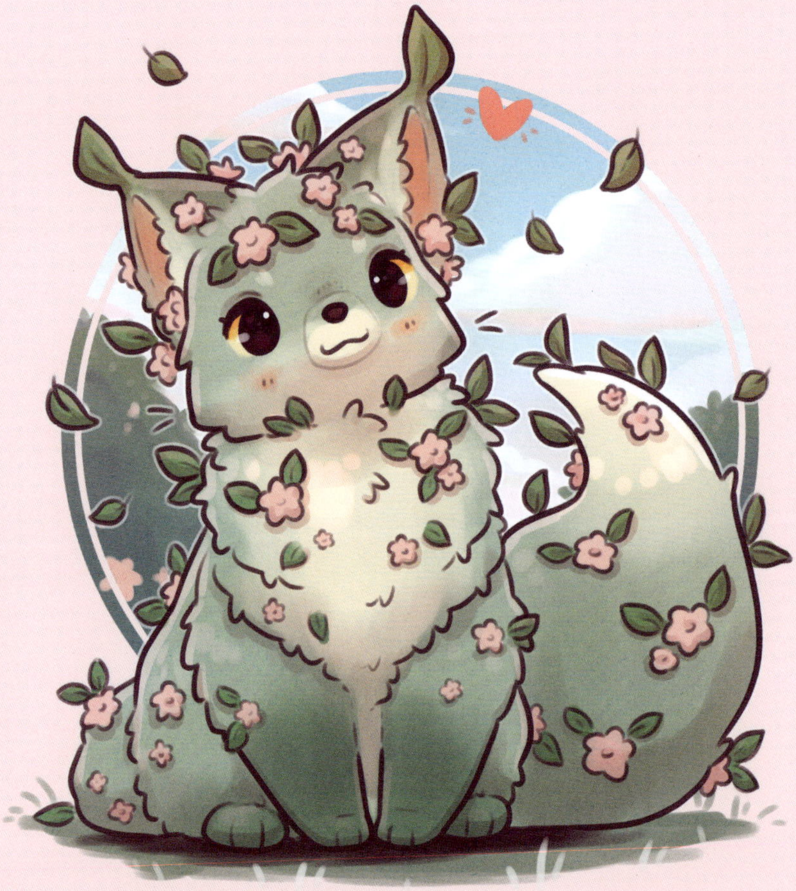

WHAT IS ANIME?

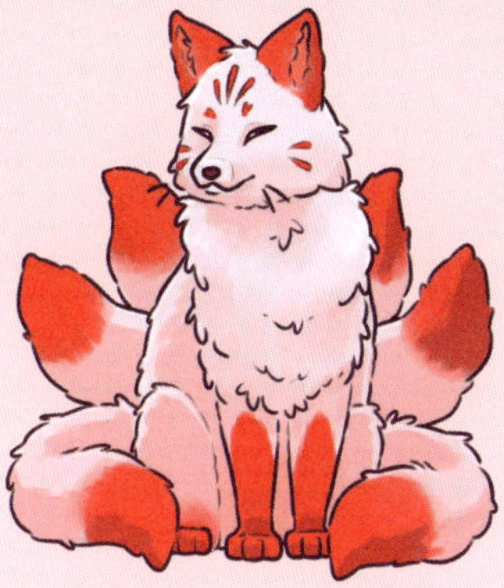

Anime is the Japanese word for "animation," but over the years it has come to refer to a specific style of art. Anime characters are known for their expressive faces and exaggerated features, with many subgenres to dive into. One, for example, you will notice in this book, as most of the creatures are also drawn in the chibi style.

Again, chibi means "small and cute" in Japanese, which is why characters drawn in this style are smaller, rounder versions of the real thing. They also have oversized heads (Hello Kitty is a popular example). However, there is no particular set of rules or limitations, so everyone should feel free to try it out for themselves. As long as your character is cute, use those creative instincts to make it your own! For me, I usually stick with big eyes, pastel colors, and lots of sparkles.

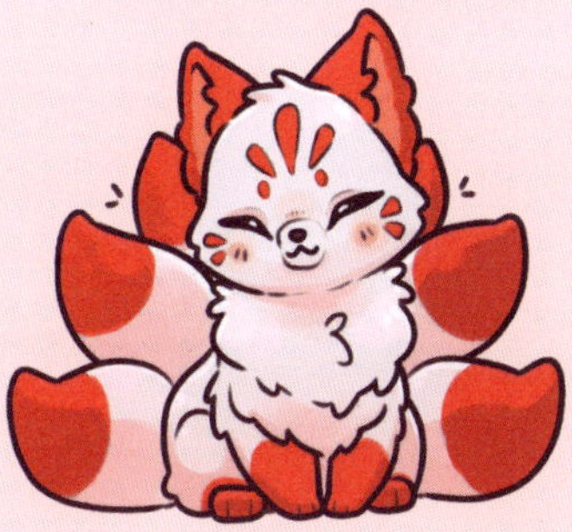

HOW TO USE THIS BOOK

First, I will share helpful information and advice to get you going, including recommended tools and techniques for drawing and coloring. Then a Creature Key will introduce you to the beasties that you will learn how to draw in this art class.

With fifty-seven step-by-step tutorials, this book is divided into five chapters: Land Walkers: Hooves, Toes, and Paws; Air Gliders: Feathers, Wings, and Scales; Sea Splashers: Fins, Flippers, and Tails; Night Dwellers: Horns, Fangs, and Claws; and a Bonus: Mythical Combos section. Each chapter has lessons that go from easy to more complex. The tutorials come with fun facts and are beginner-friendly, with room for a challenge for those who desire it.

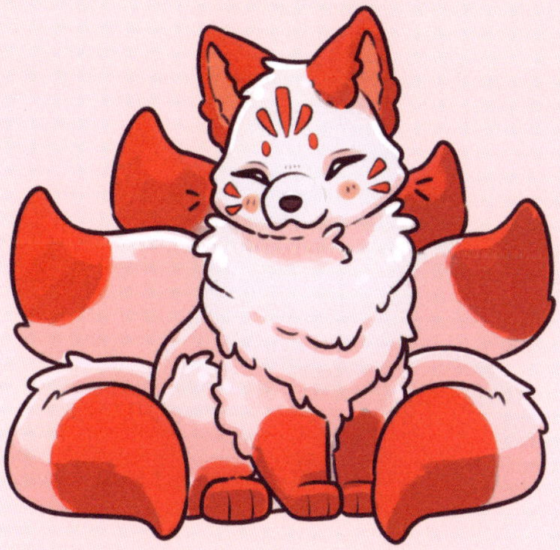

TOOLS

To create these lessons, I used a digital tablet and the Clip Studio Paint program for Windows PC, but you can use any medium you like or whatever you have on hand! For those who are interested in learning about what I use, here are a few suggestions.

Traditional

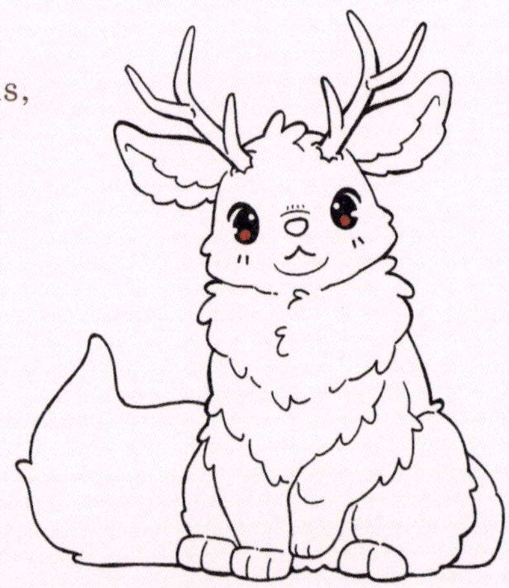

Traditional mediums are basically anything like pencils, pens, and paints. If you are using traditional tools, I recommend starting with a pencil and scrap paper and sketching each drawing very lightly. Once you are comfortable, start the final illustration. You can purchase a light box, too, which allows you to trace your sketch onto a fresh sheet of paper. Make the new sketch and use a black ink pen to define the line art. When the ink is completely dry, gently erase the sketch underneath for a clean look.

Digital

Digital art means working on tablets that connect to a desktop computer or laptop, or standalones, such as an iPad. Digital gives you a lot more flexibility and control thanks to the Undo tool that's at your disposal. You should also take advantage of the Layering tool found in most software, which keeps the sketch, line art, and coloring layers separated. In the tutorials, you'll see I use the Layering tool to spotlight each new line made to the drawing. Just make sure your layers are always separated—there's nothing worse than spending hours working only to realize your line art is on the sketch layer (ugh!).

When it comes to software, there is Adobe Photoshop and PaintTool SAI. For iPads, I recommend Procreate or Clip Studio Paint. If available, turn on the pen-pressure setting. You can vary the line weight and make your line art look far more dynamic by adjusting the pen pressure. The example on the right shows the difference between no pen-pressure lines with the same thickness all over (left images) compared to lines that flow smoothly between soft and thin to heavy and thick (right images).

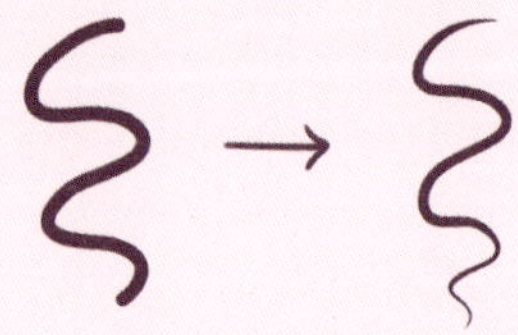

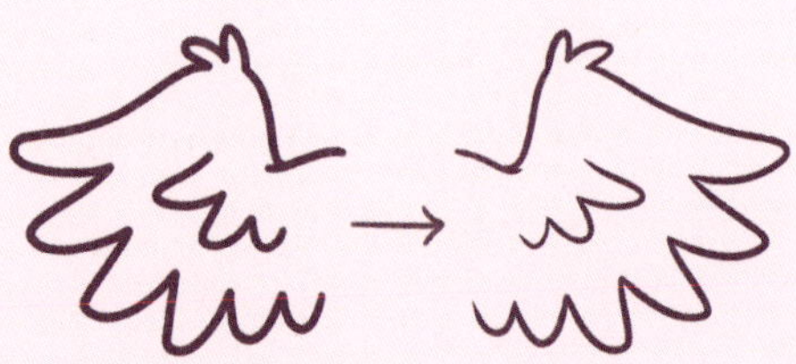

DRAWING YOUR FANTASY CREATURES

For those who want or need them, in this section you'll find tips and tricks for drawing your fantasy creatures.

Facial Features and Expressions

My tutorials all feature a specific face in the steps, but you can mix them up with those from other lessons, or create your own. A fun expression can bring a lot of life and feeling to an illustration. The main thing is to have fun and see what you can come up with.

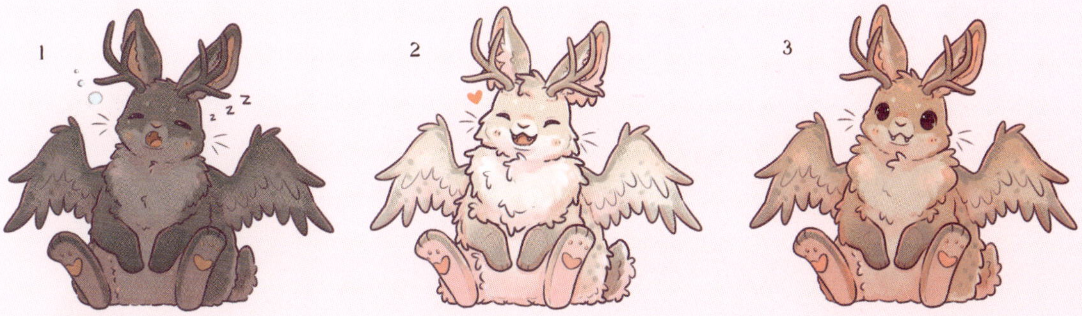

Fur Types

Many of the creatures in this book have fur, which gives you an excellent opportunity to practice adding texture. Looking at the images above, there is short fur (image 1), long fur (image 2), and all those in between (image 3). For longer fur, add extra m- and w-shaped marks for more texture, and use fewer and smaller marks for short fur. For fluffy creatures, draw the fur marks slightly farther away from the body so they take up more space.

Hair and Accessories

Some fantasy creatures are more human-like than others, especially when it comes to hair and accessories. Feel free to customize these any way you like. Just be sure you do it at the sketch stage before you start using an ink liner on the final image.

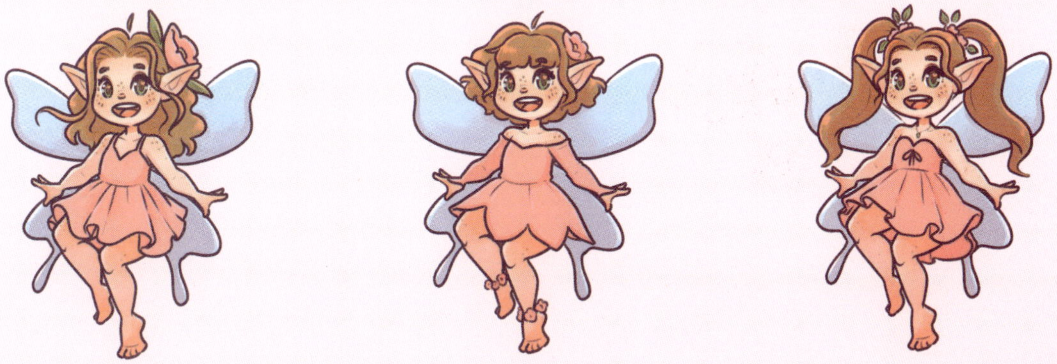

ADDING COLOR

The tutorials in this book focus more on drawing than coloring techniques. However, one of the easiest ways to enhance your drawings is by using color. As these are magical creatures, there are no right or wrong colors. You can stick with more "natural" colors for a realistic look, or use brighter, or even rainbow colors, for a magical look.

Traditional

Below you will find a quick step-by-step of coloring through traditional mediums.

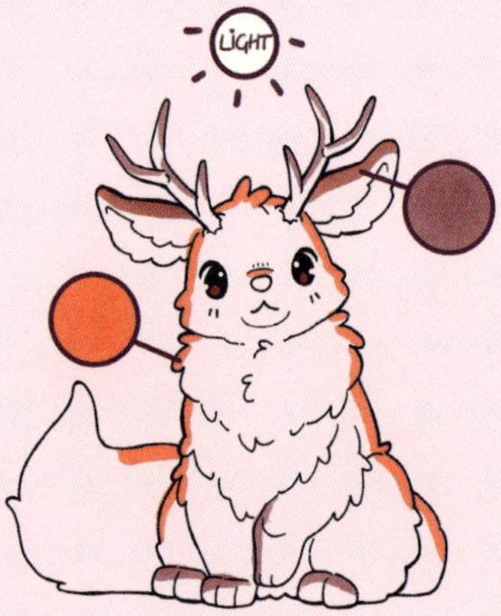

1. Start with the highlights; they're more forgiving if you make a mistake, and easier to blend out. Place highlights where the light hits the creature from above.

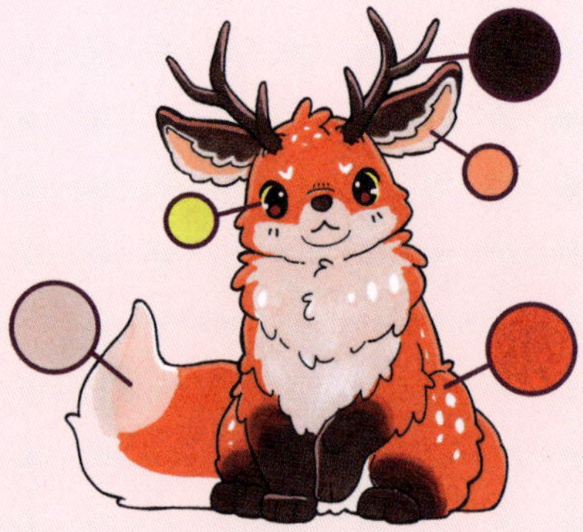

2. Fill in the main colors, leaving space for shadows. Blend lightly into the highlights for a smooth transition. Be really careful not to color over any white patches, as in the example!

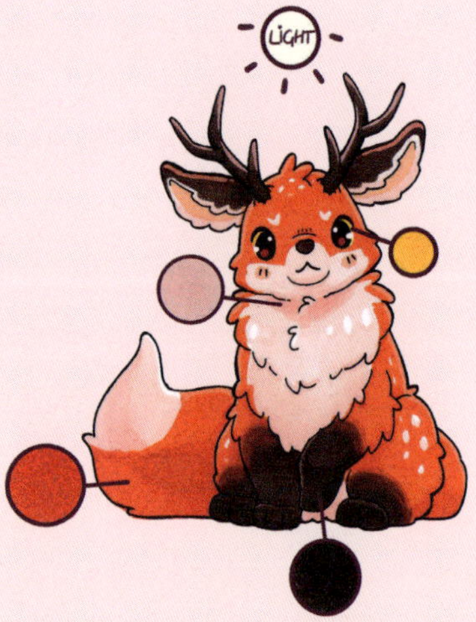

3. Add the shadows, blending them into the main colors. The shadows should be located opposite to the position of the light, usually along the bottom of the creature.

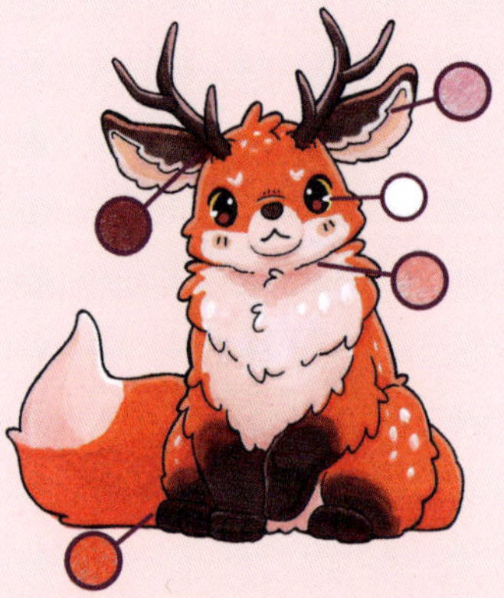

4. Add the final touches. Use white for adding highlights to the eyes. If you're using something like alcohol markers or watercolors, use colored pencils in parts to add a subtle dimension.

CUTE CREATURE ART CLASS
ENCHANTING ANIME BEASTIES

Learn to Draw OVER 50 MAGICAL MONSTERS

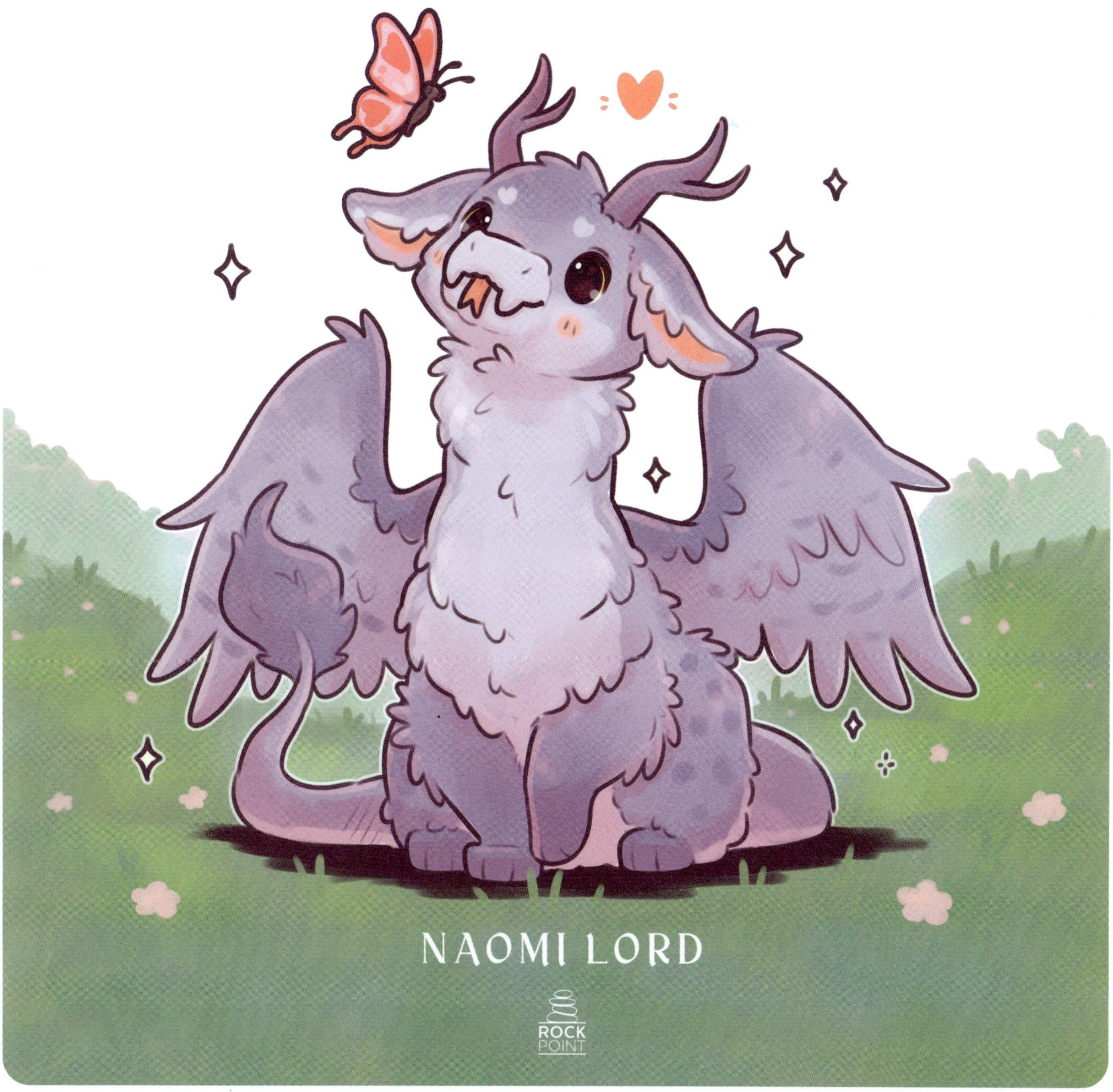

NAOMI LORD

ROCK POINT

CONTENTS

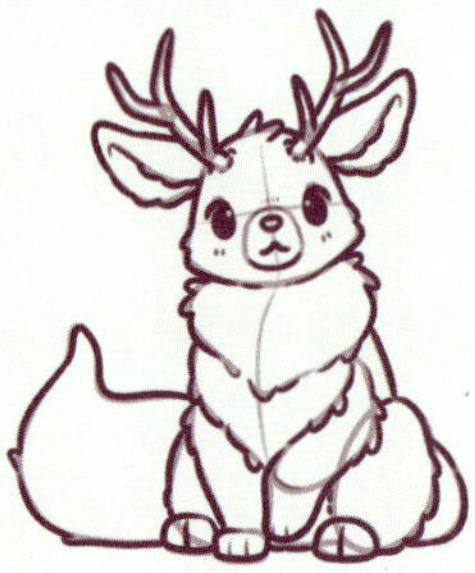

INTRODUCTION * 4

LAND WALKERS: Hooves, Toes, and Paws * 13

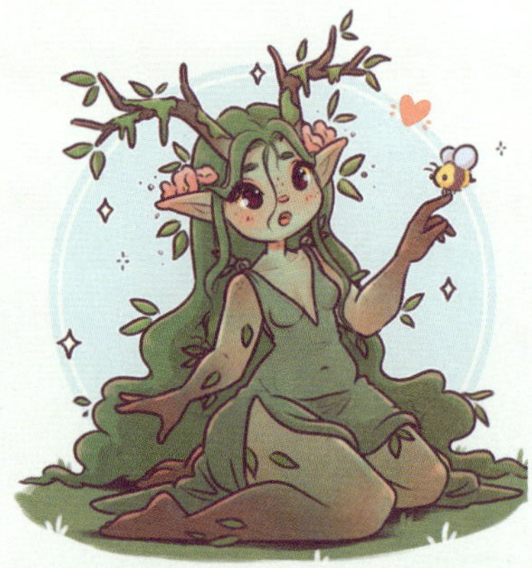

AIR GLIDERS: Feathers, Wings, and Scales * 47

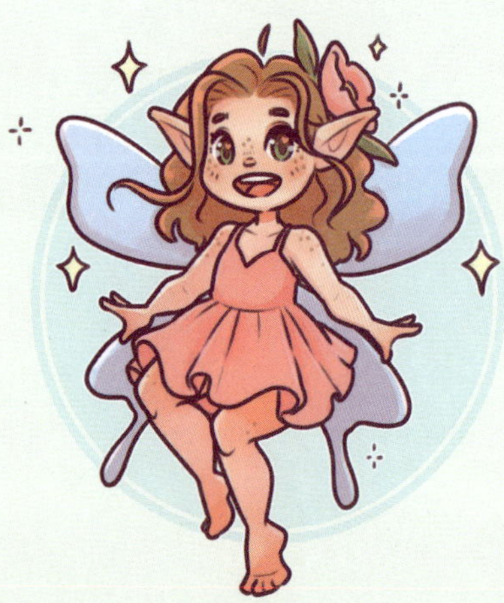

Digital

If you want to go digital, here's a step-by-step of how I color my digital illustrations.

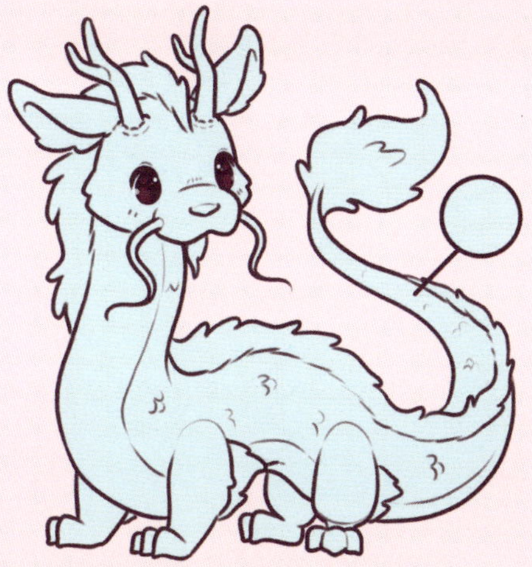

1. After you complete your line art, add a new layer underneath with the base color (the color that features most prominently on your creature).

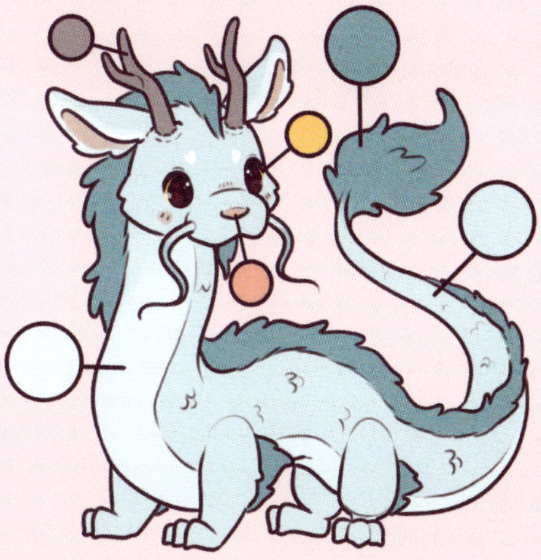

2. On top of the base color, add colors to the other features on a new layer to complete the flat colors (all the colors on the drawing before any shading is added).

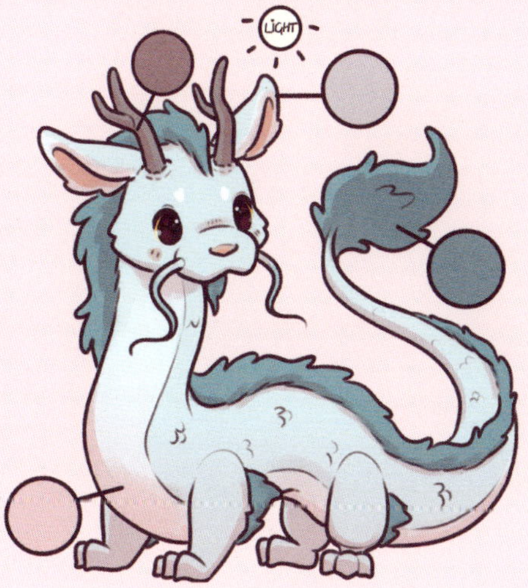

3. Add another layer on top for shadows. Shade the lower areas, such as below the head, the back, and so on. In most software you can add more shadows using the multiply layer setting at a lower opacity.

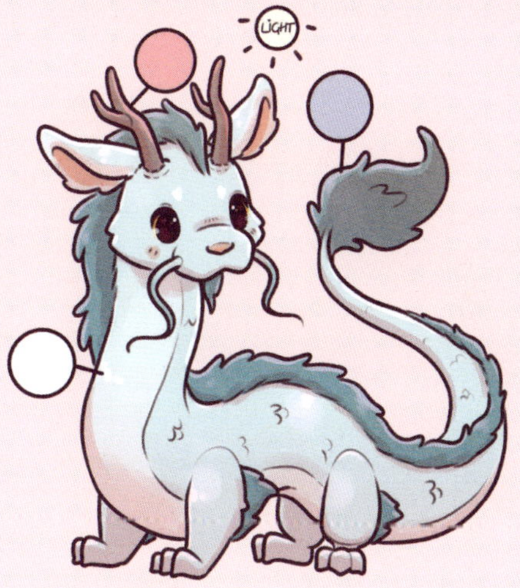

4. Add one more layer on top for highlights. The light comes from above, so your highlights should be on the top parts of your creature.

CREATURE KEY

Land Walkers: Hooves, Toes, and Paws

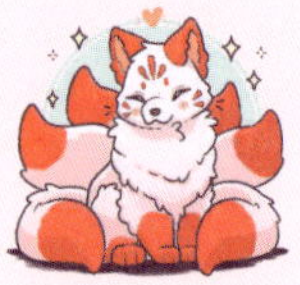

KITSUNE
Japanese folklore features these magical foxes known for having multiple tails.

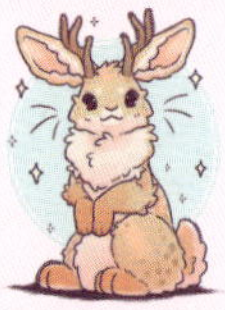

JACKALOPE
In North American folklore this is a jackrabbit with either antelope horns or deer antlers.

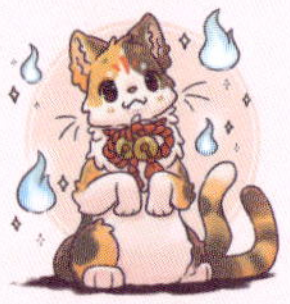

NEKOMATA
In Japanese folklore, spot this cat by its many magical traits, including a forked tail.

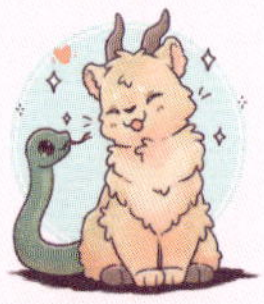

CHIMERA
An incredible fire-breathing tribrid from ancient Greek mythology.

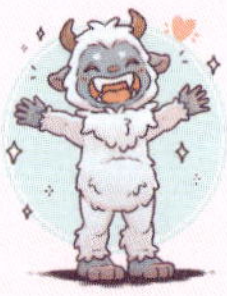

YETI
A giant, white, fluffy, and sharp-toothed beastie.

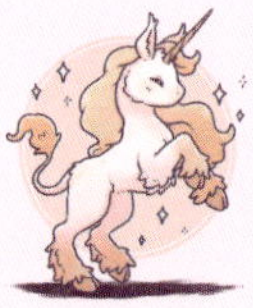

UNICORN
From European mythology comes this magically horned equine creature.

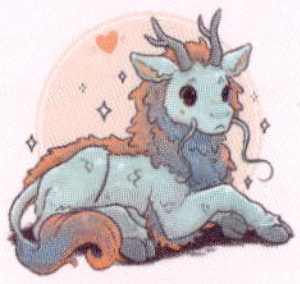

KIRIN
The kirin, or qilin, appears in many East Asian mythologies, such as Japanese and Chinese.

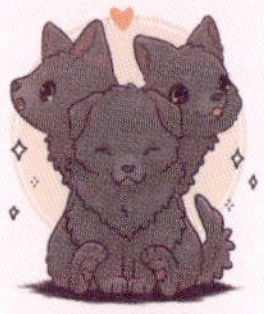

CERBERUS
In ancient Greek mythology, Cerberus is a massive three-headed dog.

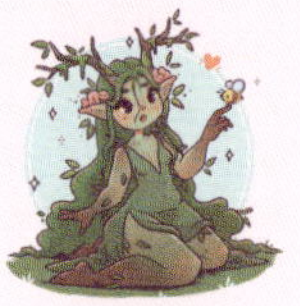

DRYAD
From Greek mythology, find this quiet nature spirit in the trees.

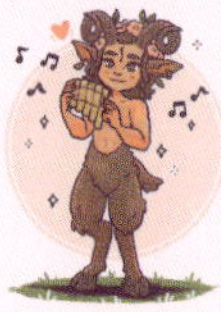

FAUN
In Roman mythology this nature spirit plays a mean panpipe.

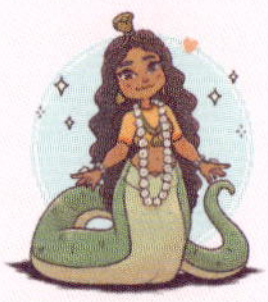

NAGA
Many South Asian cultures feature this magical serpent.

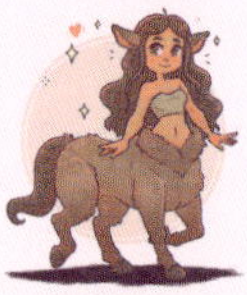

CENTAUR
Frolicking in the forest, this creature is part-human, part-horse.

Air Gliders: Feathers, Wings, and Scales

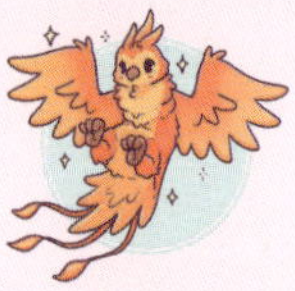

PHOENIX
Associated with the sun is this great firebird from ancient Egypt.

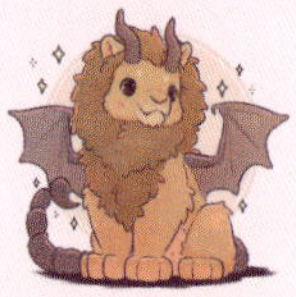

MANTICORE
From Persian mythology comes this part-lion, part-scorpion beastie.

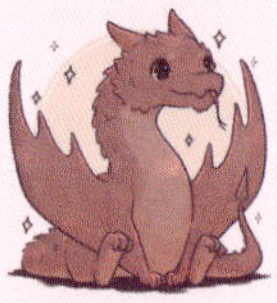

WYVERN
From Medieval European folklore comes this variant of a dragon.

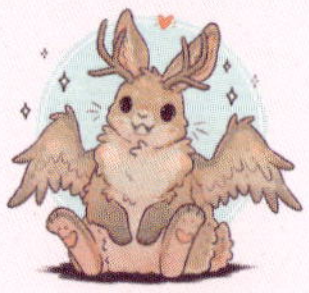

WOLPERTINGER
Originating from German folklore is this untamable hare.

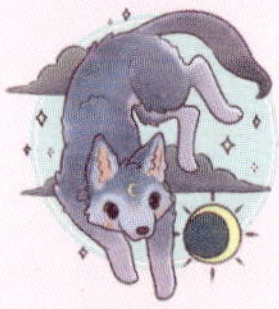

HATI (MOON WOLF)
Find this magical wolf chasing the moon across the sky.

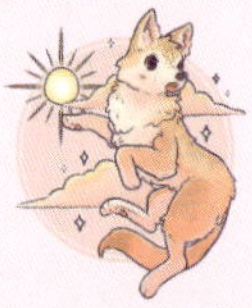

SKÖLL (SUN WOLF)
Find this magical wolf chasing the sun across the sky.

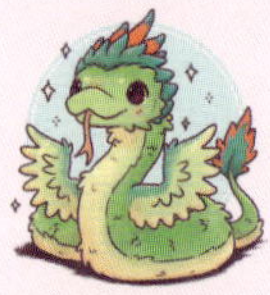

QUETZALCOATL
A powerful, flying, feathered serpent from Aztec mythology.

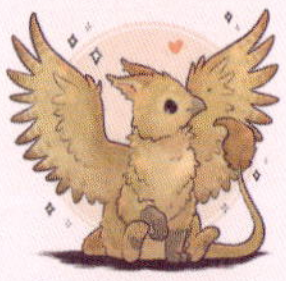

GRIFFIN
A half-eagle, half-lion creature renowned for its durability.

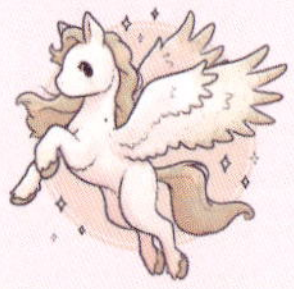

PEGASUS
An immortal winged horse from Greek mythology.

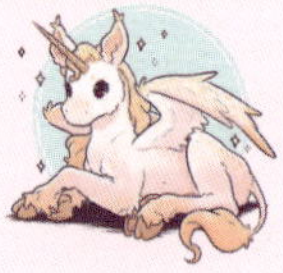

ALICORN
Informally known as pegacorn, pop culture created this winged unicorn.

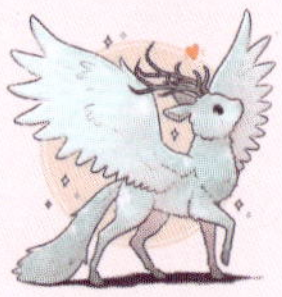

PERYTON
Originating from Europe is this winged deer.

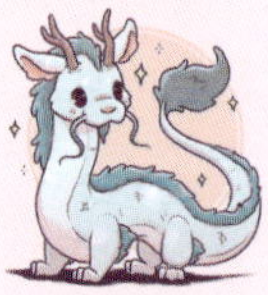

EASTERN DRAGON
A good and noble East Asian dragon that flies without wings.

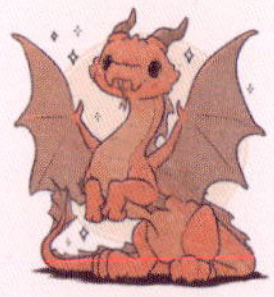

WESTERN DRAGON
This classic European dragon breathes scorching fire.

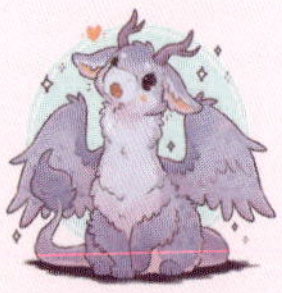

FLUFFY DRAGON
A cuddly original dragon—by me!

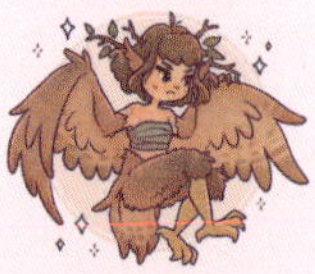

HARPY
From Greek and Roman mythology comes this half-woman, half-bird.

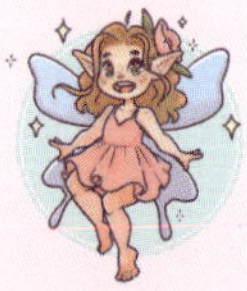

FAIRY
Watch out for this deceptively innocent-looking winged creature.

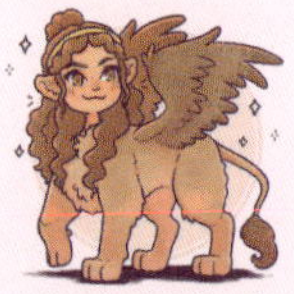

SPHINX
From Persian, Egyptian, and Greek mythology comes this deadly intelligent creature.

Sea Splashers: Fins, Flippers, and Tails

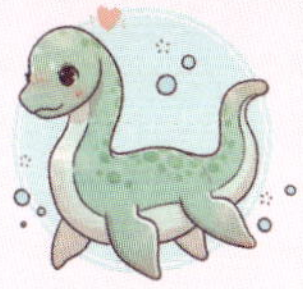

LOCH NESS MONSTER
Scottish folklore features this mysterious beastie that's elusive to the human eye.

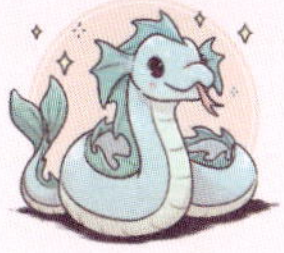

SEA SERPENT
A huge snake that appears in Norse and Greek mythologies.

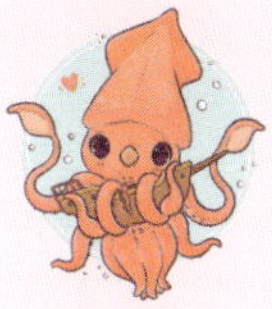

KRAKEN
From Norse mythology comes this sinister sea monster.

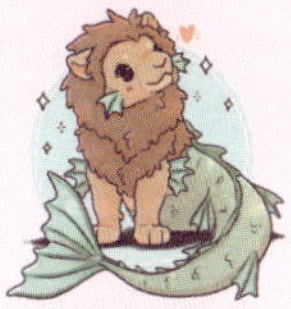

SEA LION
Find this half-lion, half-fish in many cultures' histories.

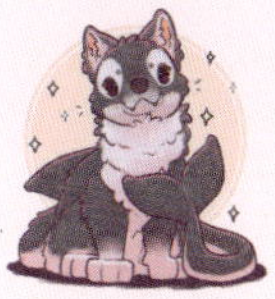

AKHLUT
In Inuit folklore, this magical creature is half-orca, half-wolf.

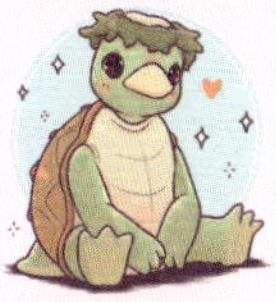

KAPPA
From Japanese folklore comes this green turtle-like creature.

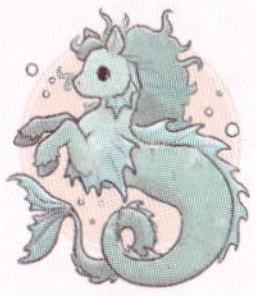

HIPPOCAMPUS
A widely known, hardworking, half-horse, half-fish beastie.

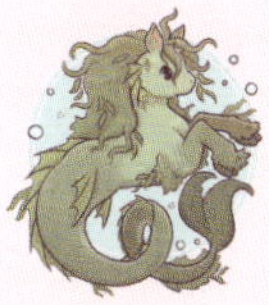

KELPIE
From Scottish mythology comes this enchanting creature of rivers and lakes.

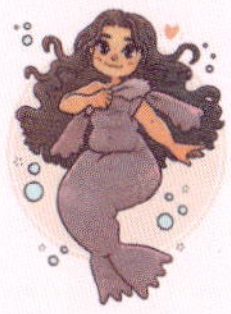

SELKIE
From Scottish folklore comes this shape-shifting sea creature.

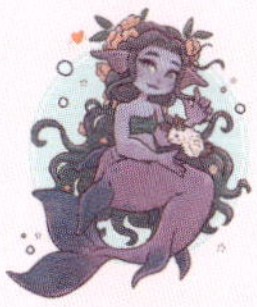

MERMAID
A whimsical half-human sea creature from an underwater kingdom.

Night Dwellers: Horns, Fangs, and Claws

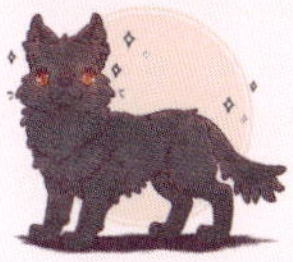

BLACK SHUCK
A great black dog from English folklore.

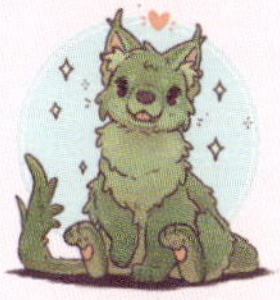

CÙ SÌTH
From Scottish folklore comes this haunting, green, fairy dog.

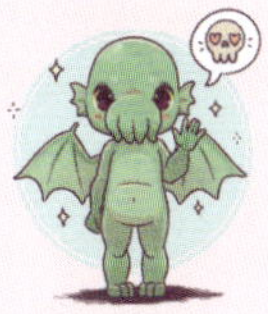

CTHULHU
From Gothic fiction comes this part-octopus, part-dragon beastie.

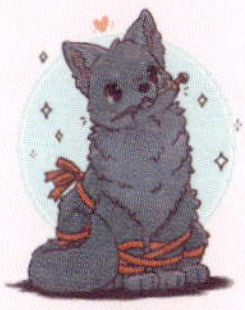

FENRIR
From Norse mythology comes this huge, shackled wolf.

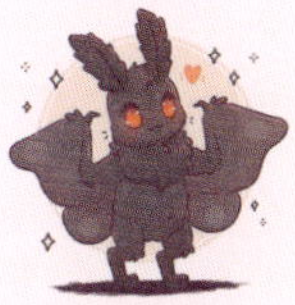

MOTHMAN
A flying humanoid from North American folklore.

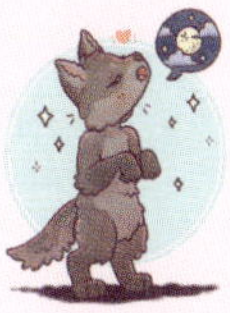

WEREWOLF
A cursed human controlled by the phases of the moon.

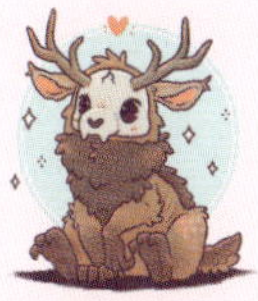

WENDIGO
An evil spirit that possesses humans.

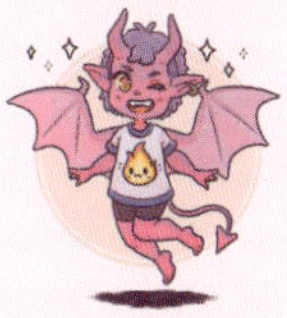

DEMON
A widely known malevolent harbinger of chaos.

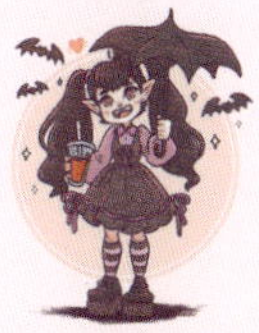

VAMPIRE
An undead beastie from European folklore.

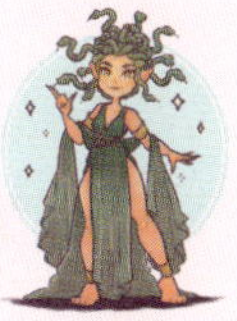

MEDUSA
A gorgon with snakes for hair from ancient Greek mythology.

Bonus: Mythical Combos

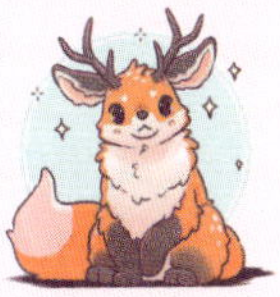

DEER + FOX
A sneaky deer.

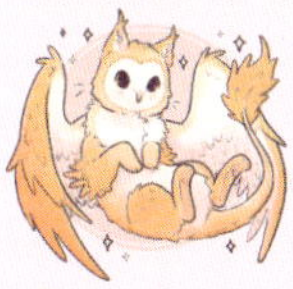

CAT + BARN OWL
A cozy flying cat.

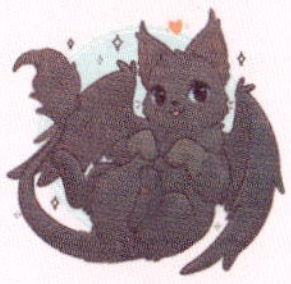

RAVEN + CAT
A flying black cat!

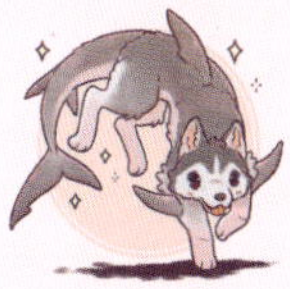

SHARK + DOG
A great white husky.

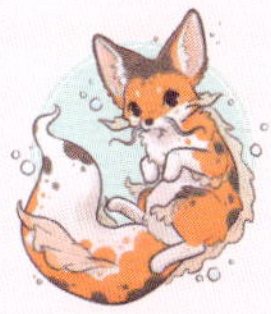

FOX + KOI
A swimming fennec fox.

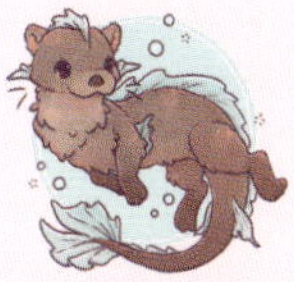

OTTER + FISH
A cute but slimy otter.

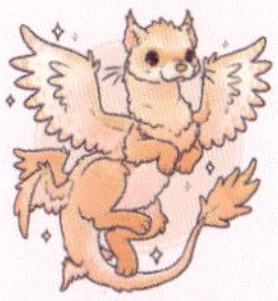

FERRET + EAGLE
A beloved winged ferret.

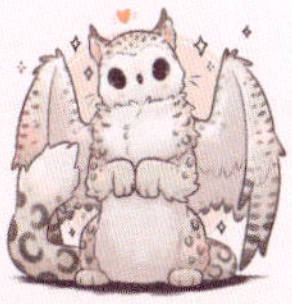

SNOWY OWL + SNOW LEOPARD
Snowy owl meets snow leopard.

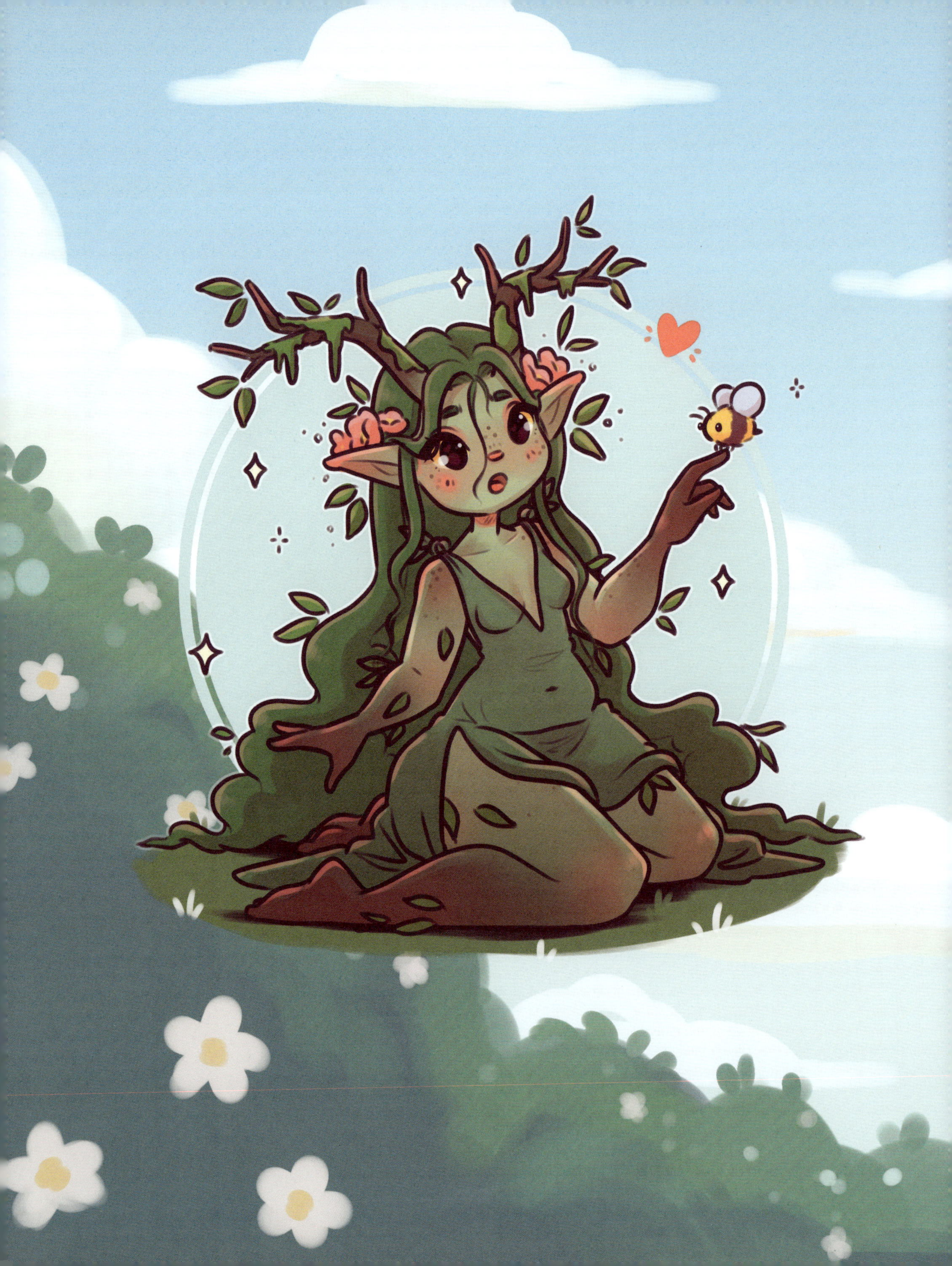

LAND WALKERS

HOOVES, TOES, AND PAWS

KITSUNE

Look toward a kitsune's tail to know their power. The older they are, the more tails they have, and the more intelligent they become, but will they use their powers for good or for mischief?

1. Lightly sketch an oval with pointed sides. Add a plus sign (+) guideline for the face.

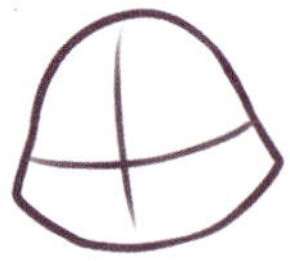

2. On top, add two rounded triangles for ears, with two smaller triangles inside.

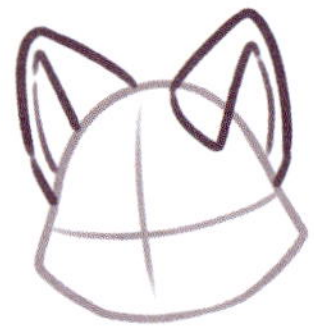

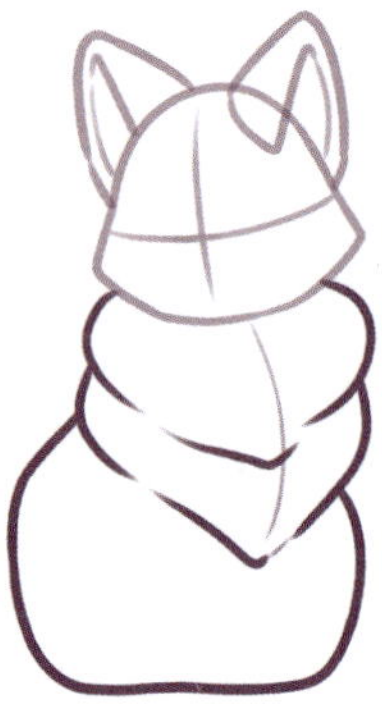

3. Add two curved V shapes for the neck with a curved square for the haunches underneath.

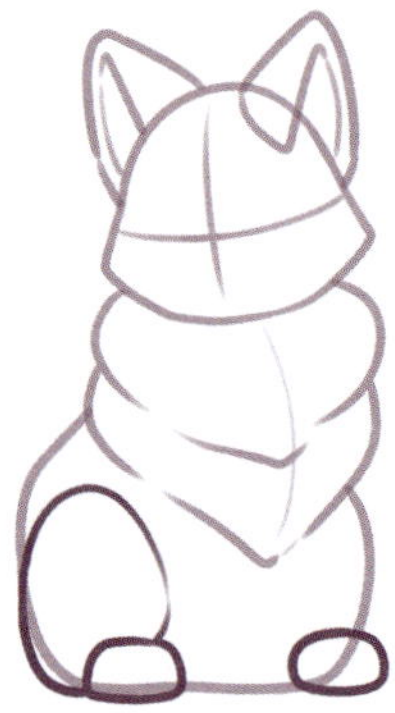

4. Add an oval back leg on the left haunch, and two small ovals for paws at the bottom of the body.

5. Under the neck, draw two front legs with a line down the center to separate them. Add two small, rounded rectangle paws.

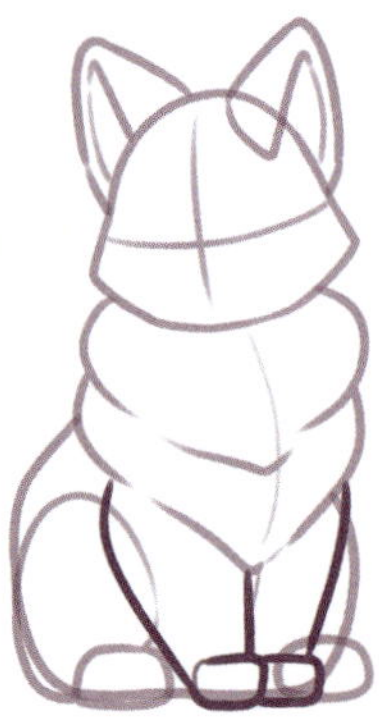

6. We only see six tails from this angle. Start by drawing the front two teardrop-shaped tails with a pointed end curling around the legs. Then draw two more tails above on both sides, getting smaller as you work up.

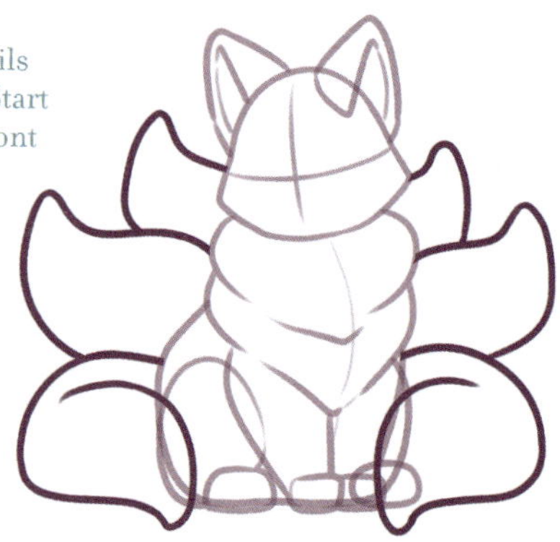

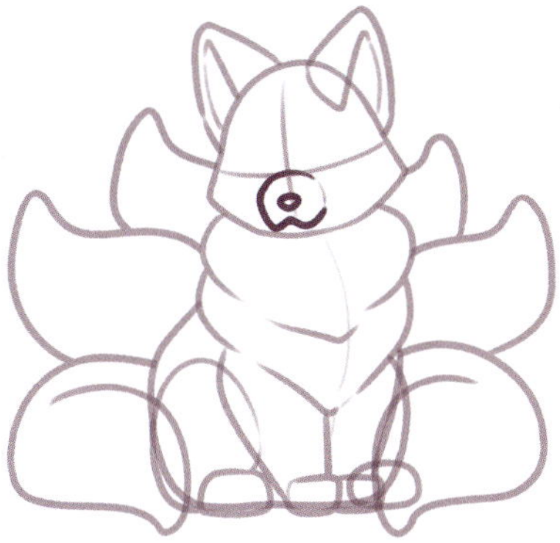

7. Draw a W-shaped mouth with a curve extending up the left side. Add a rounded triangle nose.

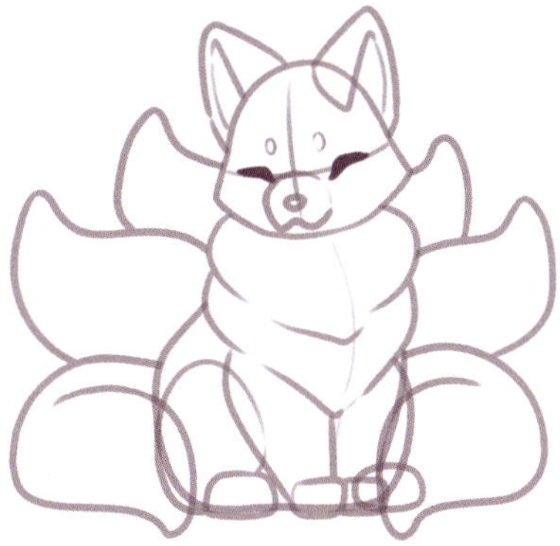

8. Draw two closed eyes with two small, oval eyebrows.

9. Lightly go over the basic sketch and add the details. Use soft W shapes for the fur. Add face markings with elongated triangles and dashes for whiskers and blush. Don't forget the toe lines.

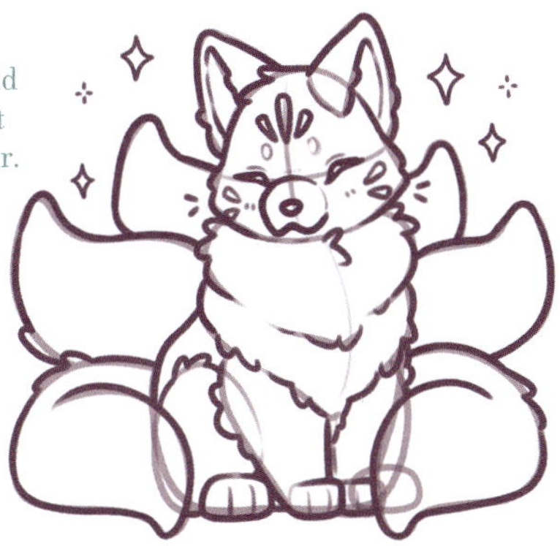

10. Neatly draw the line art over the sketch, leaving a little space inside the eyes for highlights. Add some sparkles, then erase the sketch underneath.

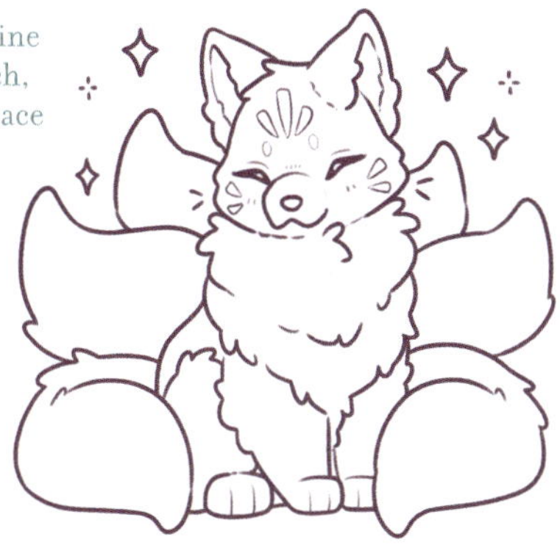

11. Finish with color! The traditional color scheme is a white body with red-tipped tails, legs, and face markings. Add a little bit of pink to the inner ears and on the cheeks for blush.

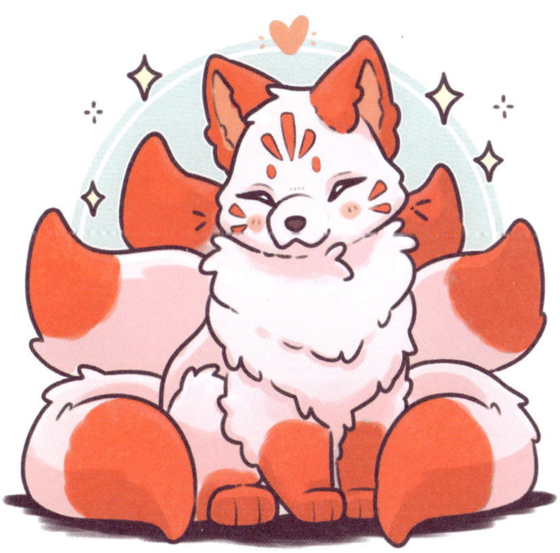

JACKALOPE

Ask any skilled hunter and they'll know this sneaky beastie. Jackalopes are devious, with the ability to mimic the human voice so well that only the best knows how to tell their cries apart.

1. Lightly sketch an oval with pointed sides. Add a plus sign guideline for the face.

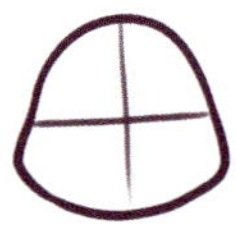

2. Add two long, pointed ears on top of the head, each with a curved line inside.

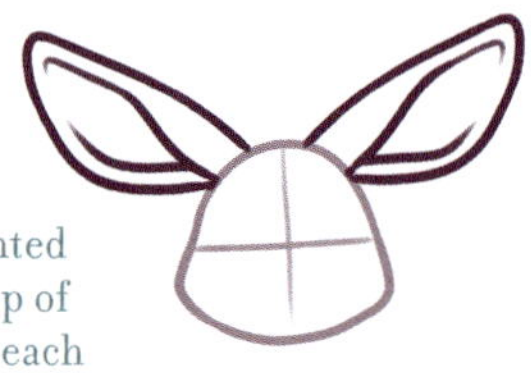

3. Add a round V-shaped neck with a smaller V underneath. Add a curved guideline down the center.

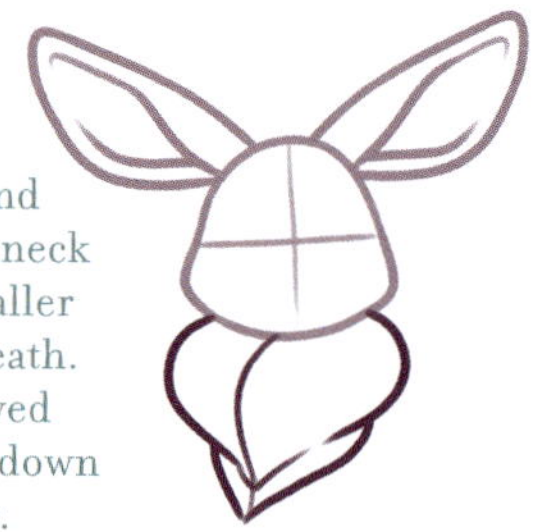

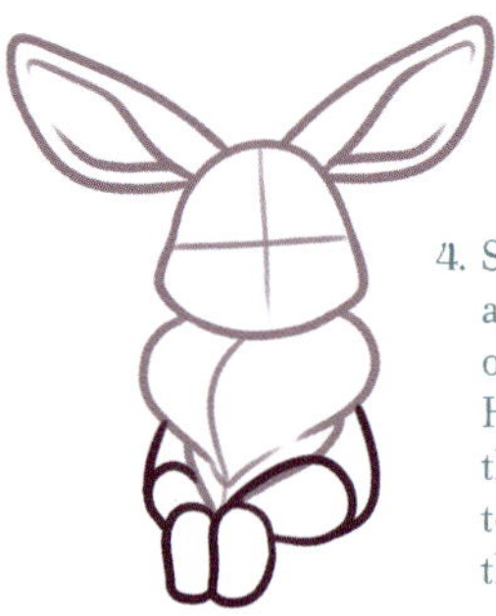

4. Sketch the arms with an oval forearm and an oval paw pointed down. Have the paws meet in the middle. Add curves to connect the arms to the body.

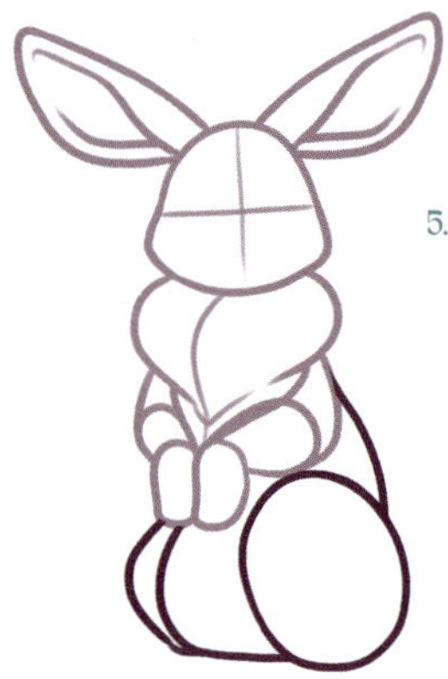

5. Add a large oval haunch beneath the right arm. Add two curved lines for the back and between the paws. Then add a smaller curved haunch below the left paw.

6. Add two flat-bottomed oval feet and a curved tail on the back of the right haunch.

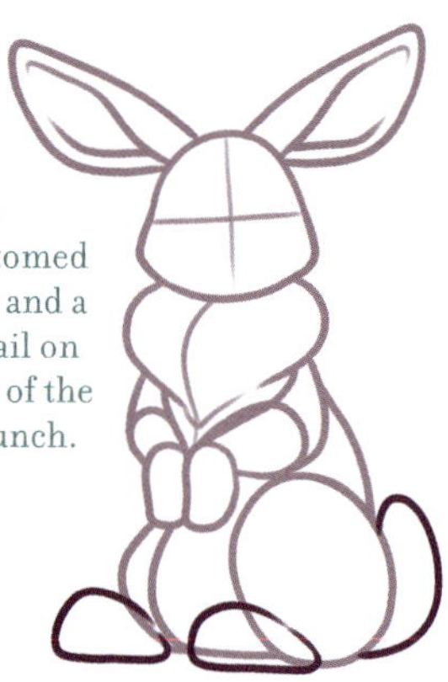

7. Draw two curved pointy antlers where the ears meet the head. Make them roughly symmetrical.

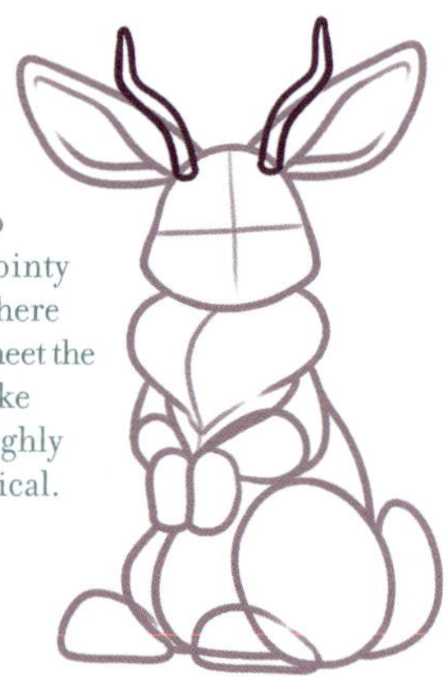

8. Add two small prongs coming out of each antler. Again, try to keep it symmetrical.

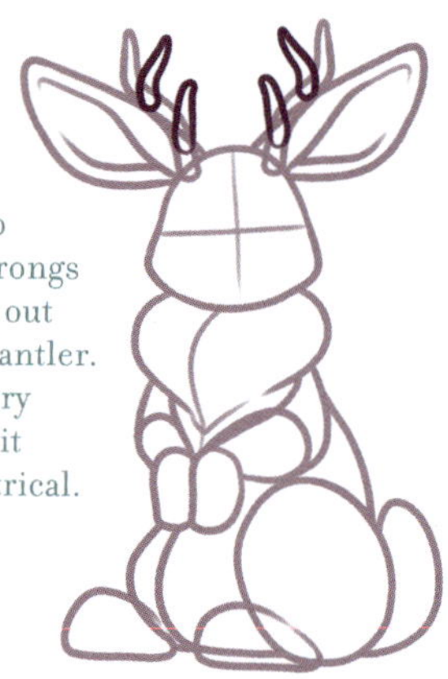

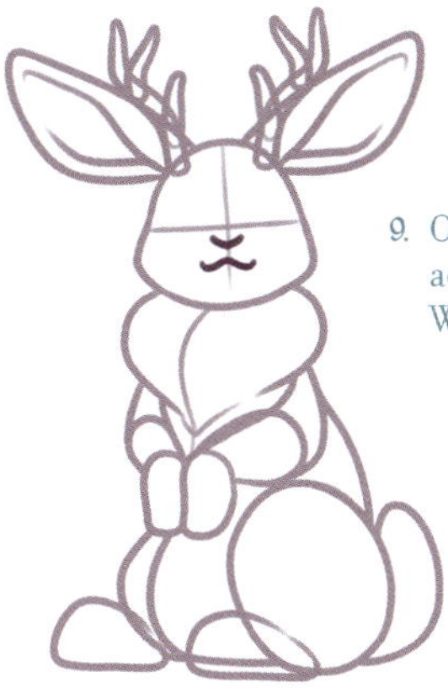

9. On the bottom of the face, add a V-shaped nose and a W-shaped mouth.

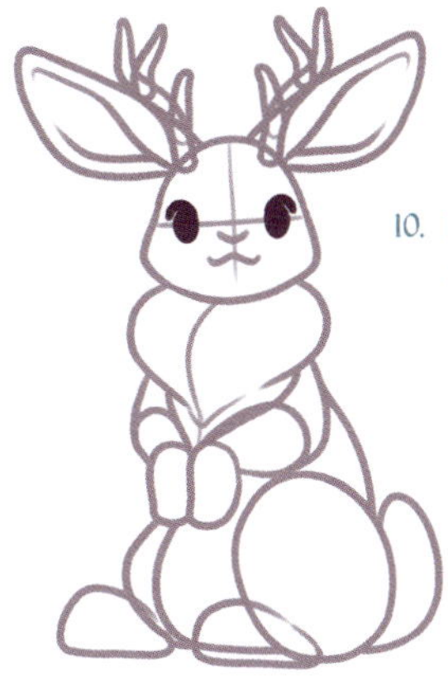

10. Draw two oval eyes with a curve around the top.

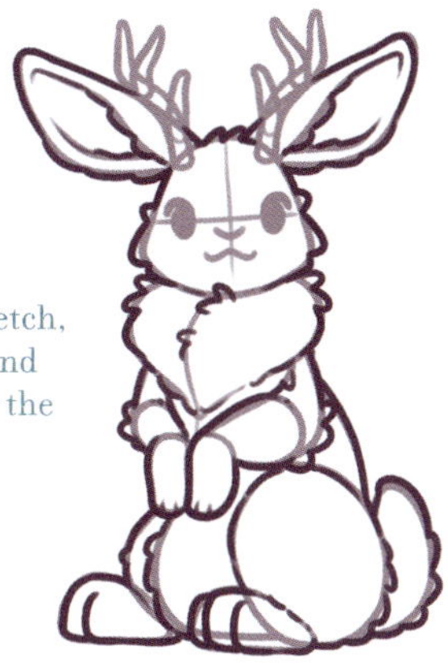

11. Lightly go over the basic sketch, adding details of the head and body. Use soft W shapes for the fur and add the toe lines.

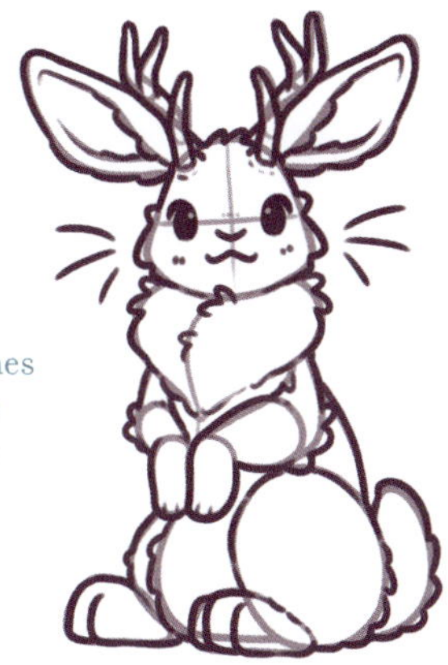

12. Sketch the antlers and the face. Add small dashes on the cheeks and three curved lines around the cheeks for whiskers.

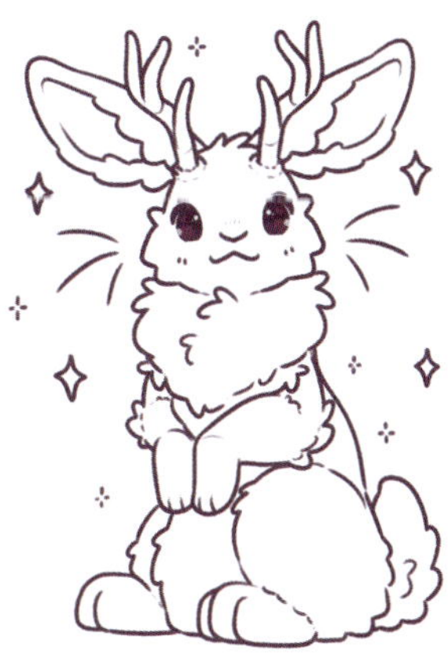

13. Neatly draw the line art over the sketch, leaving a little space inside the eyes for highlights. Add some sparkles if you'd like! Then erase the sketch underneath.

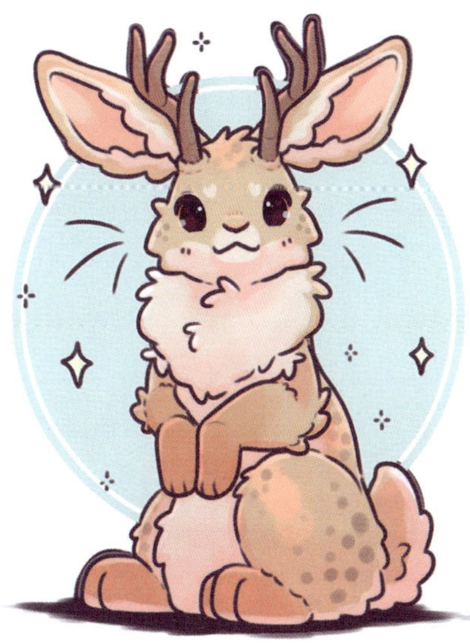

14. Time to color! I used tan for the fur with a white stomach, lower face, and around the inner ears. Add brown spots on the back legs and pink above the nose and on the cheeks for blush.

NEKOMATA

The legend goes that as domestic cats grew old, more and more turned into nekomatas, gaining magical powers that enabled them to create fires, and of necromancy.

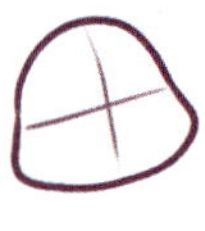

1. Lightly sketch an oval with pointed sides. Add a plus sign guideline for the face.

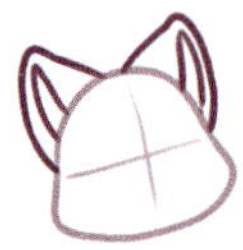

2. Add two rounded triangle ears on top with two smaller triangles inside.

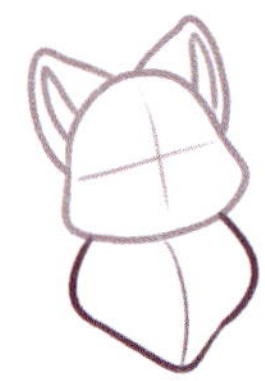

3. Add a rounded, diamond neck with a guideline down the middle.

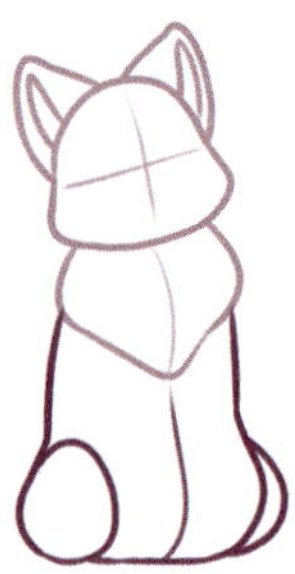

4. Add a rectangle body and continue the guideline down the middle. Add small oval haunches on the bottom with only a partial right haunch.

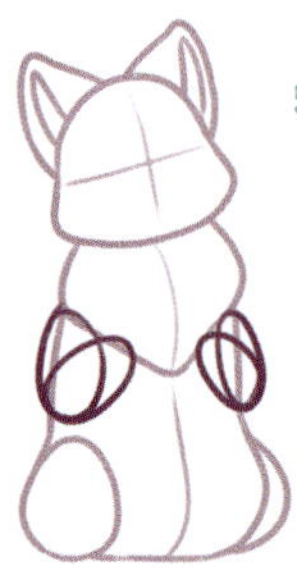

5. Draw two oval arms where the body meets the neck. Then add another oval on top to create a V shape.

6. Add two curved flat-bottomed ovals for the front paws. Then draw two soft rectangle feet at the bottom of the haunches.

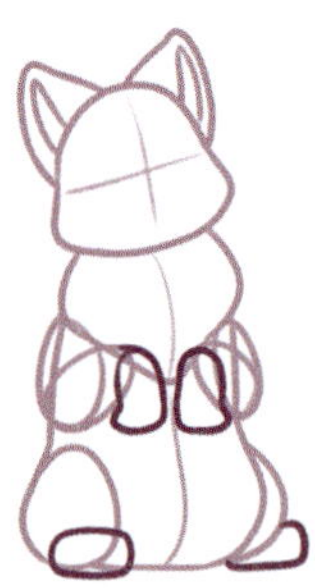

7. For the tail, add a C curve to the left leg. Then add two wavy ovals to the right leg.

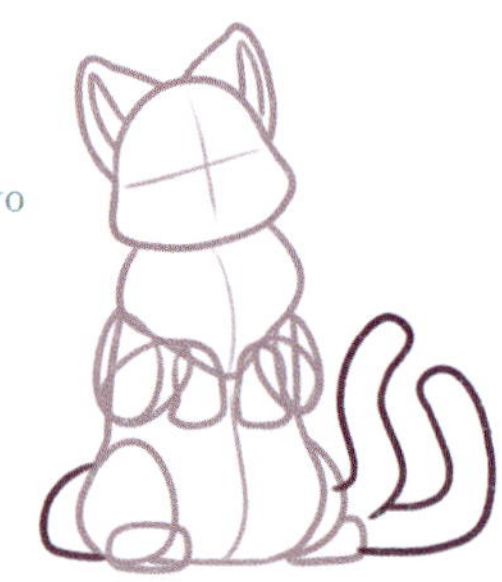

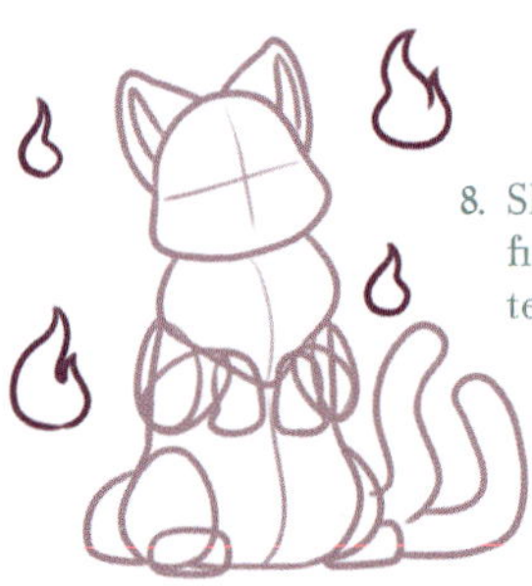

8. Sketch a few floating fireballs with wavy teardrops.

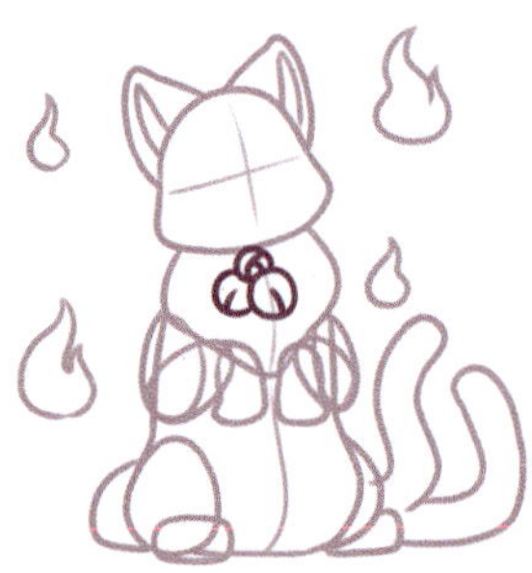

9. Add bells with three small circles under the head. Add a small line in the bottom circles, and two curved lines inside the top circle for a ring.

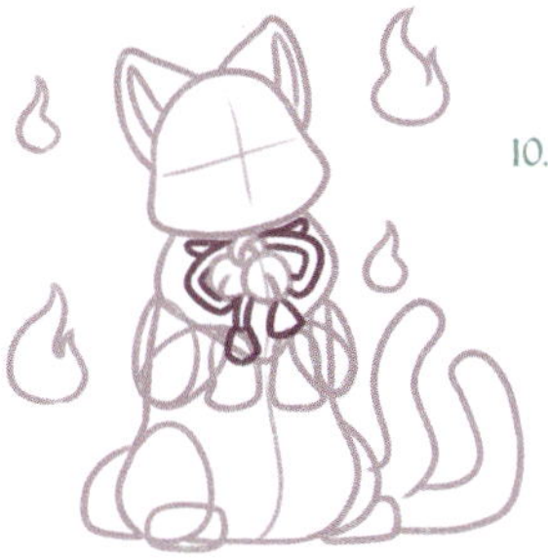

10. Around the circles, sketch the bow with two rectangular loops, two pointed ends above, and two hanging ends with polygon-shaped tips.

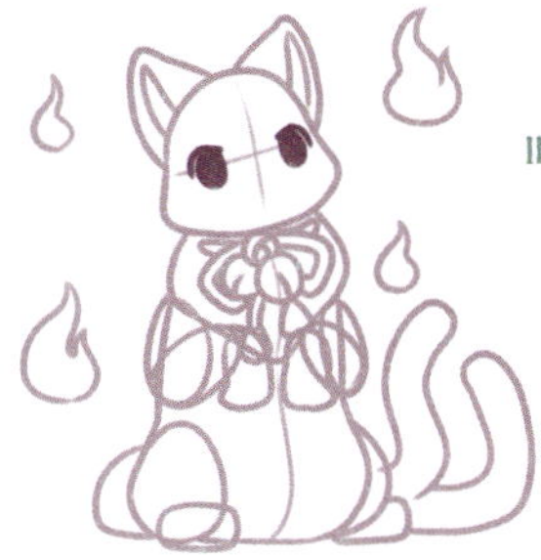

11. Add two oval eyes with a curve around the top. Tilt the curve down a bit towards the middle to create slightly angry eyes.

12. Add a small triangle nose with a curved W mouth.

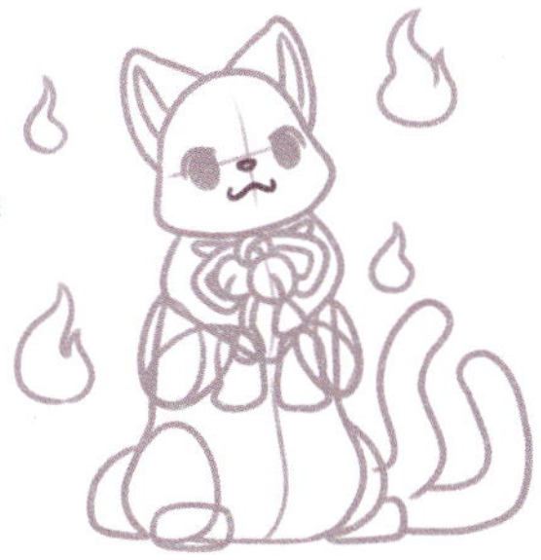

13. Lightly go over the basic sketch, adding details of the head and body. Add soft W shapes for the fur and small toe lines.

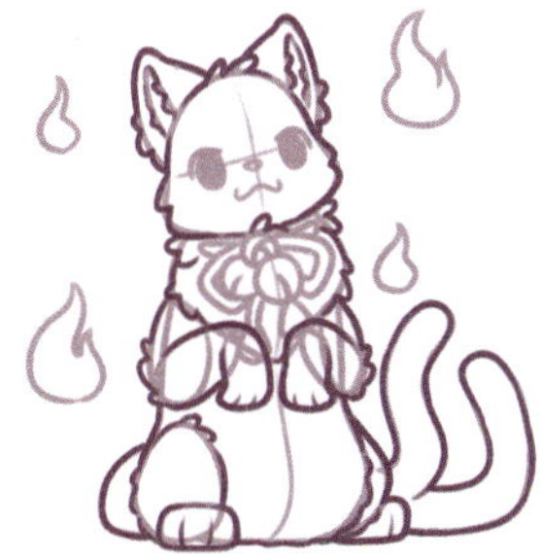

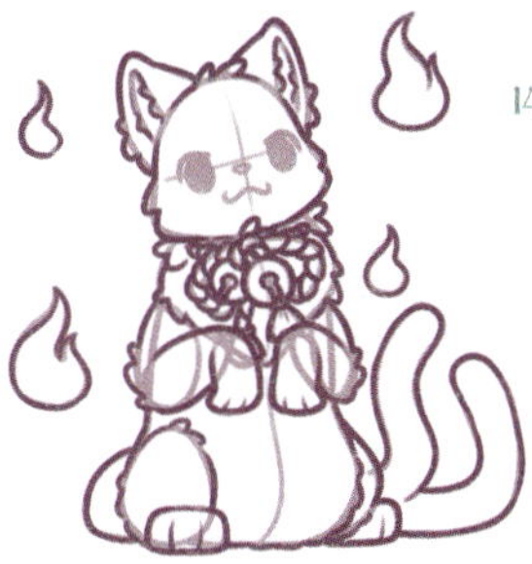

14. Add curved lines along the bow to create a rope texture and add the bells' details.

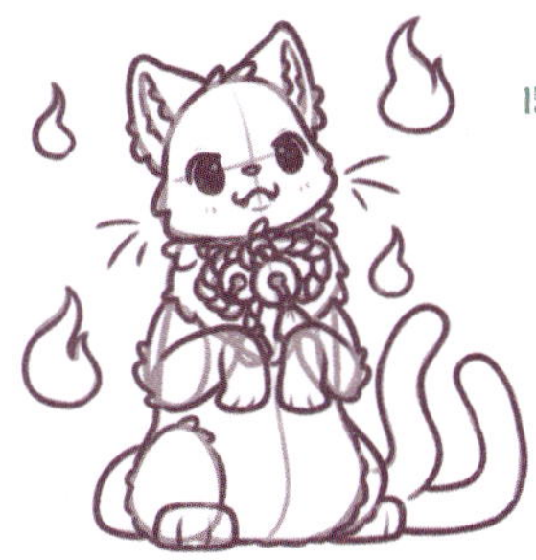

15. Sketch the face detail, adding dashes for blush marks on the cheeks and little triangle fangs. Leave space for highlights in the eyes. Add three lines around the cheeks for whiskers.

16. Neatly draw the line art over the sketch. Add some sparkles if you'd like! Then erase the sketch underneath.

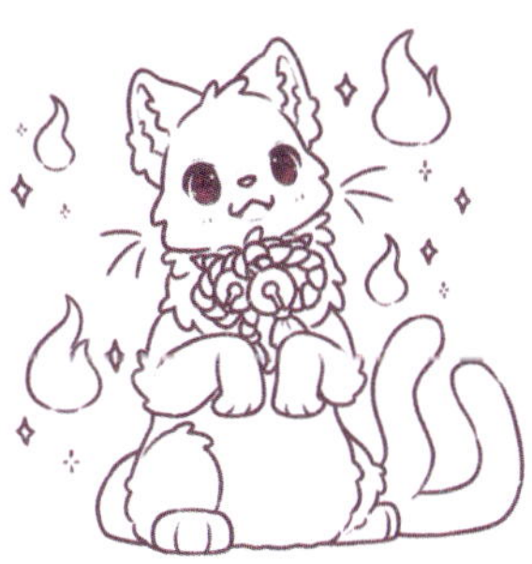

17. Let's color! I mimicked a calico cat with brown and black patches along the body. Add pink to the nose, inner ears, and cheeks. Make the bow a bright red with red face markings. Lastly, color the flames.

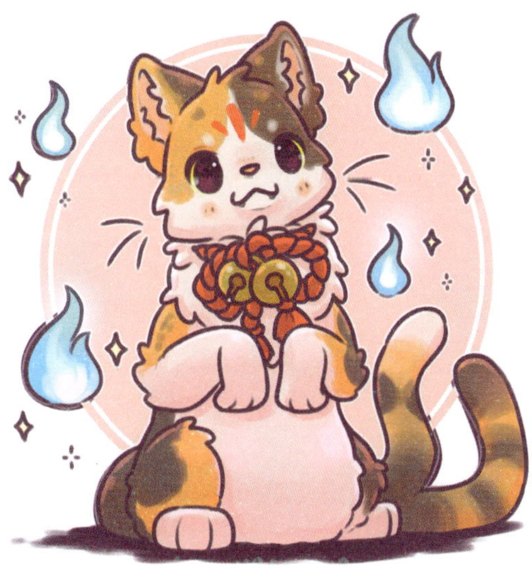

CHIMERA

Most notably, this monster is female, and it should not be forgotten that, in her most impressive form, she appears with three animal heads: those of a lion, a goat, and a snake.

1. Lightly sketch an oval with pointed sides. Add a plus sign guideline for the face.

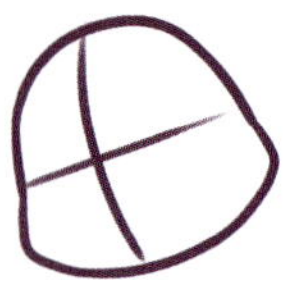

2. Add two small ears on top with two curved lines inside.

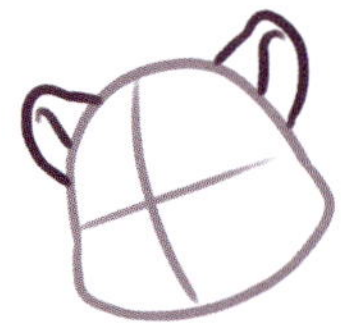

3. Add two curved V shapes for the neck.

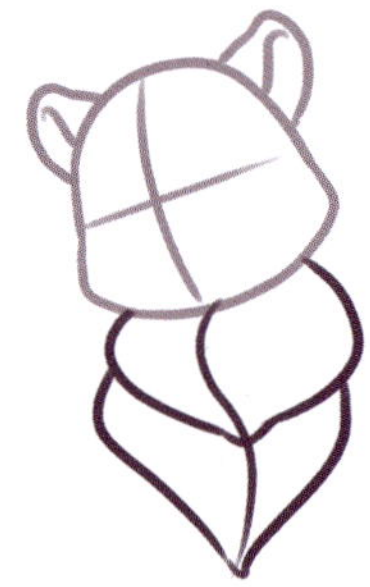

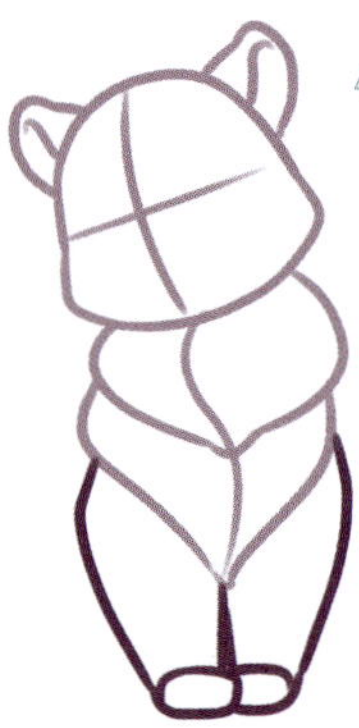

4. Sketch the front legs on either side of the neck with two rounded rectangle paws.

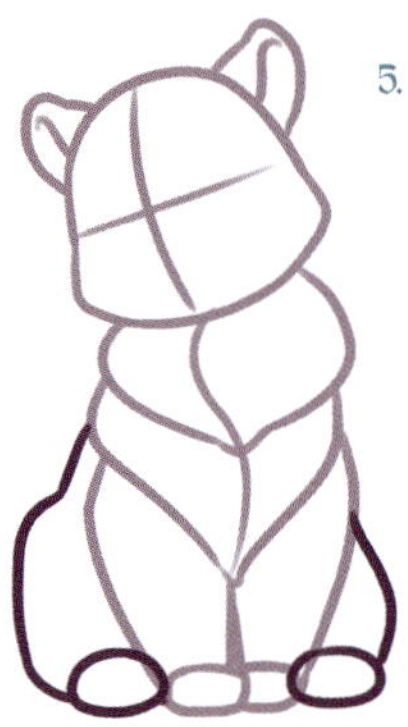

5. Draw a curved line around the left leg that ends with an oval paw. Beside the right leg, do the same with a smaller haunch.

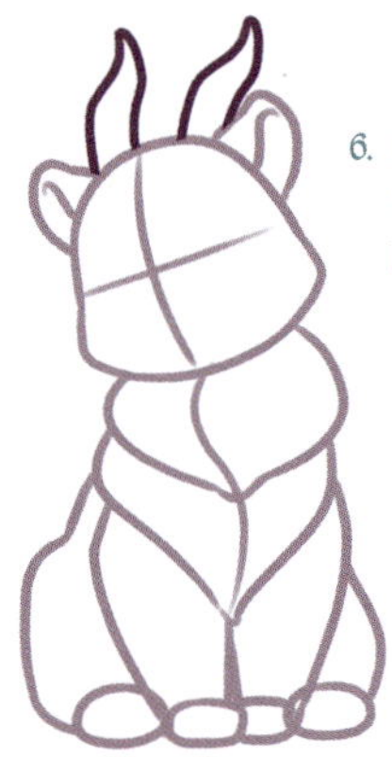

6. Between the ears, add two curved pointy horns.

7. For the snake tail, add two parallel curving lines from the left haunch moving up, ending in an egg-shaped head.

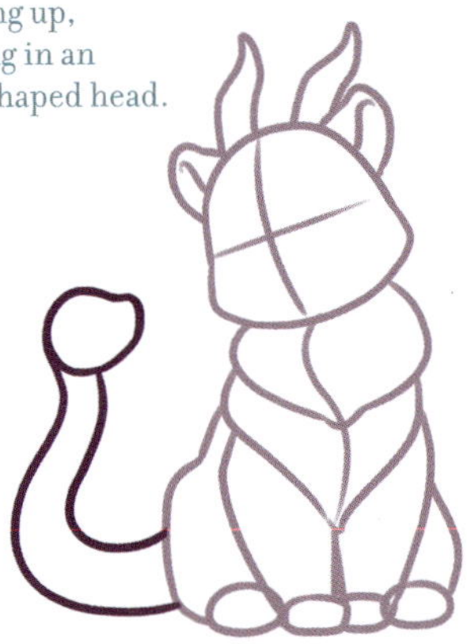

8. Add the snake's face with an oval eye, then add a curve around the top and a wiggly tongue coming out the mouth.

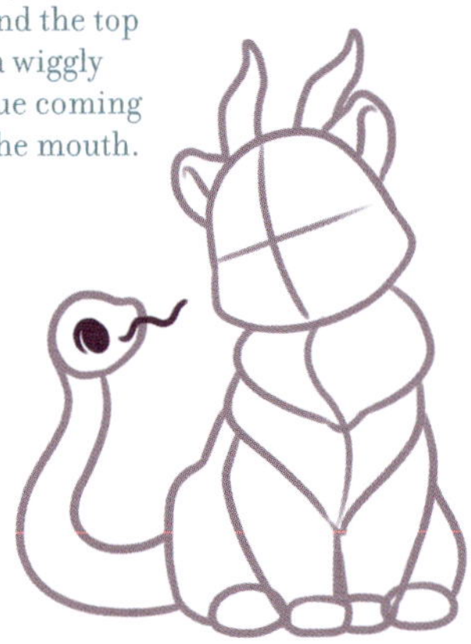

9. At the center of the chimera's head, add a small V nose and W mouth.

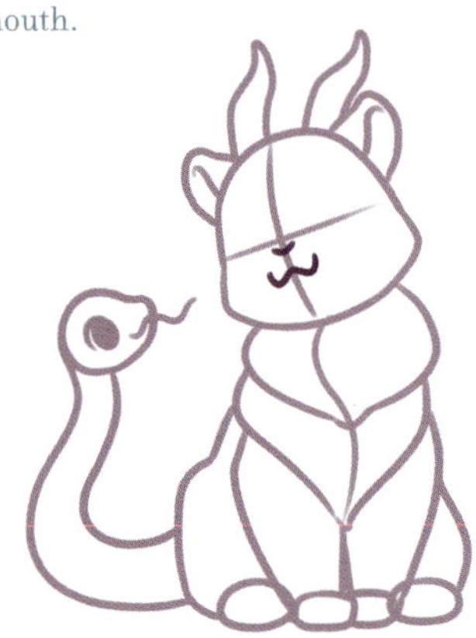

10. Draw two closed eyes with curved lines. Then, under the center of the mouth, draw a tiny U-shaped tongue.

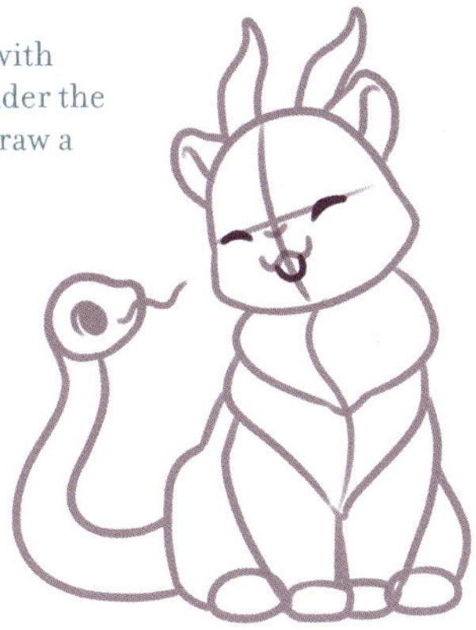

11. Lightly go over the basic sketch, adding details for the head and body. Use soft W shapes for the fur and mark the small toe lines on the paws and hooves.

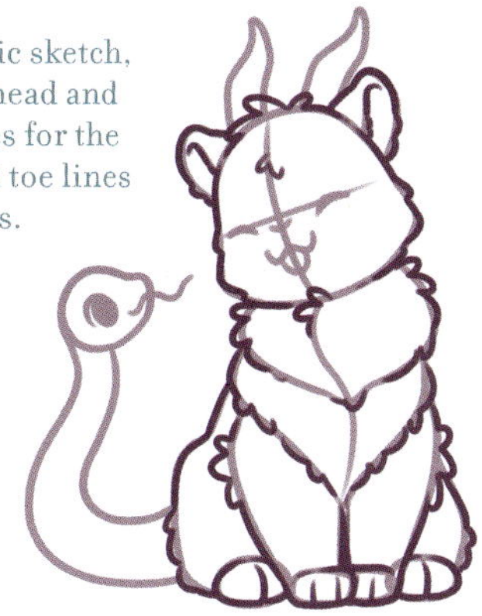

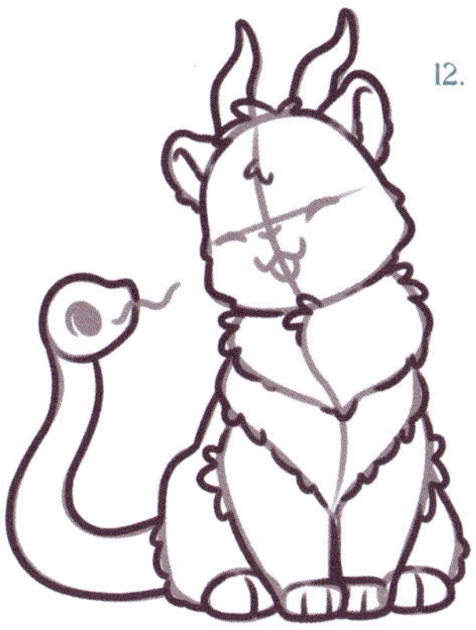

12. Sketch the snake tail and horns.

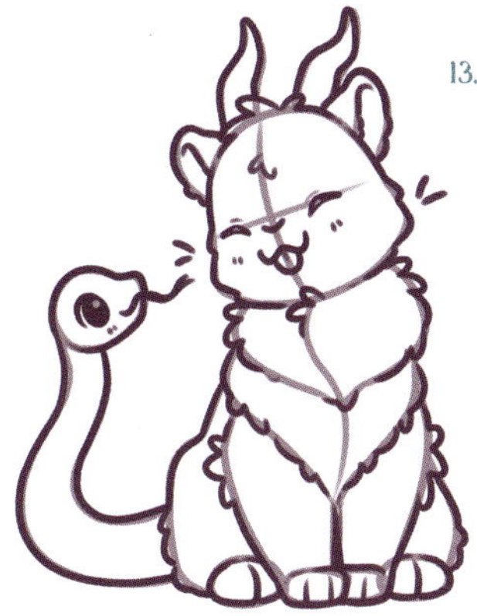

13. Add details for both faces with dashes on the cheeks for blush. Draw two lines around the chimera's cheeks for whiskers. Add the snake's forked tongue.

14. Neatly draw the line art over the sketch, leaving a little space inside the eyes for highlights. Add some sparkles if you'd like! Then erase the sketch underneath.

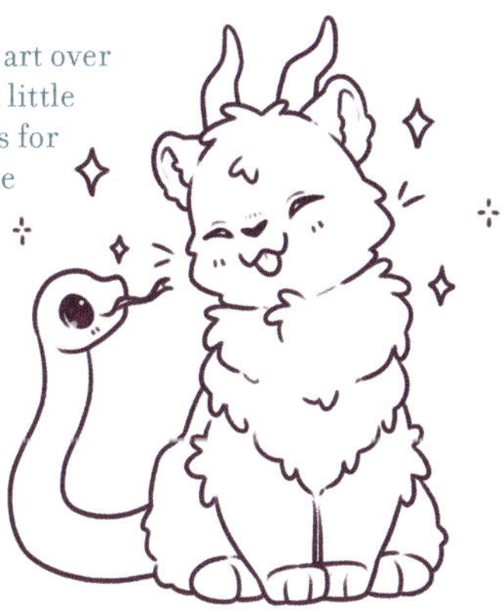

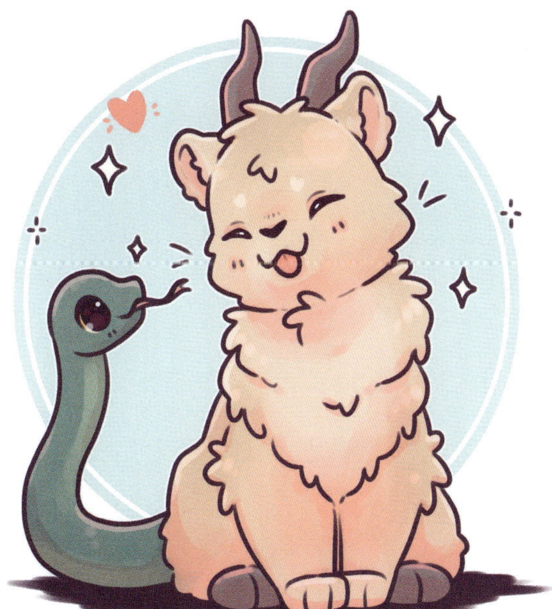

15. Now add color! Use a light tan for the lion's fur and green for the snake tail. Add pink to the inner ears and cheeks, and a dark brown for the hooves and horns.

YETI

Well known by its popular-culture name, the Abominable Snowman, this apelike creature can be found wandering the snowy Himalayas.

1. Lightly sketch an oval head. Add a plus sign guideline for the face.

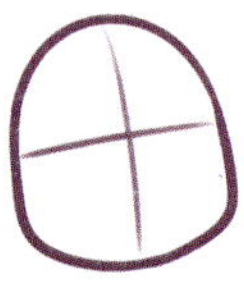

2. Draw two hook-shaped horns on top. Then add two rounded rectangle ears on the sides of the head with a line inside.

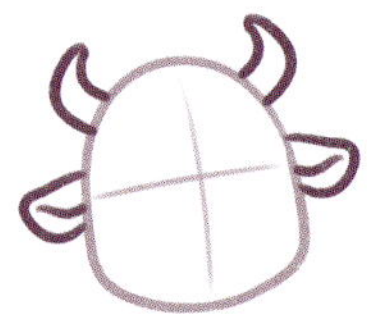

3. Draw a rounded V neck with a curved guideline down the middle.

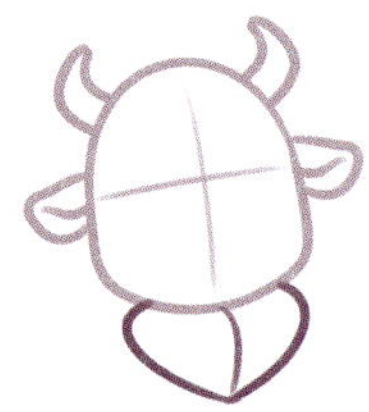

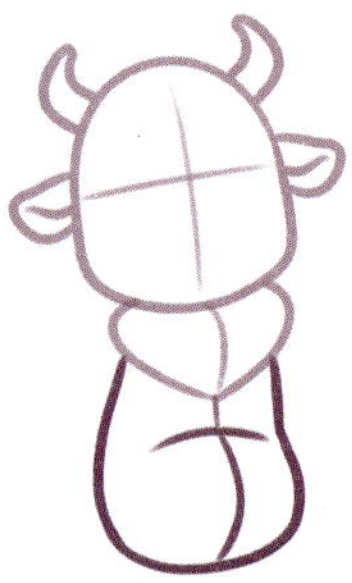

4. Add a U-shaped body with a little curve on the right for the pudgy stomach. Continue the guidelines down the middle.

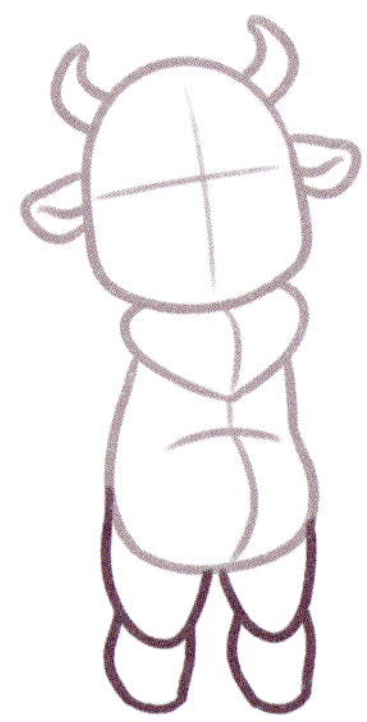

5. Sketch the legs with U shapes. Then attach two more U shapes underneath.

6. Sketch the feet with triangles and a rectangle in front for both.

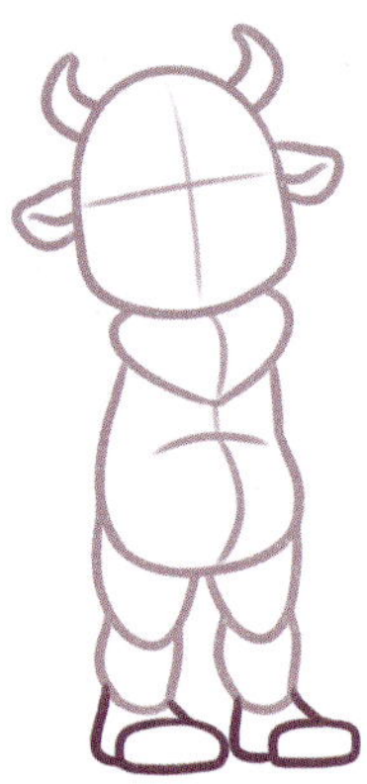

7. Draw two U-shaped upper arms where the body meets the neck. Attach rounded triangles at the ends.

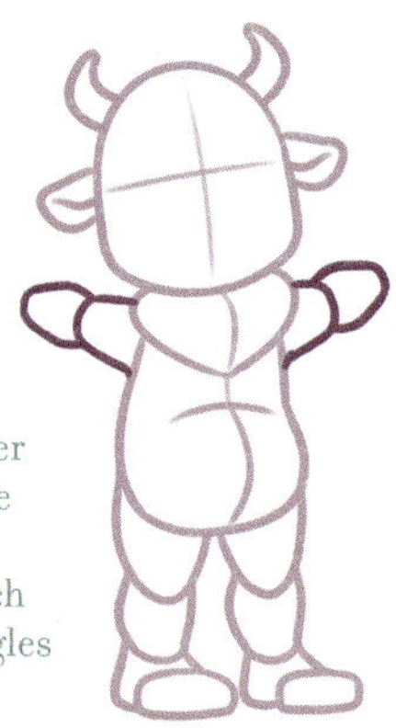

8. Start the hands with square palms and five fingers coming out of them.

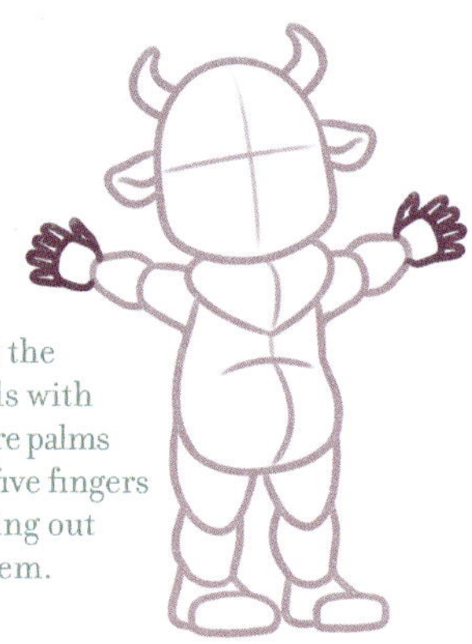

9. On the lower half of the face, draw a large bean-shaped mouth.

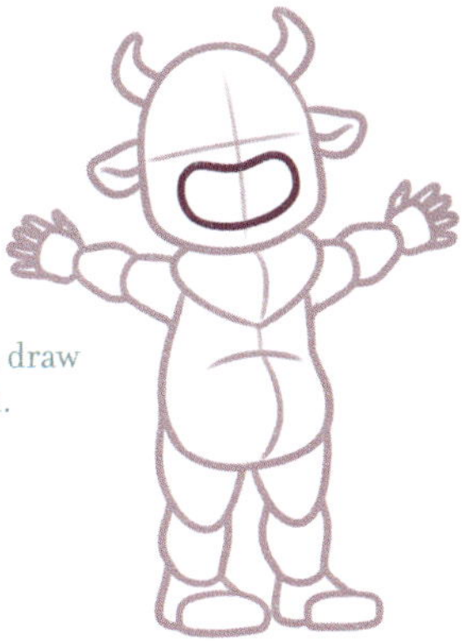

10. Add an oval nose and two curved lines for the eyes.

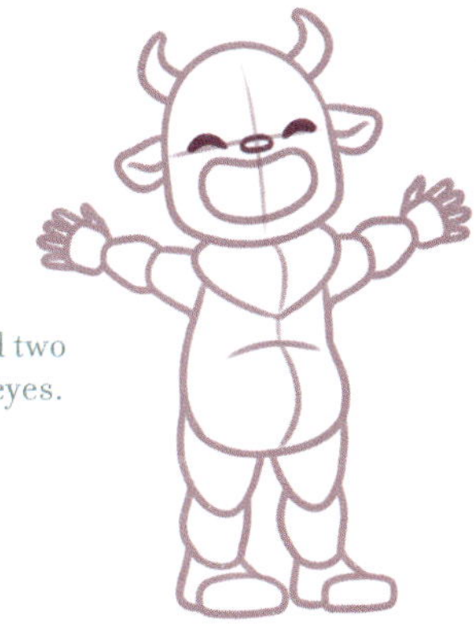

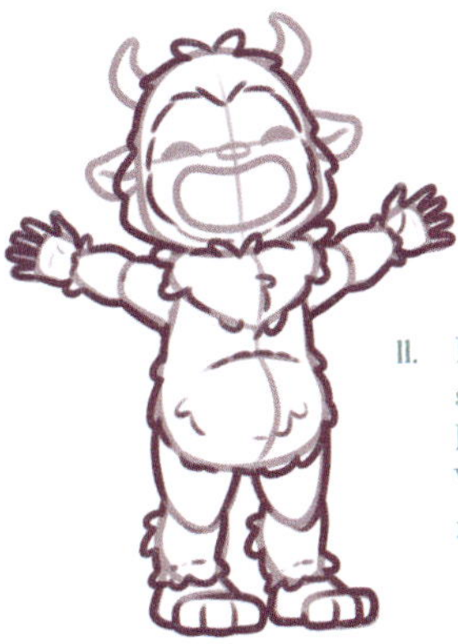

11. Lightly go over the basic sketch, adding details of the head and body. Use soft W shapes for the fur and mark the toe lines.

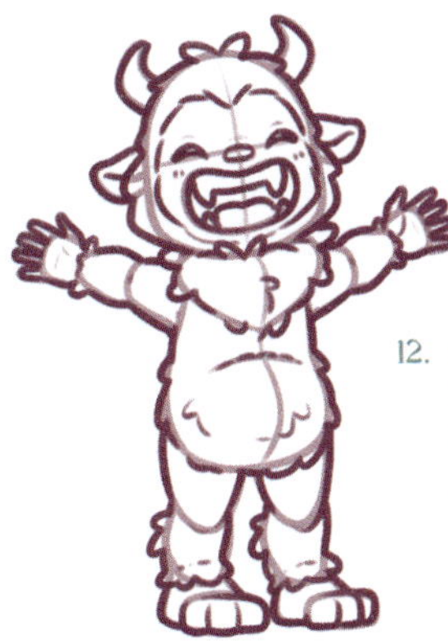

12. Sketch the horns and ears. Add more details to the face with big fanged teeth and a tongue.

13. Neatly draw the line art over the sketch, leaving a little space inside the eyes for highlights. Add some sparkles if you'd like! Then erase the sketch underneath.

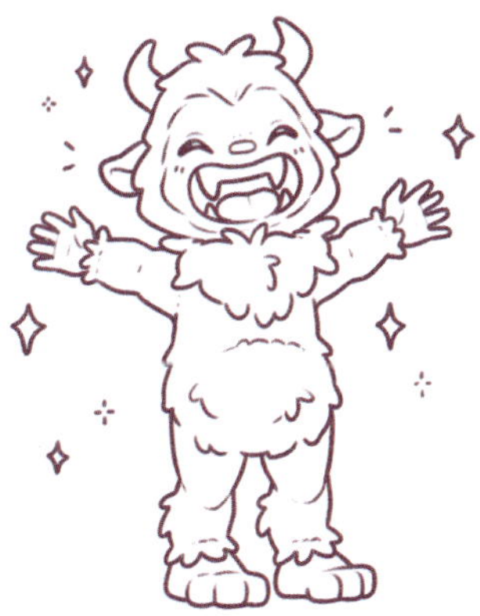

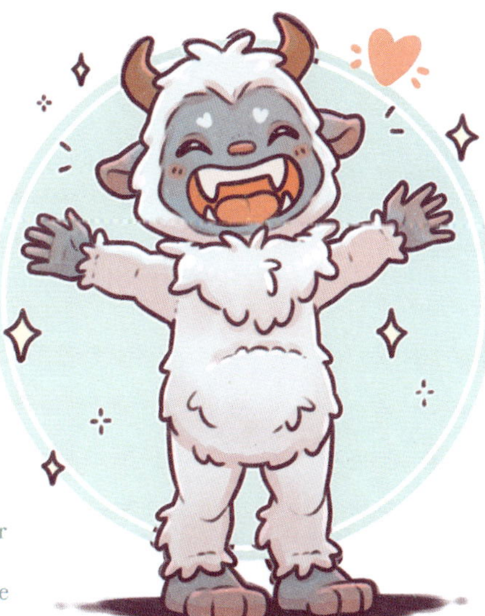

14. Finally, add color! Keep the fur white or a very, very pale blue. Make the hands, feet, and face dark blue. Add pink to the mouth, tongue, nose, and cheeks.

UNICORN

This majestic creature is as miraculous as a rainbow, with its special horn that some believe can cure any sickness.

1. Draw a circle head with a curved snout coming out of the right side. Add a line pointing out of the top of the head.

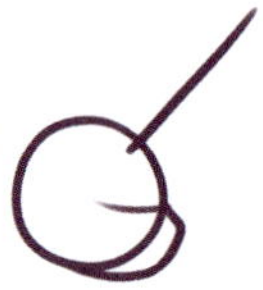

2. Add two teardrop-shaped ears with a curved line inside the left one.

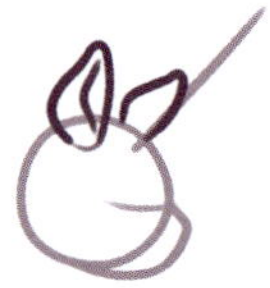

3. Draw two S-shaped lines coming down from the left ear and under the snout.

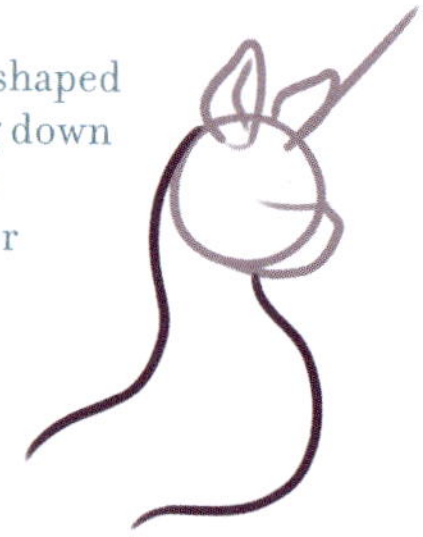

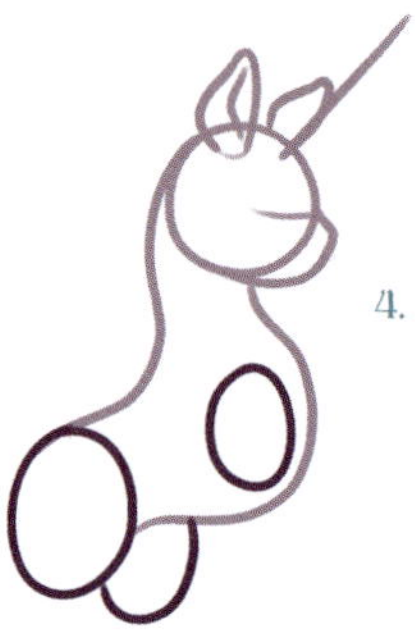

4. Add an oval at the front of the chest and two more at the end of the body.

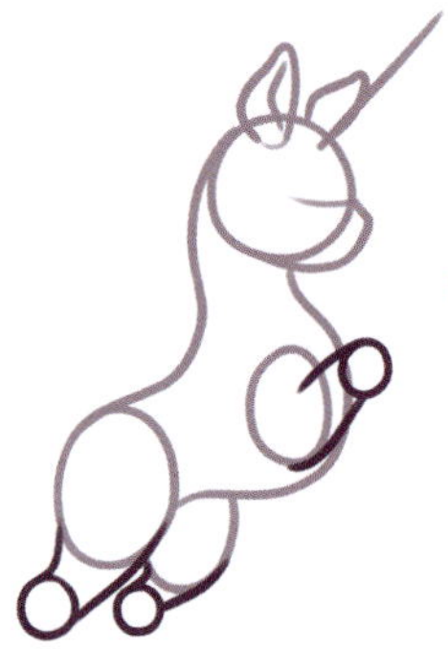

5. Draw a circle near each of the ovals and join them together with two curved lines.

6. Add two circles beneath the lower circles and join them with two lines. Then add V-shaped hooves to the bottom circles.

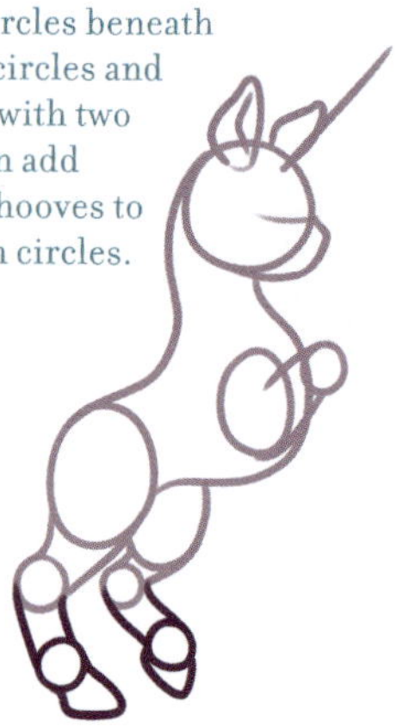

7. Repeat step 6 for the front legs, with the right leg covering part of the left.

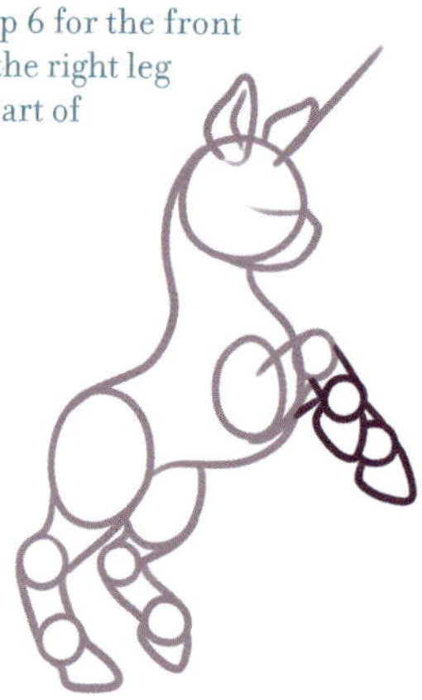

8. Attach a U-shaped line on top of the back haunch that ends in a wiggly teardrop-shaped tuft of hair.

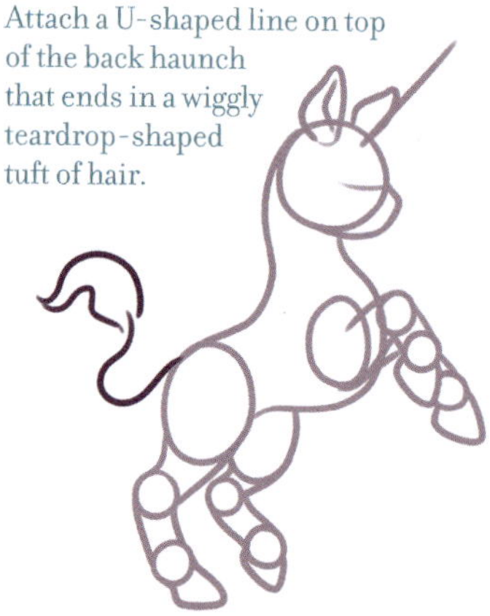

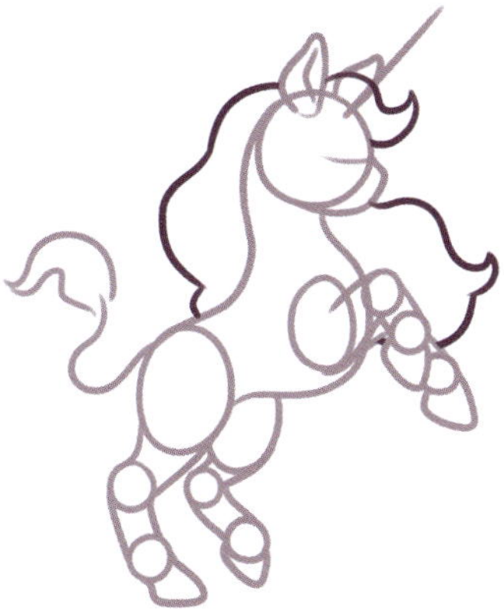

9. Add a flowing mane around the head and neck with some curved points.

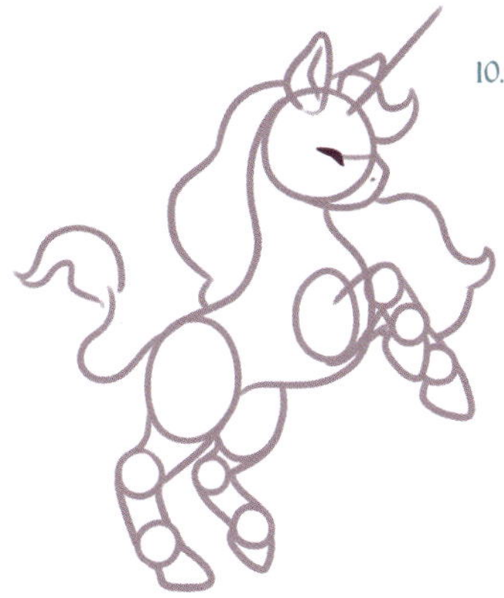

10. Sketch a curved line for the eye at the center of the head, and a small dot at the tip of snout.

11. Lightly go over the basic sketch, adding details of the head and body. Use soft W shapes for the fur around the legs. Add a line at the point of the hooves and sketch the horn.

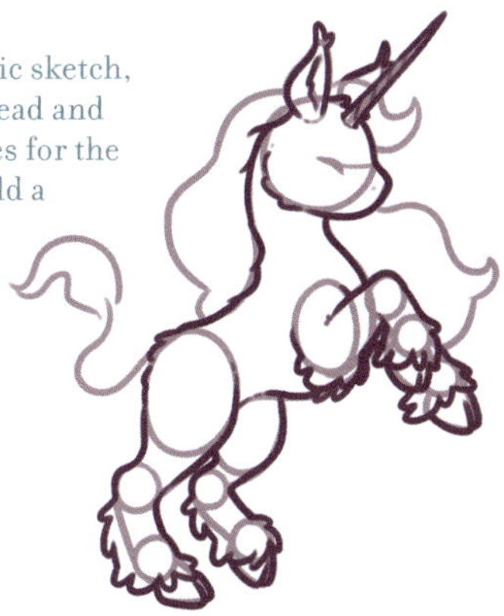

12. Sketch the mane and tail, adding more curved lines to give the hair dimension.

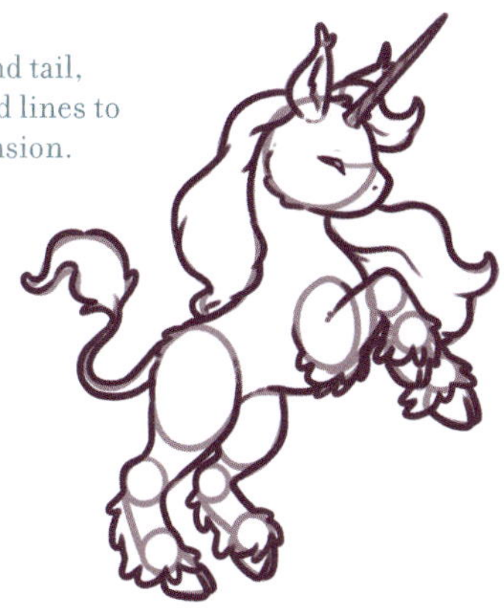

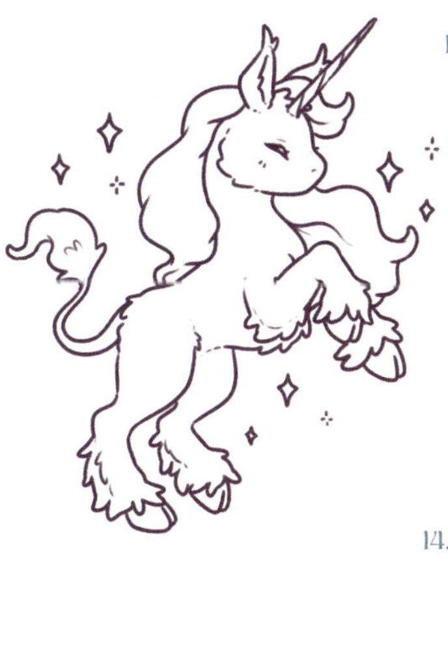

13. Neatly draw the line art over the sketch, leaving a little space inside the eyes for highlights. Add some sparkles if you'd like! Then erase the sketch underneath.

14. Add some color! I kept it traditional with a white body and slightly golden hair on the mane and tail. Add pale gold spots to the back and more gold to the bottom of the legs.

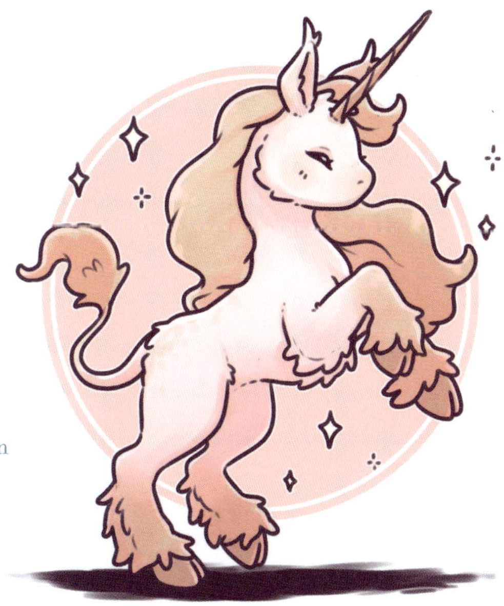

KIRIN

Appearing either as a horse or deer creature with cloven hooves, dragon scales, and one or two horns, kirins are widely known to be benevolent and noble creatures.

1. Lightly sketch a circle with a plus sign guideline. On the bottom-right side of the face, add a blocky square snout.

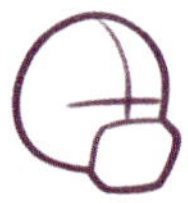

2. Add teardrop-shaped ears on the sides of the head with lines inside. Then add two wiggly whiskers on the sides of the snout.

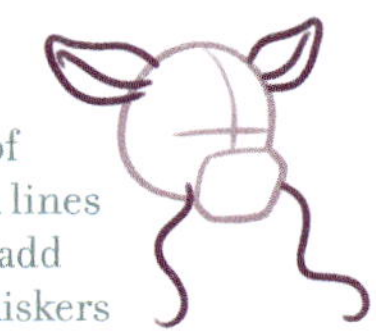

3. Between the ears, draw two forked horns.

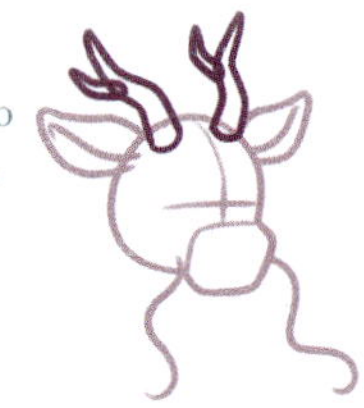

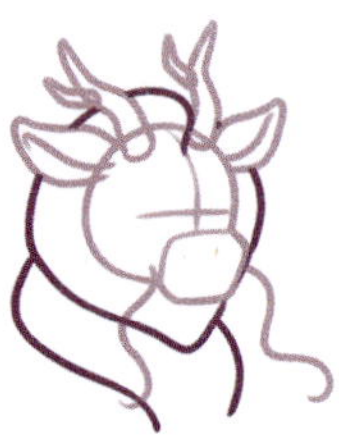

4. Draw a large teardrop-shaped mane around the head. Add two curving lines below the mane for the neck.

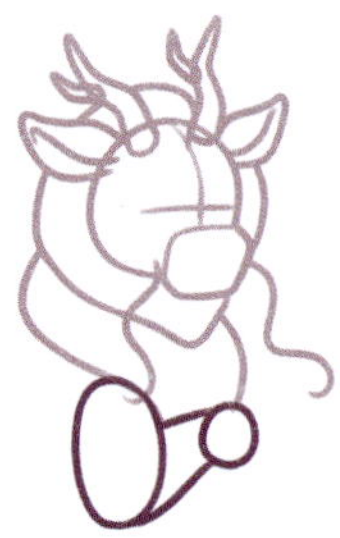

5. Under the neck, add an oval with a small circle to the right, then connect them with two lines.

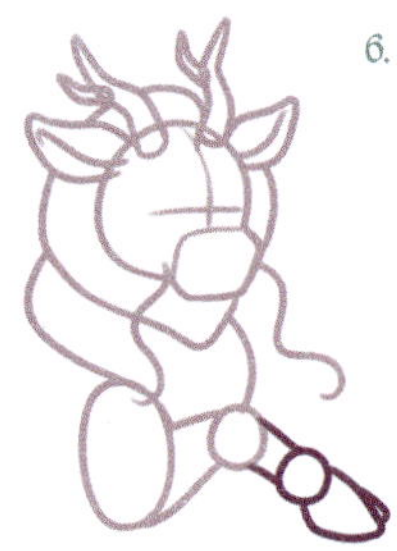

6. Add another circle slightly below the first and connect with lines. Then attach a V-shaped hoof with a defined toe.

7. Under the front leg, sketch an oval hoof with a line down the middle and a few lines for the arm around it.

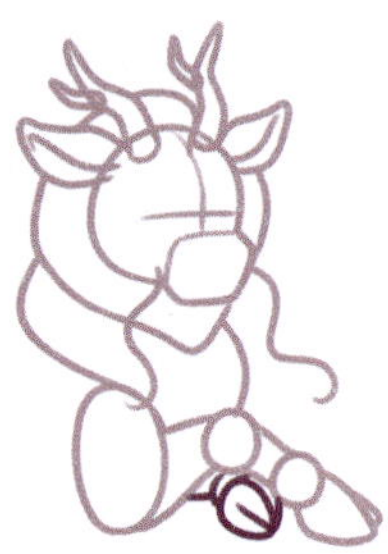

8. Draw an oval back haunch. Connect the top to the mane with a line. Add a small circle at the bottom of the haunch.

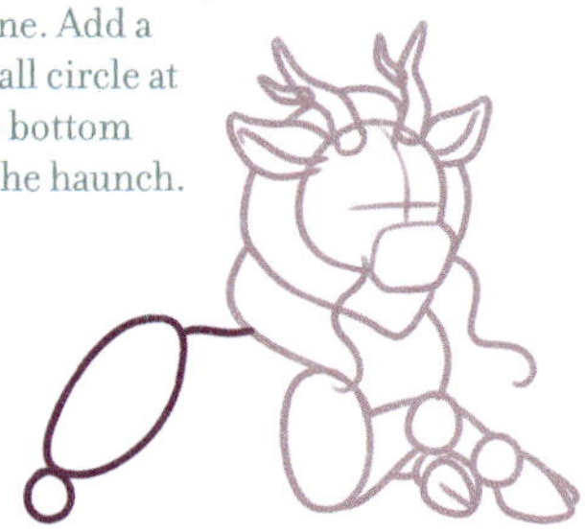

9. At the bottom-middle of the body, draw a small circle and connect it to the haunch. Attach another hoof with defined toes to the circle.

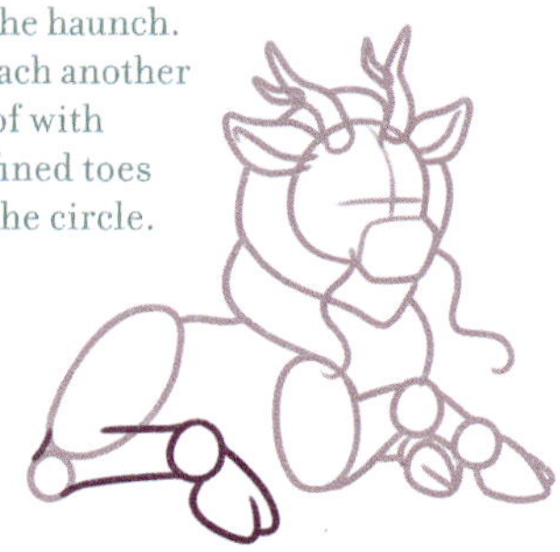

10. Add a curved line to the back of the haunch. Then, next to the back hoof, draw a partial hoof.

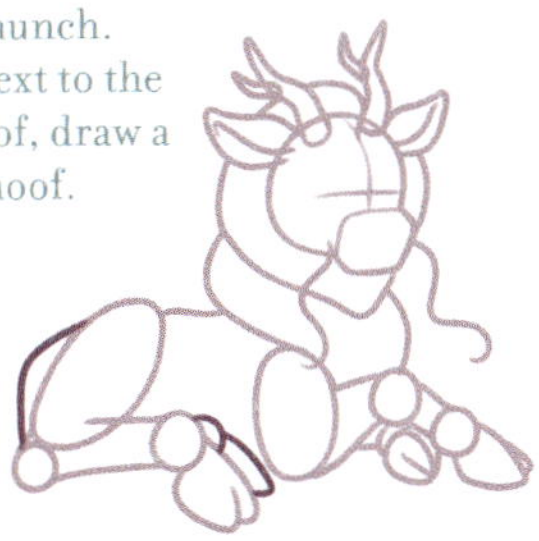

11. Draw curved parallel lines for a tail coming out of the backside. Add a large swirling length of hair around the back leg.

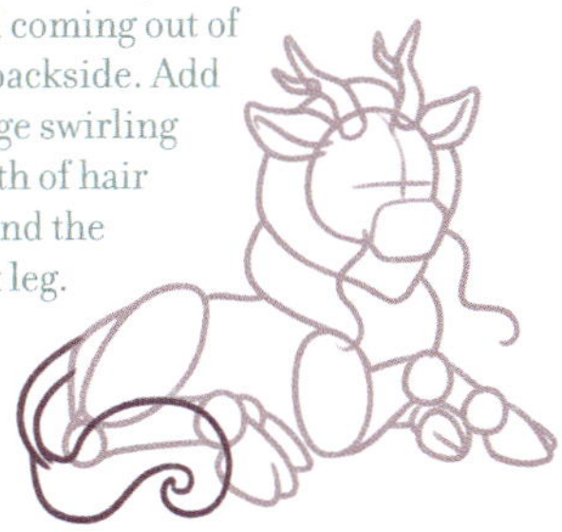

12. Add a curved line along the back. Attach a V shape under the shoulder.

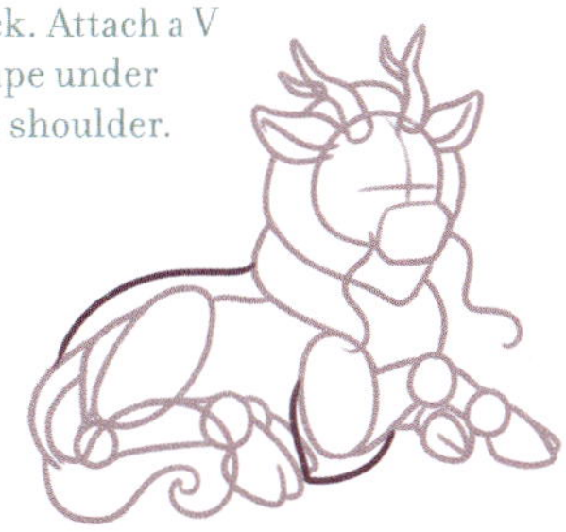

13. Sketch the face with an upside-down V mouth and two dots for the nostrils on the snout. Then draw two oval eyes with a curve around the top.

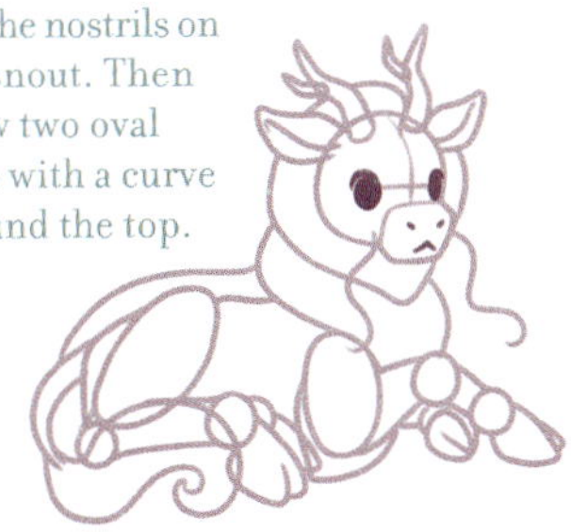

14. Lightly go over the basic sketch, adding soft W shapes on the mane, ears, and tail.

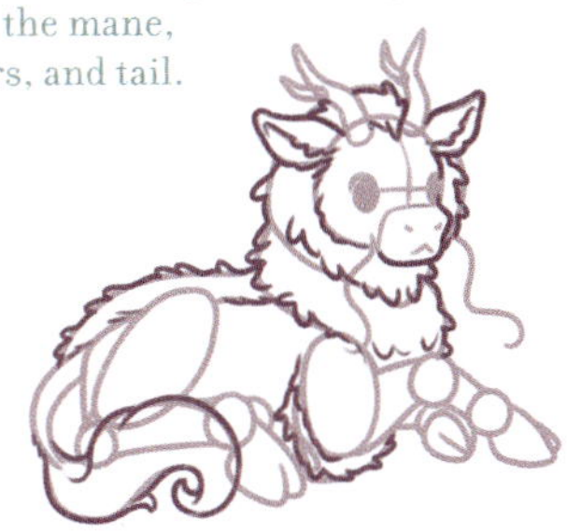

15. Lightly sketch the rest of the body. Make sure not to draw the back leg where the tail overlaps it.

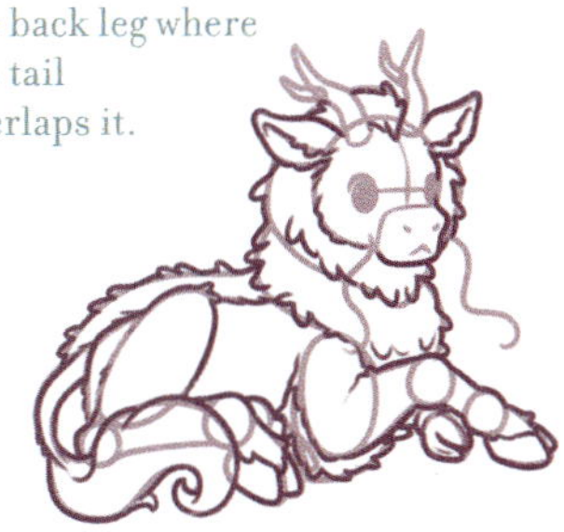

16. Sketch the face detail, including the thick whiskers and the horns. Add dashes for blush marks and small N-shaped eyebrows.

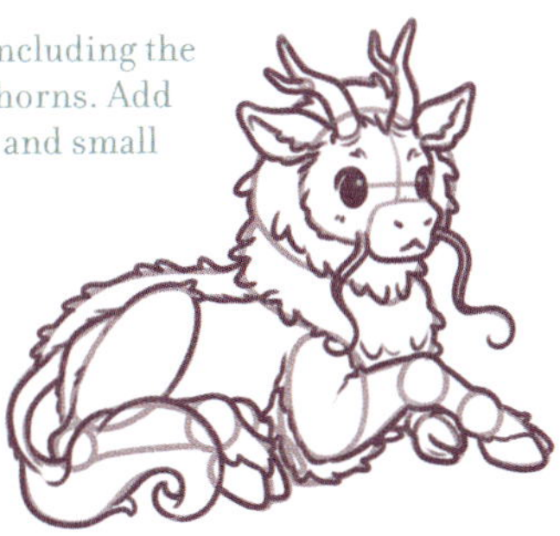

17. Neatly draw the line art over the sketch, leaving a little space inside the eyes for highlights. Use M and U shapes along the body for scales. Add some sparkles if you'd like! Then erase the sketch underneath.

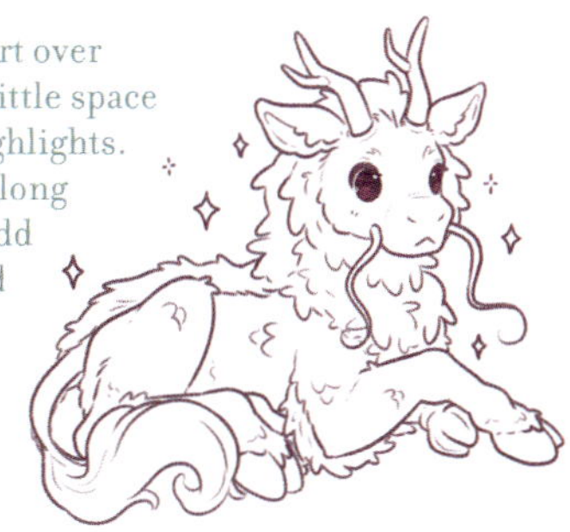

18. Lastly, add color! I used light turquoise for the body and a mix of red and blue for the hair. Add pink to the inner ear and cheeks for blush.

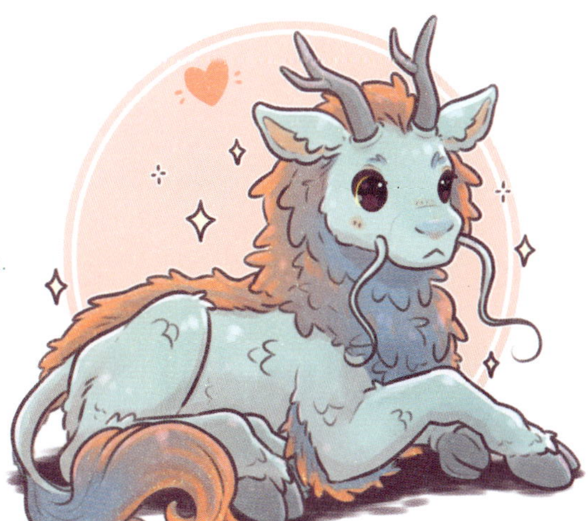

CERBERUS

Hades' personal watchdog, Cerberus, roams the Underworld with the important job of preventing the dead from leaving and the living from entering.

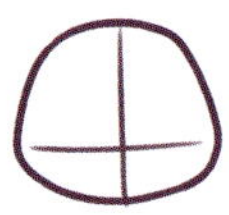

1. Lightly sketch an oval with pointed sides. Add a plus sign guideline for the face.

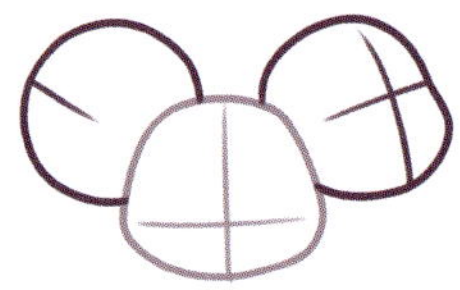

2. On the sides of the head, draw two more similar-sized circles for the other two heads. Add face guidelines.

3. On the center and right head, draw oval snouts. On the left head, draw a pointed C-shaped snout.

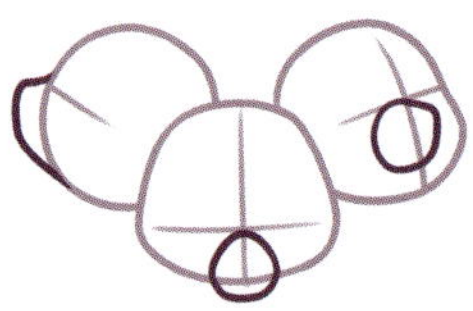

4. On the left and right heads, draw two triangle ears, each with a line inside.

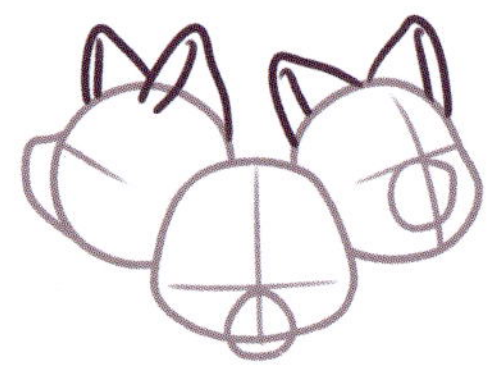

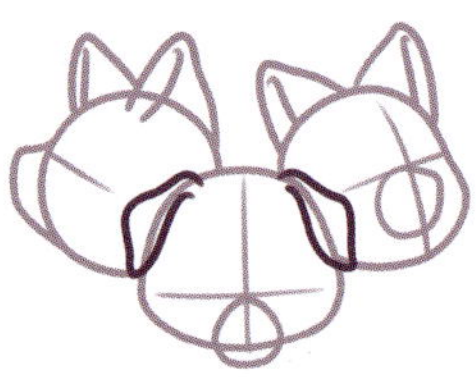

5. On the center head, draw floppy downward-triangle ears.

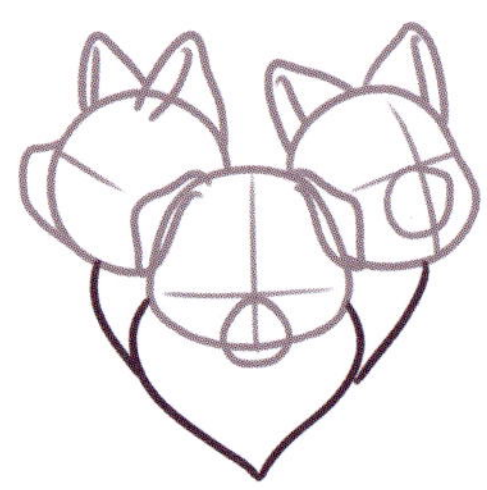

6. Draw a rounded V neck coming down from the center head. Connect the other two heads to the neck with two curved lines.

7. Underneath the joined neck, draw two small rectangle paws right next to each other and connect to the neck with two lines each.

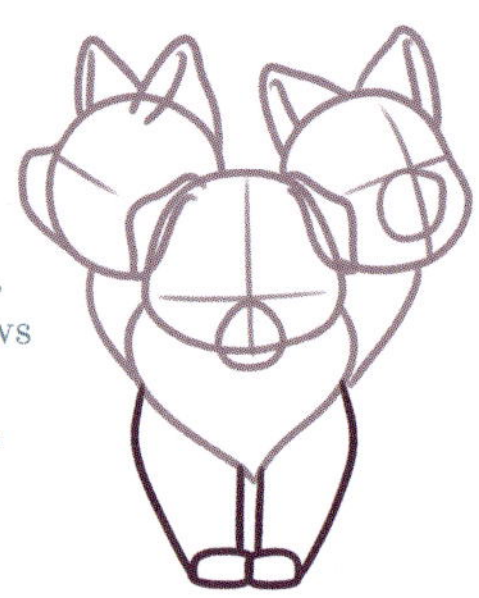

8. Draw curved haunches around the front legs, starting where the necks meet. Add two curved ovals for the back paws around the front paws.

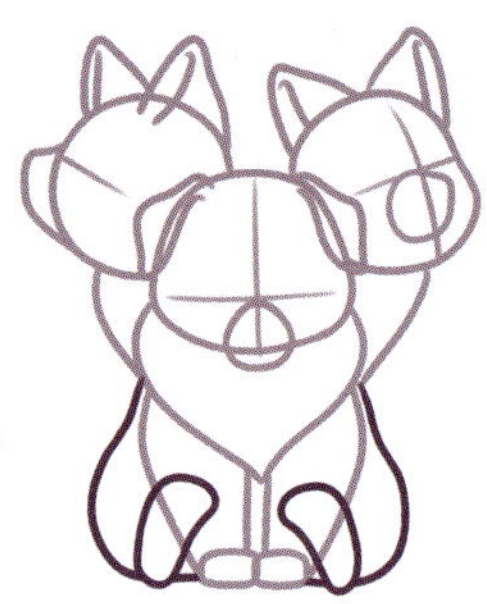

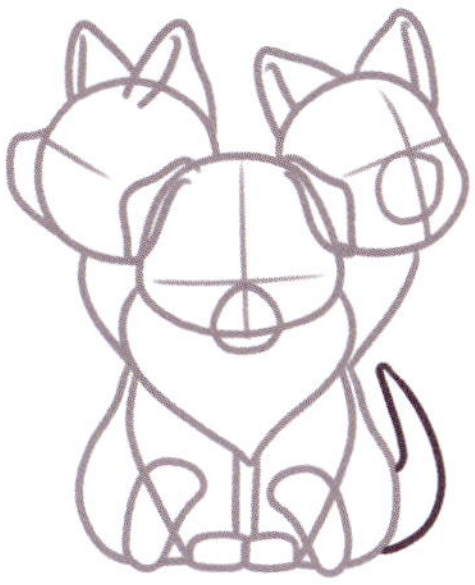

9. Add a curved pointy tail off the right haunch.

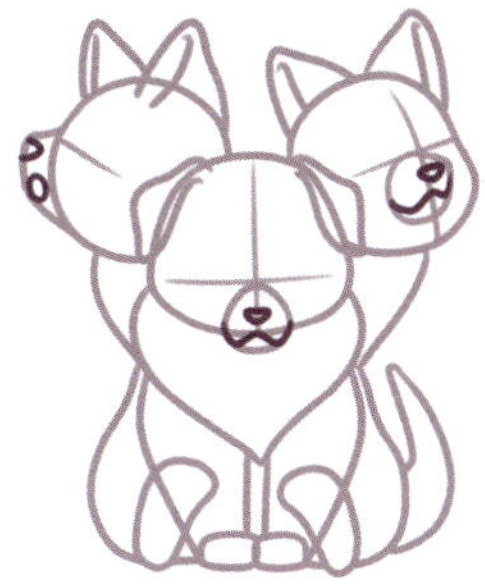

10. On the center and right heads, draw triangle noses and W mouths. On the left head, draw half of a triangle nose and an O mouth.

11. On the right head, draw two oval eyes with a curve around the top. On the left head, only draw one eye. For the center head, draw two curved lines for closed eyes.

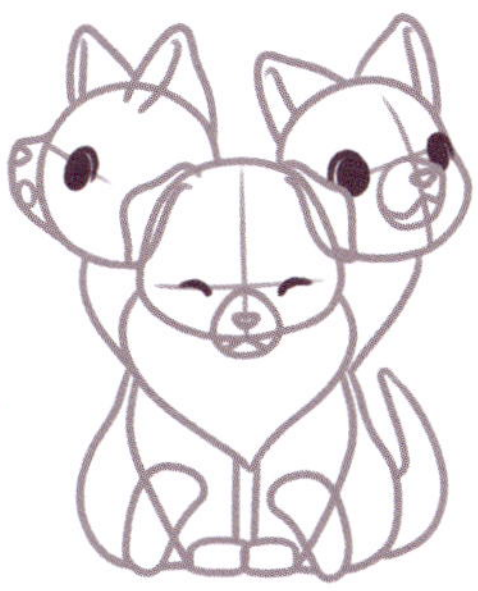

12. Lightly go over the basic sketch, adding detail to the head and body. Define the fur with soft W shapes.

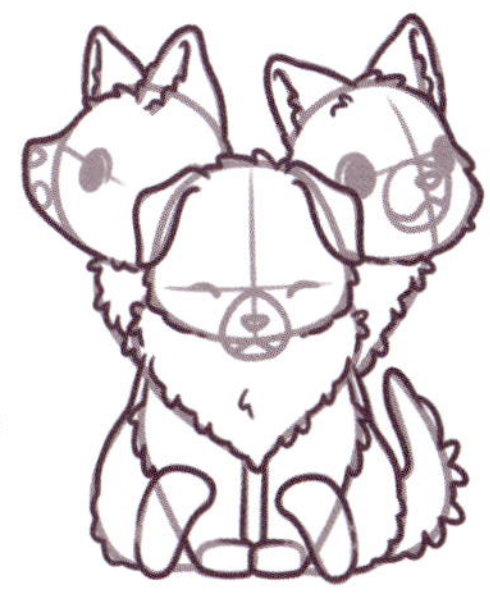

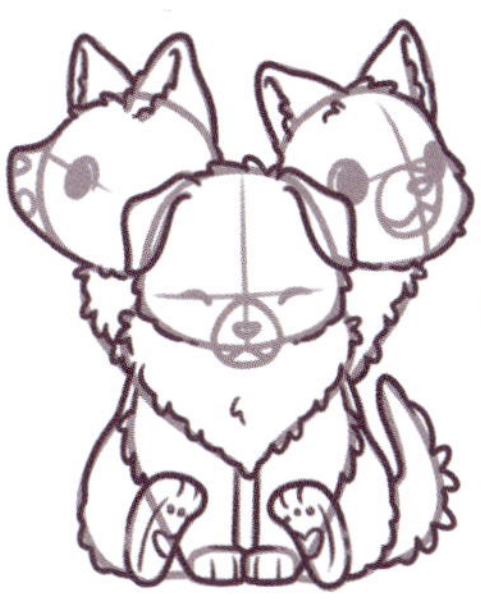

13. Sketch the details on the back paws, adding toe beans and paw pads.

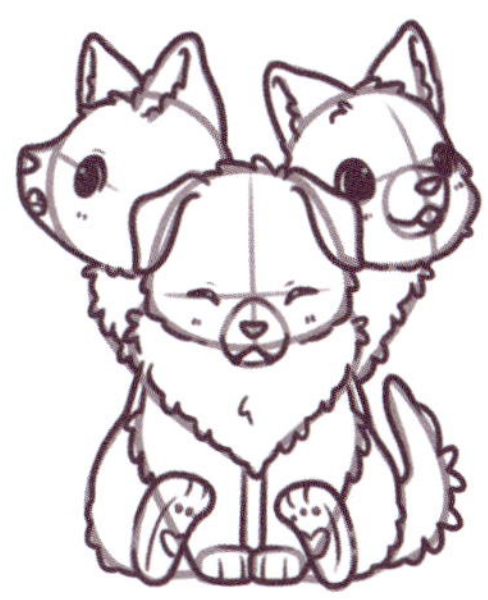

14. Sketch the face details with dashes on the cheeks and highlights in the eyes.

15. Neatly draw the line art over the sketch. Add some sparkles if you'd like! Then erase the sketch underneath.

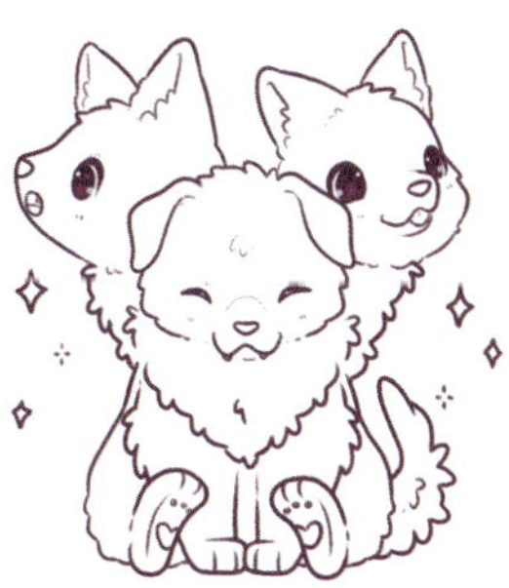

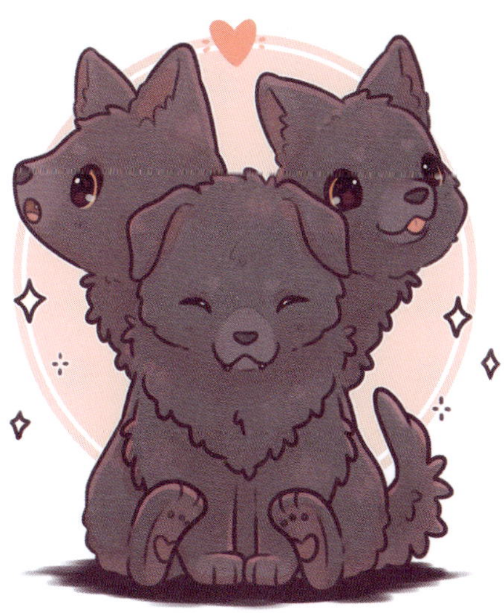

16. Let's color! I went with black fur with a slightly lighter color on the snouts and little heart-shaped eyebrows.

DRYAD

An enchanting nature spirit or nymph, the dryad usually takes on the appearance of a shy, beautiful woman and has the same life span as the tree she resides in.

1. Sketch a flat-bottomed oval with a slight dip on the right side. Add a plus sign guideline for the face.

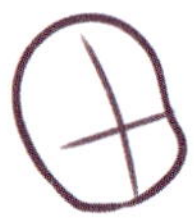

2. Draw two rounded triangle ears on the sides of the head, each with a curved line inside.

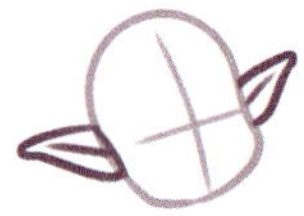

3. Add a small U neck below the head and a diamond shape to the bottom.

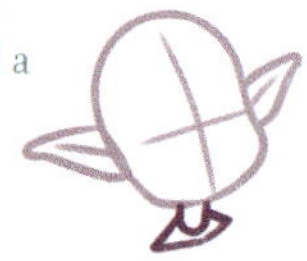

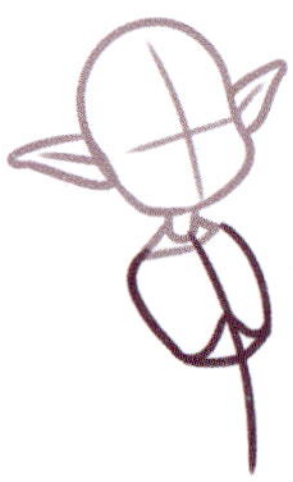

4. Add a soft W-shaped upper body. Connect the tips of the W with a curve. Then draw a long, curved guideline down the middle.

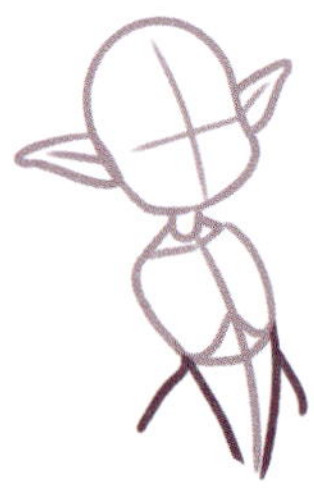

5. On either side of the line, add an upside down V.

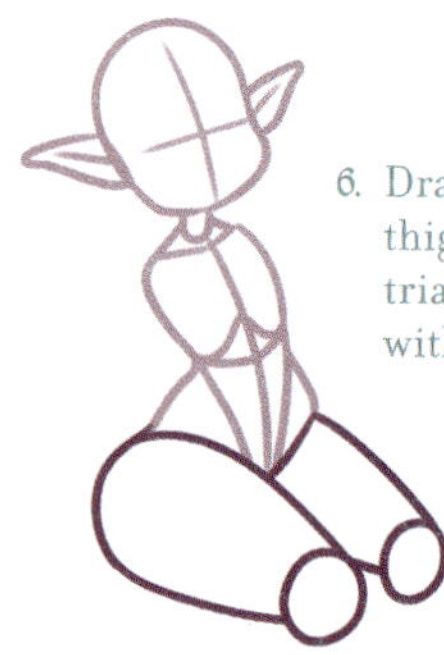

6. Draw two large oval thighs below the triangles that end with circle knees.

7. Under the thighs, sketch a rounded triangle-shaped calf. At the ankle, add the two triangles of the foot. Don't forget the partial right leg and foot.

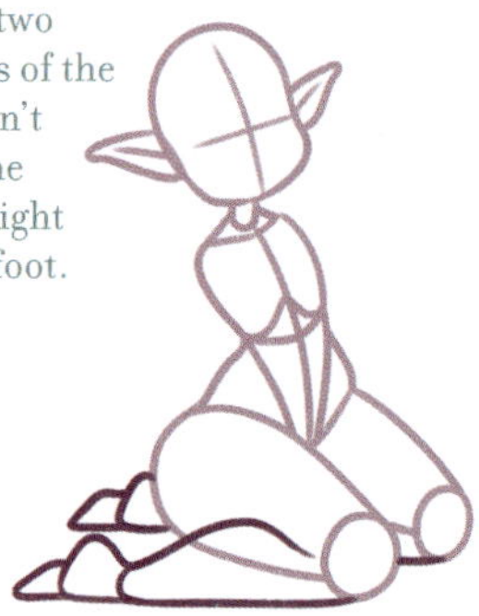

8. On the sides of the chest, draw a circle shoulder with a U connected under it.

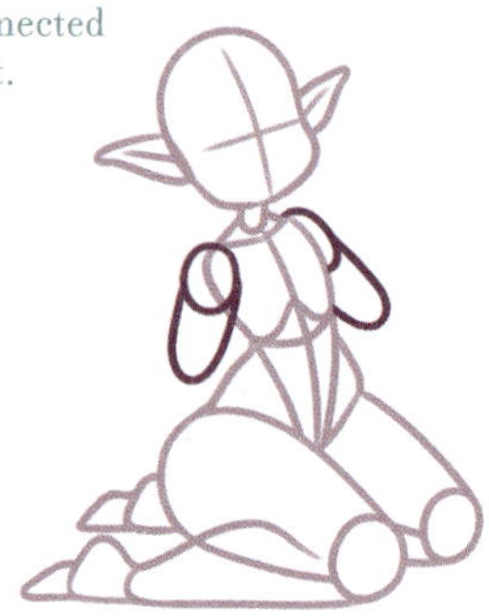

9. At the end of the arms, add two long, teardrop forearms—angle the left side slightly down with the right slightly up. At the ends, draw a flat-topped triangle.

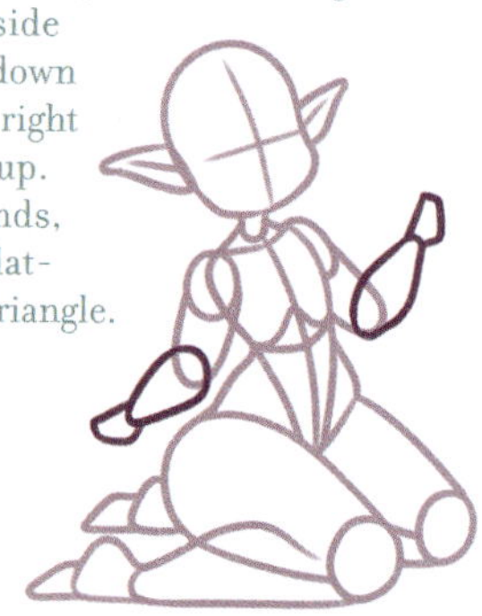

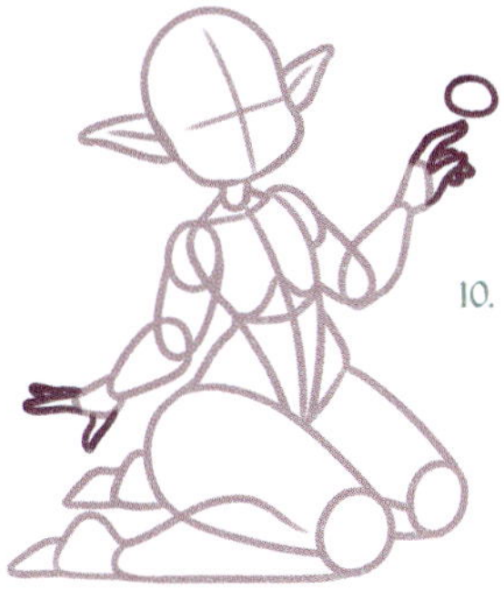

10. Sketch some fingers. Above the right hand, add a little oval for a bee.

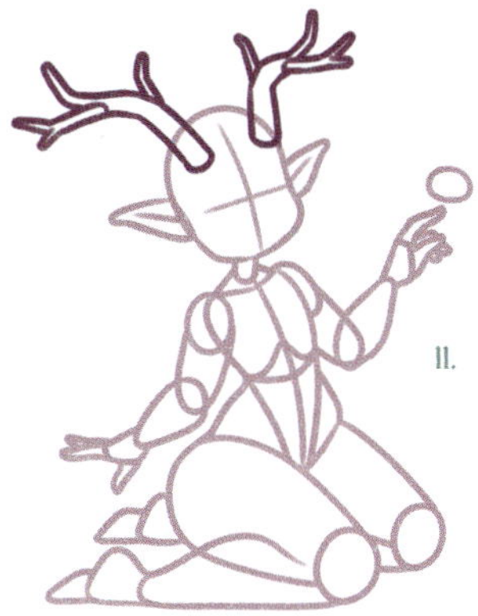

11. Sketch branch-shaped antlers coming out the top of the head. Make them relatively symmetrical.

12. Add two oval eyes with a curve around the top. Taper the line inward so it is thicker at the ends, for fuller eyelashes.

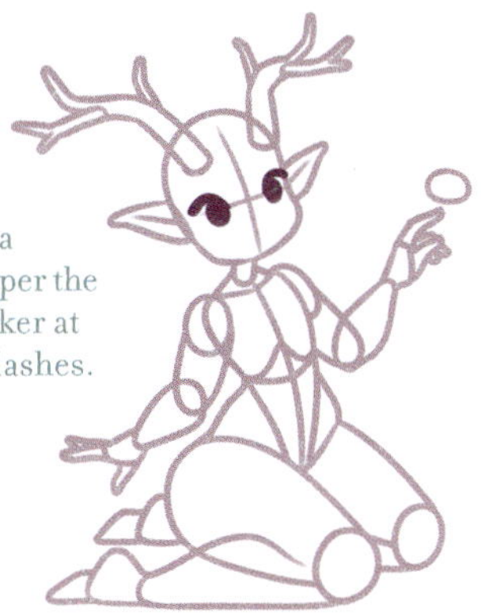

13. Draw a small oval nose with a circle mouth.

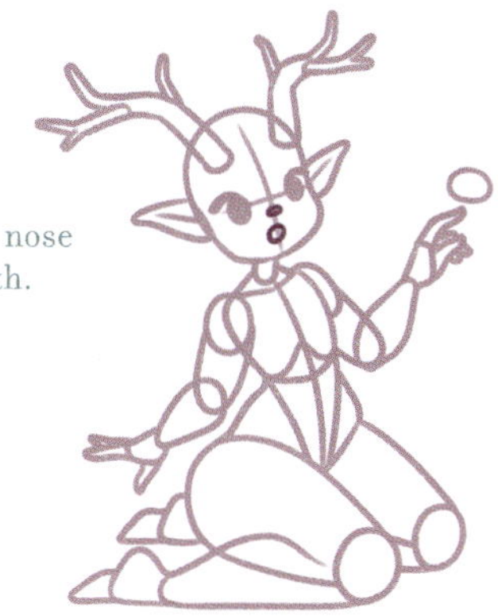

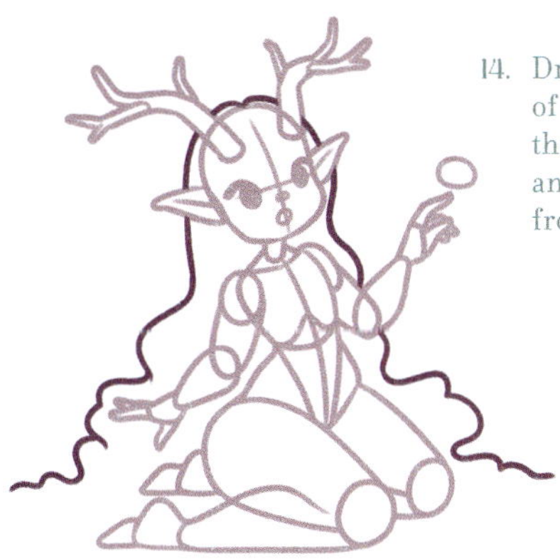

14. Draw two wavy lines of hair coming from the crown of the head and moving away from the body.

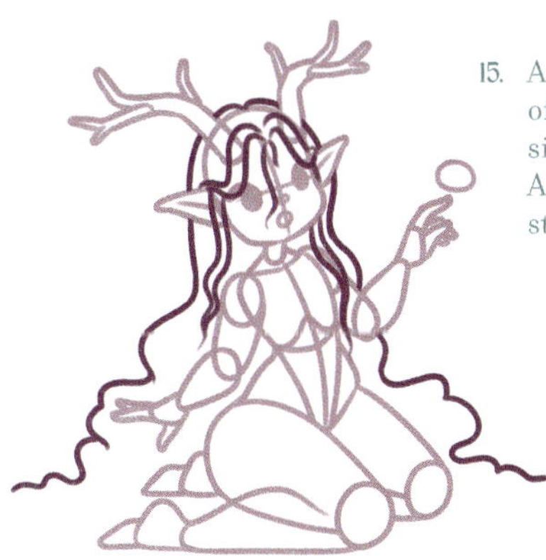

15. Add two wavy pieces of hair on both sides of the face. Add a couple of loose strands on the face.

(continued)

DRYAD

(continued)

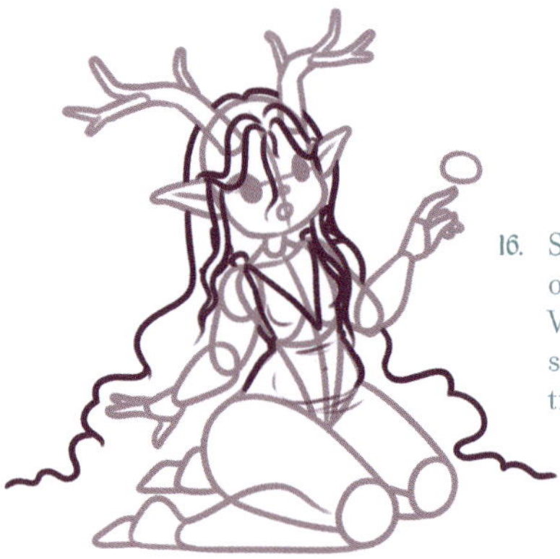

16. Sketch the top half of the dress with a V neckline. Add two small circles for the ties at the shoulders.

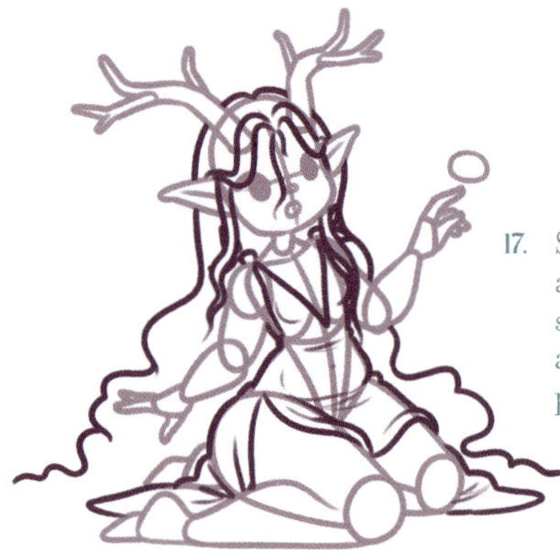

17. Sketch the skirt, adding folds where the stomach meets the legs and where the dress pools on the ground.

18. Sketch the legs and feet, but don't draw the thigh where it is hidden beneath the skirt.

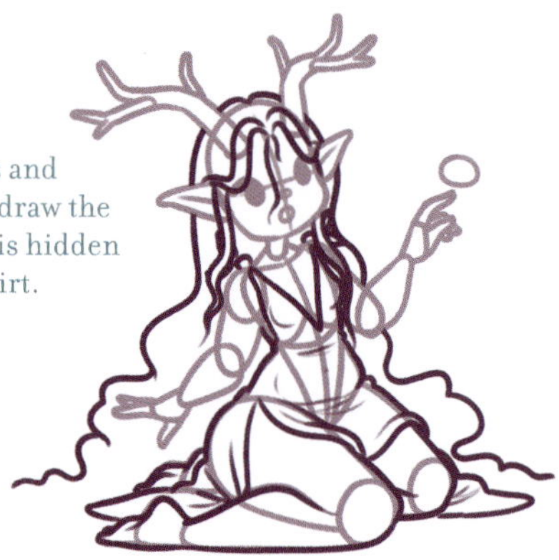

19. Sketch the arms and fingers, adding a little striped bee at the tip of the right hand with wings, an eye, two antennae, and a tiny stinger.

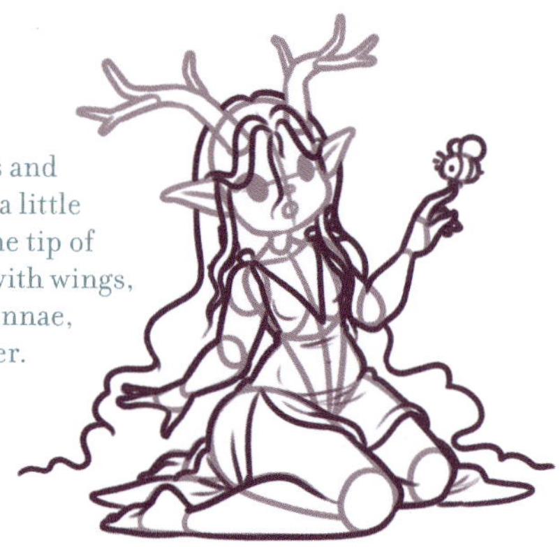

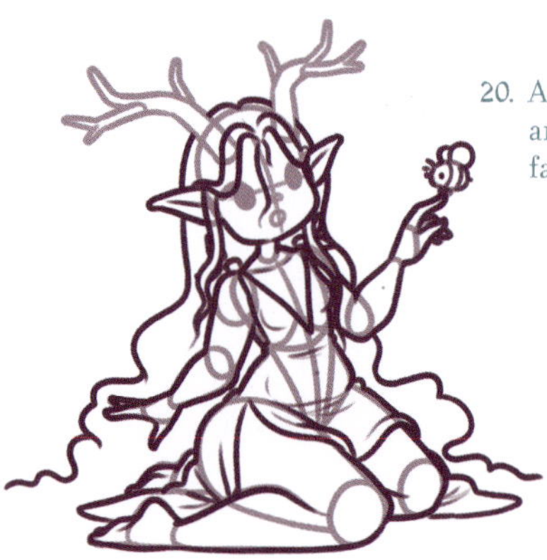

20. Add the shoulders and outline the face and ears.

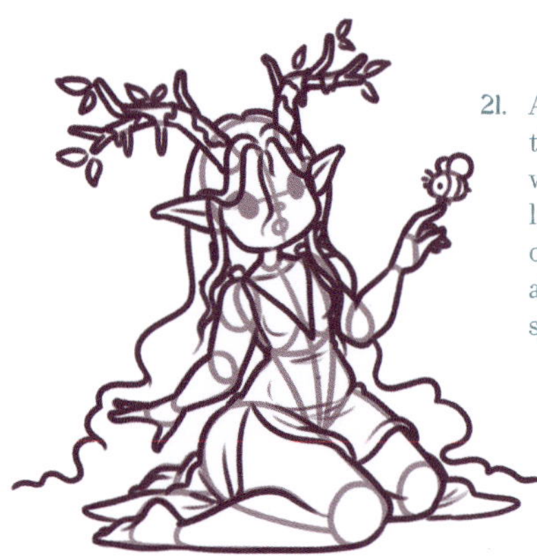

21. Add extra detail to the branch antlers, with moss and leaves hanging off. Don't worry about making it symmetrical.

22. Add leaves and flowers like they're growing out of the hair and body.

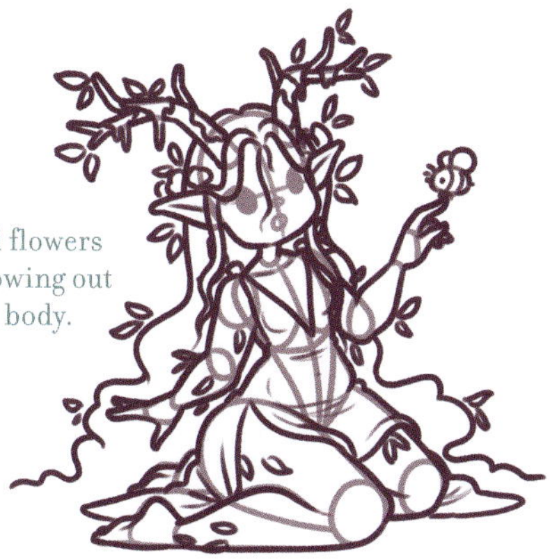

23. Sketch the face detail, including dashes of blush on the cheeks and small eyebrows.

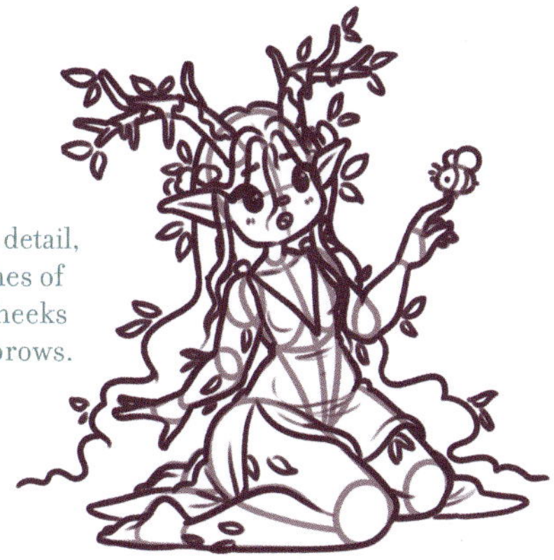

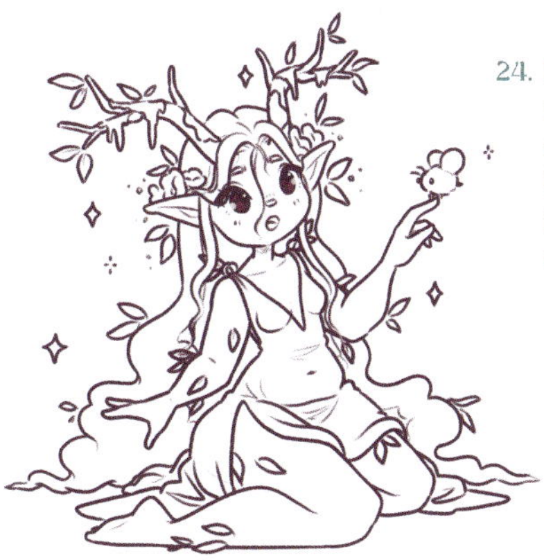

24. Neatly draw the line art over the sketch, leaving a little space inside the eyes for highlights. Add some sparkles if you'd like! Then erase the sketch underneath.

25. Time to add color! Use light green for the skin, fading to dark brown at the hands and feet. Use dark green for the dress and the hair. And, of course, yellow and black for the bumblebee.

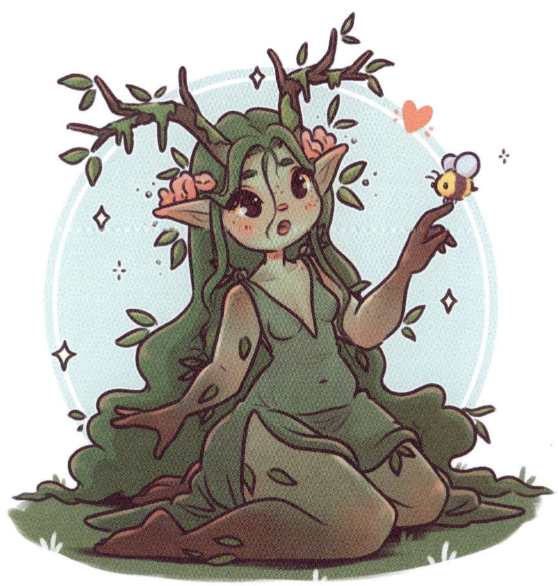

FAUN

These nature spirits are jovial creatures, many of which are talented musicians of lively woodland music.

1. Sketch an oval head with a slight dip on the left side. Add a plus sign guideline for the face.

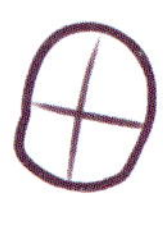

2. Add two pointed teardrop ears coming out the sides of the head with small Vs inside.

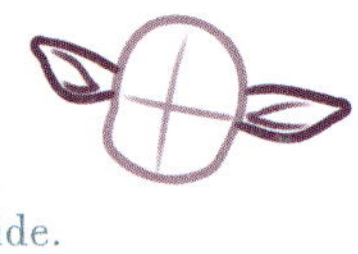

3. Add a small U neck with two thin triangles coming out the sides for the shoulders.

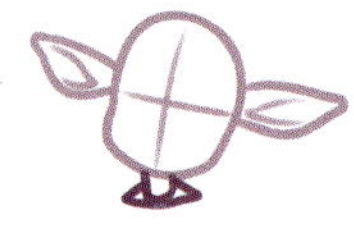

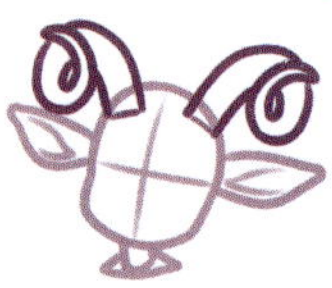

4. Add two spiral horns coming out the top of the head. Watch out where the horn overlaps itself!

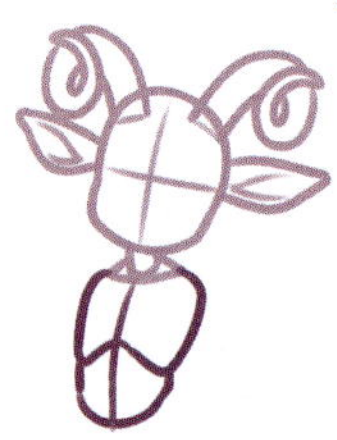

5. Draw a soft W-shaped upper body. Connect a U under the points of the W and add a guideline down the middle.

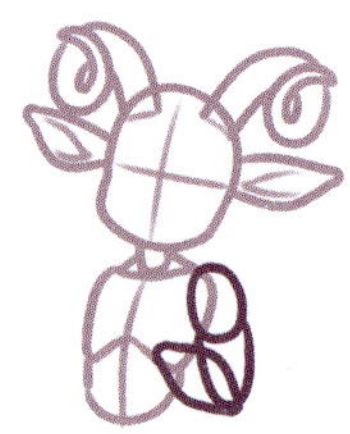

6. On the right side of the neck, draw a circle shoulder with a U upper arm. Add a rounded diamond forearm so that the arm forms a V shape.

7. Repeat step 6 on the other side. Make the left arm point away from the torso.

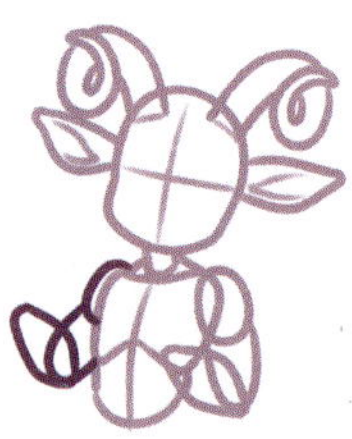

8. On the left side of the body, draw a square with a pointed corner between the head and forearm.

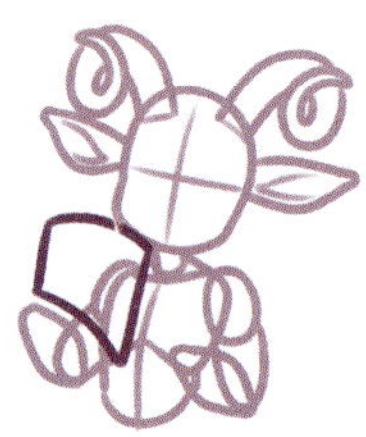

9. Connect the hands to the arms so that the fingers wrap around the square.

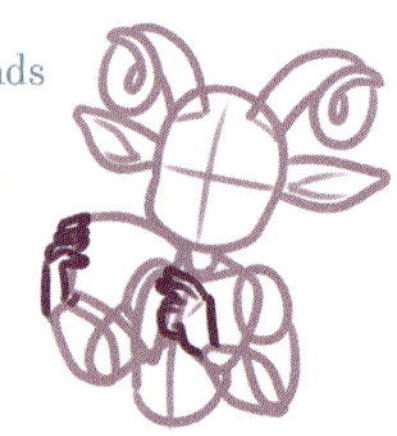

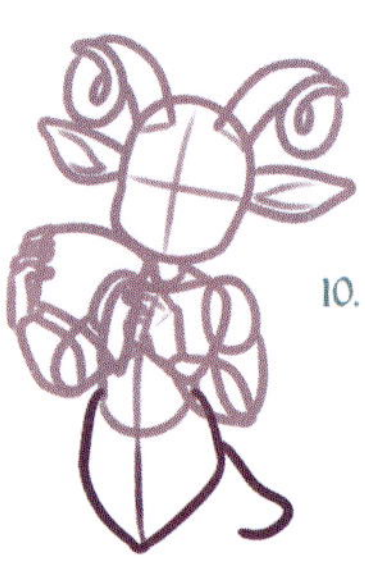

10. Under the torso, sketch a V-shaped lower body. Start the tail with a line on the bottom-right that curves at the end.

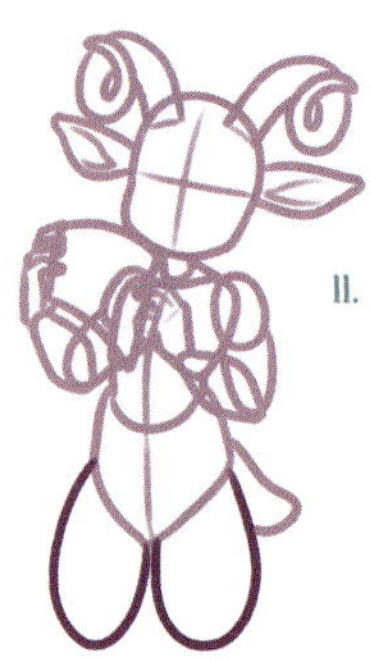

11. Draw two large U-shaped thighs on the bottom of the V.

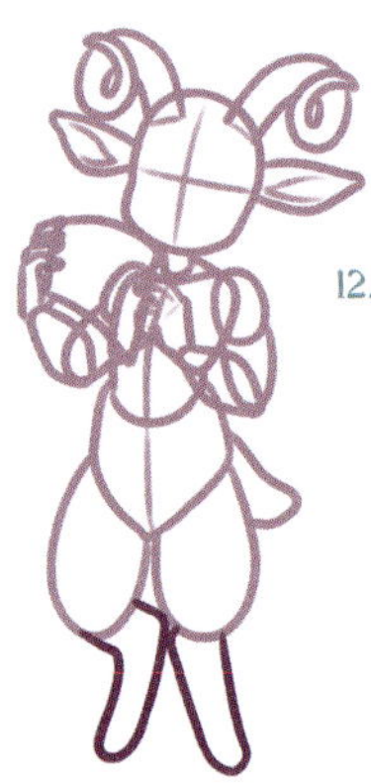

12. Draw flat-topped ovals to complete the goat legs. Remember, the legs bend slightly backwards at the knee.

13. Sketch cloven hooves at the end of each leg with a little triangle heel.

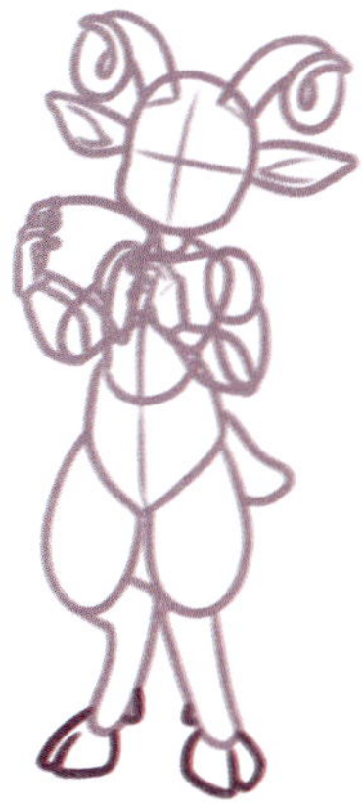

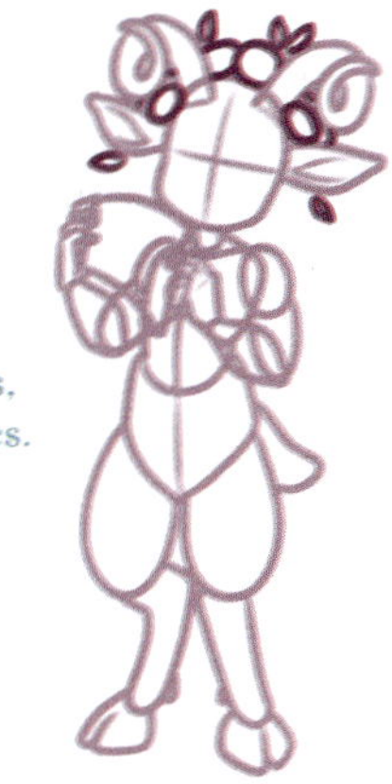

14. Around the horns and ears, add small circles and leaves.

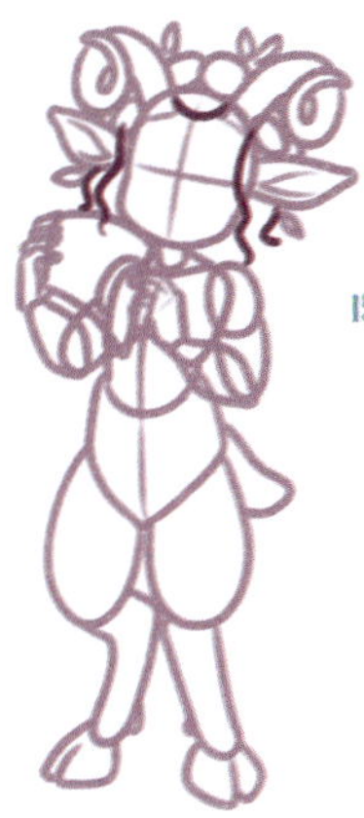

15. Add wavy strands of hair around the face and ears.

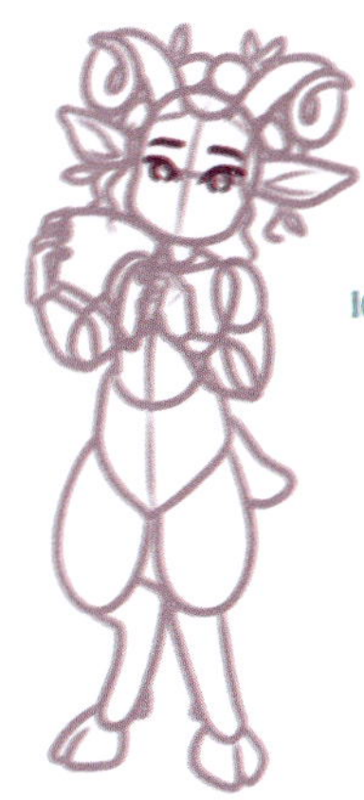

16. Sketch the eyes with a circle and a curved line around the top. Add two eyebrows above.

17. Add a small V nose and a very soft W mouth.

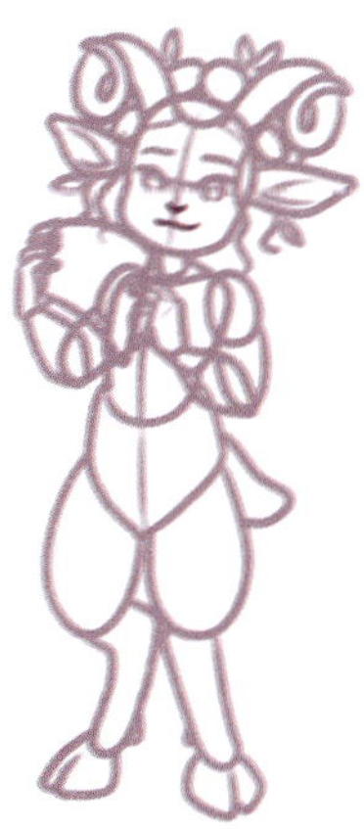

18. Add texture to the horns with lightly sketched lines.

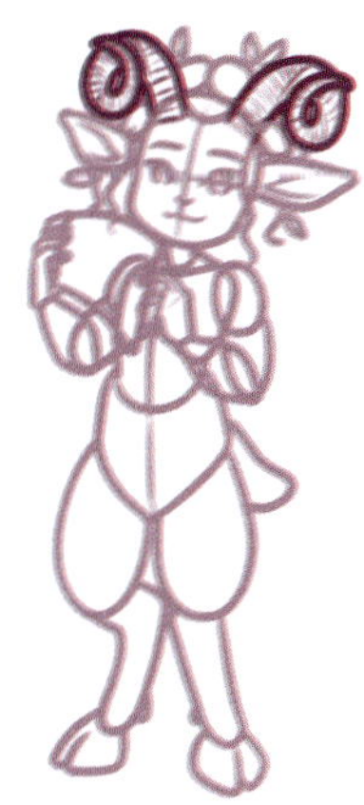

(continued)

FAUN

(continued)

19. Add the flowers and leaves to the flower crown around the horns and ears.

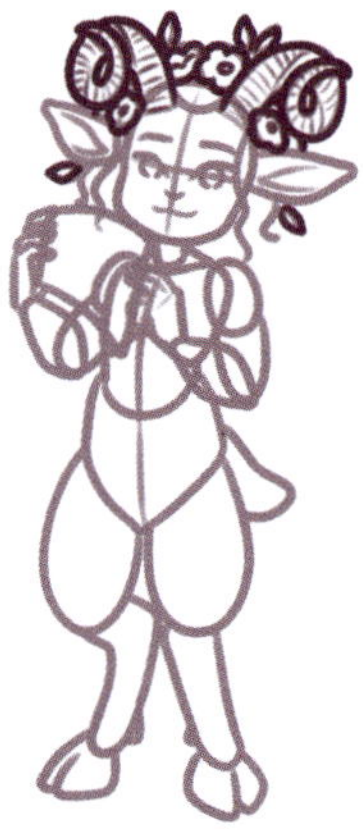

20. Sketch the strands of hair.

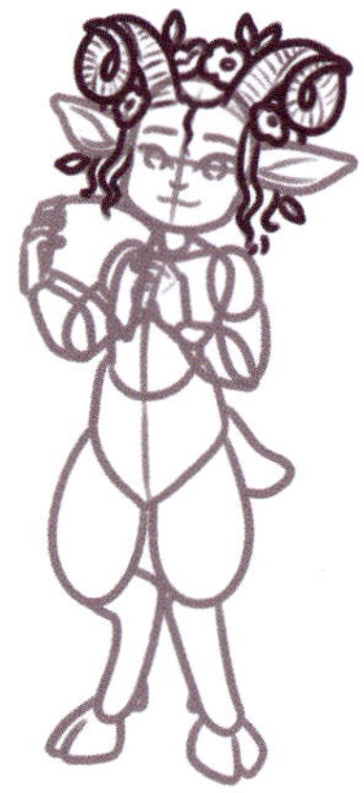

21. Sketch the outline of the face and ears. Add fluffy detail inside the ears and a hoop earring in the right ear.

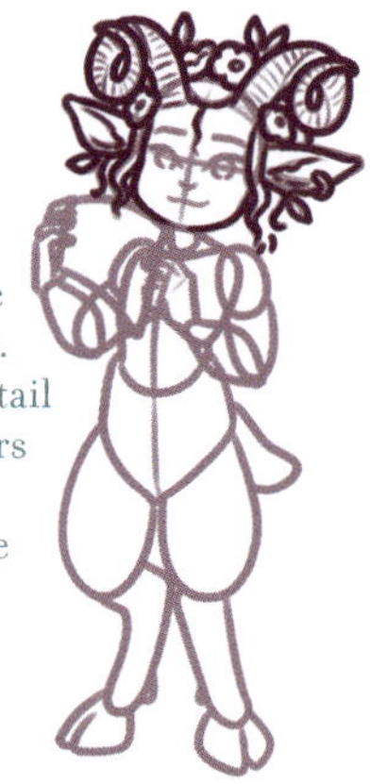

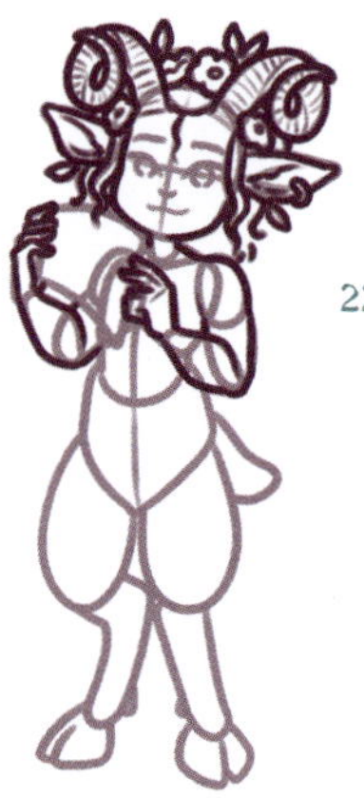

22. Sketch the arms and hands, but do not draw the left shoulder where the square overlaps it.

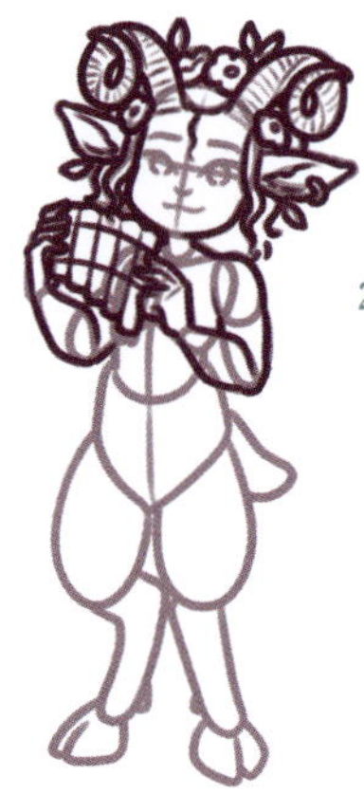

23. Sketch details on the square to make panpipes. Divide the square with repeating cylinders that get longer to the right. Draw a line across the top and bottom.

24. Sketch the abdomen and add a dot for a belly button. Then add fluffy texture to the lower body.

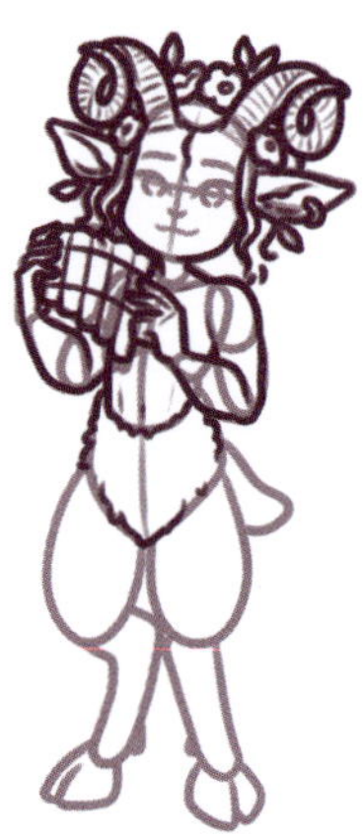

25. Sketch the tail and the thighs. Add more fluffy texture with soft M shapes.

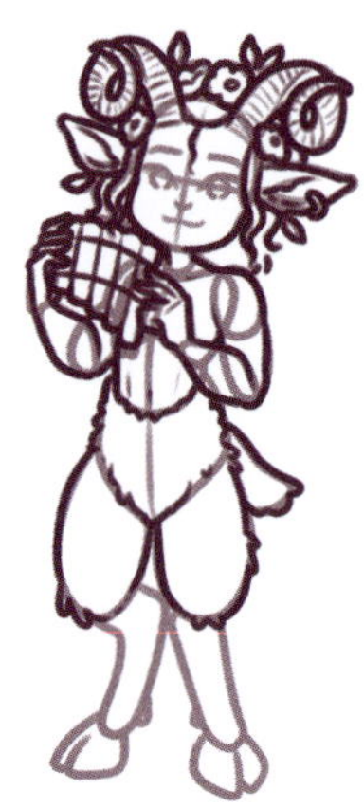

26. Sketch the lower legs and hooves. This part doesn't need to look fluffy.

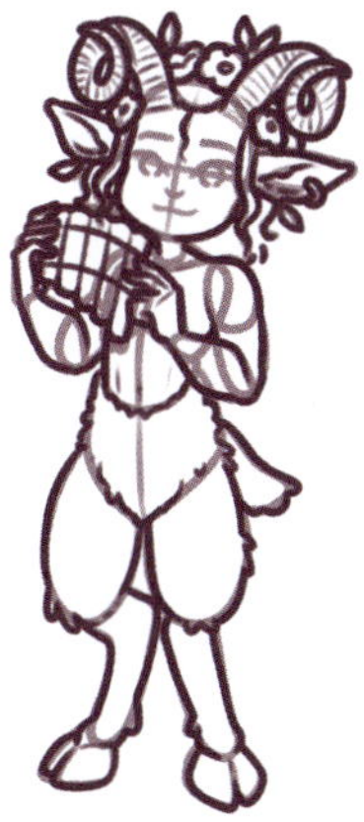

27. Sketch the face with dashes of blush on the cheeks.

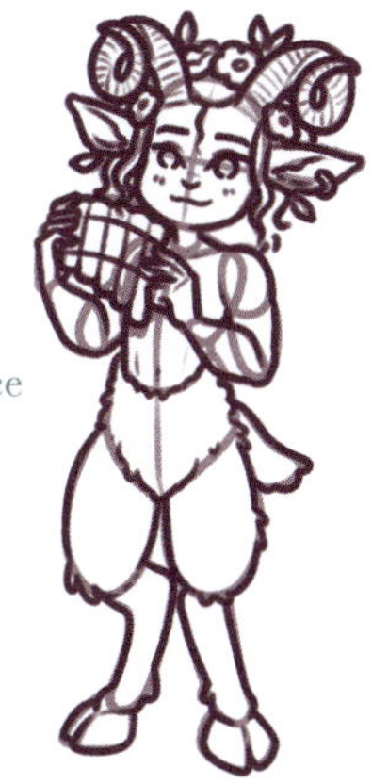

28. Add musical notes floating around the panpipes!

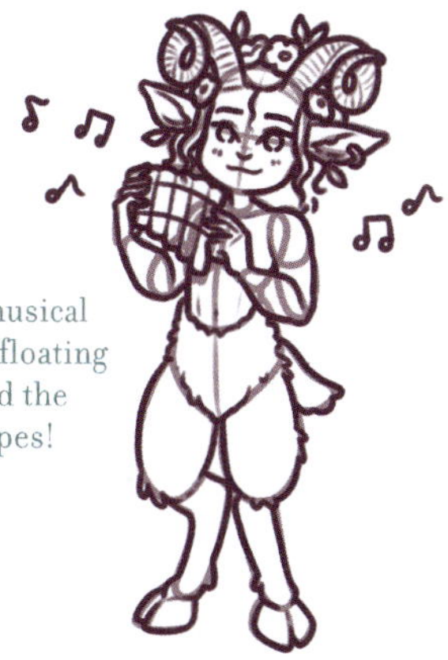

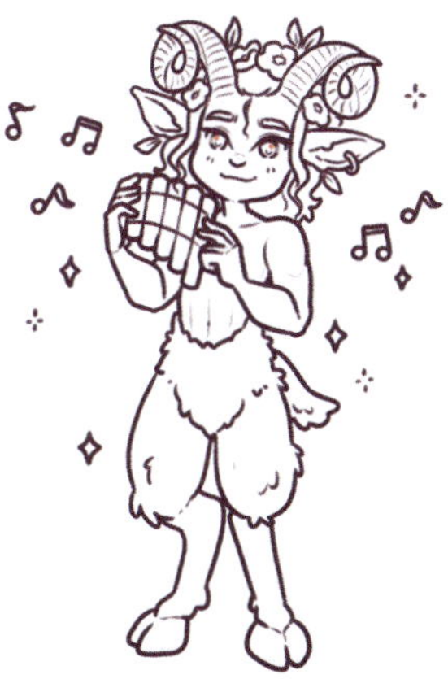

29. Neatly draw the line art over the sketch, adding white dots in the eyes for highlights. Add some sparkles if you'd like! Then erase the sketch underneath.

30. Last step: the color! You can give them any skin tone; I went with olive-toned skin, green eyes, and brown hair and fur. I also added a small patch of grass to stand on.

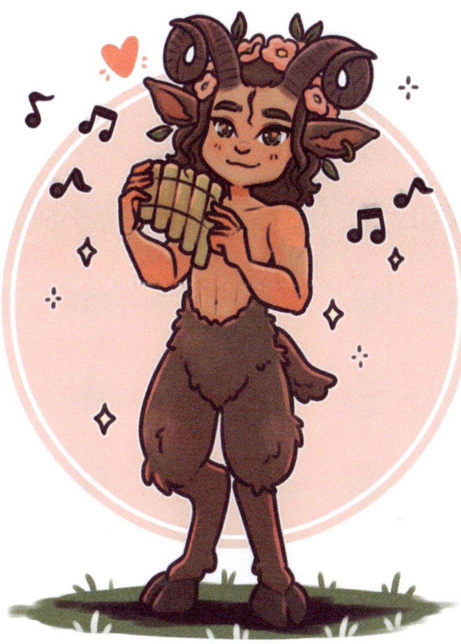

NAGA

Skilled in camouflage, nagas can embody both forms of a fully fledged human and a large serpent, but sometimes they appear as a hybrid of the two.

1. Sketch an oval head with a slight dip on the right side. Add a plus sign guideline for the face.

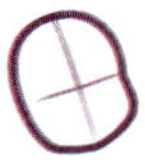

2. Add a small U neck with two thin triangles coming out the sides.

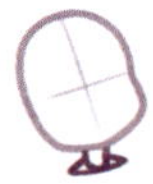

3. Draw a soft W-shaped upper body with a curved guideline down the middle.

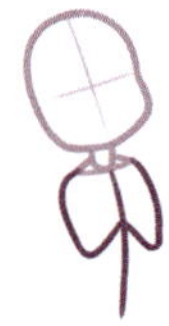

4. Complete the torso so that it makes a wide diamond. Below, connect a V shape that is a little wider.

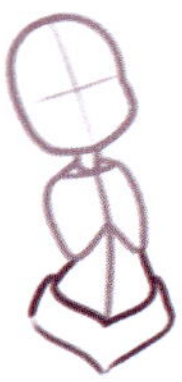

5. Draw a large U lower body. Then add a long oval coming off the bottom-left of the body.

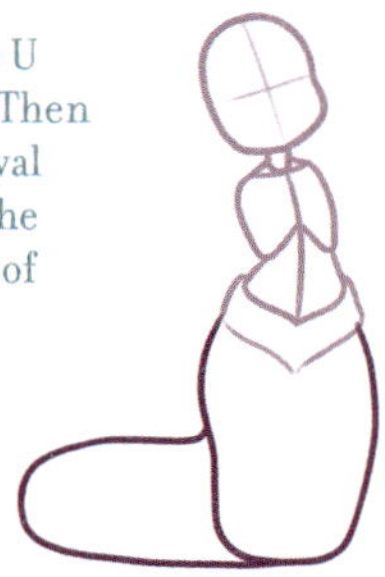

6. Finish the curvy tail so that it passes through the body and curls upwards.

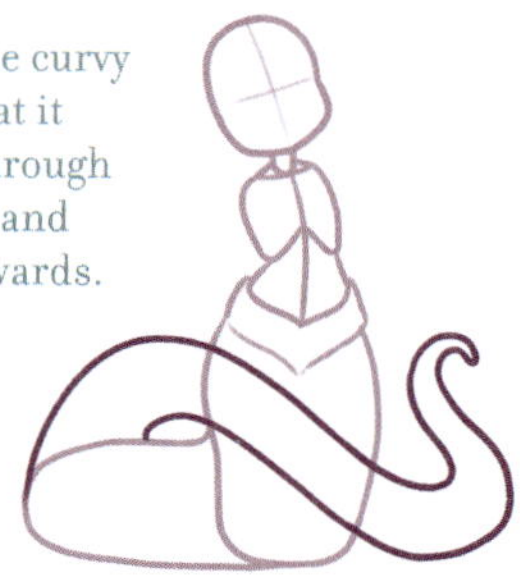

7. Draw two circles for shoulders with U upper arms.

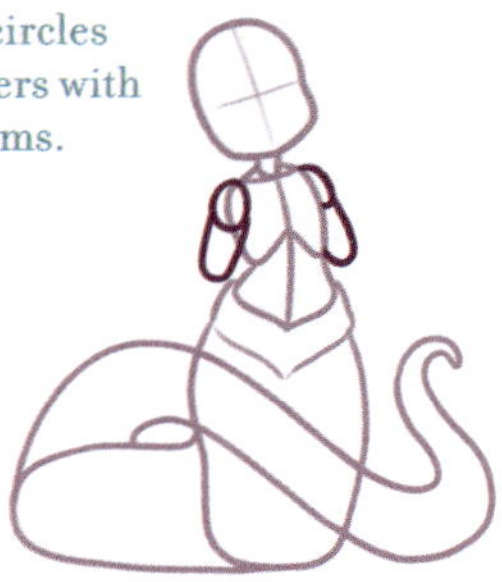

8. Add teardrop forearms, each with a triangle at the ends. Have the tips aimed away from the body.

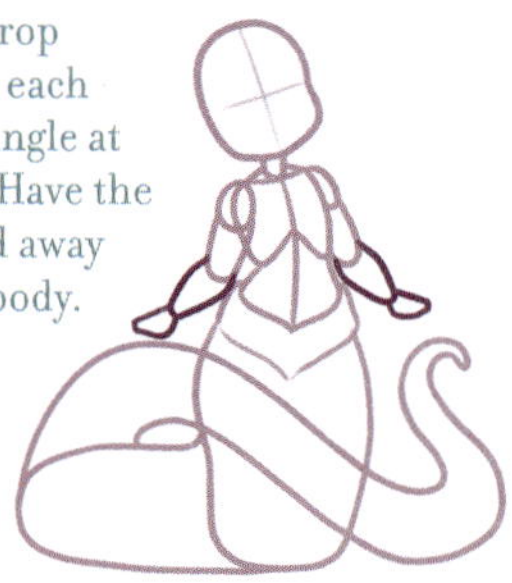

9. Draw fingers on each hand.

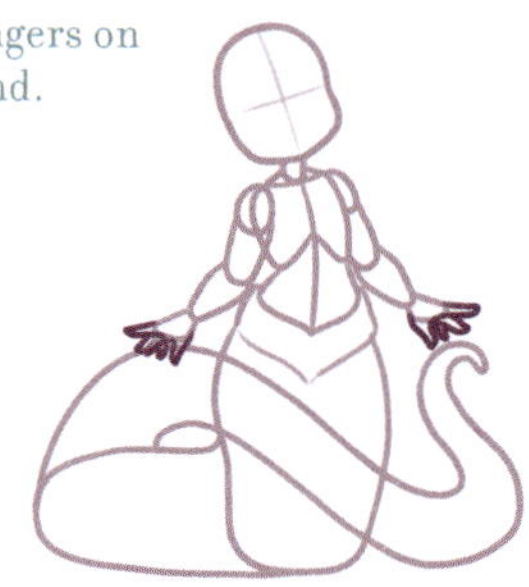

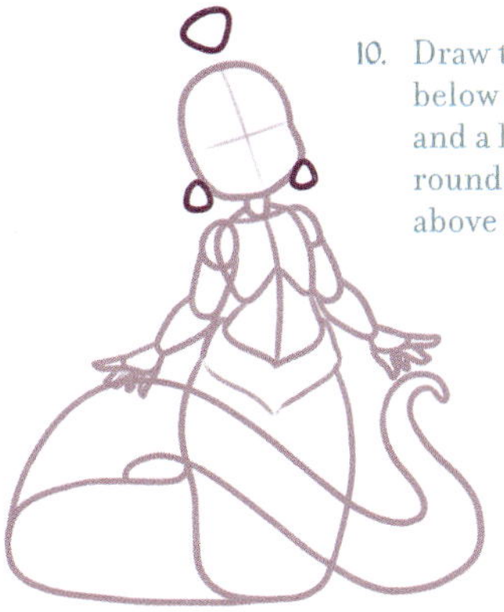

10. Draw two rounded triangles below the sides of the head, and a larger upside down rounded triangle slightly above the head.

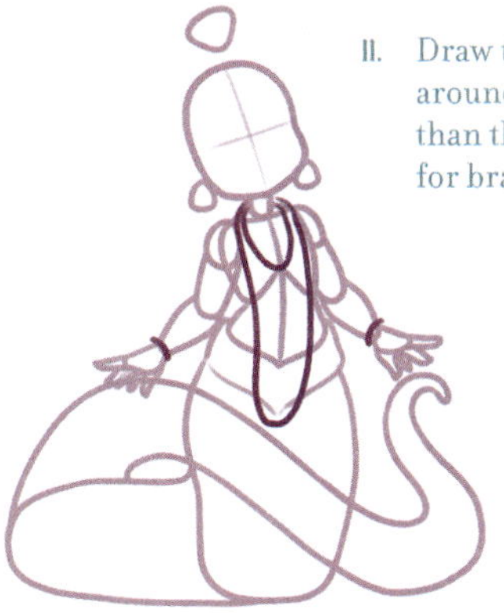

11. Draw two looped necklaces around the neck, one shorter than the other. Add two lines for bracelets at the wrists.

12. Sketch the eyes with a circle and a curved line around the top. Add two curved eyebrows.

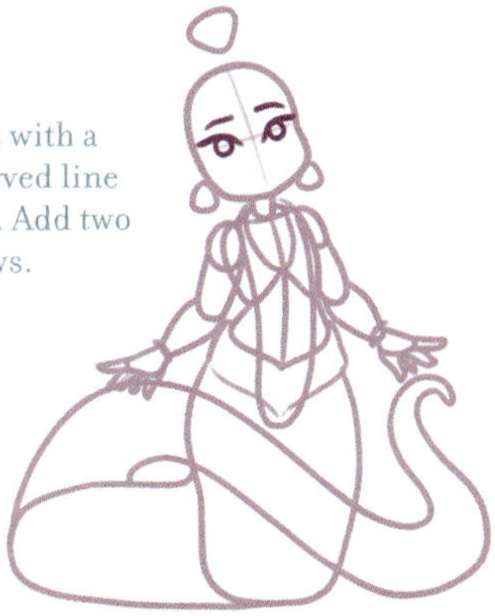

13. Draw a small oval nose and an almost flat W mouth.

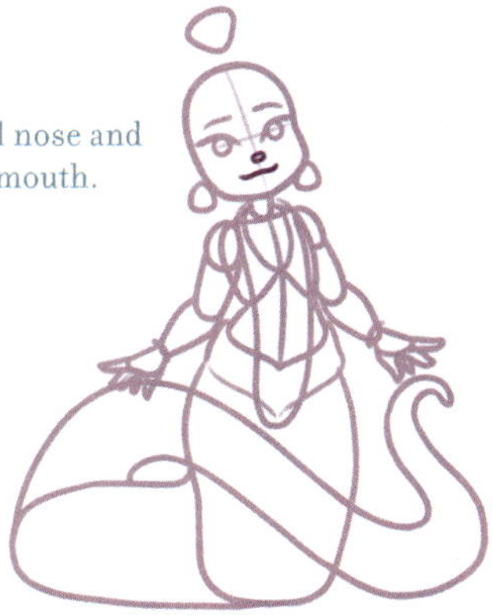

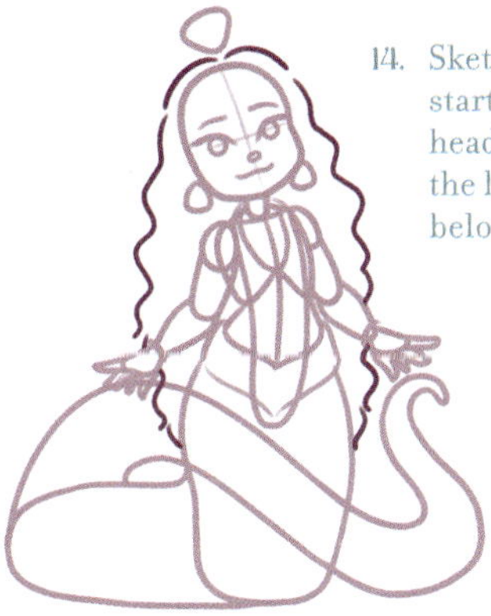

14. Sketch two wavy lines of hair starting at the crown of the head and flowing down to the lower body. Leave a space below the large triangle.

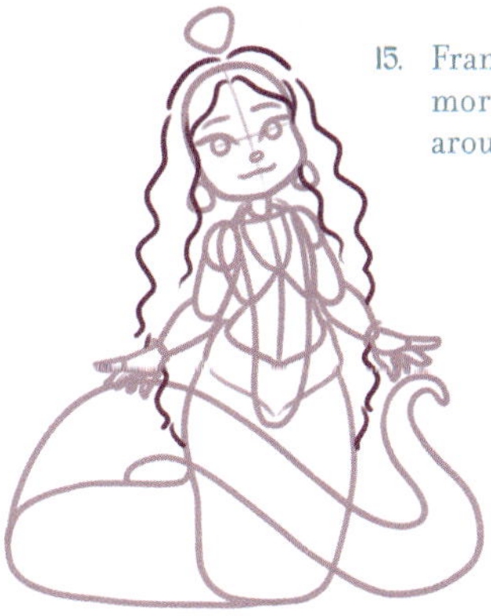

15. Frame the face with two more strands of hair around the shoulders.

(continued)

NAGA

(continued)

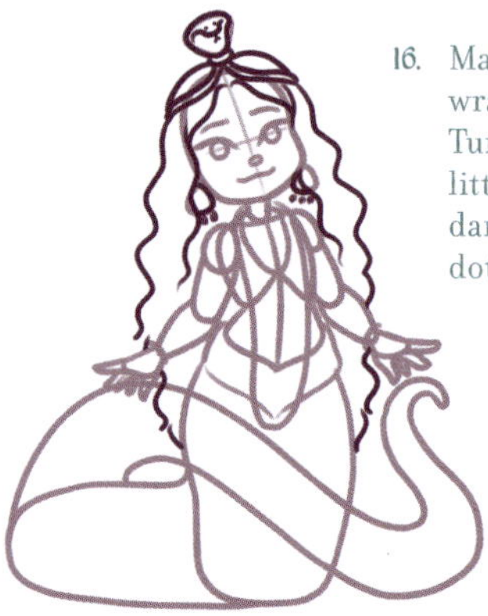

16. Make a headdress with lines wrapping around the head. Turn the top triangle into a little cobra head. Add two dangling earrings with tiny dots for beads.

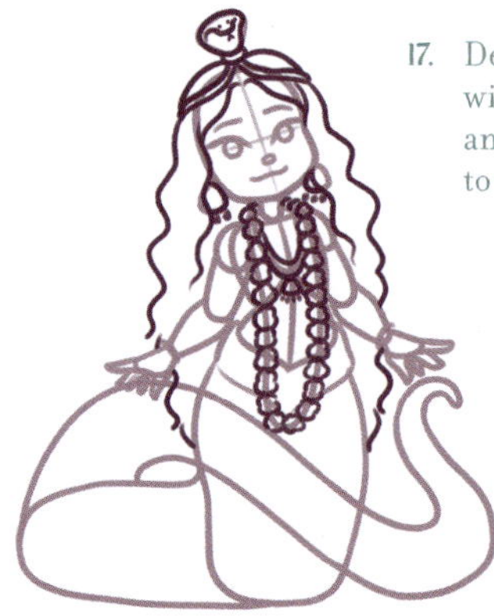

17. Decorate the longer necklace with circles. Add another line and a matching round triangle to the shorter necklace.

18. Add small circles to the bracelets and a flower on top of the hands.

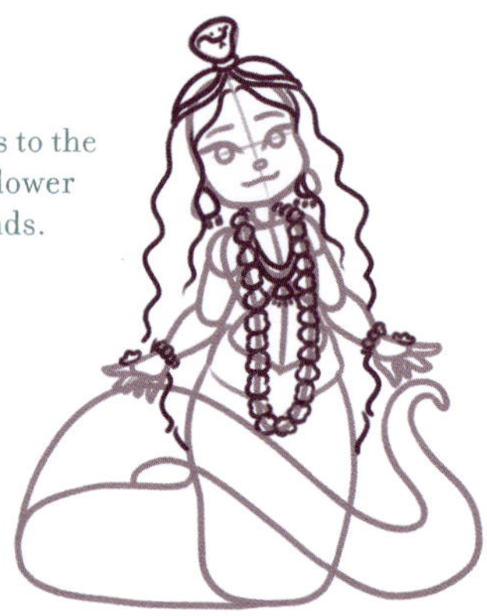

19. Outline the face. Draw the sleeves just above the elbows and cut the shirt off at the midriff.

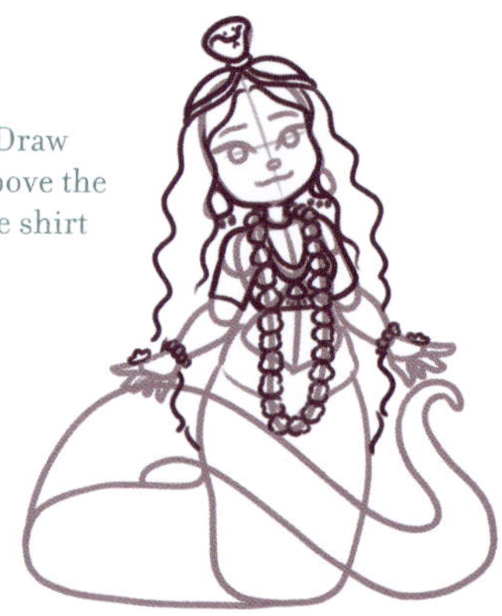

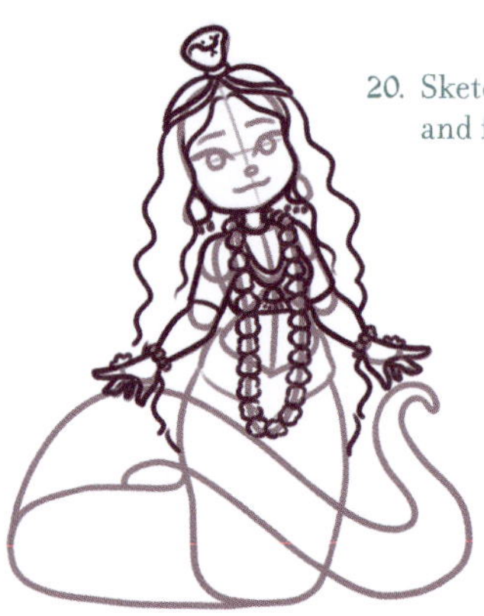

20. Sketch the arms and fingers.

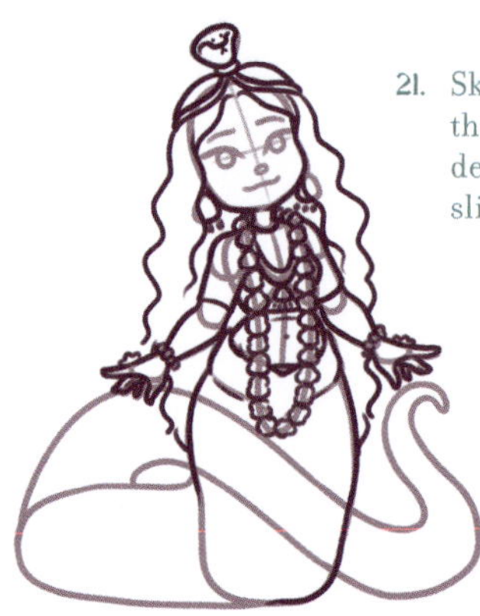

21. Sketch where the body meets the snake tail, adding a little detail where the stomach slightly overlaps.

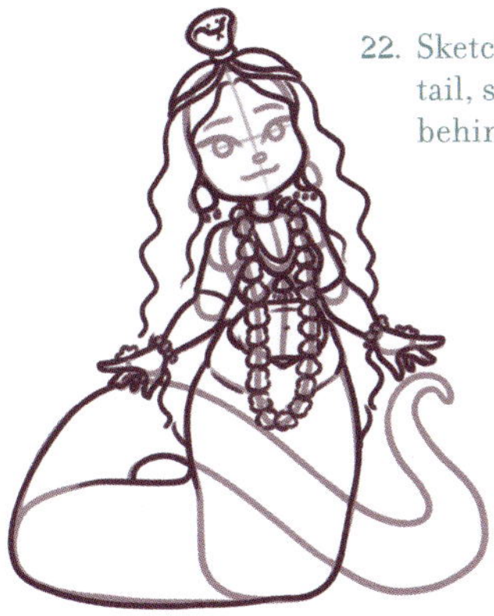

22. Sketch the left side of the tail, stopping where it passes behind the hair and body.

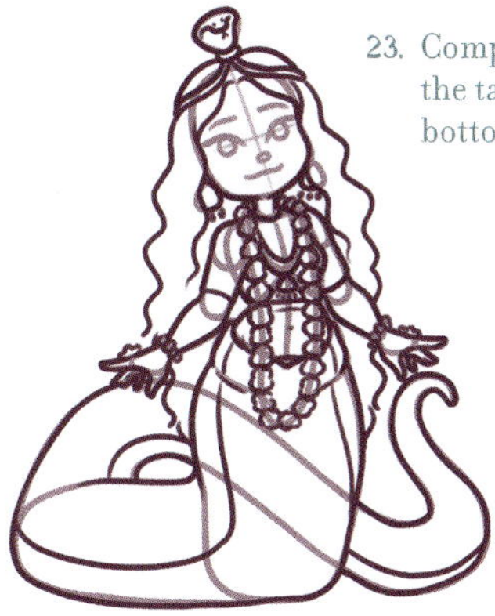

23. Complete the right side of the tail, adding a line along the bottom for the underbelly.

24. Sketch the face detail, adding dashes of blush on the cheeks.

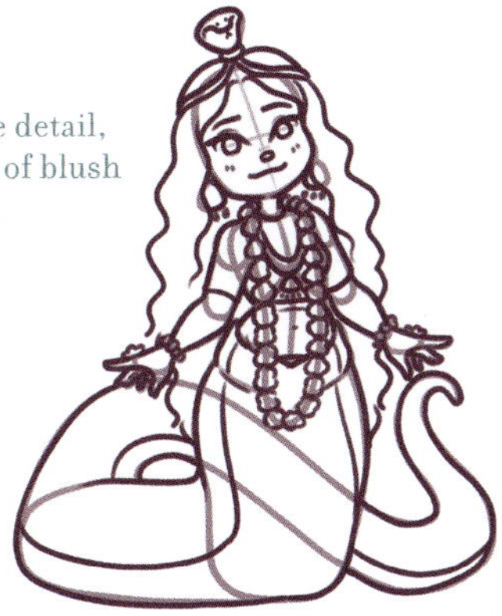

25. Neatly draw the line art over the sketch, adding little white dots in the eyes for highlights. Add some sparkles if you'd like! Then erase the sketch underneath.

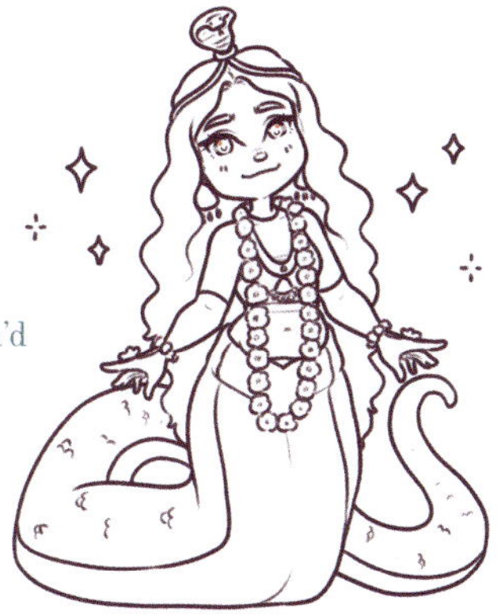

26. Finally, add color! Use gold for the jewelry and orange for the shirt. I chose a green snake tail with a pale green underbelly.

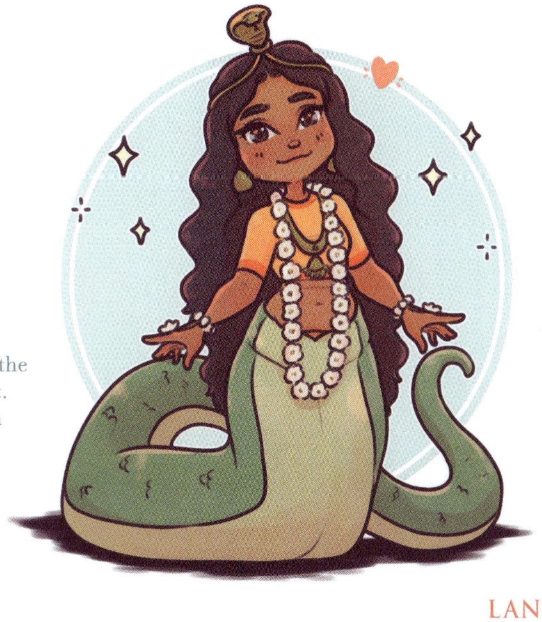

CENTAUR

In Greek mythology, centaurs are known to be wild, passionate characters who live in the forests of Thessaly.

1. Lightly sketch a circle head with a dip on the right side. Add a plus sign guideline for the face.

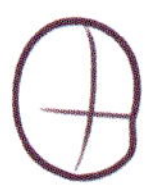

2. Add a small U neck with two thin triangles coming out the sides.

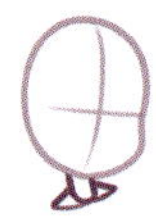

3. Draw a W-shaped torso with a curve connecting the tips of the W. Add a guideline down the middle of the body.

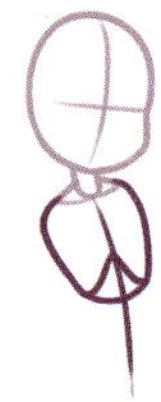

4. Draw two upside down Vs on either side of the guideline.

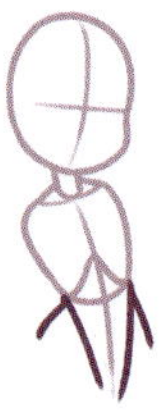

5. Add two curved Vs, one on top of the other, underneath.

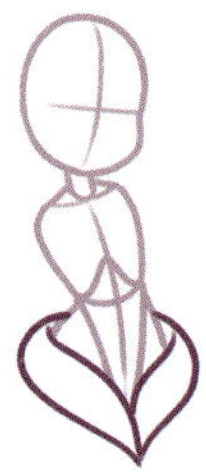

6. Under the left side of the V draw a U. Add a curve to the left and right, making the right slightly pointed.

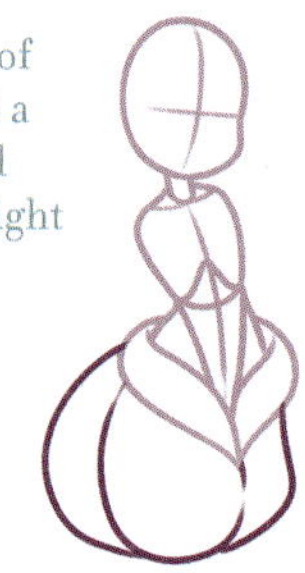

7. Draw an oval to the left with two curves connecting them together.

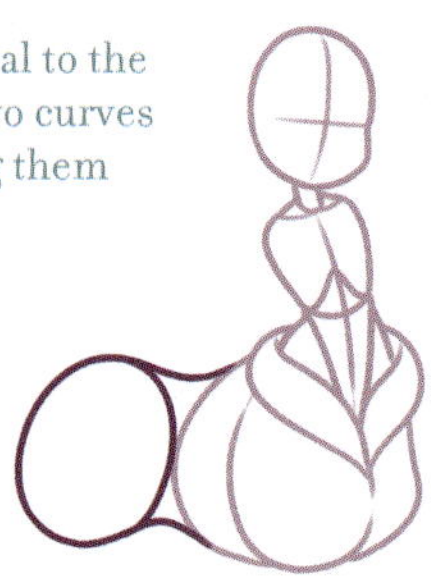

8. Draw two ovals onto the oval and the U, with the back one slightly larger.

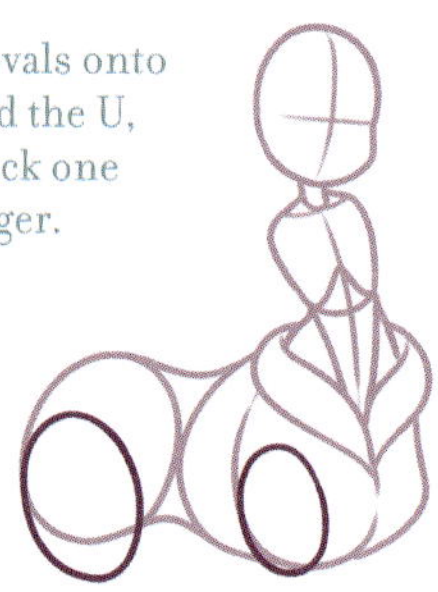

9. Below the front of the body, draw two small circles. Connect the circles to the body with two lines.

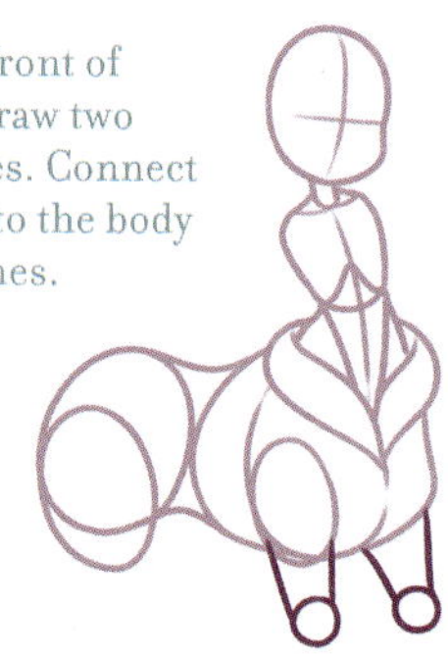

10. Add a circle below the left circle and two connecting lines. Then draw a circle slightly to the left of the right circle. Connect with two lines.

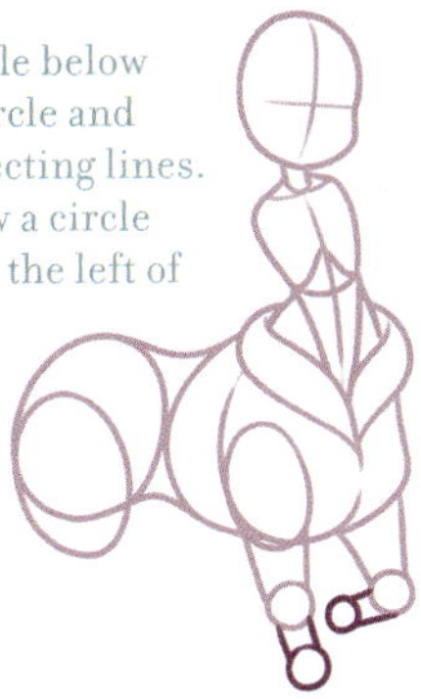

11. Draw triangle hooves below the circles with the right one slightly hidden by the left leg.

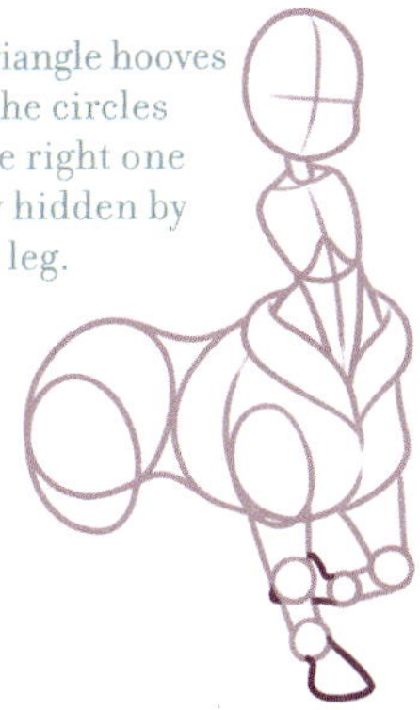

12. Start the back legs with two circles to the left and right of the oval and two connecting Us.

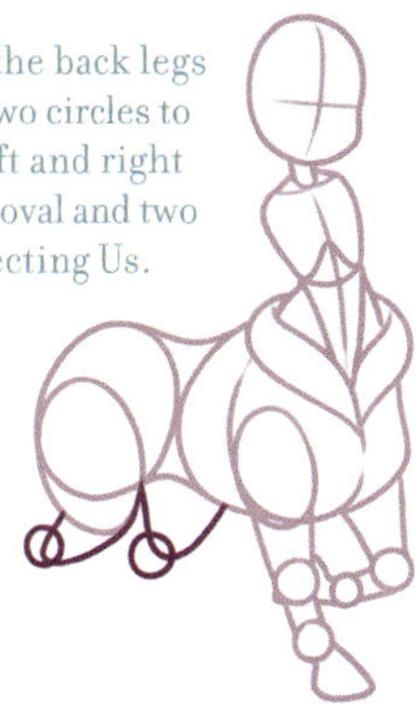

13. Draw two more circles beneath the last two with two lines each connecting them to the top of the legs.

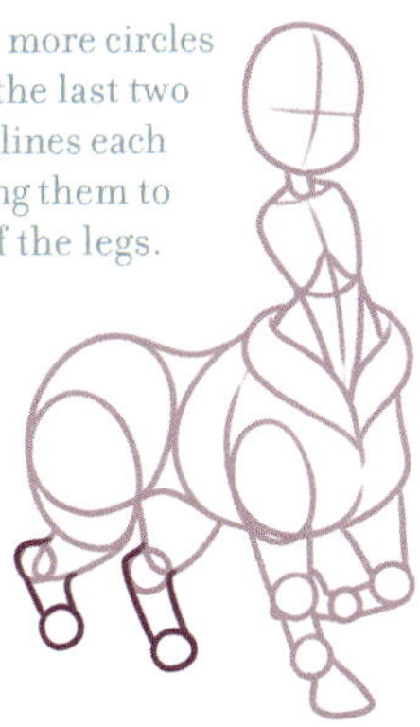

14. Below the back right leg, draw the triangle hoof flat on the ground with the left leg lifted at an angle.

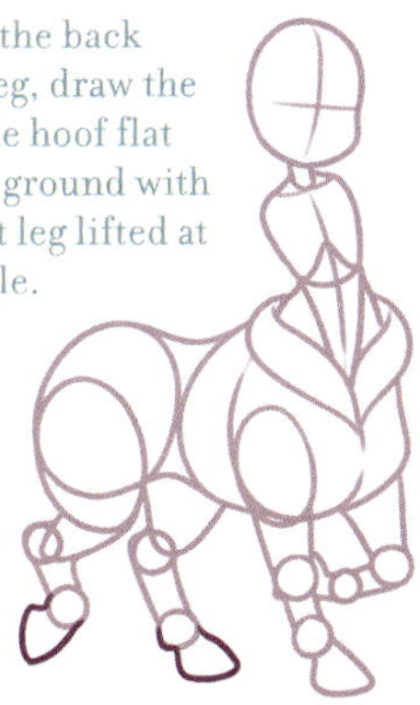

15. Draw two circle shoulders with two oval upper arms.

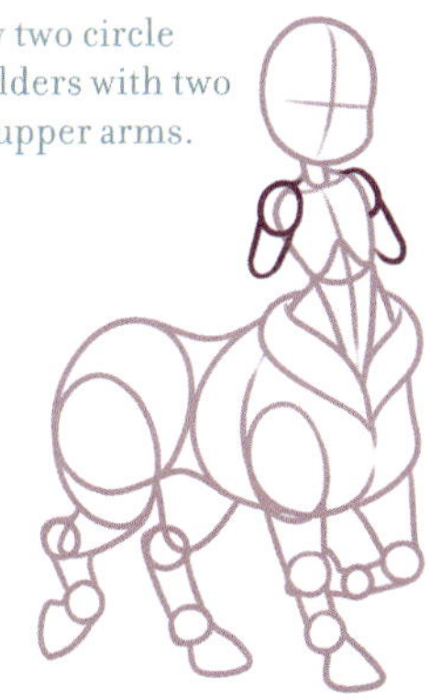

16. Add two teardrop forearms below with two smaller teardrops coming out of the ends.

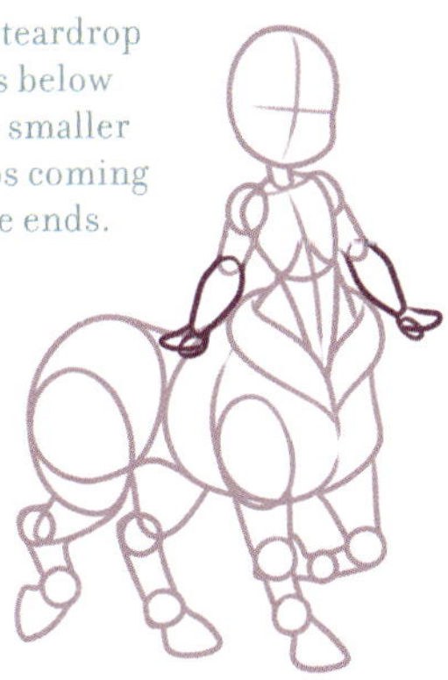

17. Add the fingers to the teardrop-shaped hands.

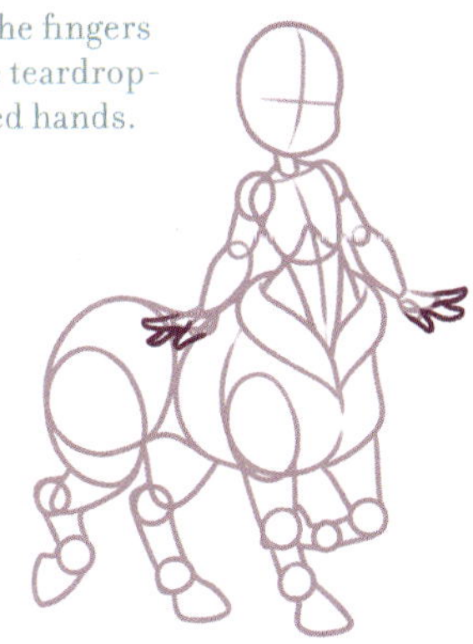

18. Draw two pointed ears coming out the sides of the head with a curved line inside each.

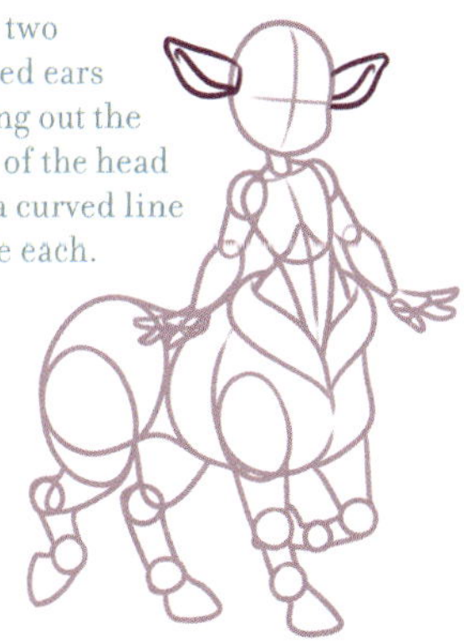

(continued)

CENTAUR

(continued)

19. Add the eyes with two ovals and a curved line around the top.

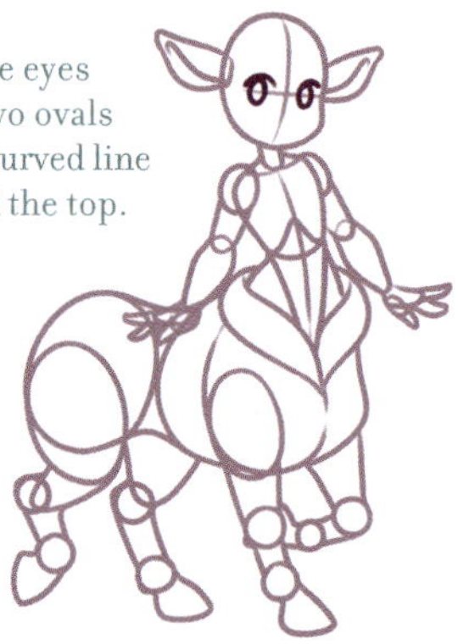

20. Draw a small oval nose and a curved mouth.

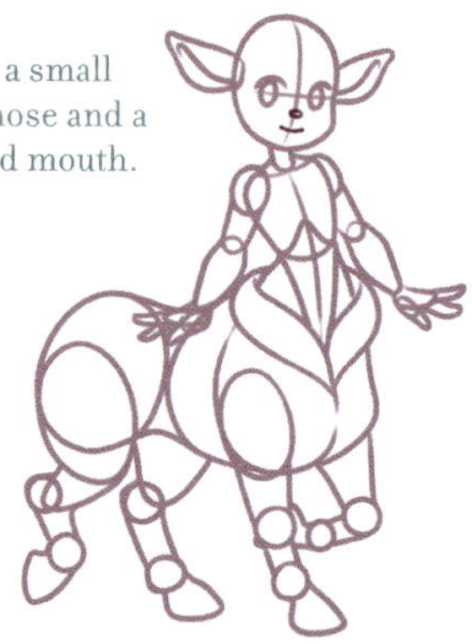

21. Add two wavy strands of hair going from the crown of the head down to the hands.

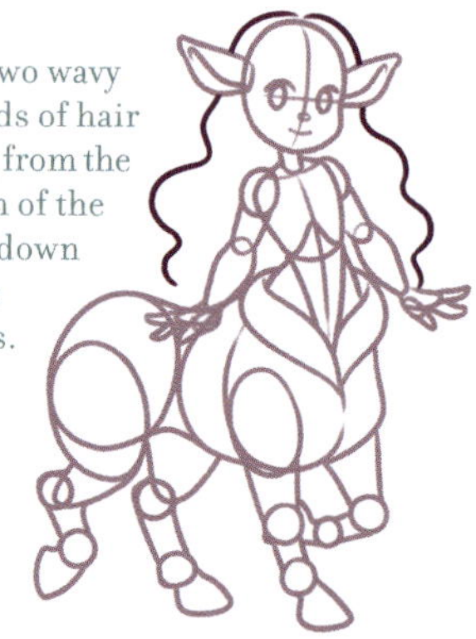

22. Add two more wavy strands of hair going down from the crown of the head, then around the ears and down to the shoulders.

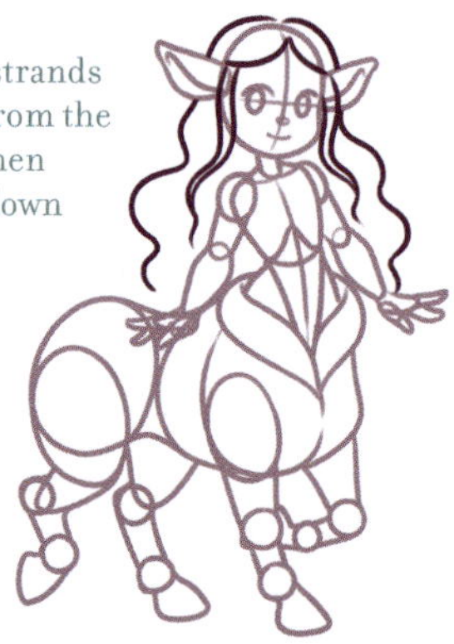

23. Make the tail with a wavy shape and a curved point at the back of the horse body.

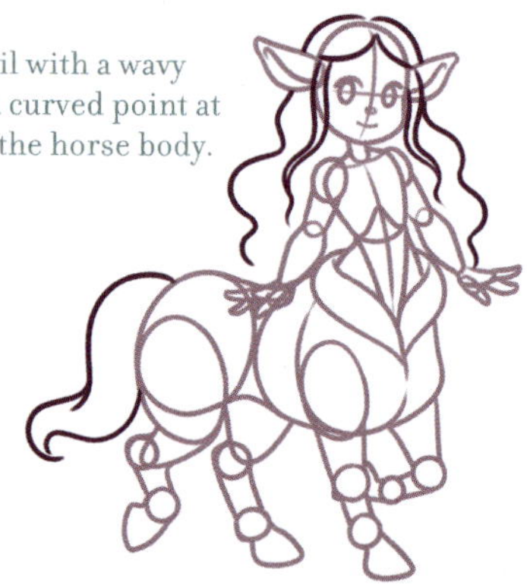

24. Lightly draw the ears, head, and neck. Add some curves to the chest.

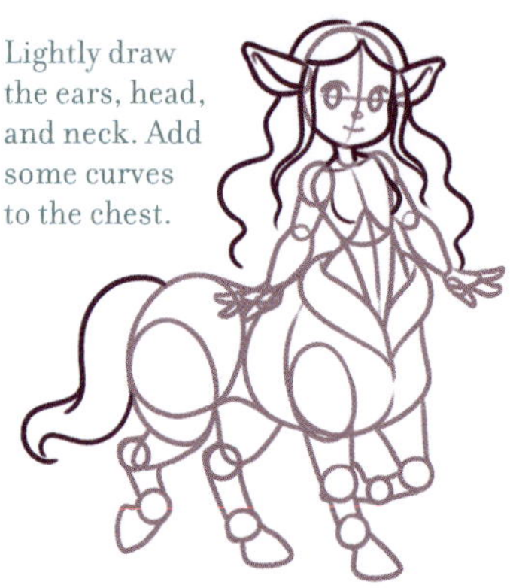

25. Sketch the arms and hands and add a belly button.

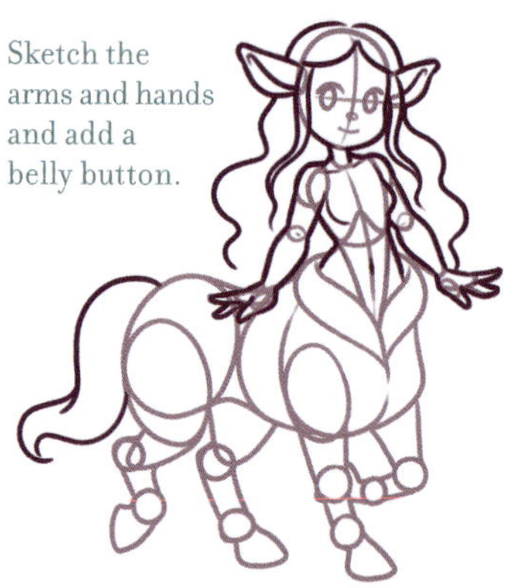

26. Go over the face, adding dashes of blush on the cheeks.

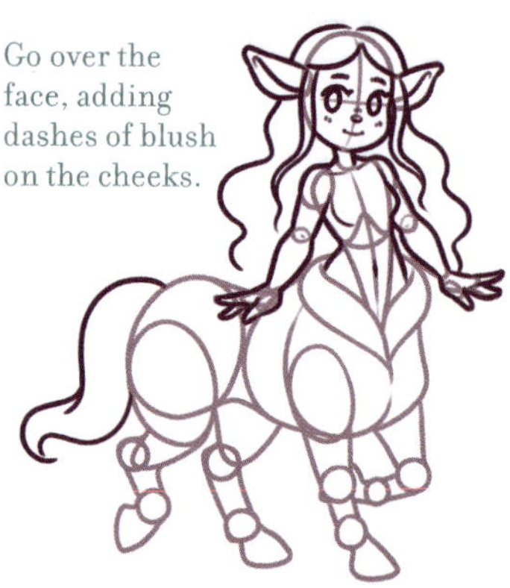

27. Go over the body of the horse with fluffy details.

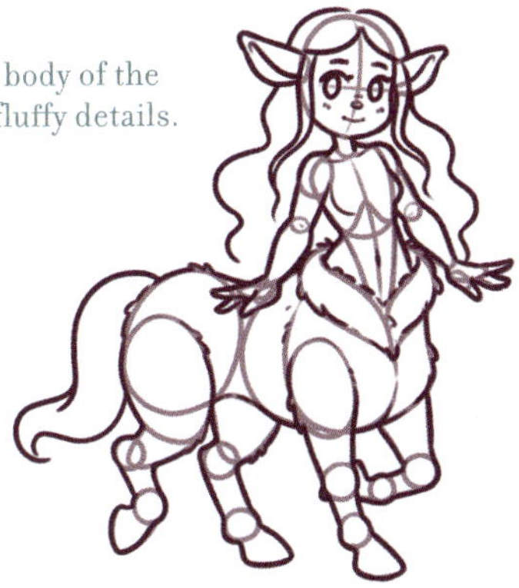

28. Add two curved lines on the torso for a bandeau top. Then add a line to the hooves to separate it from the rest of the leg.

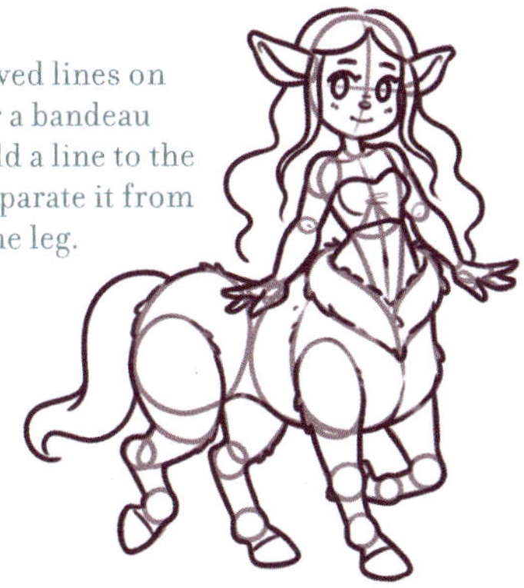

29. Neatly draw the line art over the sketch, leaving a little space in the eyes for highlights. Add two Us for the pupils and some sparkles if you'd like! Then erase the sketch underneath.

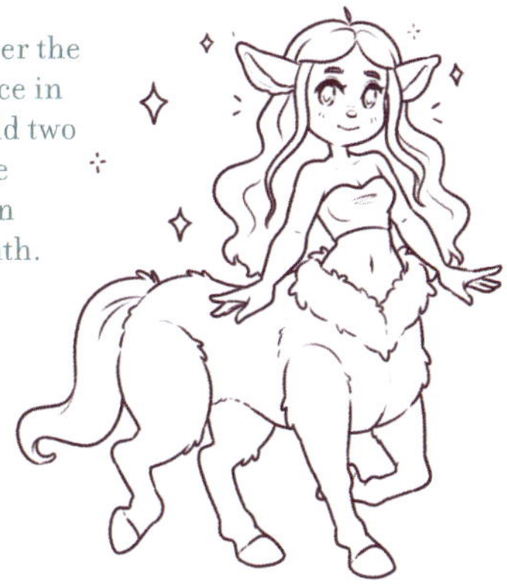

30. Finish up with color! I went with a brown color scheme: a mid-brown for the horse body with a dark brown tail, hair, and hooves, then a mid-toned skin with brown eyes, and of course a little bit of pink for the cheeks.

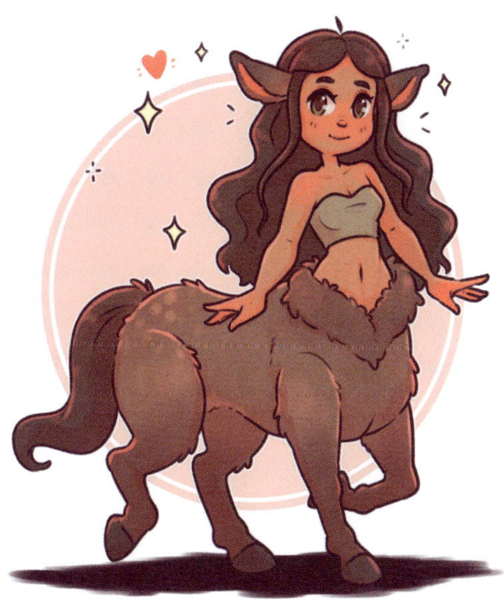

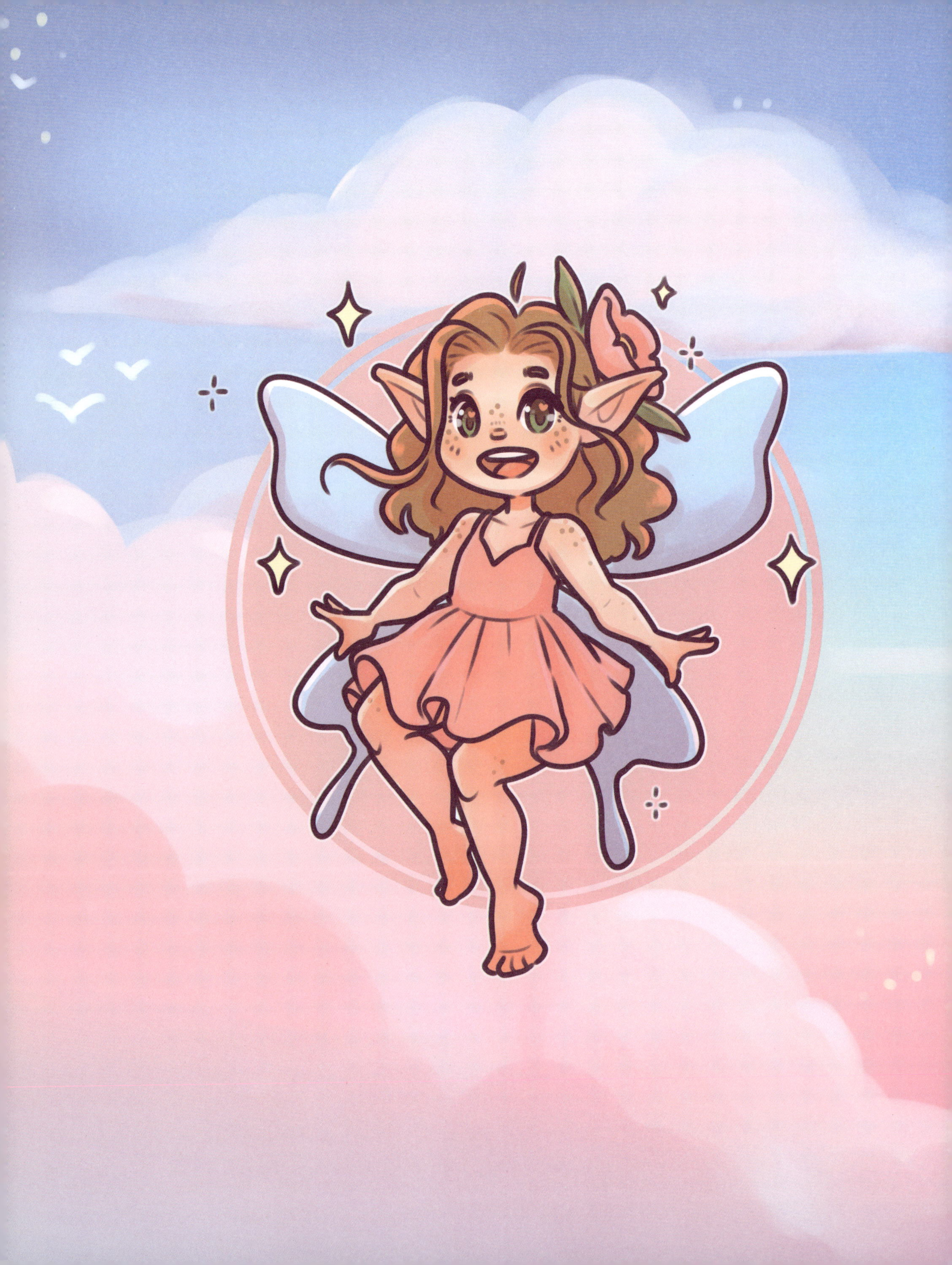

AIR GLIDERS

FEATHERS, WINGS, AND SCALES

PHOENIX

Some believe only one phoenix can exist at any given time. When that phoenix dies, consumed by fire, a new phoenix will rise from the ashes to take its place.

1. Lightly sketch an oval with pointed sides. Add a plus sign (+) guideline for the face.

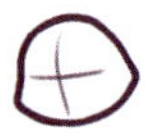

2. Add two curved V shapes for the neck. Draw a guideline down the middle.

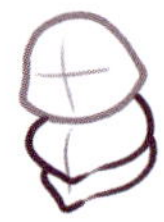

3. Sketch a circle below the V and connect them with a curved line, making a roughly jelly bean shape.

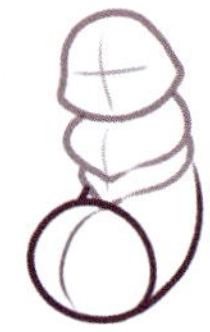

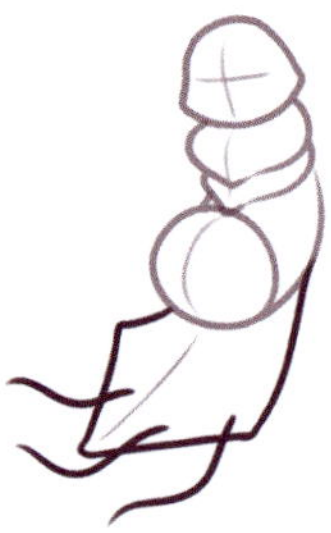

4. Connect a large diamond-shaped tail. Add three wavy lines to the end.

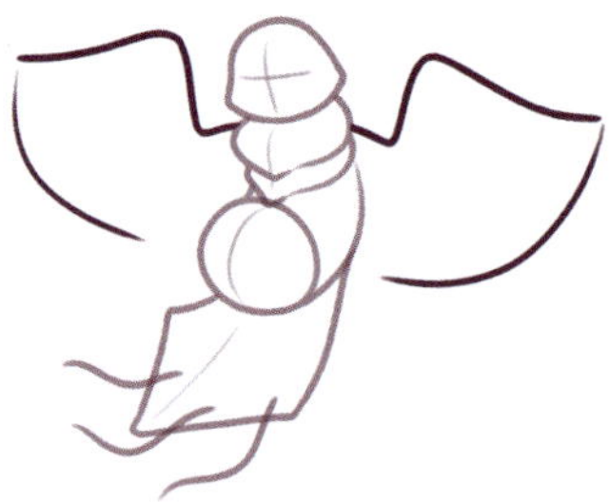

5. Sketch two Z-shaped wings starting at the neck, with each line getting longer as it goes away from the body. Then connect with an arc from the tip of the wing to the body.

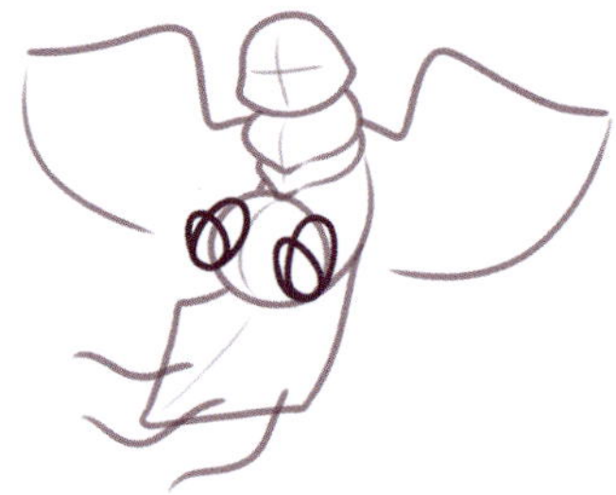

6. Draw two small ovals to the sides of the circle with a smaller oval crossing over them.

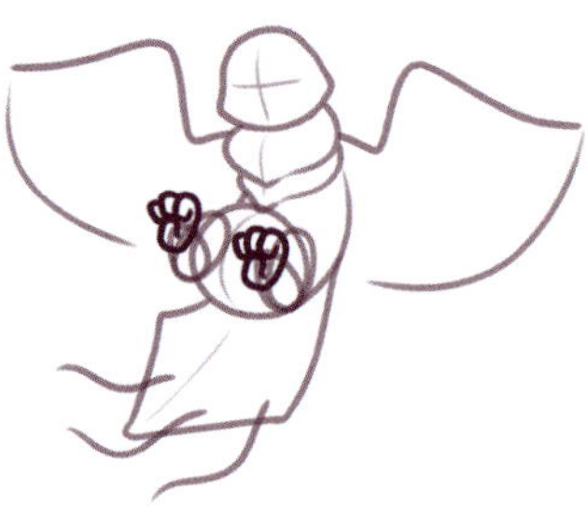

7. For the feet, draw three curled, rectangle toes with a curve connecting the bottom toe to complete the foot.

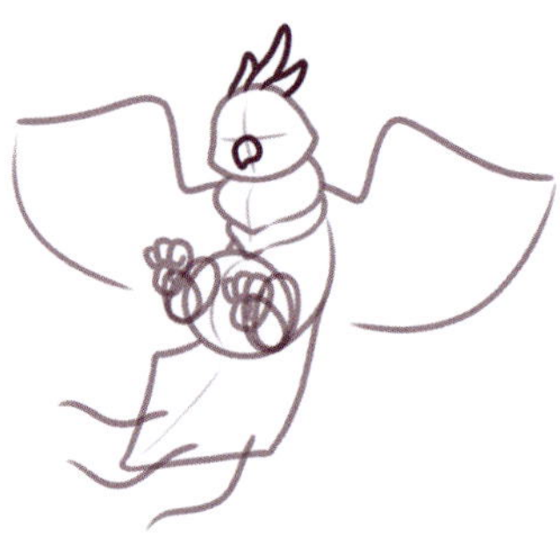

8. On top of the head, draw three tall feathers. Add a small, teardrop-shaped beak at the center of the head that curves to a point.

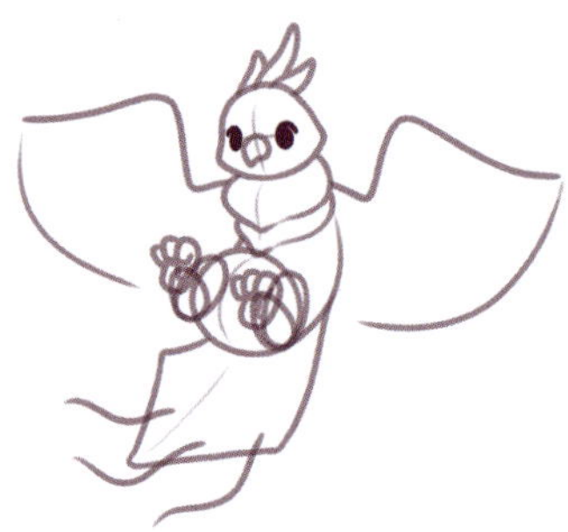

9. Add two oval eyes with a small curve around the top.

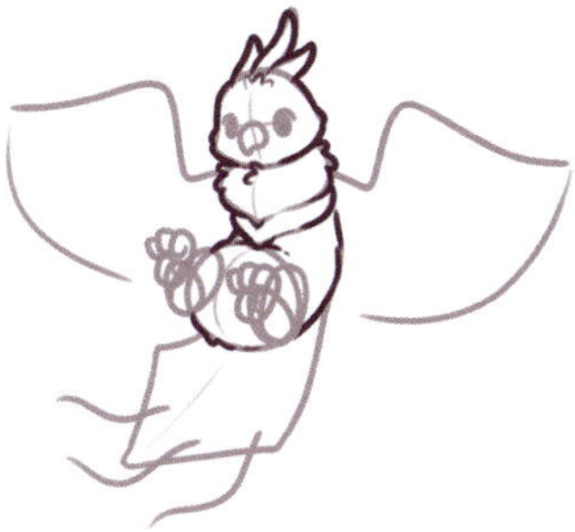

10. Lightly go over the basic sketch, adding details of the head and body. Use soft W shapes for the fluff.

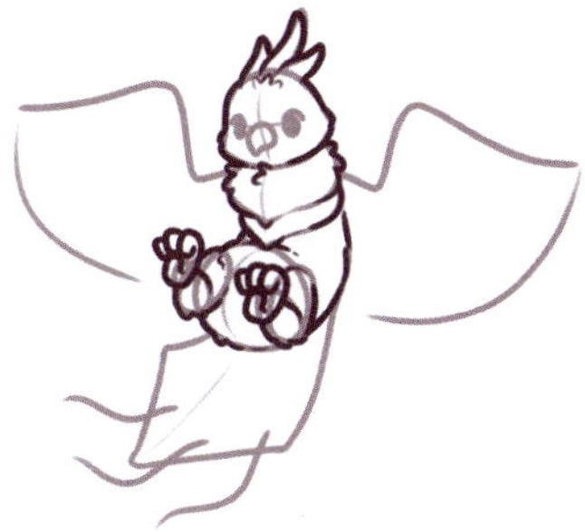

11. Go over the legs, adding fluff at the bends.

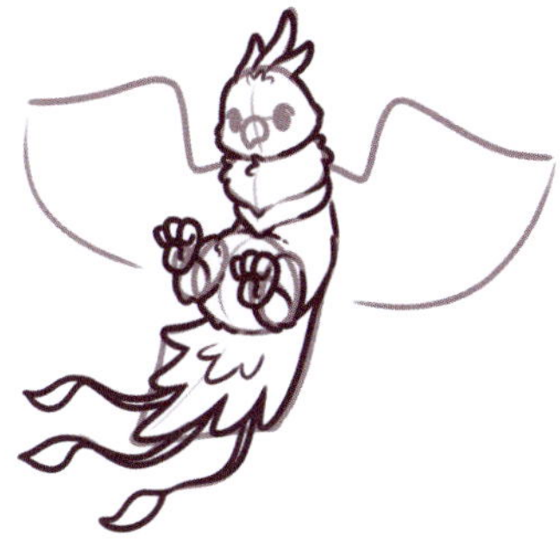

12. Sketch the tail with five long, V-shaped feathers, with the center one the longest. Thicken the wavy lines and add three curved teardrops at the ends.

13. Draw the wings using multiple U-shaped feathers along the arc that get shorter closer to the body. Add M and W shapes for fluffy details.

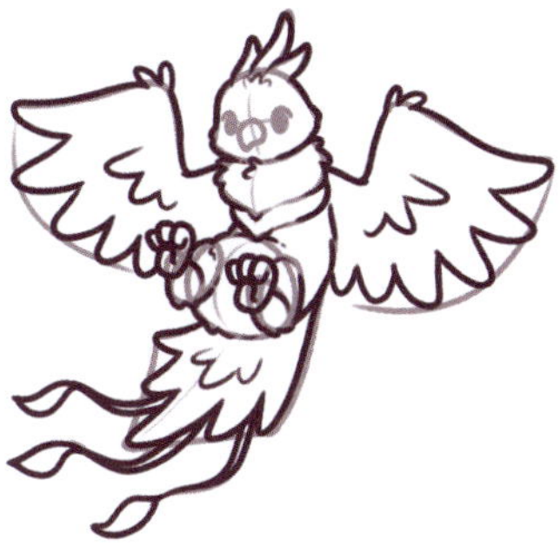

14. Sketch the face, leaving a little space in the eyes for highlights. Add dashes of blush on the cheeks.

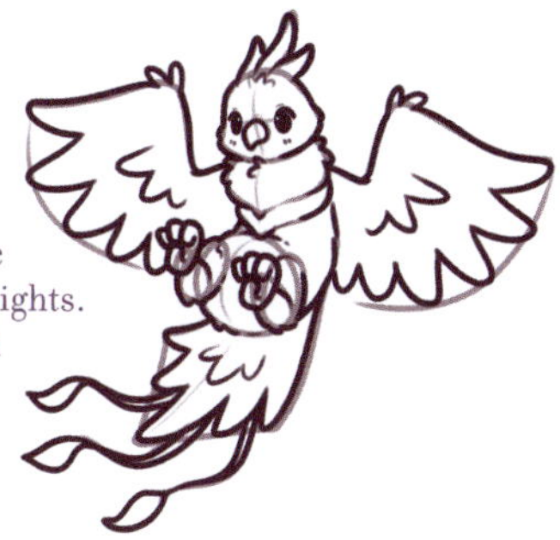

15. Neatly draw the line art over the sketch. Add some sparkles if you'd like! Then erase the sketch underneath.

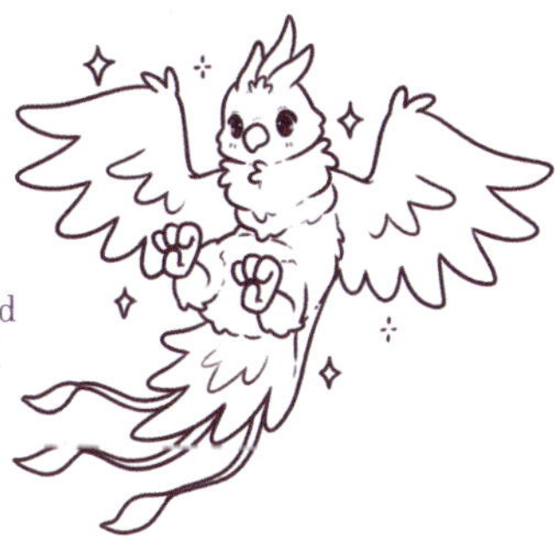

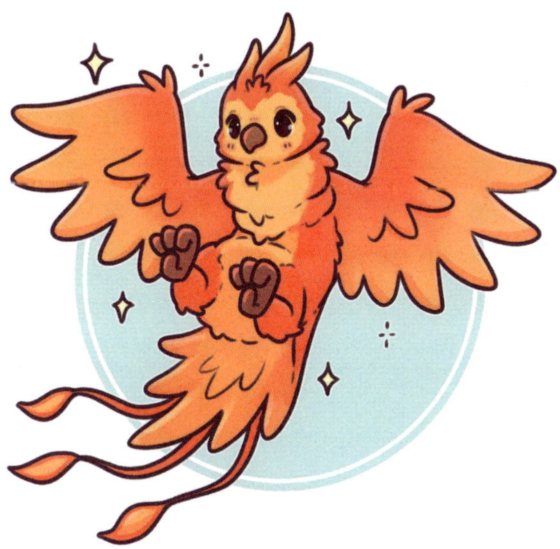

16. Time to add color! Phoenixes usually have a flame-inspired color scheme, so I used red, orange, and yellow.

MANTICORE

Carnivorous creatures, manticores are known to eat people and swallow them whole. They are especially dangerous because of their horns and scorpion tail.

1. Lightly sketch an oval with pointed sides. Add a plus sign guideline for the face.

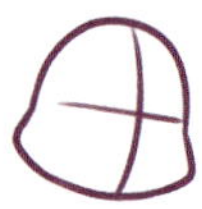

2. Draw a large teardrop-shaped mane around the head that's incomplete on the right. Add a curved guideline at the point. Add a small V to the crown of the head.

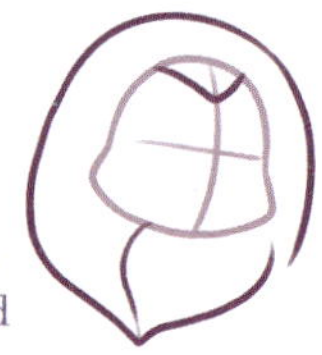

3. Add a rounded V under the mane with a guideline down the middle.

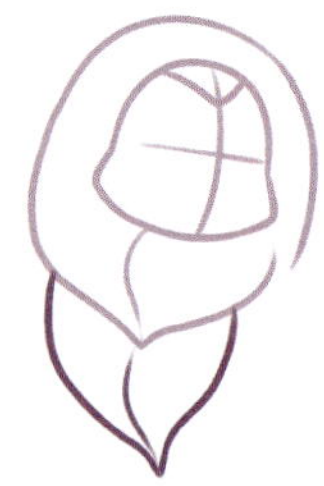

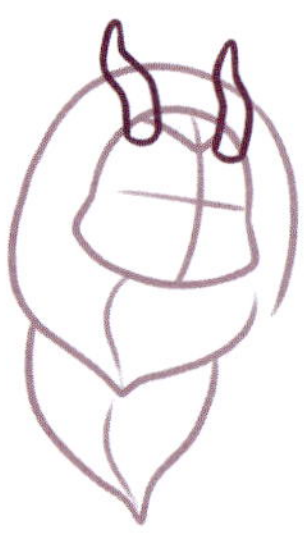

4. Draw two curvy horns to the sides of the V on the head.

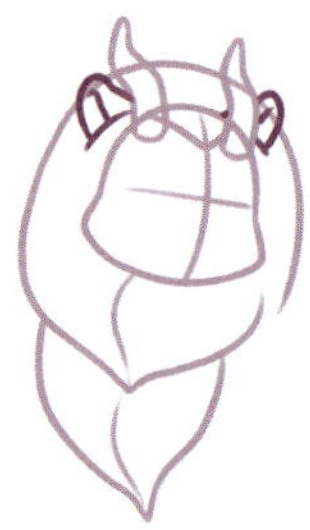

5. Add two arched ears with a curved line inside that are slightly concealed by the horns.

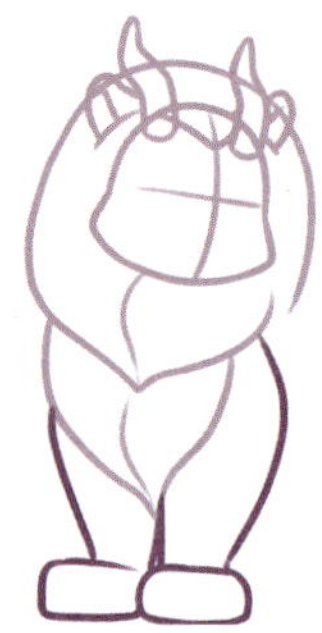

6. Add two rounded arms with rectangle paws at the bottom.

7. Draw a round triangle haunch next to the right leg with a rectangle paw. Connect the haunch to the mane with a line. Make the left back paw poke out behind the left leg with a small curve.

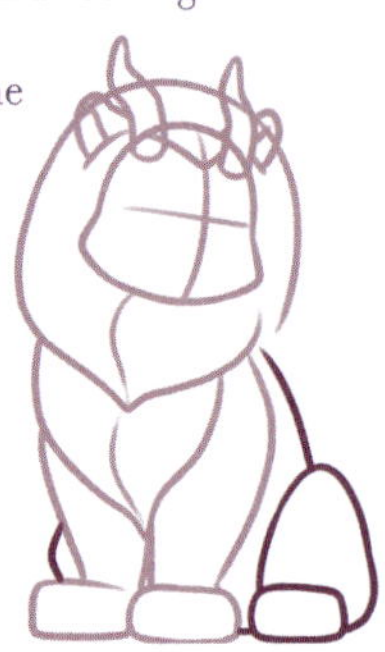

8. Draw the scorpion tail with linking rounded rectangles curving up to a teardrop stinger. Add a small curve to the right haunch.

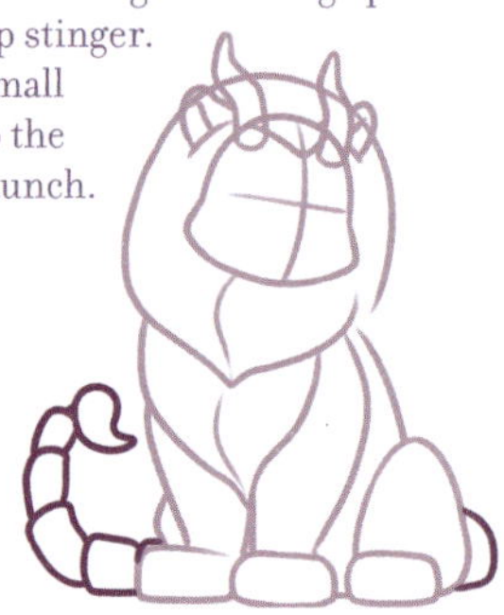

9. Sketch two Z-shaped wings where the body meets the head. Add two lines sprouting down from the wings.

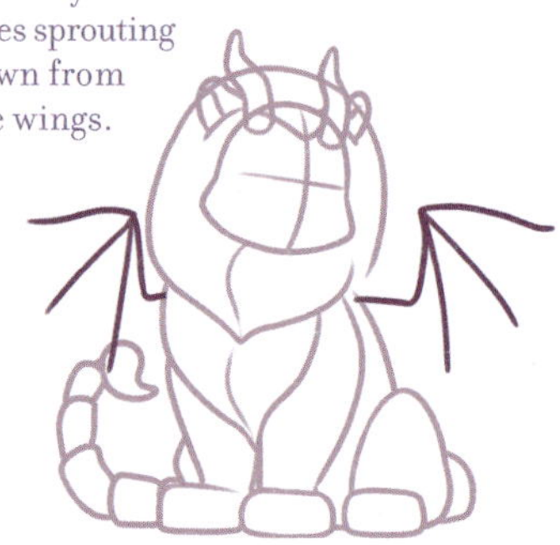

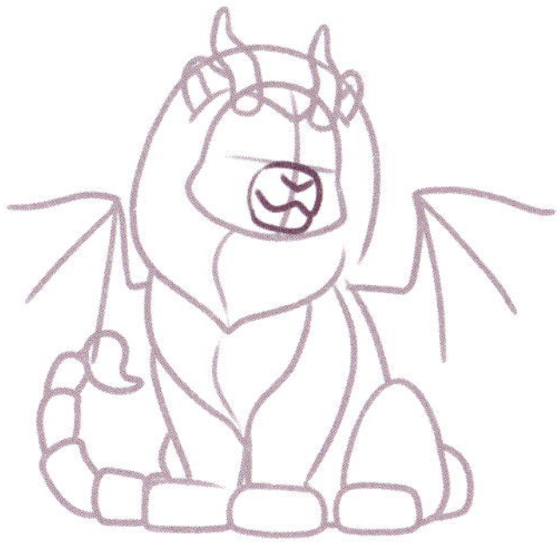

10. Draw a rounded square snout on the lower half of the face with a flat V nose and a W mouth.

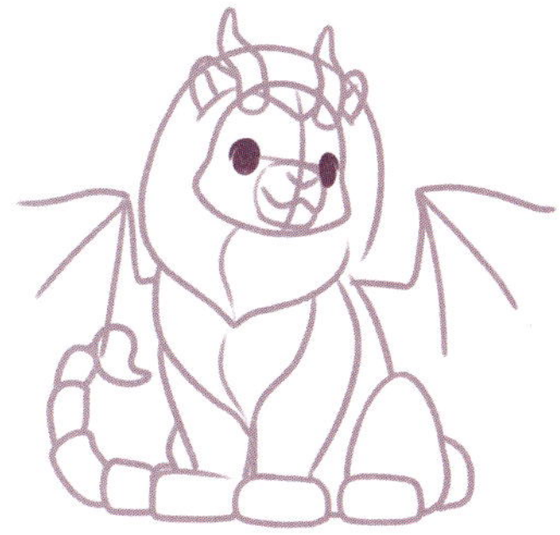

11. Draw two oval eyes with a small curve around the top.

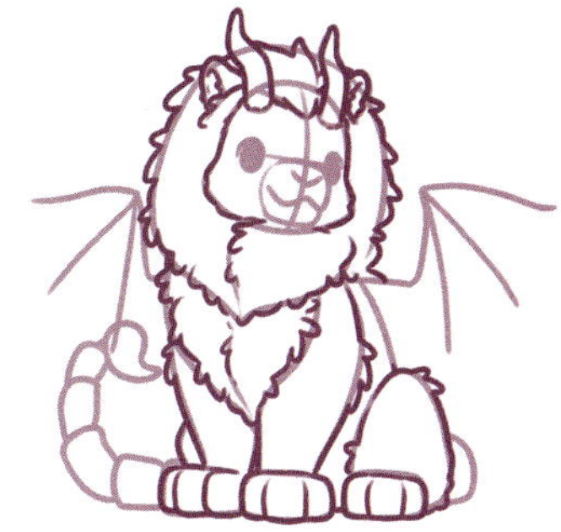

12. Lightly go over the basic sketch, adding details of the head and body. Use soft W shapes for the fur. Add the horns and toe lines.

13. Sketch the bat wings with curves connecting the points. Then sketch the tail.

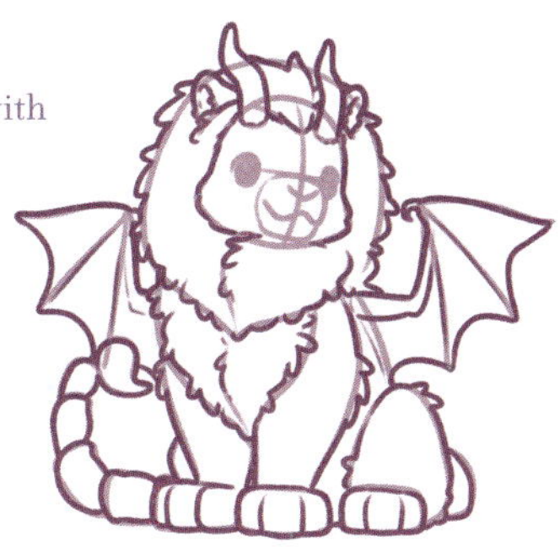

14. Sketch the face, adding highlights in the eyes and dashes on the cheeks. Add two small V fangs.

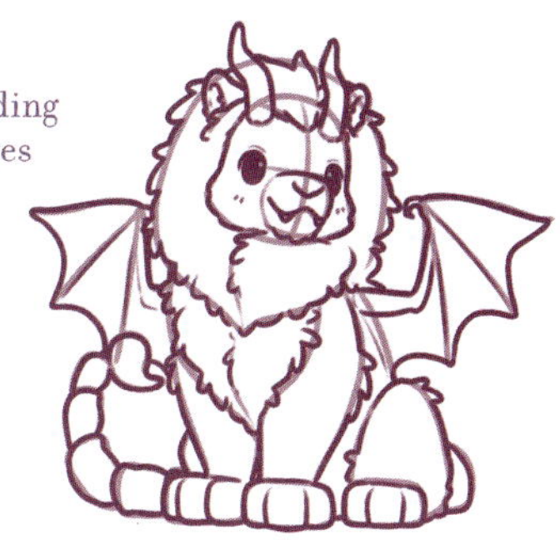

15. Neatly draw the line art over the sketch. Add some sparkles if you'd like! Then erase the sketch underneath.

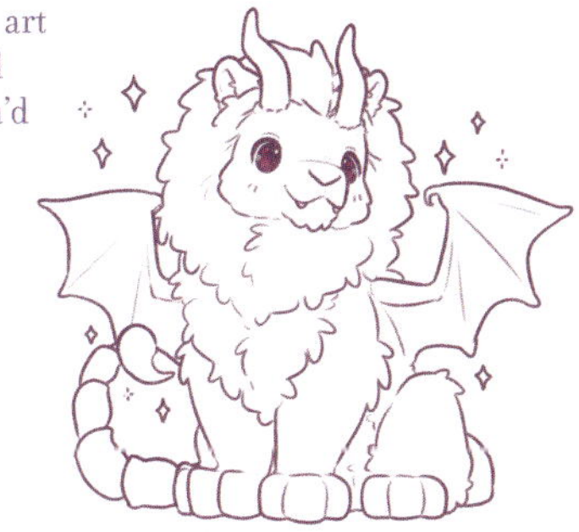

16. Finally, add color! Use mid-brown for the mane and light brown for the body. Use a very dark brown or gray for the wings, tail, and horns.

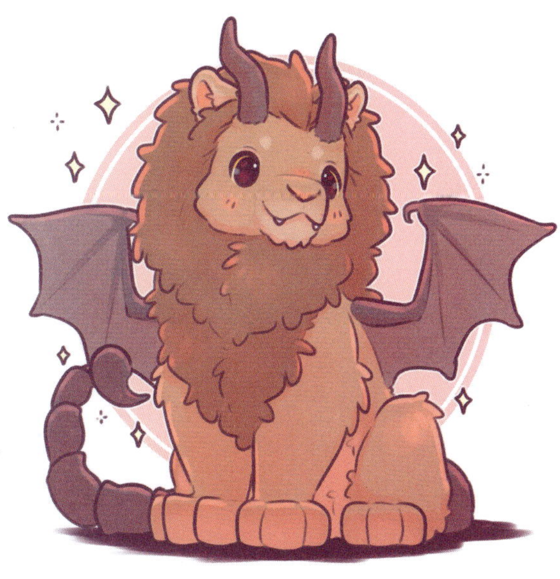

WYVERN

These vicious predators are tricky to befriend. for as cute as they may seem. they have the tendency to spit fire like their distant ancestors. dragons.

1. Lightly draw an oval head. Add a plus sign guideline for the face.

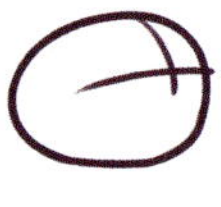

2. At the bottom-right of the head, draw a backwards C snout with a flat bottom.

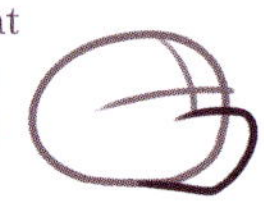

3. On top of the head, draw two triangle horns.

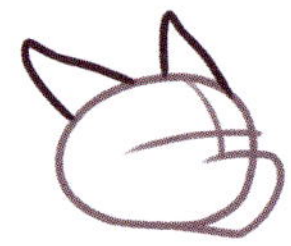

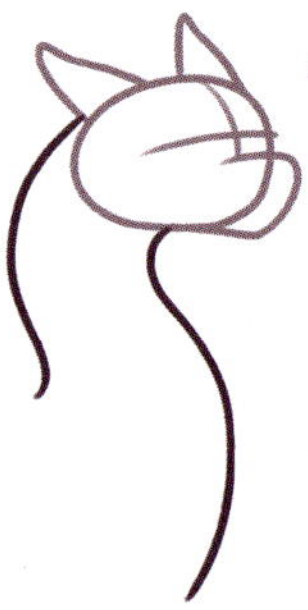

4. Draw two S-shaped lines coming down from the left horn and under the snout. Keep them parallel to each other with the right line twice as long.

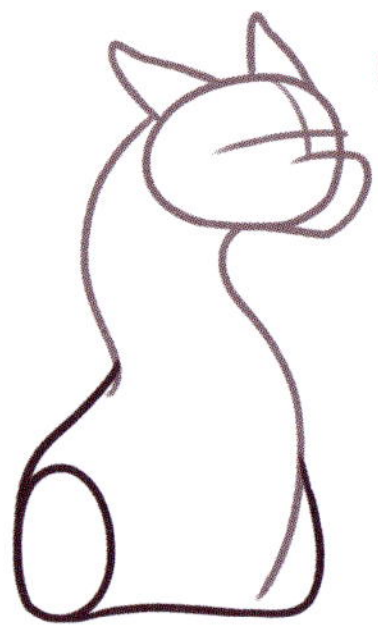

5. Draw an oval haunch on the bottom-left. Connect it to the body with curved lines, making the bottom slightly flat.

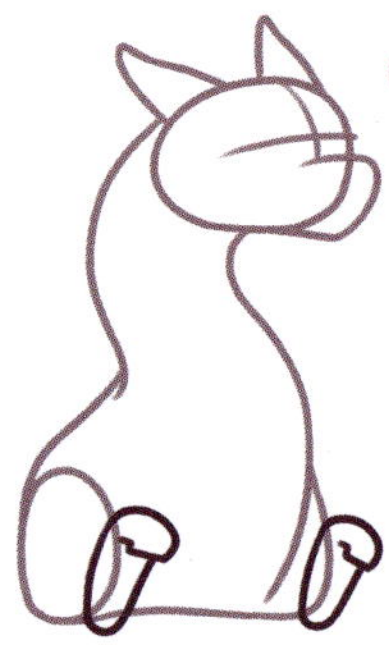

6. Draw two curved oval feet at the haunches with a lip for the toes.

7. Start the tail with a C curve to the left leg. Beside the right foot, draw the tail curved up and ending with an arrowhead.

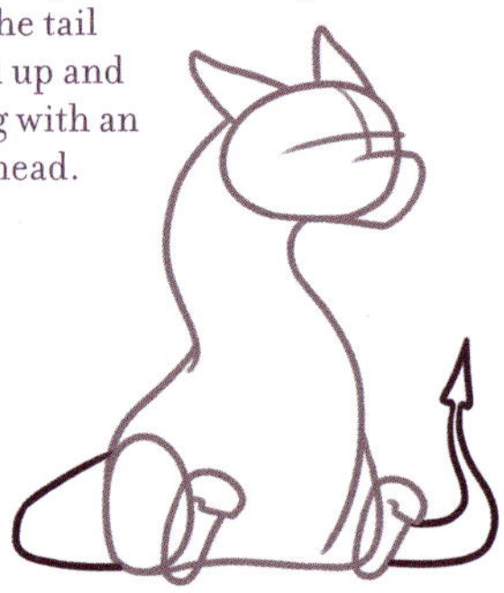

8. Where the body dips in on the left, draw the arm with an oval and a narrower oval angled to the right. Draw a partial right arm slightly concealed by the body.

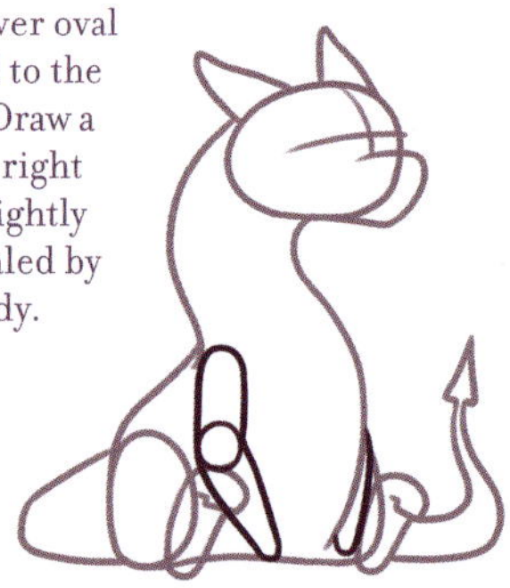

9. At the end of the arms, draw small, jagged rectangle claws.

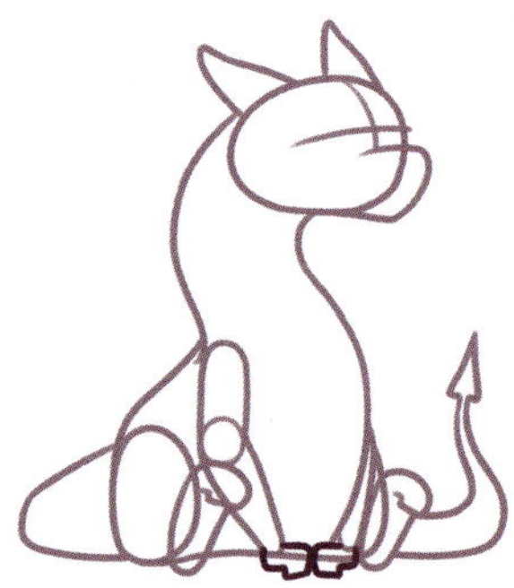

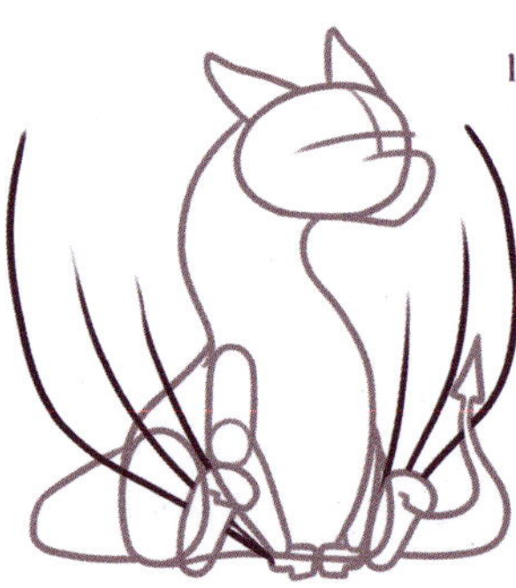

10. Starting at the left claw and the right foot, draw three lines arcing upwards.

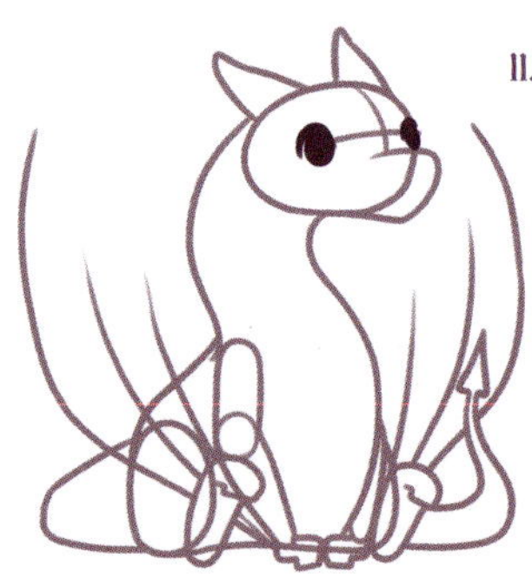

11. Draw two oval eyes with a curve around the top.

12. Following the bottom of the snout, draw a mouth with two V fangs.

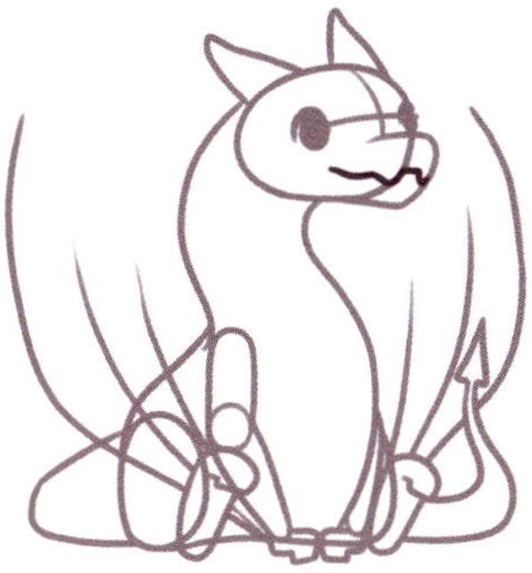

13. Lightly sketch the wing details, joining each point with a narrow U. Add the front and back claws.

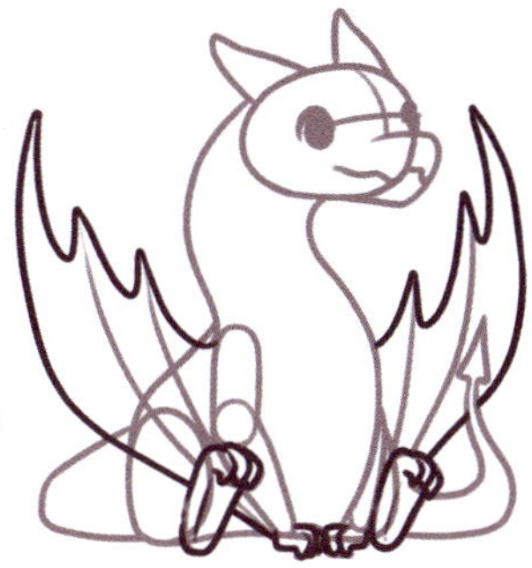

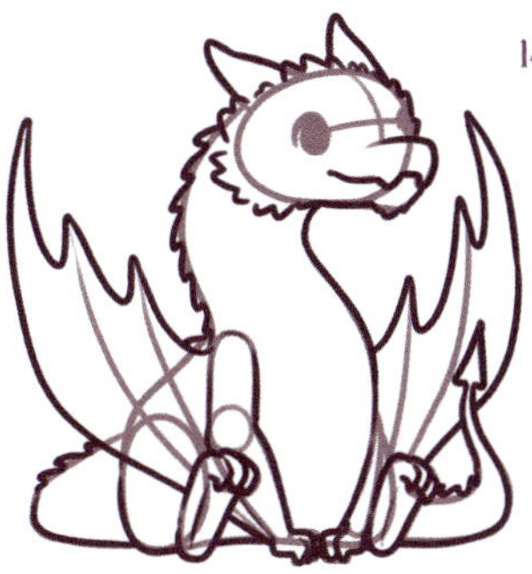

14. Sketch the rest of the body, adding small spines along the head and back.

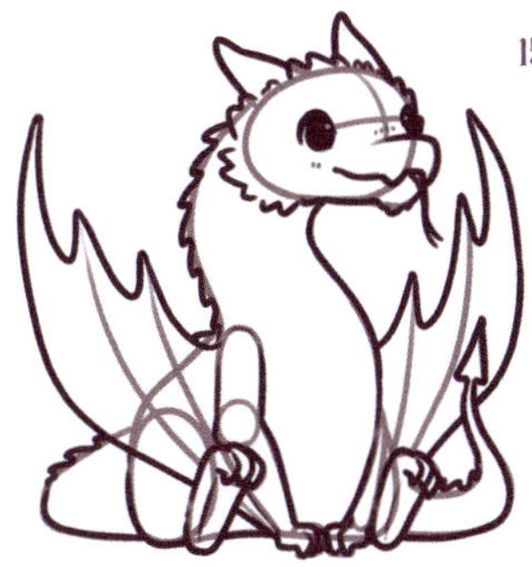

15. Sketch the face detail, leaving a space for the eye highlights. Add dashes to the cheeks and a forked tongue coming out the mouth.

16. Neatly draw the line art over the sketch. Add some sparkles if you'd like! Then erase the sketch underneath.

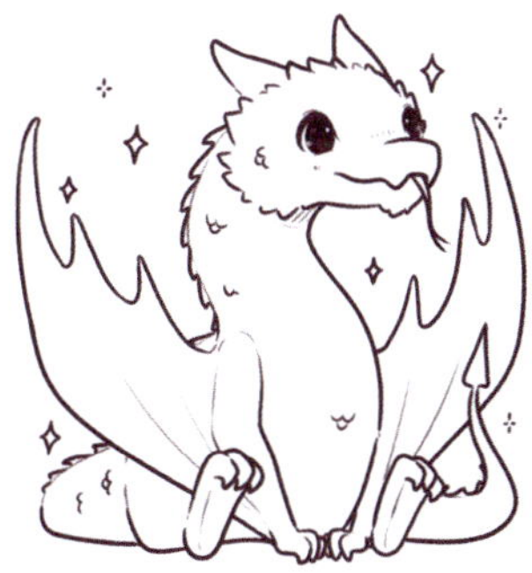

17. Lastly, let's add color! I used a dark red with a paler shade along the underbelly, but any jewel tone would look lovely!

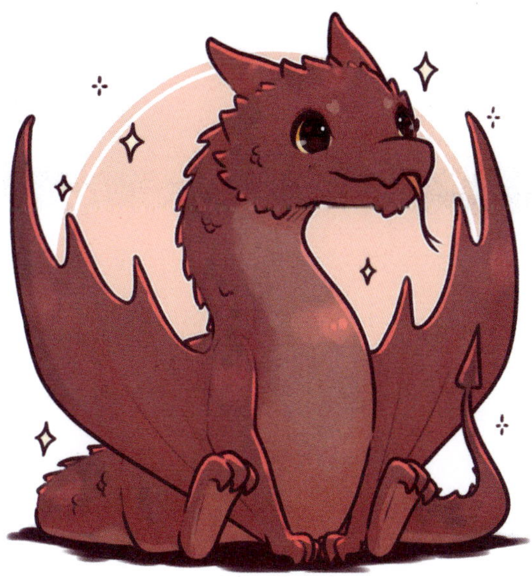

WOLPERTINGER

Found flying or hopping around the forests of Bavaria, the wolpertinger is a magnificent hybrid of a hare and a deer with fluffy wings, antlers, and fangs.

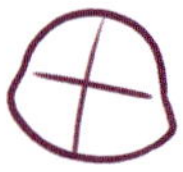

1. Lightly sketch an oval with pointed sides. Add a plus sign guideline for the face.

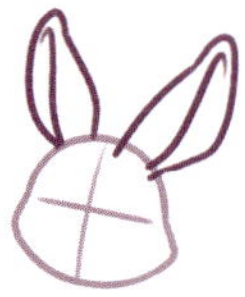

2. Add two long, teardrop-shaped ears on top with two curved lines inside.

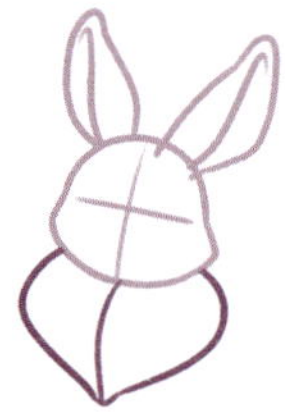

3. Add a curved V neck below with a curved guideline down the middle.

4. On either side of the neck, start the arms with an oval. Overlap another oval angled inward. At the ends, draw a U shape pointed down.

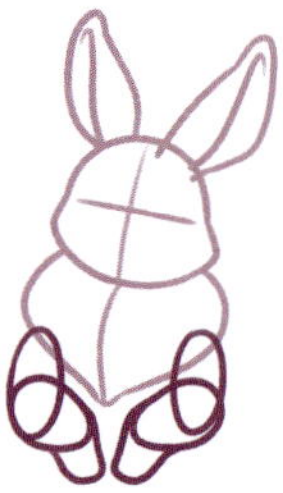

5. Draw a wide U-shaped body with a slightly flat bottom. At the bottom-right, attach a small, curved bunny tail.

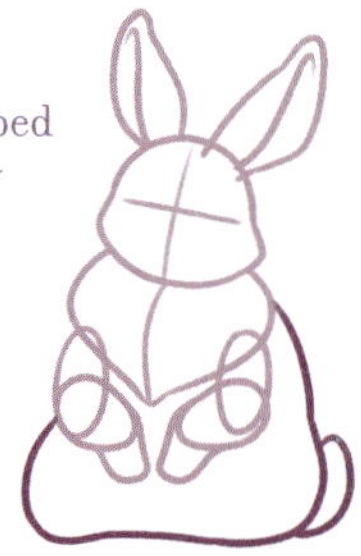

6. Draw two long oval feet below the arms, angled outward.

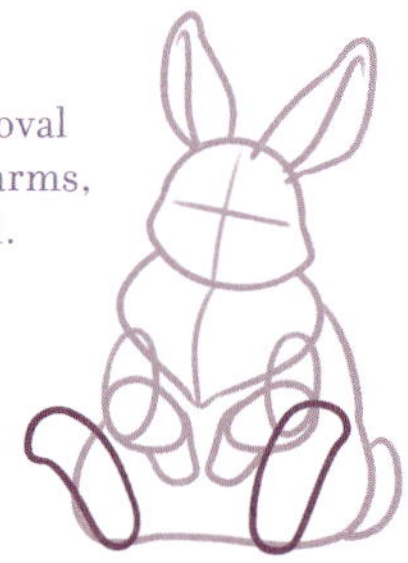

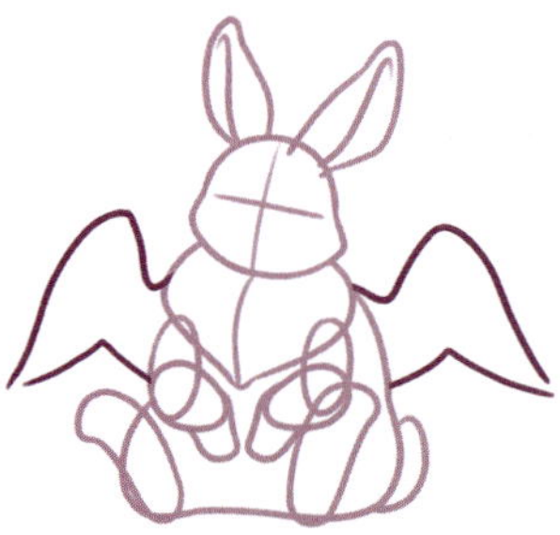

7. Sketch two Z-shaped wings on the sides of the body, with each line getting longer as it moves away from the body. Connect the wings to the body with an upside down V.

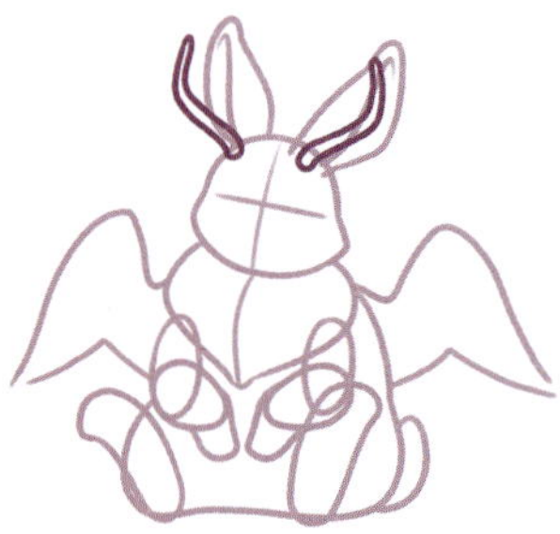

8. Draw two thin, curved antlers in front of the ears. Make them roughly symmetrical.

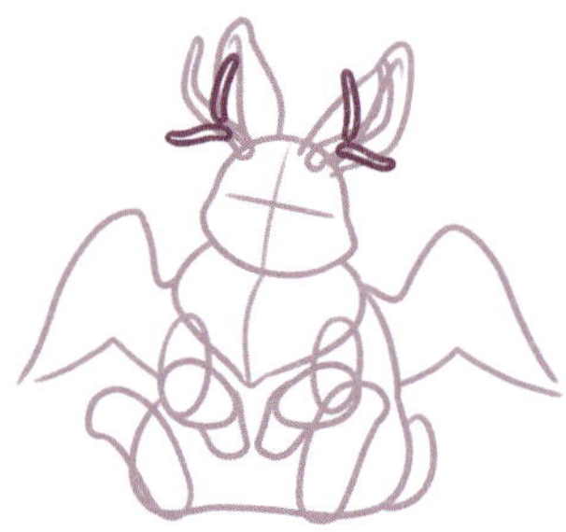

9. Add two short prongs to each antler. Again, keep these symmetrical.

10. On the bottom of the face, draw a rounded square snout. Inside, draw a flat V nose and a W mouth.

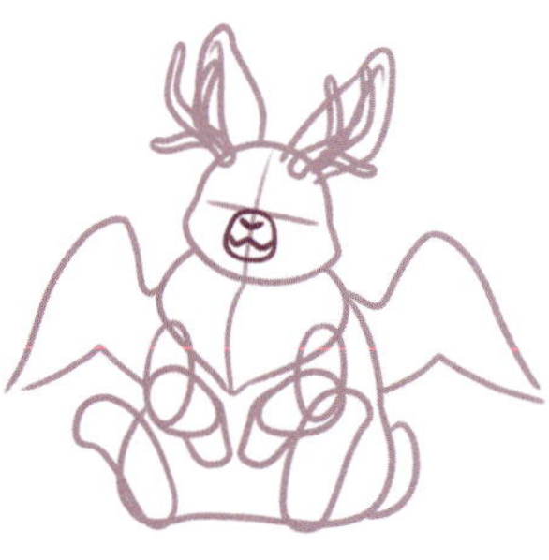

11. Draw two oval eyes with a curve around the top.

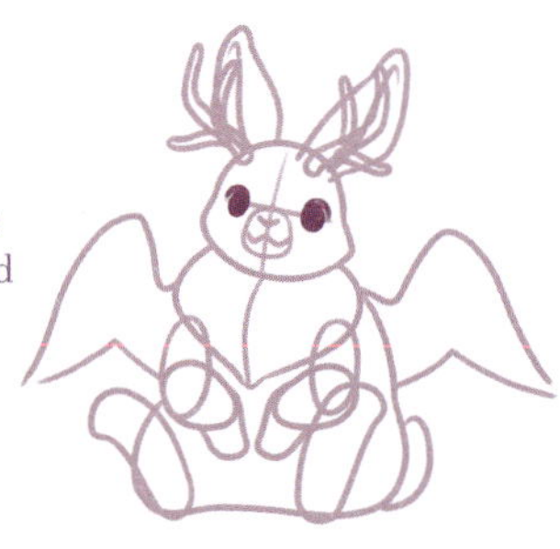

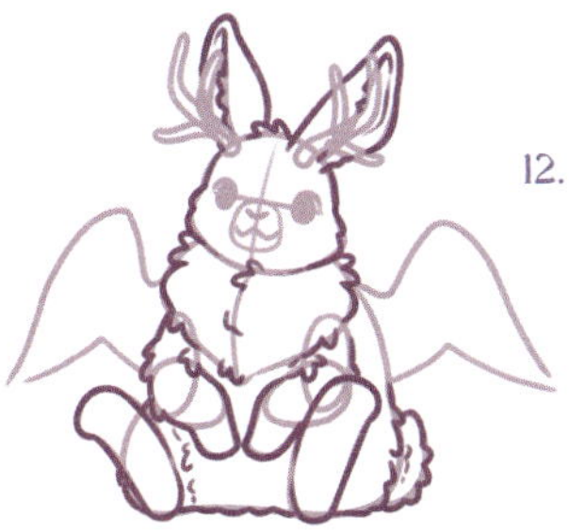

12. Lightly go over the basic sketch, adding details of the head and body. Use soft W shapes for the fur.

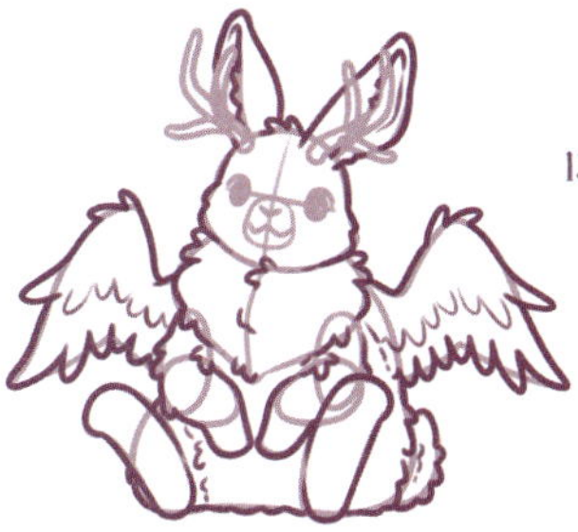

13. Sketch the wing detail using long U shapes along the bottom.

14. Sketch the antlers. Draw the toe beans with heart-shaped paw pads.

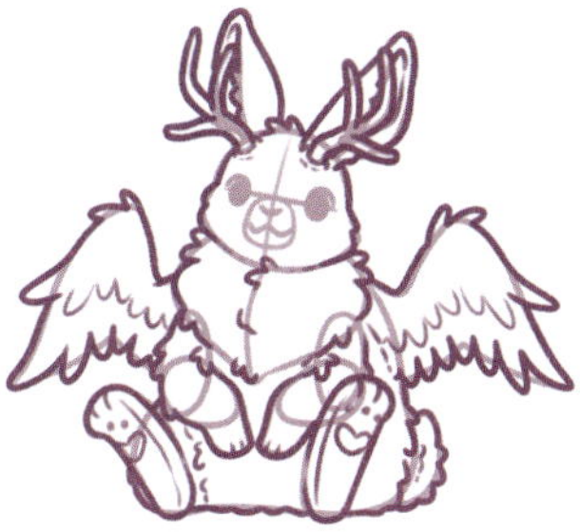

15. Add the face detail, leaving space for highlights in the eyes. Add dashes on the cheeks and above the nose, and two V fangs.

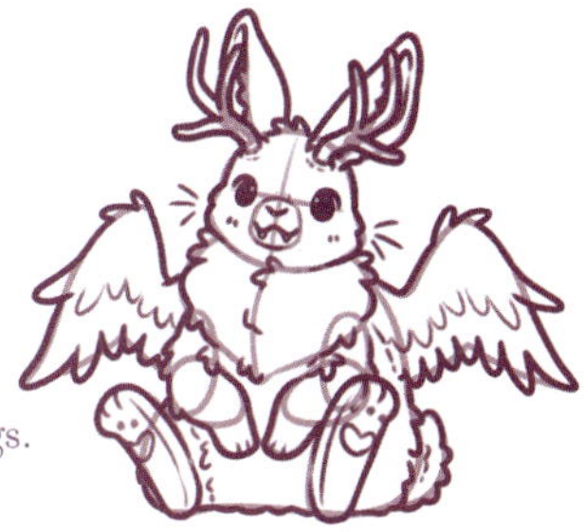

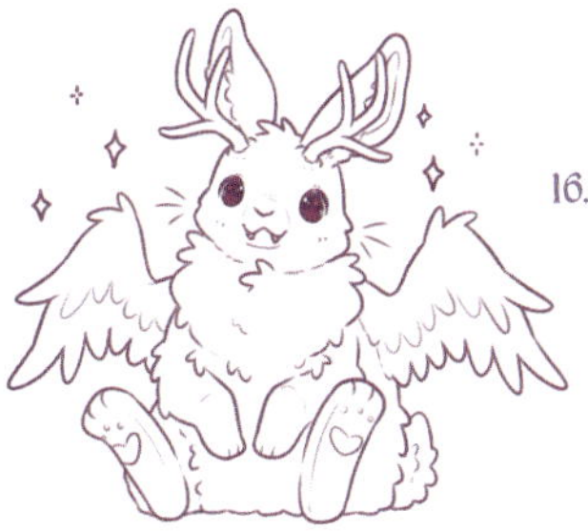

16. Neatly draw the line art over the sketch. Add some sparkles if you'd like! Then erase the sketch underneath.

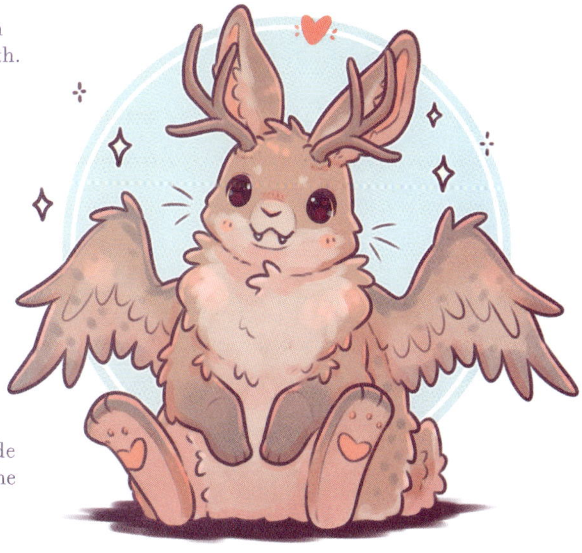

17. Finish with color! I went for light brown for the body with a paler shade on the face and chest. Add pink to the toe beans for an extra-cute look!

HATI (MOON WOLF)

From Norse mythology, Hati's mission is to continuously chase the moon until Ragnarök (the end of the world), when he is foretold to swallow it whole.

1. Lightly sketch an oval with pointed sides. On the bottom, add a trapezoid snout with a rounded top. Add a plus sign guideline for the face.

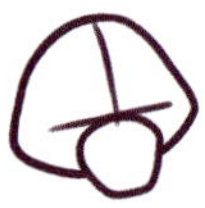

2. Add two triangle ears on top with two smaller triangles inside.

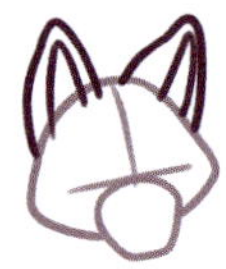

3. Sketch an oval shoulder next to the left ear. Use a U to connect the arm to below the left side of the snout. Add a smaller U underneath. Repeat on the right with the shoulder partially concealed and the leg extended slightly lower.

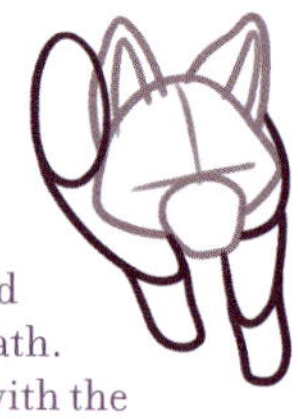

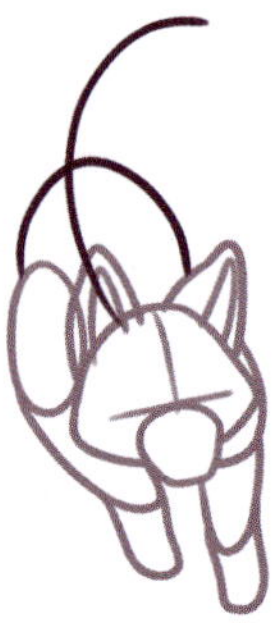

4. Draw a curved line from the top of the left ear arcing over to the right. Then draw an arch from the left shoulder to the right ear.

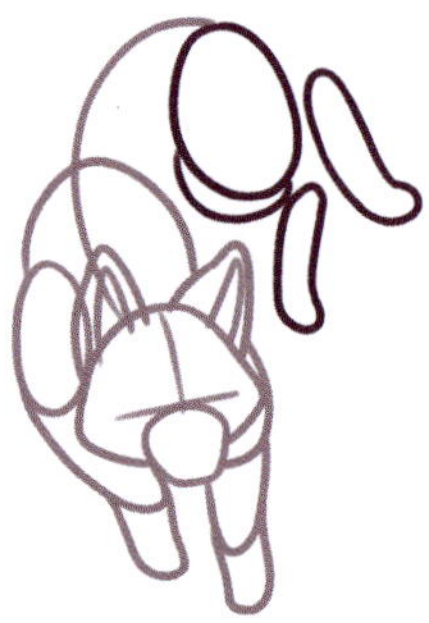

5. At the end of the curved line, draw an oval haunch with a curved line underneath. Add two long oval feet below and to the right.

6. Connect the back haunch to the body with curved lines. Then connect the back feet with curved lines.

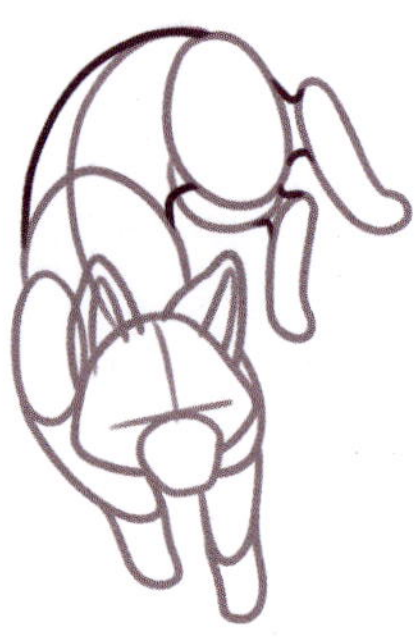

7. At the back of the body, draw a long, pointed tail.

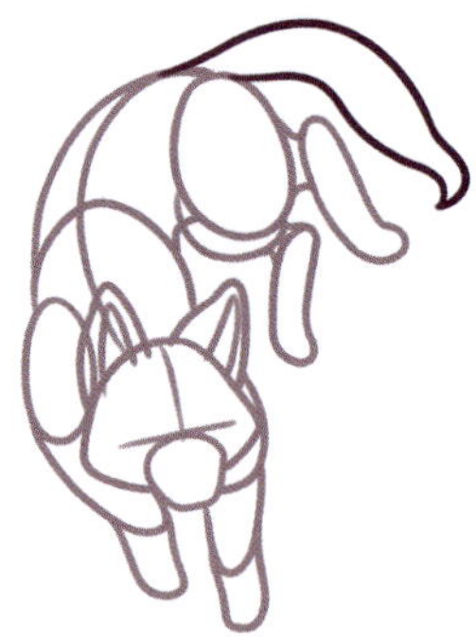

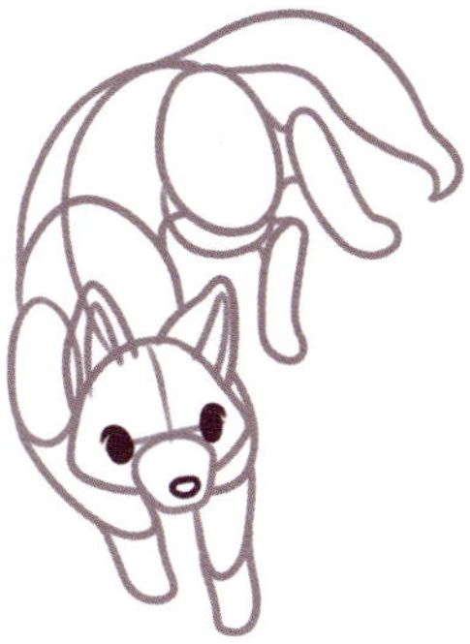

8. Draw a small oval nose at the tip of the snout. Then add two oval eyes with a curve around the top.

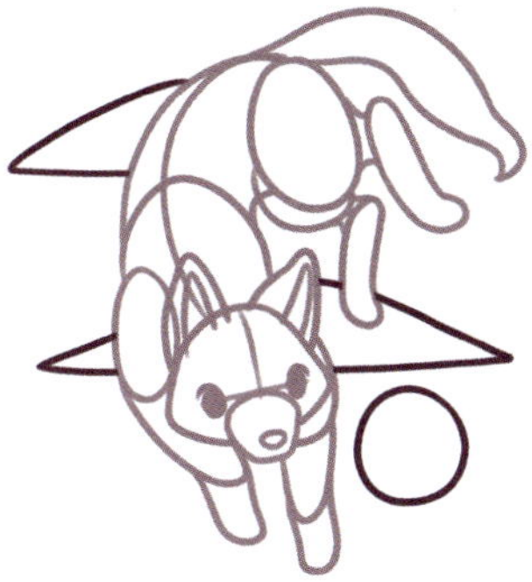

9. Around Hati, sketch two slightly rounded triangle clouds and a small, circle moon.

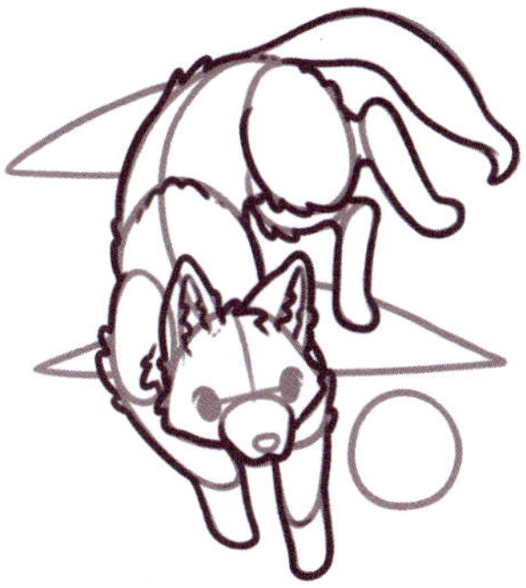

10. Lightly go over the basic sketch, adding details of the head and body. Use soft W shapes for the fur.

11. Leave space in the eyes for highlights. Add dashes on the cheeks. Draw a crescent moon on the forehead.

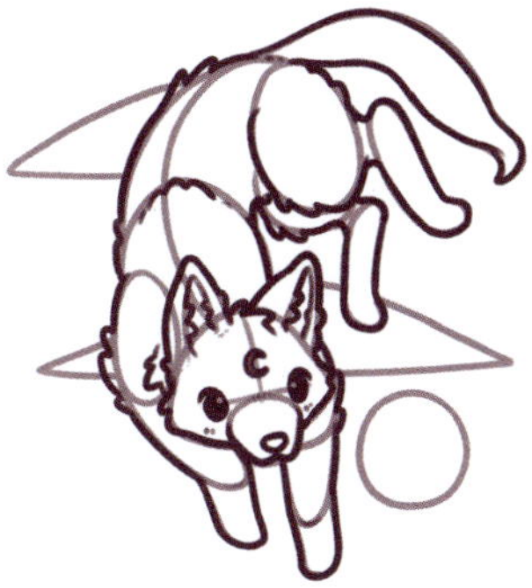

12. Detail the clouds with flat bottoms and soft M shapes along the top. Make a crescent shape in the circle and add small dashes around it.

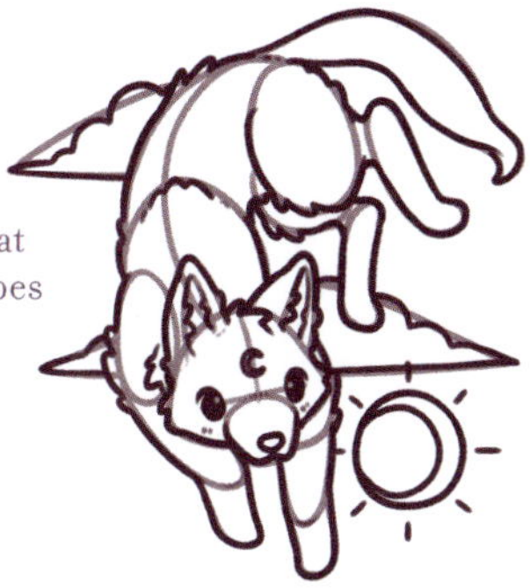

13. Neatly draw the line art over the sketch. Add some sparkles if you'd like! Then erase the sketch underneath.

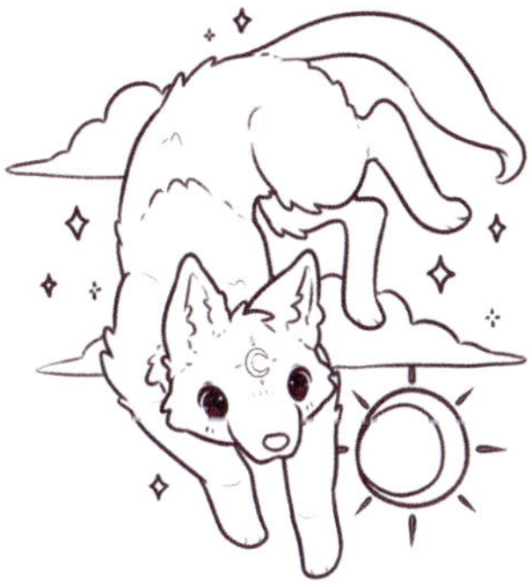

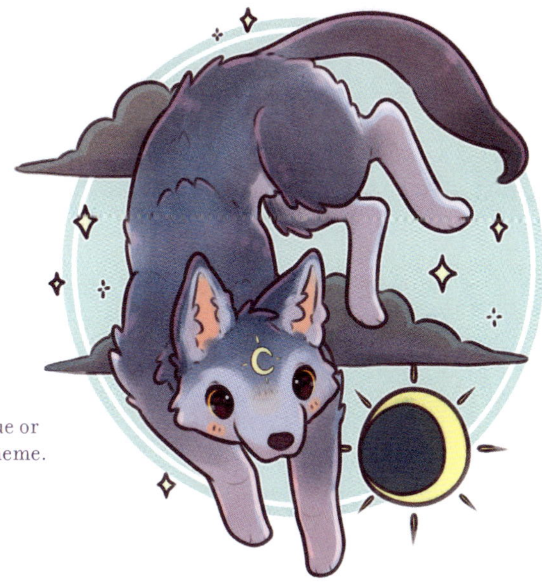

14. Make Hati a dark color like blue or gray to match the nighttime theme. Add pale yellow to the moons.

SKÖLL (SUN WOLF)

Sköll is the brother of Hati (page 56). Like his sibling, he is said to never cease his chase of the sun until Ragnarök, when it will be his job to swallow it whole.

1. Lightly sketch an oval with pointed sides. Add a plus sign guideline for the face.

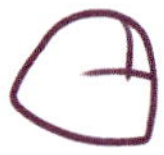

2. On the lower right of the face, add a rounded square snout with a point.

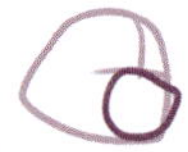

3. Add two triangle ears on top of the head, with two smaller triangles inside.

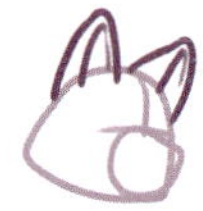

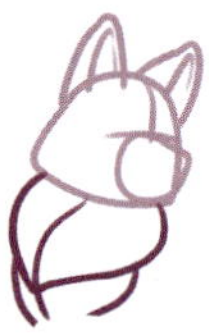

4. Add a rounded V neck and an incomplete one underneath. Add a curved guideline down the middle.

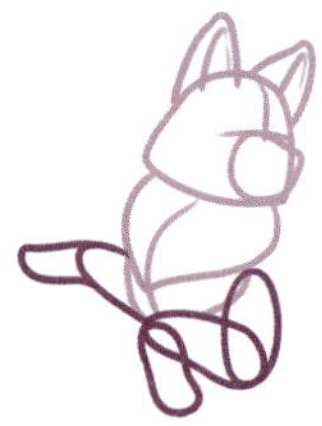

5. Draw three interlocking ovals that create an N shape for the right arm. On the left arm, draw two Us pointing away from the body.

6. Draw a large U shape from the neck to the bend in the right arm. Then draw a curved line for the back.

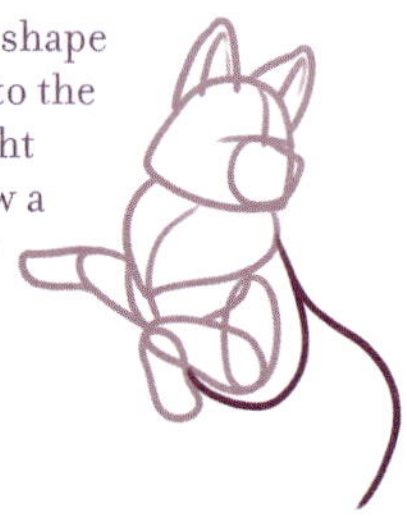

7. At the end of the curved line, draw an oval and a semicircle to the left that's nestled under the arm. Add two long oval feet below, leaving a gap between the big oval and foot.

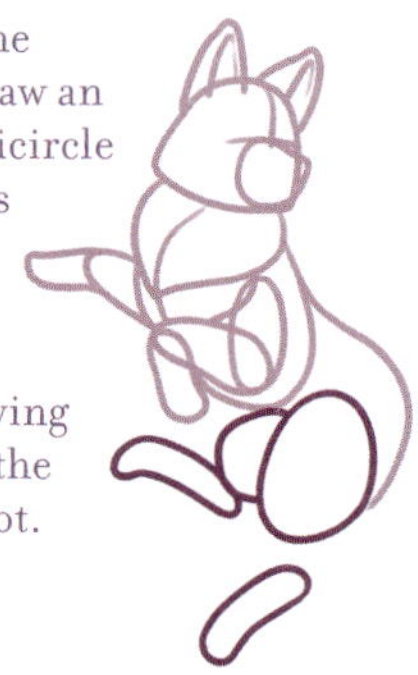

8. Connect the feet to the body with curved lines.

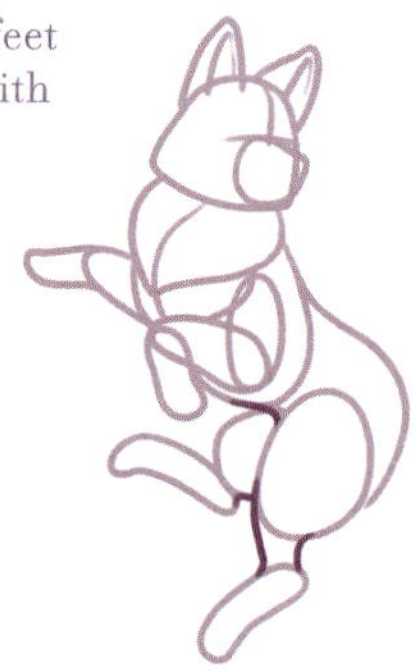

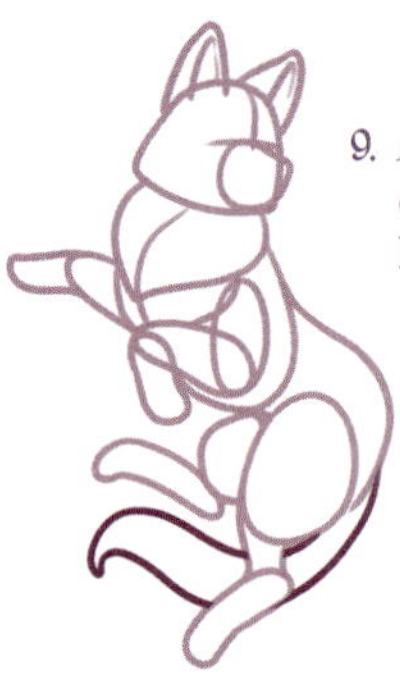

9. At the end of the body, start a curved, pointy tail that curls between the feet.

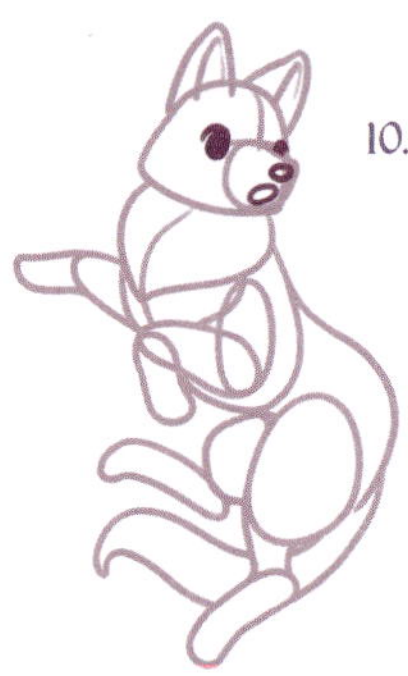

10. On the snout, draw a rounded triangle nose and an oval mouth. Then draw two oval eyes, each with a curve around the top.

11. Around Sköll, sketch two round triangle clouds and a small circle sun.

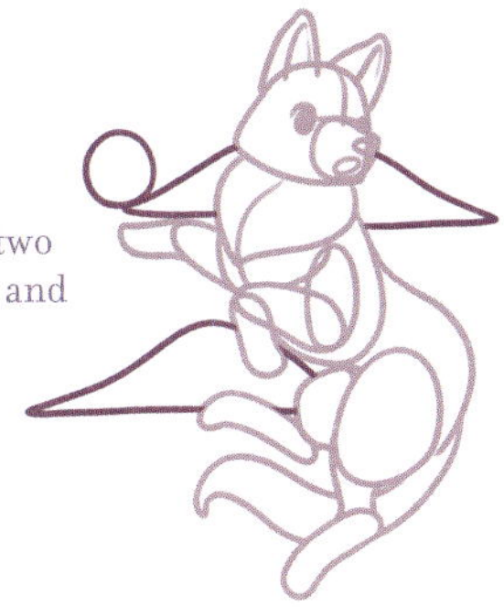

12. Lightly go over the basic sketch, adding details of the head and body. Use soft W shapes for the fur.

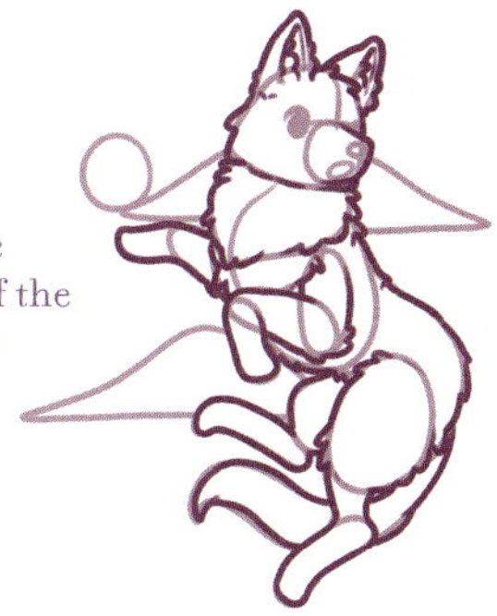

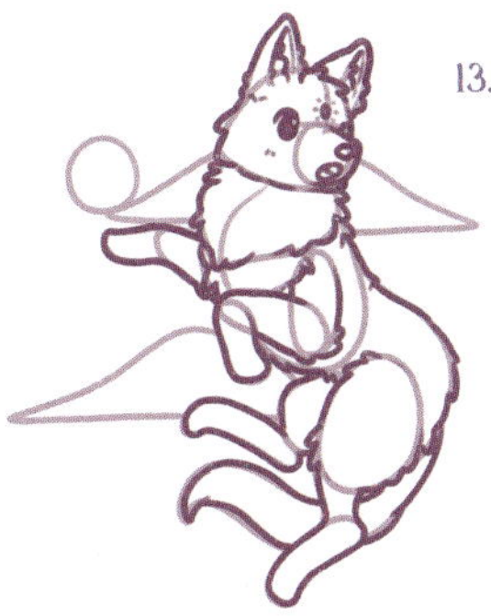

13. Leave space in the eyes for highlights. Add dashes of blush on the cheeks. Draw a small circle sun with dashes around it on the forehead.

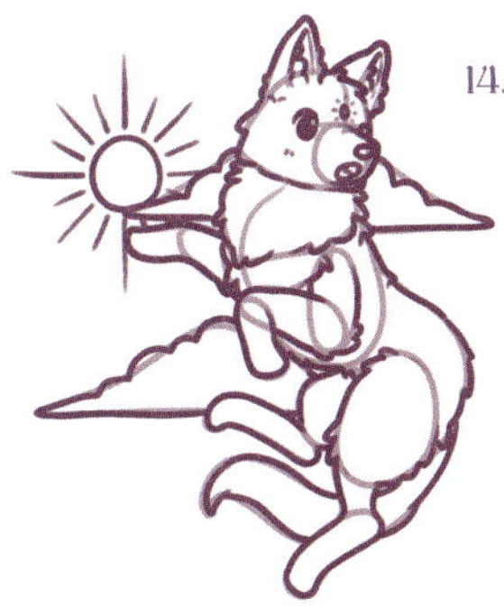

14. Detail the clouds, making the bottoms flat with soft M shapes along the top. Add light beams around the circle for a sunny look.

15. Neatly draw the line art over the sketch. Add some sparkles if you'd like! Then erase the sketch underneath.

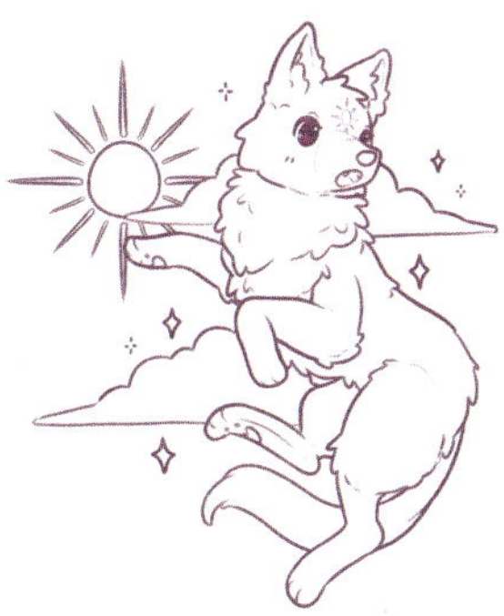

16. Make Sköll golden to enhance the sun theme. Color the sun on the forehead and in the background a light yellow.

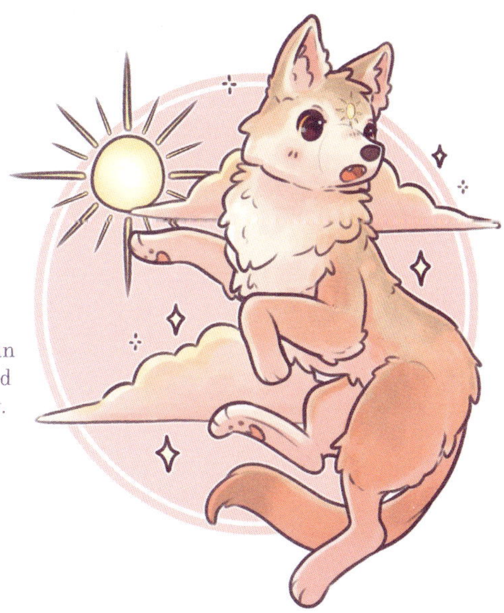

QUETZALCOATL

A powerful deity ruling over many entities, such as the wind and the planet Venus, this beastie also stands as a formidable symbol of death.

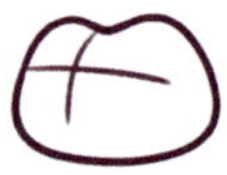

1. Lightly sketch an oval head with a soft dip on the top. Add a plus sign guideline for the face.

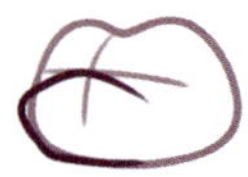

2. On the bottom-left of the face, draw a wide C-shaped snout.

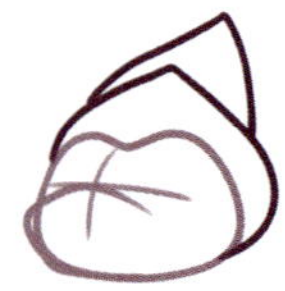

3. Draw a curved triangle around the head with a narrow triangle on top.

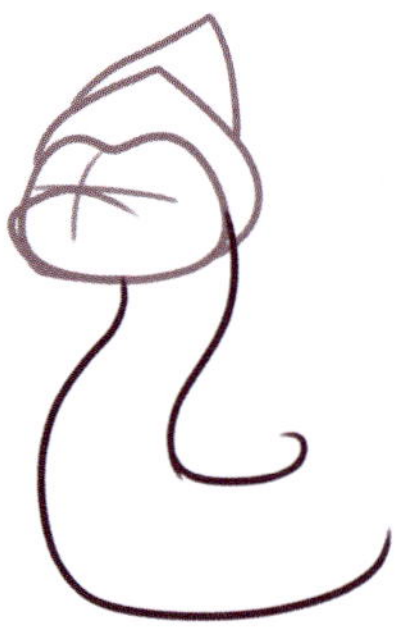

4. Draw two parallel curved lines so that the body resembles a number two.

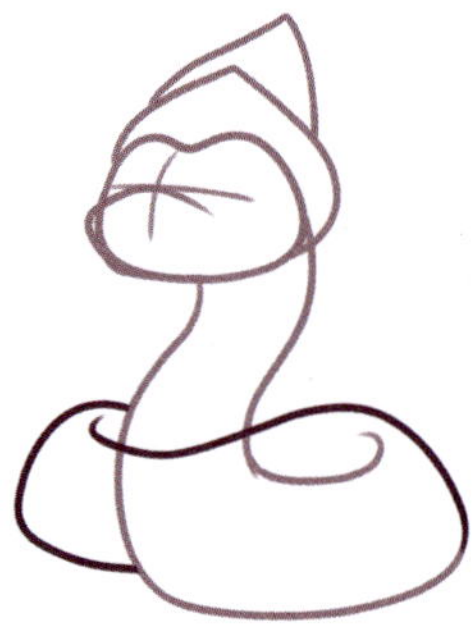

5. Draw a rounded rectangle on the bottom-left of the body. Then complete the tail with a curve crossing over from right to left.

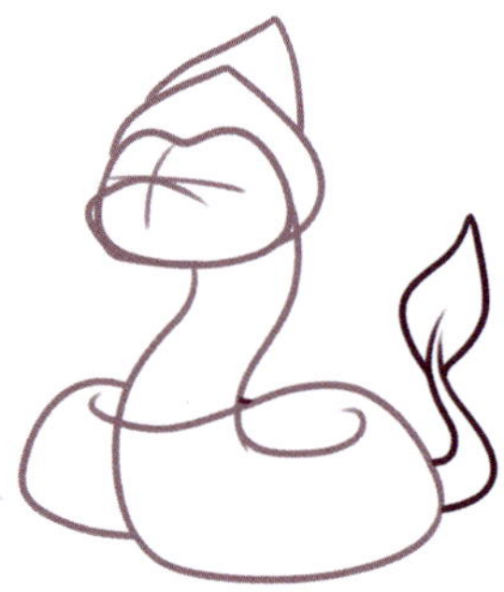

6. At the bottom-right, draw the end of the tail in a curve that narrows to a pointed teardrop.

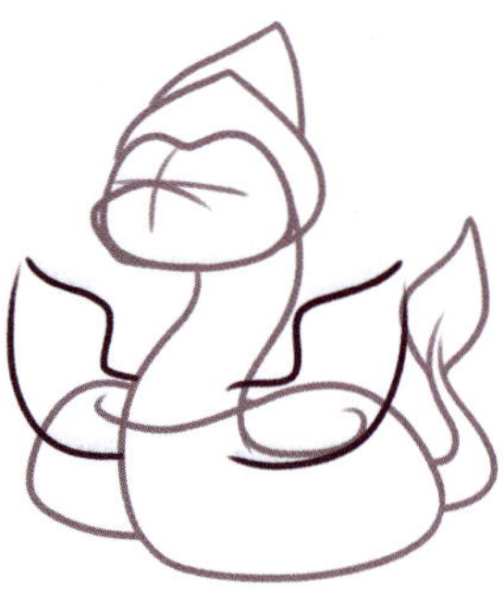

7. Draw soft Z-shaped wings on the sides of the neck. Connect an arc from the wing tips to the body.

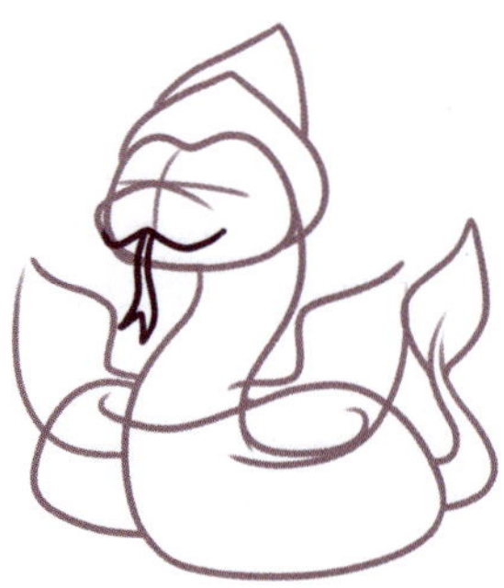

8. Draw a wide W-shaped mouth with a long, forked tongue coming out.

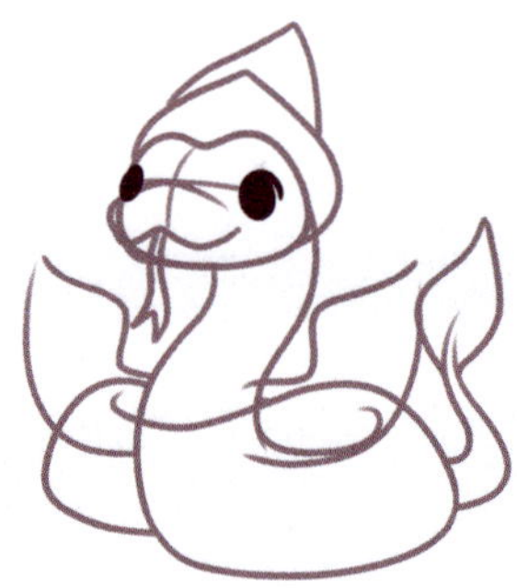

9. Draw two oval eyes with a curve around the top.

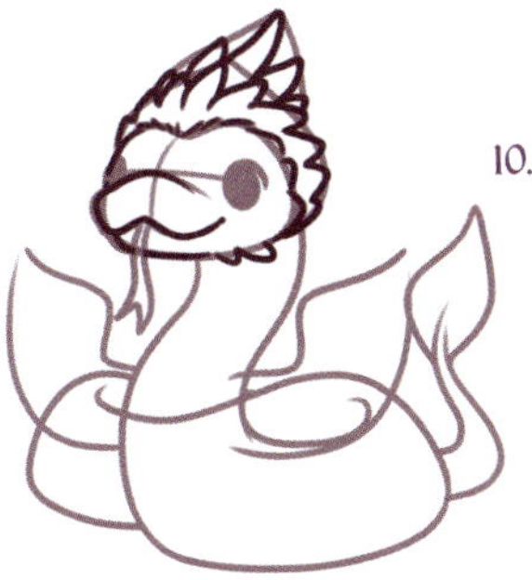

10. Lightly sketch the head and its feathers. In the top triangles use long, thin Vs that grow in height toward the middle.

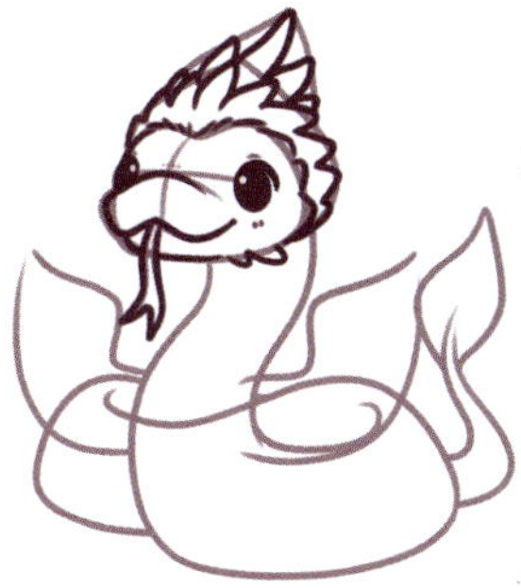

11. Sketch the face detail, adding highlights to the eyes and dashes on the cheeks.

12. Draw the body using soft M shapes for the fur. Use the arrowhead guideline of the tail to make a feather. Leave space where the wings overlap the body.

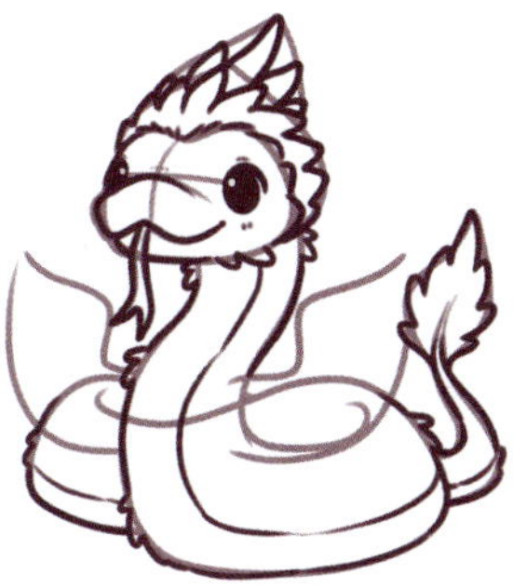

13. Sketch the wings with more thin U shapes along the bottom and across the middle.

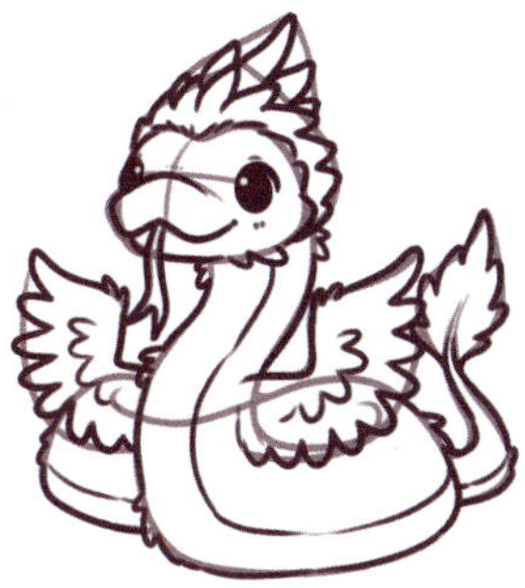

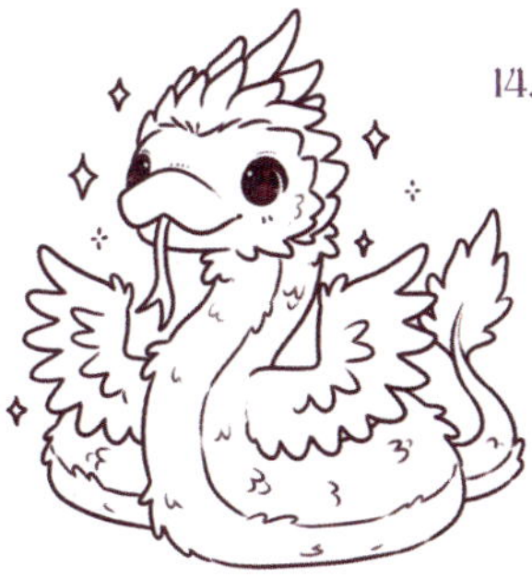

14. Neatly draw the line art over the sketch. Add some sparkles if you'd like! Then erase the sketch underneath.

15. Time for color! Make the body a vibrant green with a pale-yellow underbelly. Color the feathers a mixture of teal and bright red.

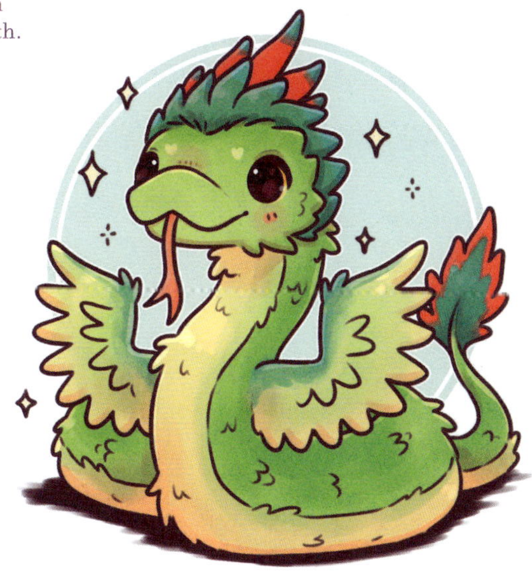

GRIFFIN

Griffins have a penchant for gold, and they also mate for life—should one mate die, the other would never find another.

1. Draw a flat-bottomed circle head with a curved V-shaped beak on the bottom-right side. Add a guideline across the head, starting at the top of the beak.

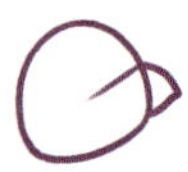

2. On top of the head, draw two triangle ears, one behind the other. Make a line in the left ear.

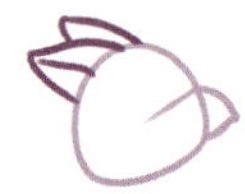

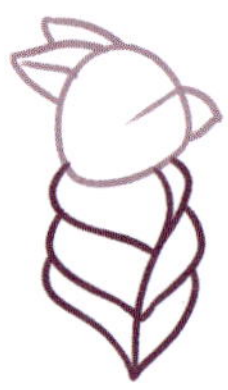

3. Draw three curved Vs, one under the other, for the neck and chest. Add a guideline down the middle.

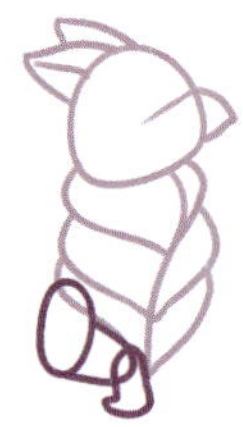

4. On the bottom-left, draw an oval shoulder with a U connected at a right angle for the arm. Overlap an oval at the end with a small hook.

5. Draw the right arm with a U and two lines that connect to a rectangle talon at the bottom.

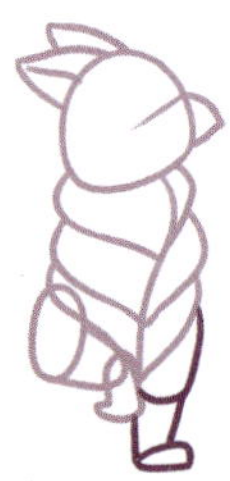

6. Draw a curved line from the left side to the right talon. Add two curved oval feet next to the arms.

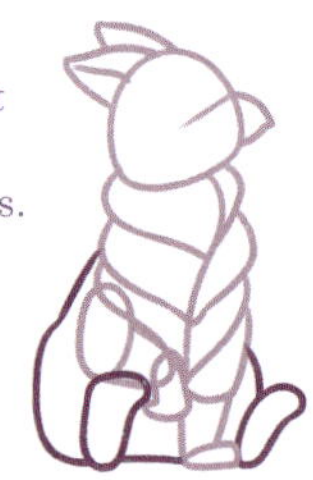

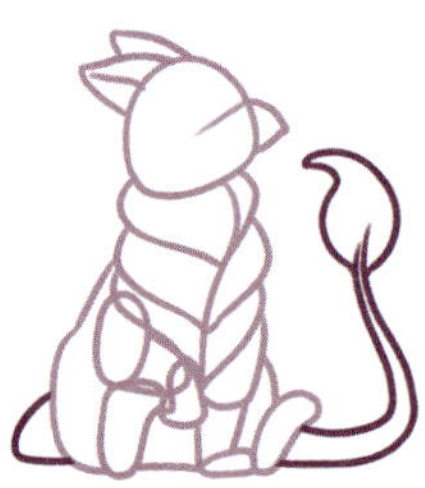

7. Start the tail with a C curve on the bottom-left of the body. Continue the curve on the right so that it narrows upwards to a teardrop-shaped tuft.

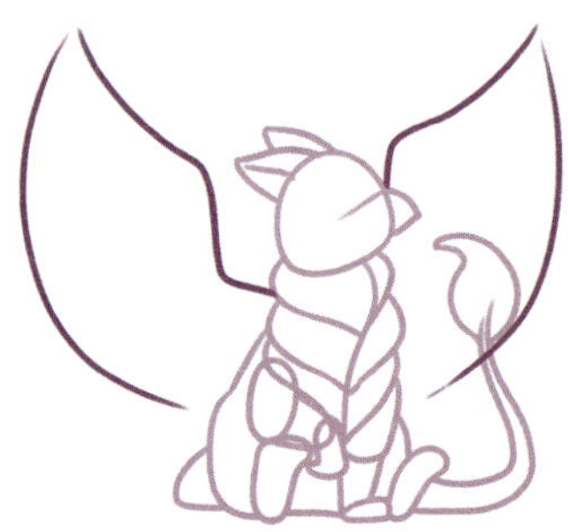

8. Draw two wide Z-shaped wings on the sides of the body. Connect an arc from the wing tips to the body.

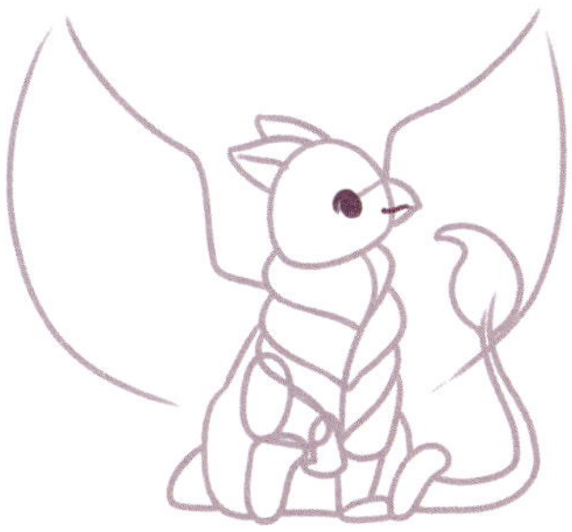

9. Sketch an eye with a curved line around the top. Draw a small, slightly curved mouth on the beak.

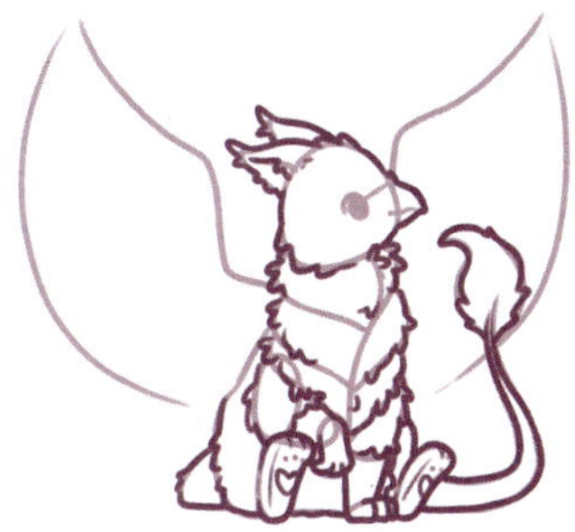

10. Lightly go over the basic sketch, adding details of the head and body. Use soft W shapes for the fur. Add the toe beans with heart-shaped paw pads.

11. Sketch the wings with thin U shapes along the bottom and across the middle.

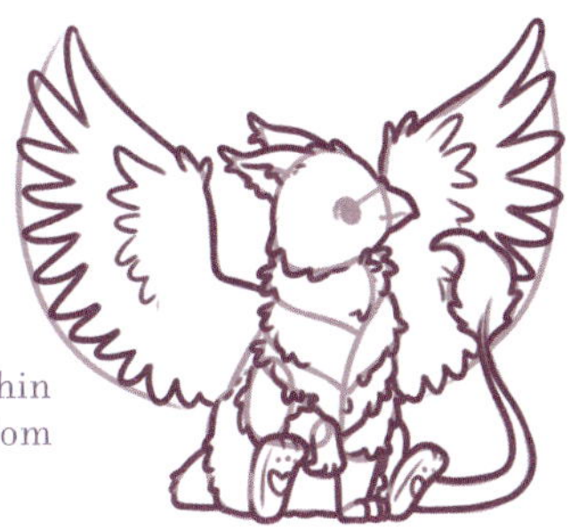

12. Sketch the face, leaving space in the eyes for highlights and dashes on the cheeks.

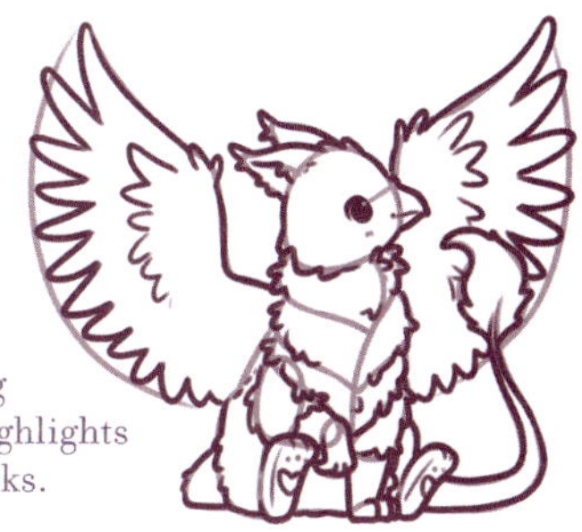

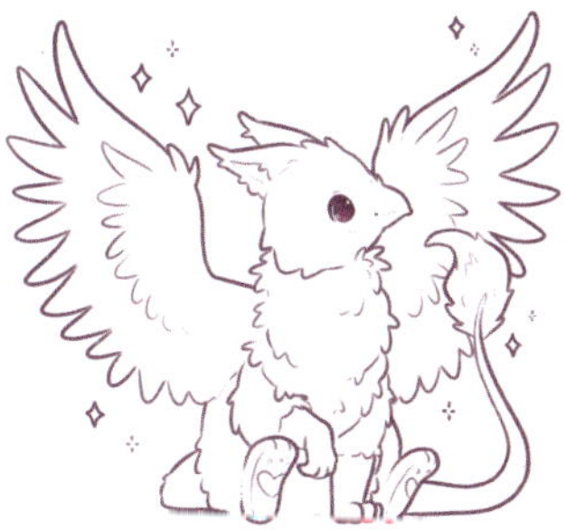

13. Neatly draw the line art over the sketch. Add some sparkles if you'd like! Then erase the sketch underneath.

14. Color your griffin! I went with golden fur with a bright brown for the tip of the tail and a dull brown for the beak and talons.

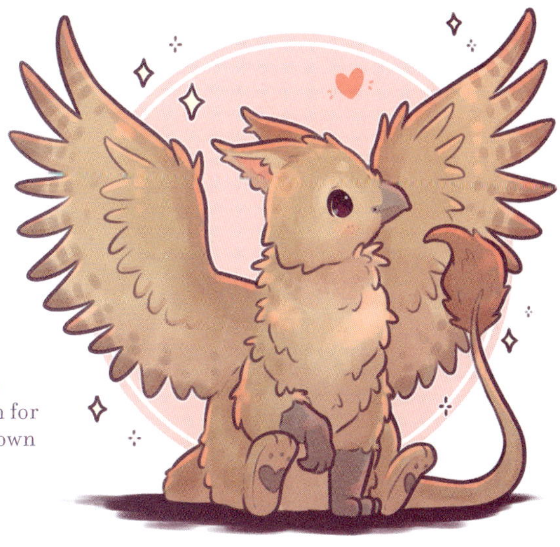

PEGASUS

Emerging from the severed neck of Medusa, Pegasus is a mighty flying warhorse for the gods on Mount Olympus in ancient Greece.

1. Sketch a circle head with a curved shape on the left side for the snout. Add a guideline across the head.

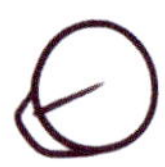

2. Add two teardrop ears on the top of the head with curved lines inside.

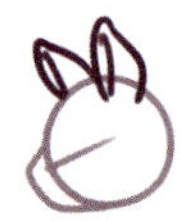

3. Draw two curved lines below the head for the neck and body.

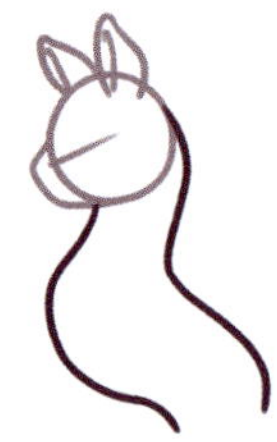

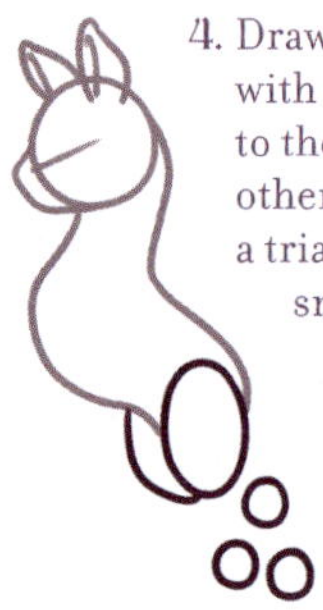

4. Draw an oval haunch with a curved line to the left for the other leg. Then draw a triangle of three small circles below the legs.

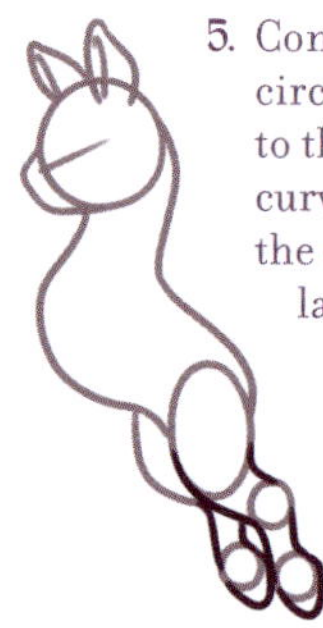

5. Connect the two circles on the right to the haunch with curved lines, doing the same for the last circle for the other leg. Attach two V-shaped hooves.

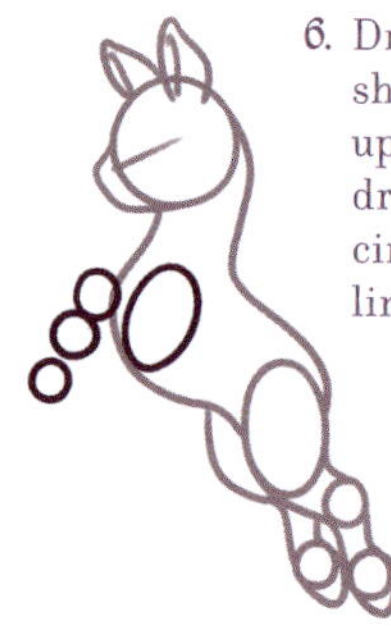

6. Draw an oval shoulder on the upper body, then draw three small circles in a diagonal line to the left.

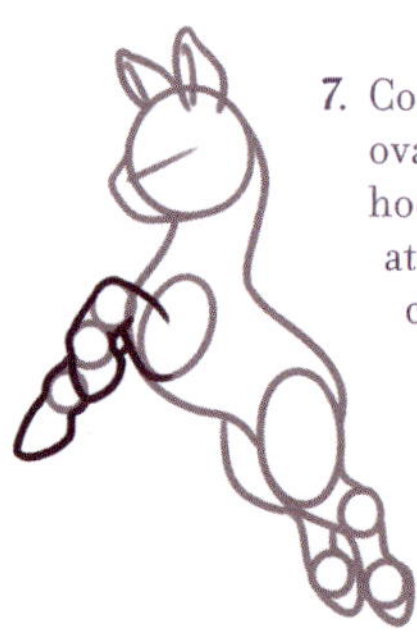

7. Connect the top two circles to the oval with lines. Attach a triangle hoof curved toward the body. Then attach another hoof to the last circle that is pointed out.

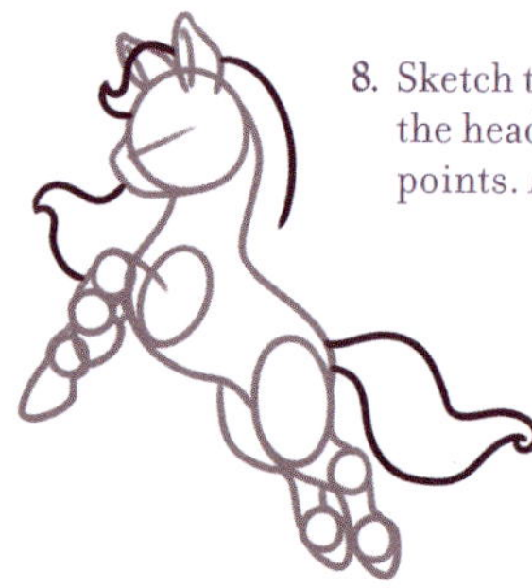

8. Sketch the flowing mane around the head and neck with curved points. Add a curvy tail.

9. Draw a wing with a stretched-out W and a curved line. Then draw a curving line from the tip of the wing toward the body. Make a second partial wing on top.

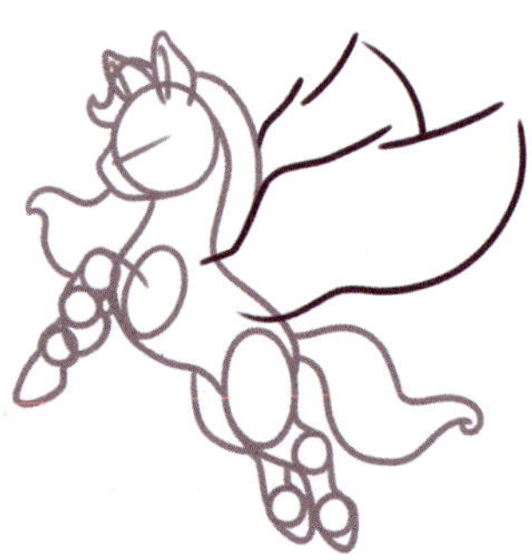

10. Draw a dot at the top of the snout for a nostril. Add an oval eye with a curved line around the top.

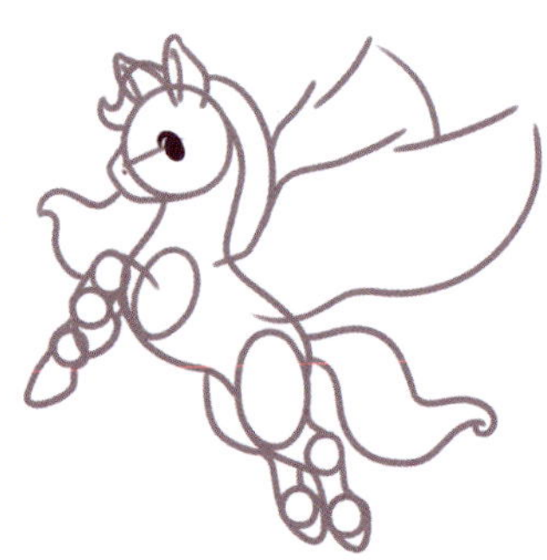

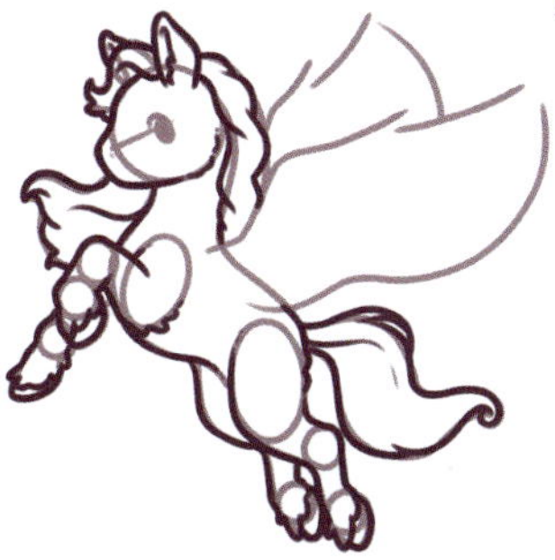

11. Lightly go over the basic sketch, adding details of the head and body. Define the fur with soft W shapes. Add curved lines to the mane and tail.

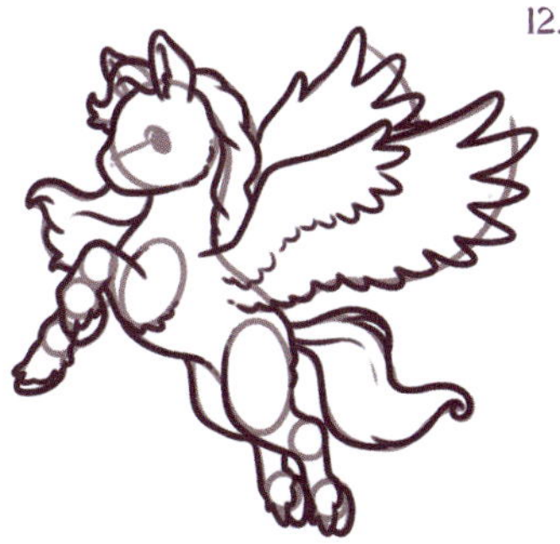

12. Sketch the wings with thin U shapes along the bottom and across the middle.

13. Sketch the face detail, adding highlight to the eye and a small eyelash on top of the eye, and dashes on the cheek.

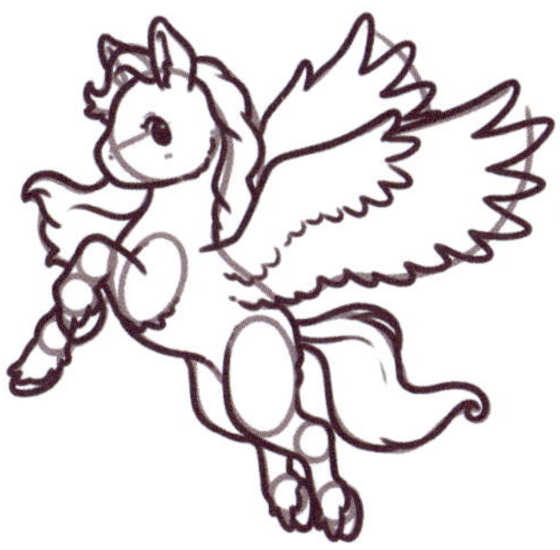

14. Neatly draw the line art over the sketch. Add some sparkles if you'd like! Then erase the sketch underneath.

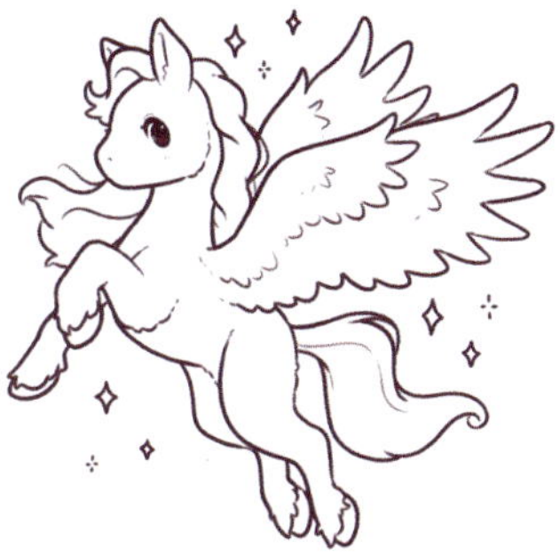

15. Lastly, add the color! I did a classic white body with a pale gold mane and tail, and a touch of pink in the ear.

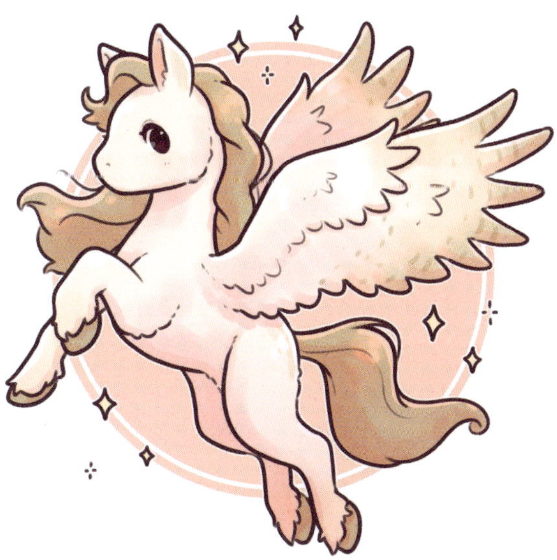

ALICORN

Born from the crossbreeding of Pegasus (page 64) and a unicorn (page 24), alicorns look physically similar but are lesser-known legacies and not often found in classic mythology.

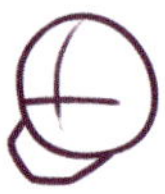

1. Lightly sketch a circle head with a plus sign guideline. On the bottom-right, add a blocky nose.

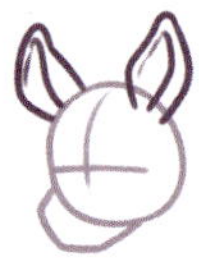

2. Add two teardrop ears on the top of the head, with smaller partial teardrops inside.

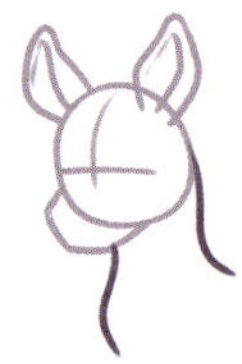

3. Add two curved lines for the neck, starting on the right side of the head and under the snout.

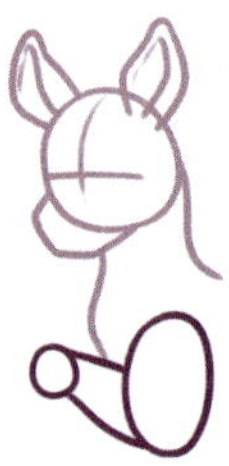

4. Draw a large oval shoulder between the curved lines. Add a small circle to the left and connect it to the shoulder with two lines.

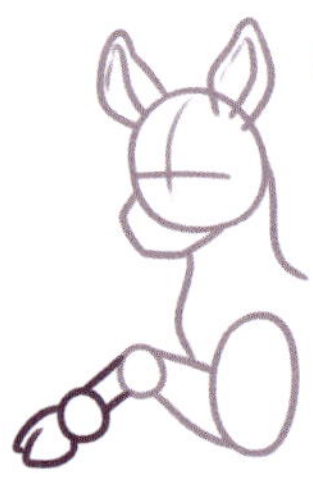

5. Draw another circle for the ankle, down and to the left. Connect it to the rest of the leg with lines. Add two rounded V shapes for a cloven hoof.

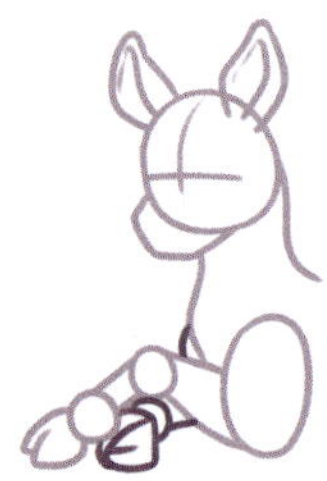

6. Draw a backwards D for another hoof to the right of the first. Use a curve and lines to connect it to the body.

7. Draw a large oval for the back haunch with space between it and the neck. Draw a small circle at the end and another circle to the left.

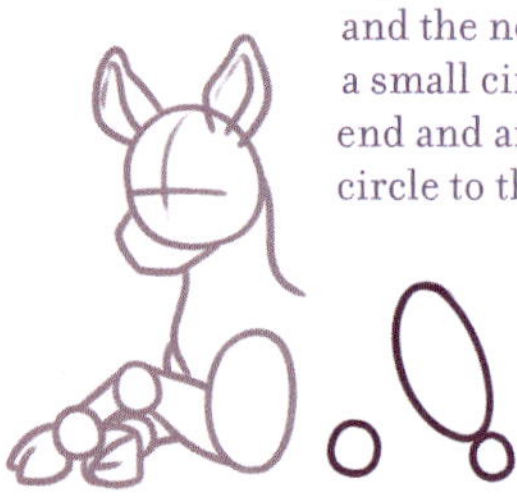

8. Connect the two circles to the haunch with lines. Attach a cloven hoof.

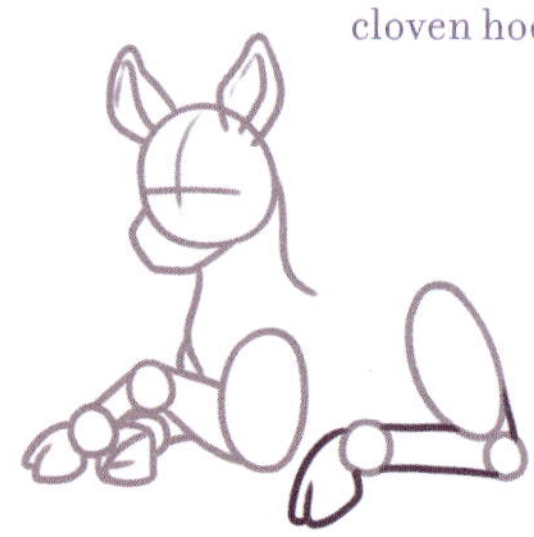

9. Draw a partial hoof between the hoof and shoulder. Add a curved line to the haunch for the back side.

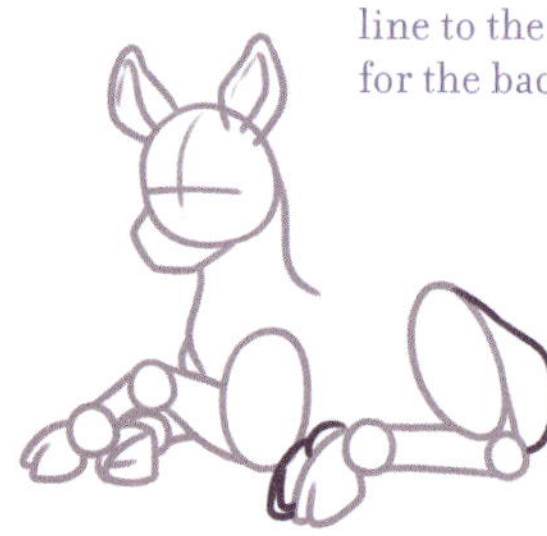

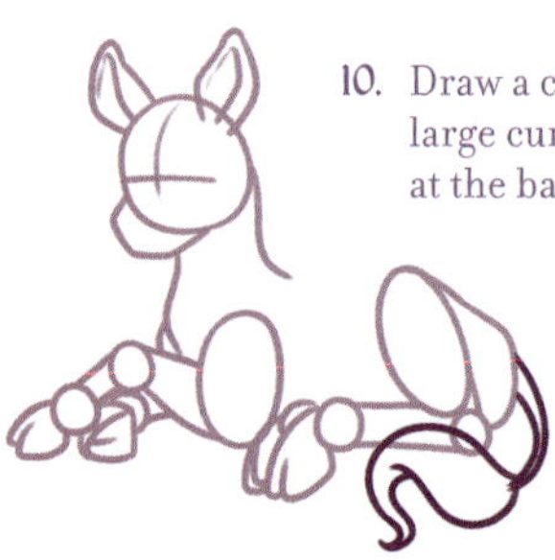

10. Draw a curved tail that narrows to a large curving tuft of fur that is wide at the base and narrows to a point.

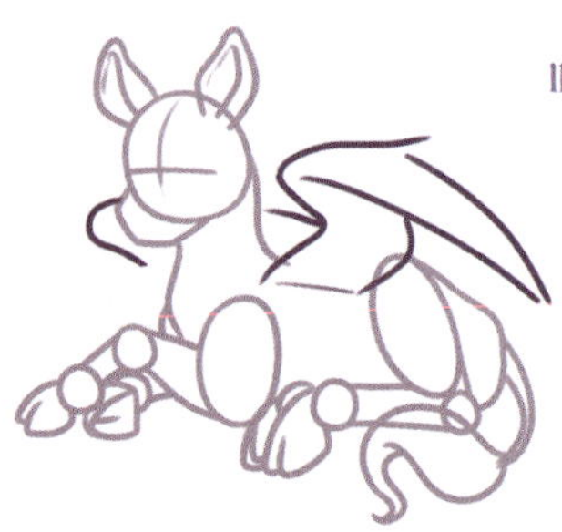

11. Draw a soft Z shape to start a wing. Attach a long, curved V pointing slightly down. Connect the wing to the body with a curved line. Draw a curve that hooks behind the head for a partial second wing.

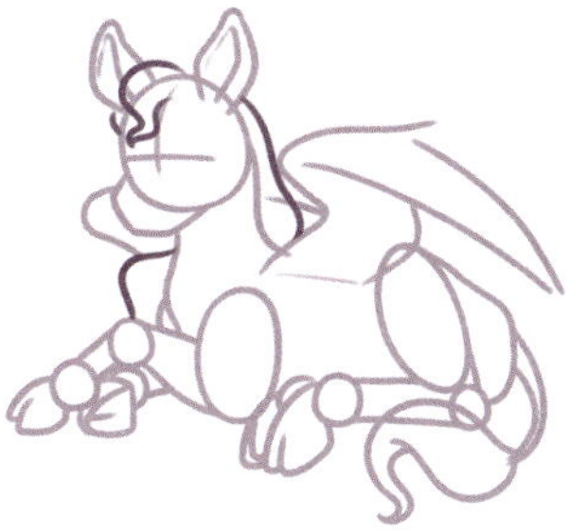

12. Sketch the mane with curving lines around the head and neck. Add a wiggly teardrop tuft of hair between the ears.

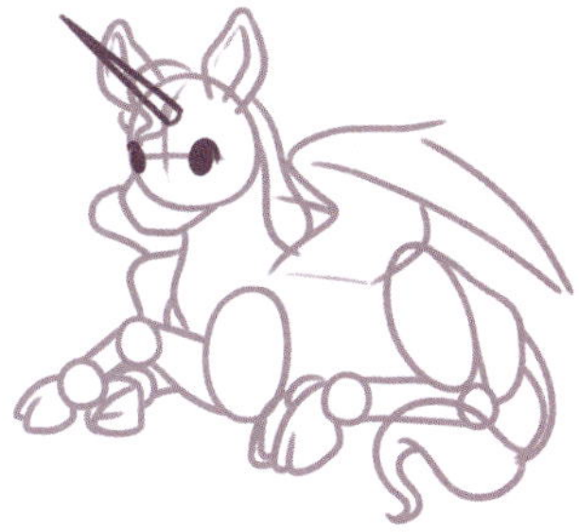

13. Add a thin pointed horn coming out of the center of the forehead. Draw two oval eyes with a curve around the top.

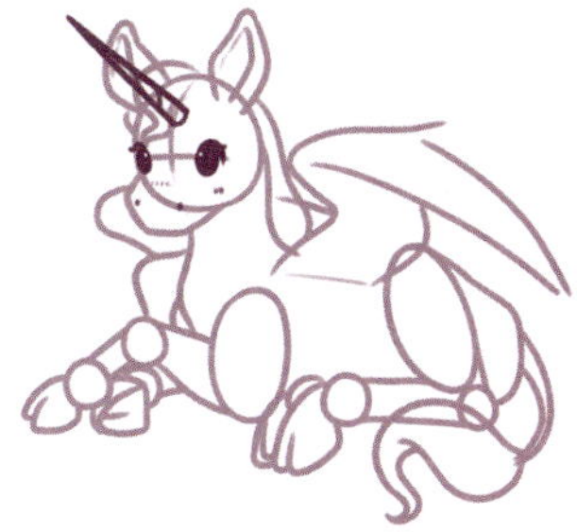

14. Lightly sketch the face detail, adding highlights in the eyes, a dot on the cheek, and two nostrils. Add some curves along the horn.

15. Go over the basic sketch, adding details of the head and body. Define the fur with soft W shapes. Add more detail to the mane and tail.

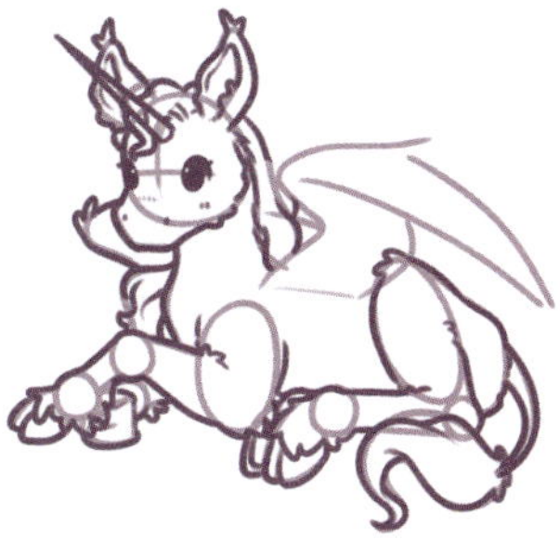

16. Sketch the wings with thin V shapes for feathers.

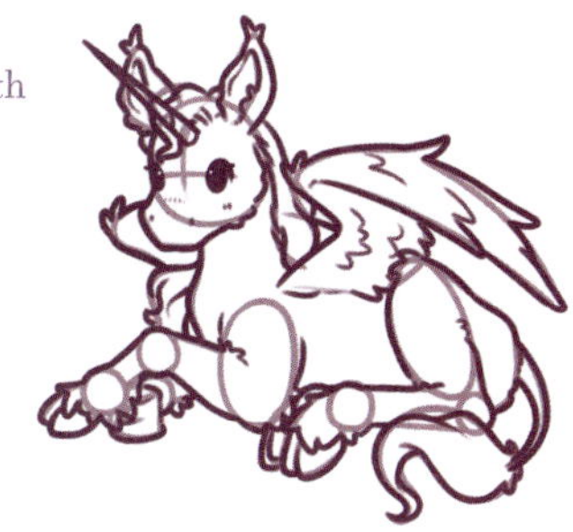

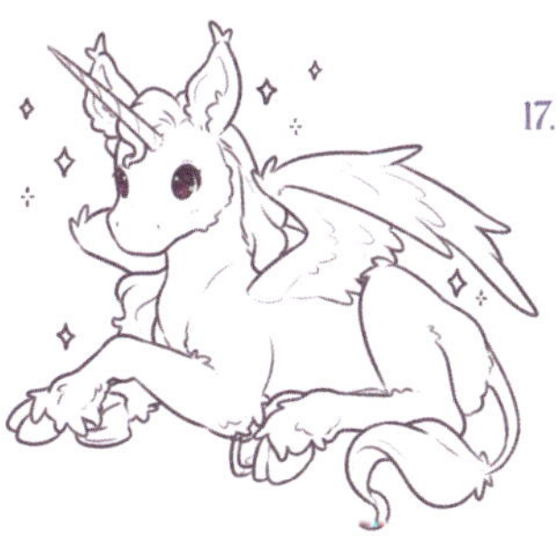

17. Neatly draw the line art over the sketch. Add some sparkles if you'd like! Then erase the sketch underneath.

18. Finally, add color! I did a white and pale gold color scheme, with pale pink in the inner ears and on the cheeks. Feel free to get creative!

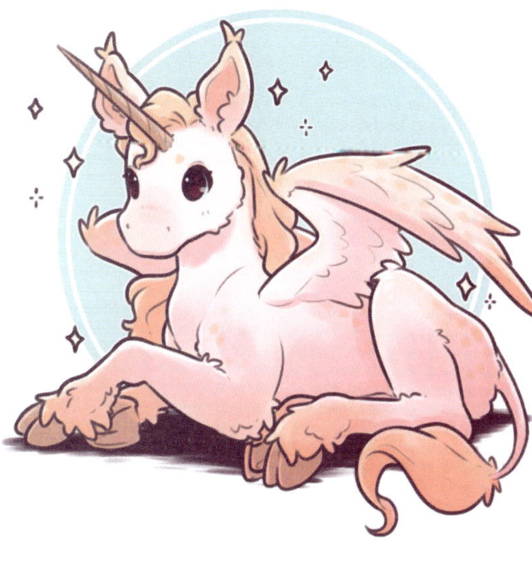

PERYTON

Find these mesmerizing creatures traipsing through the sky with the antlers and body of a stag and the giant, majestic wings of a bird.

1. Draw a circle head with a curved snout on the right side. Add a guideline across the head at a diagonal.

2. Add two overlapping teardrop ears on the left side of the head with a line inside one.

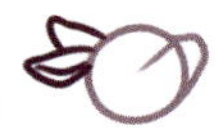

3. Sketch two curved lines for the neck, then add an oval shoulder. Continue the curved line to the left of the shoulder.

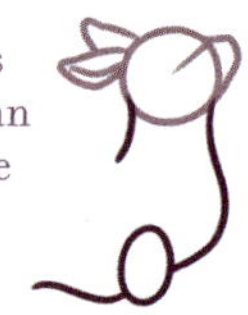

4. Below the shoulder, draw a small circle with a smaller circle underneath. To the right of that draw two more circles.

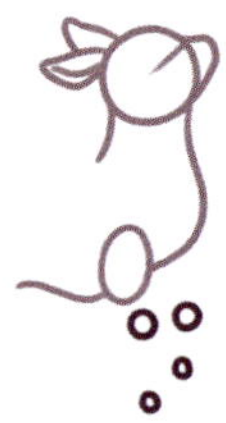

5. Connect the shoulder to the top-right circle with lines, continuing to the circle below that and ending in a V-shaped hoof. Do the same to the remaining circles.

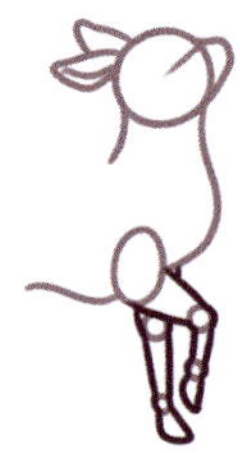

6. Draw a large oval back haunch with another to the right. Below the haunches, draw a small circle with a smaller circle going in opposite directions below.

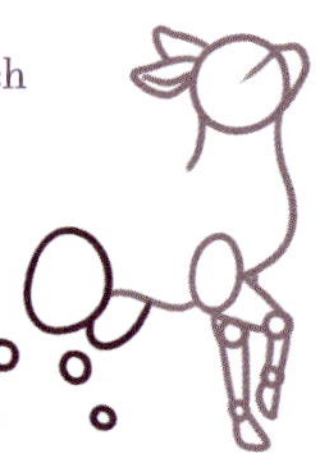

7. Connect the two left circles to the oval haunch with lines. Attach a triangle hoof at the end. Do the same for the remaining leg.

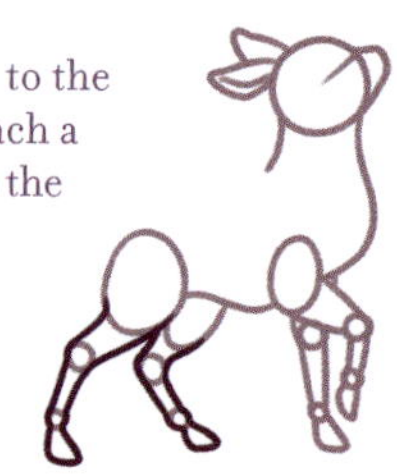

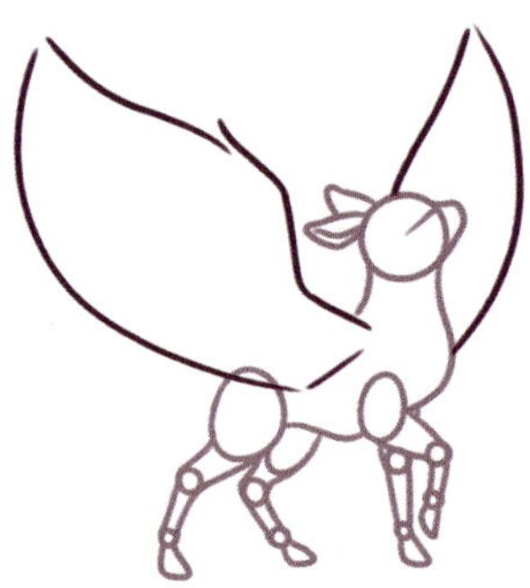

8. Sketch a stretched Z shape to start the wings. Add a long, curved line to the end and connect to the body with a curved line. For the right wing, draw a curved V around the head.

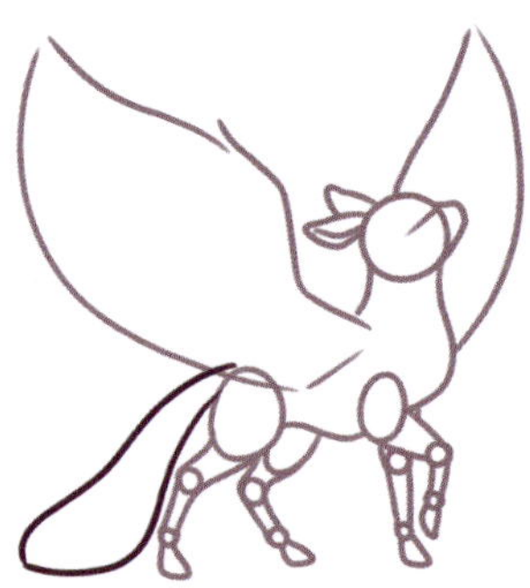

9. Starting at the top of the haunch, draw a tail that widens as it flows down to the ground.

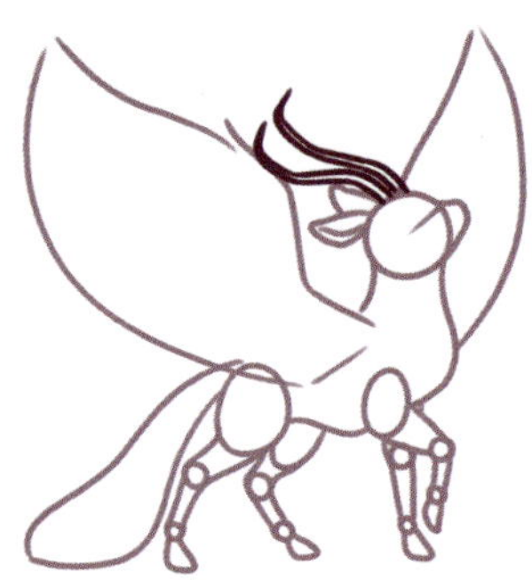

10. Draw two thin curved antlers on top of the head that narrow to a point.

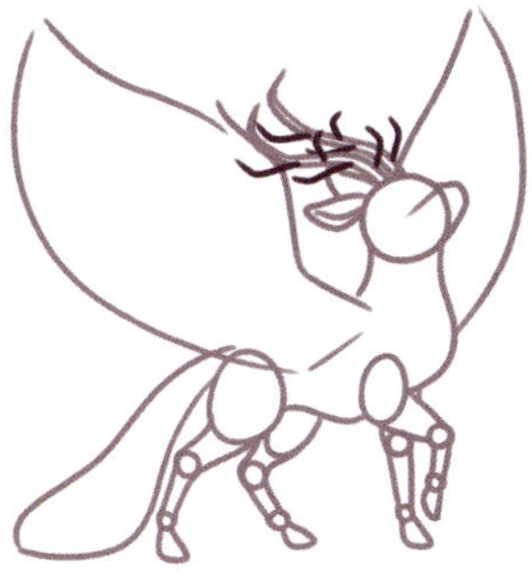

11. Add four angled prongs to each antler.

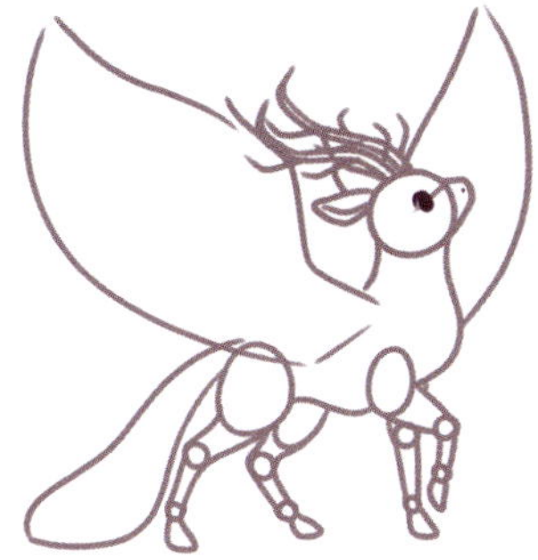

12. Draw a dot at the top of the snout for a nostril. Add an oval eye with a curved line around the top.

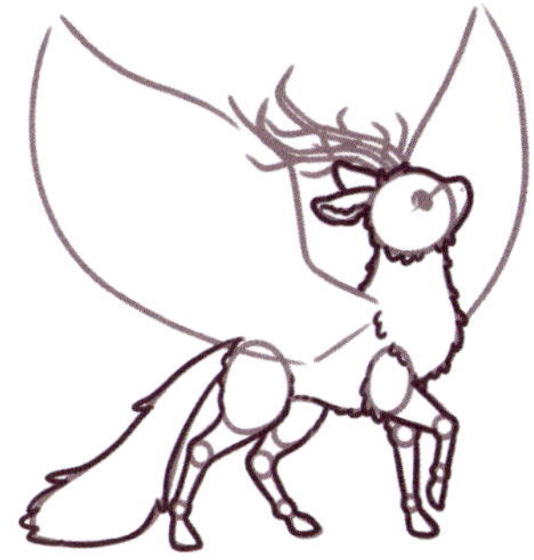

13. Lightly go over the basic sketch, adding details of the head and body. Define the fur with soft W shapes, then add more detail to the tail.

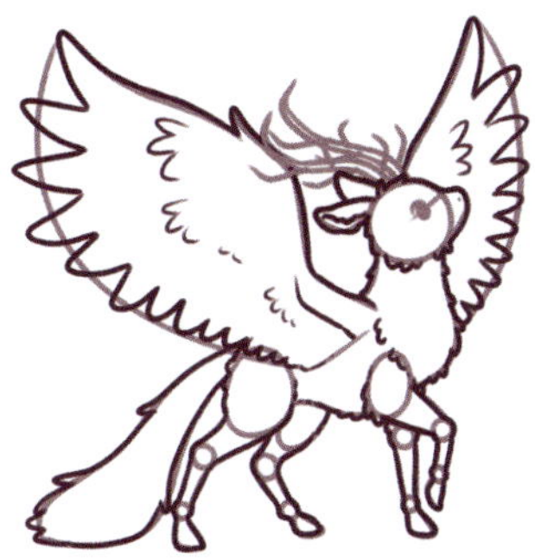

14. Sketch the wings with long V and U shapes along the bottom and the middle.

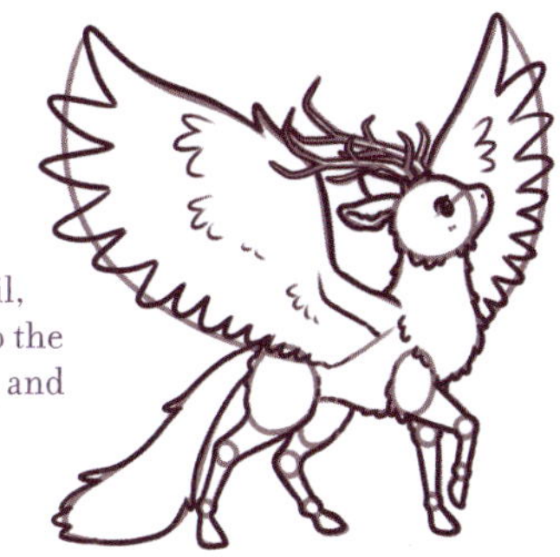

15. Sketch the face detail, adding a highlight to the eye, a small eyelash, and dashes of blush on the cheek.

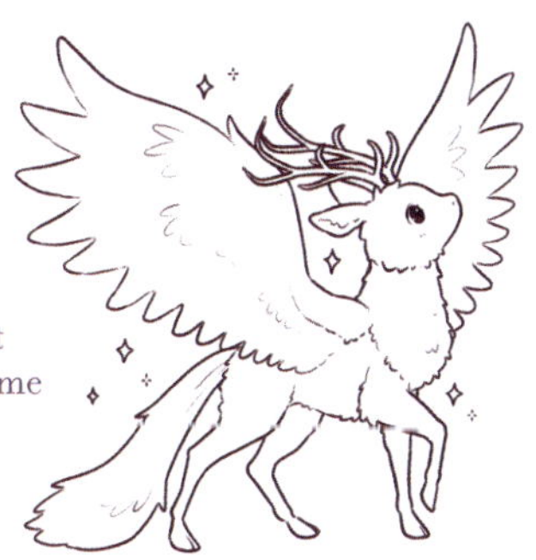

16. Neatly draw the line art over the sketch. Add some sparkles if you'd like! Then erase the sketch underneath.

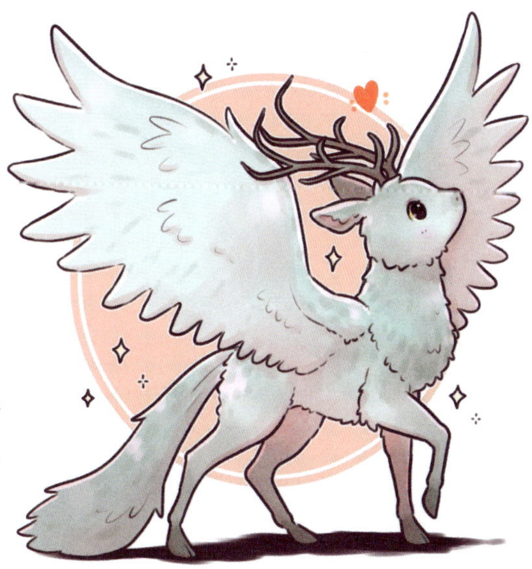

17. Time for color! I used pale blue with gray for the hooves and antlers, but you could go with a more traditional deer color scheme.

EASTERN DRAGON

Often seen or worn as a symbol of luck, the eastern dragon has a long snakelike body, four legs, and horns. Though they are often soaring through the skies, their homes are in the water.

1. Lightly sketch an oval with pointed sides. Add a plus sign guideline for the face.

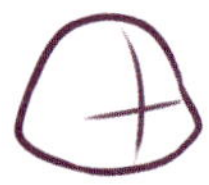

2. At the bottom of the head, add a rounded rectangle snout with a soft W shape along the bottom. Add a wide triangle nose in the middle.

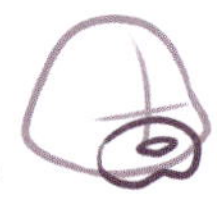

3. Add two pointed ears angled out on top of the head, with a curved line inside each.

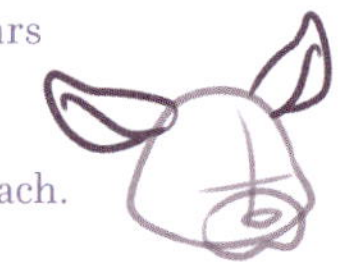

4. Draw two curved parallel lines below the head that narrow at the bottom. Add another line to the right about half as long.

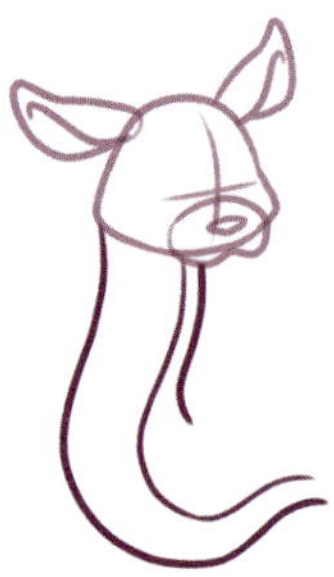

5. Continue the lines of the body with the end curling upwards and narrowing to a point.

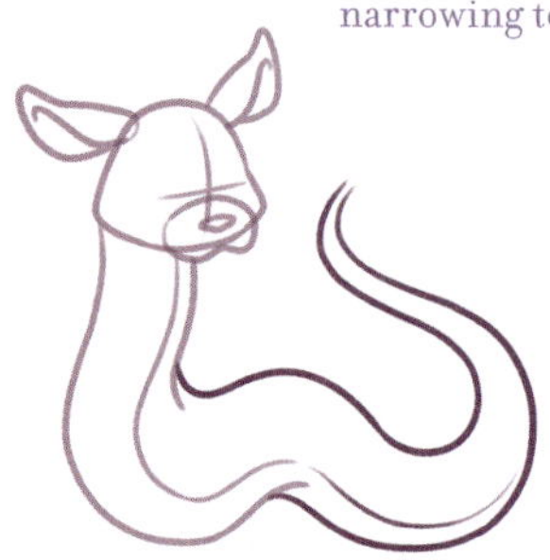

6. Draw in two ovals for the front and back legs, and two partial legs to the left of them. Then sketch four oval paws.

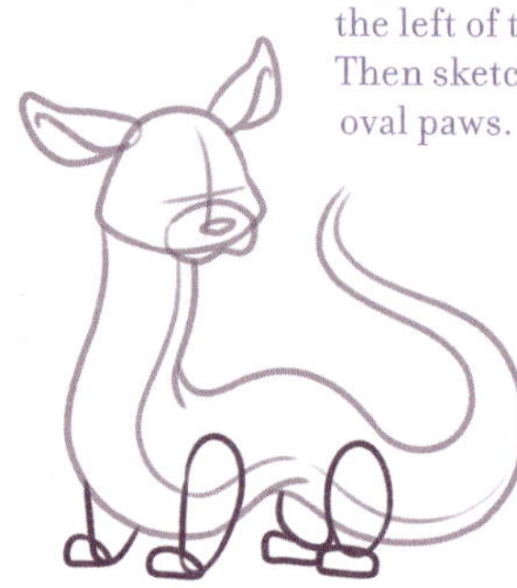

7. Draw a curved line from the top of the head that continues along the back for the fur. Add a teardrop tuft at the tip of the tail.

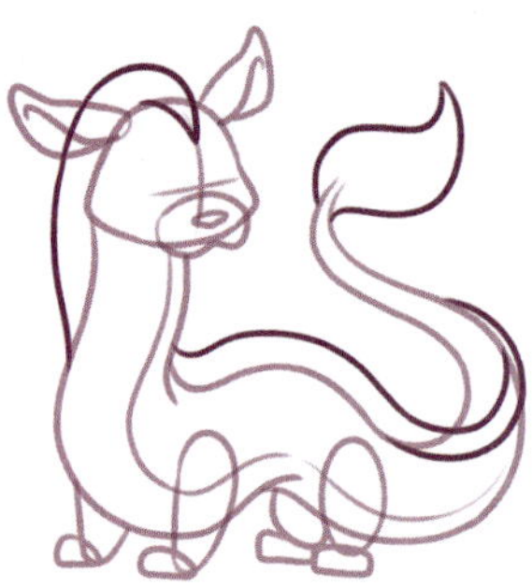

8. Add pointed ovals to the backs of the legs for more fluff.

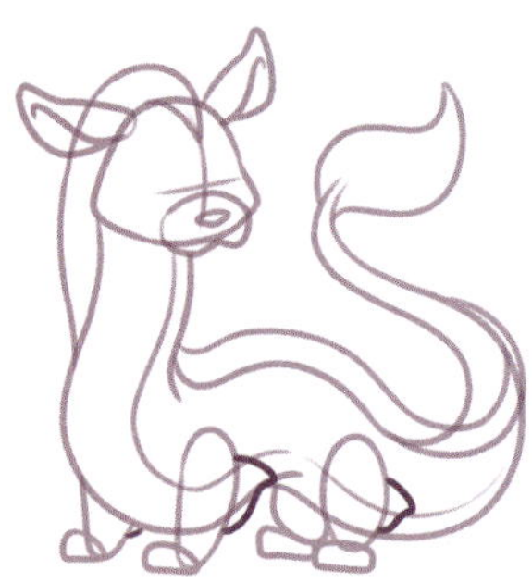

9. Sketch two wavy whiskers on the sides of the snout. Make them roughly symmetrical. Then add a small V beard under the snout.

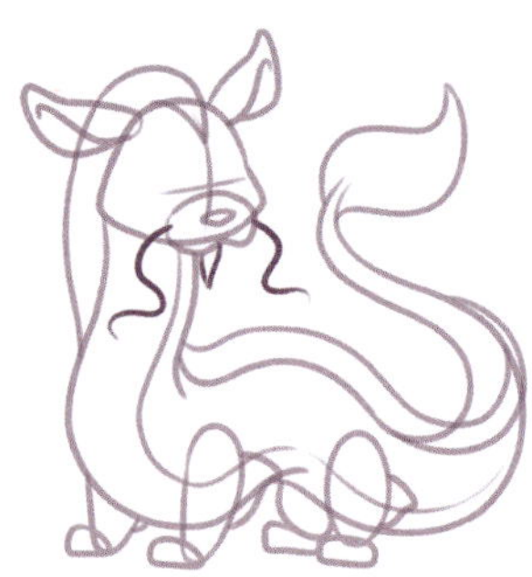

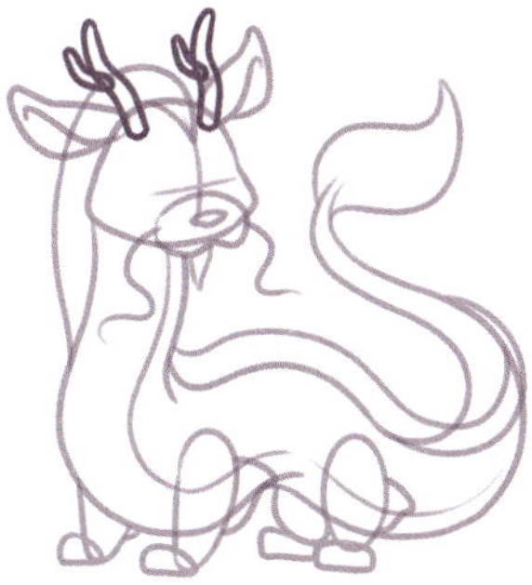

10. Add two forked antlers on top of the head with an oval at the junction of the fork.

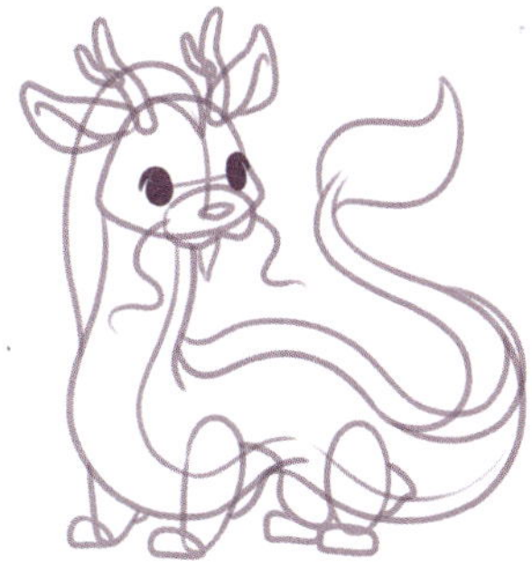

11. Add two oval eyes with a curved line around the top.

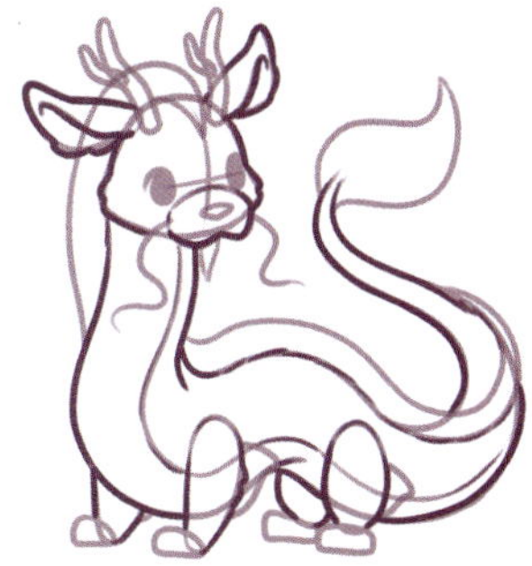

12. Lightly sketch the head and body. Add a little bit of fluff on the sides of the head and ears. Add some light lines where the fur lays on the back.

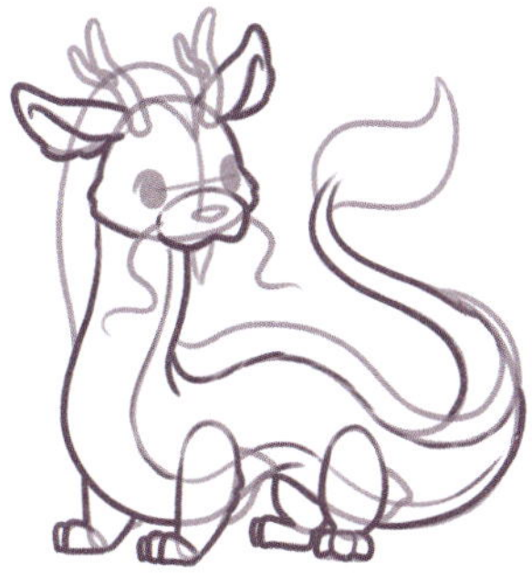

13. Sketch the paws. For the paws partially concealed by the body, draw two toes, with three toes for the paws on front side of the body.

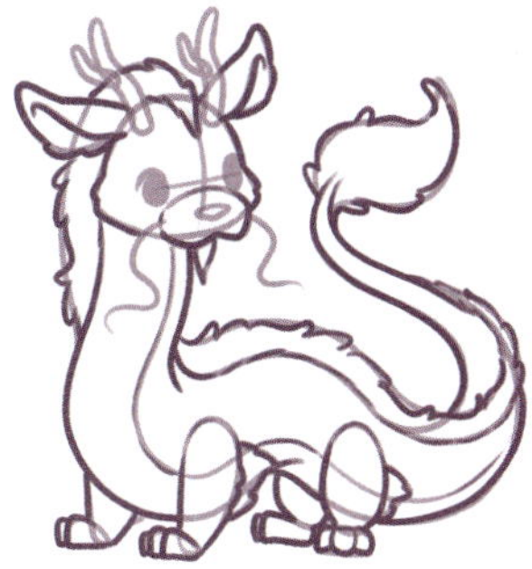

14. Sketch the fur along the back, the tip of the tail, the beard, and the backs of the legs.

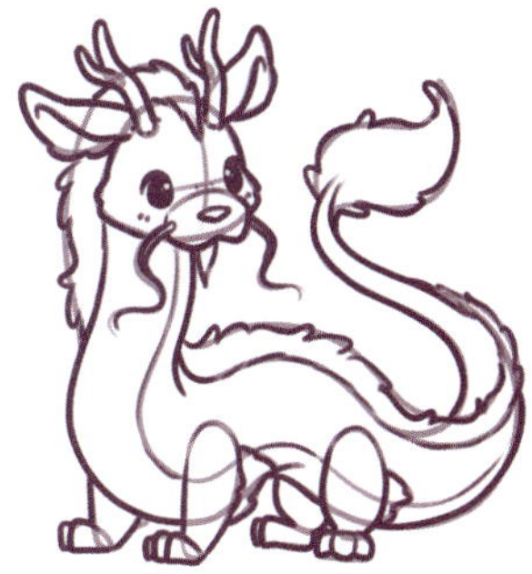

15. Add the face detail. Leave a little space in the eyes for highlights. Add dashes of blush on the cheeks. Sketch the antlers and whiskers.

16. Neatly draw the line art over the sketch. Add small W scales on the body, and some sparkles if you'd like! Then erase the sketch underneath.

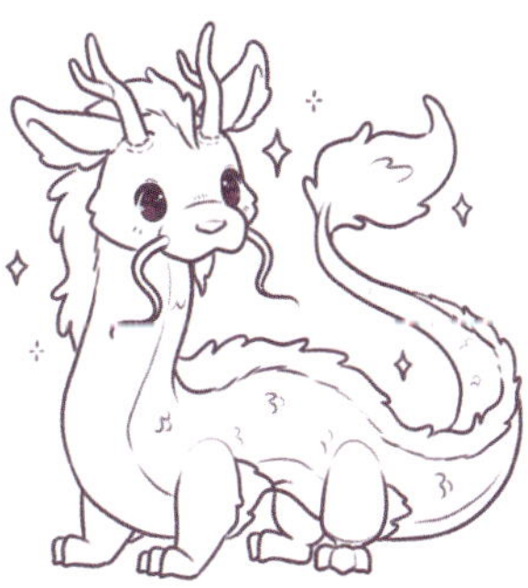

17. Finish with color! I used pale blue for the body with a lighter shade for the underbelly, and teal for the fur. Add pale pink for the inner ears and on the cheeks.

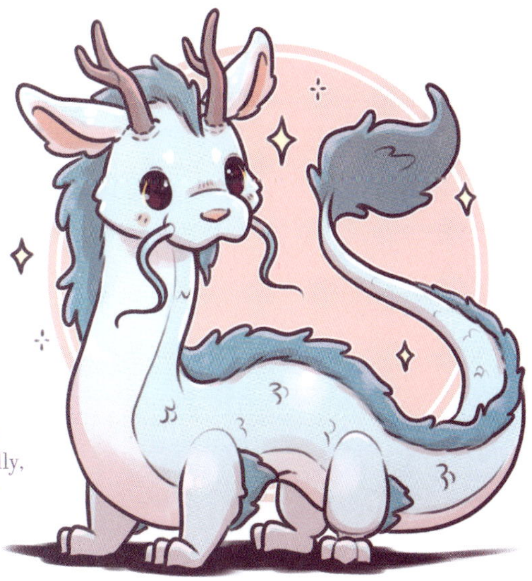

WESTERN DRAGON

Do not come between this giant scaly lizard and its love of gold as you might end up on the wrong side of its spiteful, fear–inducing temper.

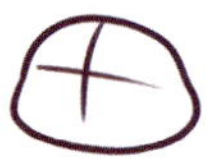

1. Lightly sketch an oval with pointed sides. Add a plus sign guideline for the face.

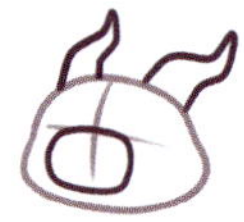

2. Add a rounded rectangle snout at the center of the face. Then on top of the head draw two pointed angled horns.

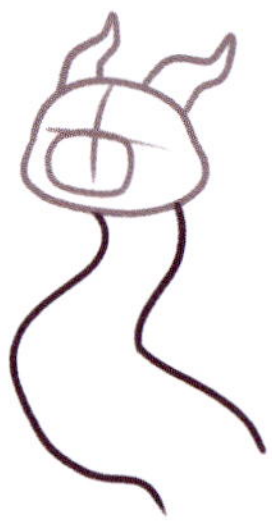

3. At the base of the head, sketch two curved lines for the neck and upper body.

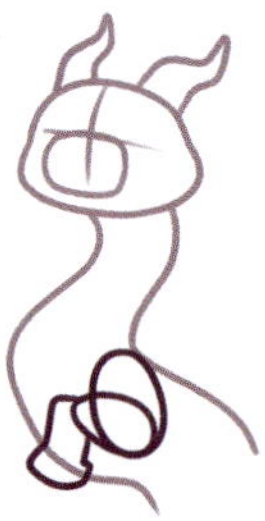

4. Sketch two overlapping ovals for the left arm, so that they create a V shape. On the tip of the oval, add a rectangle with a hooked end for the hand.

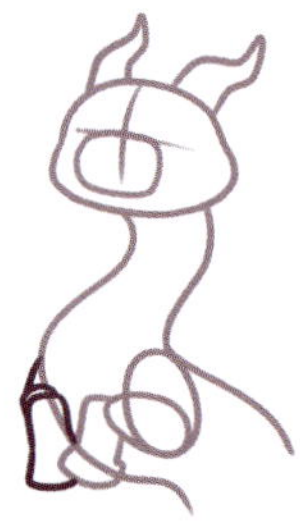

5. To the left of the hand, add the other hand. Draw two small, curved lines for the left arm.

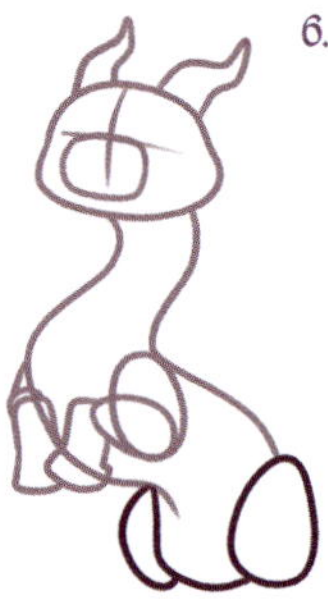

6. Draw a curve for the lower part of the body. On the sides, add oval haunches.

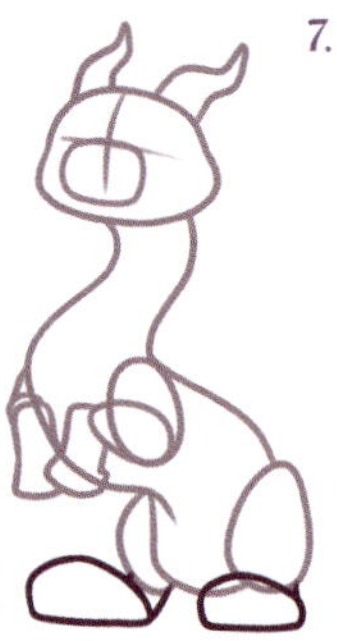

7. Below the haunches, draw two rounded rectangle feet, then connect the feet to the legs.

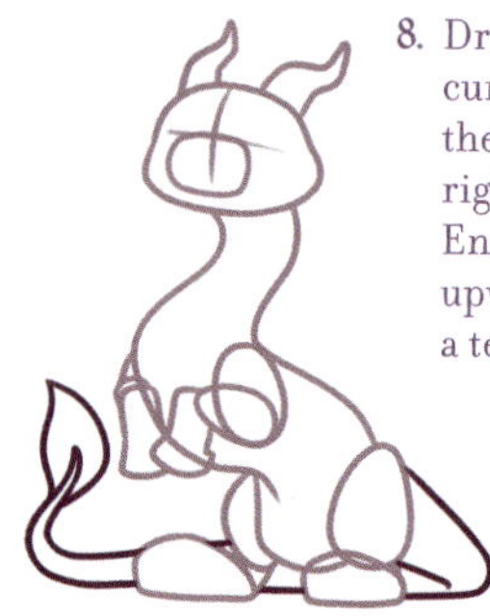

8. Draw the tail curving around the body from the right to the left. End the tail in an upward curl with a teardrop tuft.

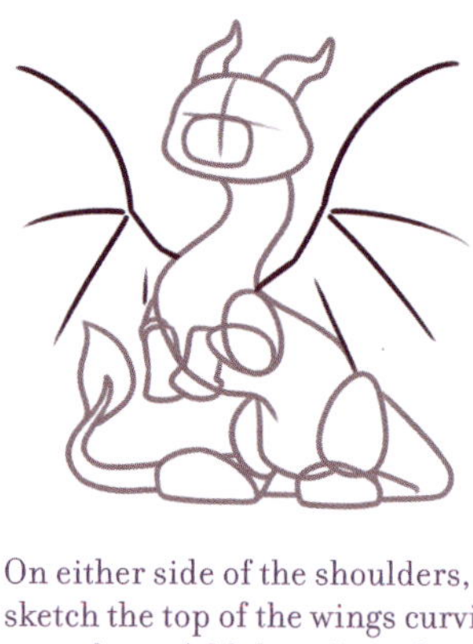

9. On either side of the shoulders, sketch the top of the wings curving up and out. Add three lines fanning out from the middle of each wing.

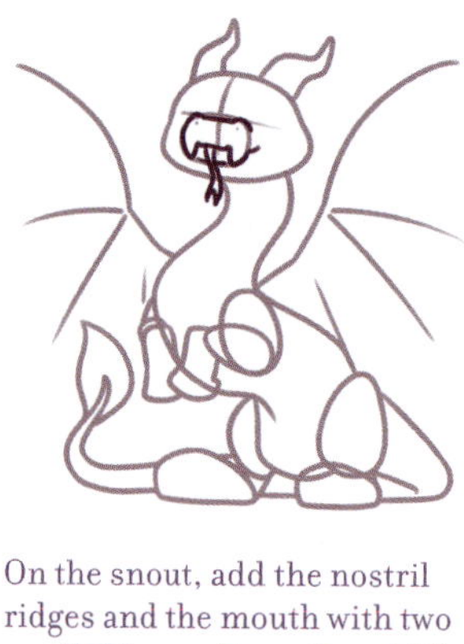

10. On the snout, add the nostril ridges and the mouth with two small V fangs. From the middle of the mouth, add a forked tongue.

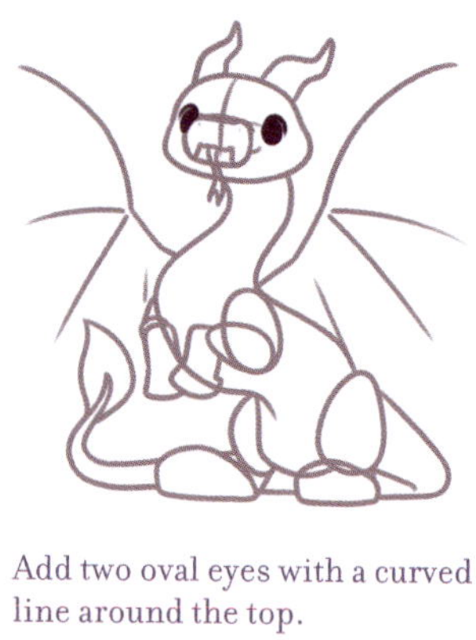

11. Add two oval eyes with a curved line around the top.

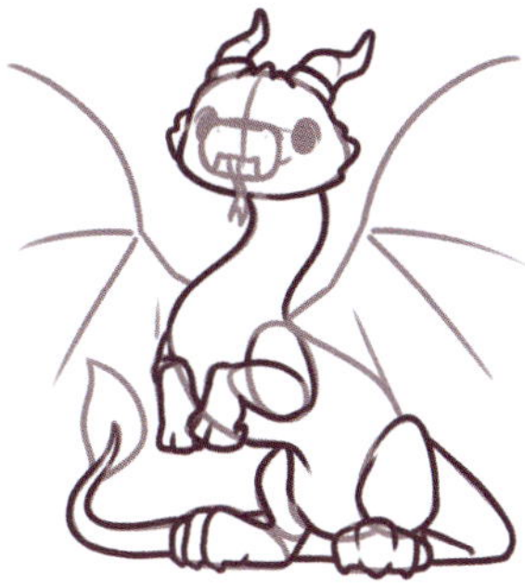

12. Lightly sketch the body and tail. Add the details of the clawed hands and feet. On the sides of the head, add small spikes.

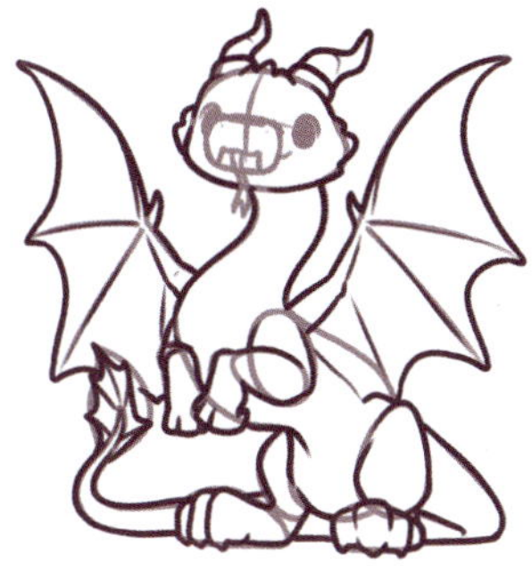

13. Sketch the details for the wings with webbing between the spines. Then add spines and webbing to the tip of the tail.

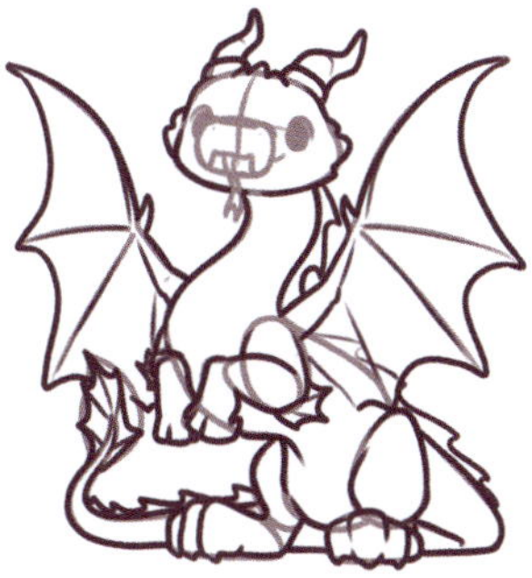

14. Draw spikes running along the back and tail, and spines coming out of the elbow.

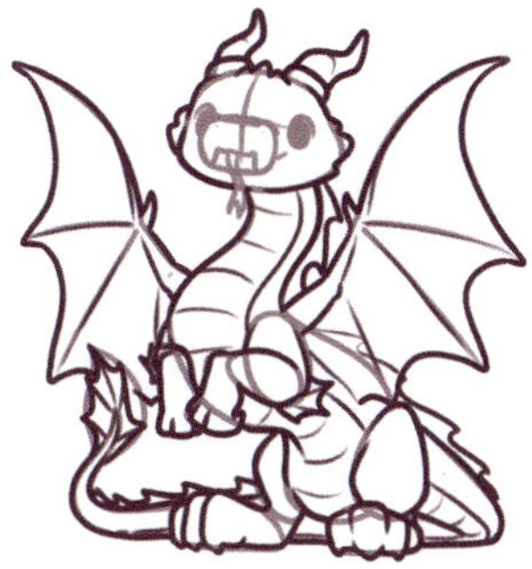

15. Draw the underbelly along the body with small, curved lines at regular intervals.

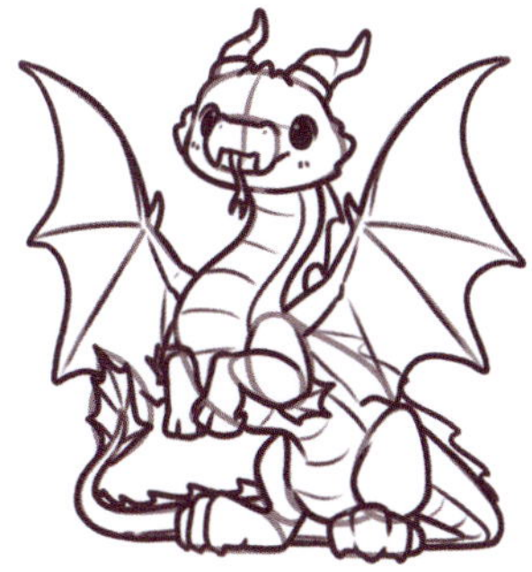

16. Sketch the face detail, leaving space for highlights in the eyes and dashes on the cheeks.

17. Neatly draw the line art over the sketch. Add some sparkles if you'd like! Then erase the sketch underneath.

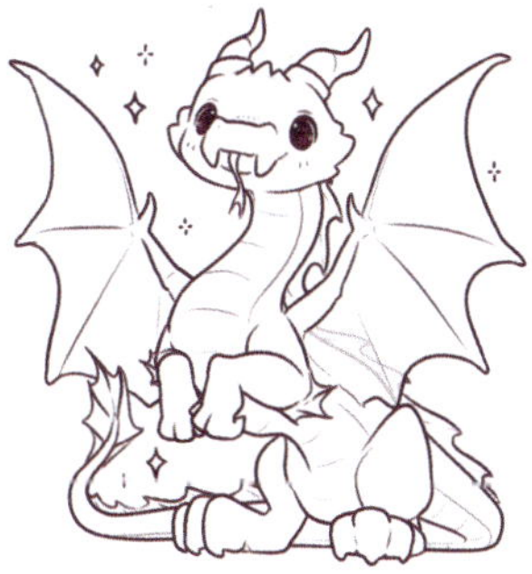

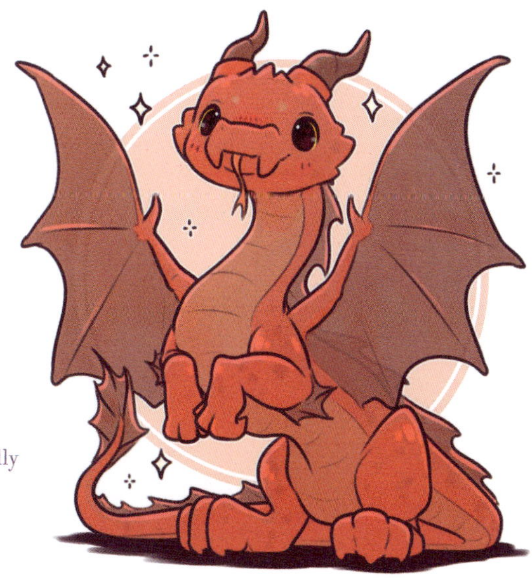

18. Lastly, add color! I made a classic red dragon, with a pale red for the underbelly and for the heart-shaped eyebrows.

FLUFFY DRAGON

Here's a cute dragon variation I created myself, with cuddly fur and feathered wings, that suits my anime-mixed-with-chibi style.

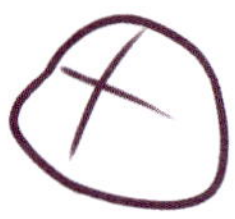

1. Lightly sketch an oval with pointed sides. Add a plus sign guideline for the face.

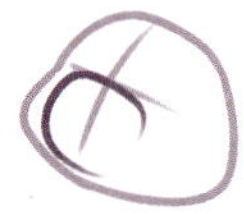

2. Sketch a C-shaped snout in the middle of the face.

3. On top of the head, add two curved, pointed horns.

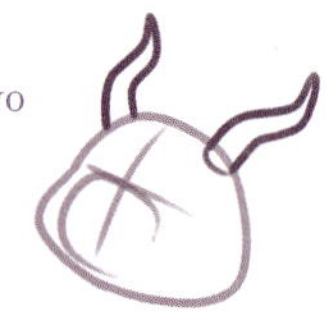

4. Under the horns, sketch the ears drooping slightly down. Add a curved line inside.

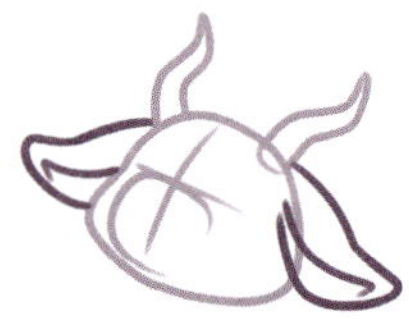

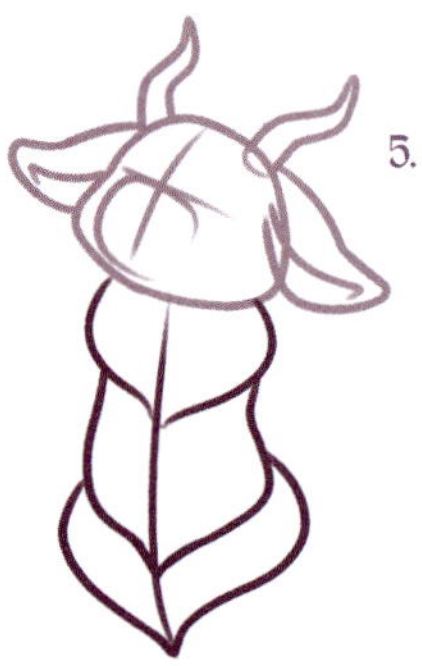

5. For the long neck and chest, draw three rounded Vs, one under the other, with the middle one being the longest.

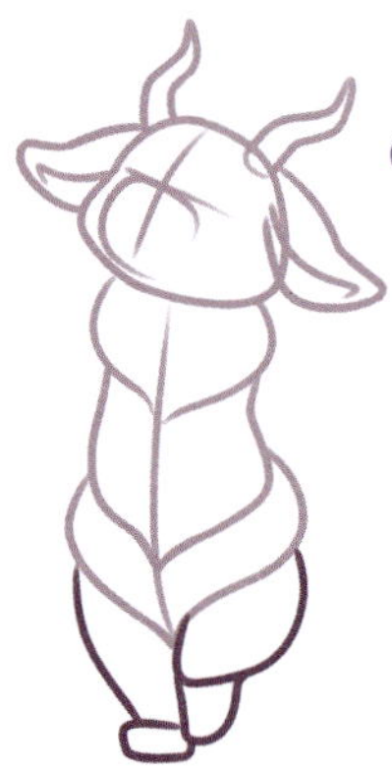

6. Sketch the two front legs with the right leg slightly raised up and a U-shaped paw. Draw a rounded rectangle for the left paw.

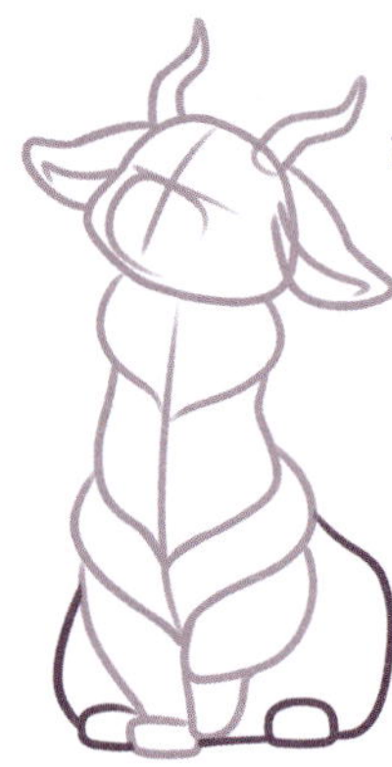

7. Draw two curved lines for the haunches on the bottom sides. Add rounded rectangle paws.

8. Add the tail beside the right haunch, continuing to the left and curving up. End with a teardrop tuft.

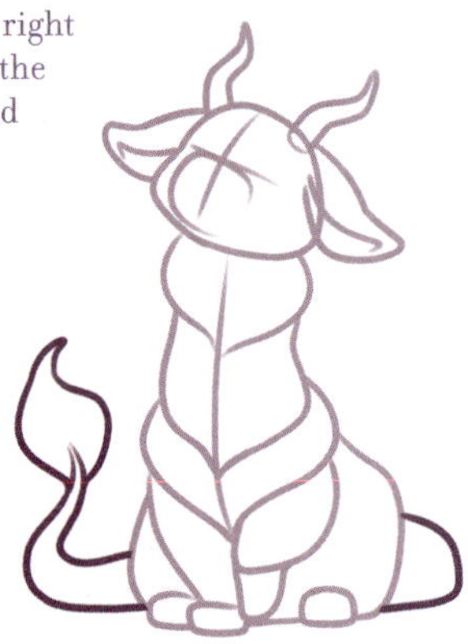

9. Sketch the wings on the sides of the shoulders. Add two soft Z-shaped wings with a line connecting at the ends. Connect the tip of the wings to the body with a curved line.

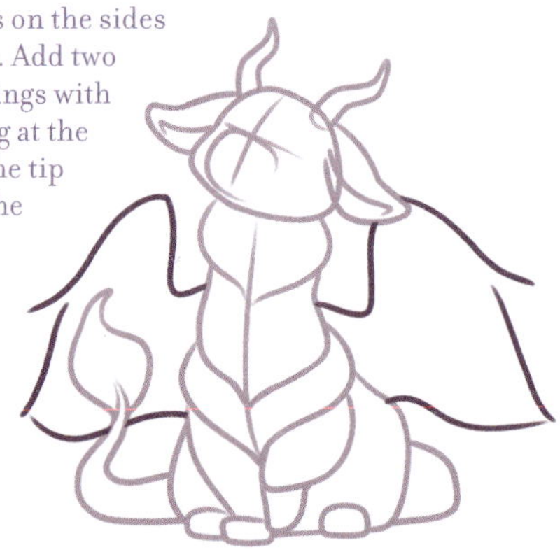

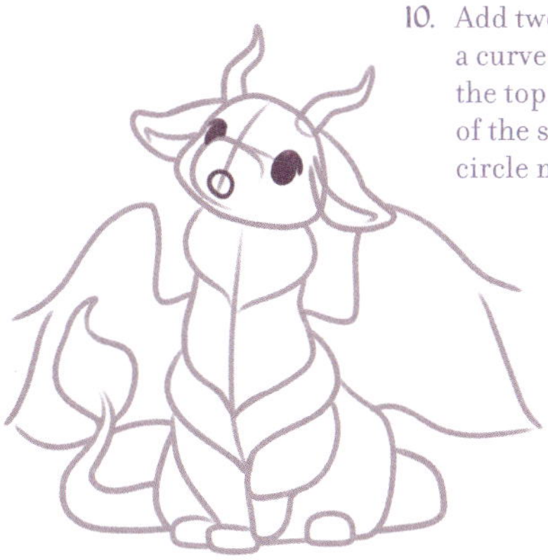

10. Add two oval eyes with a curved line around the top. At the bottom of the snout add a circle mouth.

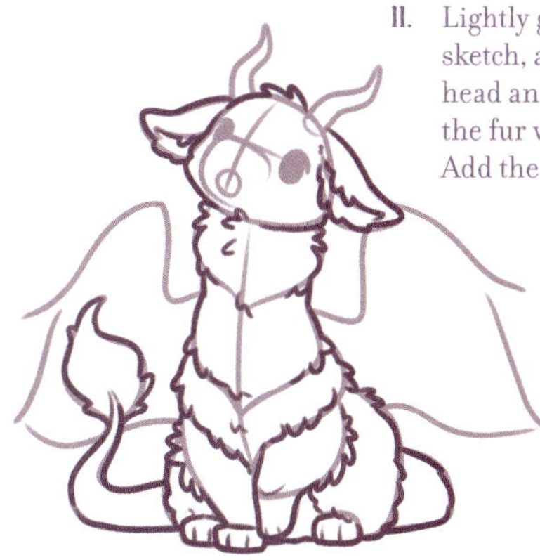

11. Lightly go over the basic sketch, adding details of the head and body. Define the fur with soft W shapes. Add the tail tuft.

12. Sketch the wings with thin U shapes for the feathers.

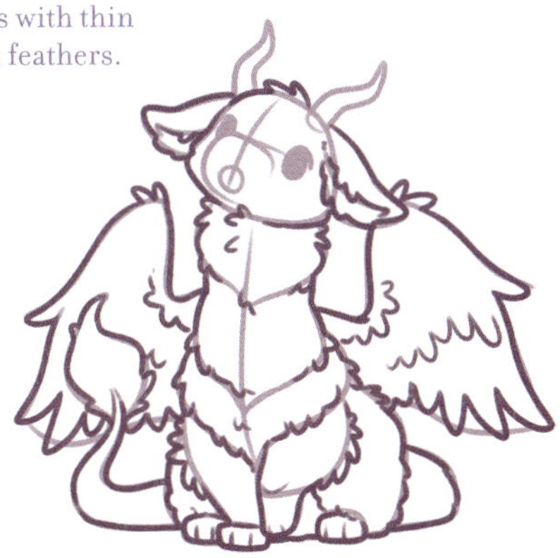

13. Sketch the face detail. Add highlights to the eyes, dashes on the cheeks, and two whiskers on the sides of the head. Add two small teeth and a tongue inside the mouth.

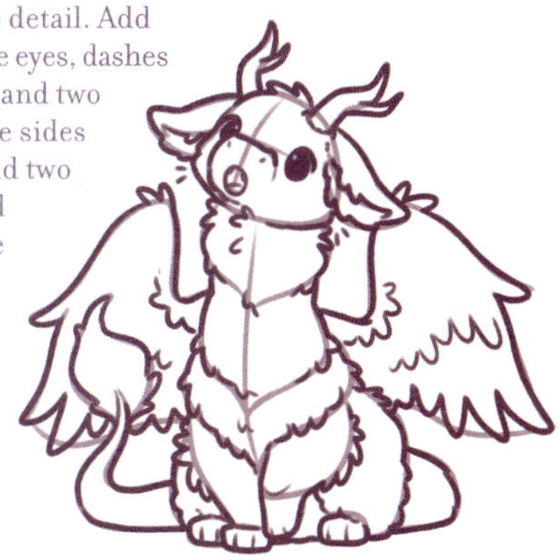

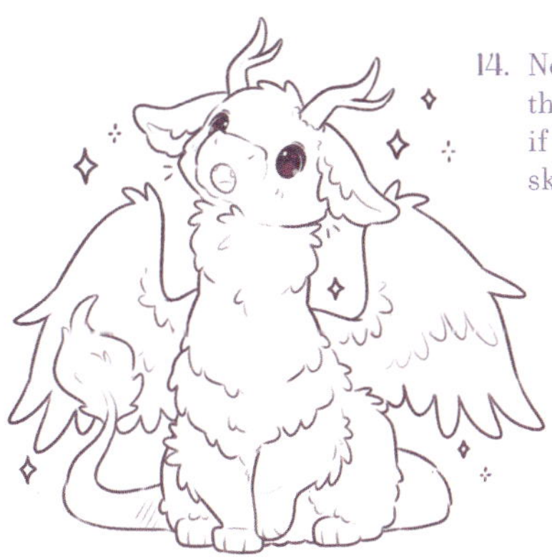

14. Neatly draw the line art over the sketch. Add some sparkles if you'd like! Then erase the sketch underneath.

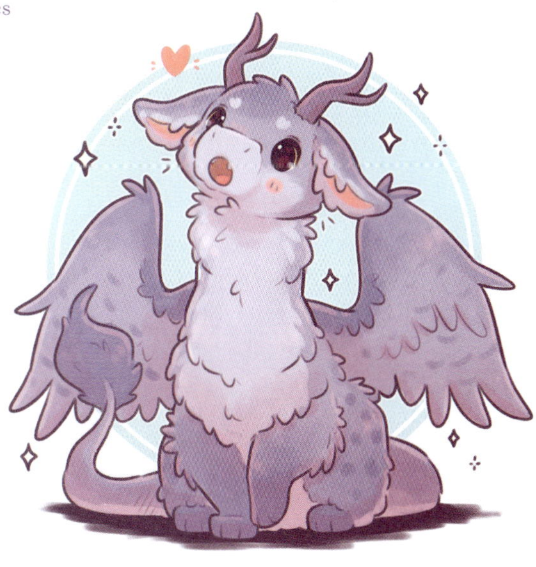

15. Color your dragon! I used a pastel-purple color scheme with a paler color on the stomach and for the heart-shaped eyebrows. But pick any color you like!

HARPY

These fluttering creatures are sometimes thought of as spirits of the wind. On the other hand, they can be quite monstrous, with a tendency to attack people.

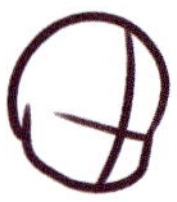

1. Lightly sketch a flat-bottomed circle head with a dip on the right. Add a plus sign guideline for the face.

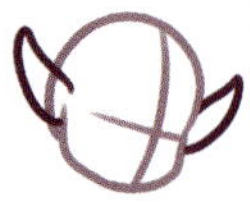

2. Draw two rounded V ears on the sides of the head.

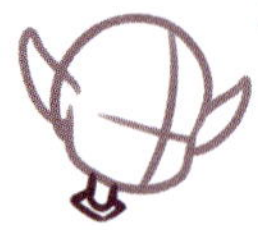

3. Add a small U neck with a diamond-shaped neckline below.

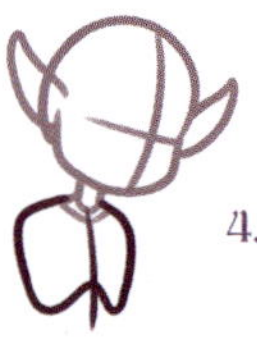

4. Draw a roughly W-shaped upper body with a guideline through the middle.

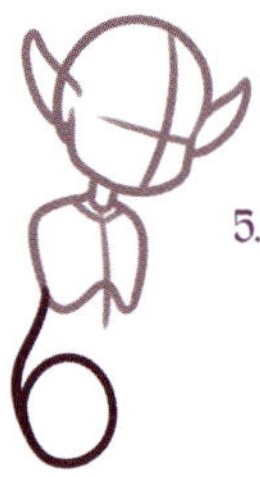

5. Draw a curving line for the back leading into a circle to start the legs.

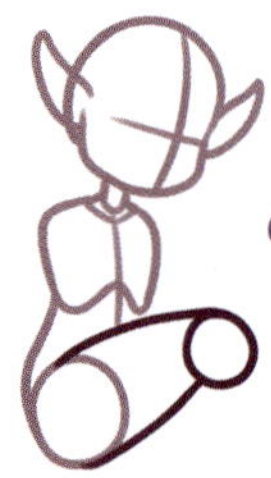

6. Slightly above and to the right of the leg, sketch a smaller circle knee. Connect the two circles with curved lines.

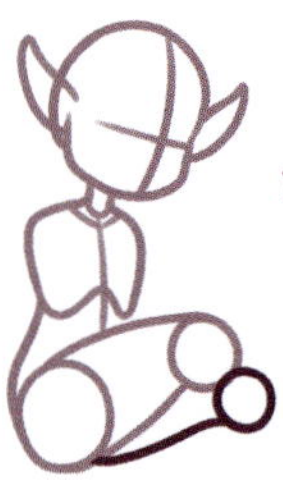

7. Draw another circle under the knee. Connect the circle to the body with a curved line.

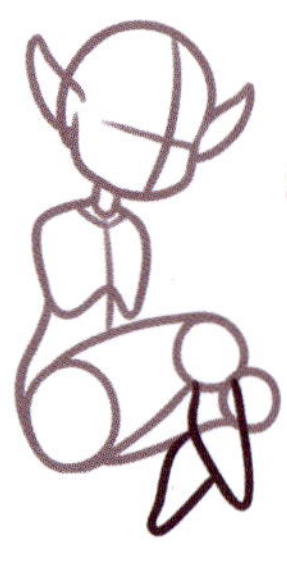

8. Draw two narrow ovals for the lower legs, so that the legs are slightly crossed.

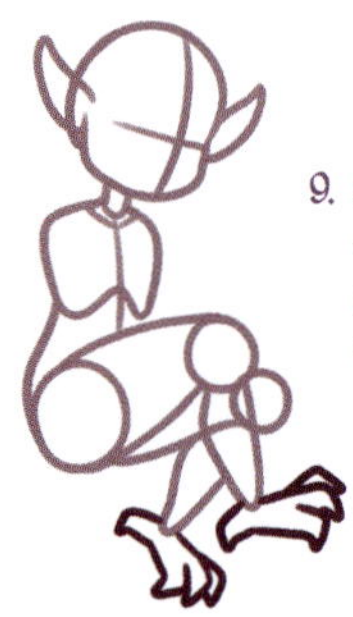

9. Sketch the bird feet with three front claws and a back claw on each foot.

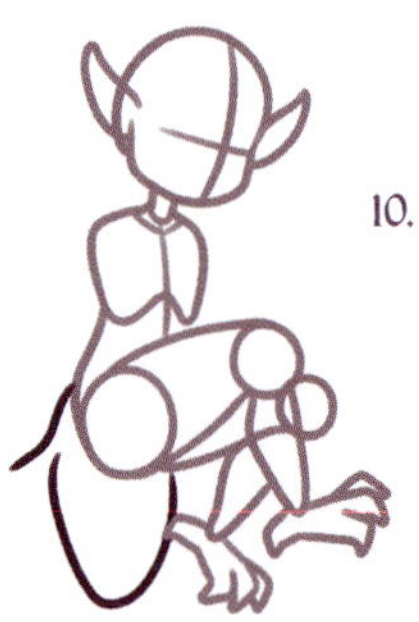

10. Below the backside, add a U-shaped bird tail with a short, curved line on the top-left.

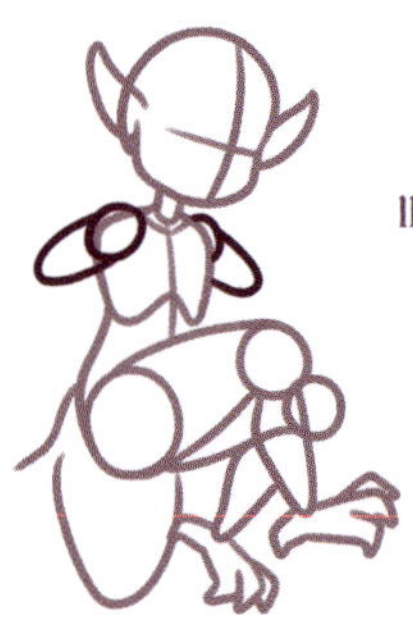

11. Draw a circle shoulder on either side with a U attached for the upper arms, angled slightly away from the body.

12. Sketch the lower arms with two narrow Vs at an upward ninety-degree angle.

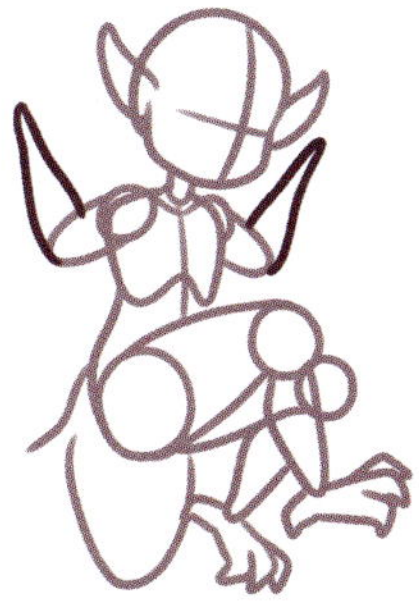

13. From the tip of the lower arms, sketch the wings with long, arcing, curved lines.

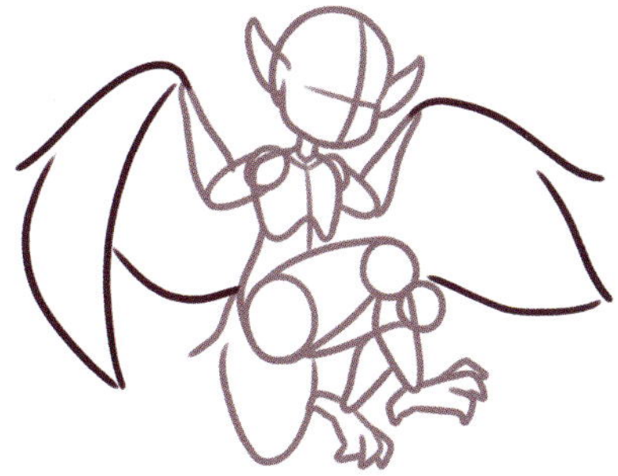

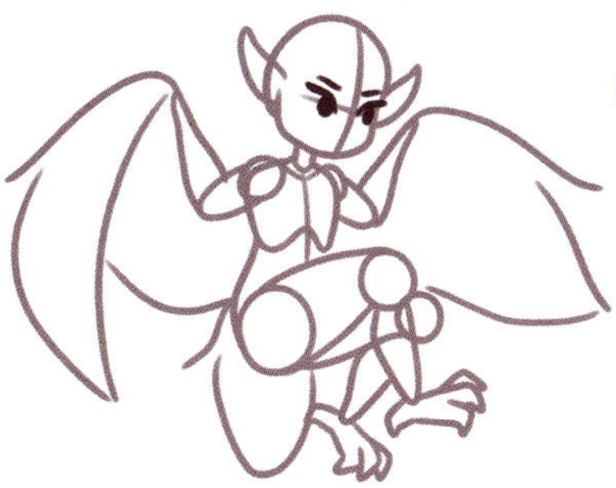

14. Add two oval eyes with a curved line around the top. Draw two small eyebrows angled slightly down.

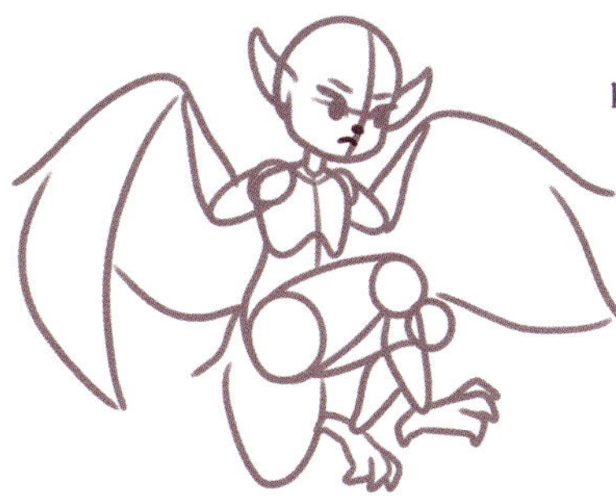

15. Draw a small oval nose and a small, upside-down V for a grumpy mouth.

16. Sketch an oval above the eyes for the front of the hair. Then add two small, wavy strands of hair on the sides of the head.

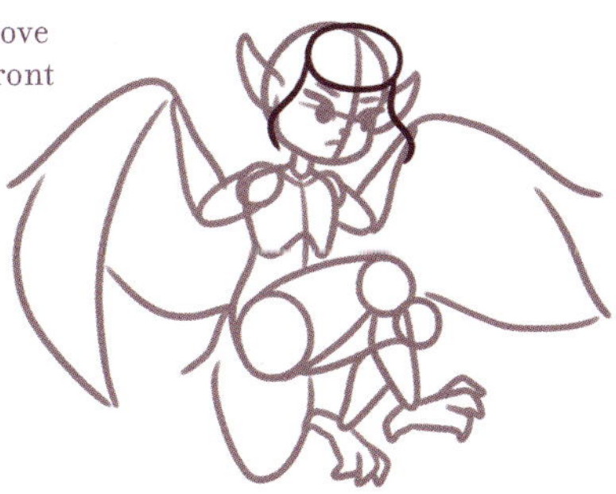

17. Draw the outline of the hair around the head in a short bob just above the shoulders.

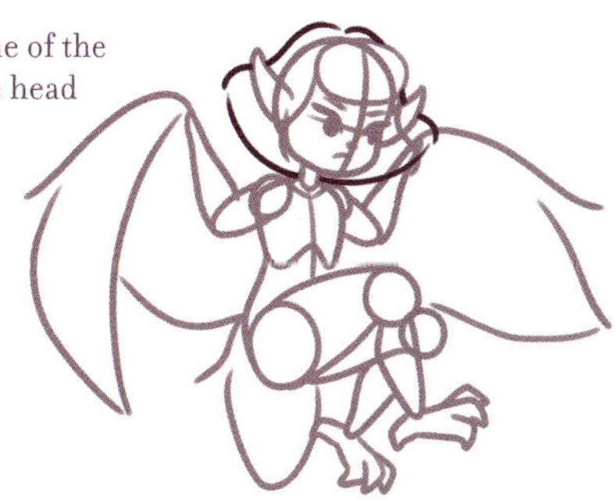

(continued)

HARPY

(continued)

18. Sketch the hair detail with fluffy edges to the ears.

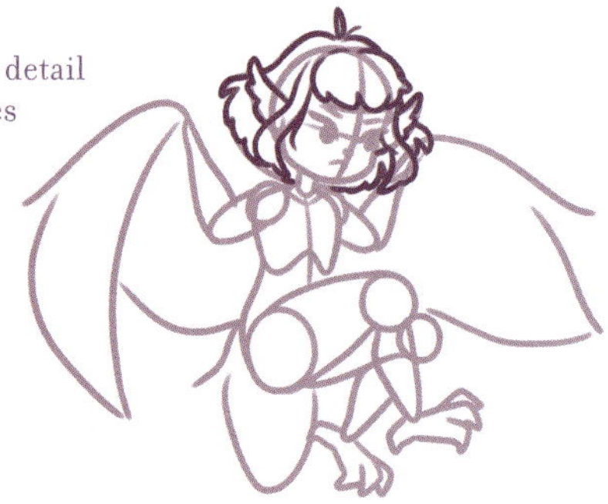

19. Draw twigs and leaves sticking out of the hair.

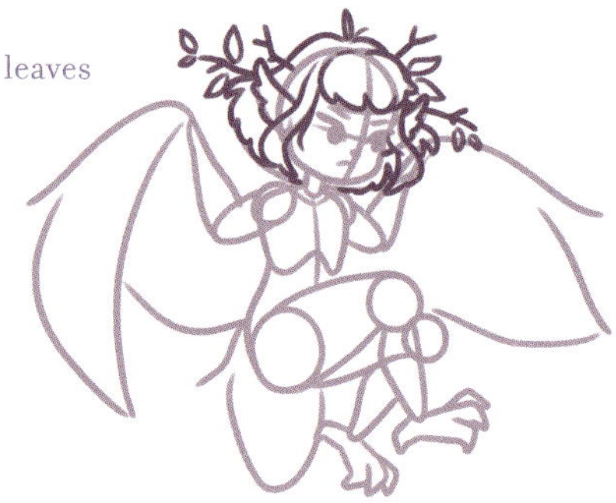

20. Sketch the outline of the neck and chest.

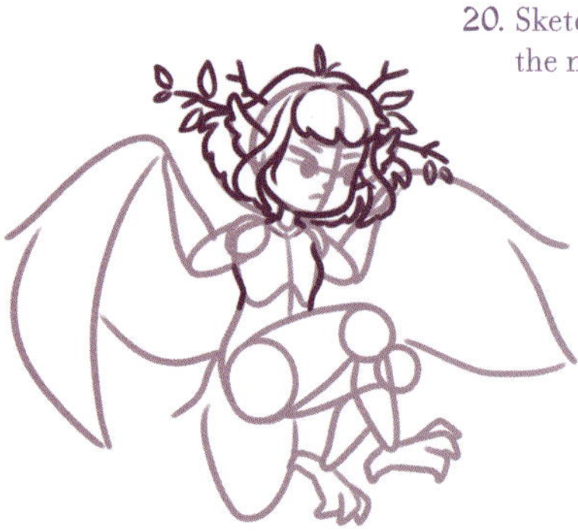

21. Draw the shoulders and arms. Add details where the feathers begin on the upper arms.

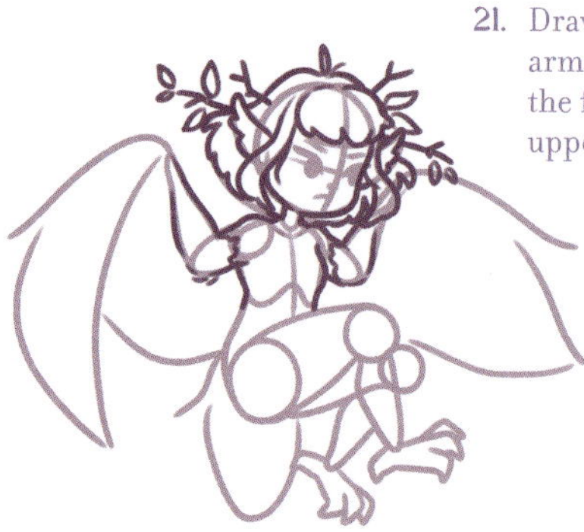

22. Sketch the wings with thin U-shaped feathers along the bottom and across the middle.

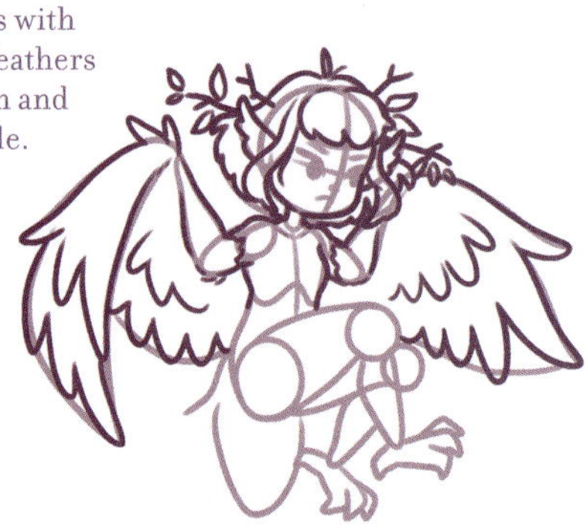

23. Add a band across the chest with lines inside to give it a wrapped look.

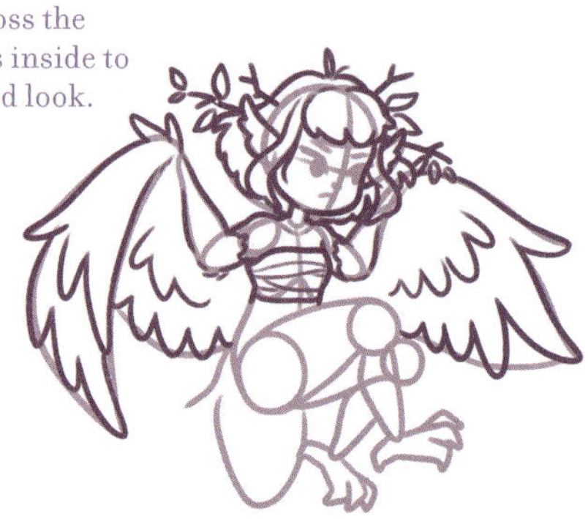

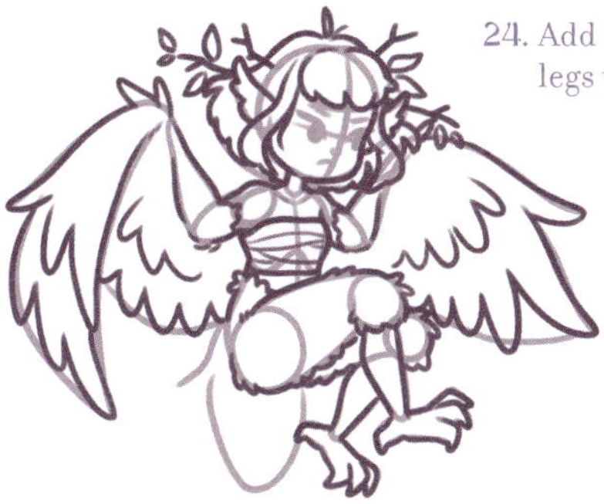

24. Add fluff around the legs up to the knees.

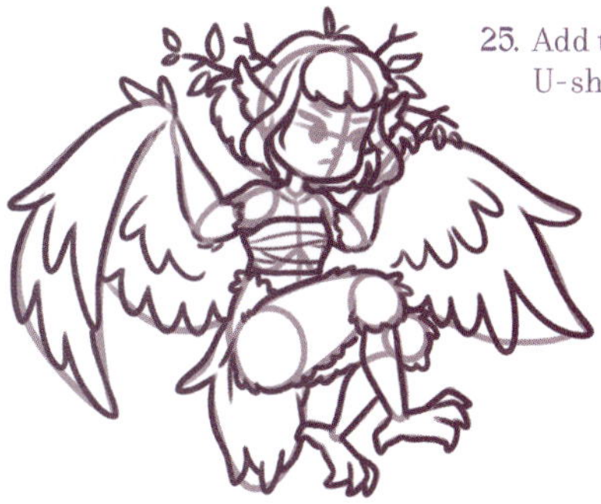

25. Add the tail details with U-shaped feathers.

26. Sketch the face detail, adding highlights to the eyes and dashes on the cheeks.

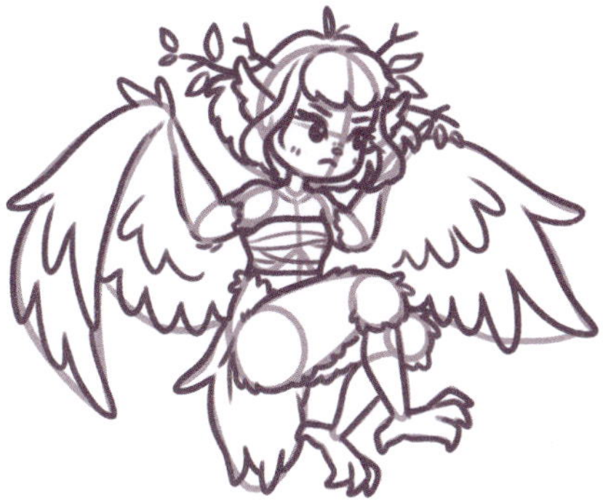

27. Neatly draw the line art over the sketch. Add some sparkles if you'd like! Then erase the sketch underneath.

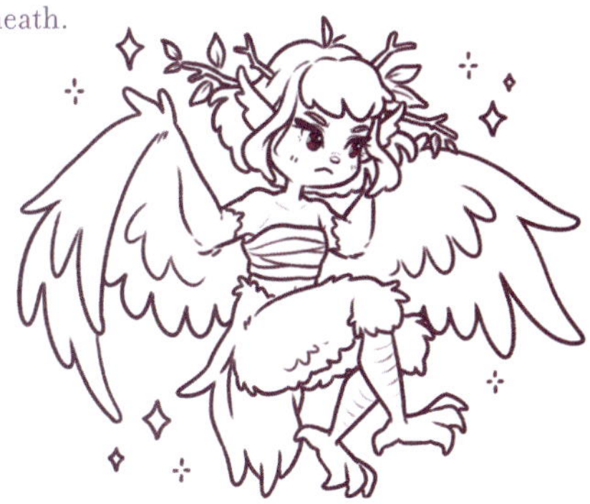

28. Time to add color! I gave them brown hair and wings with brown patches along the shoulders to show the transition of the arms to wings and around the face. I also gave them yellow eyes.

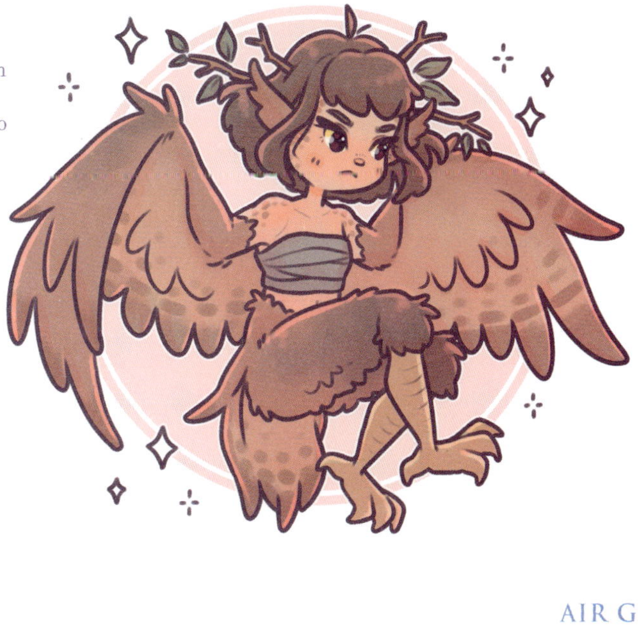

FAIRY

Found throughout European folklore, including Celtic, Slavic, and French, fairies are described as a range of magical creatures with their most common attribute being mischievous.

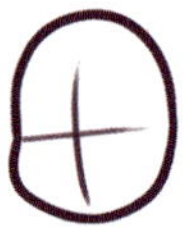

1. Lightly sketch an oval head with a dip on the left side. Add a plus sign guideline for the face.

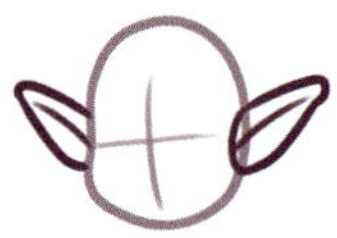

2. Add two rounded triangle ears on the sides of the head, each with a curved line down the middle.

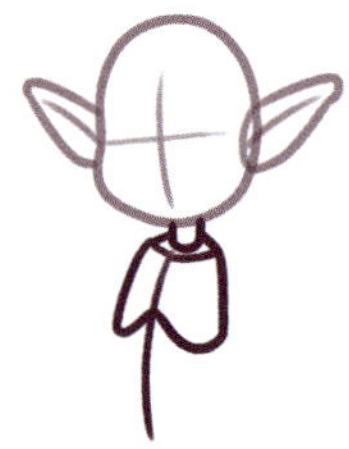

3. Draw a small, U-shaped neck with a diamond below. Then attach a W-shaped upper body with a curved guideline down the middle.

4. Using the guideline, add a triangle-shaped lower body.

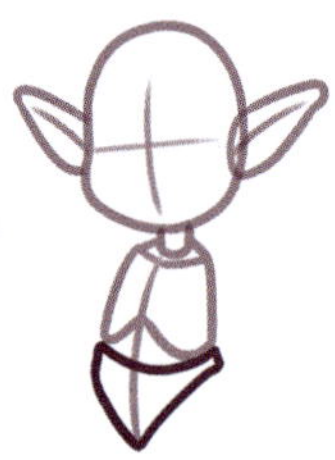

5. Add the legs with an egg shape on the bottom-right. Connect an oval thigh. Add a U-shaped left thigh.

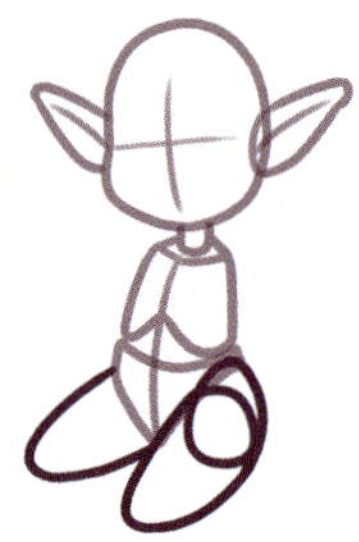

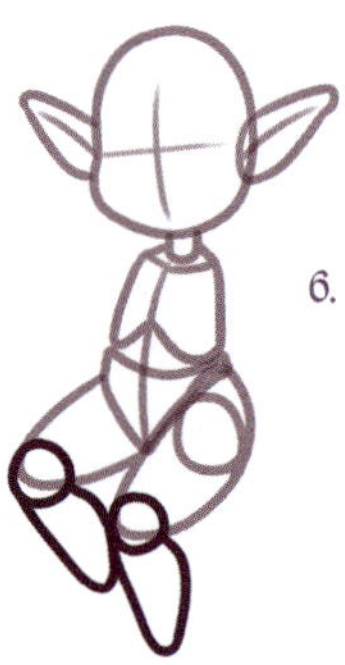

6. Attach two circle knees at the ends of the thighs. Then draw two narrow U shapes below both circles, angled right.

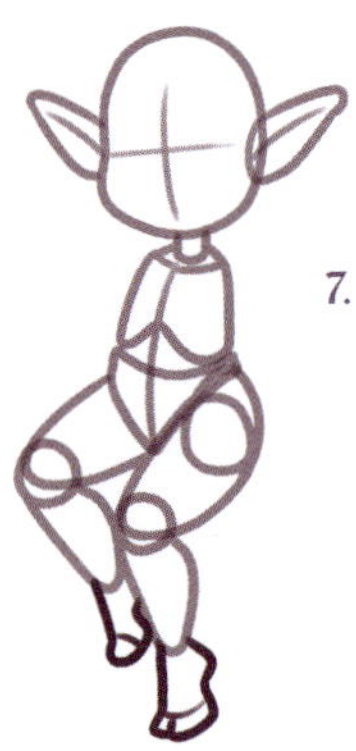

7. Sketch the feet with curved rectangles, adding guidelines for the toes.

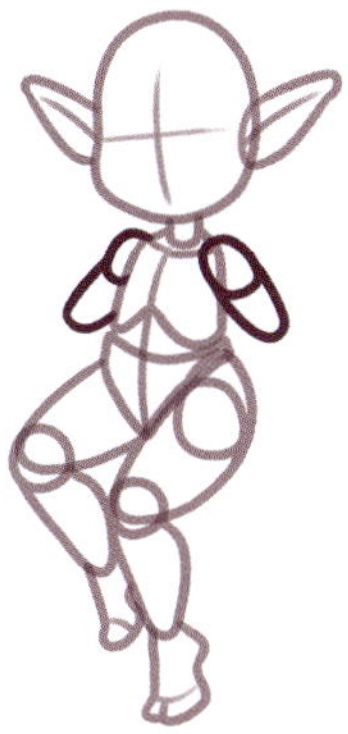

8. Draw two circle shoulders on the sides of the upper body, then connect a U.

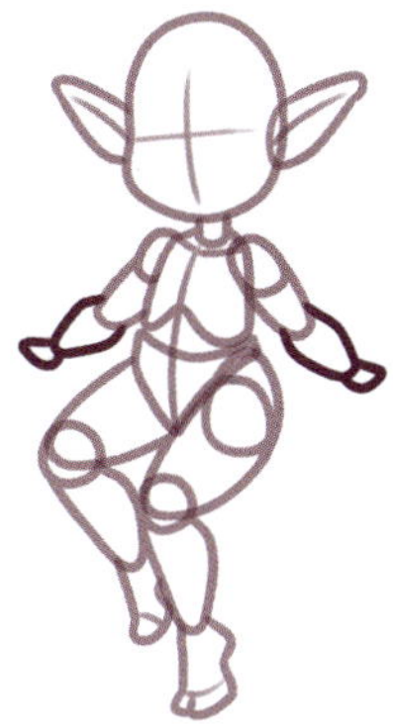

9. Connect two rounded V forearms to each upper arm and add a teardrop-shaped hand, pointed out.

10. Sketch some fingers onto both hands.

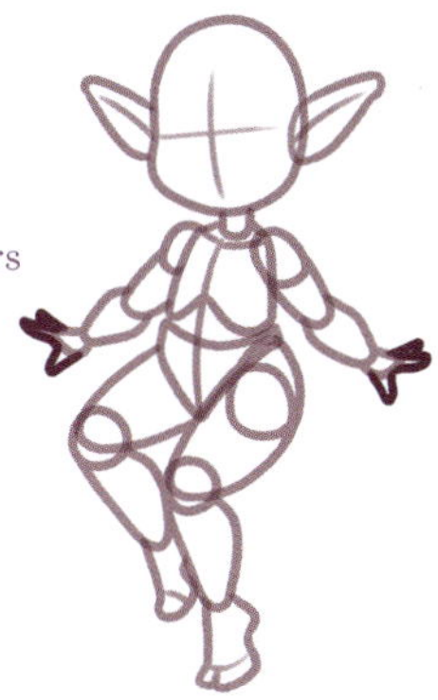

11. Next to the shoulders, draw two teardrop shapes with soft dips on the sides.

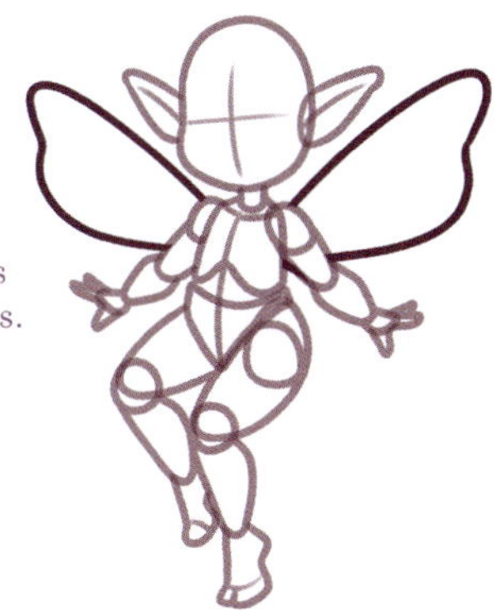

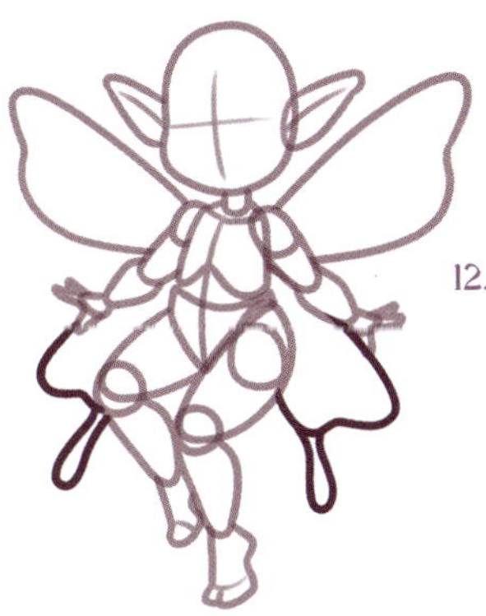

12. Add two small lower wings angled down From the bottom inner corner of the wings, add a thin droplet shape.

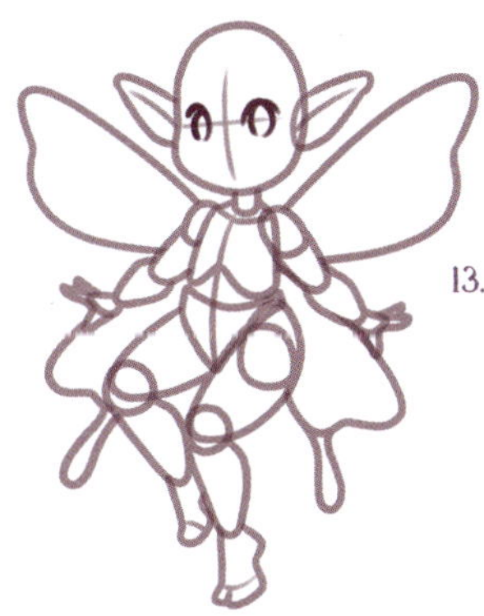

13. Add two hollow oval eyes with a curved line around the top.

(continued)

FAIRY

(continued)

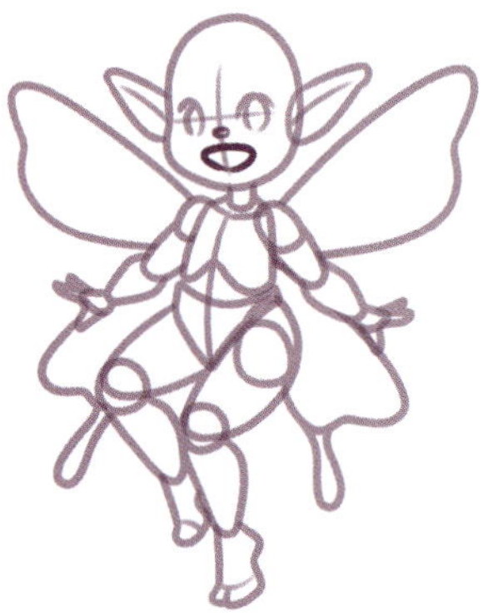

14. Add a small oval nose and a triangular mouth.

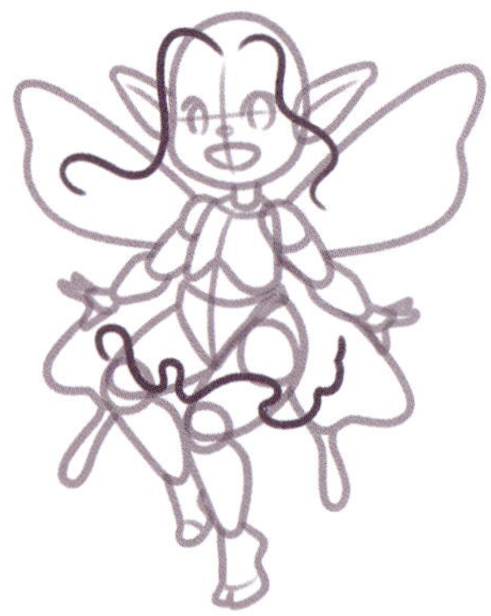

15. Draw two wavy strands of hair flowing from the crown of the head. Then add a wavy line just above the knees for the skirt.

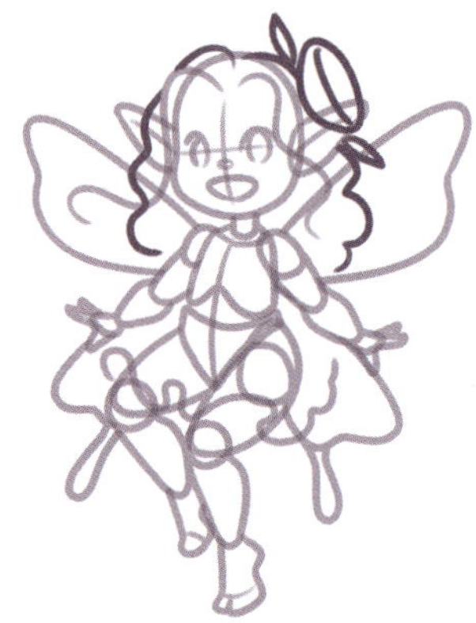

16. Add two more wavy strands of hair that frame the head. Then on the side and above the right ear, add a flower with an oval with two small, pointed ovals.

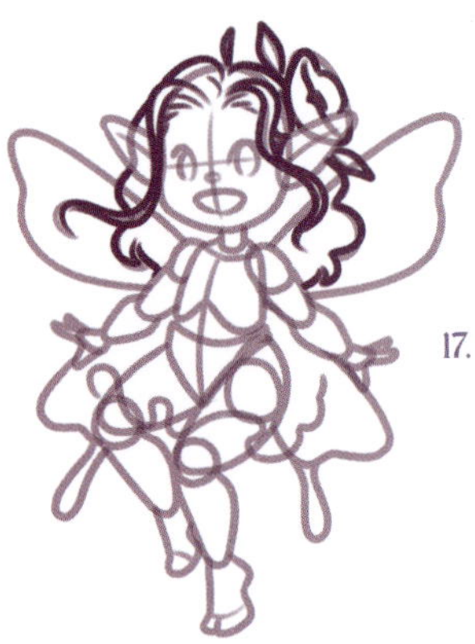

17. Sketch the hair and flower, adding detail with a little hair flick on the very top of the head.

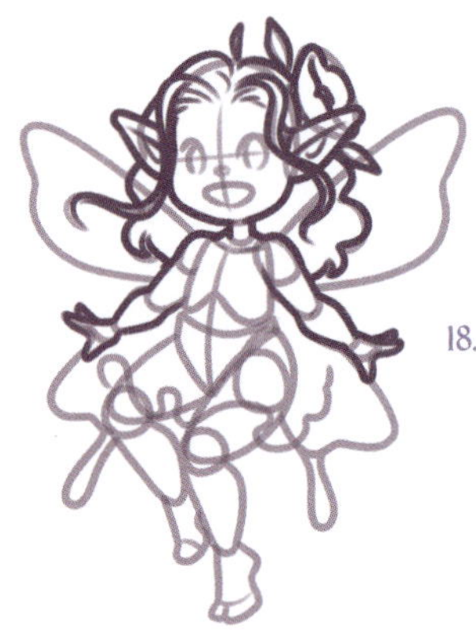

18. Lightly sketch over the head, shoulders, and arms, adding detail to the ears.

19. Outline the top of the dress with thin straps and a V-shaped neckline.

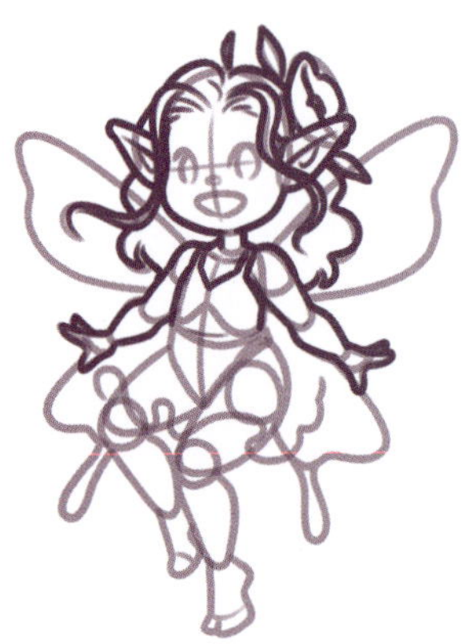

20. For the skirt, connect the wavy line to the waist of the dress, adding details where the material folds.

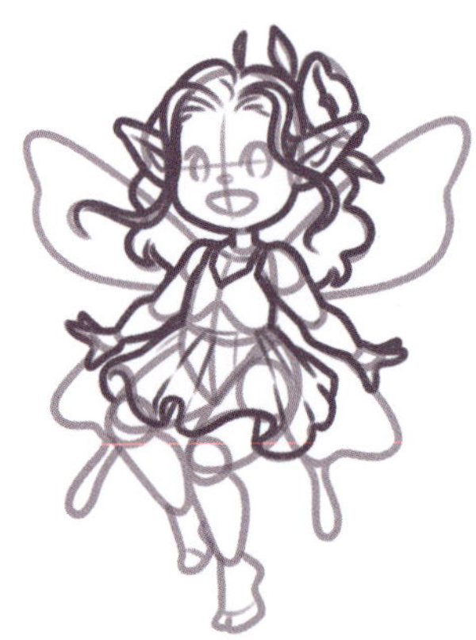

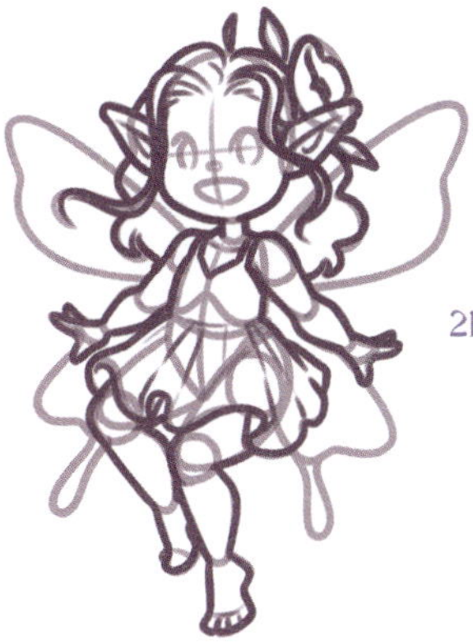

21. Sketch over the legs, adding short toe lines.

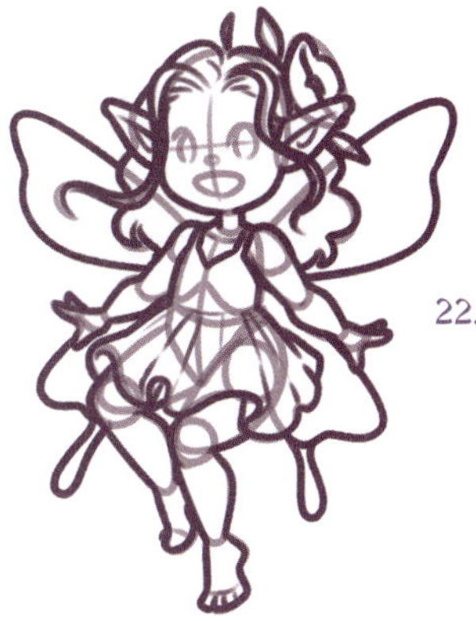

22. Add the wings, but don't draw over where the skirt or hair overlaps.

23. Go over the face, adding dashes of blush on the cheeks. Then add a curved line in the top of the mouth for teeth and a curve at the back of the mouth for the tongue.

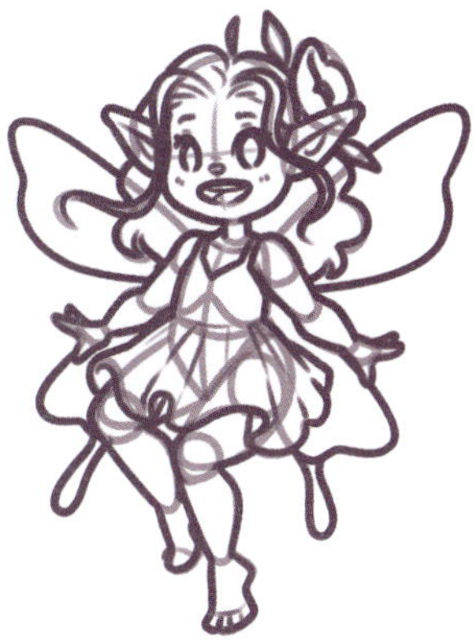

24. Neatly draw the line art over the sketch. Leave a little space in the eyes for highlights. Add some sparkles if you'd like! Then erase the sketch underneath.

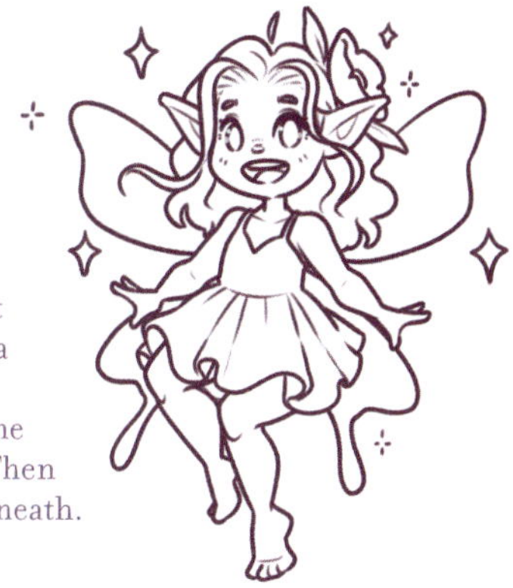

25. Finish up with color! You can use any colors for this fairy, but I used a light brown for the hair and freckles, pale pink for the dress and flower, green for the eyes and leaves, and pale blue for the wings.

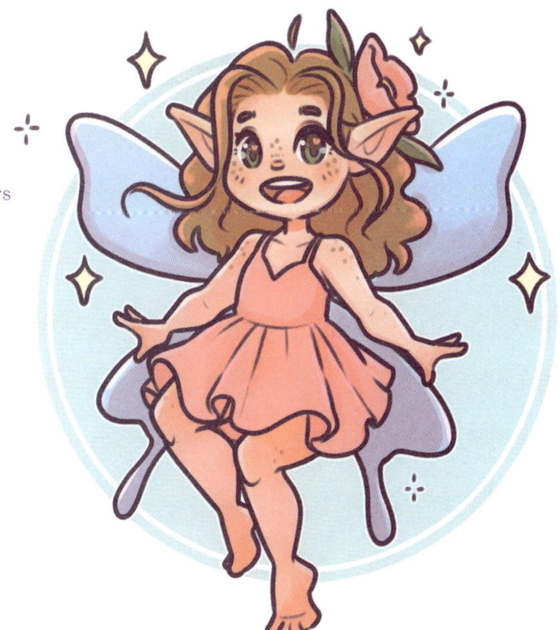

SPHINX

In myths, the sphinx has the head of a woman, the body of a lion, and the wings of a bird. Known to challenge people with a riddle, she is said to take them as a meal if they answer incorrectly.

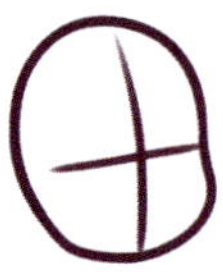

1. Lightly sketch an oval head with a dip on the right side. Add a plus sign guideline for the face.

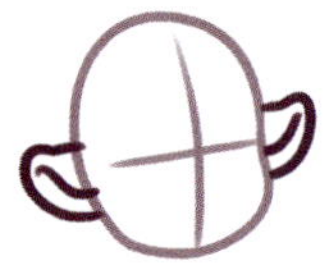

2. On either side of the head, add two semicircle ears, each with a curved line inside.

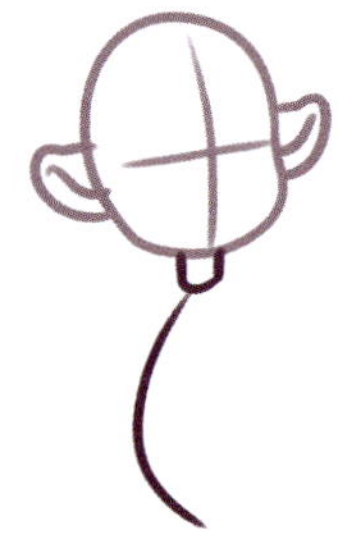

3. Add a small U neck with a guideline curving down and to the right.

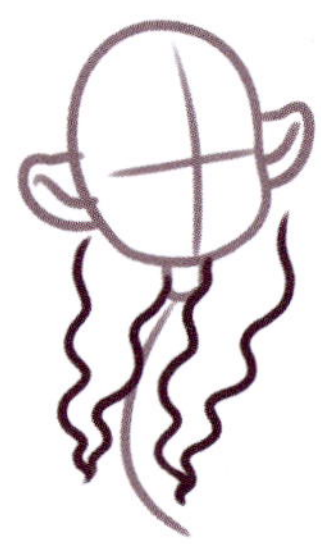

4. Around the neck and under the ears, draw two wavy pieces of hair.

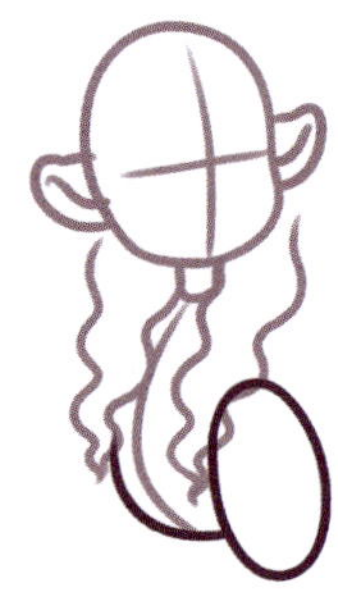

5. Using the guideline, draw a curved line across the bottom of the chest, then add a large oval for the right upper arm.

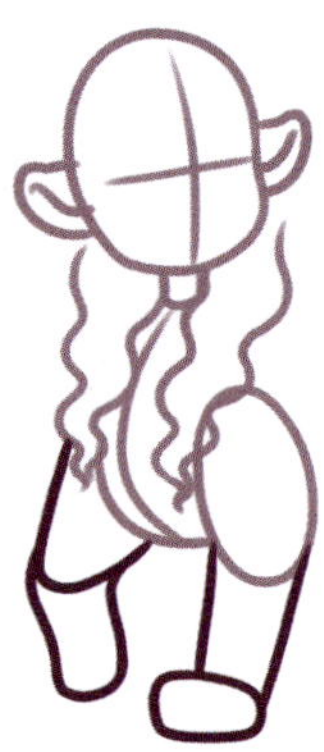

6. Draw two lines coming down the upper arm for a leg, ending in a rounded rectangle paw. For the left leg, draw two connected U shapes, making it so the leg is slightly raised.

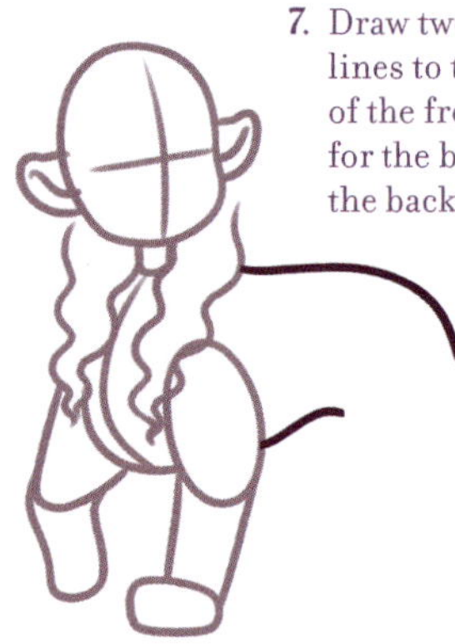

7. Draw two curved lines to the right of the front body for the belly and the back.

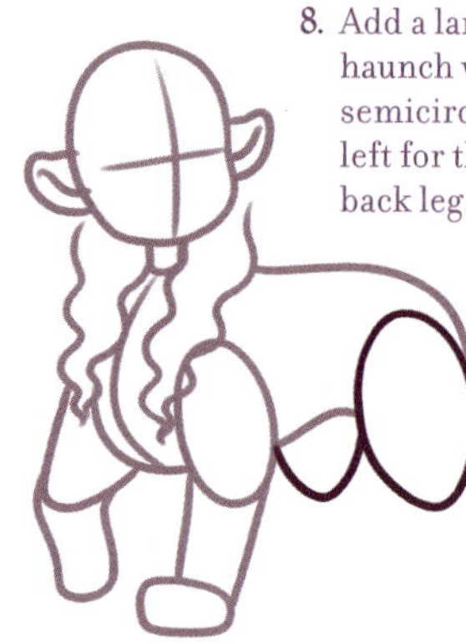

8. Add a large oval haunch with a semicircle to the left for the other back leg.

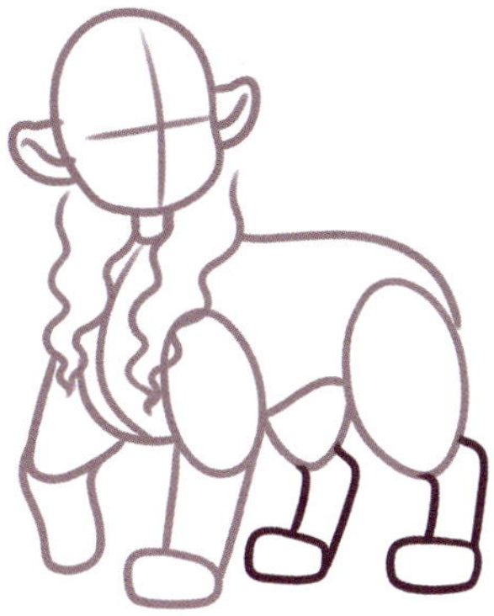

9. Draw two rounded rectangle paws with two angled lines to connect it to the haunches.

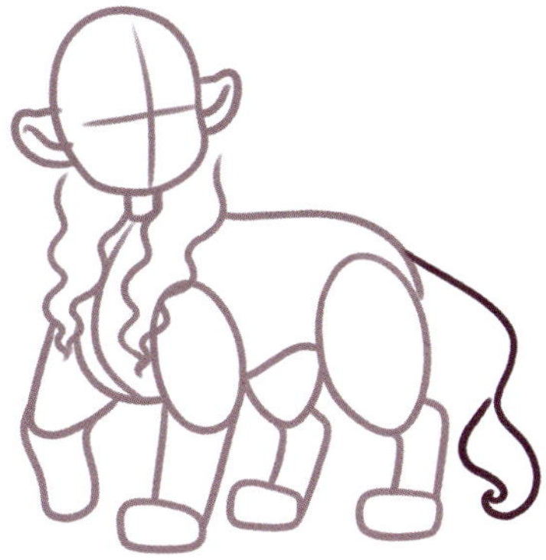

10. Draw a wavy line coming from the backside for the tail. Make a teardrop tuft at the end.

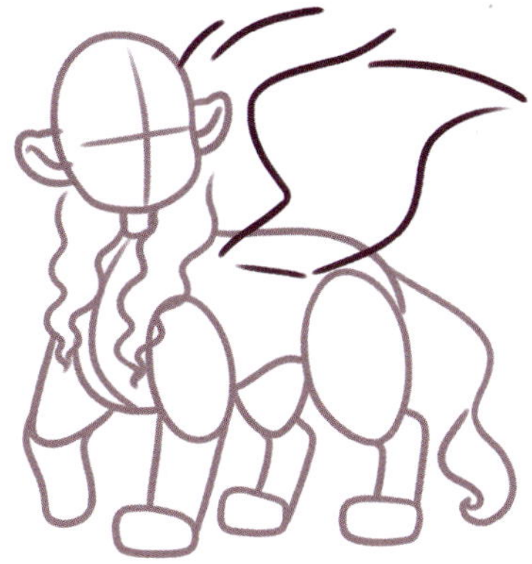

11. Sketch a wing with a soft Z and curved lines. Draw a curve connecting the tip to the back of the body. Then add two arcing lines for a partial second wing next to the head.

12. Add an arc across the top of the head to start the headband.

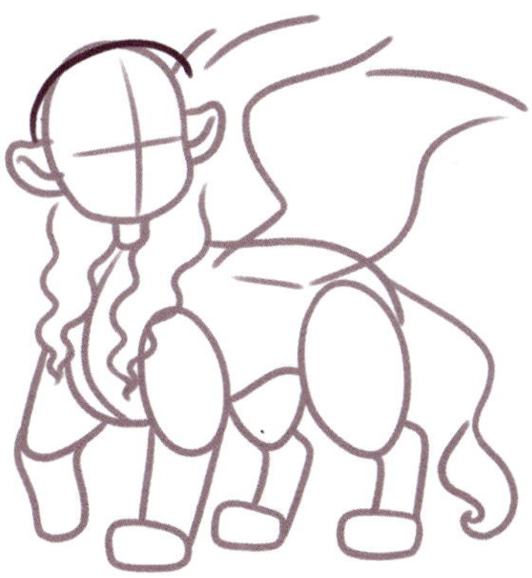

13. Sketch curly bangs on the forehead.

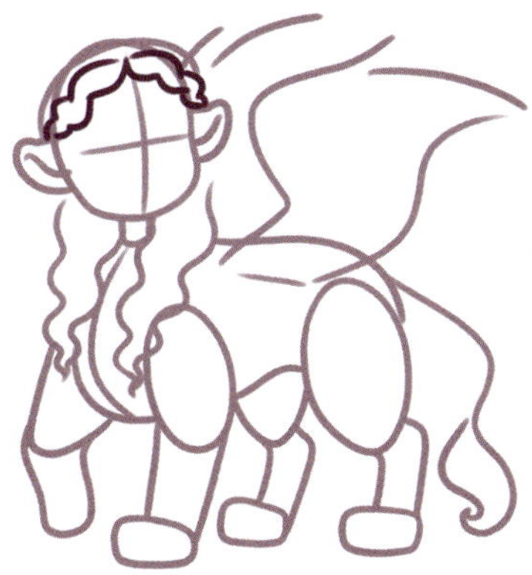

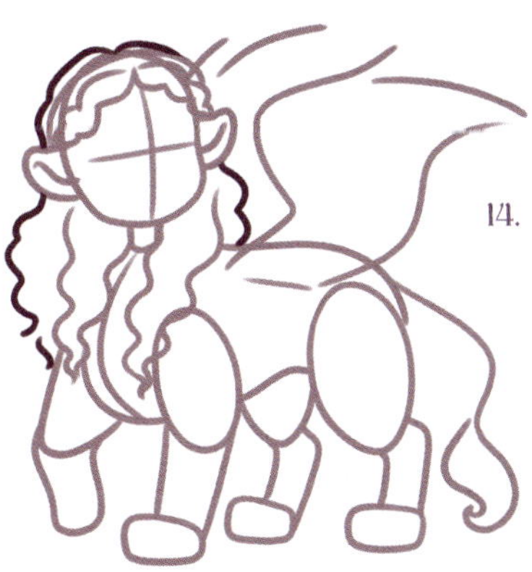

14. Start the hair from the crown of the head, falling behind the ears, and down to the chest.

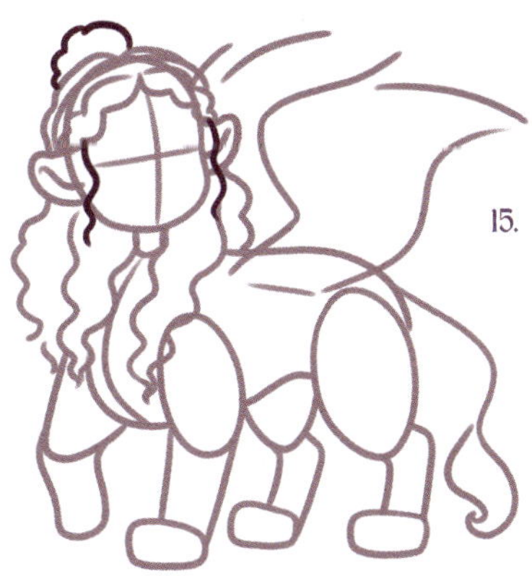

15. Add two hair strands on the sides of the face, and a small hair bun at the top of the head.

(continued)

SPHINX

(continued)

16. Add two oval eyes with a curved line around the top. Then draw two curved eyebrows.

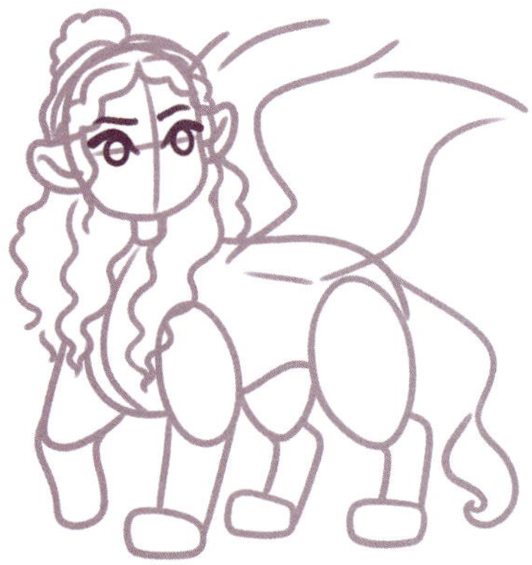

17. Draw a tiny oval nose and a flat W mouth.

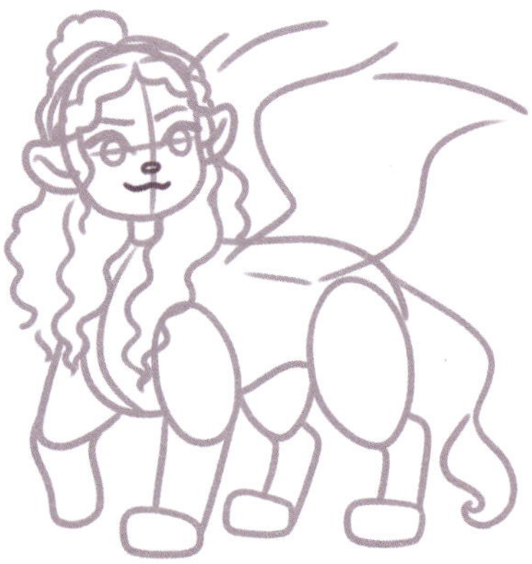

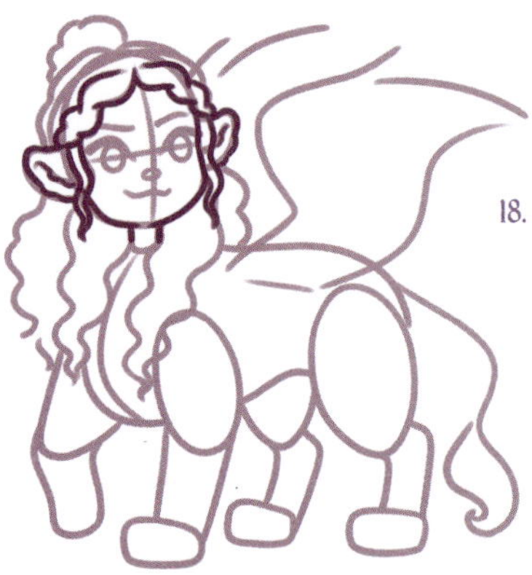

18. Lightly sketch the outline of the face, ears, neck, and hair that frames the face.

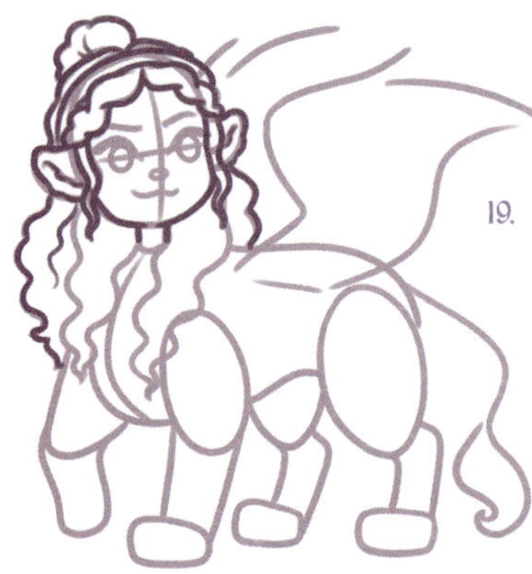

19. Sketch the back of the hair and headband.

20. Add the rest of the hair. Then sketch some fur on the chest.

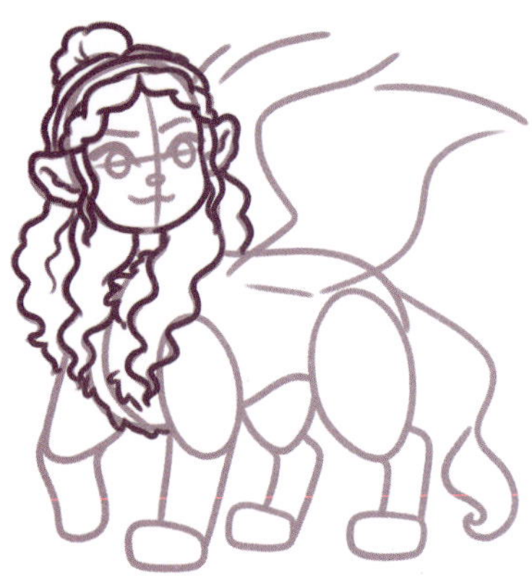

21. Add the details of the body; define the fur with soft W shapes and add the toe lines on the paws.

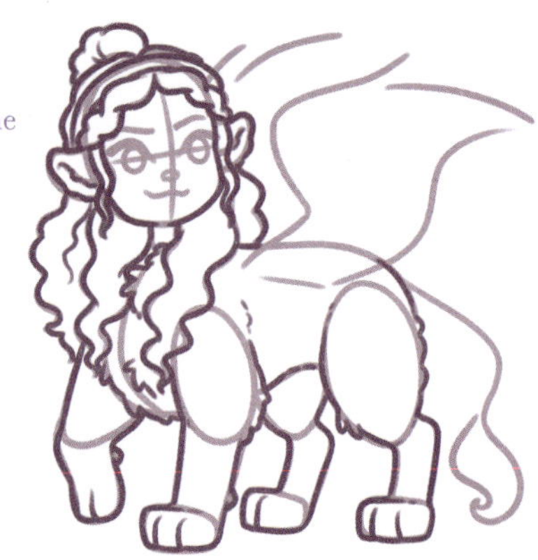

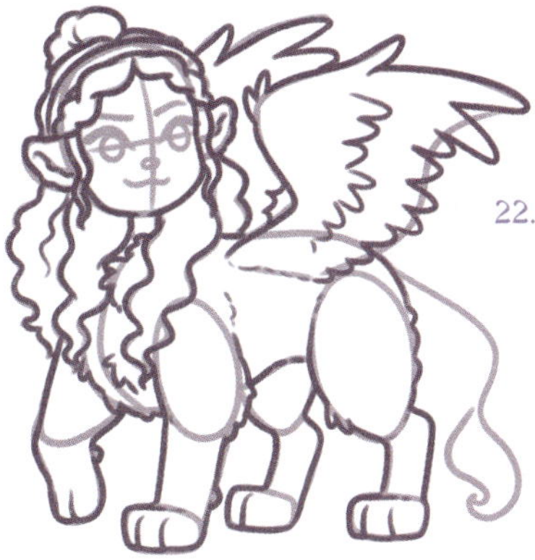

22. Sketch the wings with thin U shapes along the bottom and across the middle for feathers.

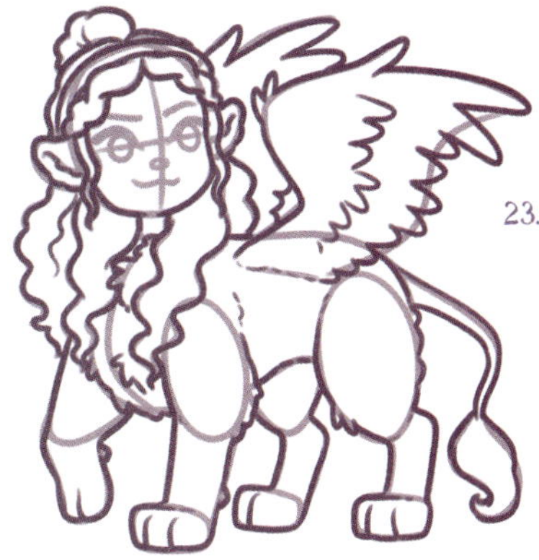

23. Make the tail with a second line and a tuft at the tip.

24. Sketch the face detail with dashes on the cheek and above the nose, and some eyelashes. Add two lines around each side of the head for whiskers.

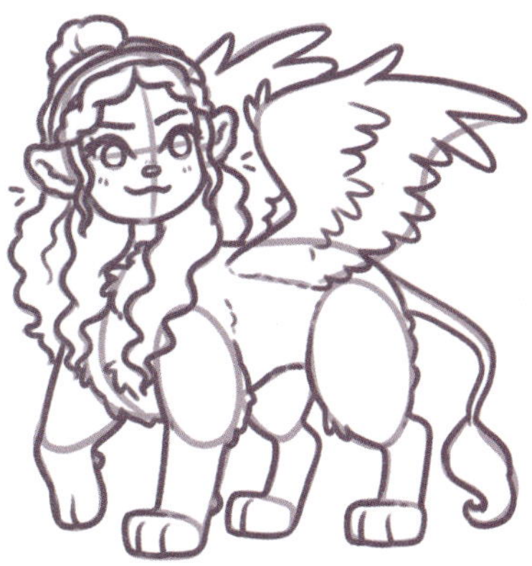

25. Neatly draw the line art over the sketch, leaving a little space inside the eyes for highlights. Add some sparkles if you'd like! Then erase the sketch underneath.

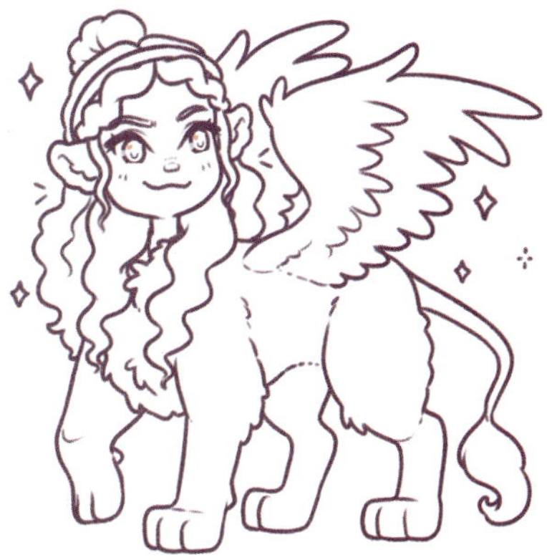

26. Add the color! Use tan for the lion's fur, and a slightly darker brown for the wings, the hair, and the tail tuft.

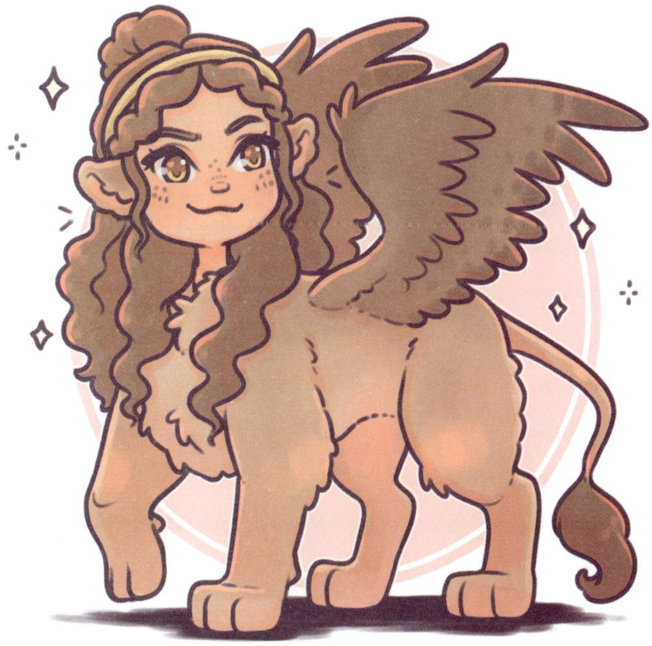

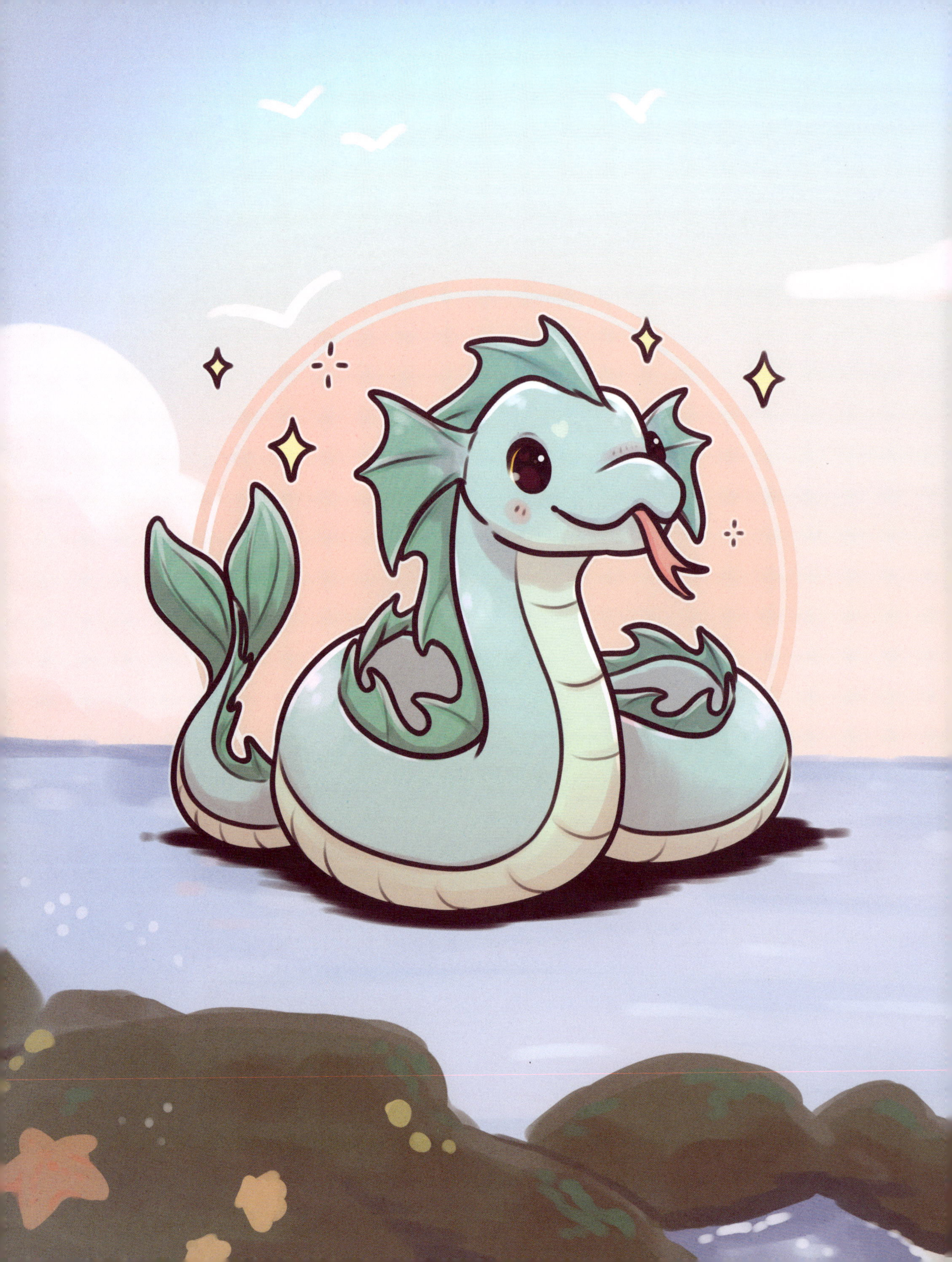

SEA SPLASHERS

FINS, FLIPPERS, AND TAILS

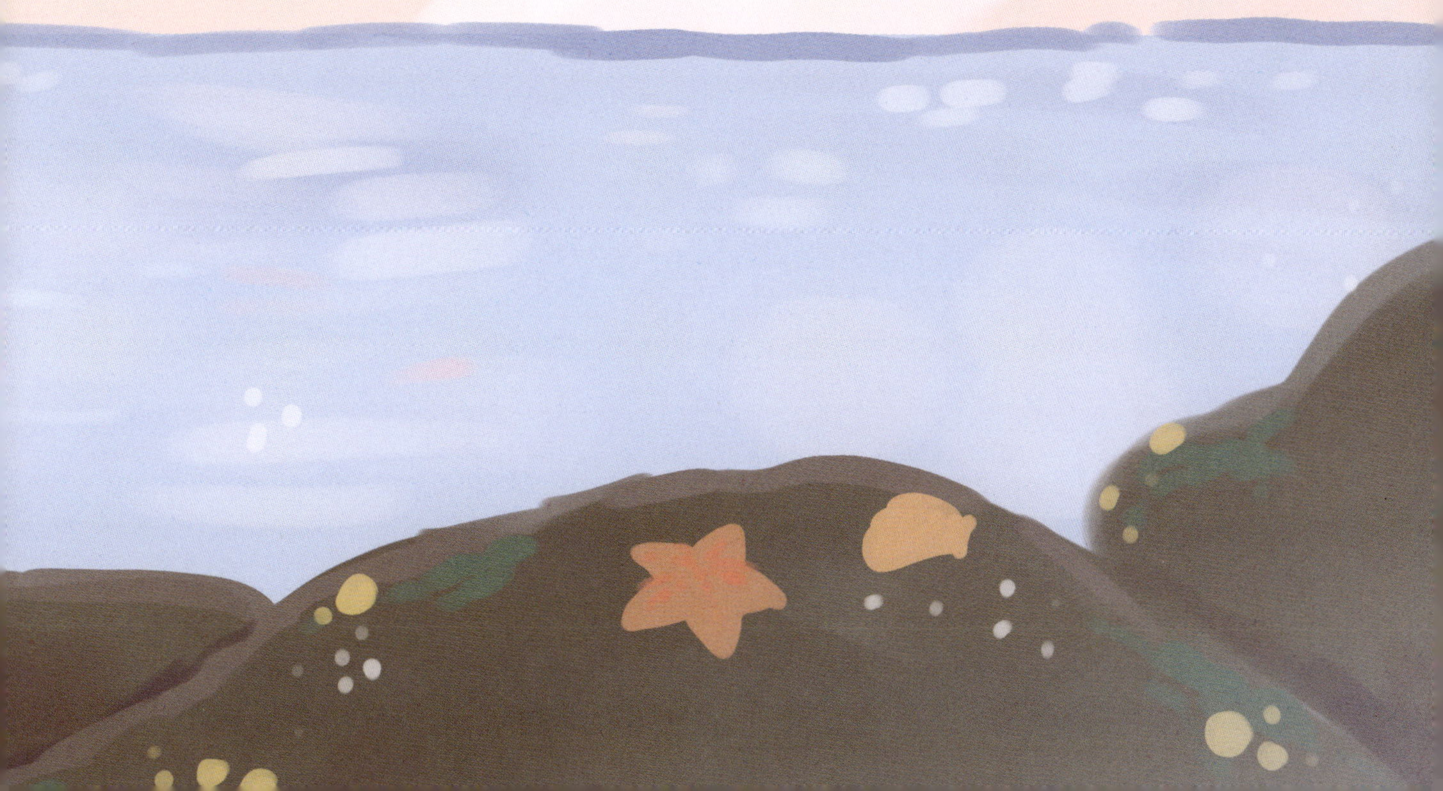

LOCH NESS MONSTER

Otherwise known as Nessie, this incredibly stealthy serpent swims unseen in the freshwater lake of Loch Ness in the Scottish Highlands.

1. Draw a circle head. Add a plus sign (+) guideline on the left side for the face.

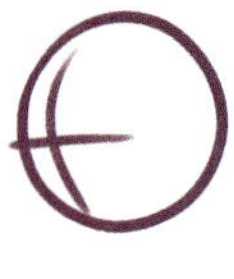

2. Add a curved snout with a top point on the lower left side of the head.

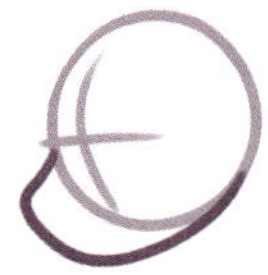

3. Add two long, curved lines from the head for the neck. Then complete the body with a big oval.

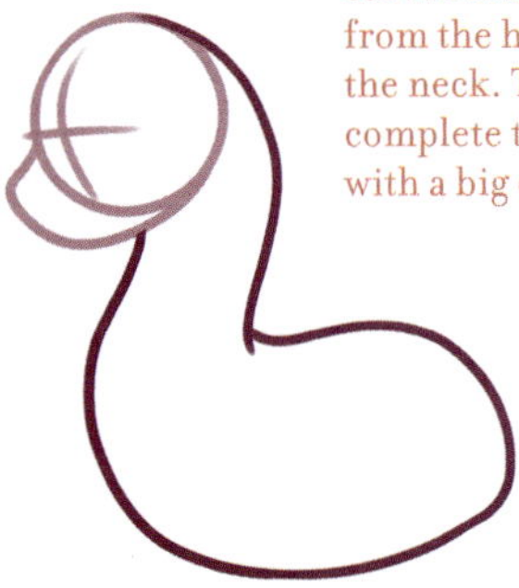

4. At the end of the body, draw a curved tail moving up.

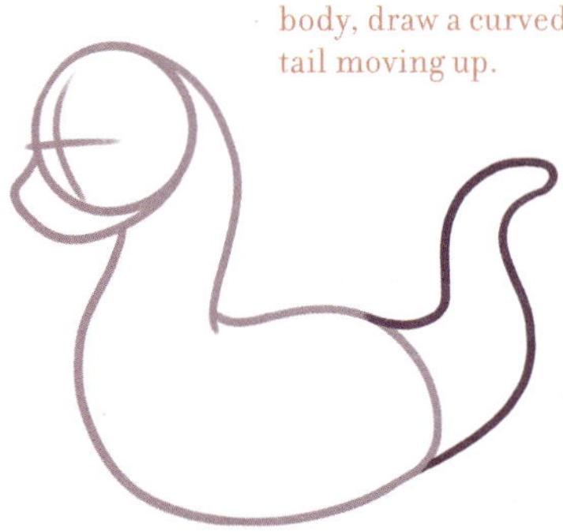

5. Draw a line curving along the body to define the underbelly.

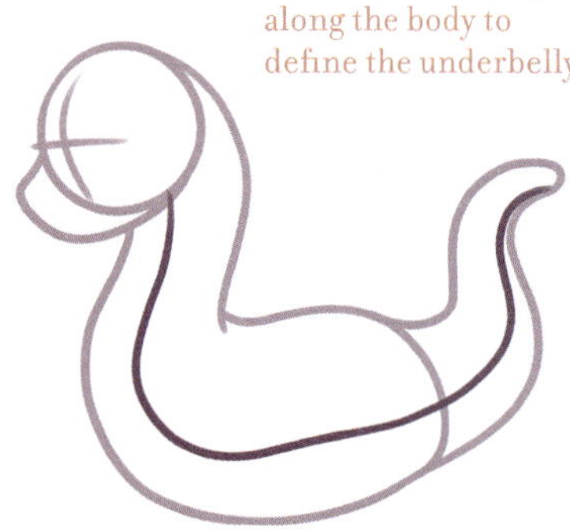

6. Just above the underbelly, draw two pointed fins.

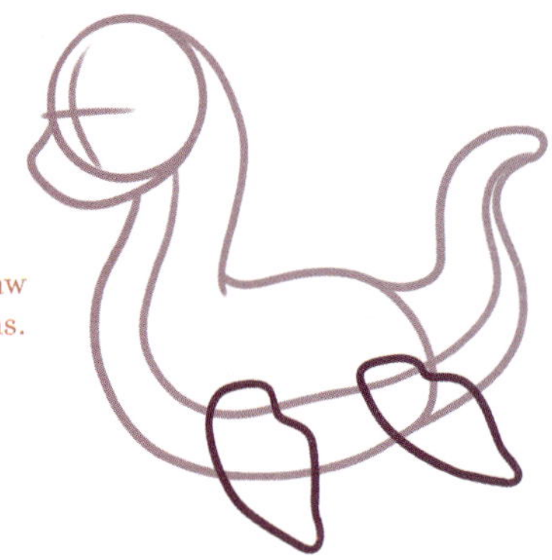

7. Draw two more partial fins to the left of the other fins.

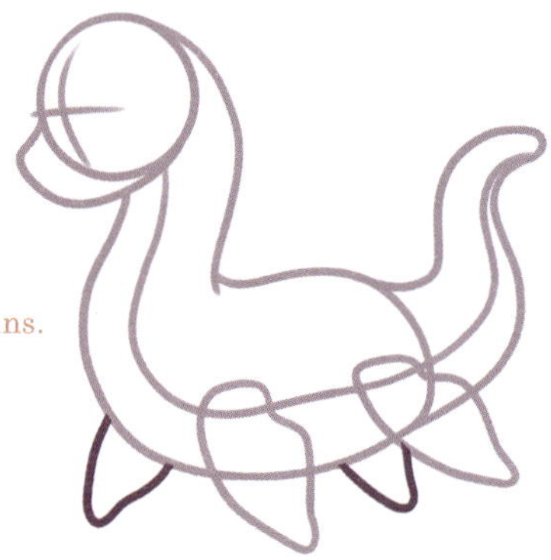

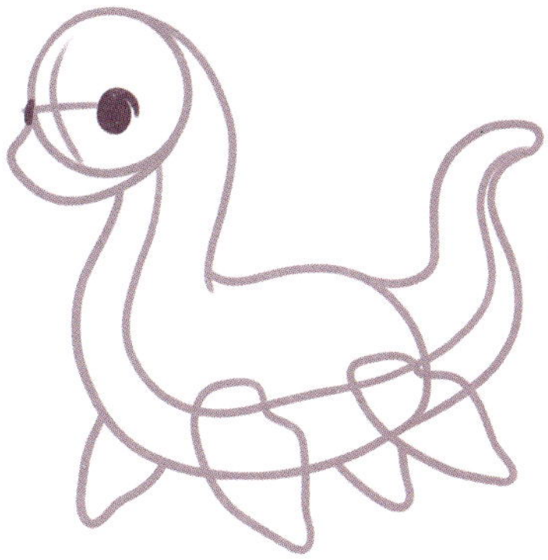

8. Add an oval eye with a curve around the top. Draw a partial left eye just above the snout.

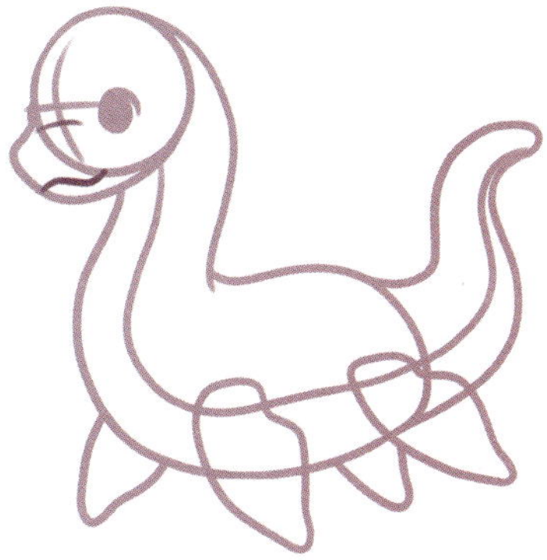

9. Draw a line marking the top of the snout on the face. Then sketch the mouth with a wavy line.

10. Lightly sketch over the outline of the body.

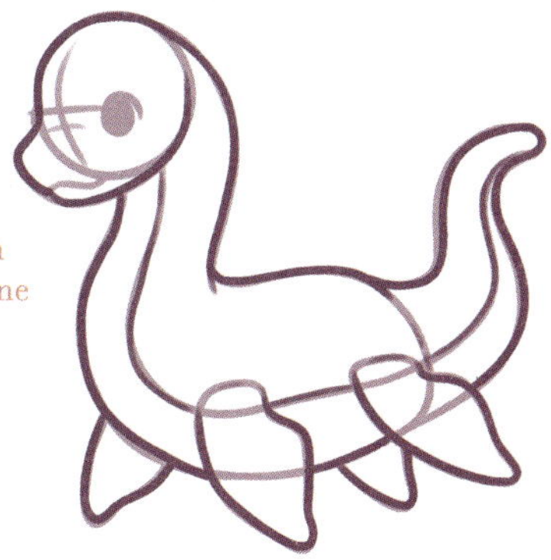

11. Add the face detail with dashes above the nose and on the cheek and highlights in the eyes.

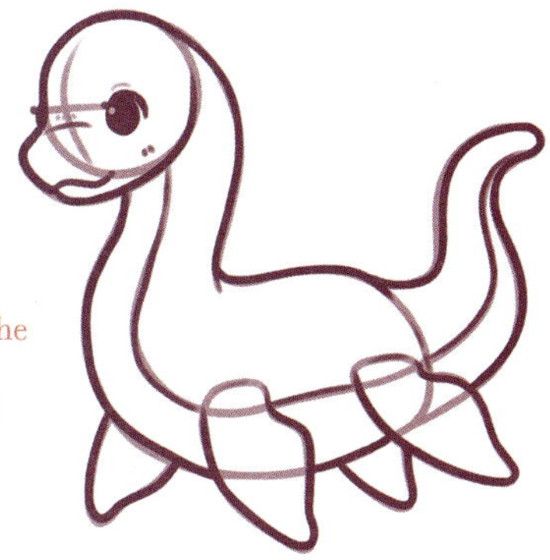

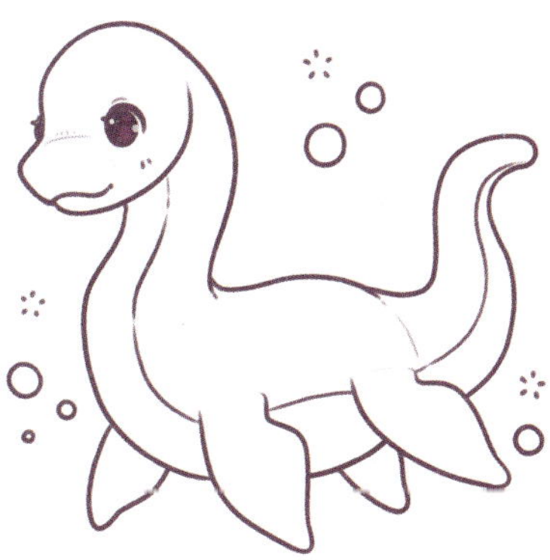

12. Neatly draw the line art over the sketch. Add some bubbles if you'd like! Then erase the sketch underneath.

13. Add the color! I chose a pale green for the body with a lighter color on the underbelly and dark green for spots along the back.

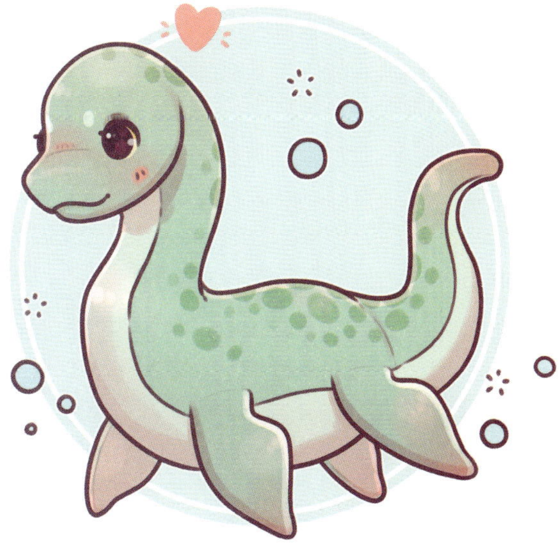

SEA SERPENT

Beware the next time you're crossing the seas, for these serpents live in the deepest parts of the ocean and are inclined to attack boats sailing past.

1. Lightly sketch a rounded square head with a dip in the top. Add a plus sign guideline on the right side for the face.

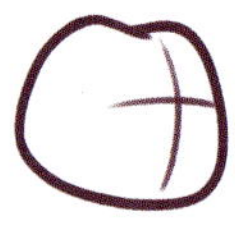

2. Add a circle snout on the bottom-right of the head. Then add a curved guideline down the middle.

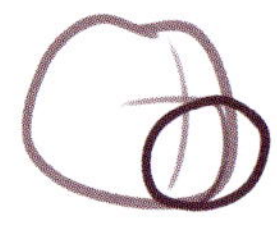

3. Sketch two parallel curved lines for the neck, one starting below the snout and one at the left corner of the head.

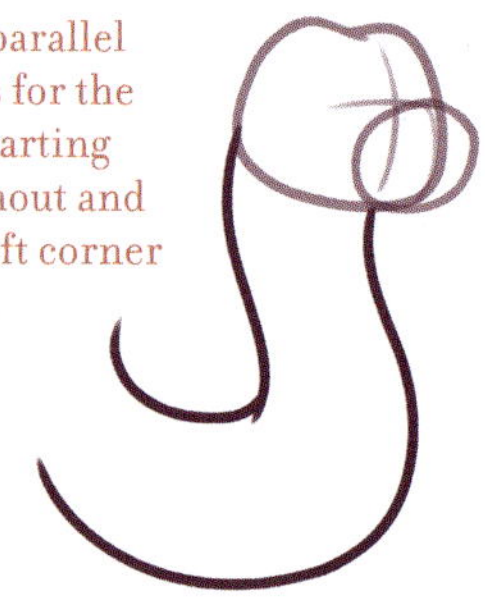

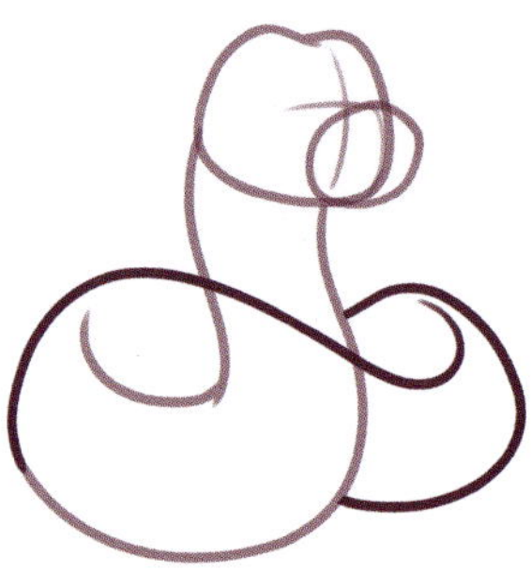

4. Complete the body with a long sideways S-line connecting to the bottom neckline. Make it pass across the neck to the other side. Then add a backwards C to finish the right side.

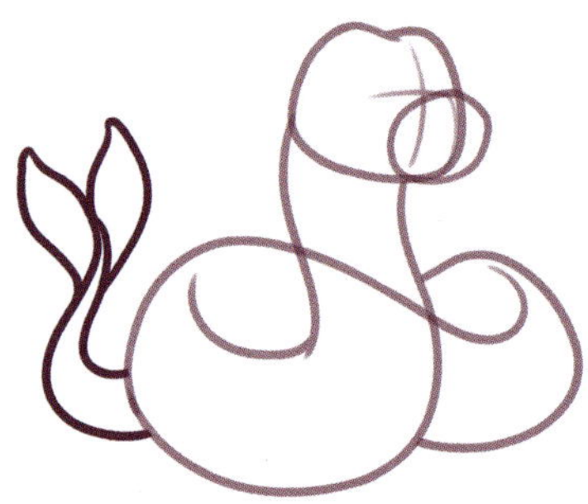

5. Draw the tip of the tail on the bottom-left of the body with two curved lines meeting at a point. Add two pointed ovals on the end to make fins.

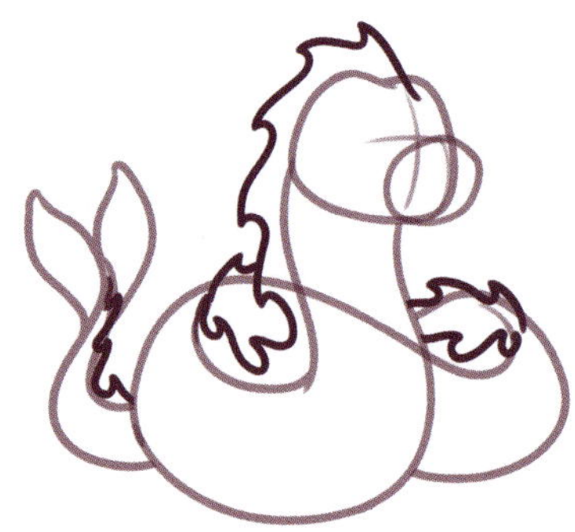

6. Add spines along the back with a curved zigzag from the top of the head to the tip of the tail.

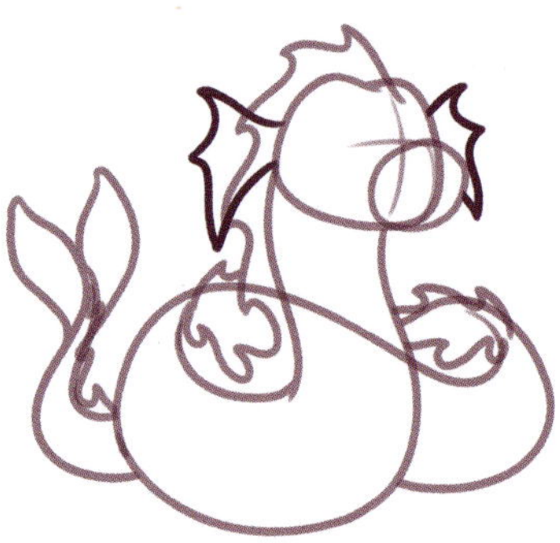

7. Draw squished number 3-shaped ear fins with two curved lines joining them to the sides of the head.

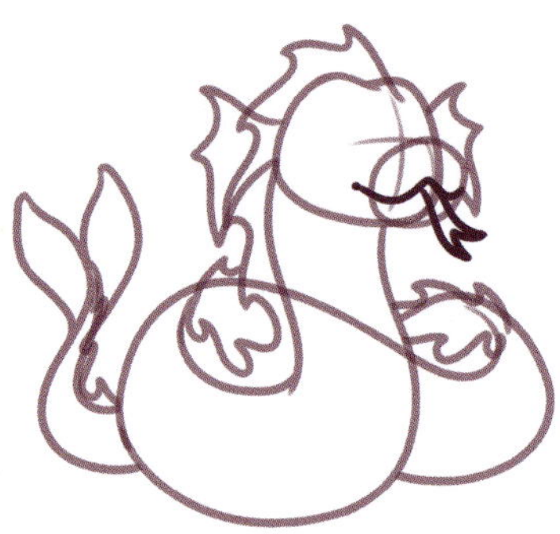

8. Add a stretched W mouth. Then add the forked tongue coming out of the middle of the W.

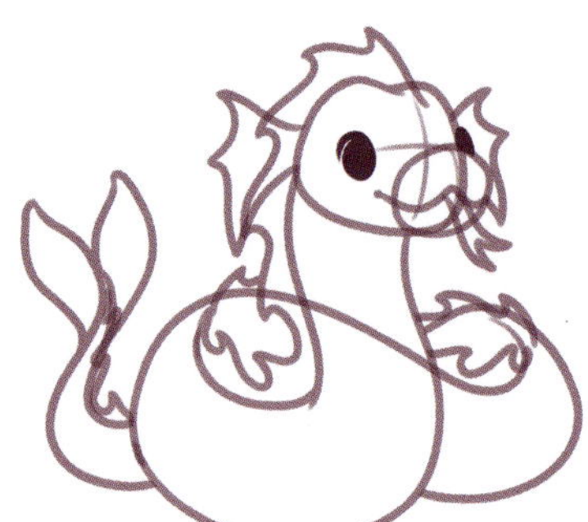

9. Add an oval eye with a curved line around the top. Then add a partial right eye above the snout.

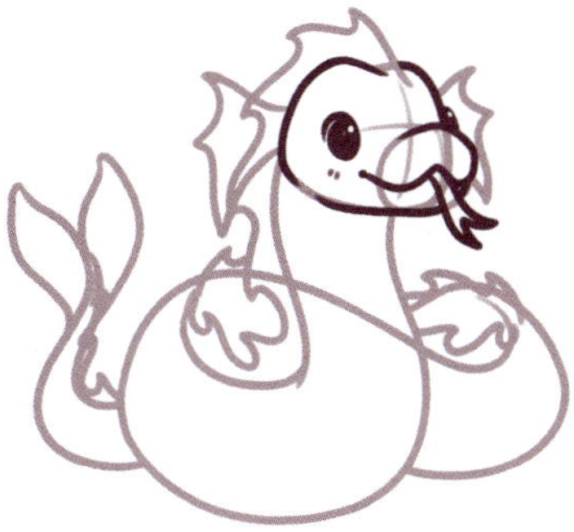

10. Lightly go over the face and head, leaving space in the eyes for highlights. Add dashes of blush on the cheeks.

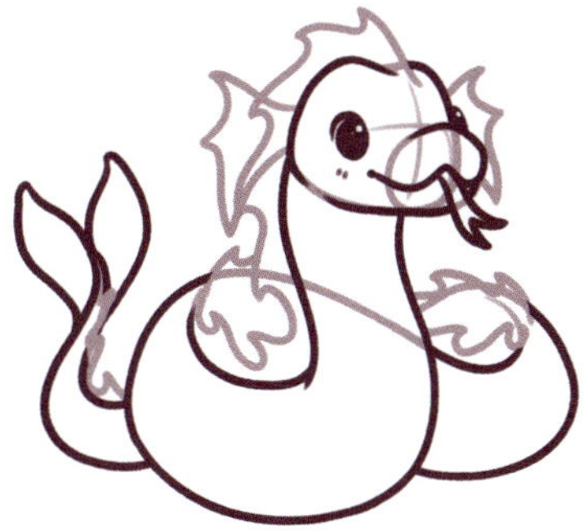

11. Sketch the body and tail, keeping an eye out for where the spines overlap the body.

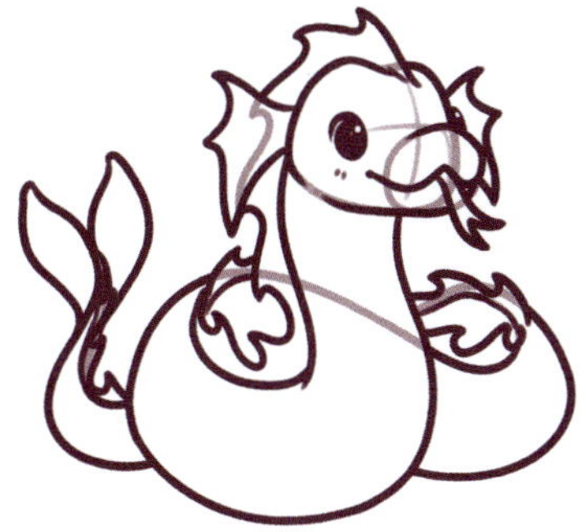

12. Draw the spines and ear fins.

13. Draw a line along the middle of the neck that narrows toward the tail for the underbelly. Add gently curved lines at evenly spaced intervals.

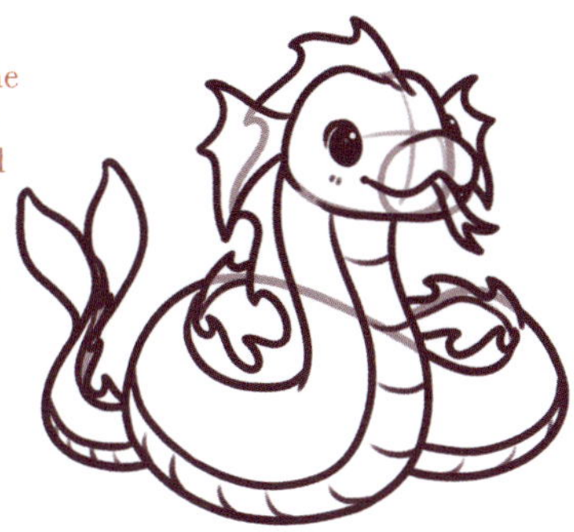

14. Add diagonal lines along the spine from the tips to the body. Also add lines on the ears and tail fins.

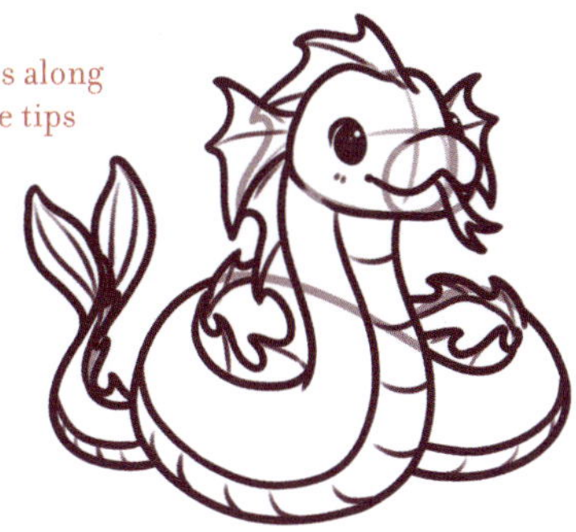

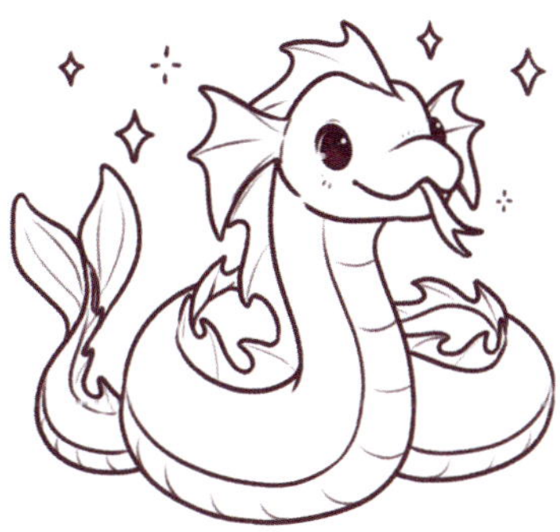

15. Neatly draw the line art over the sketch and add some sparkles if you'd like! Then erase the sketch underneath.

16. Finally, add color! I chose a watercolor palette of pale blues and teals, with pink for the tongue and cheeks, and yellow eyes.

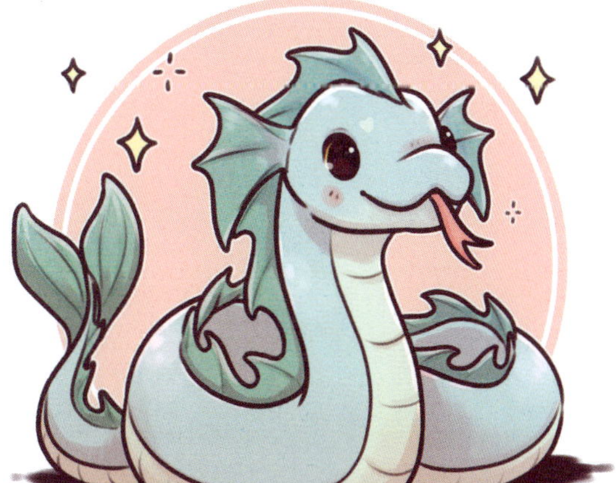

KRAKEN

Taking after the form of an octopus or squid, the kraken has a morbid history of attacking ships and dragging them to the ocean floor with its massive tentacles.

1. Draw an oval head with a plus sign guideline for the face.

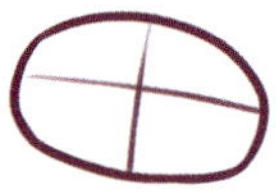

2. On top of the head, sketch a large triangle with a smaller triangle on top. Add a guideline down the middle.

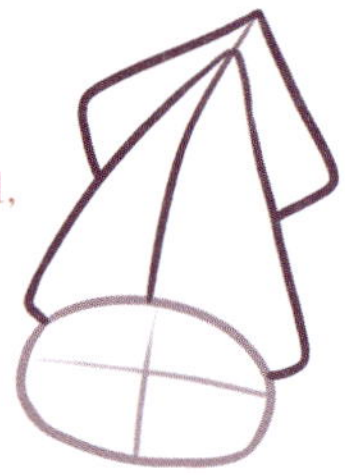

3. Below the head, sketch a boat shape with a thin V down the middle to show a crack.

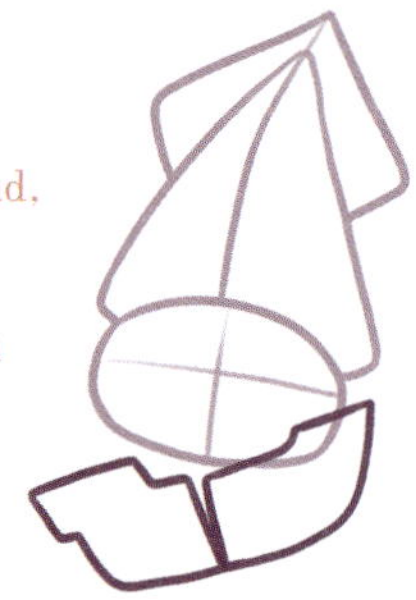

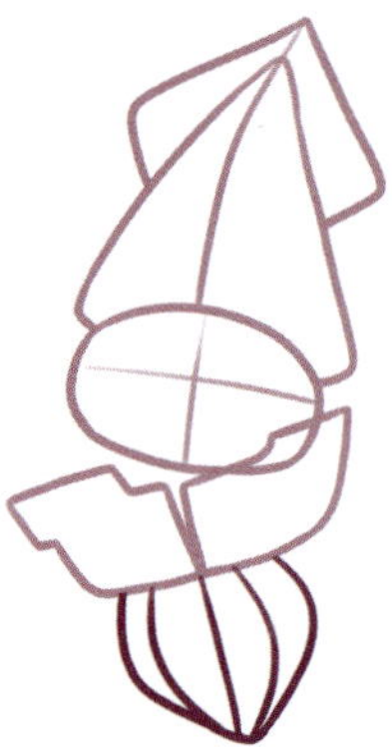

4. Under the boat, sketch a rounded V with three lines dividing it into four tentacles.

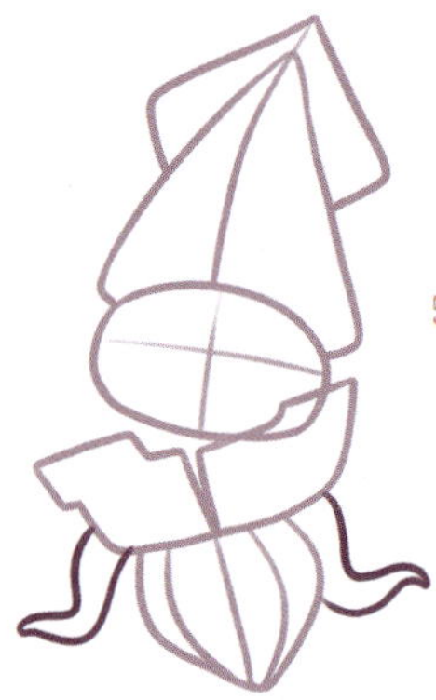

5. On the sides of the tentacles, draw a wavy tentacle pointed out.

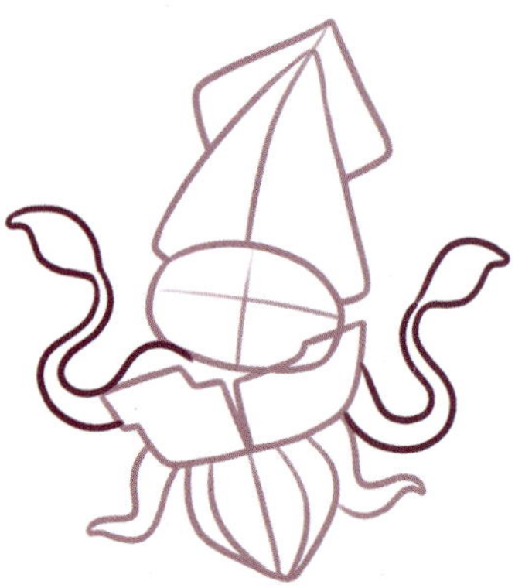

6. Around the boat, draw two large curling tentacles with teardrop-shaped ends.

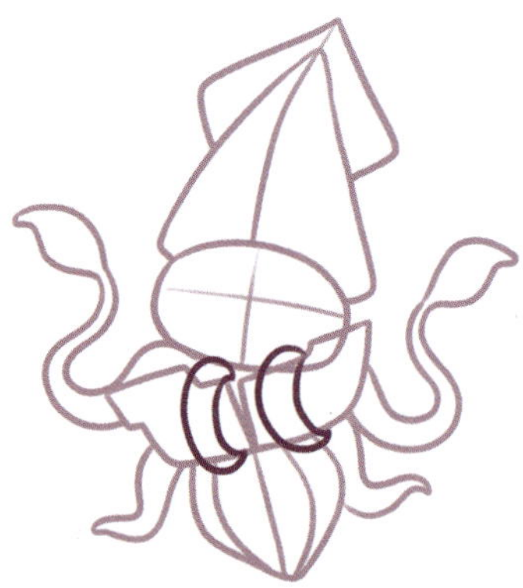

7. Add two crescent-shaped tentacles wrapped around the front of the boat on either side of the crack.

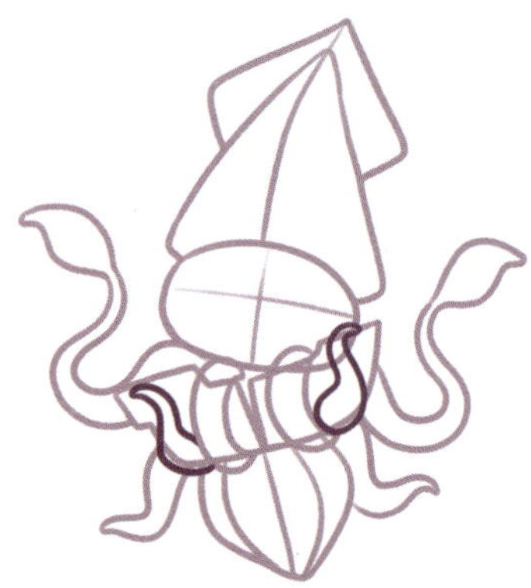

8. Add two curved tentacle tips next to the tentacles wrapped around the boat.

9. At the center of the face, draw a rounded diamond-shaped beak. Then add two oval eyes with a curved line around the top.

10. Lightly sketch the outline of the body. Add small dashes along the bottom of the tentacles for the suckers.

11. Sketch more details to the boat, like a spike coming out of the front, a rail along the back, and small, round windows along the side. Add splinters along the crack.

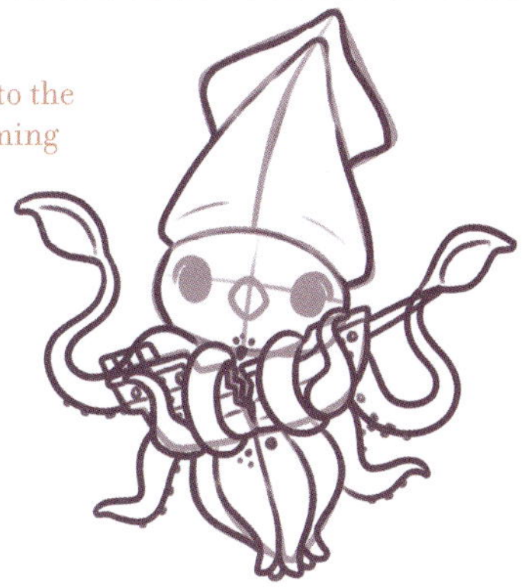

12. Sketch the face, adding highlights for the eyes and dashes above the beak, on the cheeks, and on the chin.

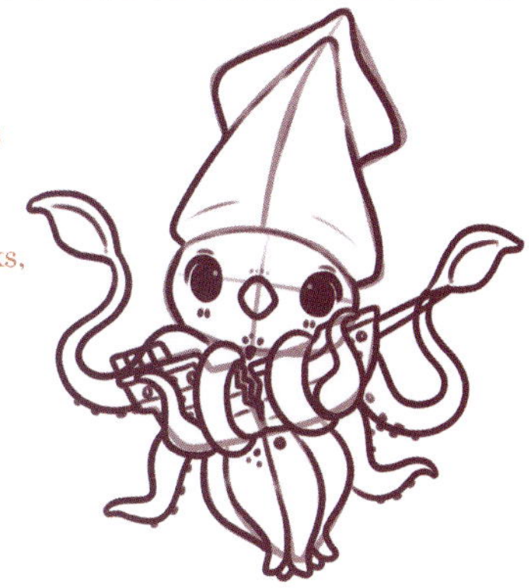

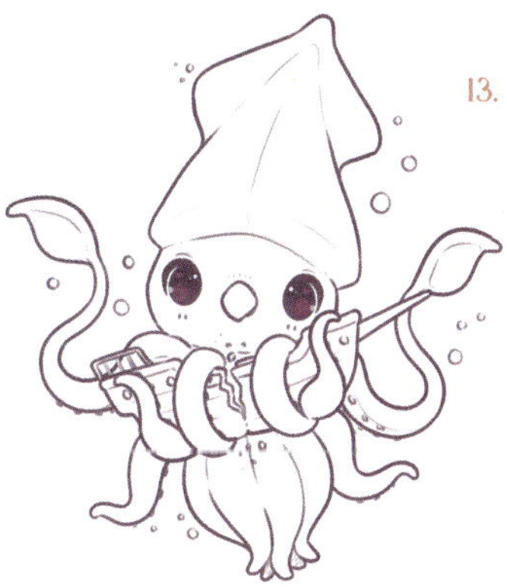

13. Neatly draw the line art over the sketch and add some bubbles if you'd like! Then erase the sketch underneath.

14. Lastly, add color! I used coral for the body and yellow for the eyes.

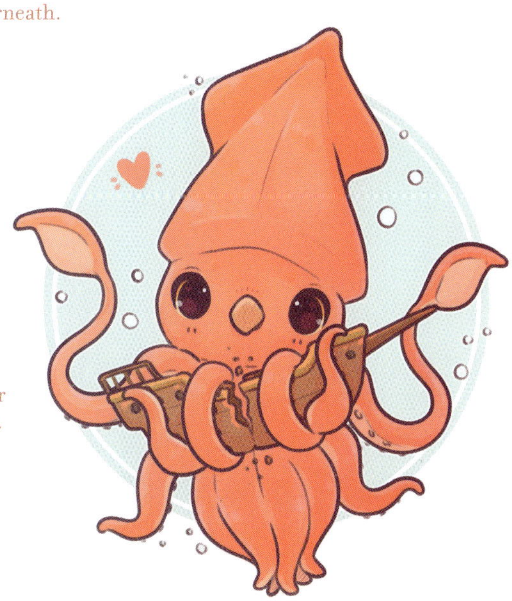

SEA LION

Not your average sea lion, this version represents many movements and cultures with its beautiful lion's mane and fish tail gracing flags and crests.

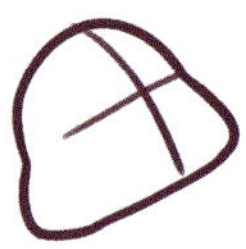

1. Lightly sketch an oval with pointed sides. Add a plus sign guideline for the face.

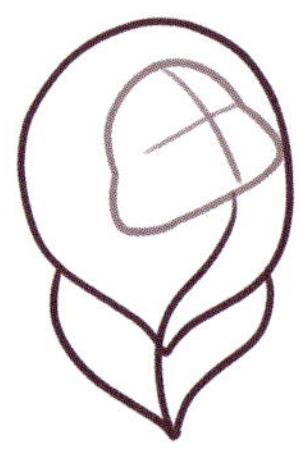

2. Draw a large teardrop mane around the head. Then draw a rounded V below where the mane continues onto the chest.

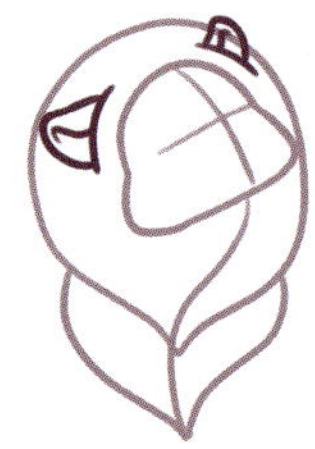

3. On the top sides of the mane, add two semicircle ears, each with a curved line inside.

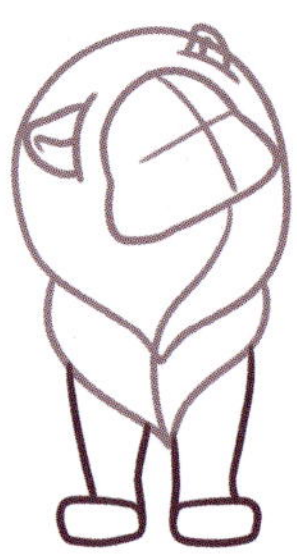

4. Draw two rounded rectangle paws with two lines connecting them to the chest.

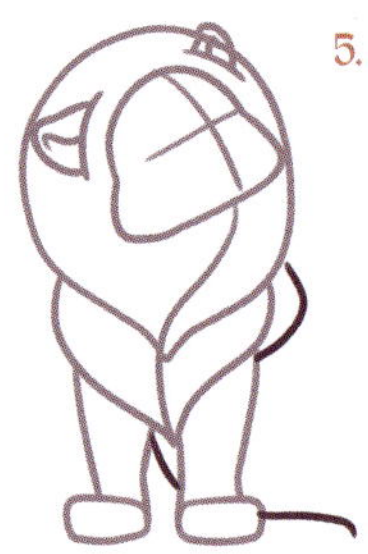

5. Draw a curve starting between the legs and continuing next to the right paw. Then add a small, curved line to the right of the chest to start the back.

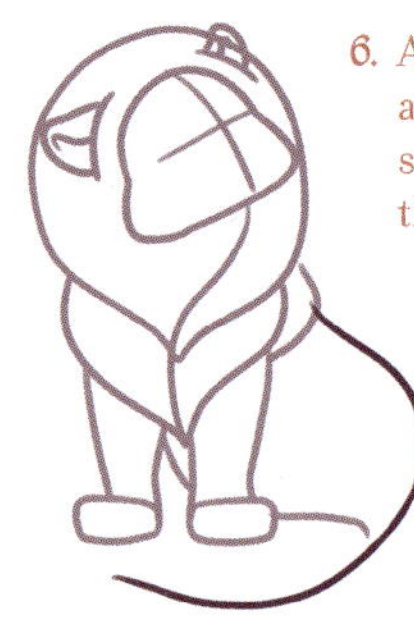

6. Add a curved line at the back and sweep below the paws.

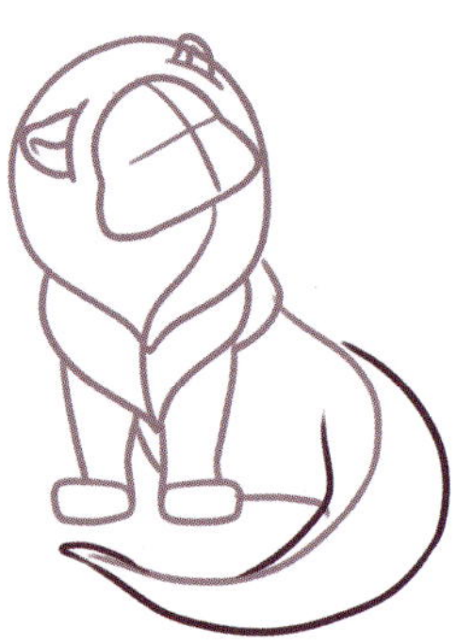

7. Draw the tail following the curved line that tapers to a point at the end.

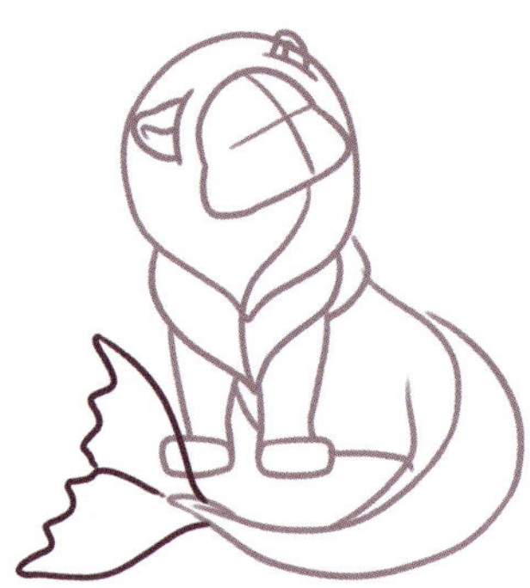

8. At the end of the tail sketch a fin with scalloped edges and a line down the middle.

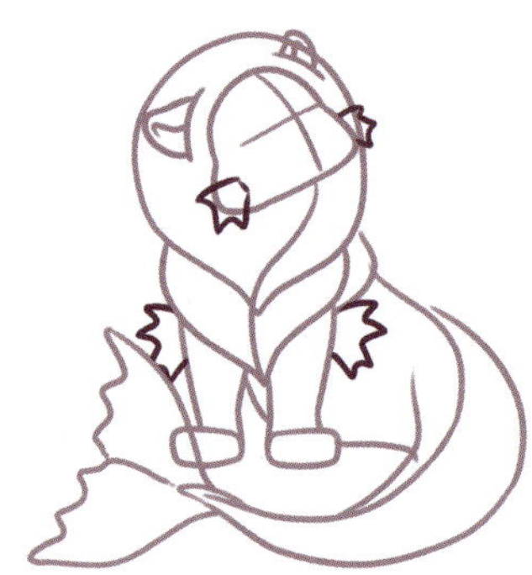

9. Add small spikey fins on the sides of the face and to the upper legs.

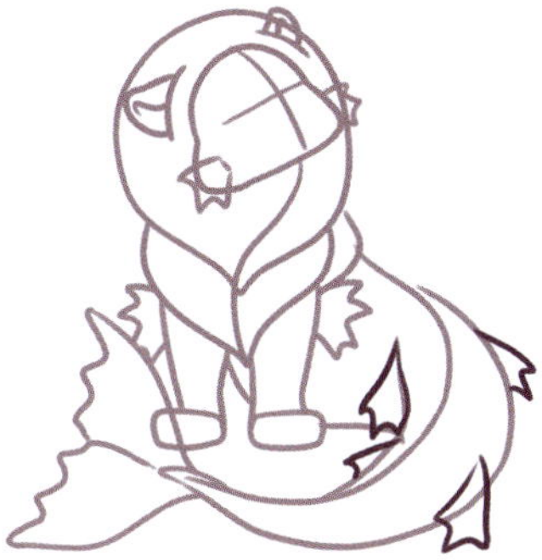

10. Draw two sets of fins—some whole, some partial—along the tail.

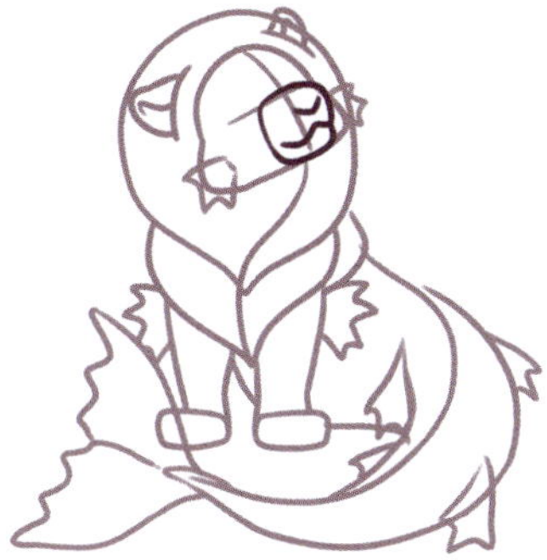

11. Draw a rounded square snout at the center of the face. Add a W mouth and a flat V nose.

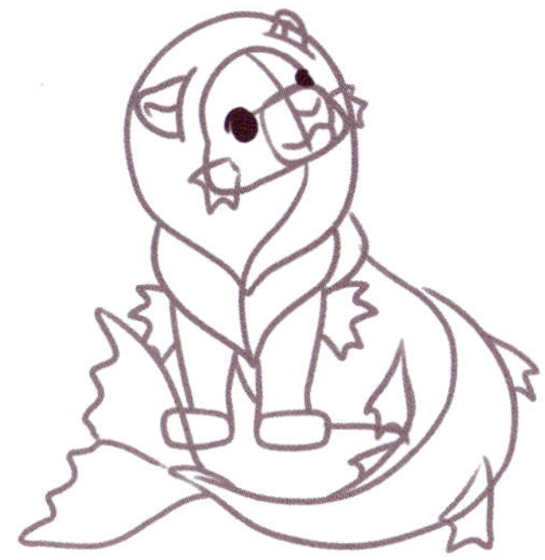

12. Add an oval eye with a curve around the top. Then add a partial right eye above the snout.

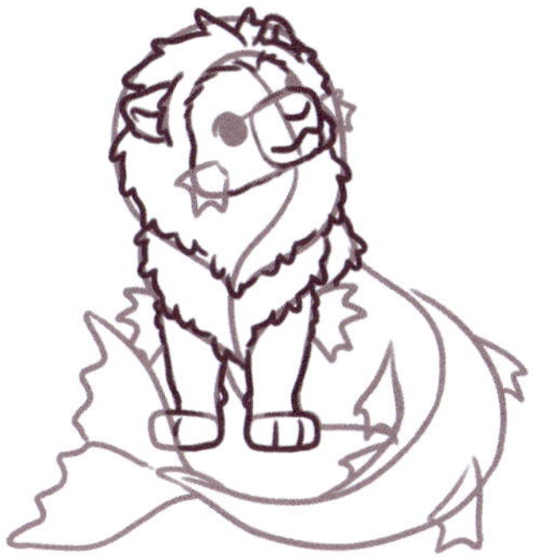

13. Add details to the body. Define the fur with soft W shapes. Add toe lines to the paws.

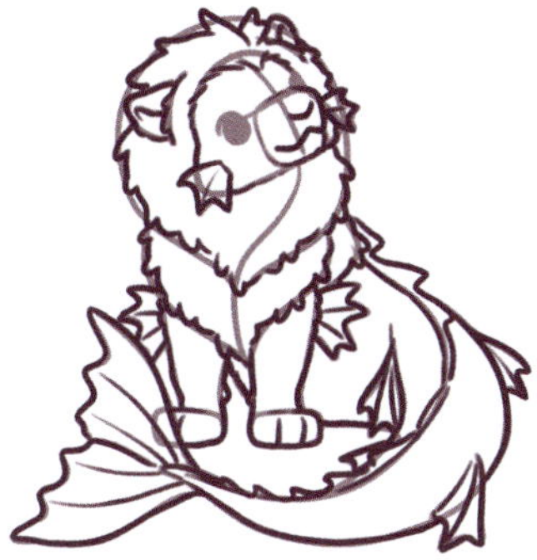

14. Sketch the fins and the tail, adding spikes along the top of the tail.

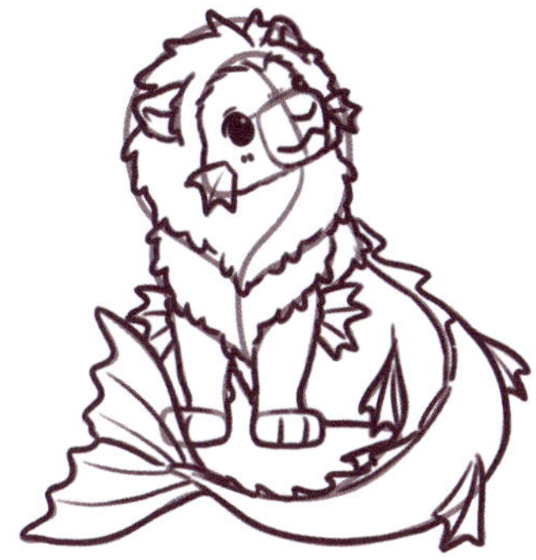

15. Draw the face detail, adding highlights to the eyes and dashes above the nose and on the cheeks.

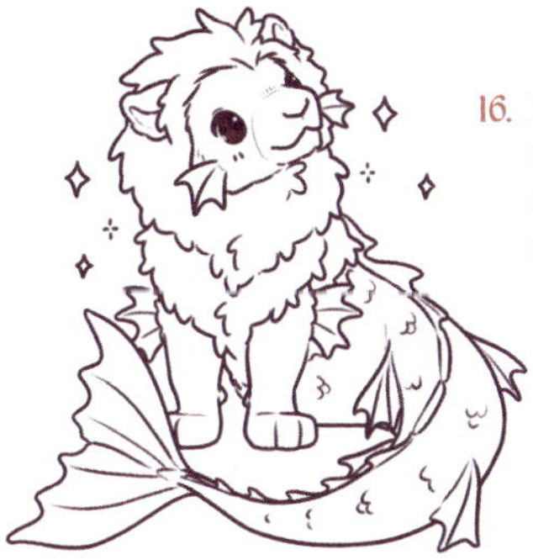

16. Neatly draw the line art over the sketch. Add some sparkles if you'd like! Then erase the sketch underneath.

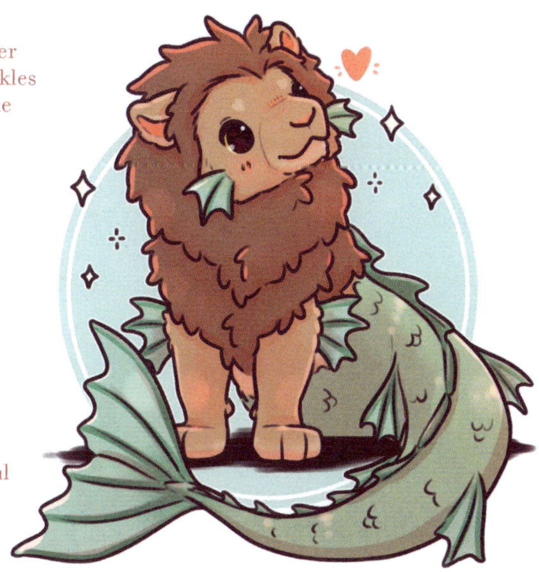

17. Color your sea lion! For the lion-half, keep it the traditional tan and brown. For the tail, I used pale green and teal.

AKHLUT

This shape-shifting creature spends half of its life on land in the form of a wolf. with the other half swimming the seas as an orca.

1. Lightly sketch an oval with pointed sides. Add a plus sign guideline for the face.

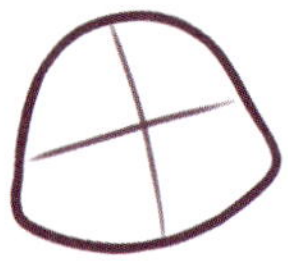

2. Add two triangle ears on top of the head, each with two smaller triangles inside.

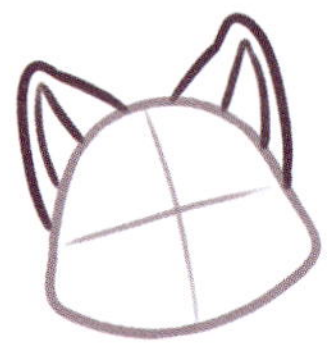

3. Draw three rounded V shapes, one under the other, for the neck and chest.

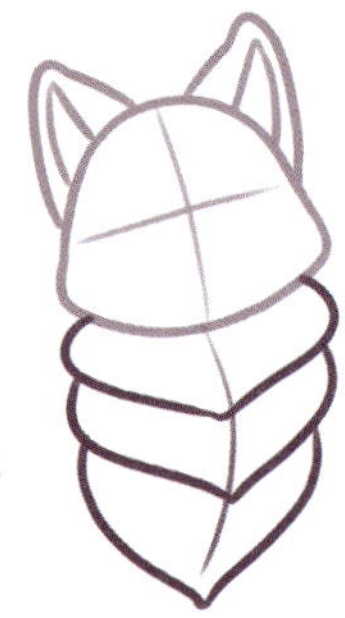

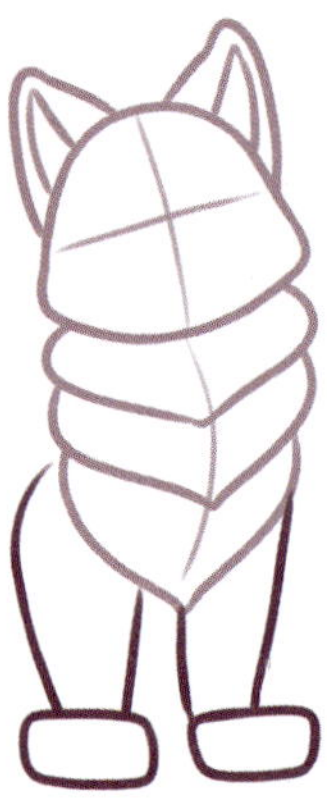

4. Draw two rounded rectangle paws and connect them to the chest with two lines.

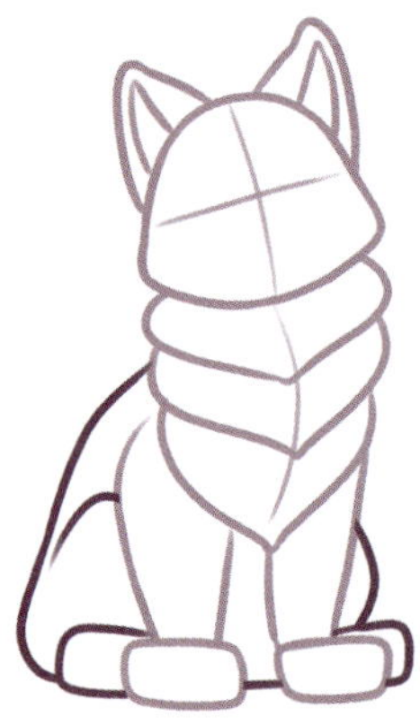

5. Sketch a curve from the neck down to the paws for the haunches. Next to the front paws, draw two partial back paws. Add a curve above the left back paw for the knee. Draw a line between the front paws.

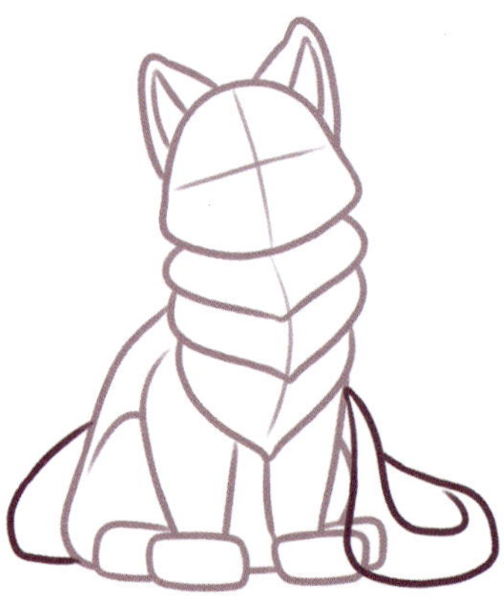

6. Start the tail with a C curve on the left and continue it with a teardrop shape on the right with a curved line inside.

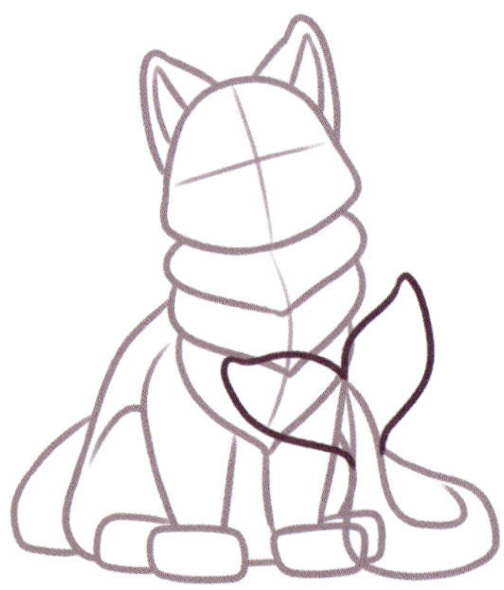

7. Add teardrop-shaped fins to the tip of the tail.

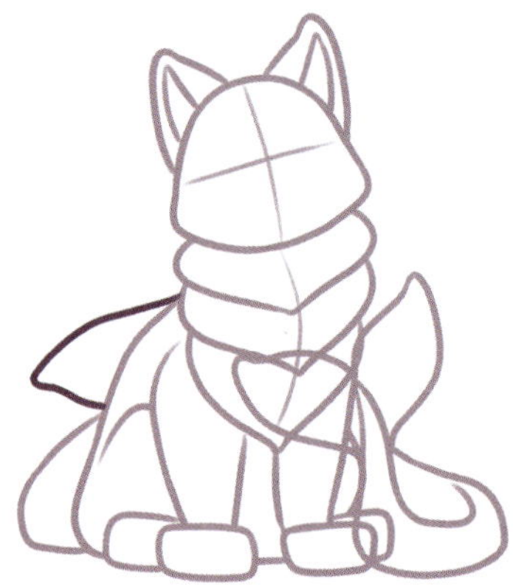

8. Add a rounded triangle dorsal fin on the back.

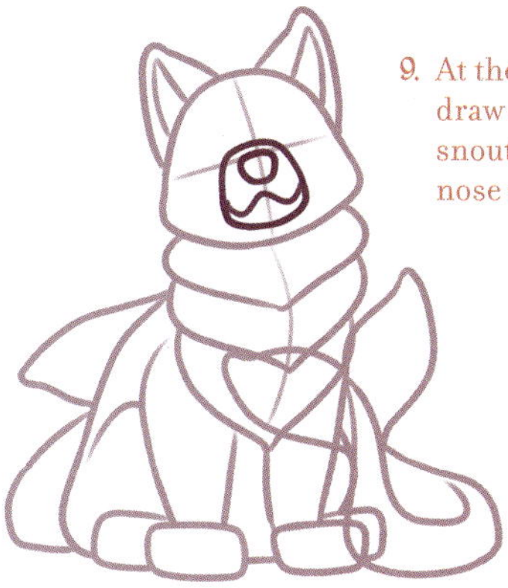

9. At the center of the face, draw a rounded square snout. Add a small, trapezoid nose and a W mouth.

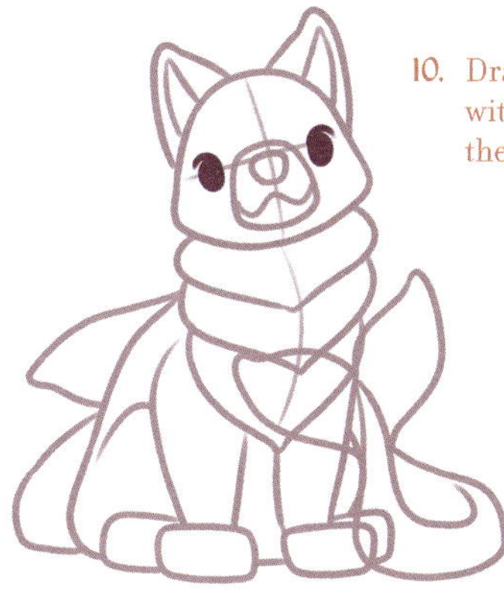

10. Draw two oval eyes with a curve around the top.

11. Draw the outline of the body and add details. Define the fur with soft W shapes. Add toe lines on the paws.

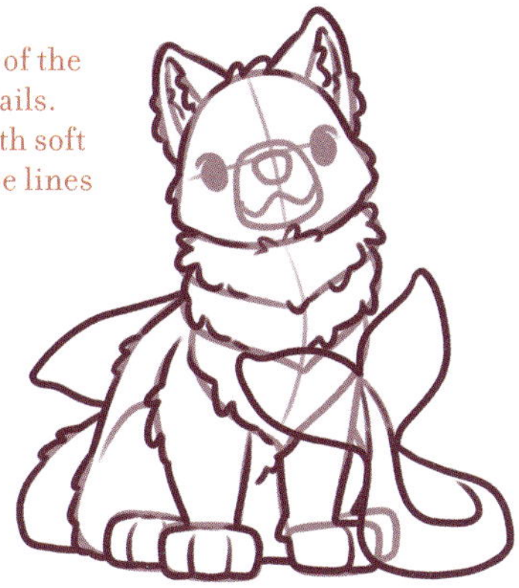

12. Sketch the face, adding highlights for the eyes and dashes above the nose and on the cheeks. Add two small V fangs and two dashes on the sides of the head for whiskers.

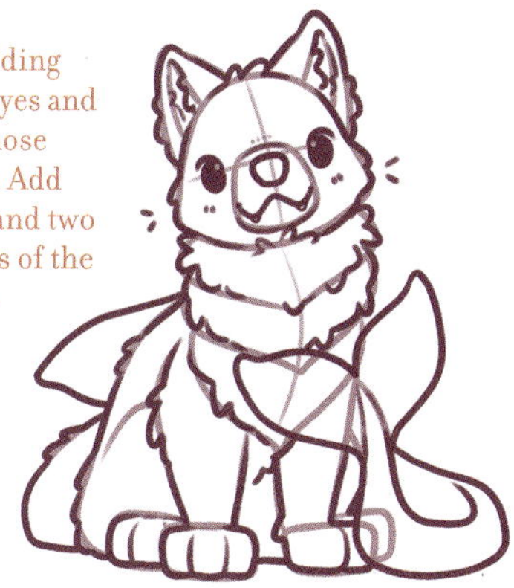

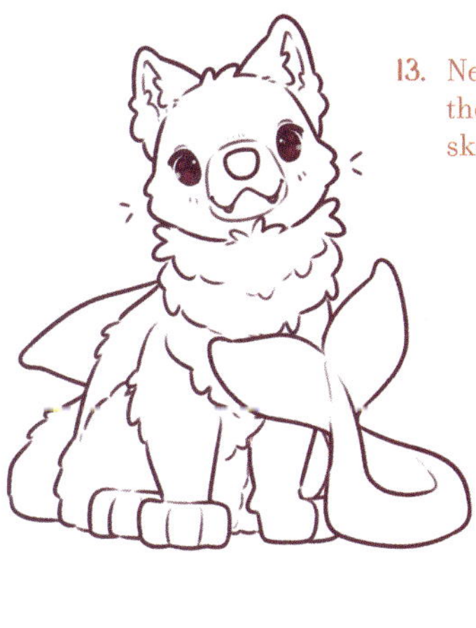

13. Neatly draw the line art over the sketch! Then erase the sketch underneath.

14. Orcas have such iconic coloring, so keep to black and white. Use black along the back and white for the chest, paws, and big patches around the eyes.

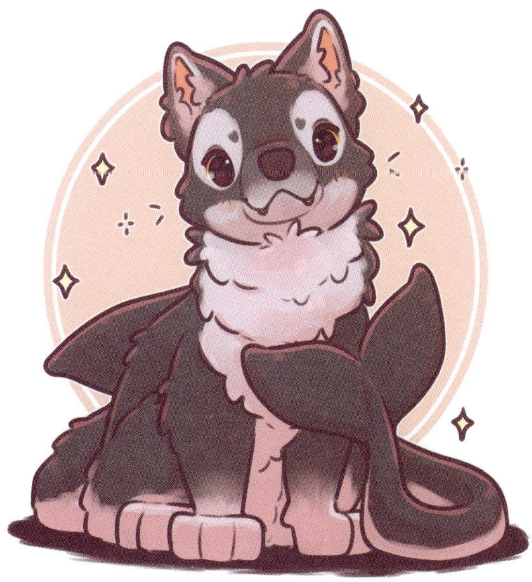

KAPPA

Physically reminiscent of turtles, these vicious beasties are known to attack humans, but it is said that you can placate them with their favorite vegetable: cucumber!

1. Lightly sketch a circle head with a dip on the right side. Add a plus sign guideline for the face.

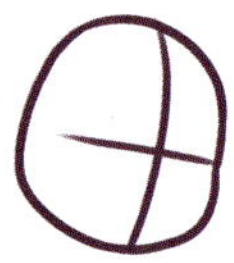

2. Draw a big, rounded rectangle for the body, with a flatter right side and a curve for the neckline.

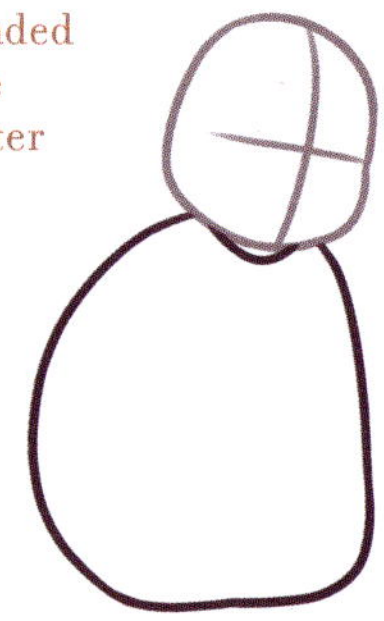

3. Draw two oval upper arms and connect rectangles for the lower arms. Angle the lower arms so the hands meet in the middle. Draw finger lines.

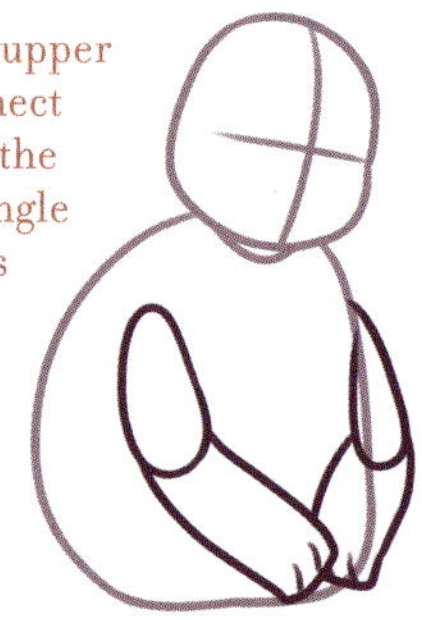

4. Draw the two webbed feet at the bottom of the body. Then connect the feet to the body with curved lines.

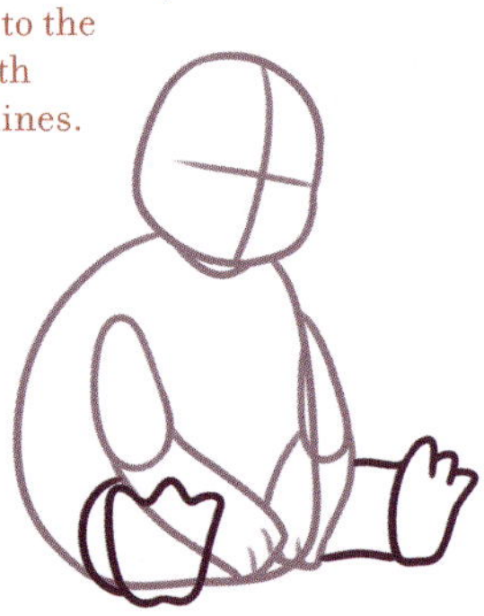

5. Define the edge of the shell with two curved lines, from the head to the leg. Add a small curve above the right arm.

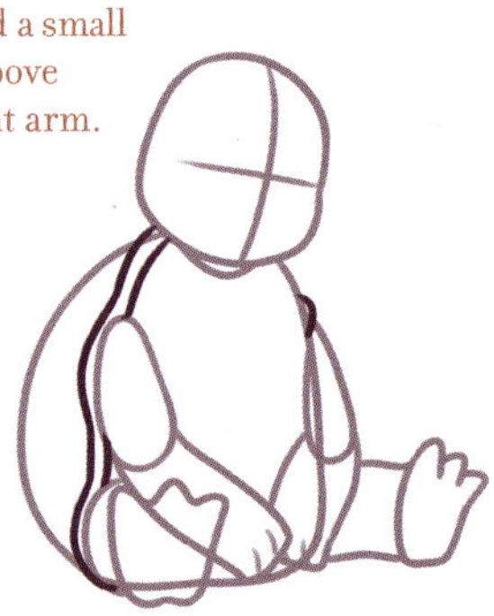

6. On the bottom-left of the shell, add a little triangle tail.

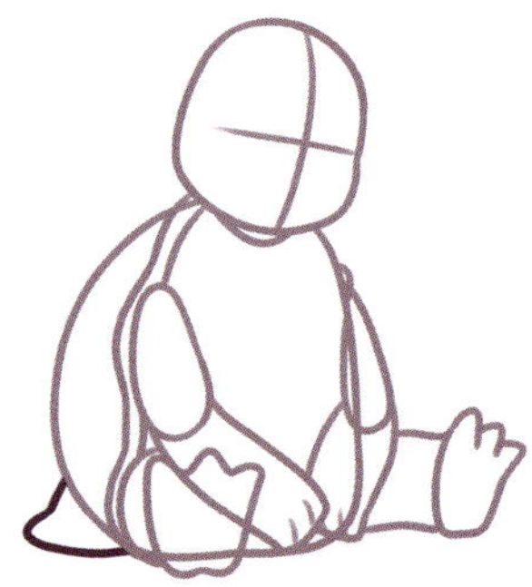

7. Draw a band around the top of the head for the hair, with two curves on the sides.

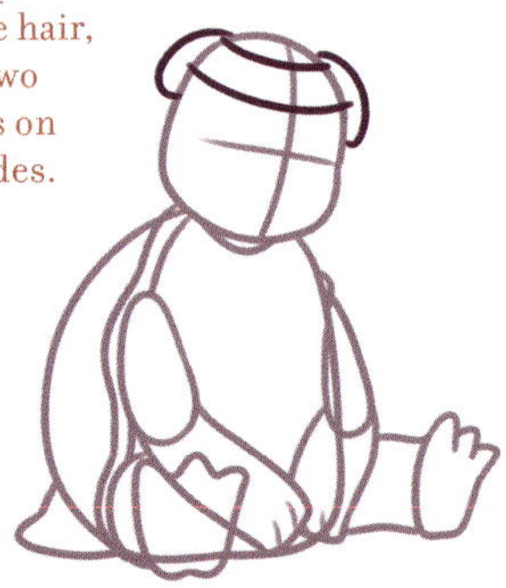

8. Draw a large, rounded diamond beak at the center of the face.

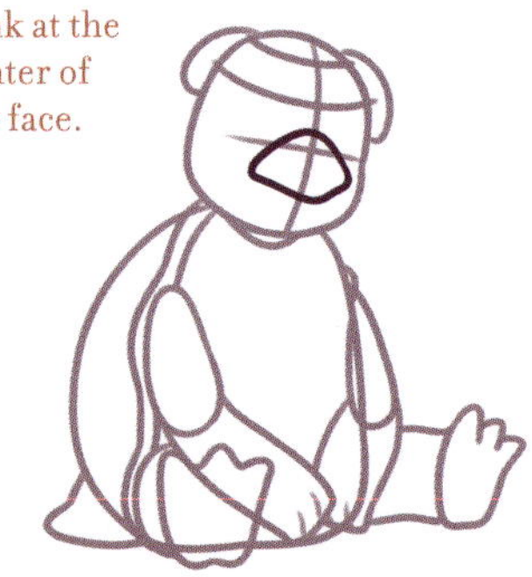

9. Add the oval eyes with a curve around the top.

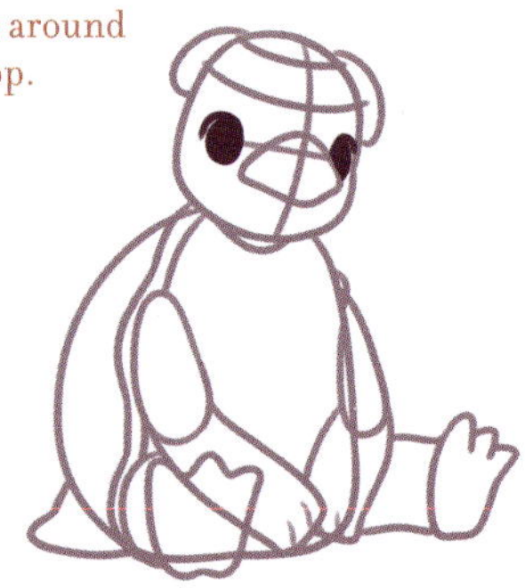

10. Lightly sketch over the shell, adding detail to the chest with horizontal lines and a line down the middle.

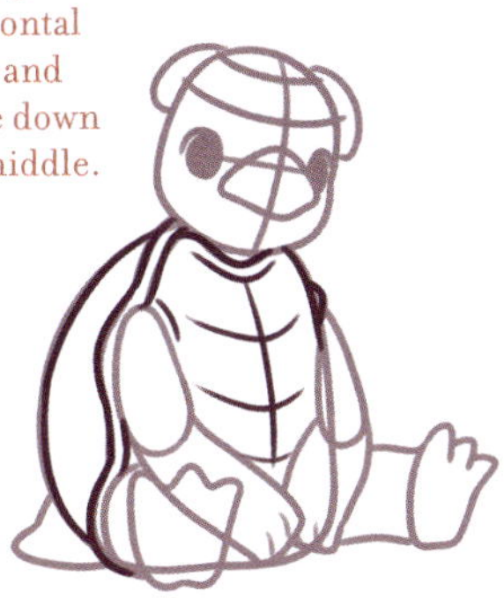

11. Add detail to the shell with arching lines along the side and four small spikes along the back.

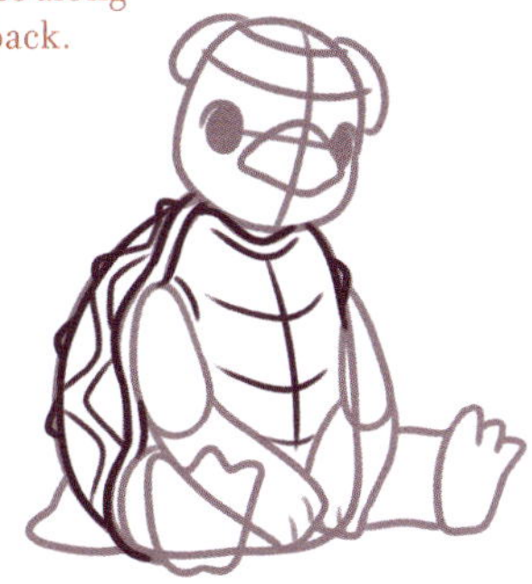

12. Sketch the arms and the legs. Define the fingers of the hands and lines of the feet. Keep an eye on where the left foot overlaps the arm.

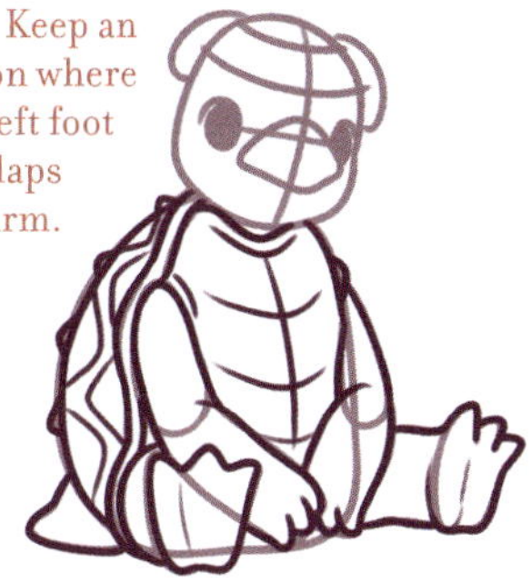

13. Draw the head, leaving a space where the hair will go. On the top of the head, draw a curve with a dip.

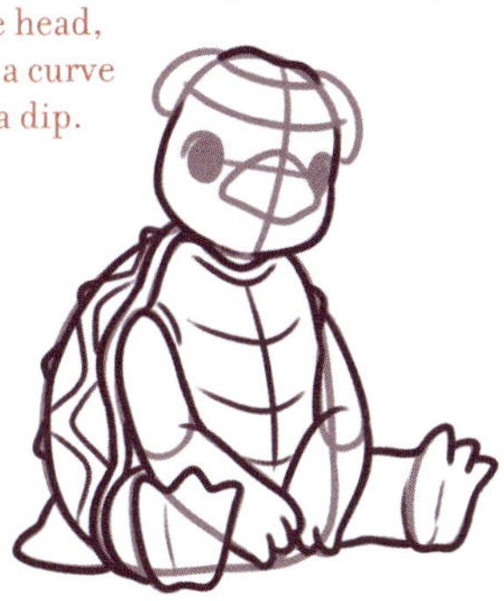

14. Sketch the hair using the band around the head with soft W shapes.

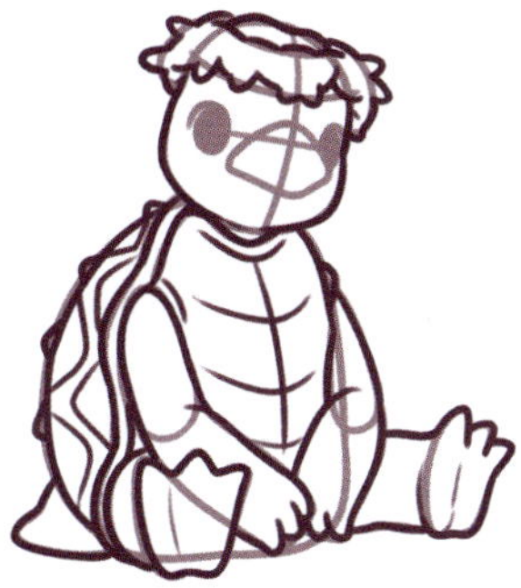

15. Sketch the face, adding highlights in the eyes and dashes on the cheeks. Add two dots at the top of the beak for nostrils.

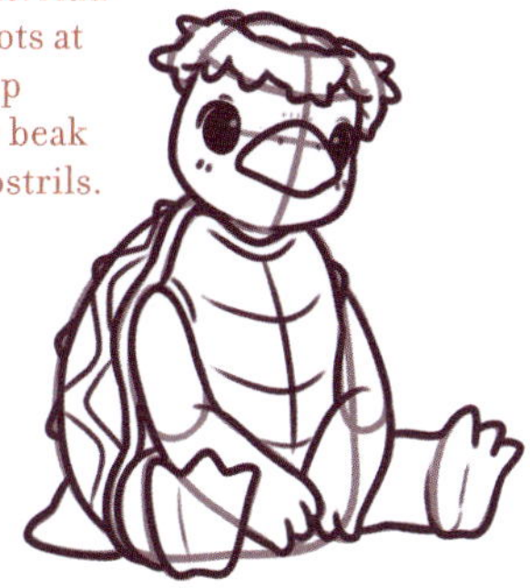

16. Neatly draw the line art over the sketch. Add some sparkles if you'd like! Then erase the sketch underneath.

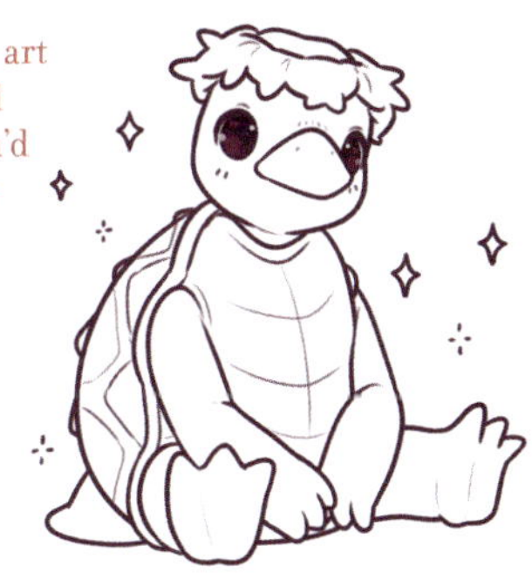

17. Add some color! Use green for the arms, face, and legs, and dark green for the hair. Use pale yellow for the top of the head, beak, and chest, and brown for the shell.

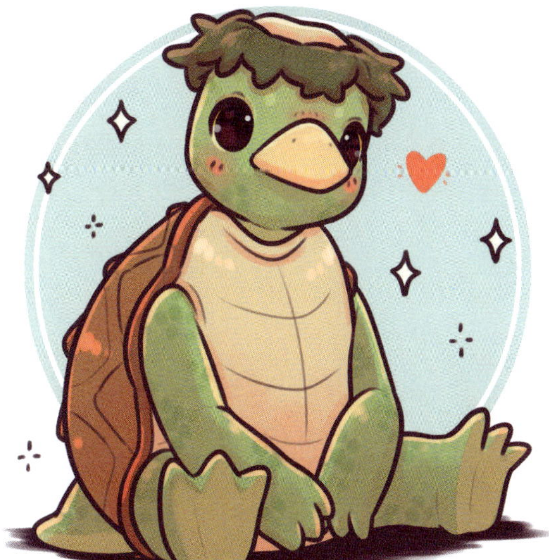

HIPPOCAMPUS

Found in many mythologies, including Greek and Roman, hippocampi are known to pull the chariot of Poseidon, the ancient Greek God of the Sea.

1. Draw a circle head with a rectangle snout on the left side. Draw a horizontal guideline across the head.

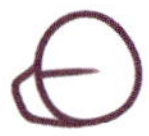

2. Add two teardrop ears on the top of the head, each with a line inside.

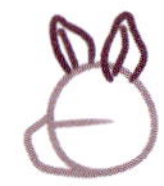

3. Draw two curved lines, starting at the right ear and under the snout for the neck and chest.

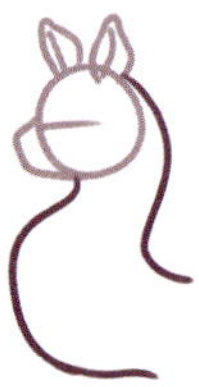

4. Continue the body with two curling lines sweeping under the chest and swirling into a tapered tail.

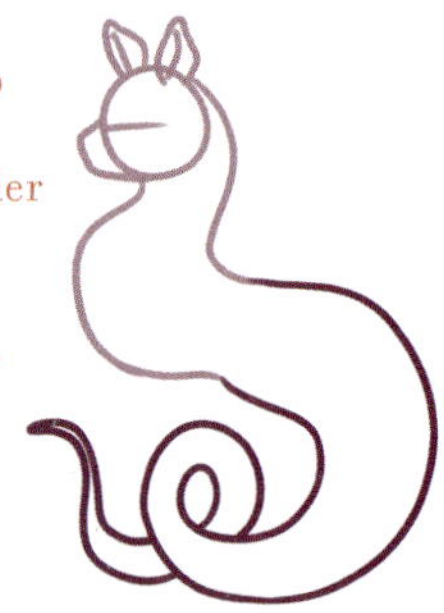

5. At the tip of the tail, draw a fish tail with two teardrop shapes in a wide V.

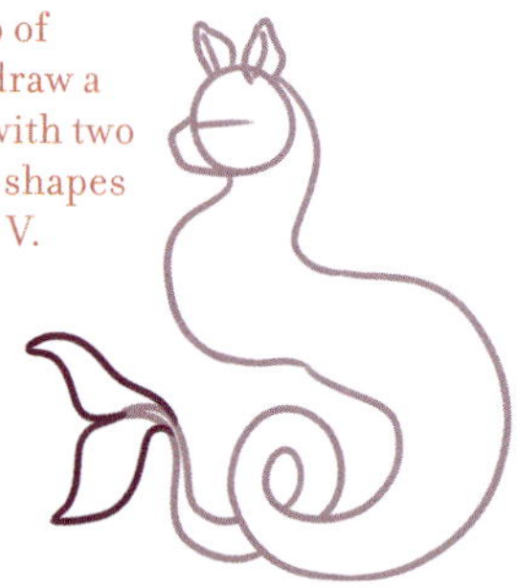

6. Draw an oval upper arm with a small circle slightly up and to the left. Connect the circle to the oval with lines.

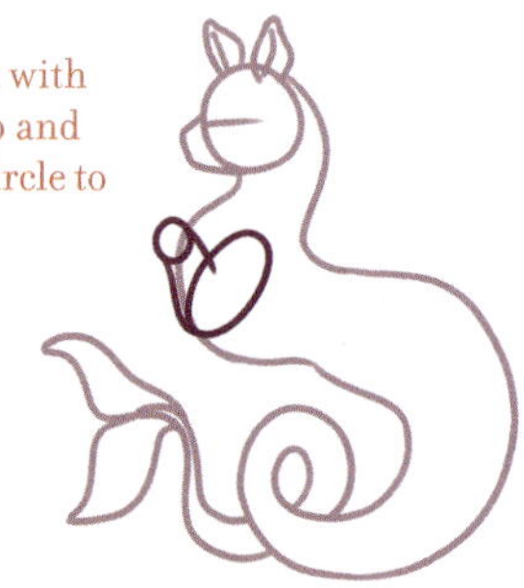

7. Slightly below the circle, draw another circle for the ankle. Attach a rounded V hoof below. Then connect the two circles with lines.

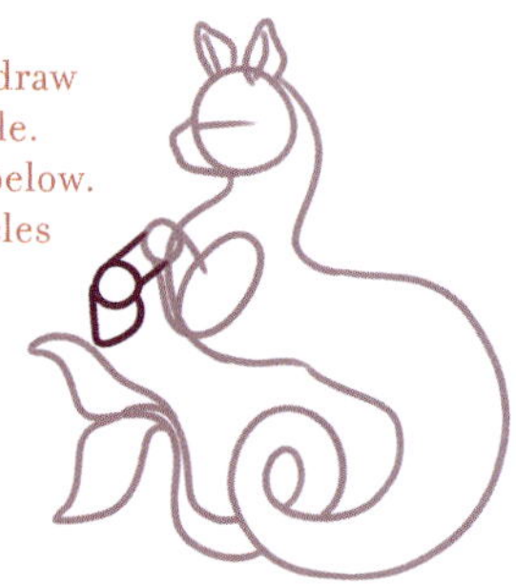

8. Above the front leg, draw a partially concealed second leg.

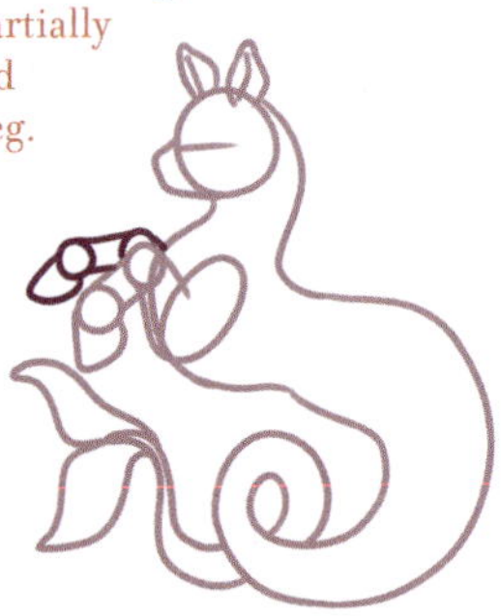

9. Draw spines along the back and tail.

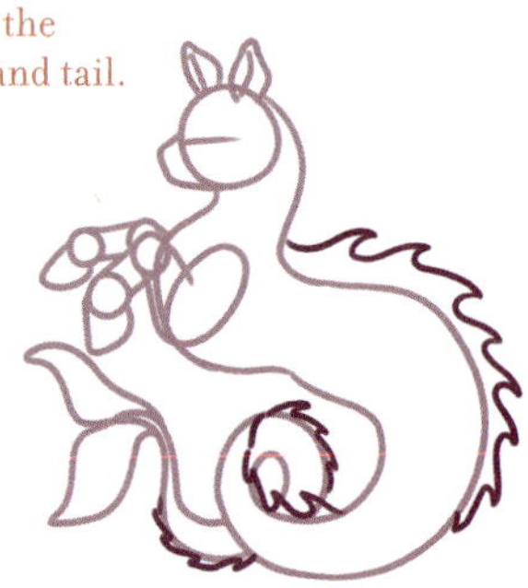

10. Add spines around the arm and the side of the head.

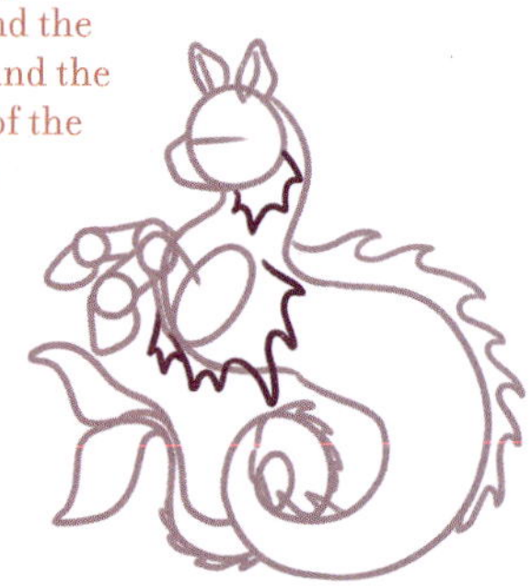

11. Sketch floating, swirly hair around the head and neck with some strands on the face and around the snout.

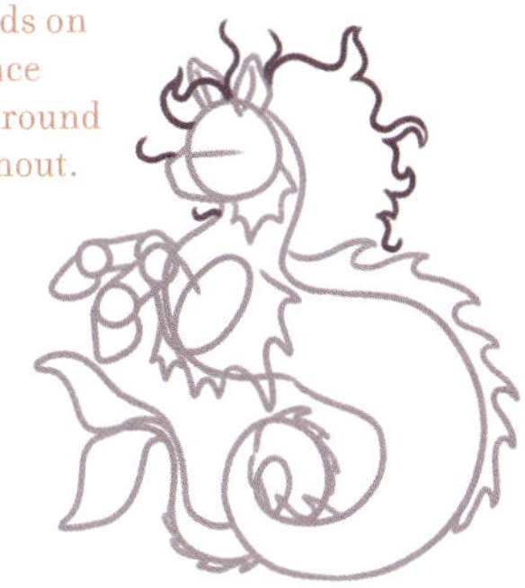

12. Draw an oval eye with a curved line around the top. Make a dot for the nostril in the top of the snout.

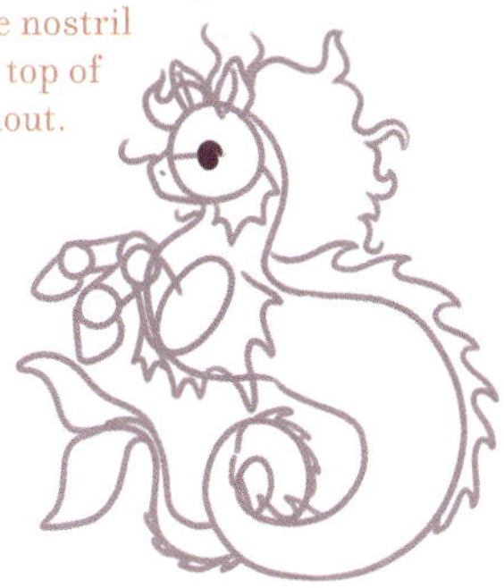

13. Lightly sketch over the body. Detail the fur at the elbow, hooves, and around the face, but keep the lines smooth along the tail.

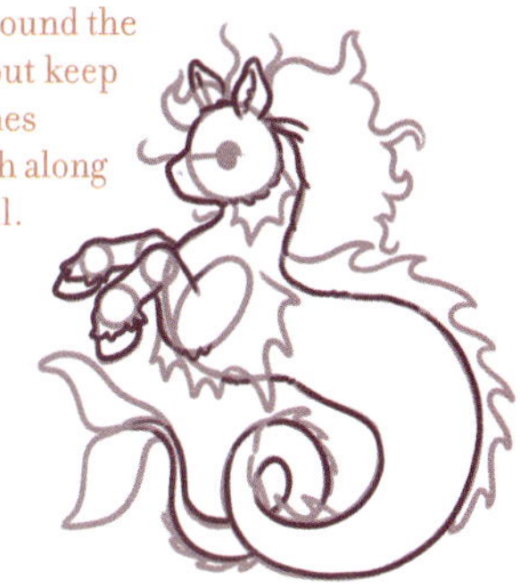

14. Sketch the fins and spines, adding webbed lines along the fins.

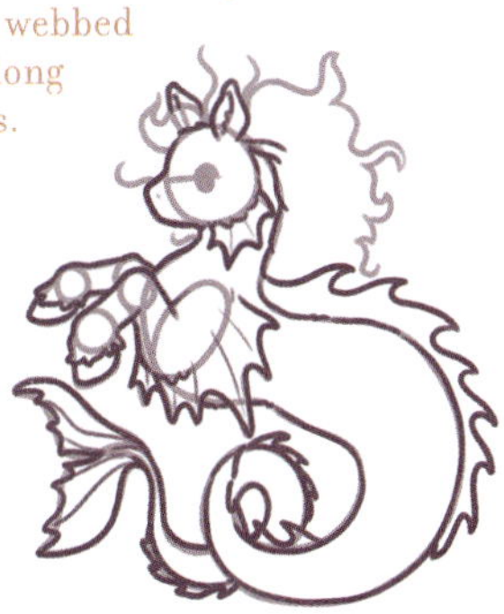

15. Lightly sketch the hair, adding a little more detail.

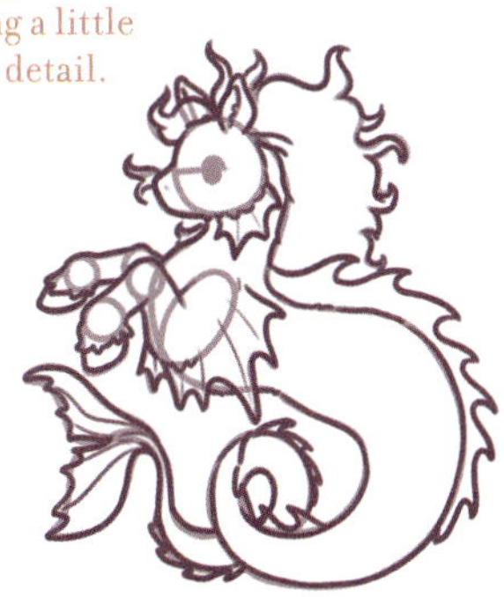

16. Sketch the face detail, adding highlight to the eye and a small eyelash and dashes on the cheek.

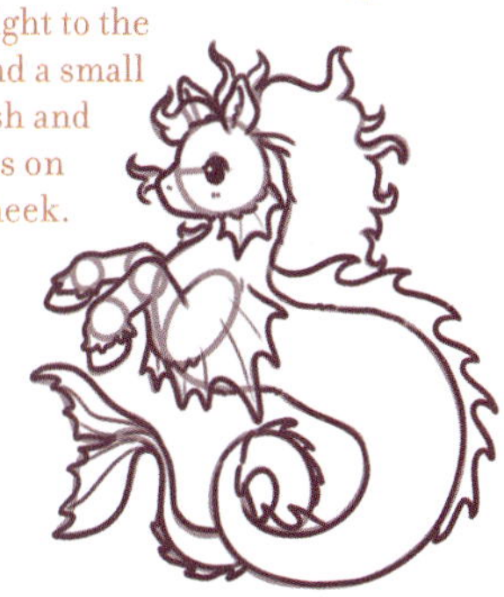

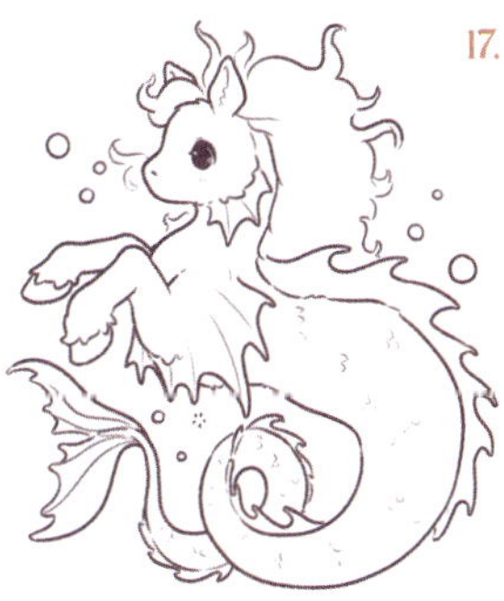

17. Neatly draw the line art over the sketch. Add bubbles if you'd like! Then erase the sketch underneath.

18. Finish with color! I went with pale blue with a slightly darker shade for the hair and tails and bright blue for the spines.

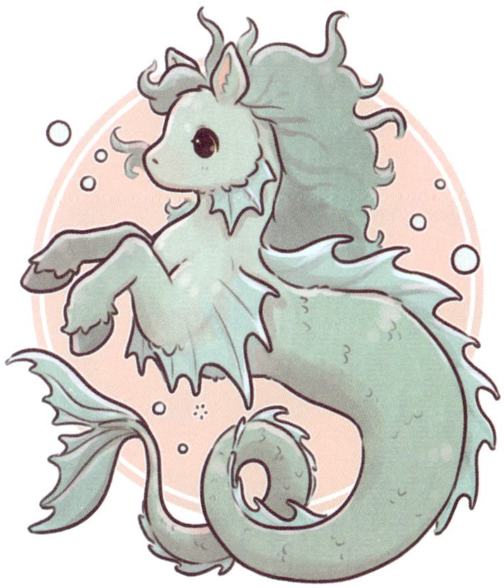

KELPIE

Beware of these insidious shape-shifting beasties, for they appear as a horse near water, to lure people in before pulling them under.

1. Draw a circle head with a rectangle snout on the right. Add a horizontal guideline across the head.

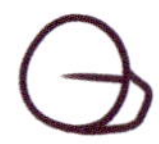

2. Add two teardrop ears on the top of the head, each with a line inside.

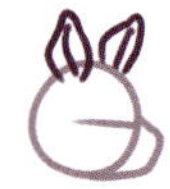

3. Draw two curved lines starting at the left ear and under the snout for the neck and chest.

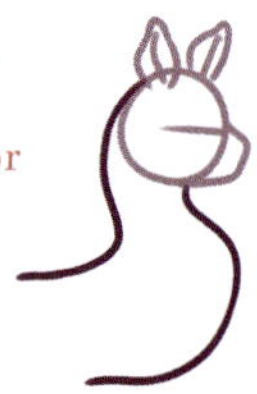

4. Complete the body with two curling lines sweeping under the chest and swirling to a tapered tail.

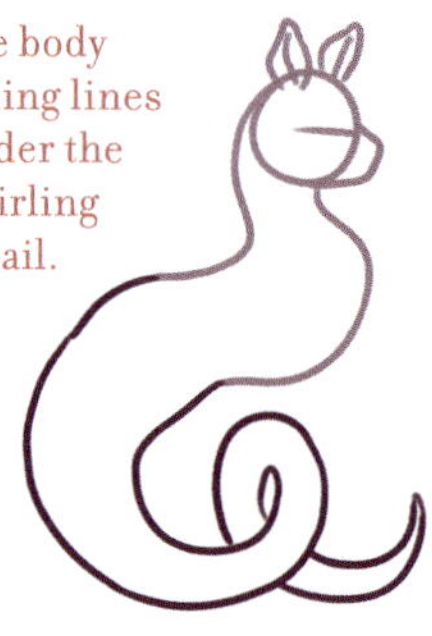

5. Draw a fish tail with two curved teardrops in the shape of a V.

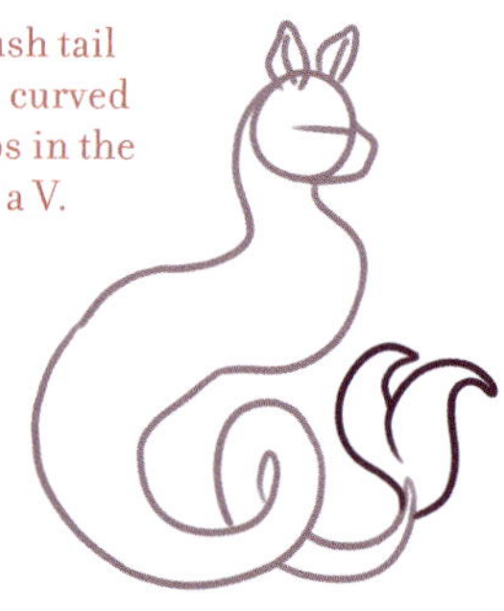

6. Draw an oval upper arm with a small circle to the right. Connect the circle to the oval with a line on either side, making a V shape.

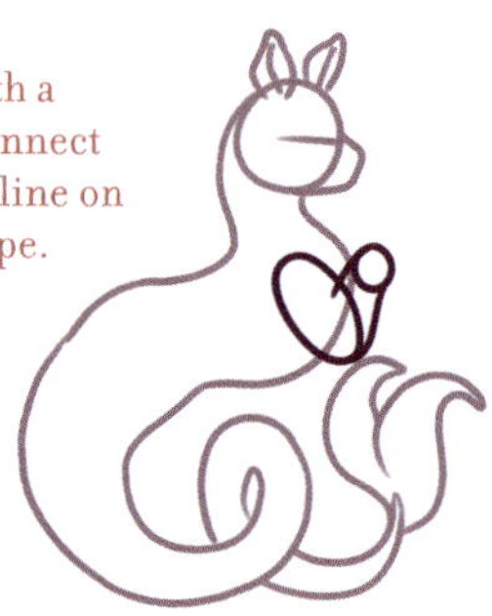

7. Below and to the right of the circle, draw another circle for the ankle. Draw two rounded V shapes for the cloven hoof. Then connect the two circles with lines.

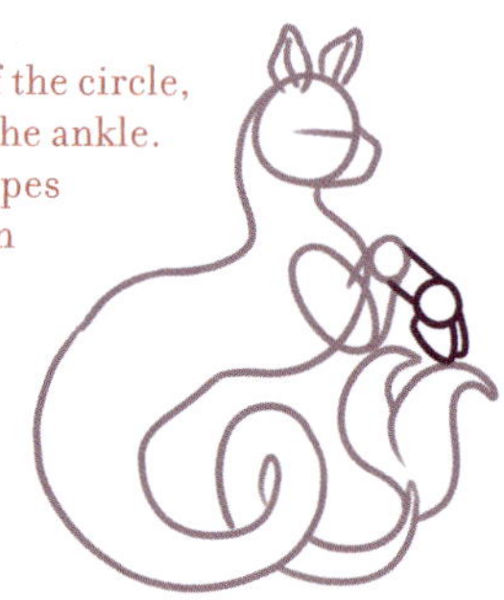

8. Draw a partial second leg above the first leg.

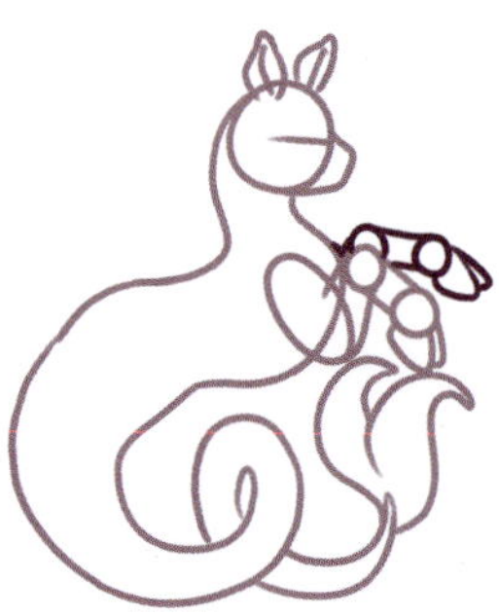

9. Draw spines along the tail and on the side of the head. Then add two spiny triangle fins on the sides of the body.

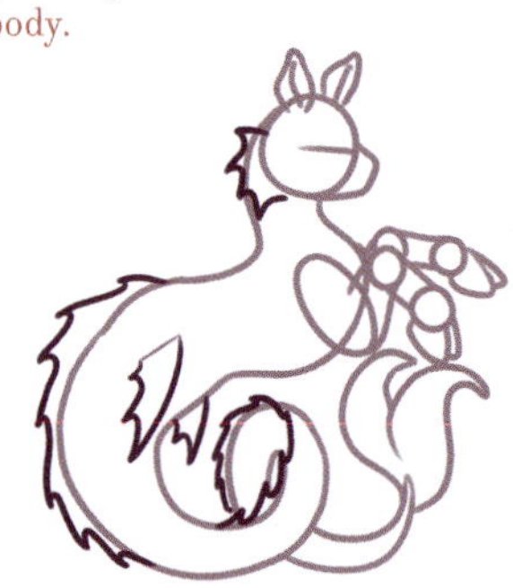

10. Sketch floating hair around the head and neck, with pieces on the face. Add a triangle tuft around the elbow and curved lines around the end of the tail.

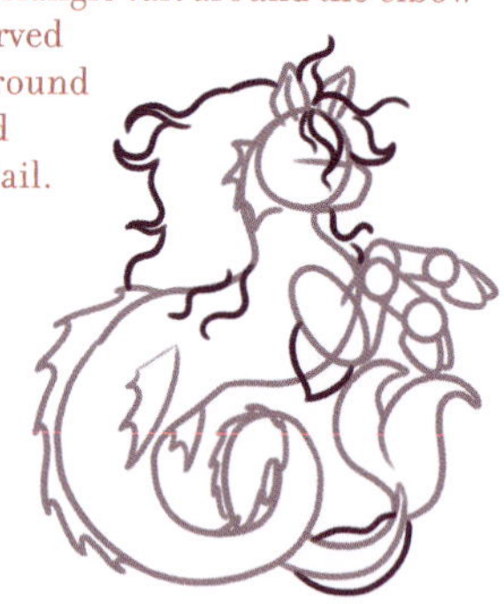

11. Using the face guideline, draw an oval eye with a curved line around the top. Add a dot at the tip of the nose for a nostril.

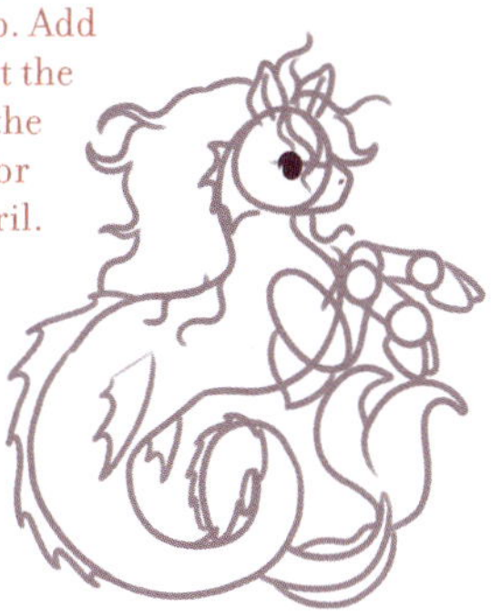

12. Lightly sketch over the body. Define the fur around the elbow, hooves, and face, but keep it smooth on the fish tail.

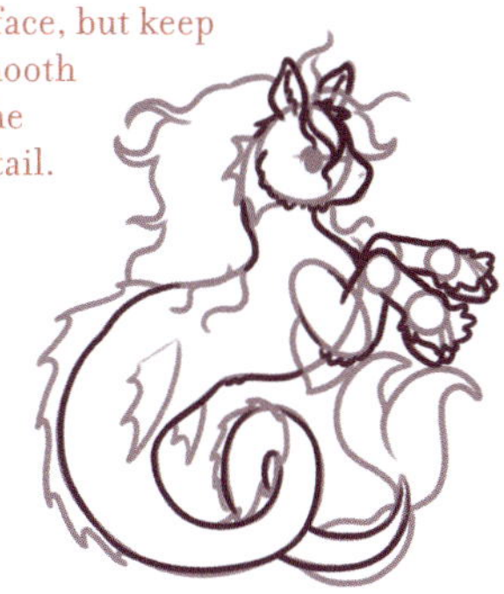

13. Sketch the spines and fins, adding lines for detail.

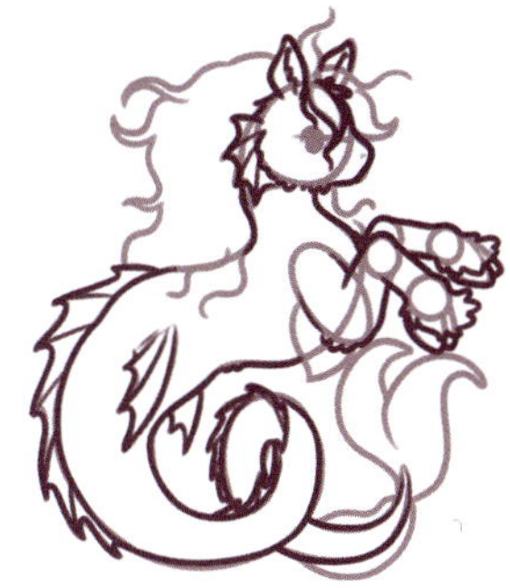

14. Sketch the detail for the tufts of fur around the elbows and near the bottom of the tail.

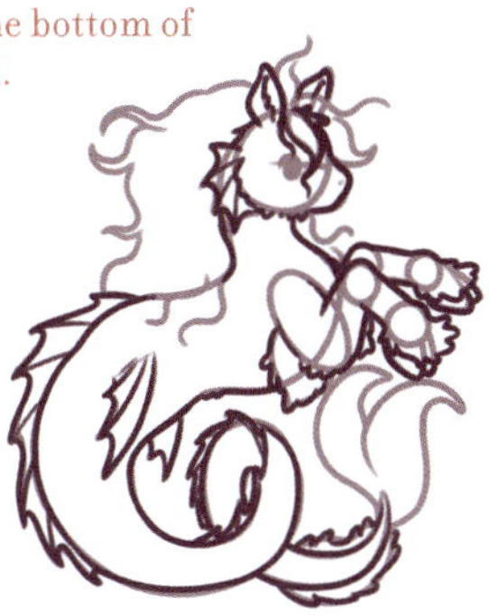

15. Sketch the hair. Add detail with thin pointed ovals for seaweed along the hair and body.

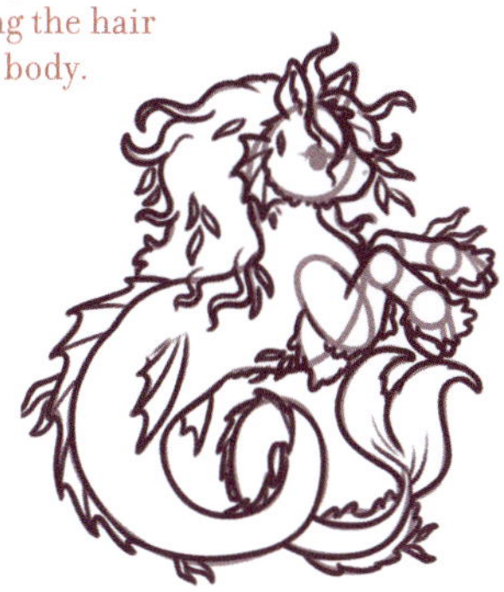

16. Sketch the face detail, adding highlight to the eye, a small eyelash, and dashes on the cheek.

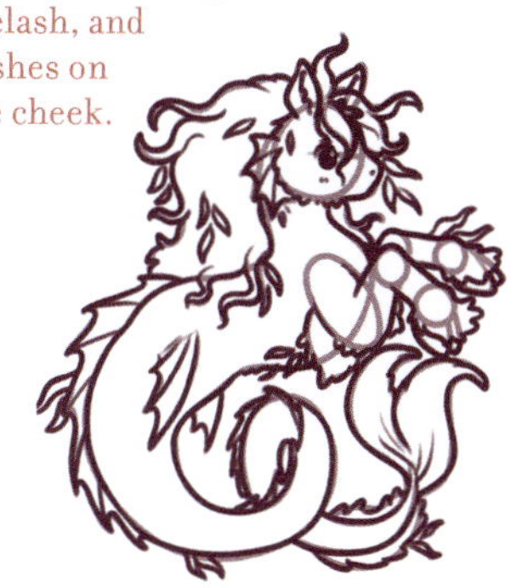

17. Neatly draw the line art over the sketch. Add some bubbles if you'd like! Then erase the sketch underneath.

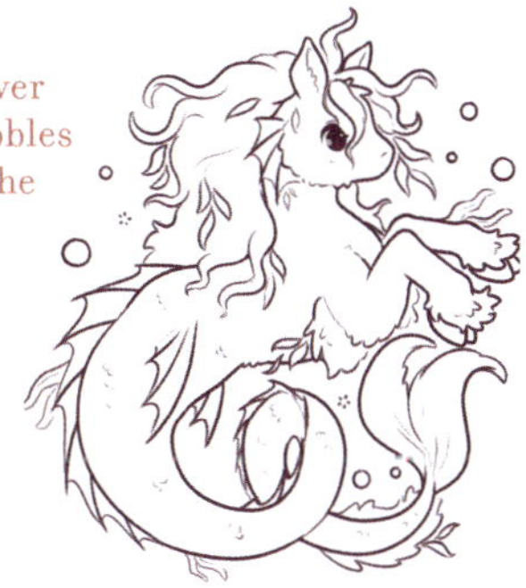

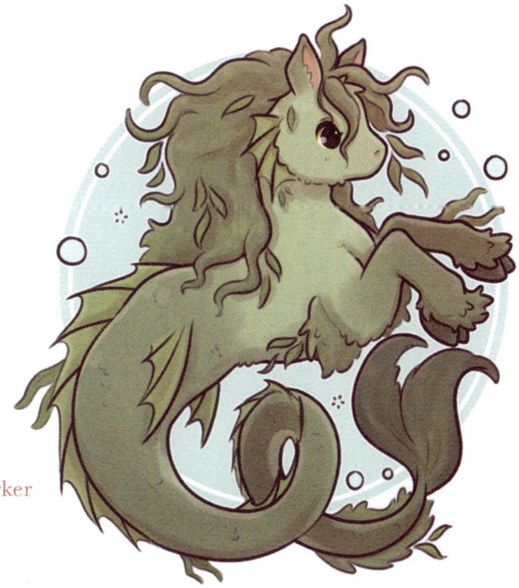

18. Finish up with color! I used pale green with a slightly darker shade for the hair and tail.

SELKIE

Friendly creatures, selkies can put on or remove their seal skin and return to their human form.

1. Lightly sketch an oval head with a dip on the left side. Add a plus sign guideline for the face.

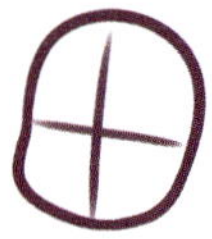

2. On either side of the head, add two small curves for ears.

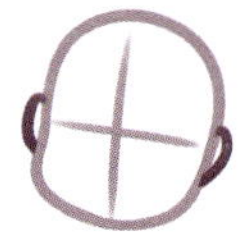

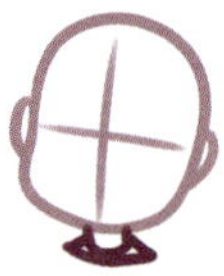

3. Add a small U neck. Then add two flat triangles on the sides for shoulders.

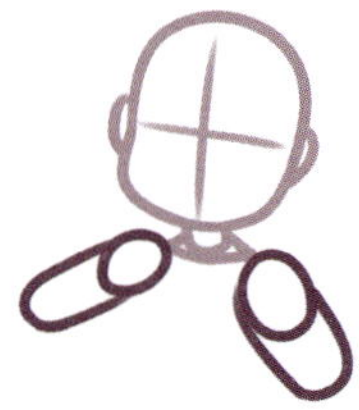

4. On the sides of the shoulders, add a small circle with a U for the upper arms. Angle the arms so they're pointed down and out.

5. Draw the lower arms with rounded diamonds. Angle the left arm toward the neck so that it overlaps the upper arm. Add squares for the hands.

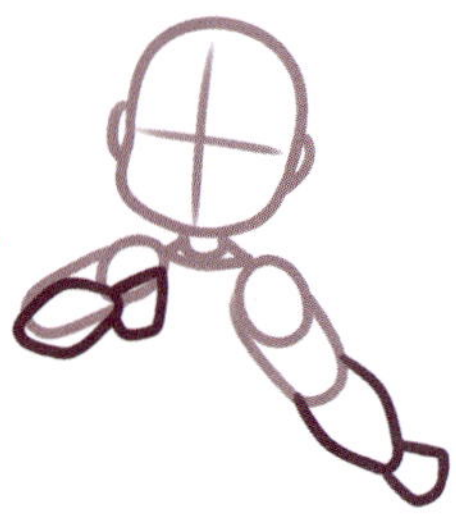

6. Sketch the fingers for both hands. Make the left hand curl into a fist and the right spread out.

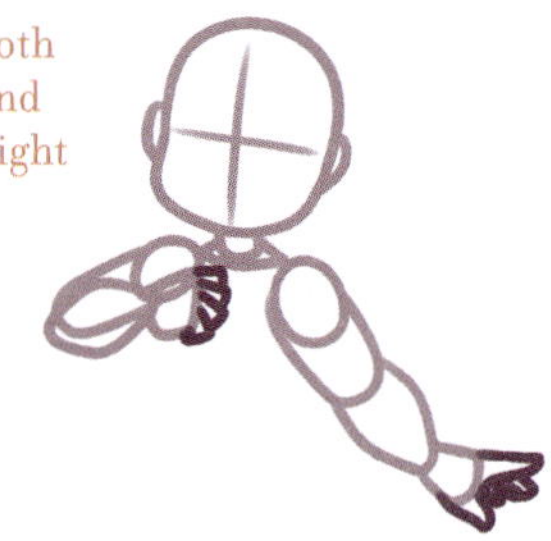

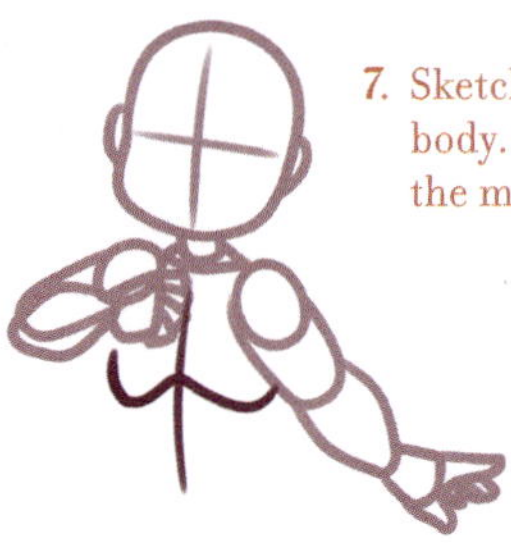

7. Sketch a W-shaped upper body. Add a guideline down the middle.

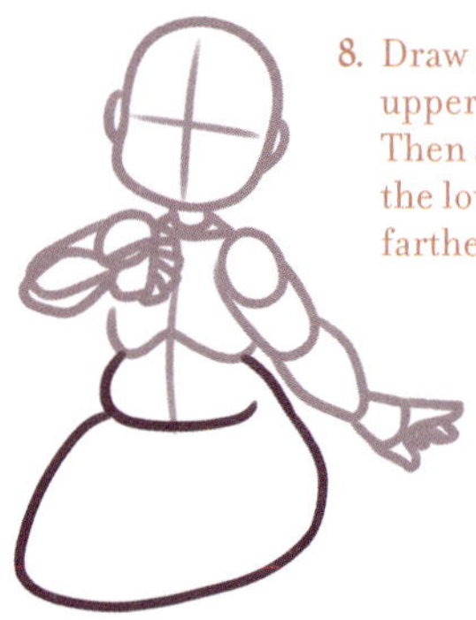

8. Draw an L curve under the upper body for the stomach. Then add an egg shape for the lower body that extends farther on the left.

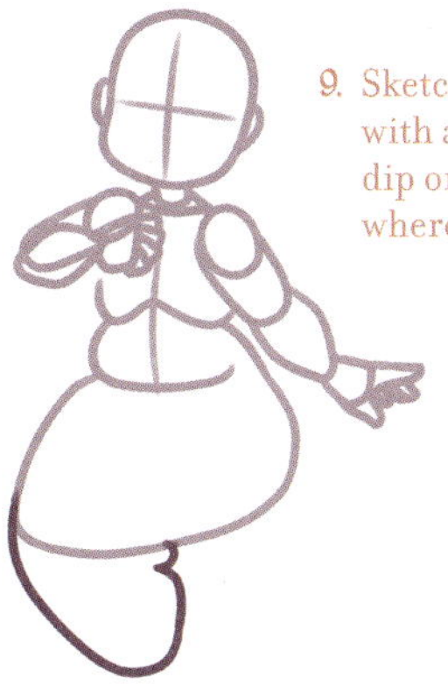

9. Sketch the end of the tail with a U shape. Add a little dip on the right to show where it bends.

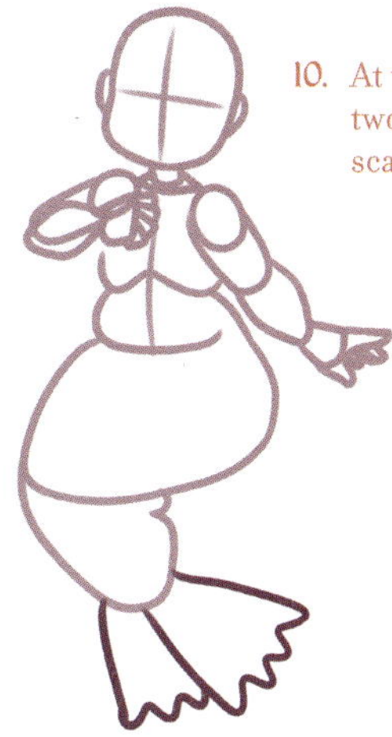

10. At the tip of the tail, add two seal flippers with scallops at the ends.

11. Draw a squished oval across the shoulders. Start under the left hand and come up to the right shoulder.

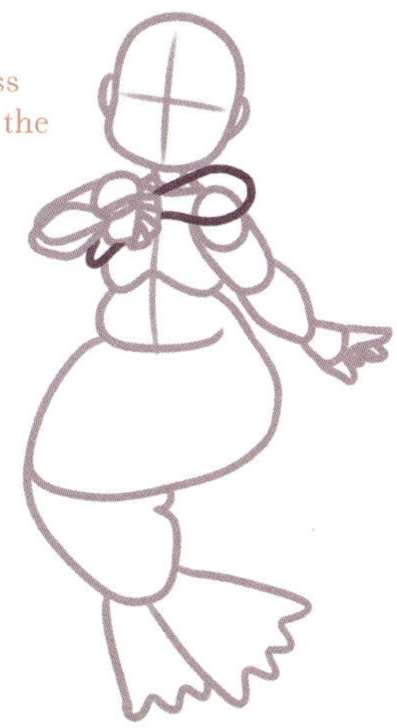

12. On the sides of the oval, draw two seal flippers.

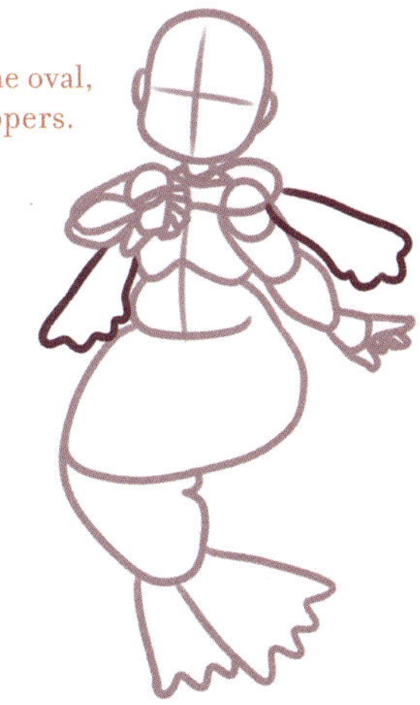

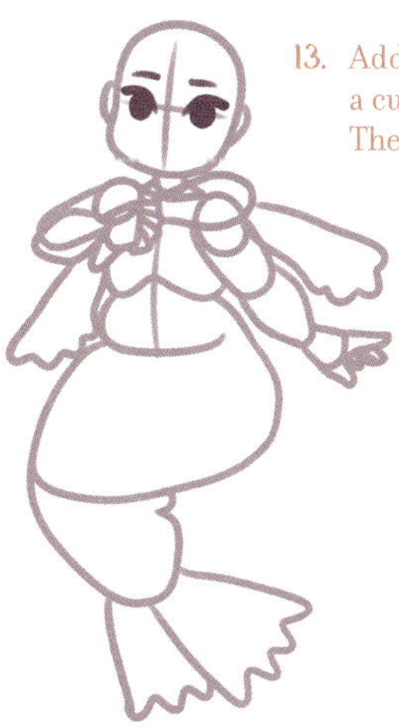

13. Add two oval eyes with a curve around the top. Then add two small eyebrows.

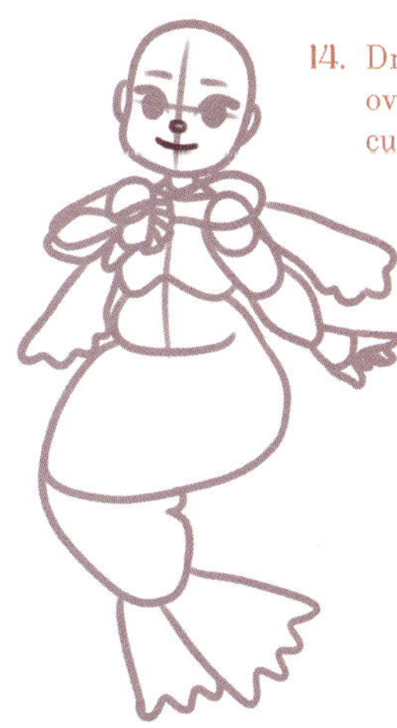

14. Draw a small oval nose and a curved mouth.

(continued)

SELKIE

(continued)

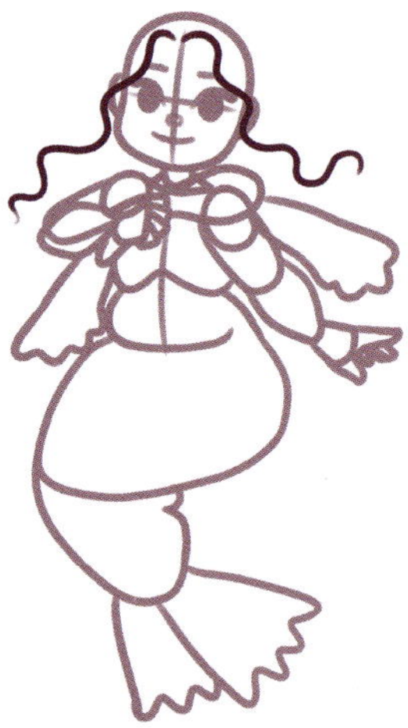

15. From the top of the face, draw two wavy strands of hair floating around the face.

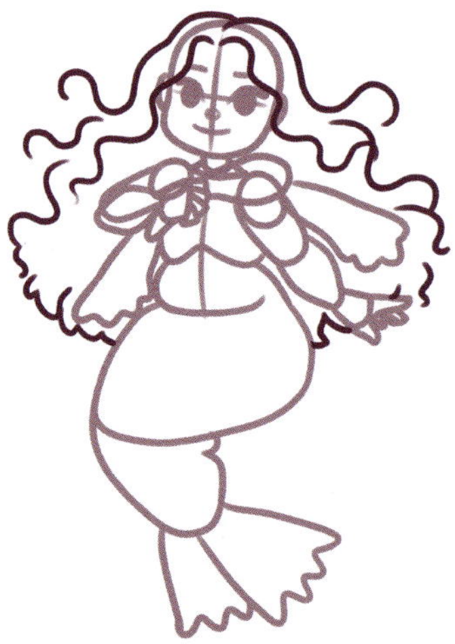

16. Add more wavy strands of hair around the head to the hands to complete the hair. Keep it flowy as the hair is underwater.

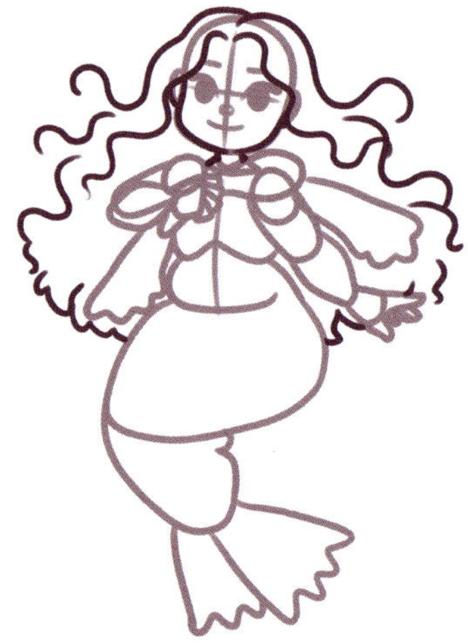

17. Sketch the outline of the face and the neck.

18. Lightly sketch a shirt sleeve and the seal flippers. Add texture to the seal flipper in their hand and stomach folds around the torso. Add a little belly button dot.

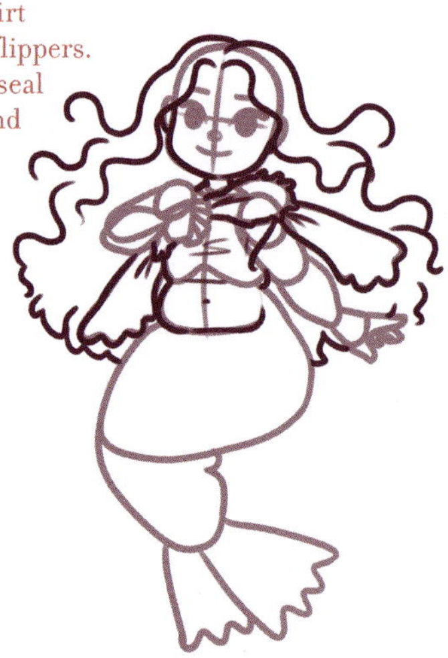

19. Sketch the arms and hands.

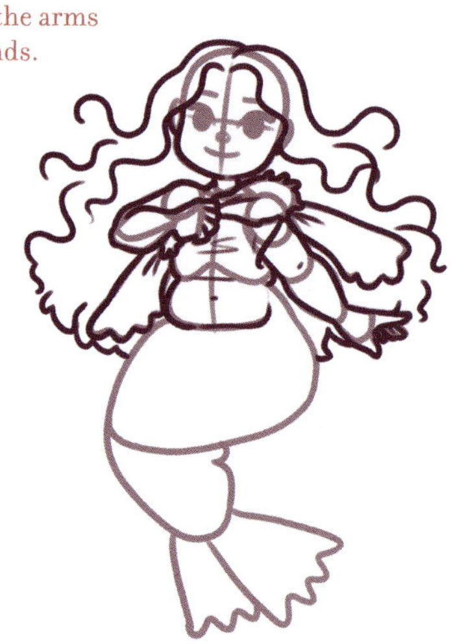

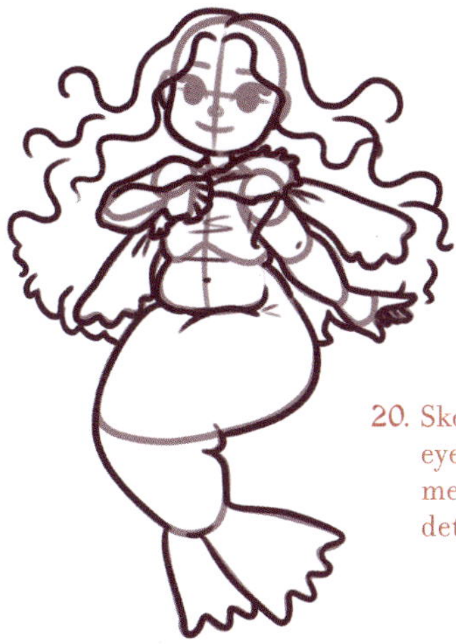

20. Sketch the tail. Keep an eye on where the stomach meets the tail and add detail there.

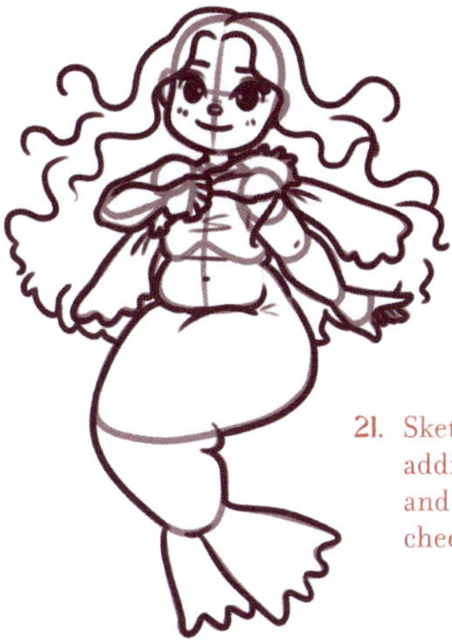

21. Sketch the face detail, adding highlights in the eyes and dashes of blush on the cheeks and above the nose.

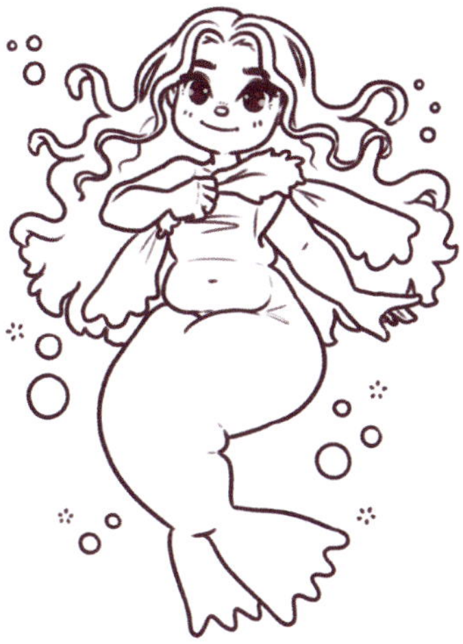

22. Neatly draw the line art over the sketch. Add some bubbles if you'd like! Then erase the sketch underneath.

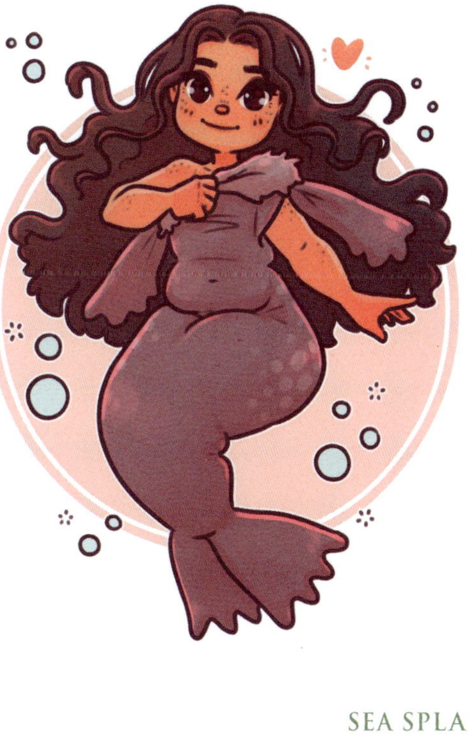

23. Lastly, add color! Keep the seal part of the body gray and add light gray spots. I chose to give them dark hair with freckles on the face and arms.

MERMAID

Appearing in mythologies worldwide, mermaids are commonly associated with shipwrecks and sea storms, but don't think too harshly of them, as there are kind merfolk out there.

1. Lightly sketch an oval head with a dip on the right side. Add a plus sign guideline for the face.

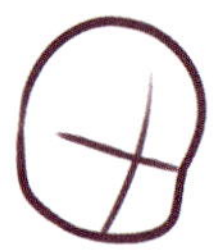

2. On the sides of the head, draw two wavy triangle ear fins.

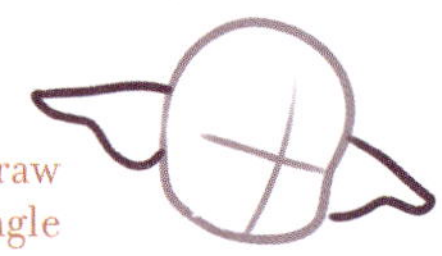

3. Draw a small U neck and connect a small diamond at the base for the shoulders.

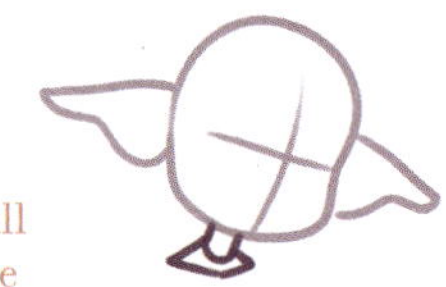

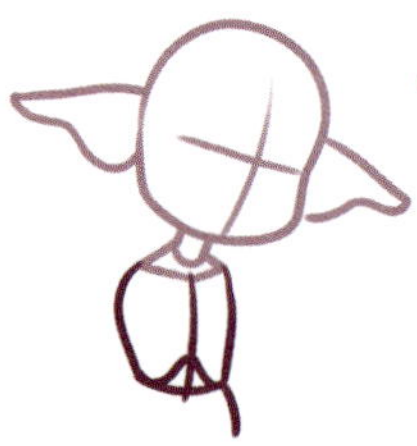

4. Draw a W-shaped torso with a guideline down the middle and across the bottom. Add a small curve on the bottom-right of the torso to start the stomach.

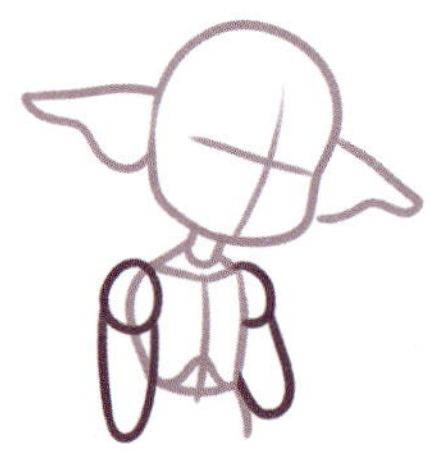

5. Add two circle shoulders with a U for the upper arms.

6. Draw the lower arms with teardrop shapes. Angle the left arm across the stomach and the right arm pointed up. Add soft rectangle hands.

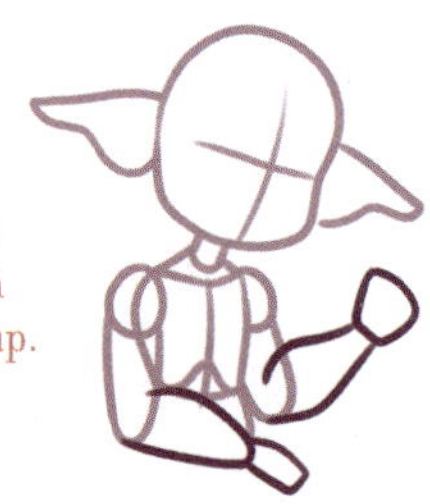

7. Sketch the fingers on the hands.

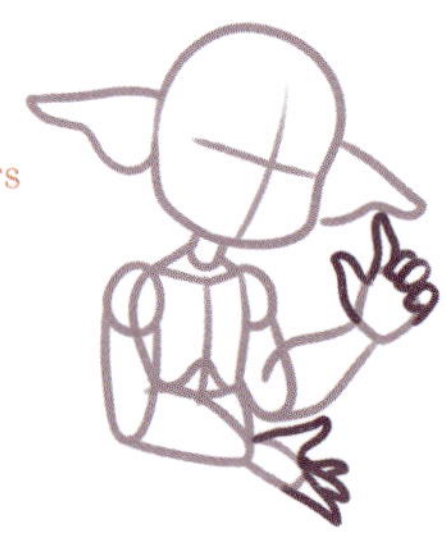

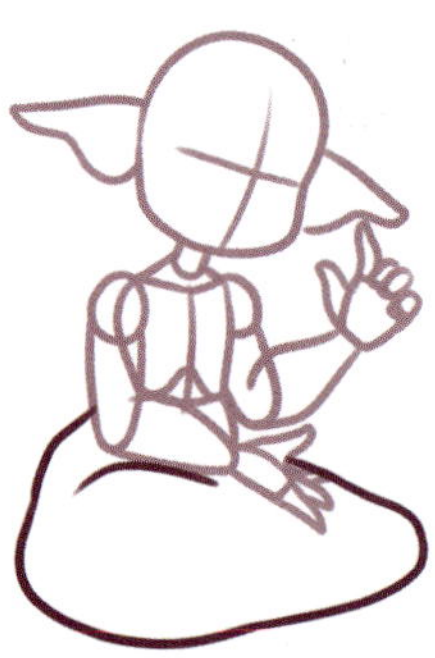

8. Draw a lumpy sideways triangle for the top half of the tail. Add a small curve where the tail meets the stomach beneath the arm.

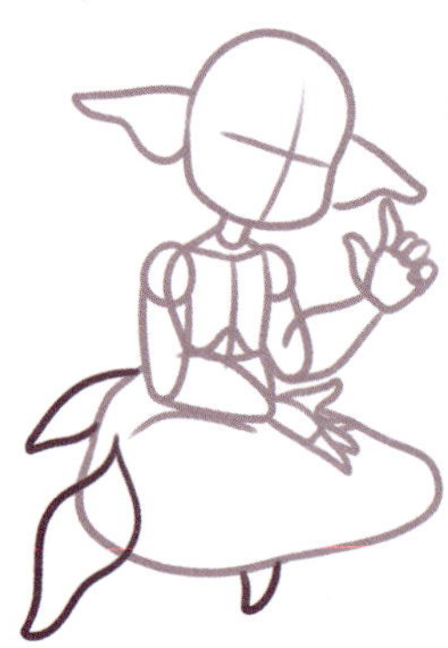

9. Draw three pointed oval fins on the sides and back of the tail.

10. Attach the end of the tail on the right that curves underneath the body and tapers at the end.

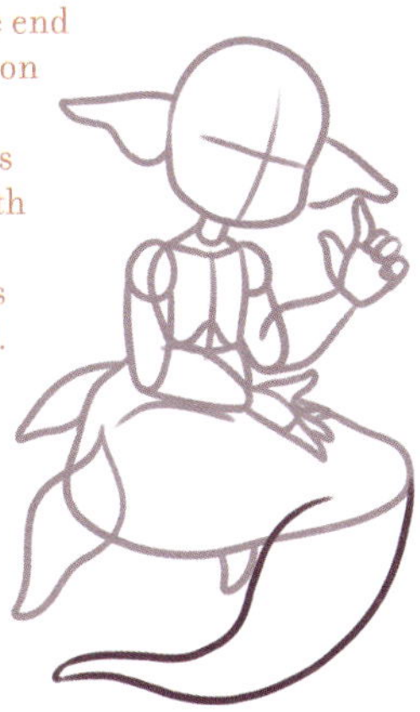

11. Add two curvy fins that end in a point on the sides of the tail.

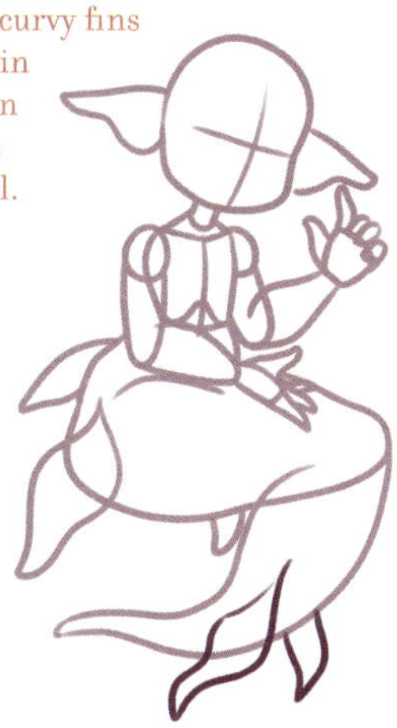

12. Draw a large fish tail with two teardrop shapes forming a V.

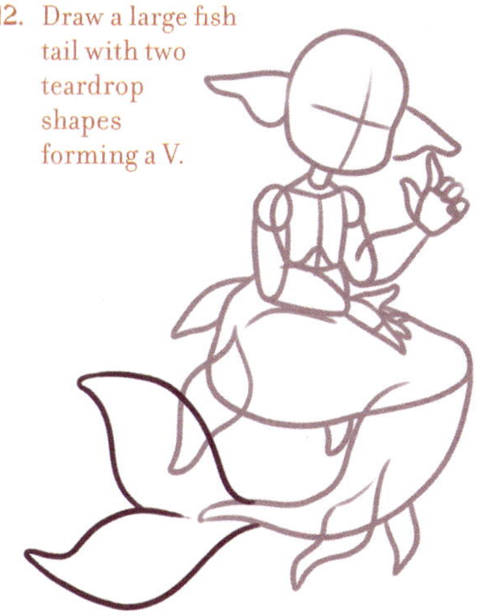

13. Between the hands, draw a small bean shape with two little oval ears on the top and a little oval tail at the back. This will be her sea bunny friend!

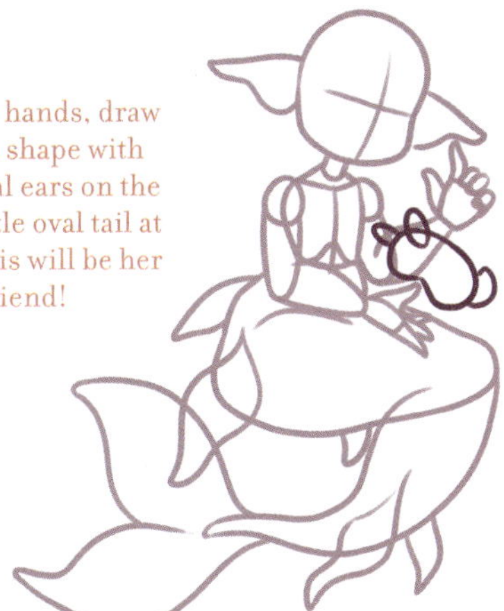

14. Add two oval eyes with a curved line around the top and two curved eyebrows.

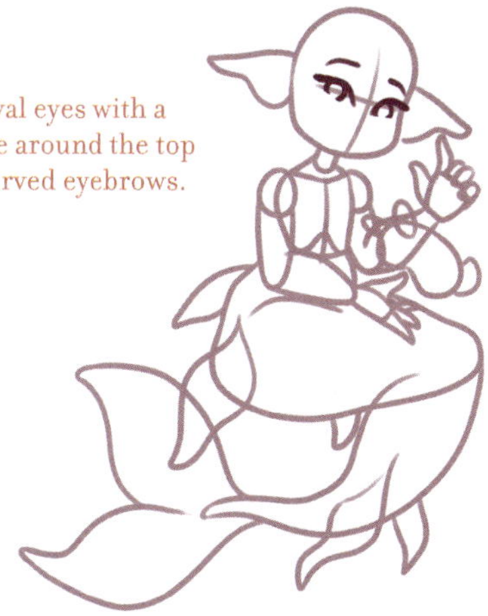

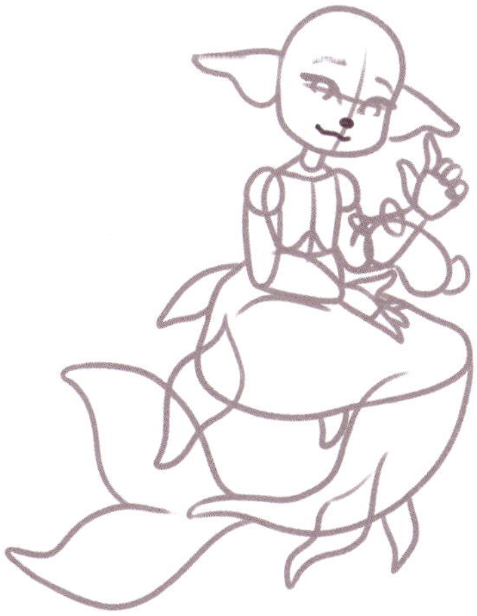

15. Draw a small oval nose and a flat W mouth.

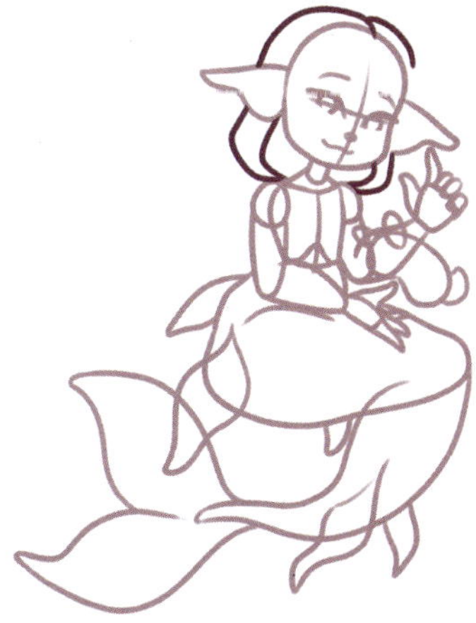

16. Draw the top of the hair coming down and curving in at the shoulders.

(continued)

MERMAID

(continued)

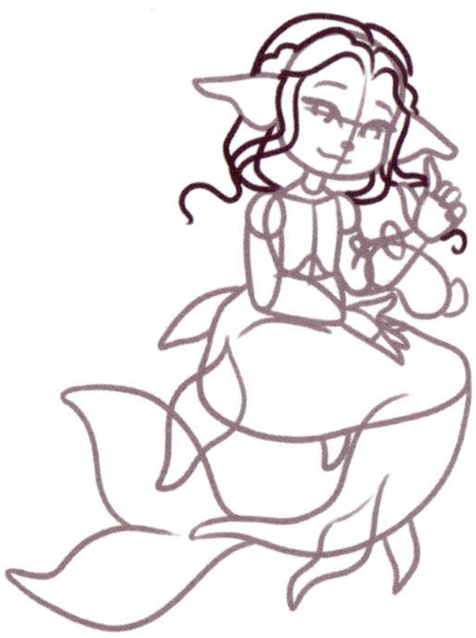

17. Draw the hair at the top of the face, tucking behind the ears, and two wavy strands framing the face.

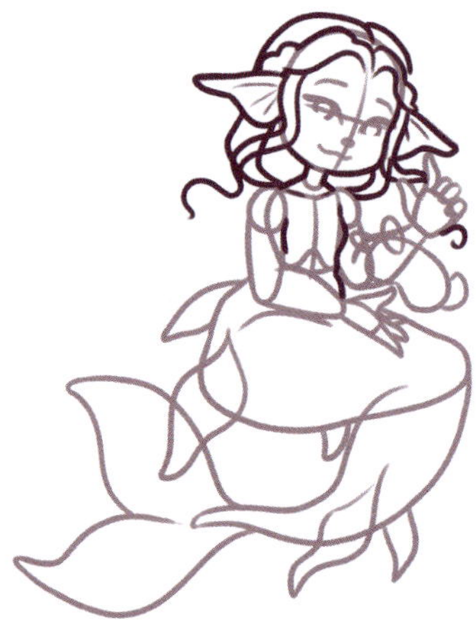

18. Lightly sketch over the ears, face, and torso.

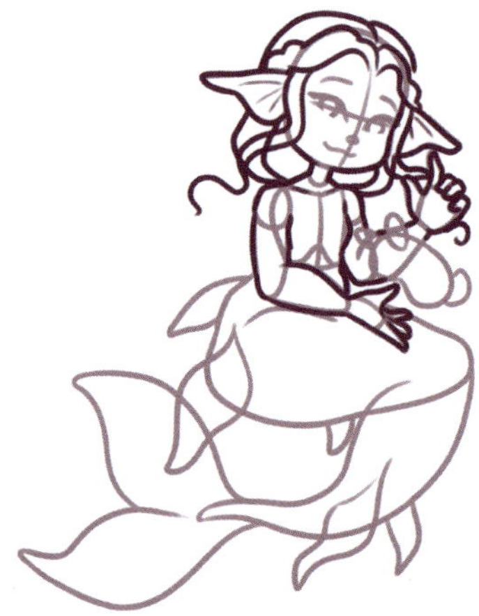

19. Sketch the arms and hands.

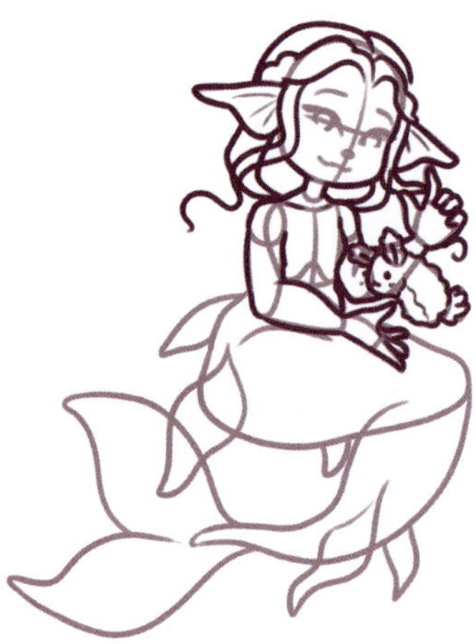

20. Draw the details of the sea bunny. Add some fluff and a tiny face.

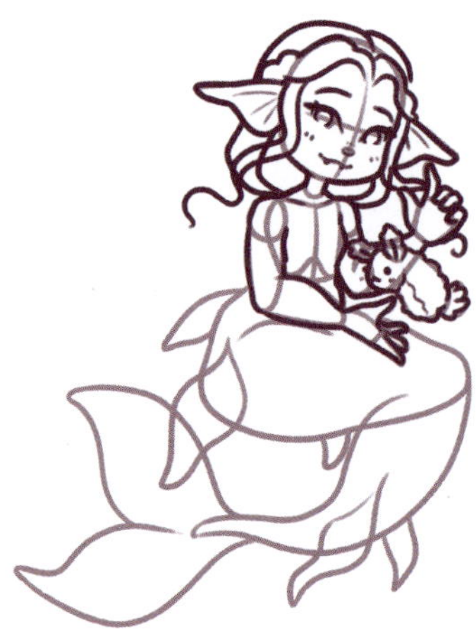

21. Sketch the mermaid's face detail, adding dashes on the cheeks and a few eyelashes. Give the mermaid two small V fangs.

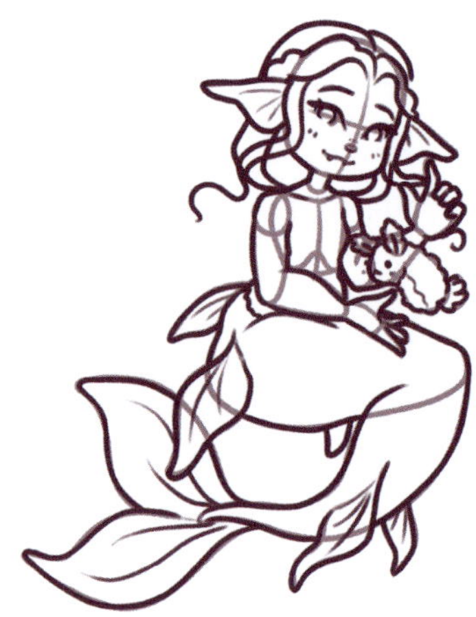

22. Lightly sketch the tail, adding lines to the fins. Add a little curve around the hip where the human-half meets the fish-half.

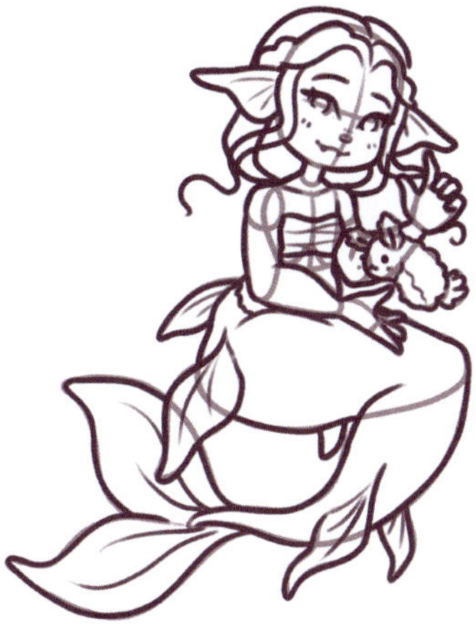

23. Draw a little wrapped bandeau across the chest with lines for detail.

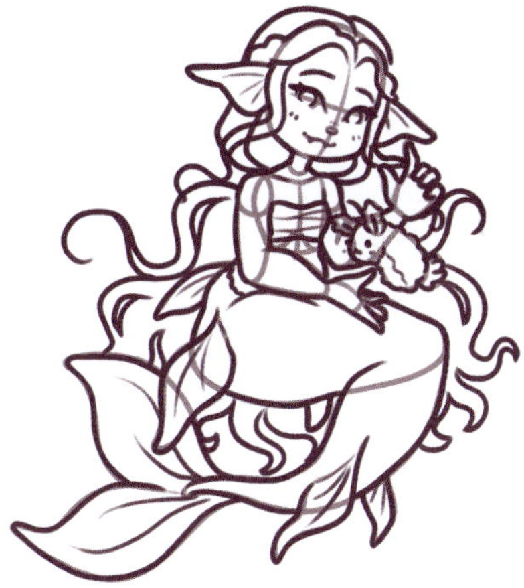

24. Around the body, draw a bunch of swirling, floating hair.

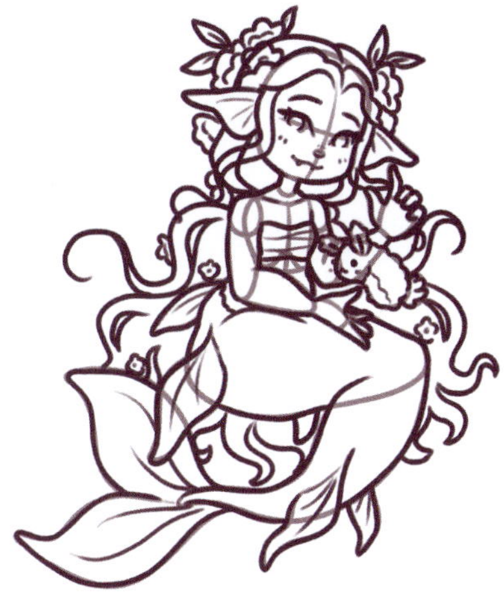

25. Sketch a bunch of flowers on top of the head where the hair tucks in at the shoulders , and scatter throughout. Add a few leaves as well.

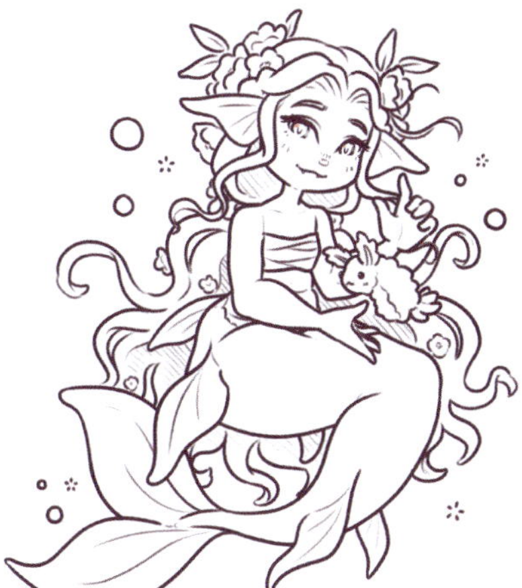

26. Neatly draw the line art over the sketch. Add some bubbles if you'd like! Add space for highlights in the eyes. Then erase the sketch underneath.

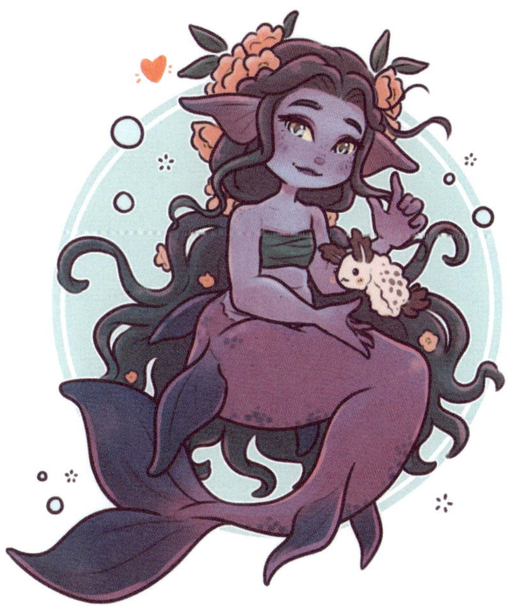

27. Finally, it's time for color! You can do any color scheme, but I chose pale purple skin and a more vibrant shade for the tail. For the fins and scale spots, I used indigo and dark teal for the hair. Make the sea bunny pop out with a light color.

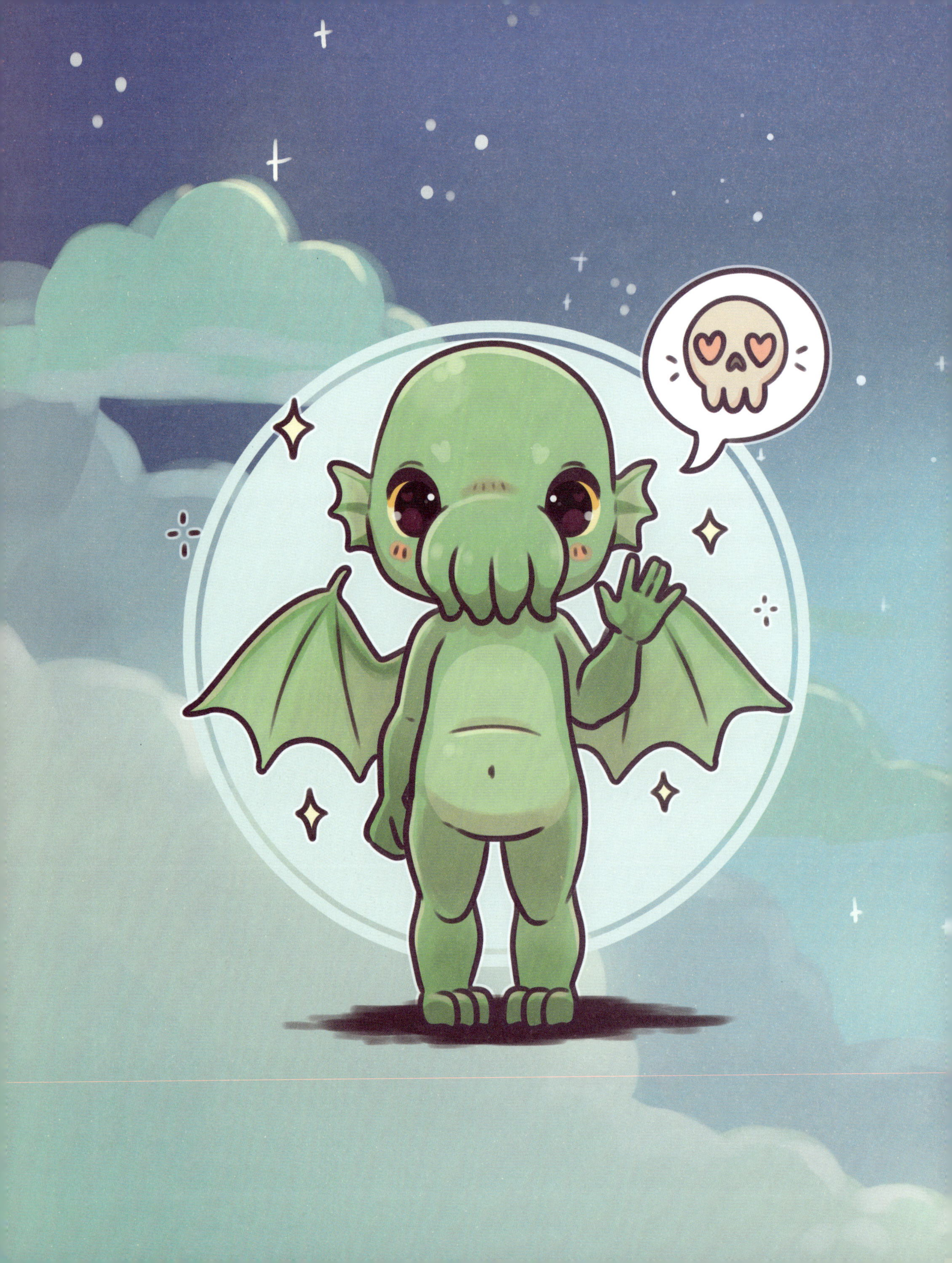

NIGHT DWELLERS

HORNS, FANGS, AND CLAWS

BLACK SHUCK

If you're out roaming the coastlines, or getting your tea leaves read, despair the day the black shuck appears, for it is seen as an omen of death.

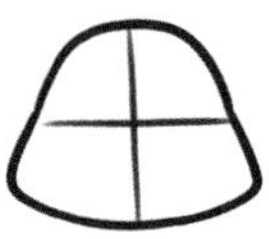

1. Lightly sketch an oval with pointed sides. Add a plus sign (+) guideline for the face.

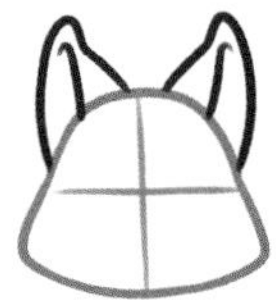

2. Add two triangle ears on top, each with a line inside.

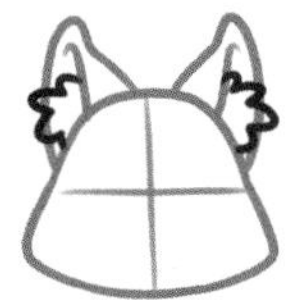

3. Draw a tuft of fur coming out of each inner ear.

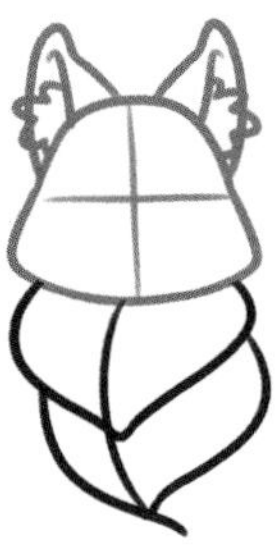

4. Draw two round Vs under the head, one under the other, for the neck and the chest.

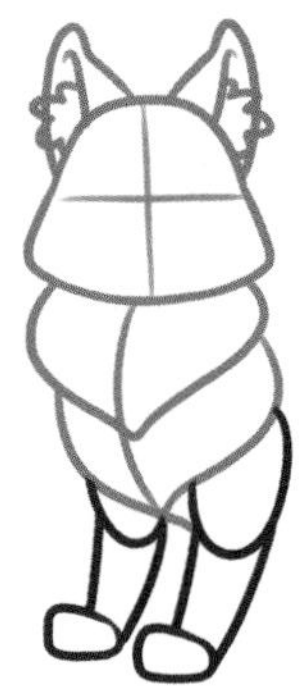

5. Add two Us for the upper arms. Below, draw two rounded rectangle paws. Connect the paws to the upper legs with lines.

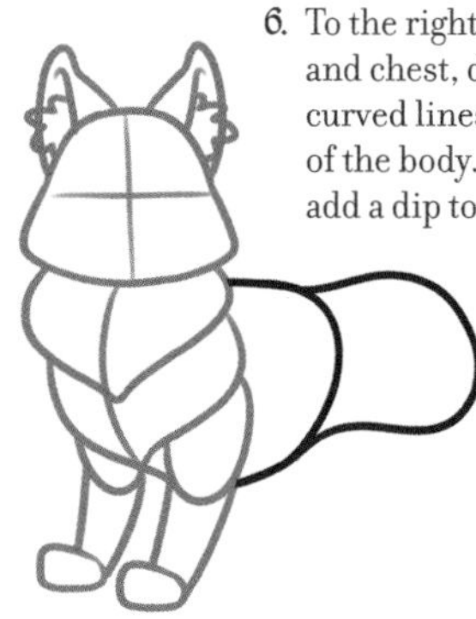

6. To the right of the neck and chest, draw two curved lines for the rest of the body. Make sure to add a dip to the stomach.

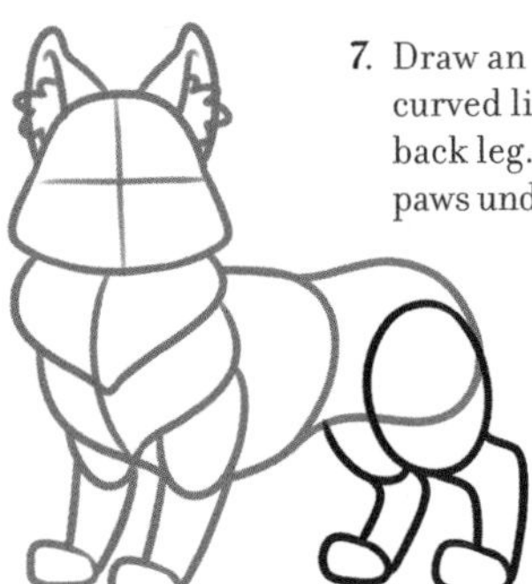

7. Draw an oval back haunch and a curved line to the left for the other back leg. Then draw the two back paws underneath and connect those to the back legs with slightly angled lines.

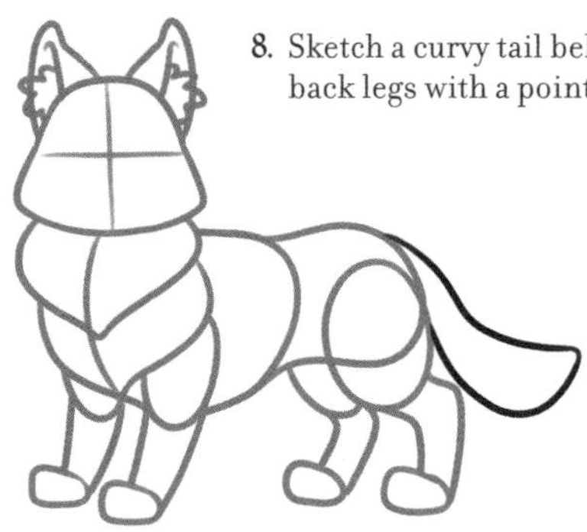

8. Sketch a curvy tail behind the back legs with a pointed tip.

9. In the middle of the face, draw a rounded square snout. Draw a small, rounded square nose and a W mouth.

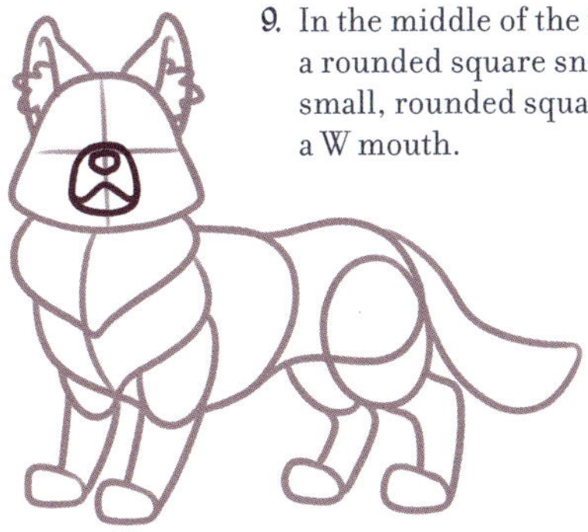

10. Draw two hollow oval eyes with a curved line around the top.

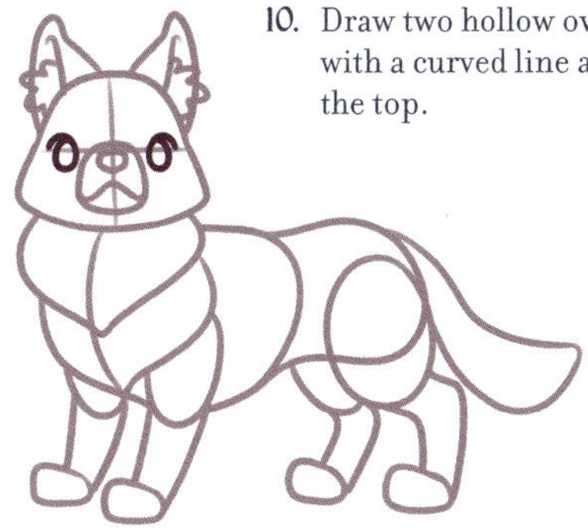

11. Add details to the body. Define the fur with soft W shapes. Add those toe lines to the paws.

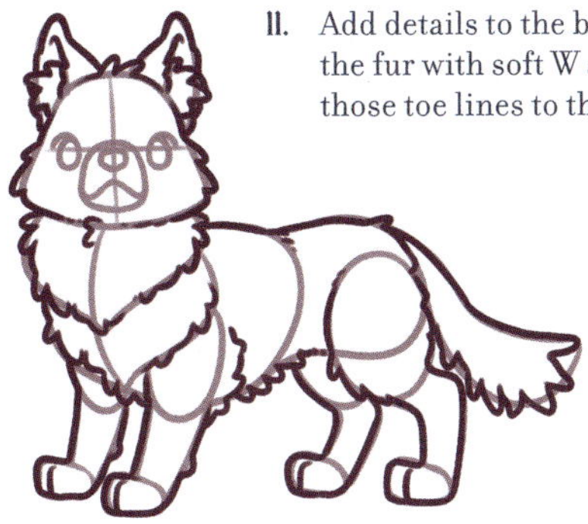

12. Sketch the face detail, adding dashes on the cheeks and on the sides of the head for whiskers. Add two small V fangs.

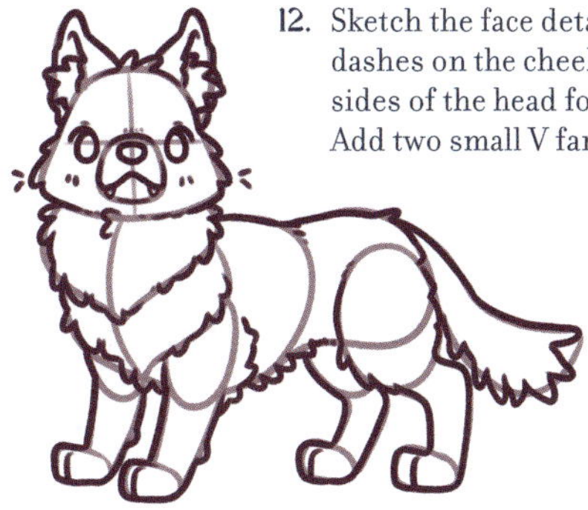

13. Neatly draw the line art over the sketch. Add white highlights to the eyes and some sparkles if you'd like! Then erase the sketch underneath.

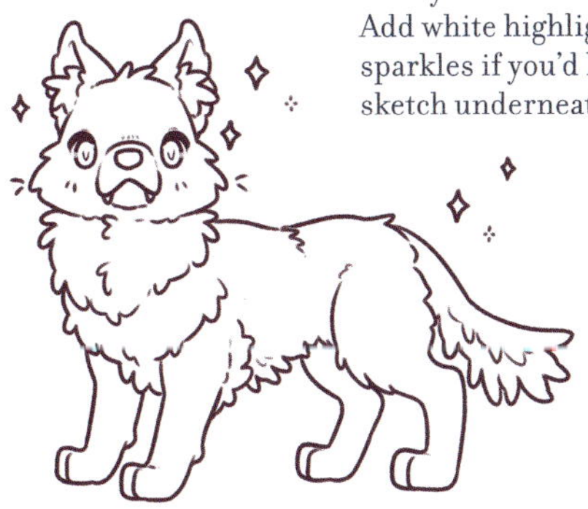

14. Color the coat black and the eyes a bright red!

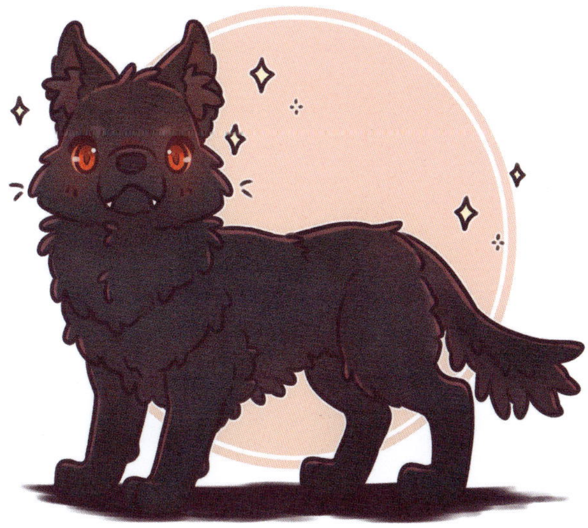

CÙ SÌTH

If a person hears cù sìth's barks and does not find a safe place to hide before the third bark, heed the omen of death and fear that the end is nigh.

1. Lightly sketch a rounded square head. Add a plus sign guideline for the face.

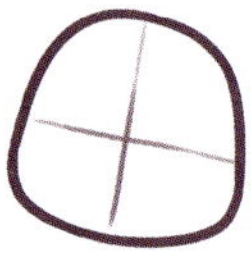

2. Add two triangle ears on top, each with a smaller triangle inside.

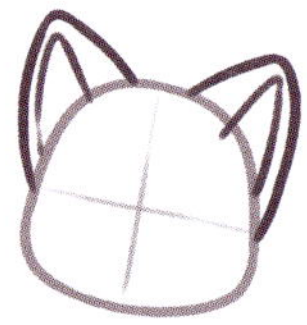

3. Draw two round Vs under the head, one under the other, for the neck and chest.

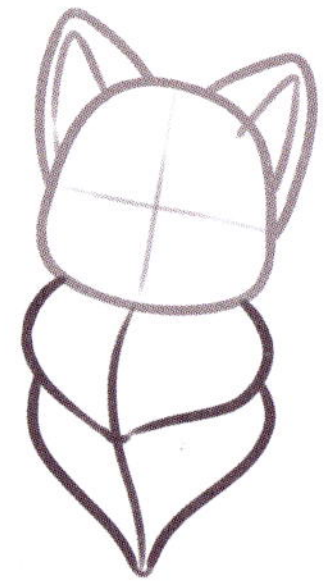

4. Draw a wiggly W shape for the back of the body. Add an oval on the bottom-right for a back haunch.

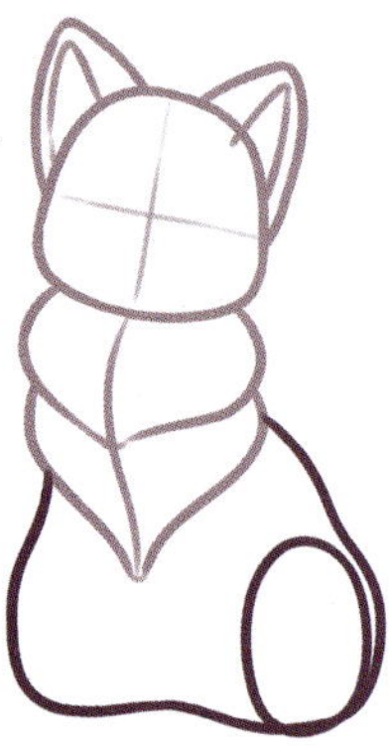

5. Draw two long U shapes for the front legs. Make the right longer and pointed down, with the left shorter and angled in. Add the paws with a U for the left paw and a rounded rectangle for the right.

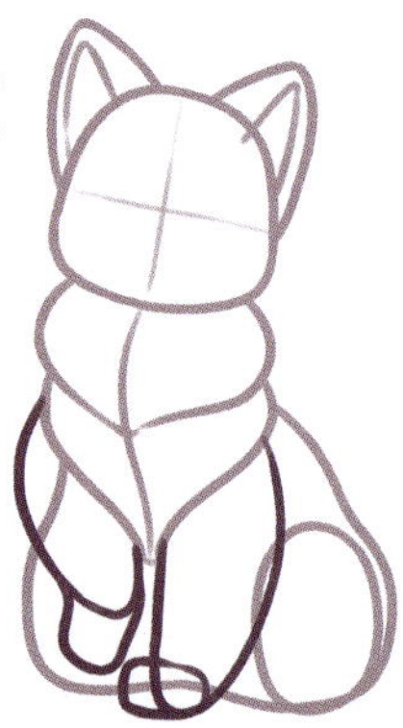

6. Draw two curved oval paws with a hooked top next to the arms.

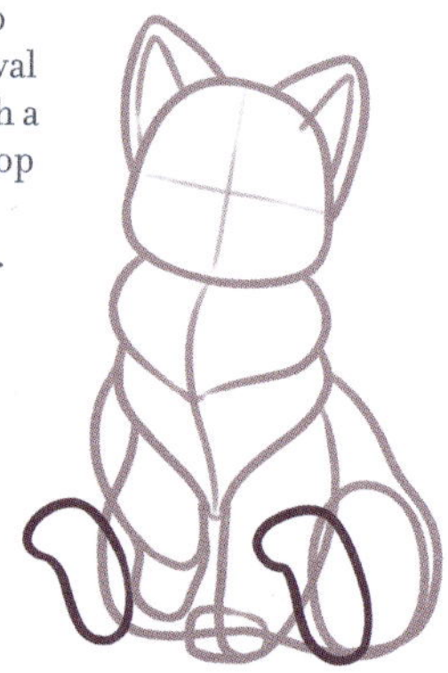

7. Draw a skinny tail curving up beside the left paw and a small curve next to the right haunch.

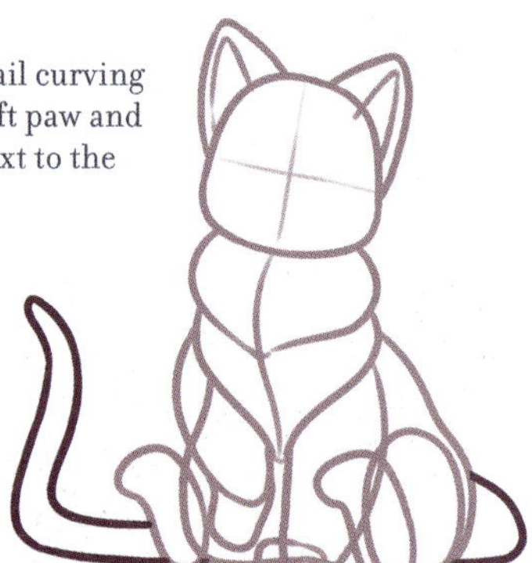

8. At the center of the face, draw a rounded square snout. Then add a small, rounded rectangle nose and a W mouth. Connect the points of the W with a line so the mouth is open.

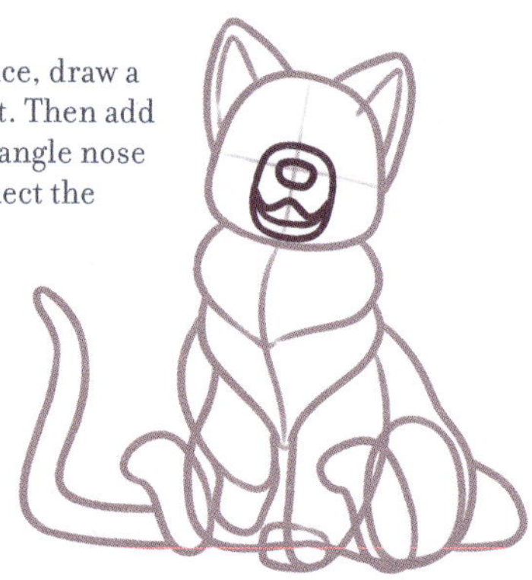

9. Draw two oval eyes with a curved line around the top.

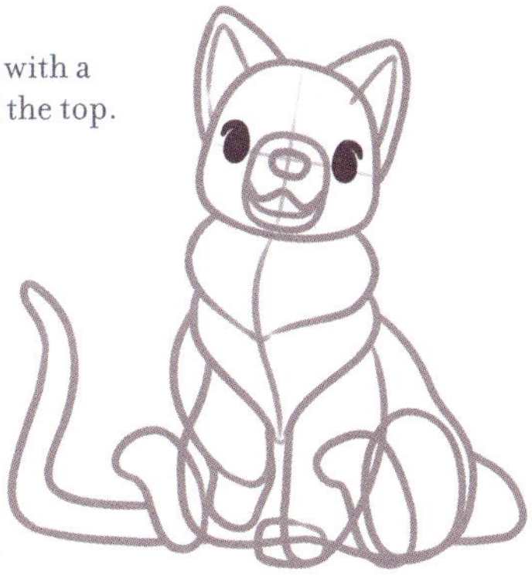

10. Define the fur along the body and inside the ears with soft W shapes.

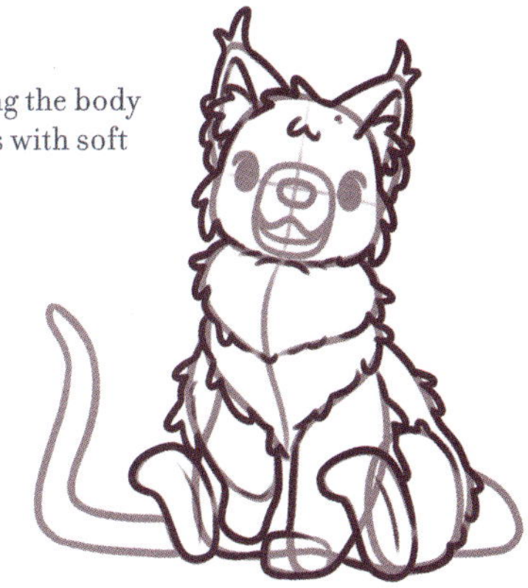

11. Add detail to the paws with toe beans and heart-shaped paw pads. Draw the tail, adding a lot of long fur toward the tip.

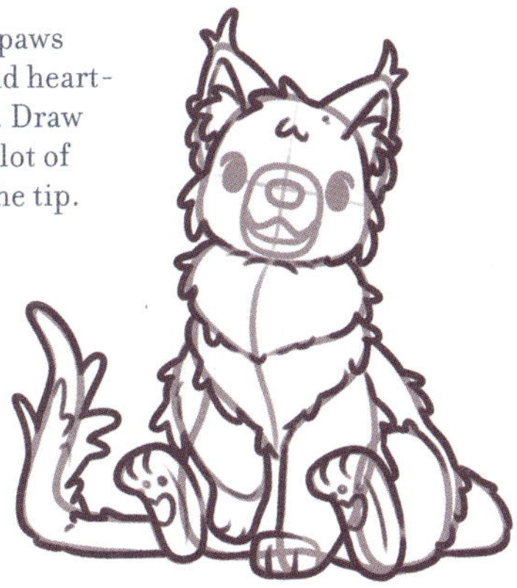

12. Sketch the face detail, adding highlights for the eyes. Add dashes on the cheeks for blush and around the sides of the head for whiskers. Also add a tongue line inside the mouth.

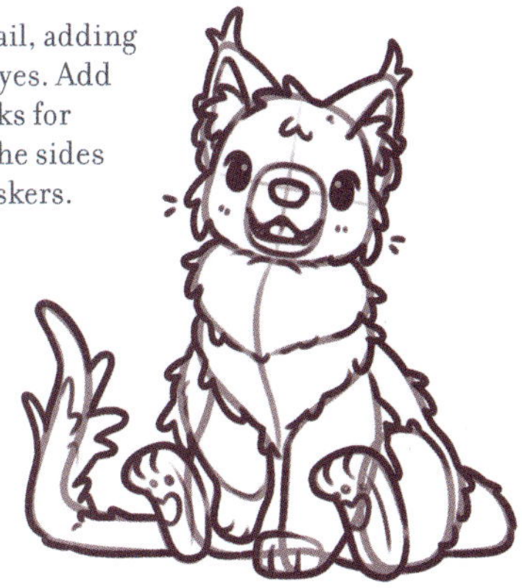

13. Neatly draw the line art over the sketch. Add some sparkles if you'd like! Then erase the sketch underneath.

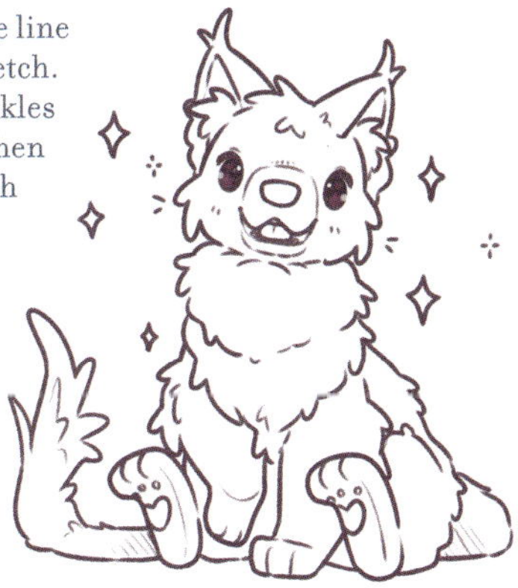

14. Make the coat green! I used a pale green on the chest and for little heart-shaped eyebrows.

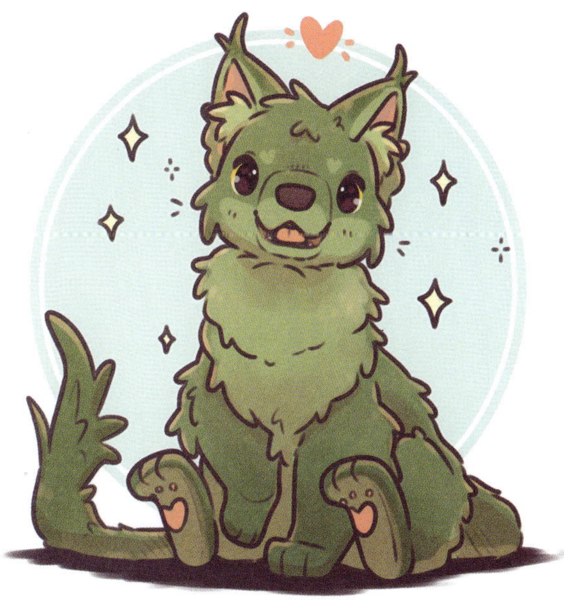

CTHULHU

Nothing slips past this great cosmic entity, with its telepathic abilities that span the universe.

1. Lightly sketch a circle head. Add a plus sign guideline for the face.

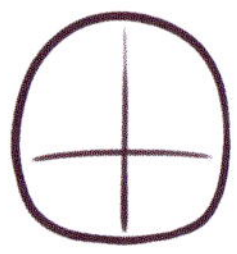

2. Draw pointy number 3-shaped ears with lines joining them to the head.

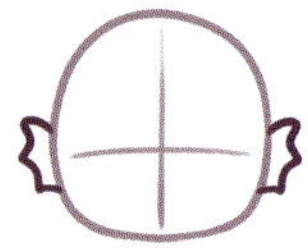

3. Sketch an egg-shaped body with a W-shaped torso and a plus sign guideline to divide the upper and lower body.

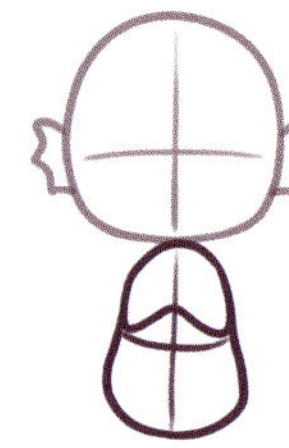

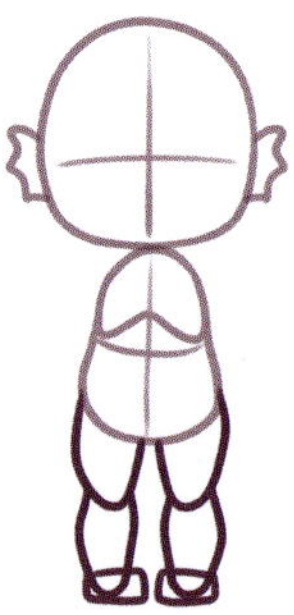

4. Add two Us and two ovals for the legs. Then add two rounded rectangle feet.

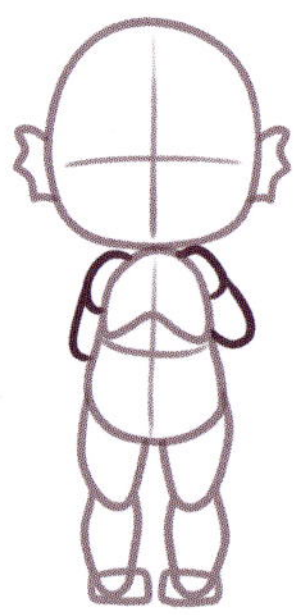

5. Add two circle shoulders with two oval upper arms partially concealed by the body.

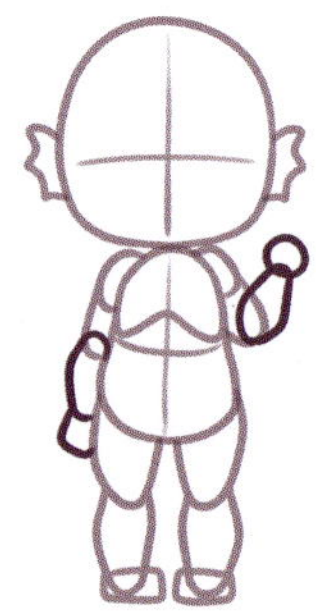

6. For the lower arms, add two rounded diamonds with the left pointed down and the right pointed up in a waving pose. Then sketch a circle at the ends of each.

7. On the right hand, sketch the fingers. Draw a small thumb line on the left hand for a closed hand.

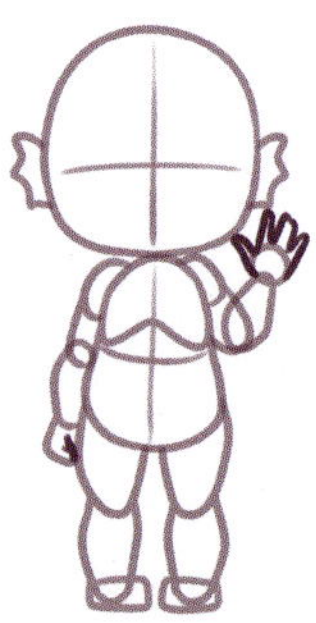

8. Add a stretched Z-shaped wing starting at the shoulders with two lines coming down from the point.

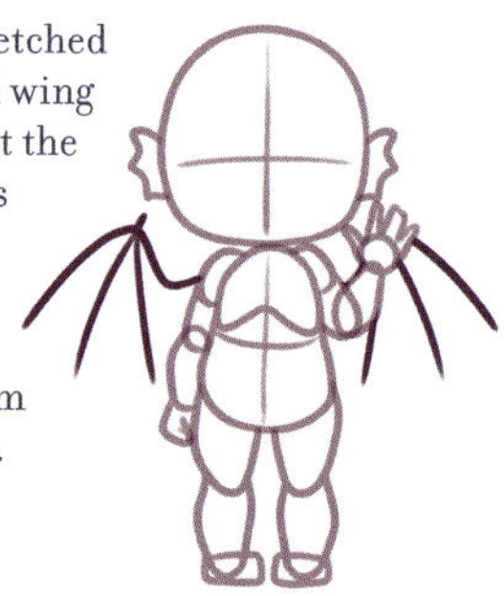

9. On the bottom of the face, add an oval with three lines dividing the lower half for the tentacle mouth.

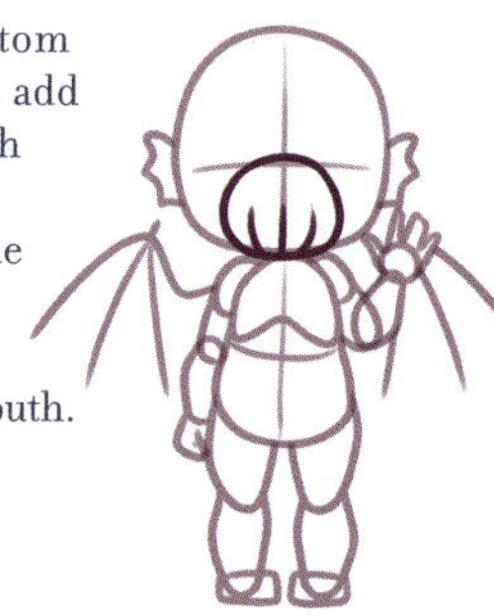

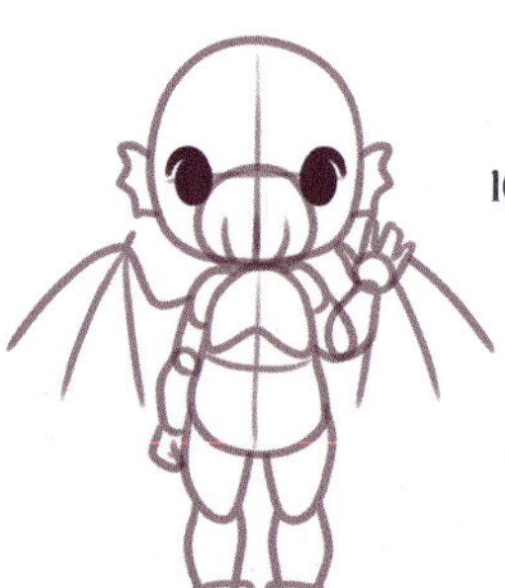

10. Add two oval eyes with a curved line around the top.

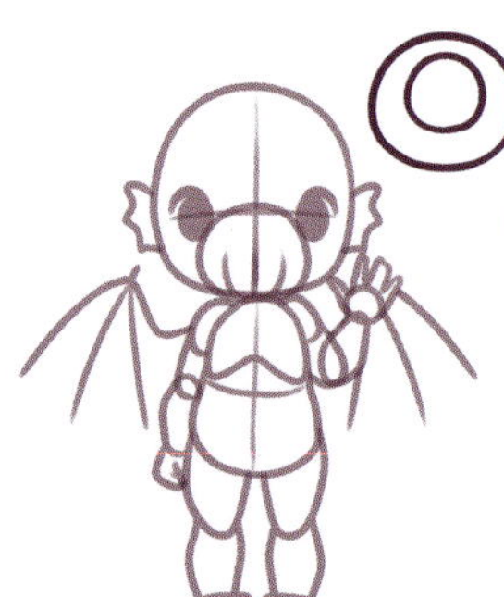

11. Above and to the right of the figure, draw a circle with a smaller circle inside it for the speech bubble.

12. Lightly go over the eyes, leaving a little space inside for highlights. Add dashes of blush on the cheeks. Define the bottoms of the tentacles.

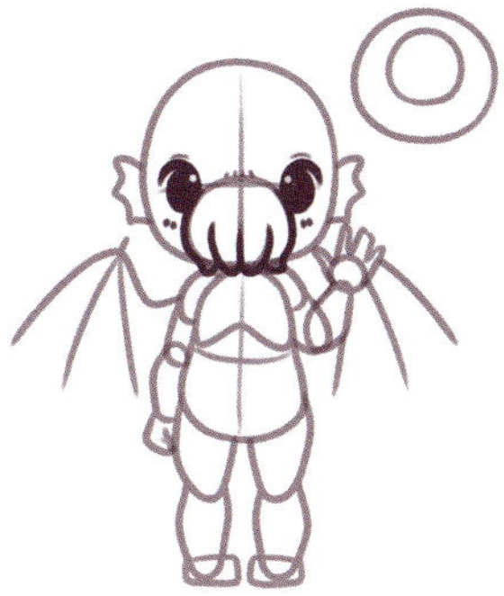

13. Sketch the head and body. Add toes to the feet, a small, curved line to show the belly, and a dot for the belly button.

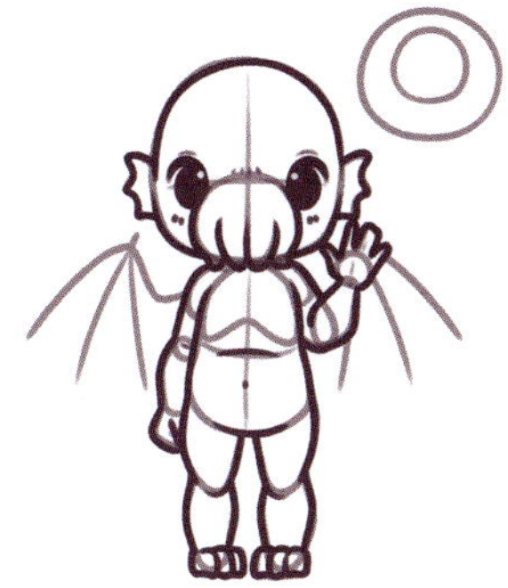

14. Draw the wings with curves, connecting the tips of the lines along the bottom for that bat-like look.

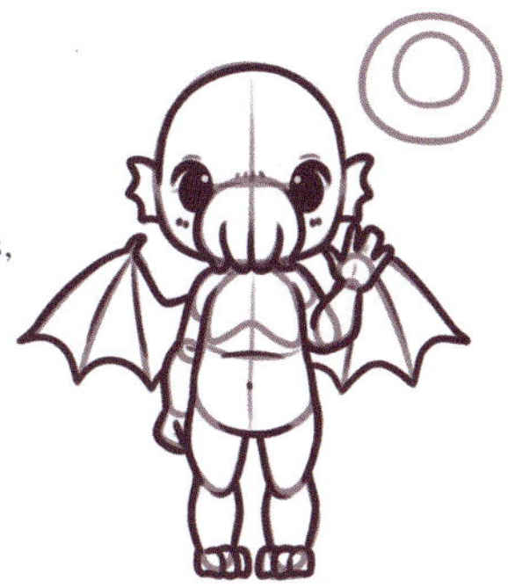

15. Add a point to the speech bubble. Then, inside the speech bubble, sketch a skull with three Us for the teeth and two hearts for eyes.

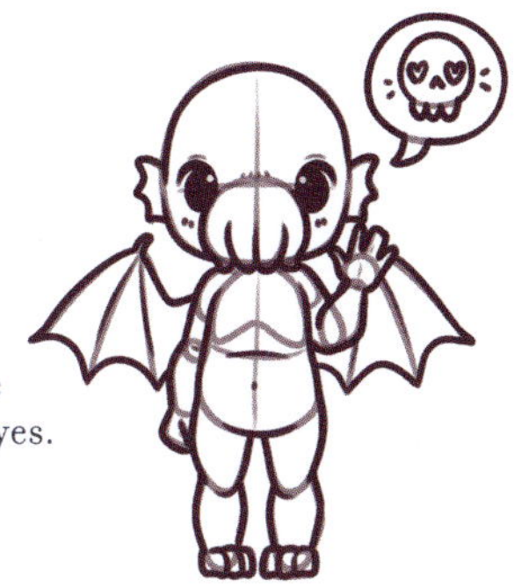

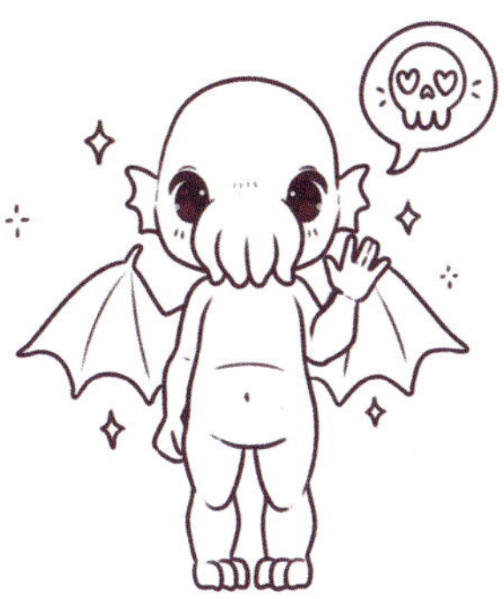

16. Neatly draw the line art over the sketch. Add some sparkles if you'd like! Then erase the sketch underneath.

17. Finish up with color! Cthulhu is usually green. I gave him a pale green belly and heart-shaped eyebrows, with yellow eyes and pale pink on the cheeks.

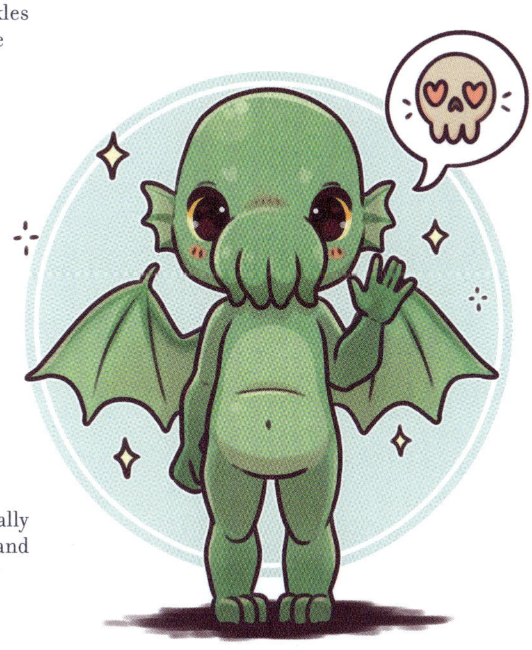

FENRIR

Bound by the gods in magical, unbreakable chains to prevent his evil doings, it would take Ragnarök for him to finally break free.

1. Lightly sketch an oval with pointed sides. Add a plus sign guideline for the face.

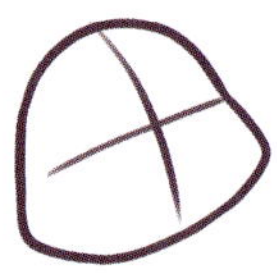

2. Add two triangle ears on top, each with a smaller triangle inside.

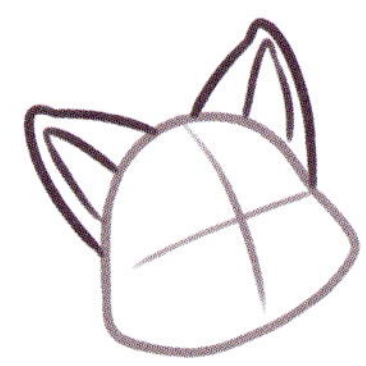

3. For the neck and the chest, draw three round Vs under the head, one under the other.

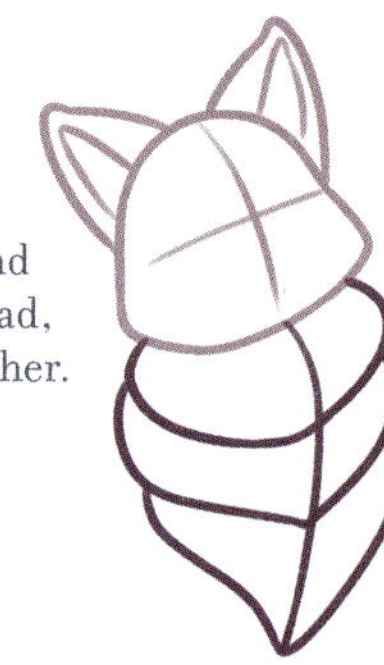

4. Draw two rounded rectangle paws and connect with curved lines to the chest.

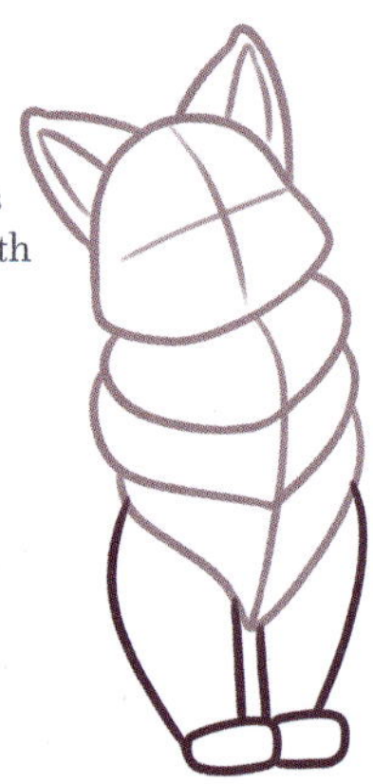

5. Draw a large curve on the left side for the back of the body, and a smaller curve on the right side. Beside the front paws, draw two more rectangle back paws.

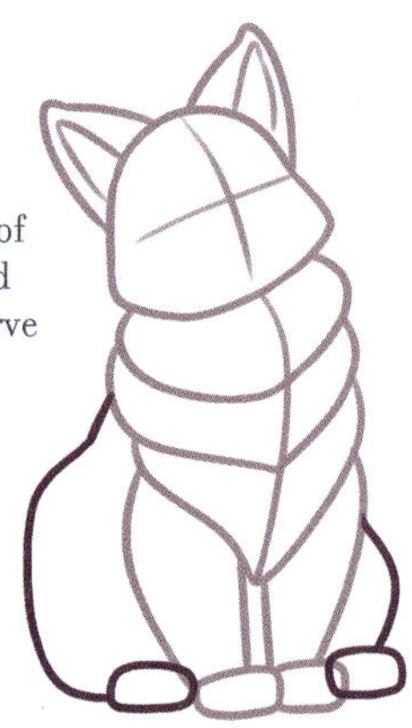

6. Draw a tail on the bottom-left of the body that curves in front of the back paw.

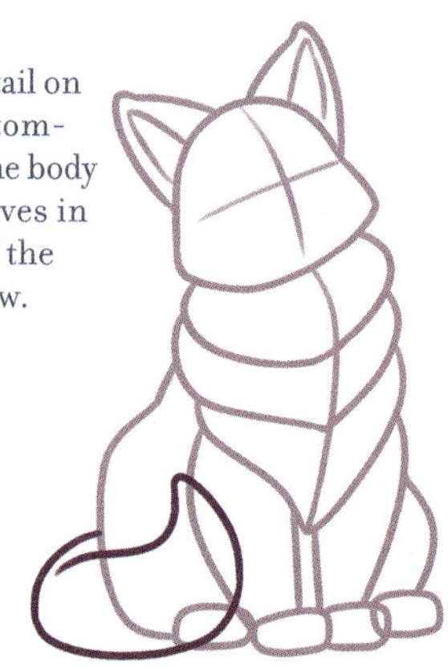

7. In the middle of the face, draw a small oval nose and a W mouth. On the right side of the mouth, curve the line above the nose. Then add a small curve beneath the mouth.

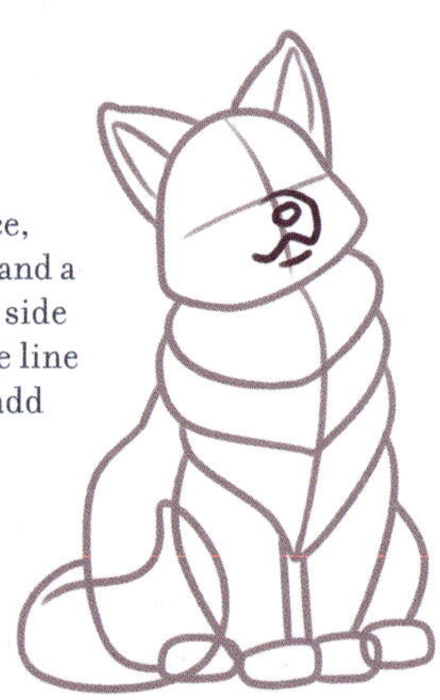

8. Draw two oval eyes with curved lines around the top that tilt down toward the middle to give them a slightly angry eye shape.

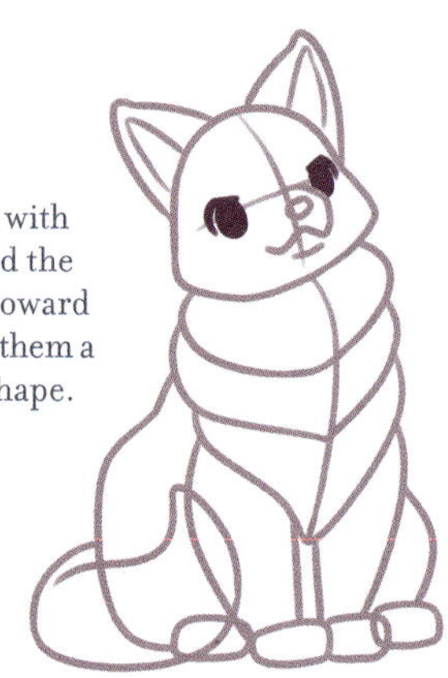

9. Draw a small sword in the mouth with the point on the left and the pommel on the right.

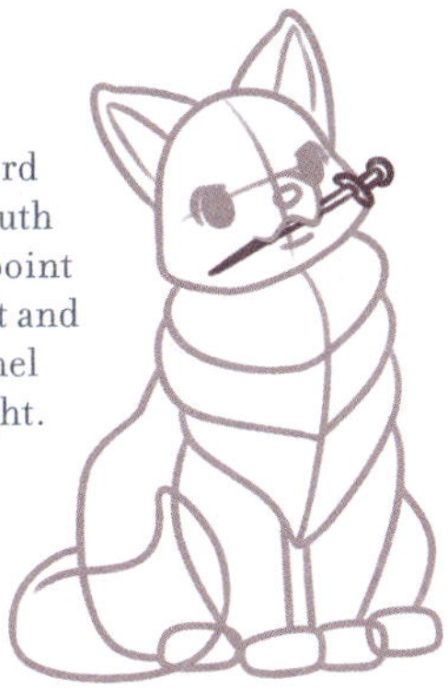

10. Draw a bunch of curved, crisscrossing lines around the legs and body. On the back, draw little bow loops.

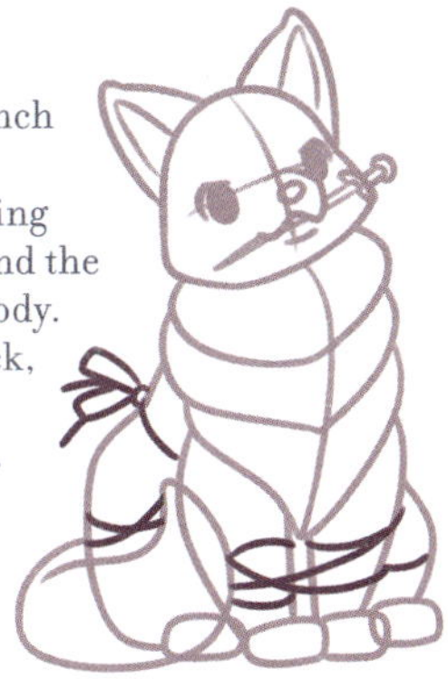

11. Thicken the curved lines so each one has two parallel lines. Make it look like they're tied up with ribbon.

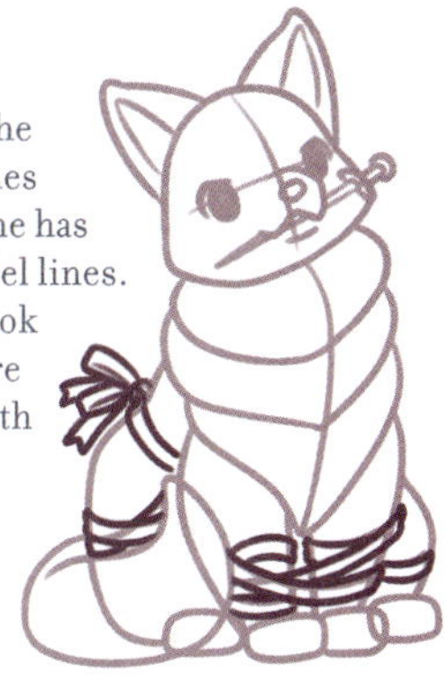

12. Add details on the body. Define the fur with soft W shapes. Add toe lines to the paws.

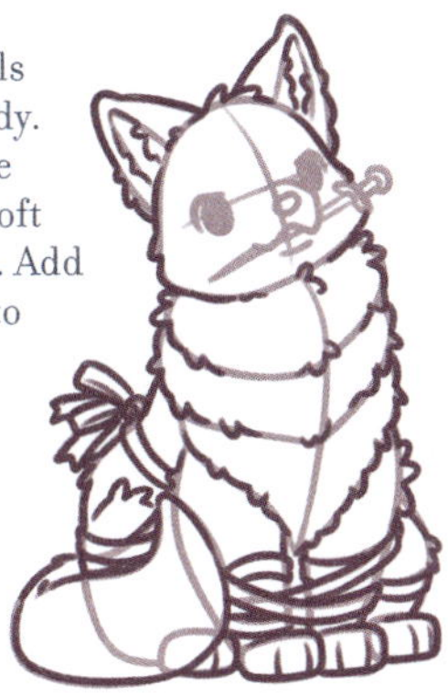

13. Sketch the face detail. Add highlights for the eyes, dashes on the cheeks for blush and on either side of the head for whiskers. Add two small V fangs.

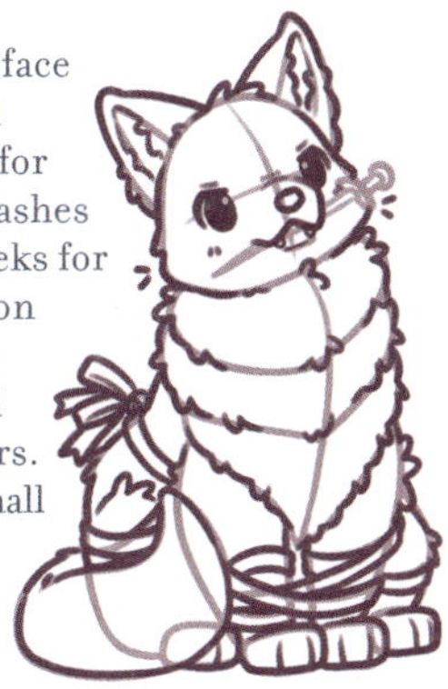

14. Sketch the sword and add drool coming out the left side of the mouth.

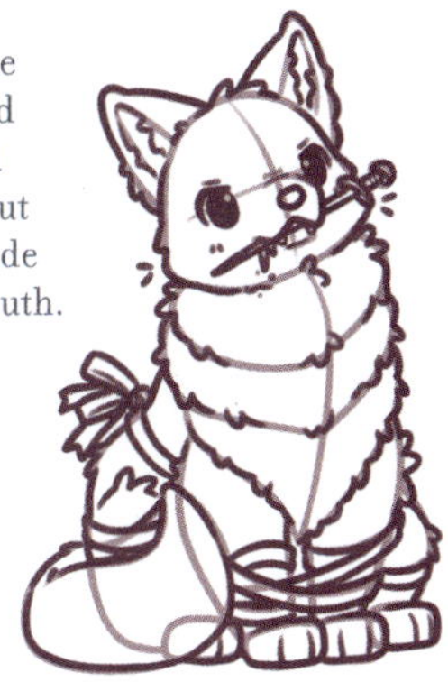

15. Neatly draw the line art over the sketch. Add some sparkles if you'd like! Then erase the sketch underneath.

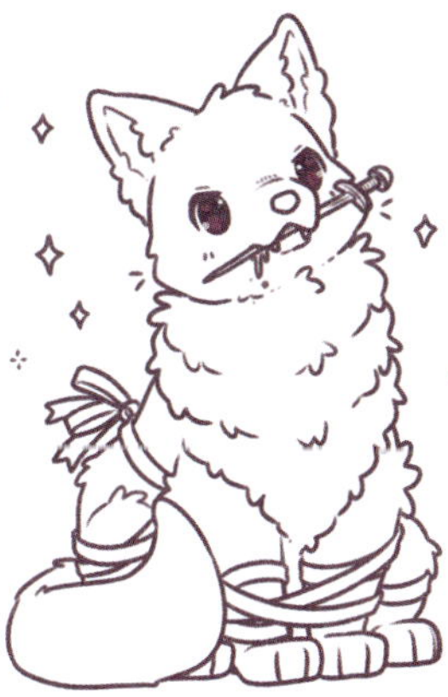

16. Now add color! I made him dark blue with a lighter shade for the chest, and bright red for the eyes and the ribbon.

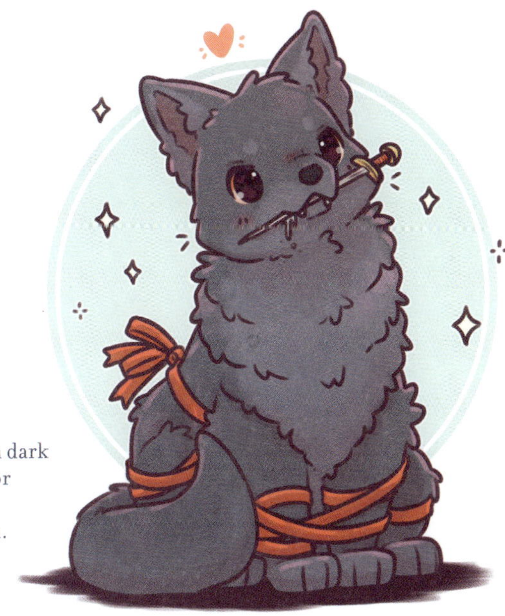

MOTHMAN

The Mothman takes the form of a dark black-winged beastie with glowing red eyes. When spotted, it is believed that it can only be an ill omen.

1. Lightly sketch an oval with pointed sides. Add a plus sign guideline for the face.

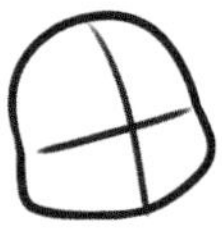

2. Add a curved V for the fluffy neck.

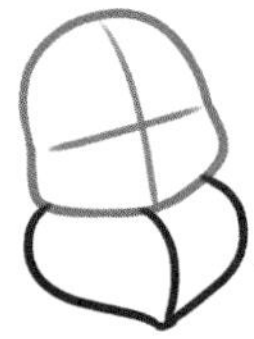

3. Draw a U for the body with a guideline along the middle.

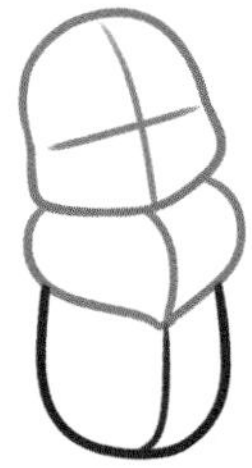

4. Add two oval legs on the bottom of the body. Leave a gap underneath and draw two rectangle feet.

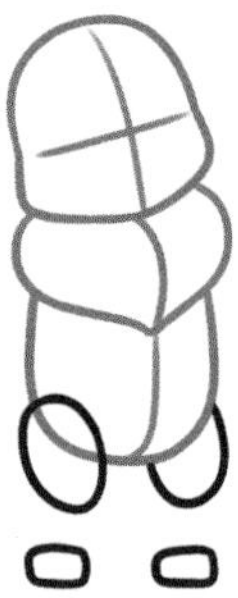

5. Connect the feet to the upper legs with bent lines.

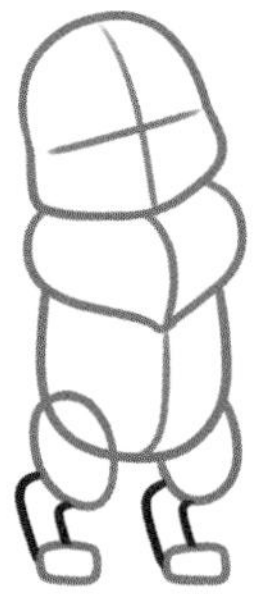

6. Sketch two triangle upper arms, then add narrow triangles at a ninety-degree angle.

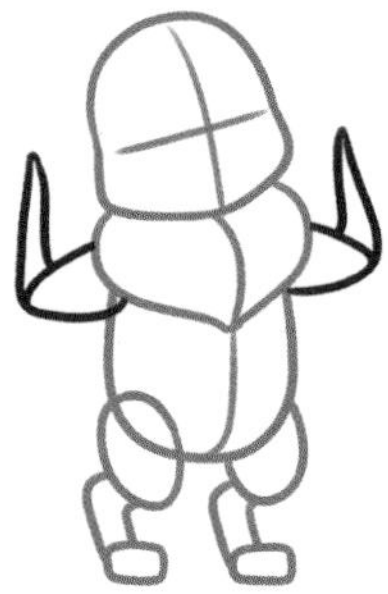

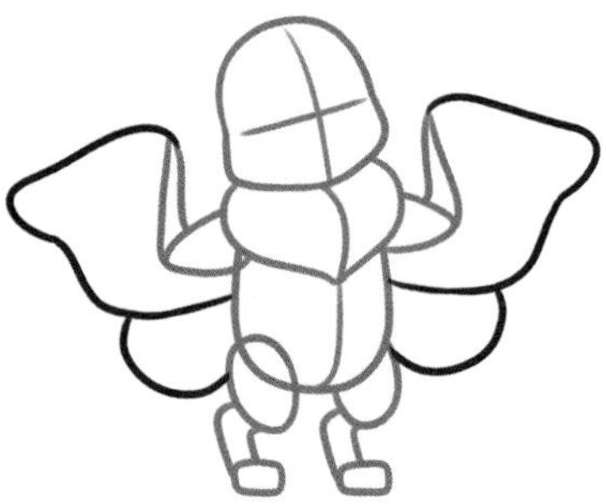

7. Sketch the wings coming out of the tips of the arms and curving underneath. Add a smaller wing underneath with a curve.

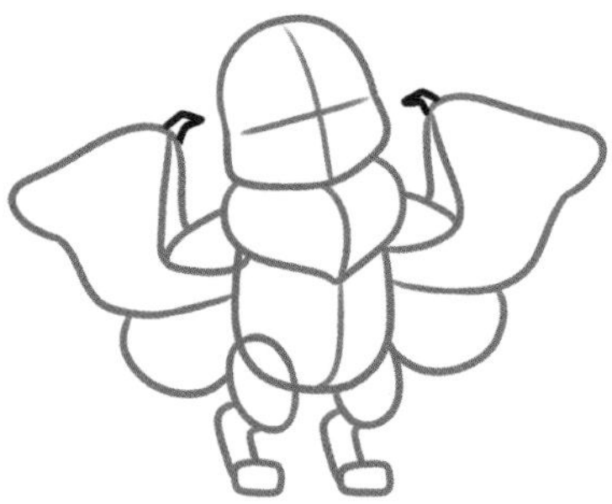

8. Add two little hooks at the tips of the arms.

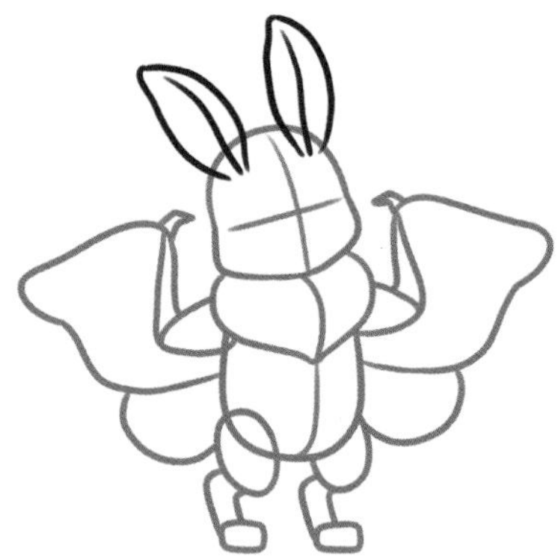

9. On top of the head, draw two pointed oval antennae with a line inside.

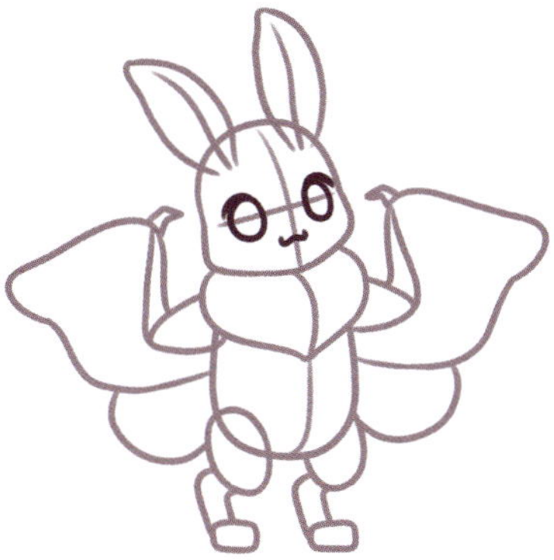

10. Draw two oval eyes with curved lines around the top. In the bottom of the face, draw a small W mouth.

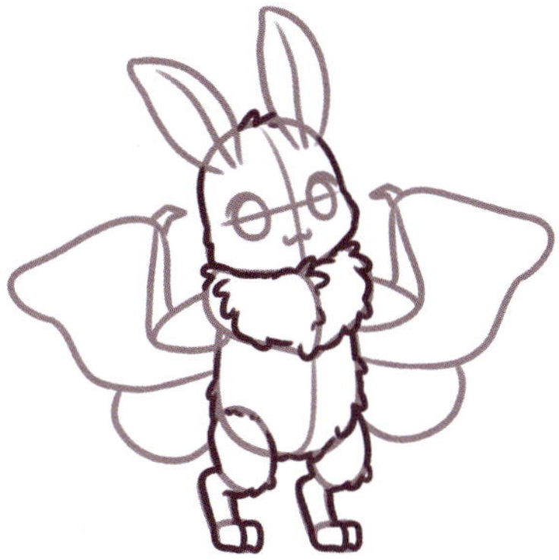

11. Add details to the body. Define the fur with soft W shapes. Draw over the feet with two defined toes.

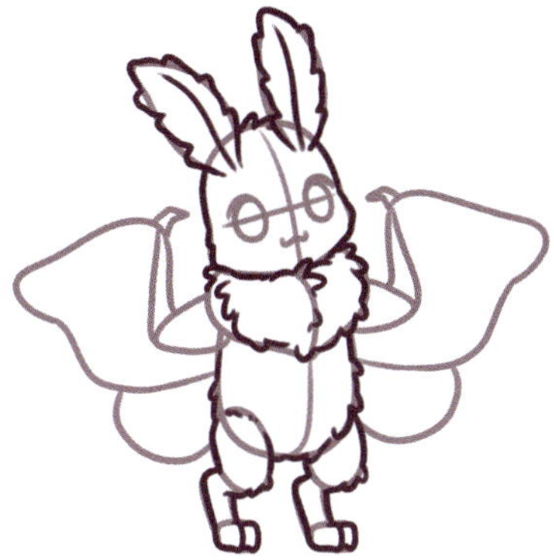

12. Sketch over the antennae. Make them a little bit fluffy.

13. Lightly go over the wings, adding a little fluff on the arms.

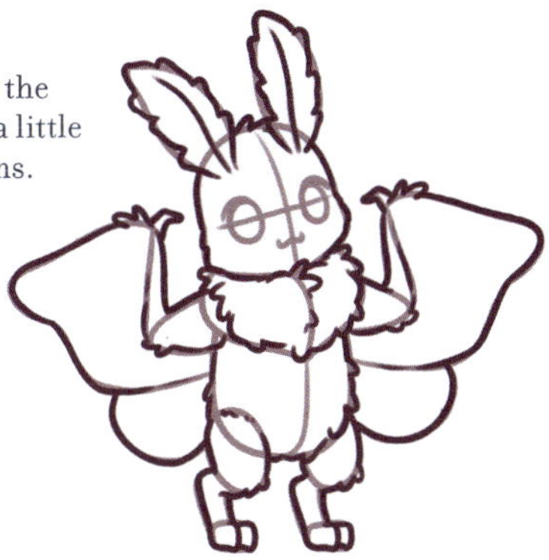

14. Sketch the face detail. Add dashes to the cheeks, and little dashes on the sides of the head.

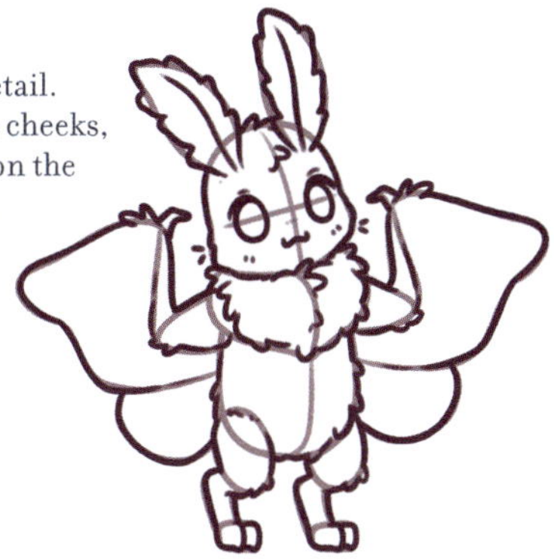

15. Neatly draw the line art over the sketch. Leave space for highlights in the eyes and add some sparkles if you'd like! Then erase the sketch underneath.

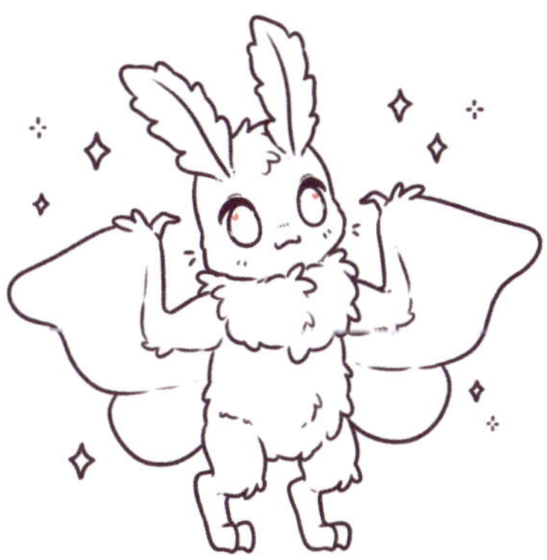

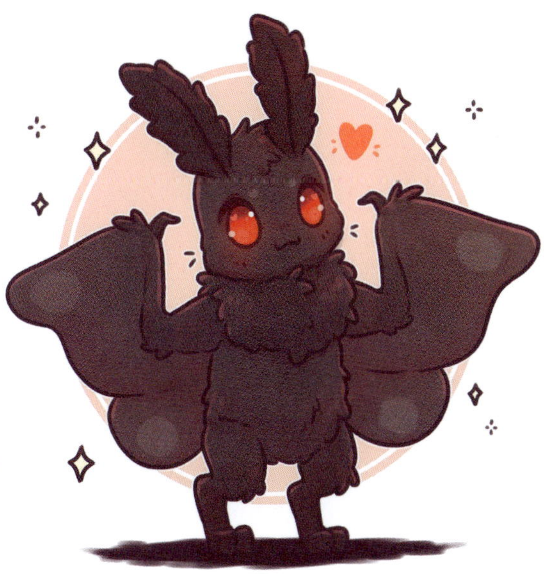

16. Lastly, add color! Use black all over with bright red eyes, and gray spots on the ends of the wings.

WEREWOLF

From European folklore, a human bitten by a werewolf is forever cursed to transform into this beastie every full moon.

1. Draw a circle head with a rectangle snout on the top-right side. Add a guideline across the head, starting at the top of the nose.

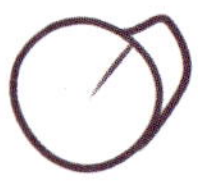

2. Add two triangle ears on the top-left of the head, each with a line inside.

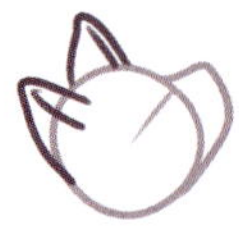

3. Add a wide V under the head for the fur. Then add two small Us under that for the neck.

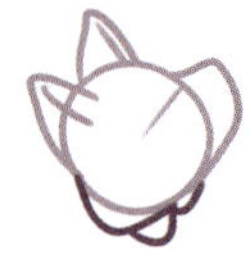

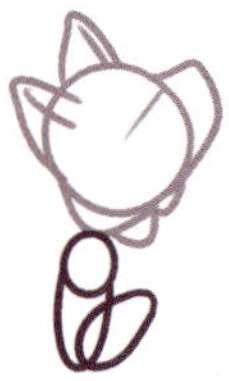

4. Below the V, draw a circle shoulder with a U upper arm. Attach an oval so the arm creates a V shape.

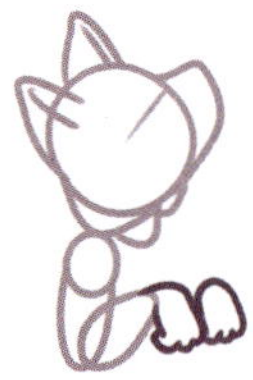

5. At the end of the arm, draw a pair of paws with the fingers defined.

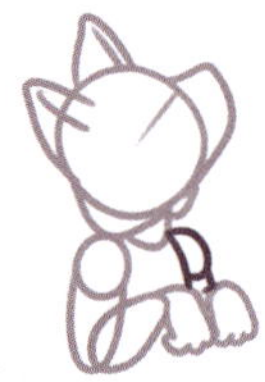

6. Above the right paw, draw a teardrop-shaped right shoulder and a partial lower arm. Then draw a line to define the chest.

7. Draw a U lower body with curved sides. Add a plus sign guideline.

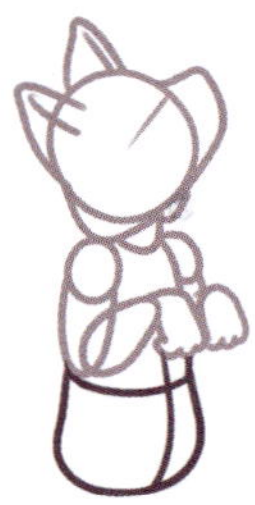

8. Add the upper legs with an oval for the left and a curve for the right.

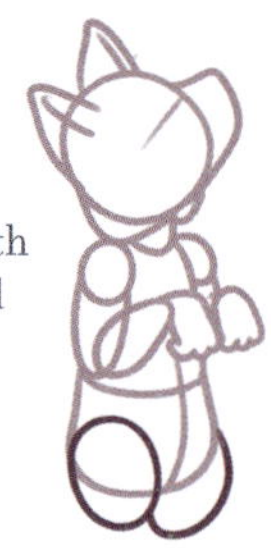

9. Draw two rounded rectangles for the back paws and connect to the upper legs with angled lines.

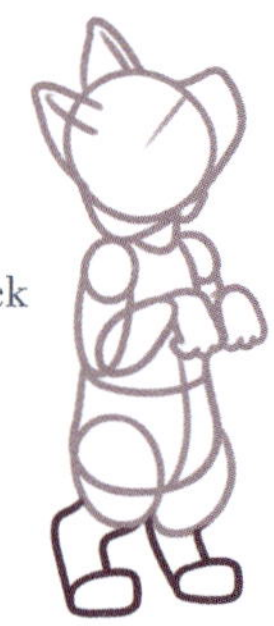

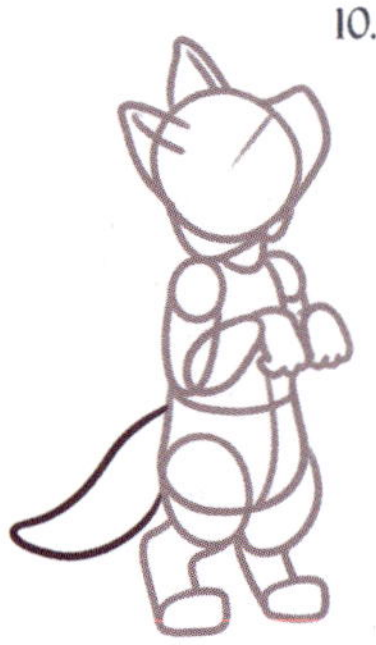

10. Next to the back haunch, add a curved tail.

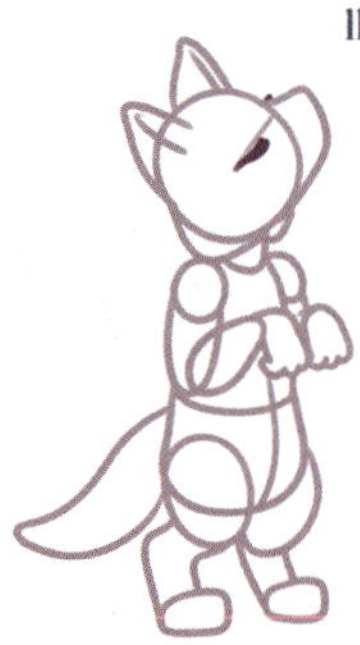

11. Using the face guideline, draw a curved line for the eye and a tiny line above the snout for the other eye's eyelash.

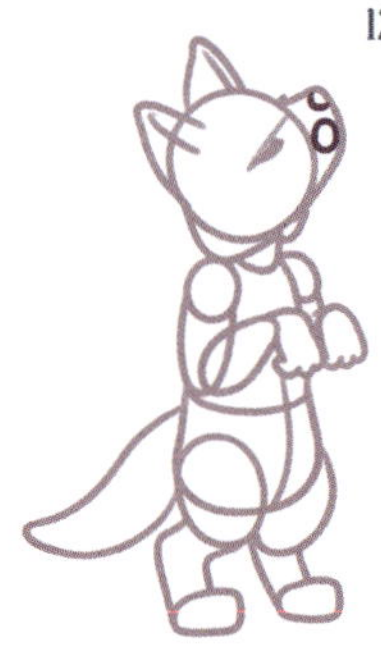

12. On the tip of the snout, draw a curve for the nose. Then, below, draw an O mouth.

13. Sketch a speech bubble to the right of the snout with a circle inside.

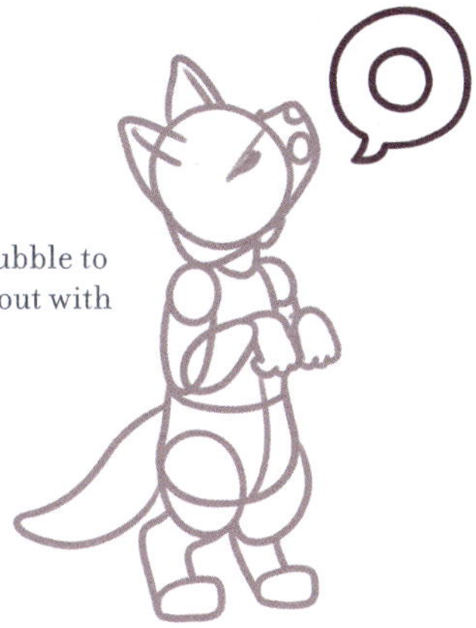

14. Add details to the body. Define the fur with soft W shapes and add toe lines on the paws.

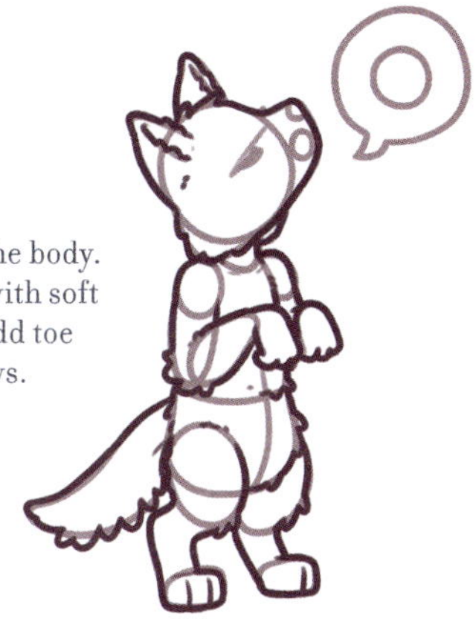

15. Sketch the face detail. Leave space for highlights on the closed eyes, dashes on the cheeks, and two dashes on the sides of the head for whiskers.

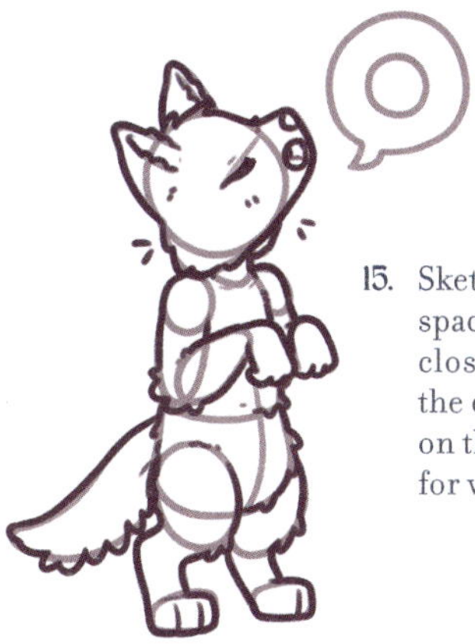

16. In the speech bubble, sketch small clouds and a couple of stars. Detail the circle to make it look like the moon.

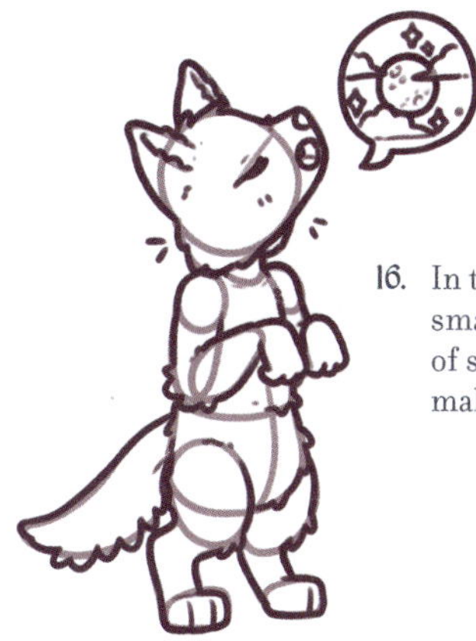

17. Neatly draw the line art over the sketch. Add some sparkles if you'd like! Then erase the sketch underneath.

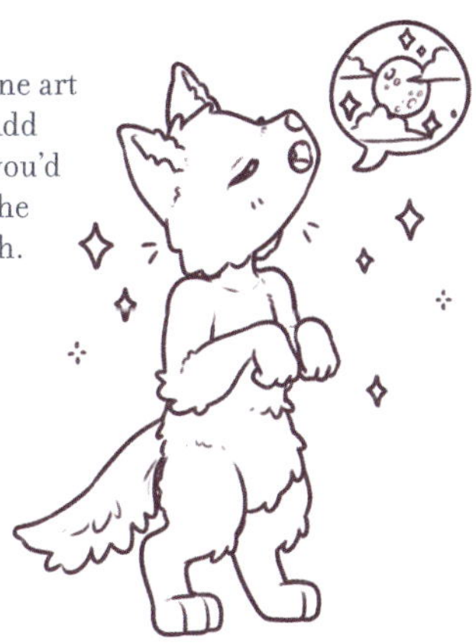

18. Lastly, add color! I gave them a gray coat with light gray on the stomach and face. Color the speech bubble dark blue or black for the night sky and make the moon and stars pale gold.

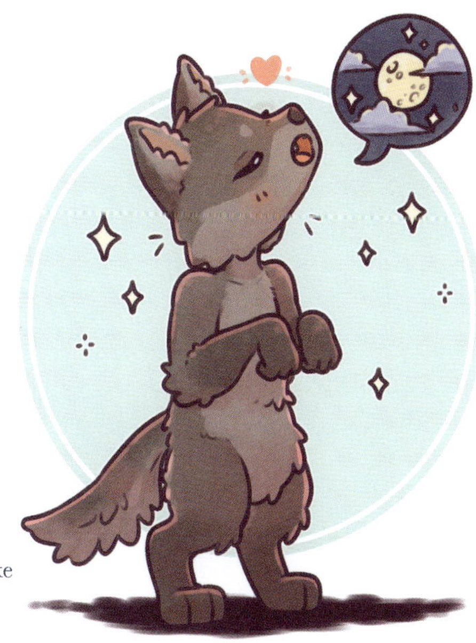

WENDIGO

Originating from Native American mythology, wendigoes are said to possess people and turn them toward cannibalism.

1. Lightly sketch a rounded square head. Add a plus sign guideline for the face.

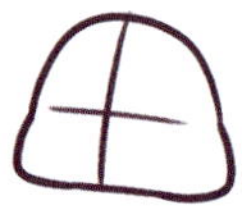

2. Sketch a smaller helmet shape inside the first with a rounded rectangle snout on the bottom of the face. Make two V fangs along the bottom.

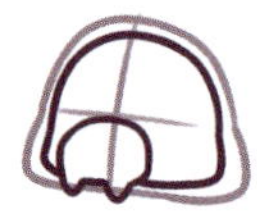

3. Draw U-shaped ears on the sides of the head. Add little lines flicking up from the tip of the ears and a curved line inside both the ears.

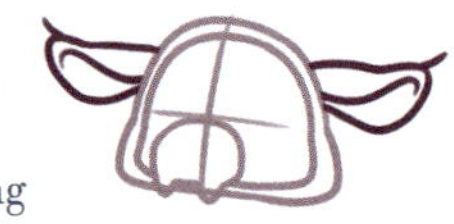

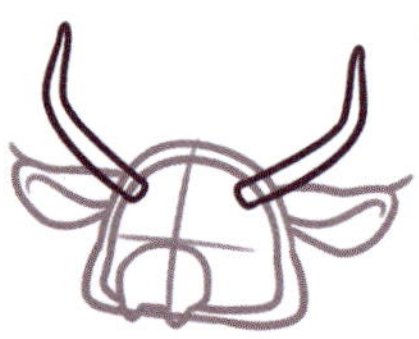

4. Draw two curved, pointed antlers above the ears. Try to keep them symmetrical.

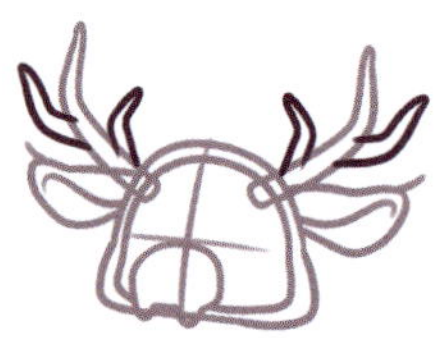

5. Add two curved, pointed prongs on both antlers.

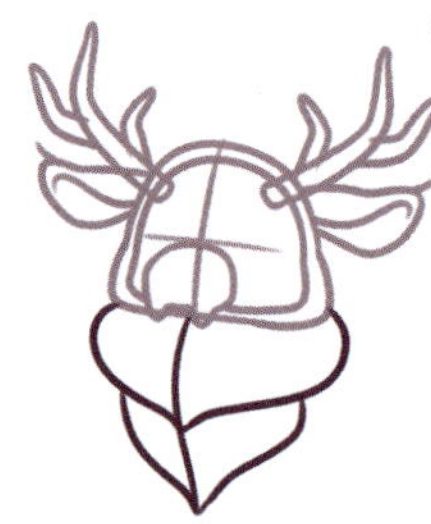

6. Draw two round Vs under the head, one under the other, for the neck and the chest.

7. Draw an oval upper right arm and a curve for the left. Attach the lower arms with long Us, keeping the right arm pulled close to the chest and the left pointing down.

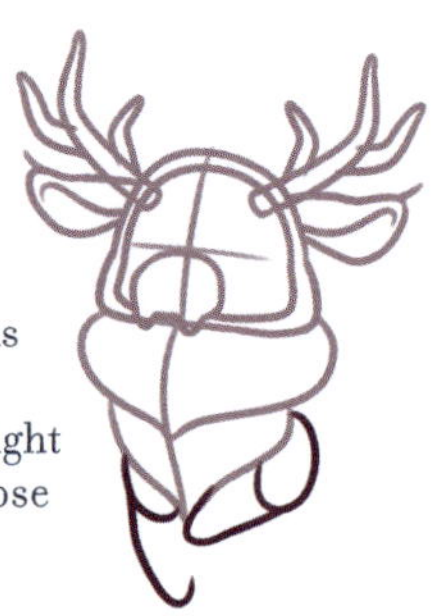

8. Add the claws with three talons each.

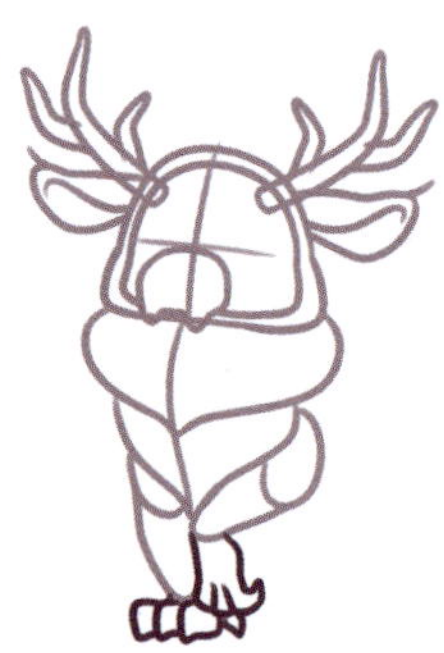

9. Sketch a curve around the chest and legs for the haunches, with an oval on the bottom-right for the back leg.

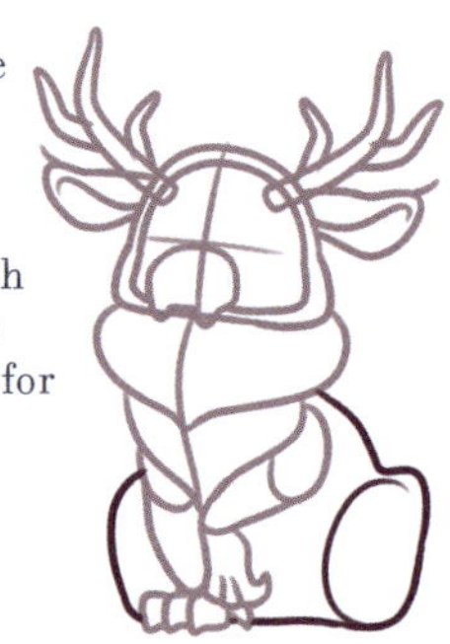

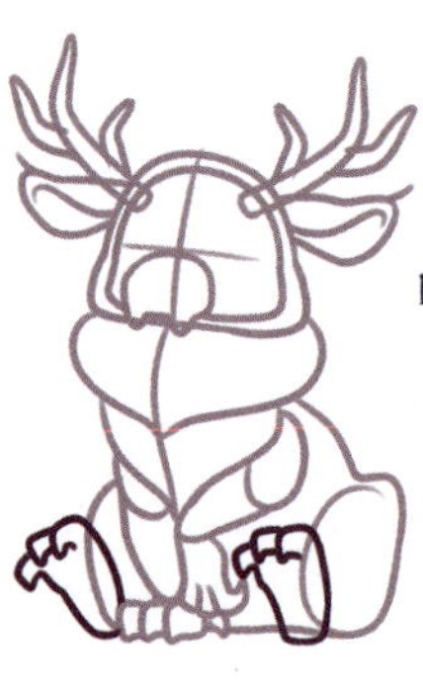

10. Next to the claws, add the two back claws with curved ovals and pointed talons.

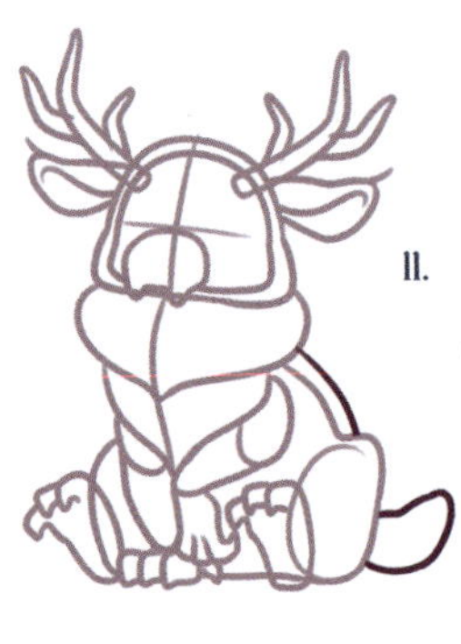

11. Next to the right haunch, add a bean-shaped tail. Then add a line running along the back.

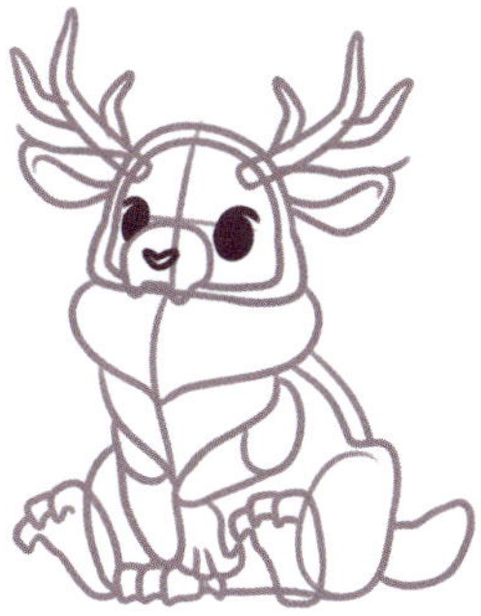

12. At the center of the snout, draw a heart-shaped nose. Then add two oval eyes with curved lines around the top.

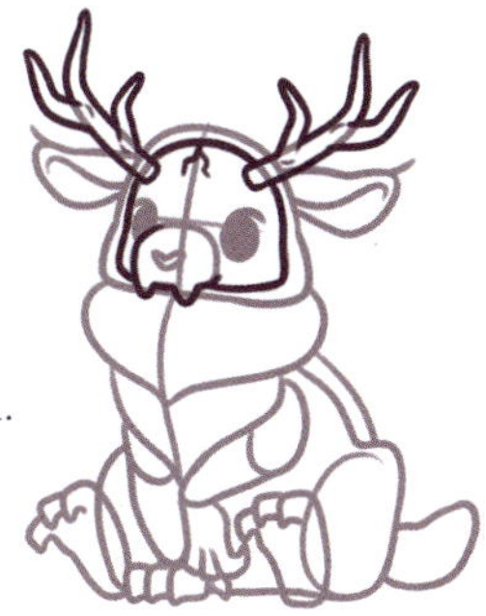

13. Draw the outline of the skull mask and antlers. Add a small, Y-shaped crack at the top of the skull.

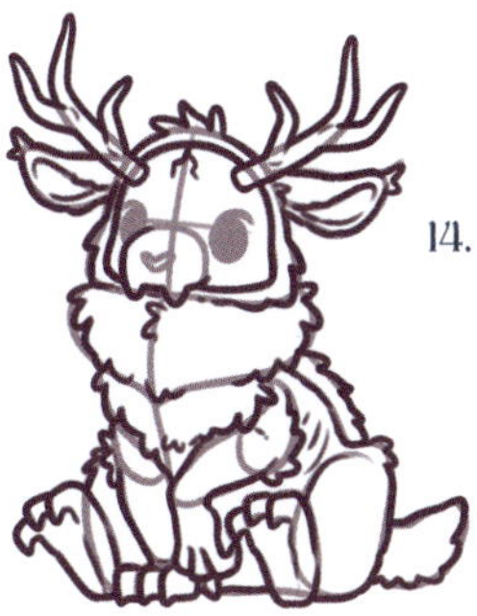

14. Add details to the body. Define the fur with soft W shapes. Add a few dashes on the body for ribs.

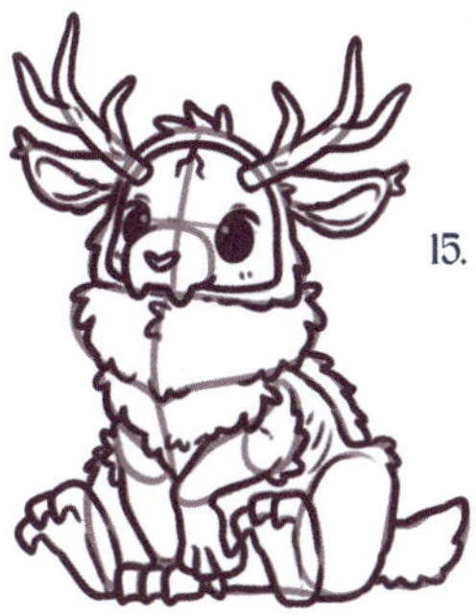

15. Sketch the face detail, adding dashes to the cheeks and highlights to the eyes.

16. Neatly draw the line art over the sketch. Add some sparkles if you'd like! Then erase the sketch underneath.

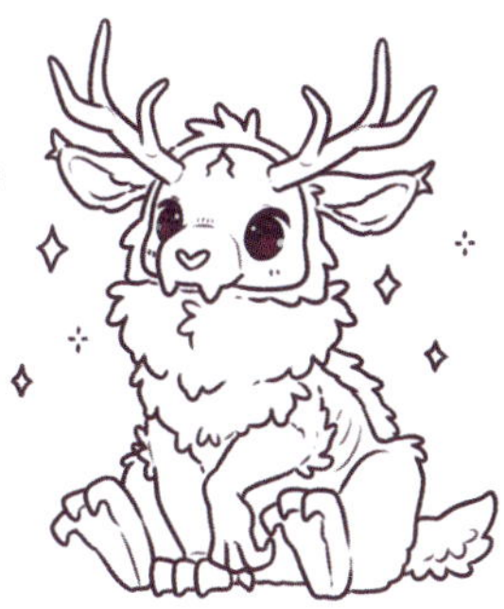

17. Now it's time for color! I used tan-brown for the body and a darker color for the fluff on the neck and fur along the back. Use off-white for the skull.

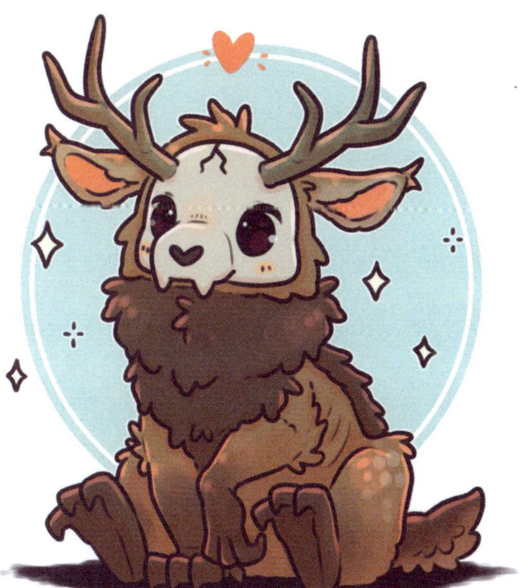

DEMON

Found throughout the world's mythologies in many forms. I've drawn a spin on the classic red demon with horns, bat wings, and a sharp, pointed tail.

1. Lightly sketch an oval head with a dip on the left side. Add a plus sign guideline for the face.

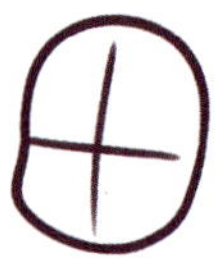

2. Add two triangle ears on the sides of the head, each with a line through the middle.

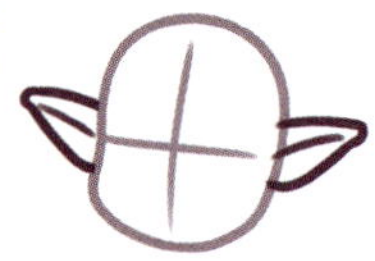

3. On top of the head, add two curved, pointed horns.

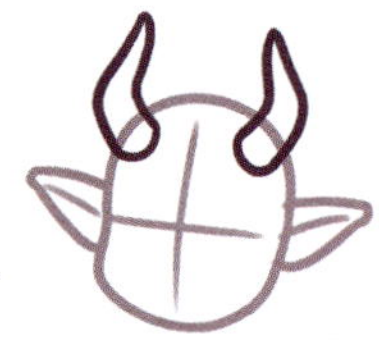

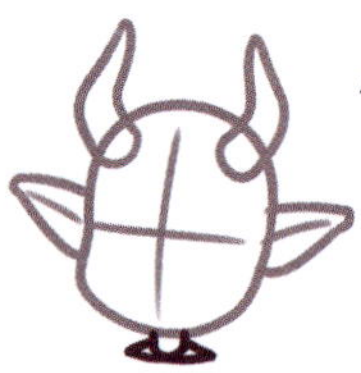

4. Add a small U neck with two small, flat triangles on the sides for the shoulders.

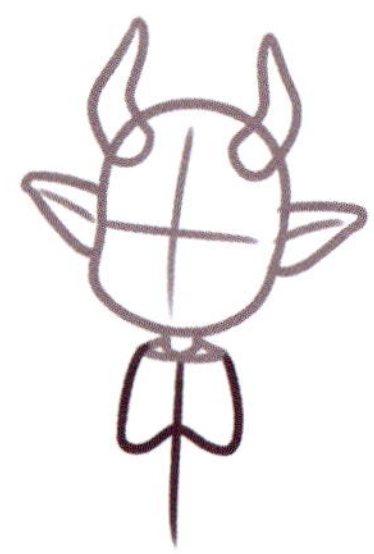

5. Under the shoulders, draw a W-shaped torso with a guideline down the middle.

6. Under the torso draw a U for the lower half of the body.

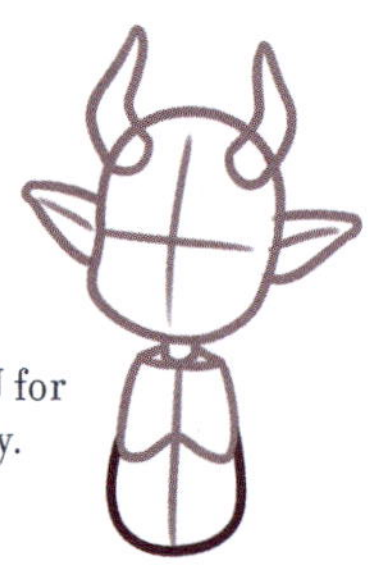

7. Draw two U thighs below the body with the right slightly pointed in.

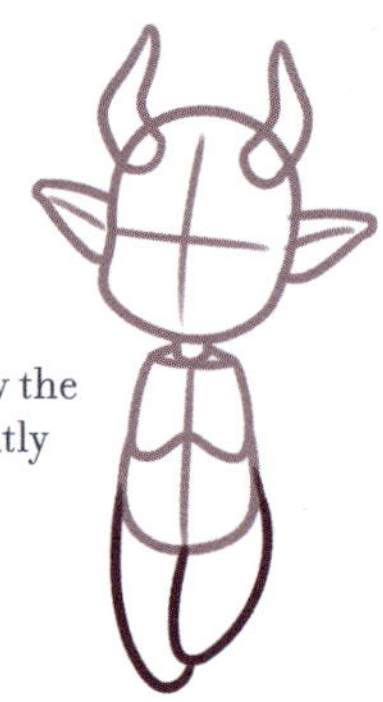

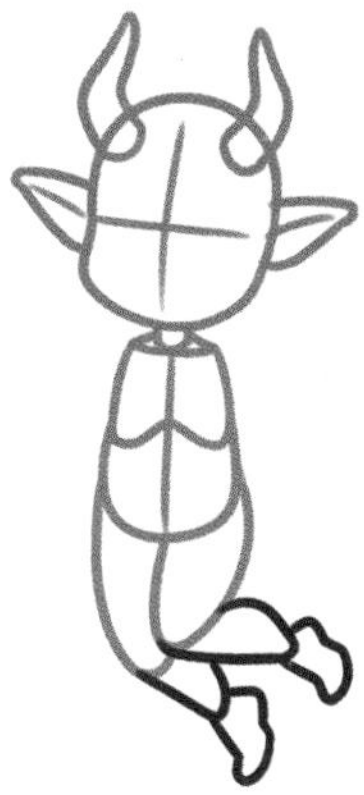

8. Draw two rounded triangles for the lower legs, angled to the right. Attach two boot-shaped feet.

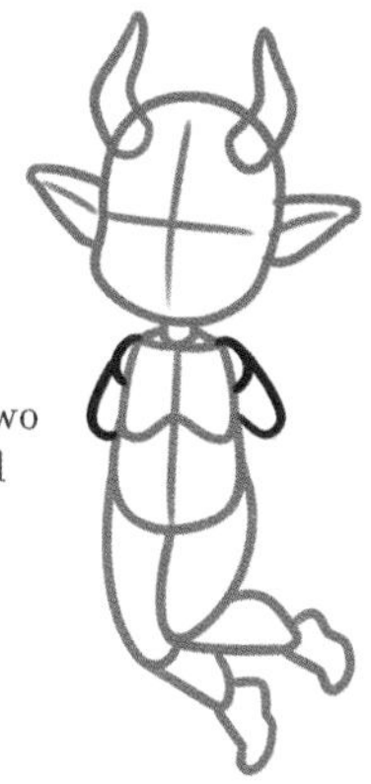

9. Draw the upper arms with two curves and two Us partially concealed by the body.

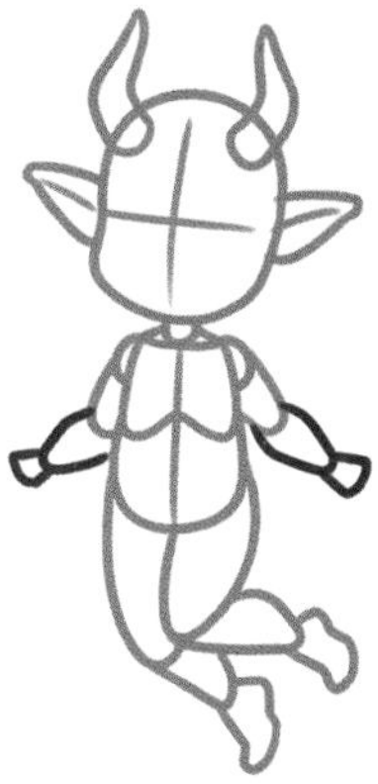

10. Add two diamond-shaped lower arms angled away from the body. Draw trapezoids for the hands.

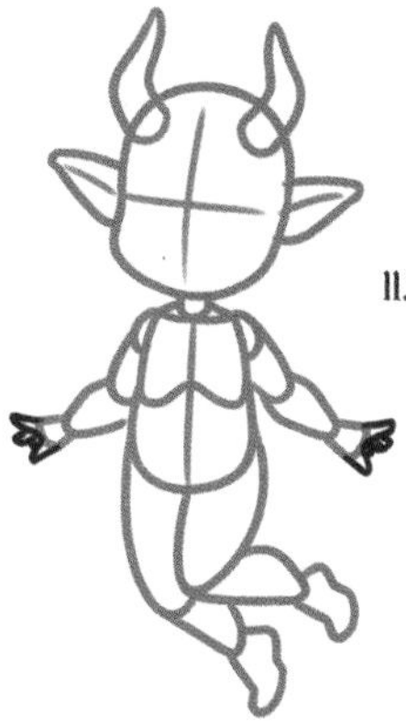

11. Sketch the fingers of both hands.

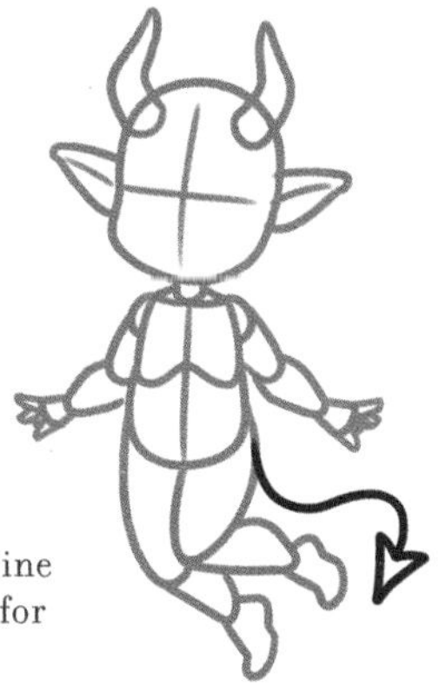

12. At the bottom-right of the body, extend an S-line with an arrowpoint tip for the tail.

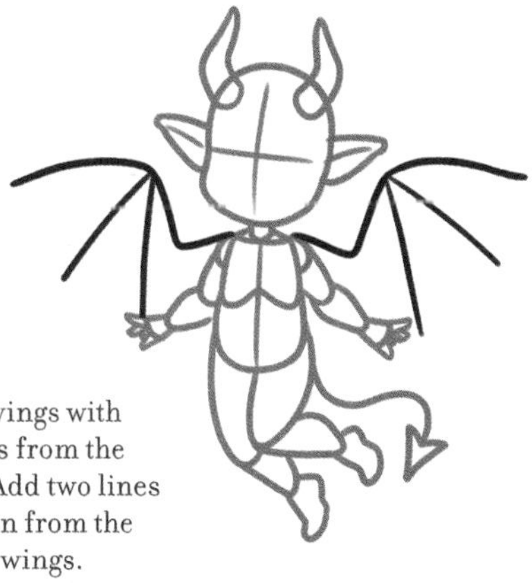

13. Sketch the wings with soft Z shapes from the shoulders. Add two lines forking down from the point of the wings.

(continued)

DEMON

(continued)

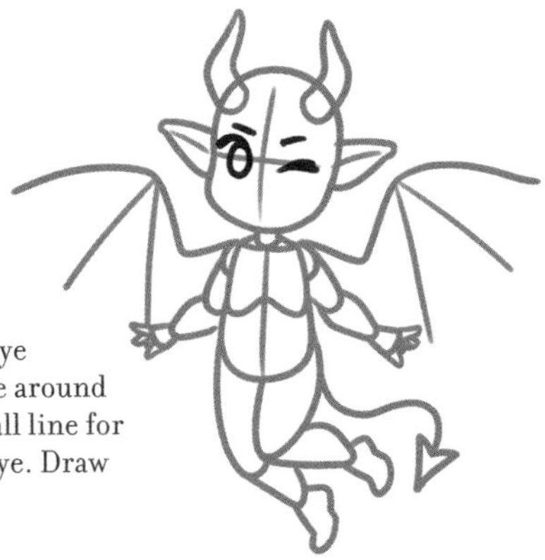

14. Add an oval left eye with a curved line around the top and a small line for a winking right eye. Draw two eyebrows.

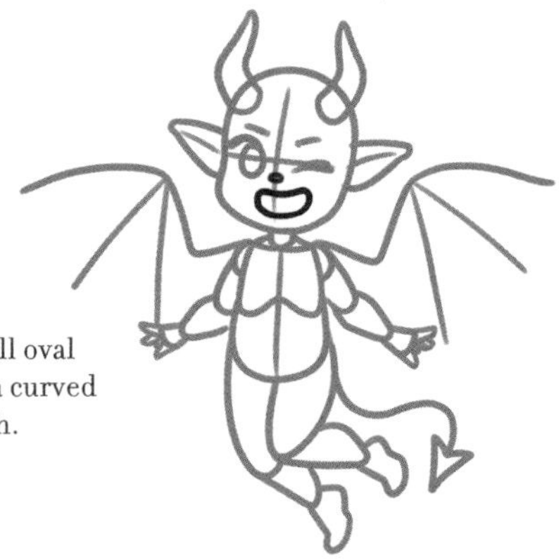

15. Add a small oval nose and a curved oval mouth.

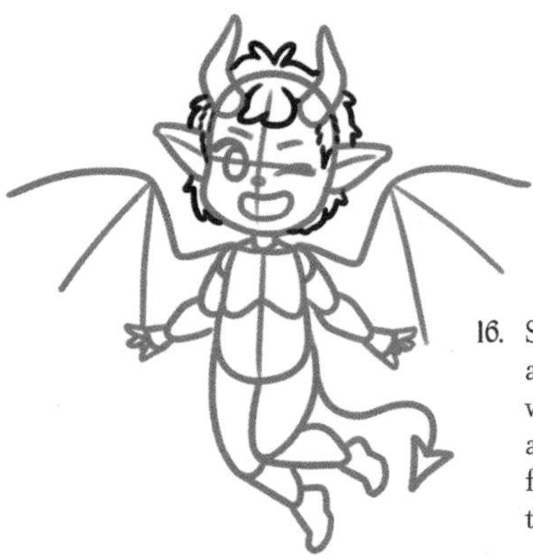

16. Sketch the hair around the head with pointed ends and bangs on the forehead between the horns.

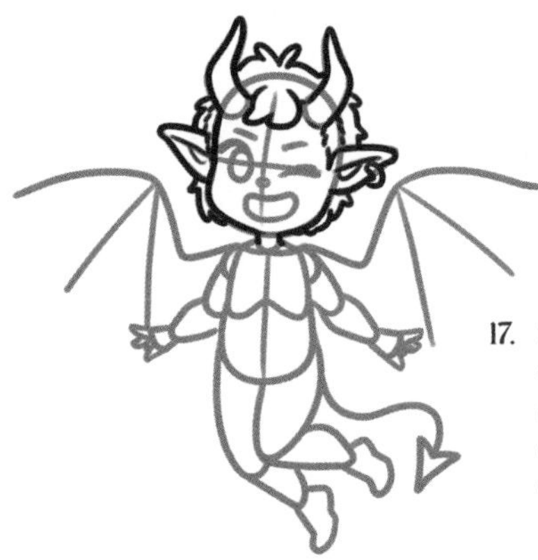

17. Sketch the outline of the head, horns, and ears with a curve on the right ear for an earring.

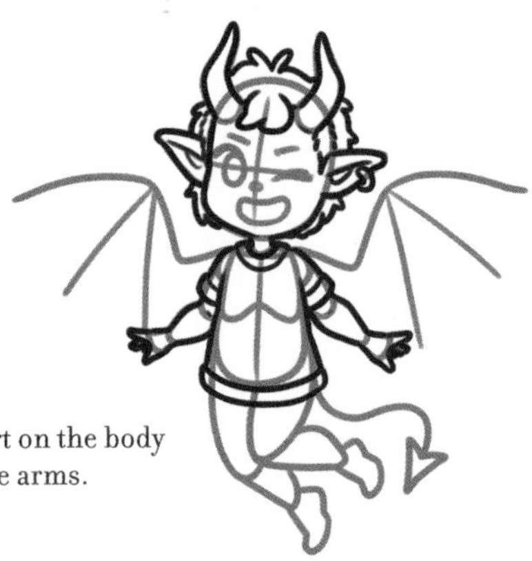

18. Draw a T-shirt on the body and sketch the arms.

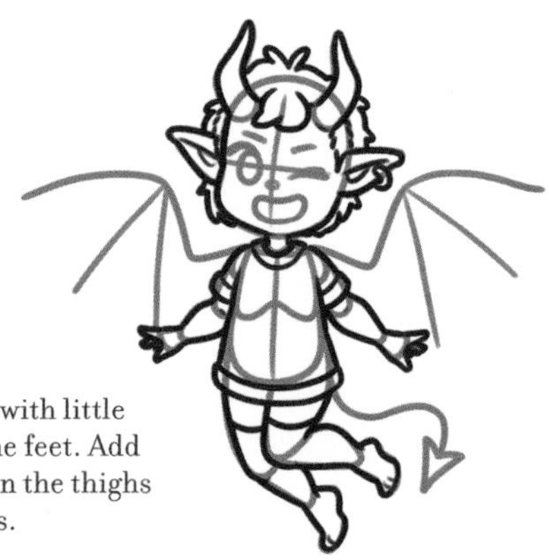

19. Draw the legs with little toe lines on the feet. Add curved lines on the thighs for bike shorts.

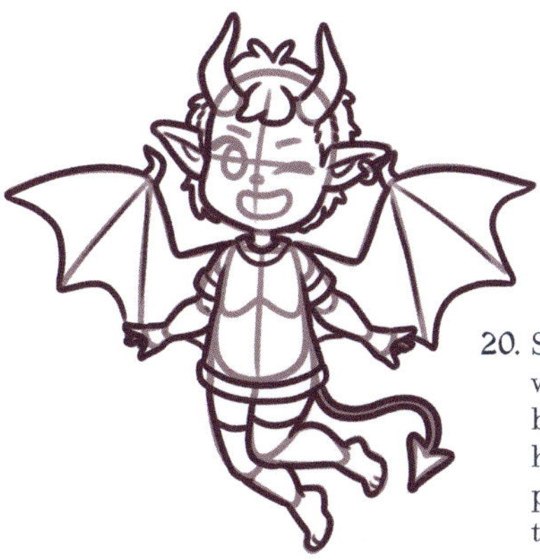

20. Sketch the wings with arcs along the bottom and little hooks at the top points. Thicken the tail.

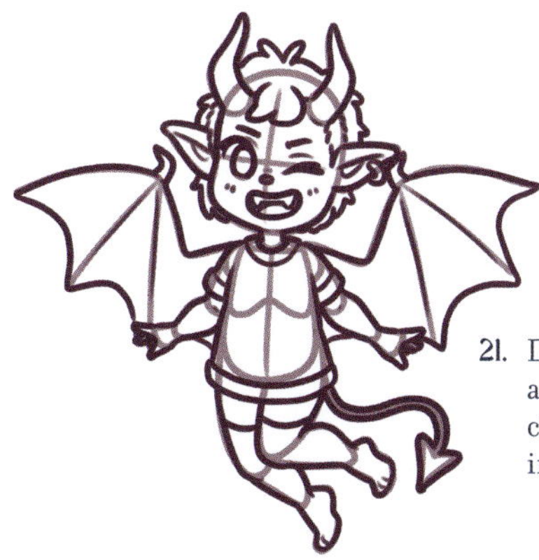

21. Draw the face detail, adding dashes on the cheeks and V fangs in the mouth.

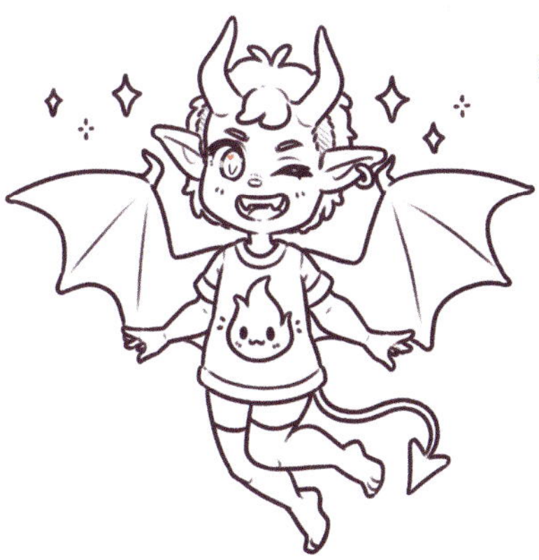

22. Neatly draw the line art over the sketch. Leave space for highlights in the eyes and add some sparkles. If you'd like, make a design on the T-shirt! Then erase the sketch underneath.

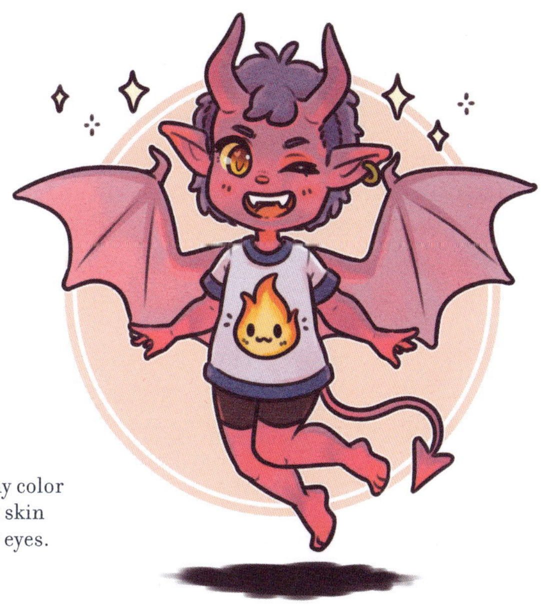

23. You can make the demon any color you'd like! I did bright pink skin with purple hair and yellow eyes.

VAMPIRE

Surviving off the blood of the living, vampires usually appear with pale skin and wicked sharp fangs and have an extreme aversion to sunlight.

1. Lightly sketch an oval head with a dip on the left side. Add a plus sign guideline for the face.

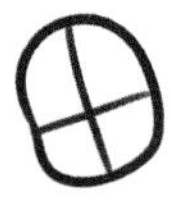

2. Add two triangle ears on the sides of the head, each with a line inside.

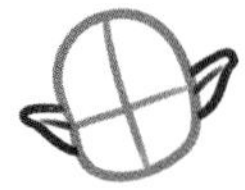

3. Draw a small U neck with two small, flat triangles on the sides for the shoulders.

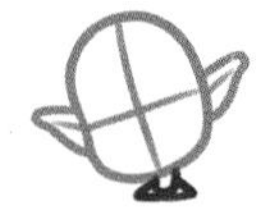

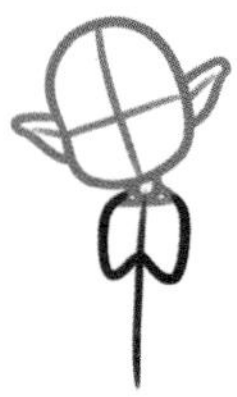

4. Draw a W-shaped torso with a guideline down the middle.

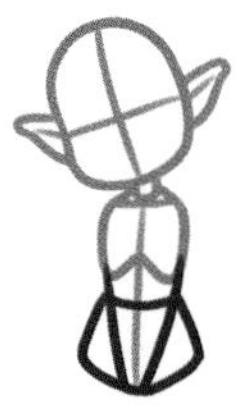

5. Add a V to the end of the guideline with two triangles on the sides for the hips.

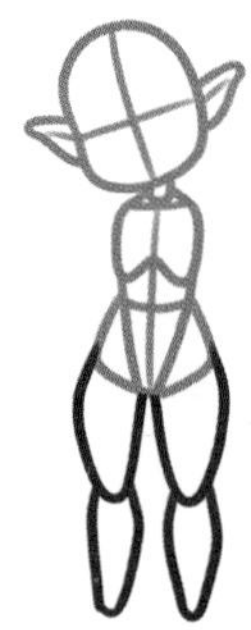

6. Draw U-shaped thighs and diamond-shaped lower legs.

7. Sketch the feet with a triangle and a rectangle in front of it.

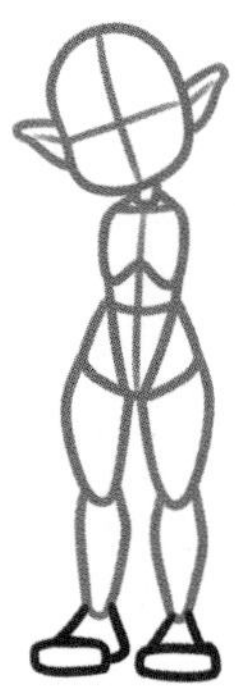

8. Add partial circles for the shoulders and Us for the upper arms. Angle the arms away from the body.

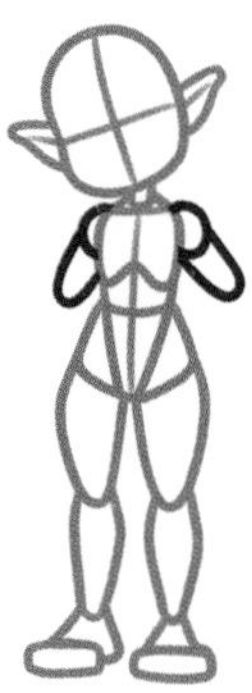

9. Draw round triangles for the lower arms. Angle the left arm left and the right pointed up. Draw the left hand with a triangle and rectangle. Draw a rectangle for the right hand with a small circle on top.

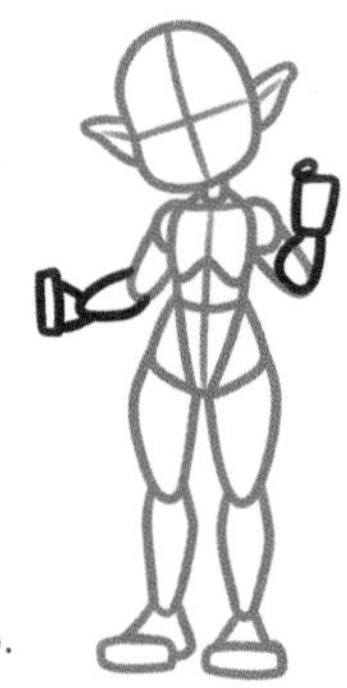

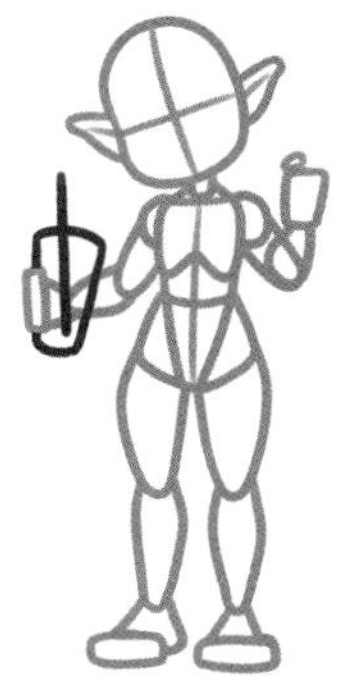

10. Between the rectangle of the left hand and the upper arm, draw a cup shape with a straight line for the straw.

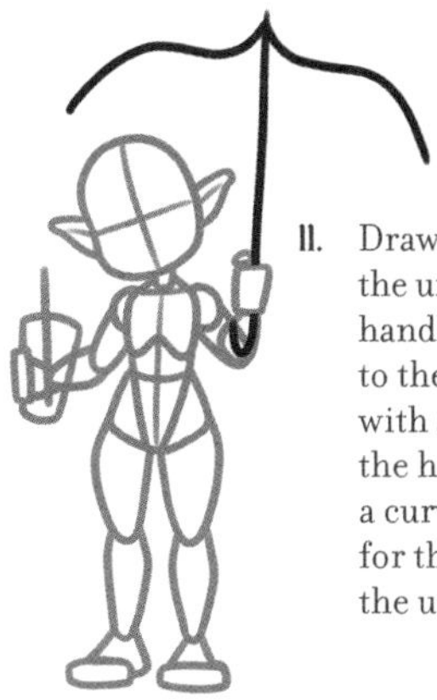

11. Draw the line of the umbrella's handle connected to the right hand with a J under the hand. Draw a curved arrow for the top of the umbrella.

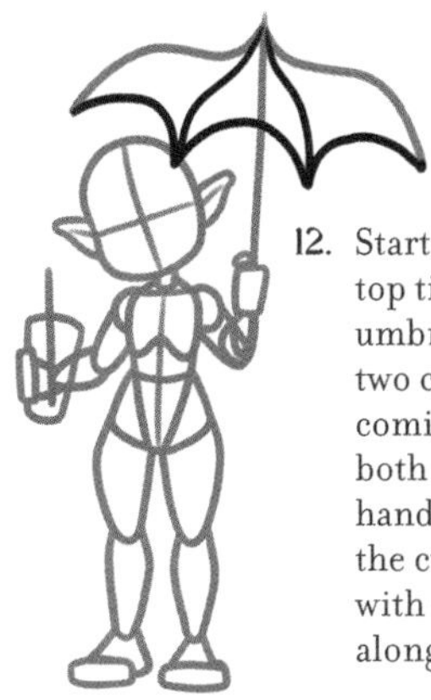

12. Starting at the top tip of the umbrella, draw two curved lines coming down on both sides of the handle. Connect the curved lines with three arcs along the bottom.

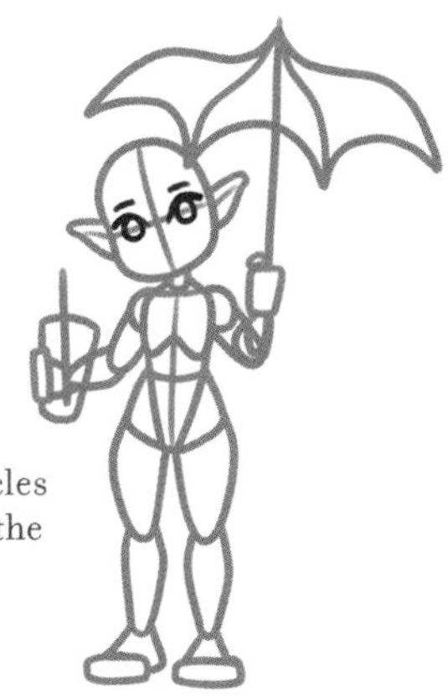

13. Add the eyes with two circles and a curved line around the top. Draw two eyebrows.

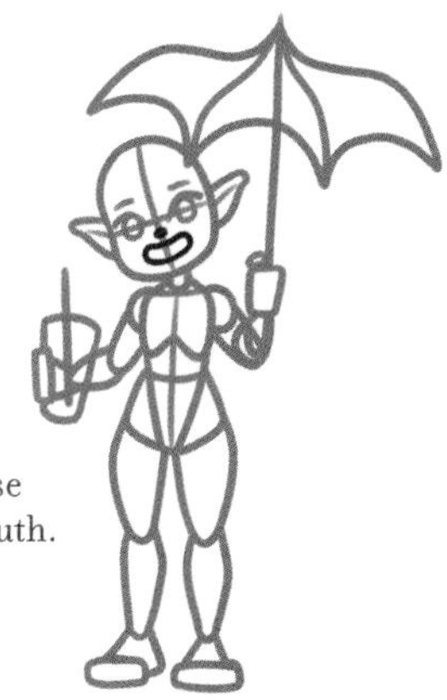

14. Draw a small oval nose and a curved oval mouth.

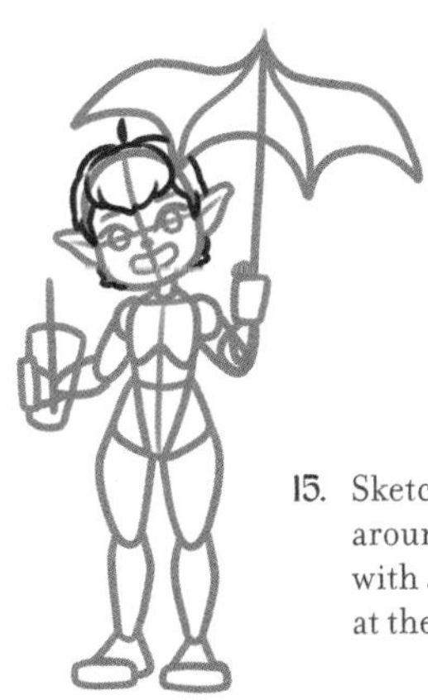

15. Sketch the hair around the head with a tiny flick at the top.

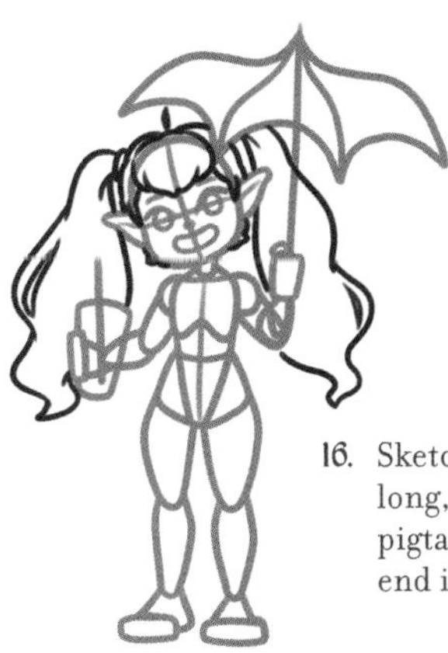

16. Sketch two long, wavy pigtails that end in points.

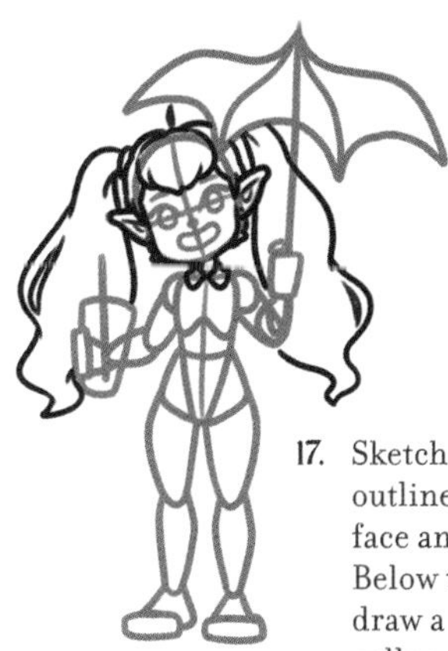

17. Sketch the outline of the face and ears. Below the neck, draw a small collar with two diamonds.

(continued)

VAMPIRE

(continued)

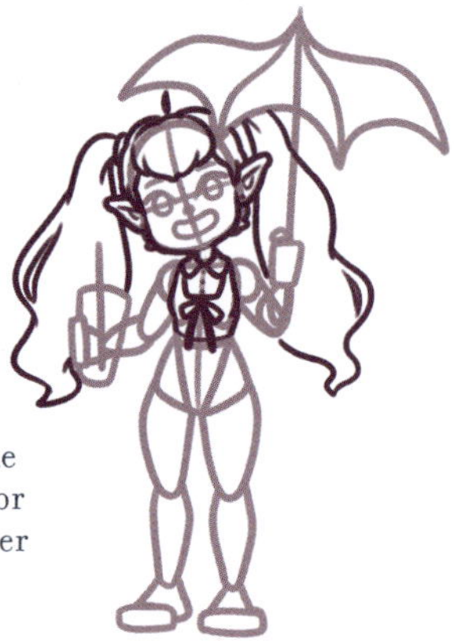

18. Sketch the bodice of the dress with three dots for buttons and a bow under the square neckline.

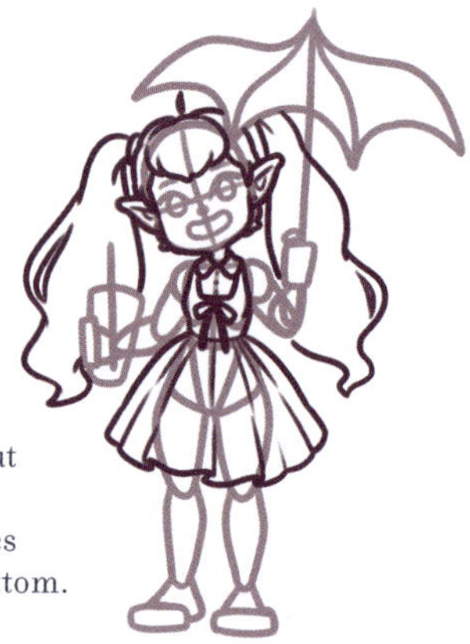

19. Draw the skirt flaring out to just above the knees. Add little folds with lines and curves along the bottom.

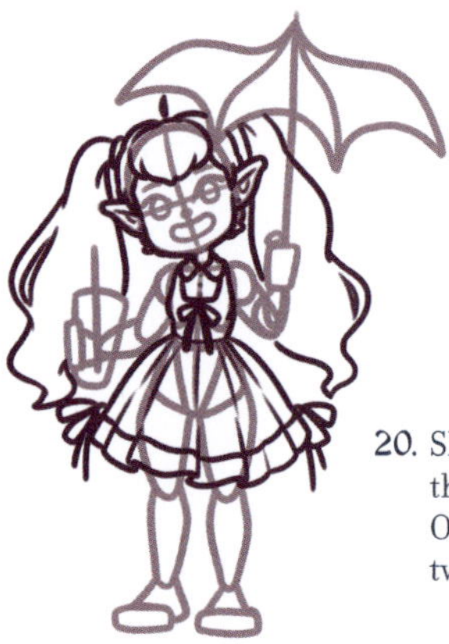

20. Sketch a ring around the bottom of the skirt. On the bottom sides, add two bows.

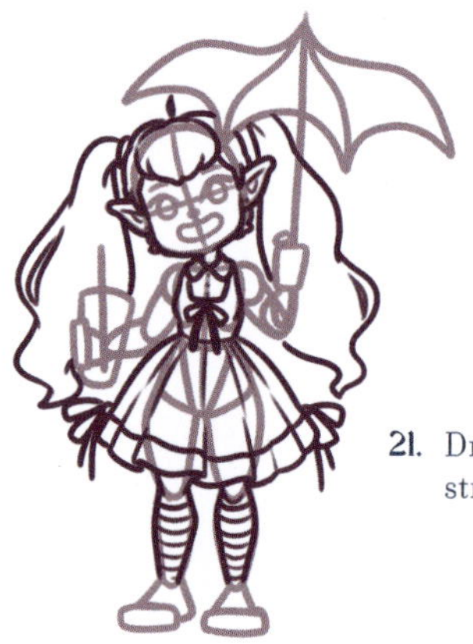

21. Draw the legs and add stripey socks.

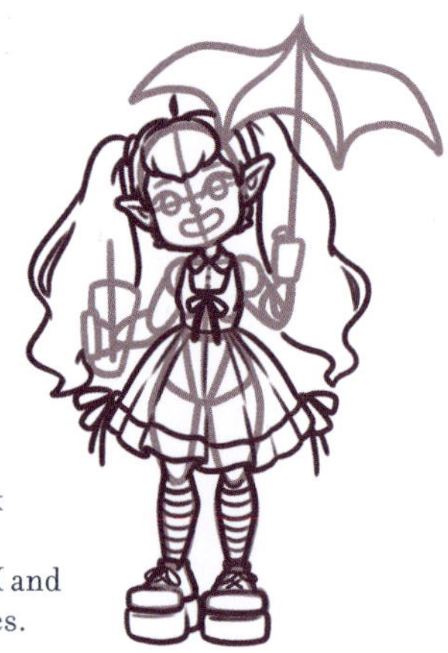

22. Sketch platform shoes by adding another block underneath the foot's guideline. Add a small X and a bow on top for the laces.

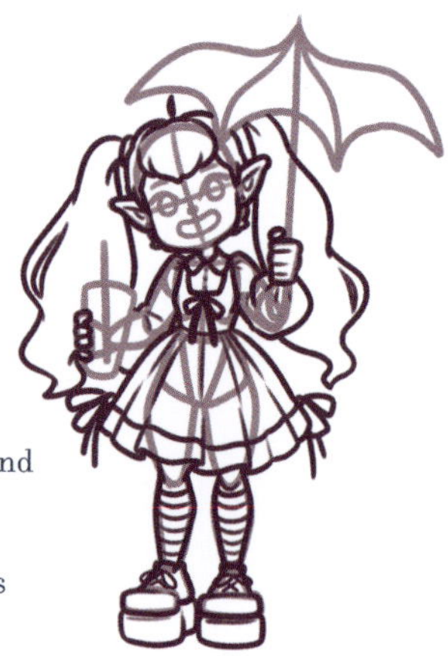

23. Sketch puffy sleeves around the arms. Add the hands, keeping an eye on where the left hand and sleeve is concealed by the cup.

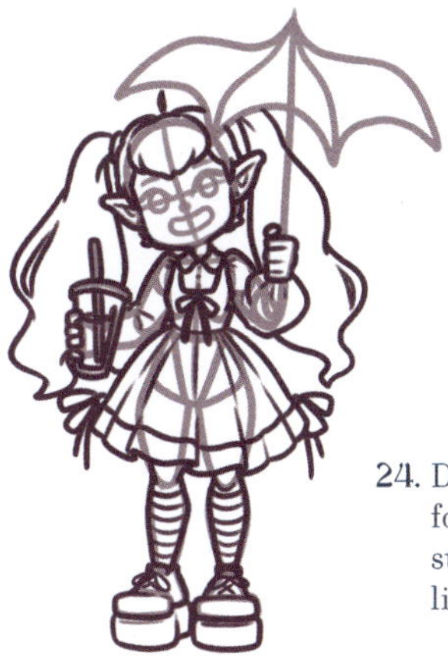

24. Draw the cup with a rim for the lid, a thin oval straw, and a line of liquid inside.

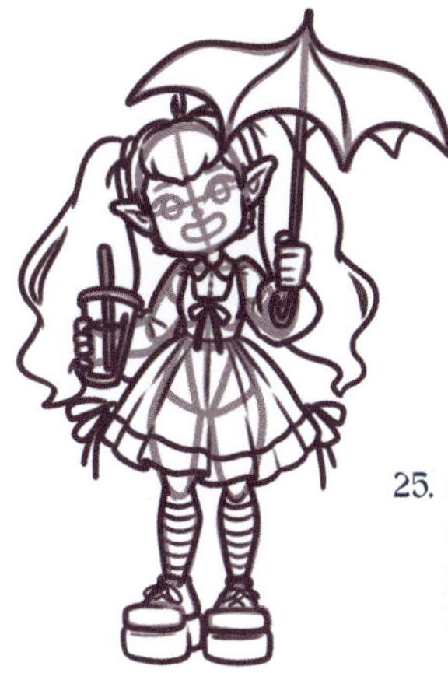

25. Sketch the umbrella, adding three more prongs between the front four.

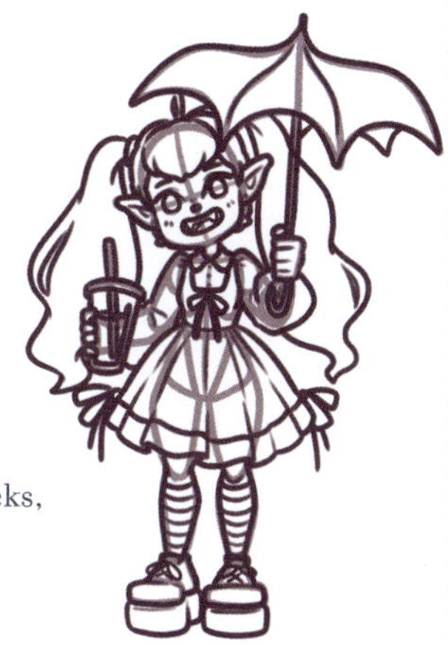

26. Sketch the face detail. Add dashes of blush on the cheeks, and fangs and a tongue in the mouth.

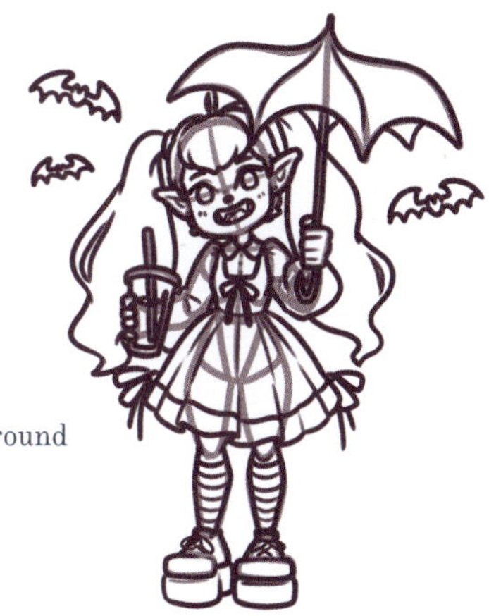

27. Sketch little bats around the figure!

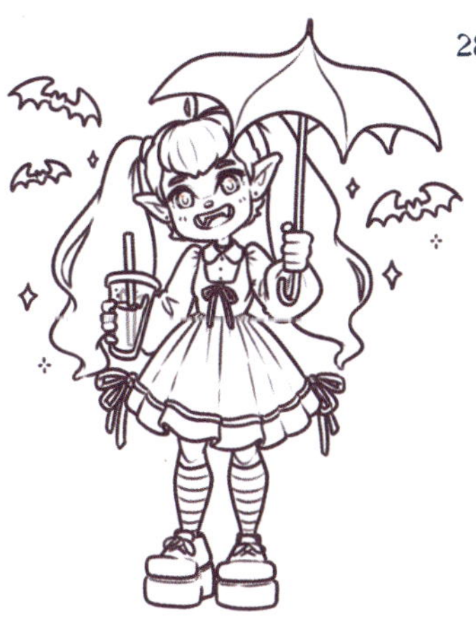

28. Neatly draw the line art over the sketch. Leave space for highlights in the eyes and add some sparkles if you'd like! Then erase the sketch underneath.

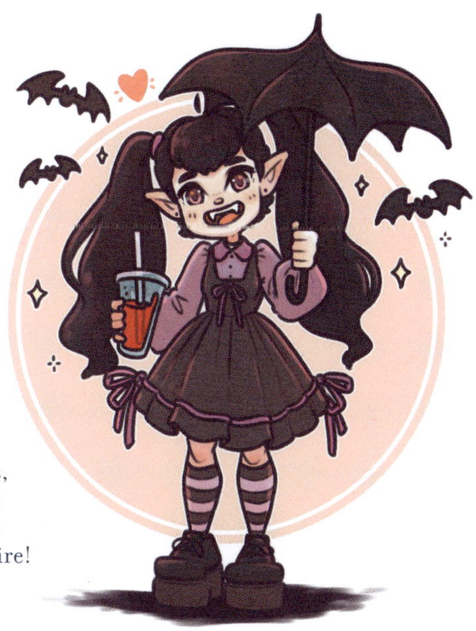

29. Lastly, add color! I went with a gothic aesthetic with a black dress, umbrella, and shoes, and a purple blouse. Make the liquid in the cup bright red because they're a vampire!

MEDUSA

Avoid the stare of Medusa, for it is said that if anyone looks her directly in the eye, they will be petrified and turned into a stone statue for her garden.

1. Lightly sketch an oval head with a dip on the left side and a slightly pointed bottom. Add a plus sign guideline for the face.

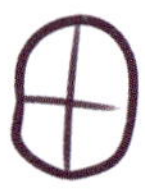

2. Add two triangle ears on each side, each with a line inside.

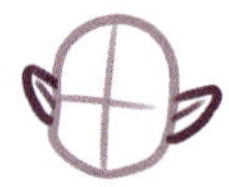

3. Draw a small U neck with a small diamond shape for the shoulders.

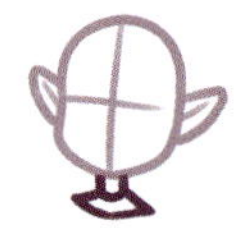

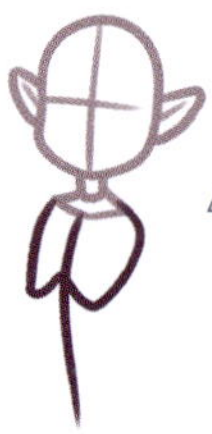

4. Draw a W-shaped torso with a guideline down the middle.

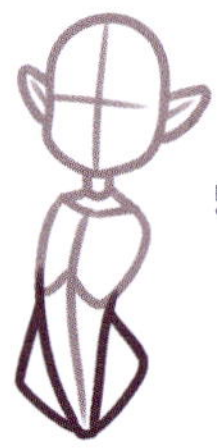

5. Add a V to the length of the guideline with two triangles on either side for the hips.

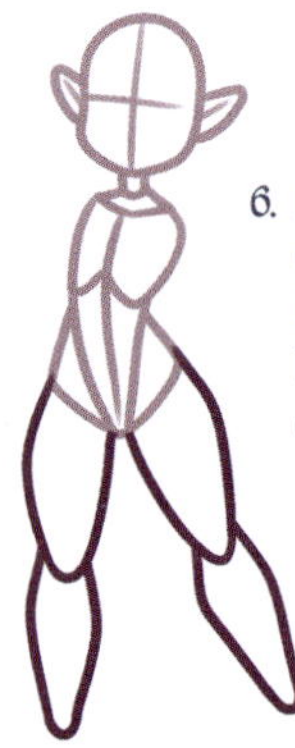

6. Draw two U thighs and diamond lower legs. Make the right leg angled slightly away from the body.

7. Sketch the shape of the feet with a triangle and a rectangle in front of it. Slightly raise the right foot with an arch in the triangle bottom.

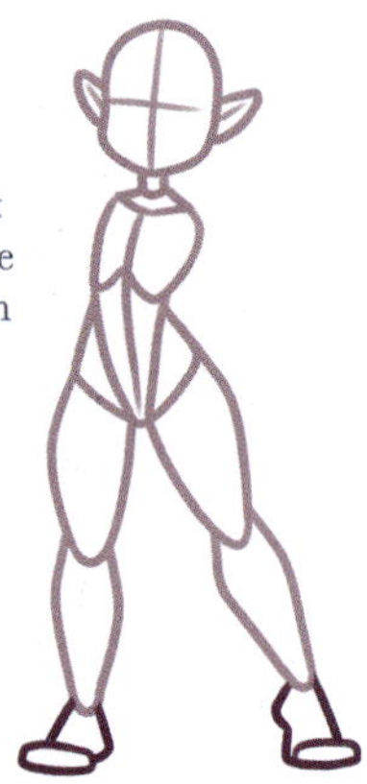

8. Draw a circle at the right shoulder with a U slightly angled out. Draw a partial left arm.

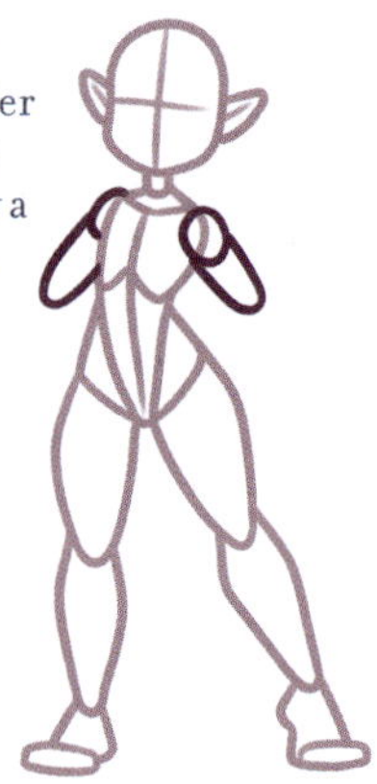

9. Draw the lower arms with teardrops. Make the right arm pointed out to the right and the left pointed up. Use a triangle for the right hand and a rectangle for the left.

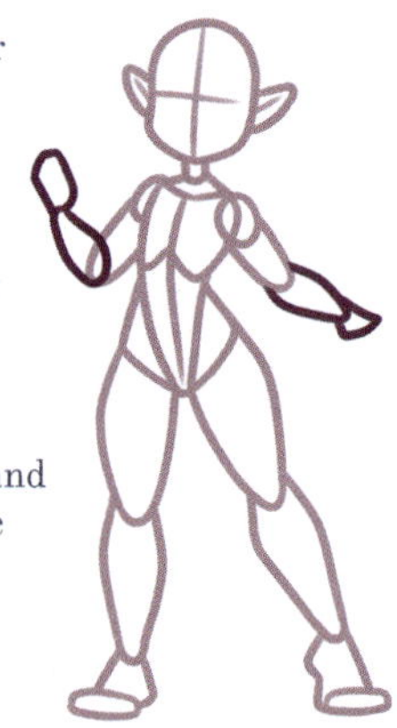

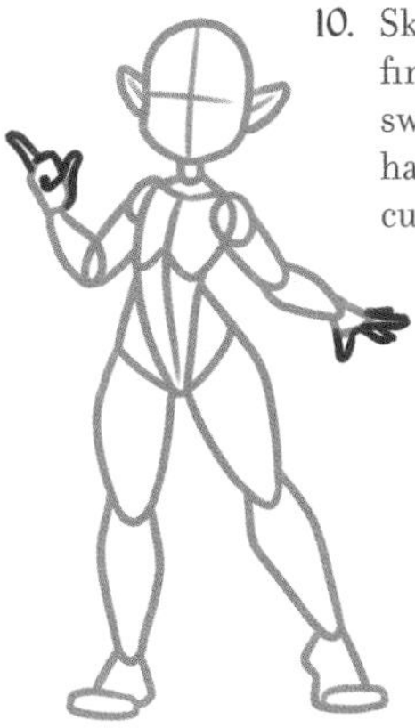

10. Sketch the fingers with a swirl on the left hand to show curled fingers.

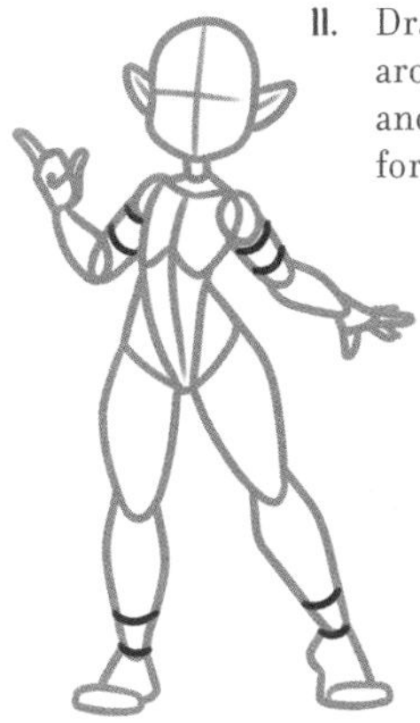

11. Draw rings around the ankles and upper arms for the jewelry.

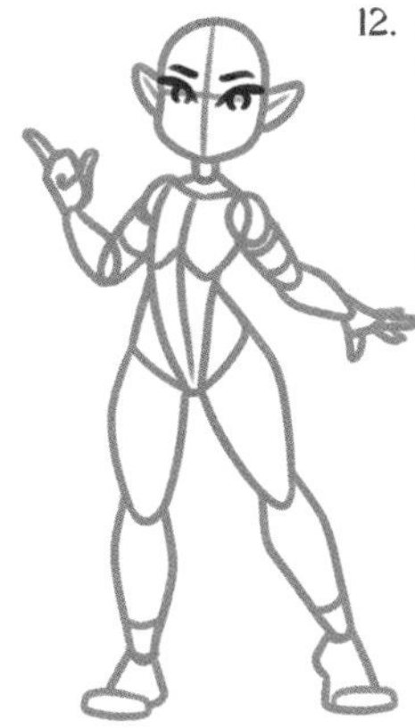

12. Add the eyes with two circles and a curved line around the top. Draw two eyebrows.

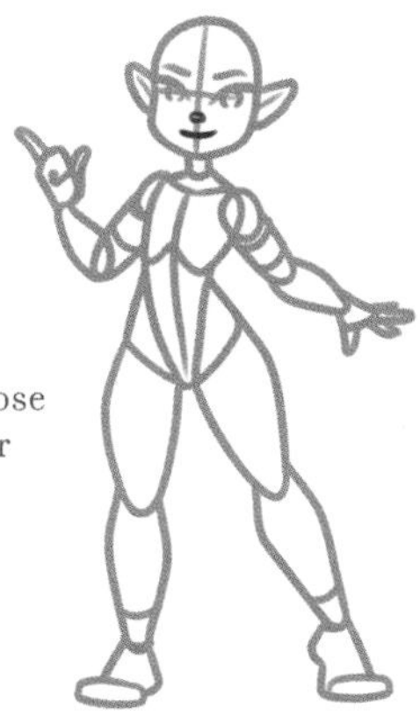

13. Draw a small oval nose and a curved line for the mouth.

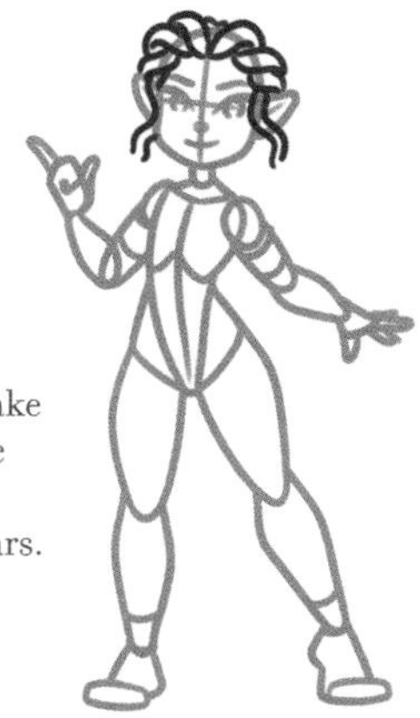

14. Sketch the roots of the snake bodies along the top of the face with curved lines and wavy parallel lines by the ears.

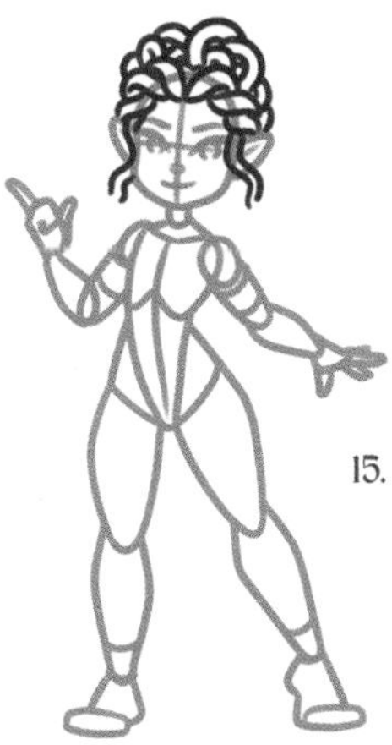

15. Draw more twisting curved lines above for more snake bodies.

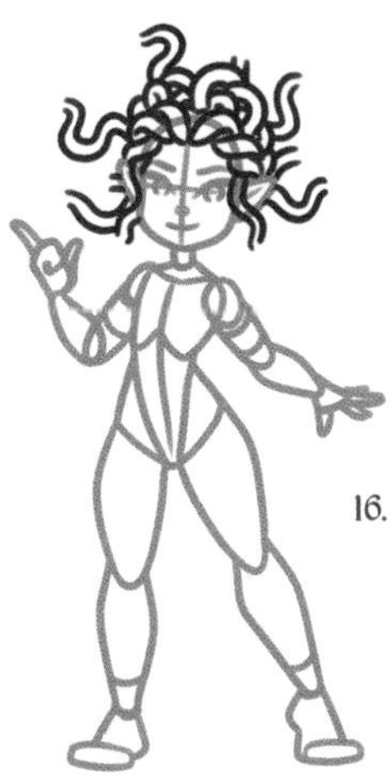

16. Extend S-shaped parallel lines coming out of the hair in all directions.

(continued)

MEDUSA

(continued)

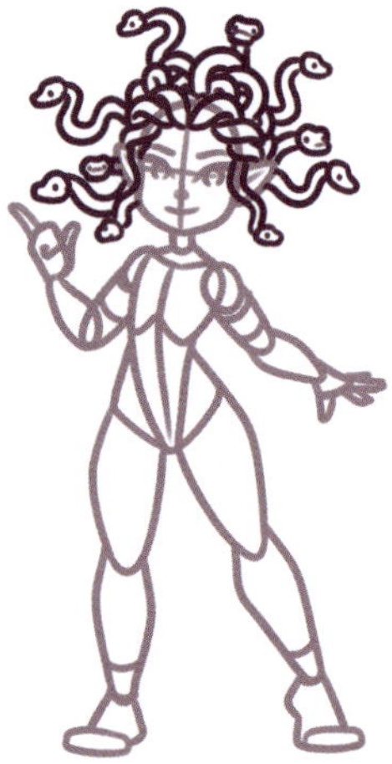

17. At the end of each S-line, draw a triangle snake head with an eye.

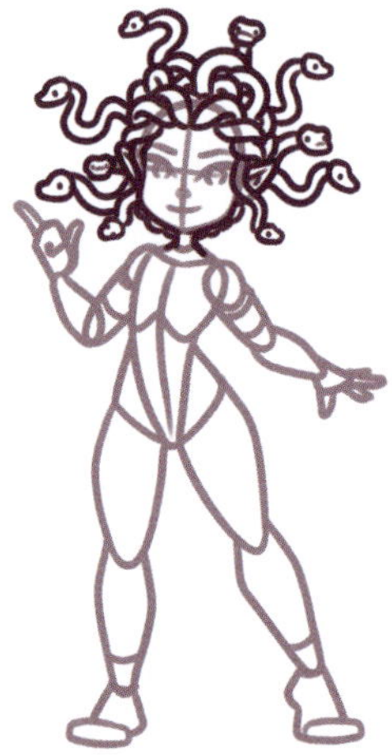

18. Sketch the outline of Medusa's head and ears.

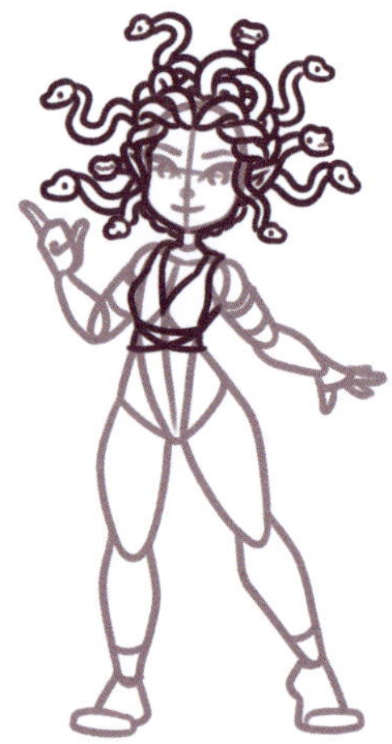

19. Draw the top of the dress with a low V neckline and a thin belt crisscrossing around the waist.

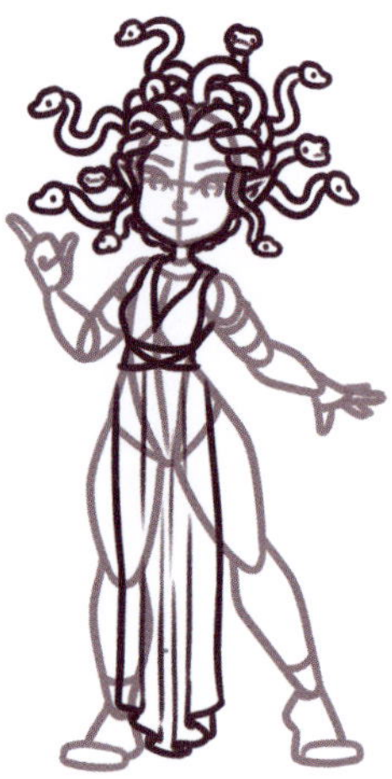

20. Draw the front of the dress hanging between the legs. Add folds with lines along the front and curves along the bottom.

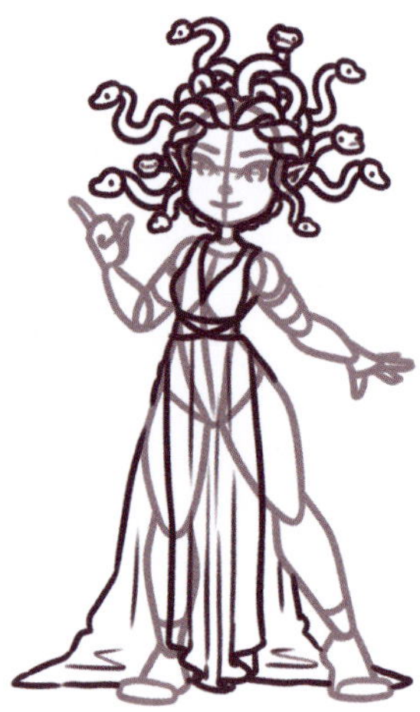

21. Draw the back of the skirt on the left, pooling on the floor. Keep most of the right leg visible.

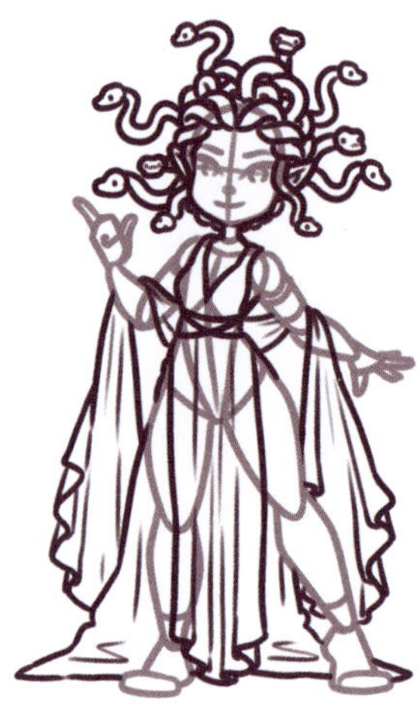

22. Draw the shawl draped over the elbows and hanging down to the floor. Draw lines for folds and curves along the edges.

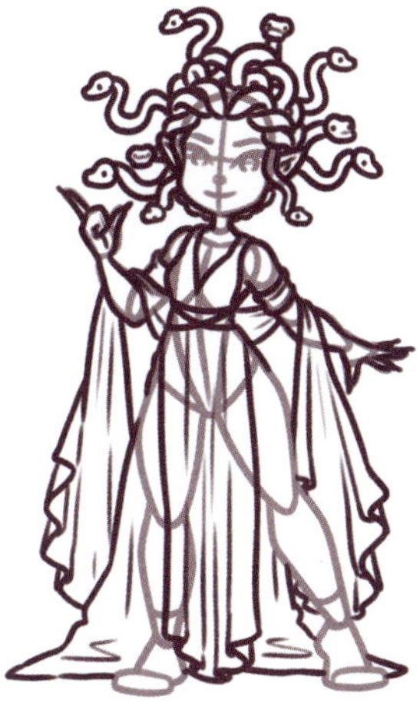

23. Sketch the arms with sharp points at the tips of the fingers for the nails. Add the arm cuffs.

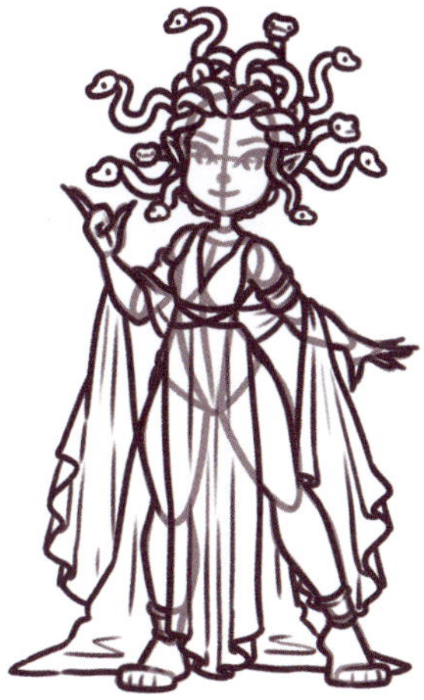

24. Sketch the legs, adding toe lines and the cuffs on the ankles.

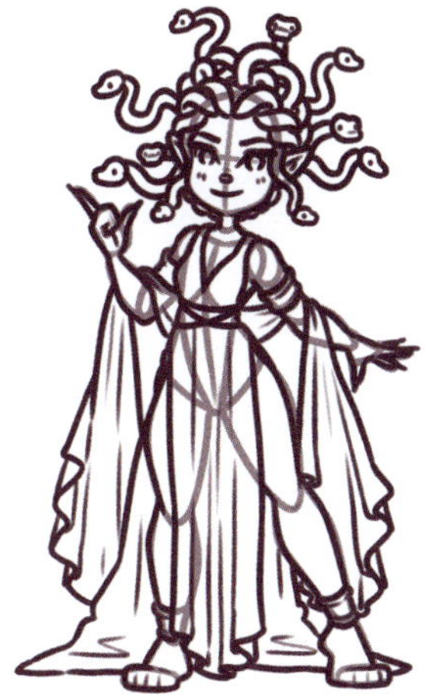

25. Sketch the face detail, adding dashes of blush on the cheeks.

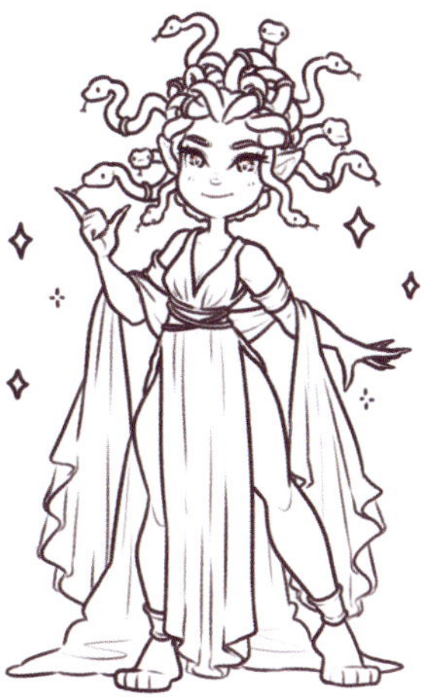

26. Neatly draw the line art over the sketch. Leave space for highlights in the eyes. Add little tongues sticking out of the snake heads and little rings around some of the snake bodies. Add some sparkles if you'd like! Then erase the sketch underneath.

27. Lastly, add color! Make the belt and jewelry gold, the dress and snakes an emerald green. Make her eyes a bright yellow.

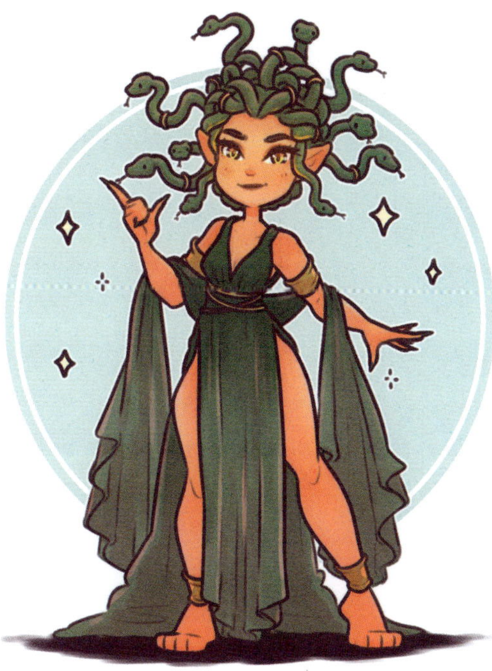

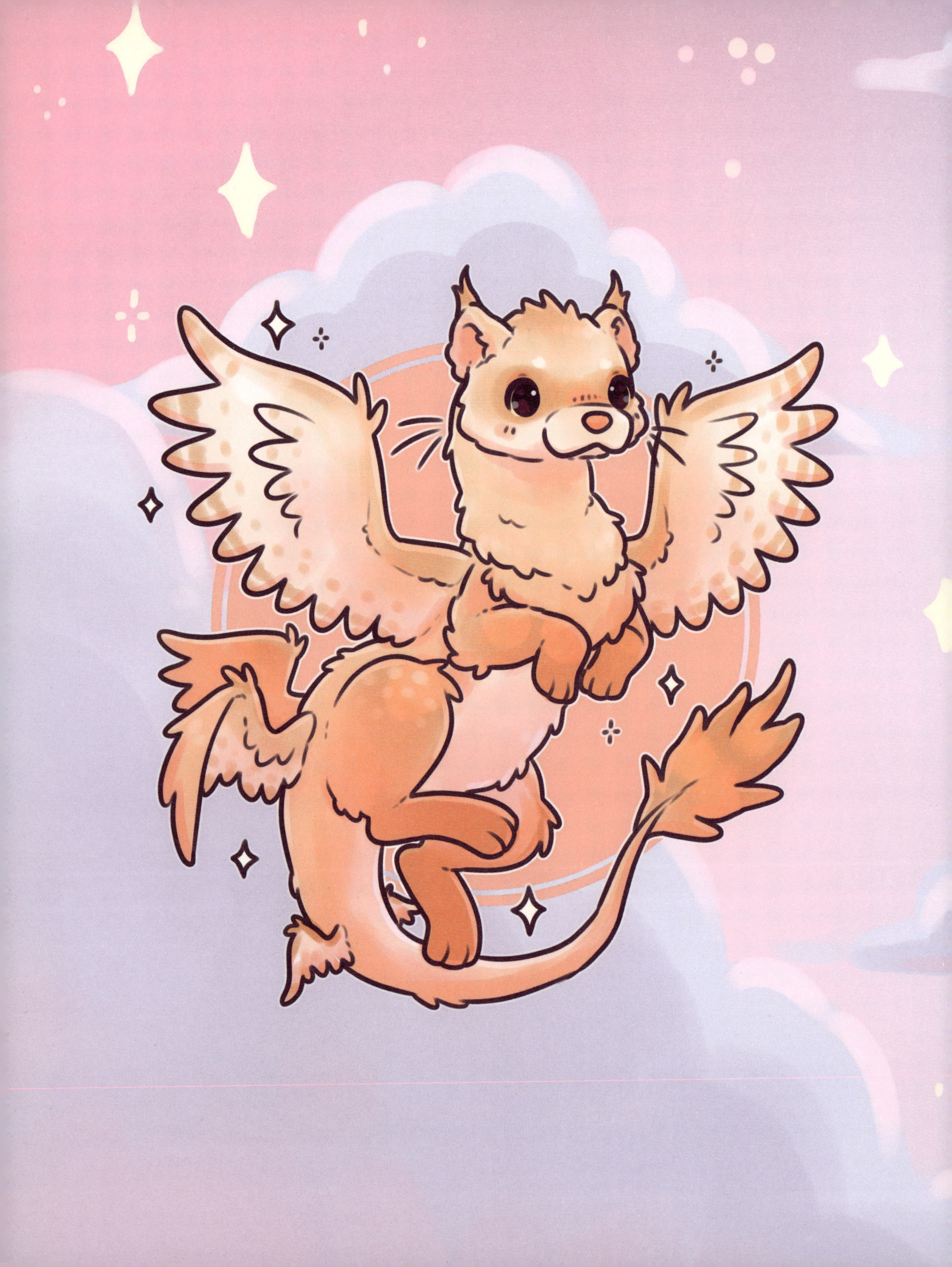

BONUS

MYTHICAL COMBOS

DEER + FOX

I've combined a deer and a red fox by giving it the antlers and hooves of a deer and the body and tail of a fox.

1. Lightly sketch a rounded square head. Add a plus sign (+) guideline for the face.

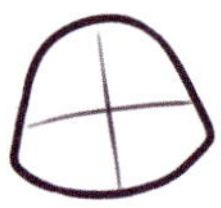

2. Add two pointed ears on either side of the head, each with a curved line inside.

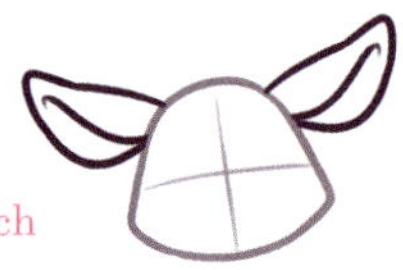

3. Add two curved Vs for the upper body and a curved guideline through the middle.

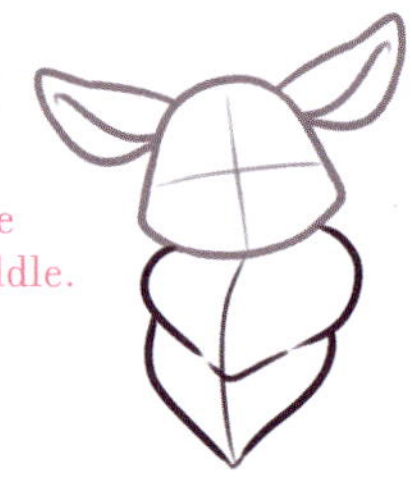

4. Draw a small, rounded rectangle left paw and connect it to the body with two lines.

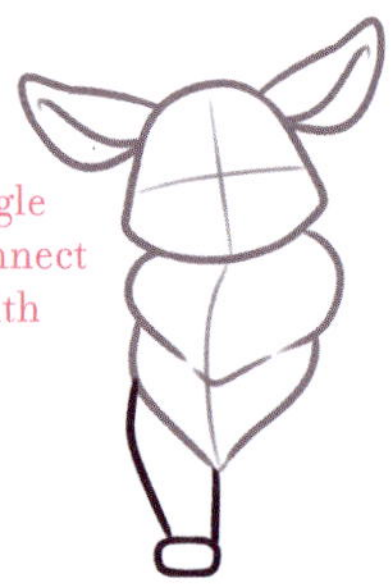

5. On the bottom-right of the V, draw a curved line moving towards the center. Then add a U-shaped paw.

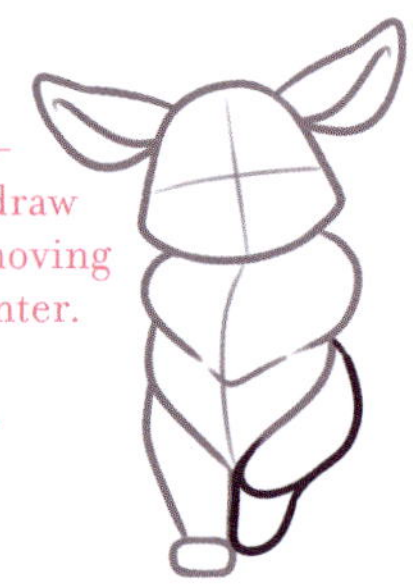

6. Draw a large, roughly U-shaped lower body, keeping an eye on where it passes in front of the front paw. Add an oval haunch next to the right leg.

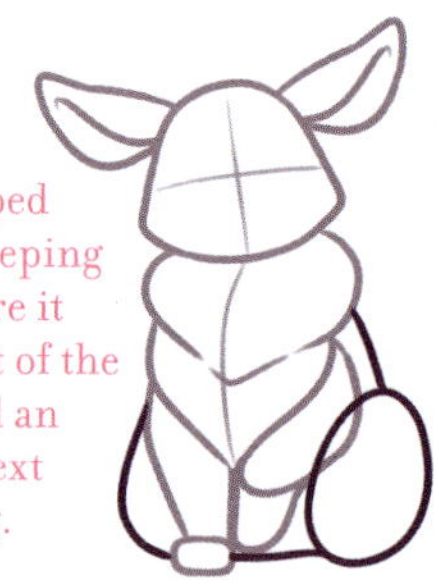

7. Draw two ovals on the bottom of the body for the back hooves.

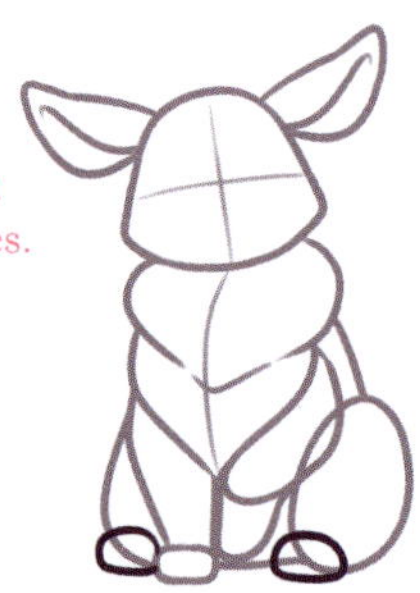

8. Add a curve to the right haunch to start the tail. Then, on the left, draw a wide teardrop-shaped tail curving up to a point.

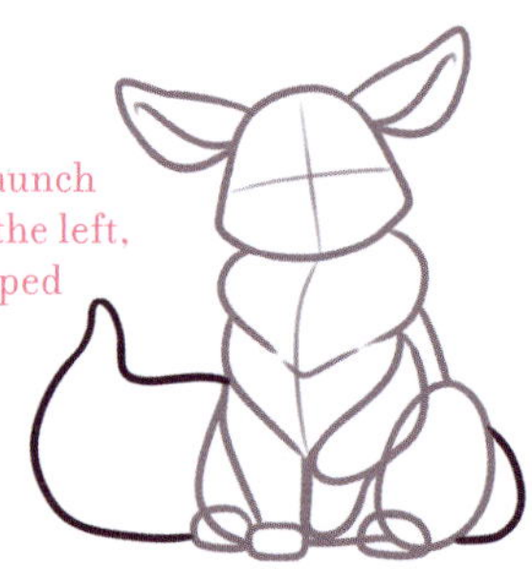

9. On top of the head, draw an angled antler coming to a point. Mirror this on the other side.

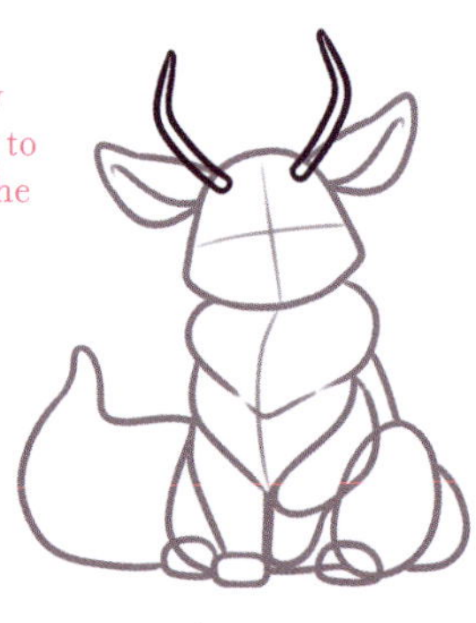

10. Add two prongs on the antlers, with a straight one near the base and an angled one near the tip. Make the antlers roughly symmetrical.

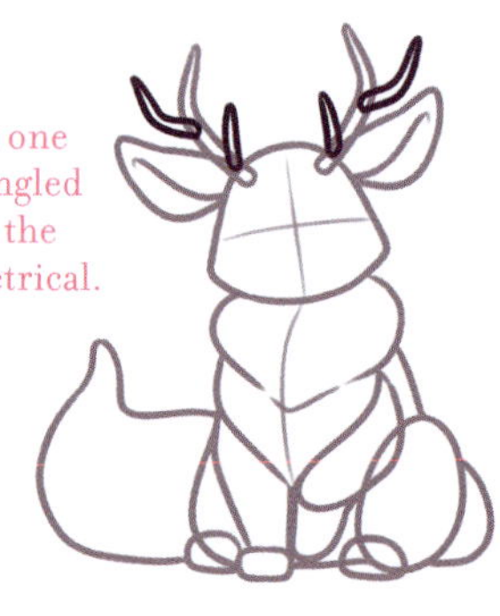

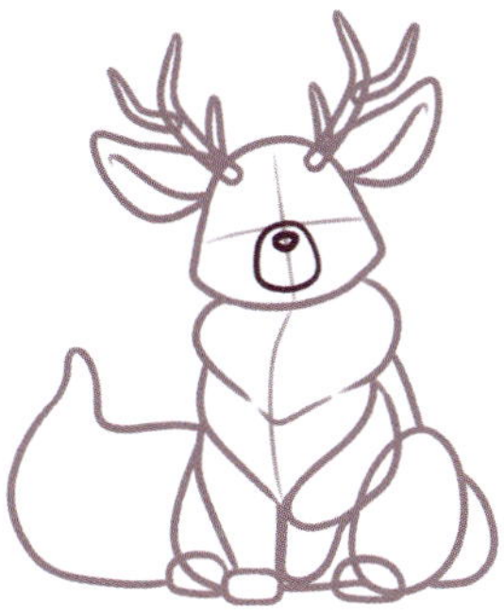

11. On the bottom-middle of the face, draw a rounded square snout. Then add a triangle nose at the top of the snout.

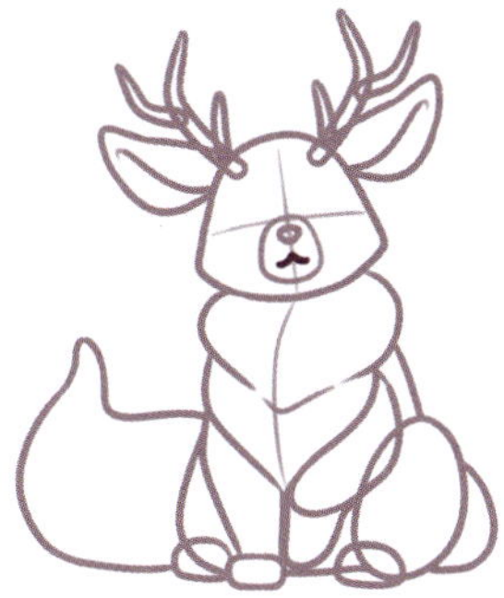

12. Add a gentle W mouth, but don't extend the sides up.

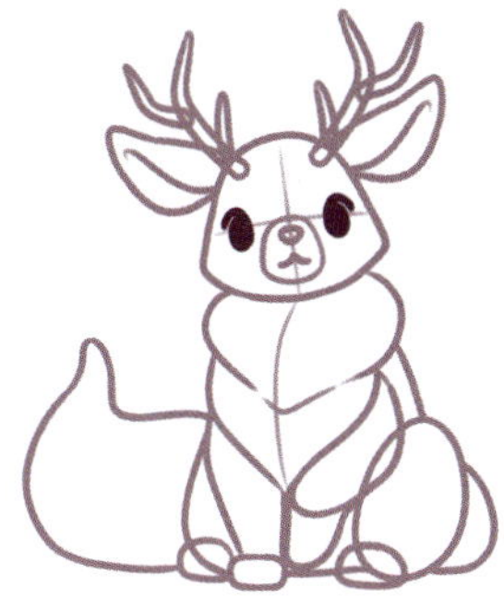

13. Draw two oval eyes with a curved line around the top.

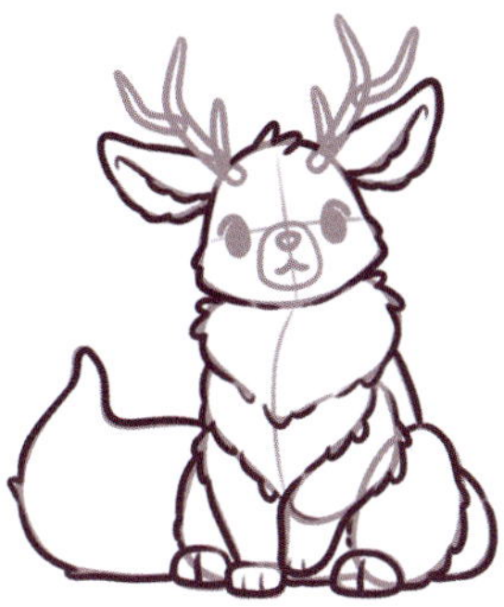

14. Lightly go over the basic sketch of the body and add details. Define the fur with soft W shapes. Add toe lines to the paws and the back hooves.

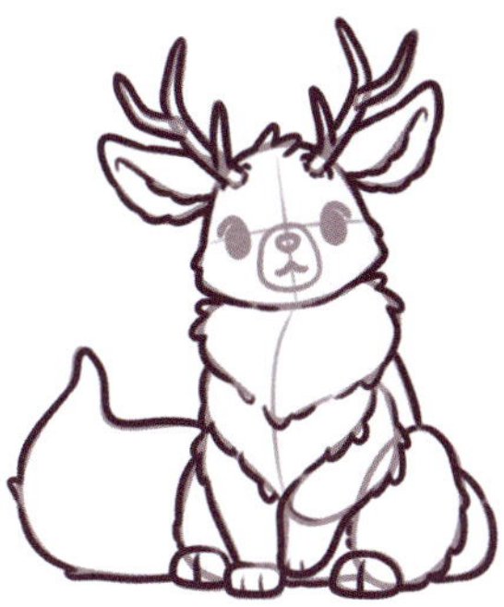

15. Sketch the antlers and add fluff at the base where they meet the head.

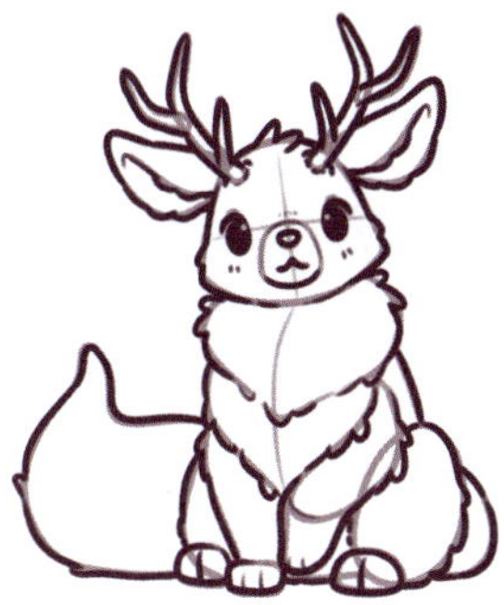

16. Go over the face, leaving a little space inside the eyes for highlights. Add dashes of blush on the cheeks.

17. Neatly draw the line art over the sketch. Add some sparkles if you'd like! Then erase the sketch underneath.

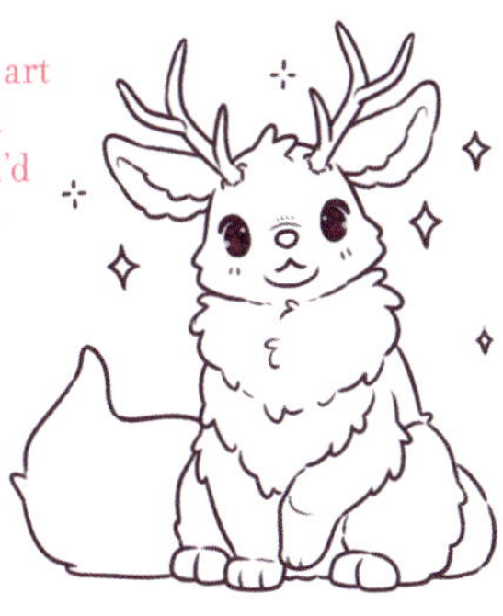

18. For the coat use orange, then use dark brown for the legs, the tops of the ears and antlers. Use a pale cream for the chest, lower face, and spots, and pale pink for the inner ears and on the cheeks, with yellow for the eyes.

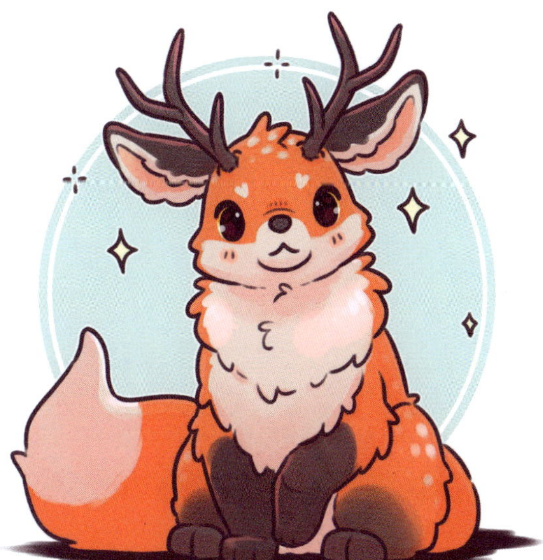

CAT + BARN OWL

A fun spin on a griffin, this creature has the body and ears of a house cat and the head and wings of an owl.

1. Lightly sketch an oval with pointed sides. Add a plus sign guideline for the face.

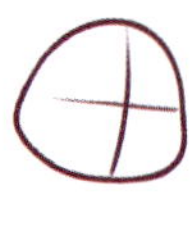

2. Draw two rounded triangle ears on top. Add little flicks at the tip of each ear with an arch inside the left and a line in the right.

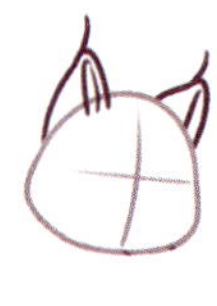

3. Draw a rounded V neck with a curved guideline down the middle.

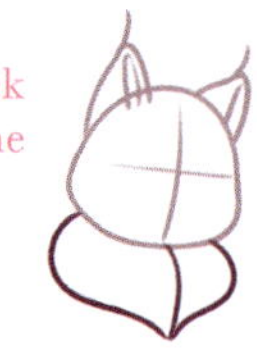

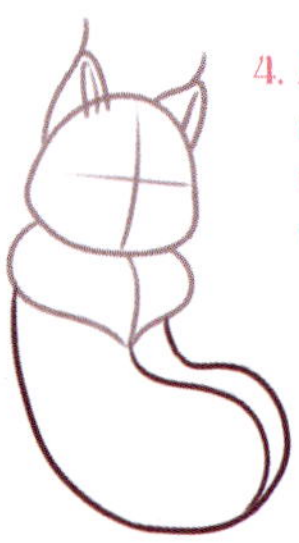

4. Add a large bean-shaped body. Continue the guideline down the right side.

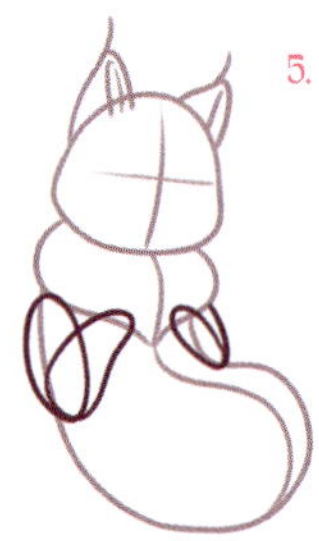

5. Under the neck on either side, draw two ovals in a V shape for the arms.

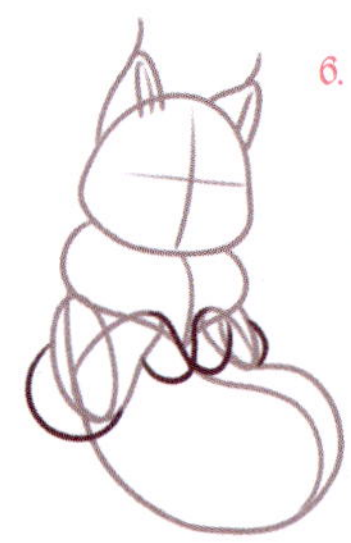

6. Draw U-shaped paws pointed to the center of the body. Around the elbows draw a curve for the feathers.

7. At the lower end of the body, draw a circle for the back leg. For the right leg, draw a curve.

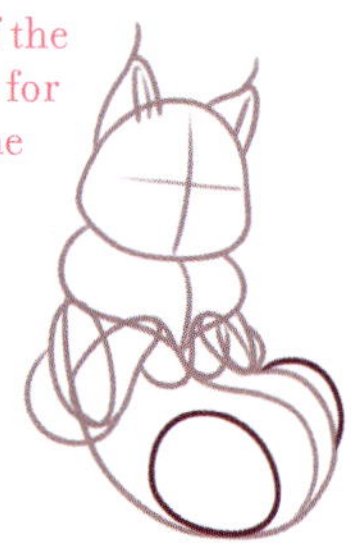

8. Draw two long, curved ovals at the end of the legs for the back paws.

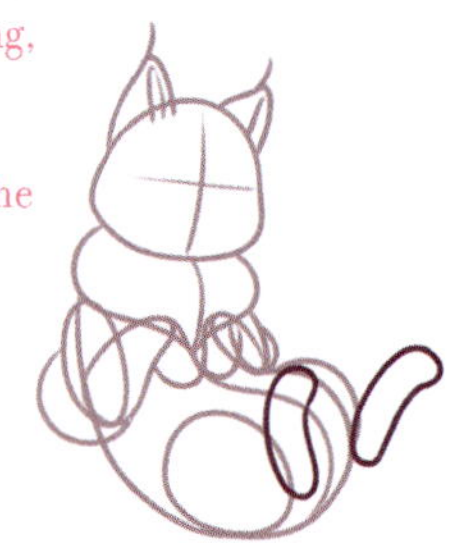

9. Sketch the tail curling out from the end of the body. Add a teardrop-shaped tip.

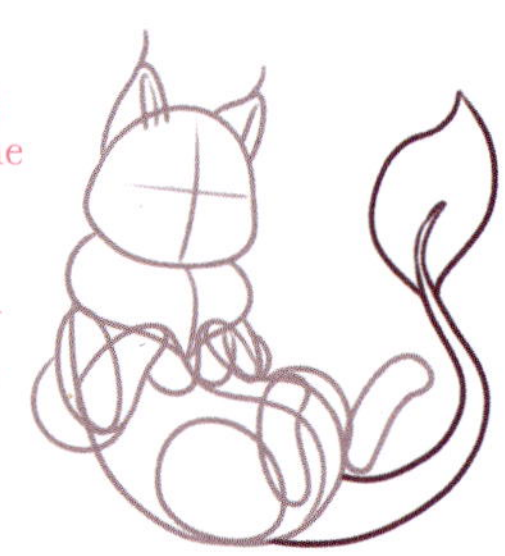

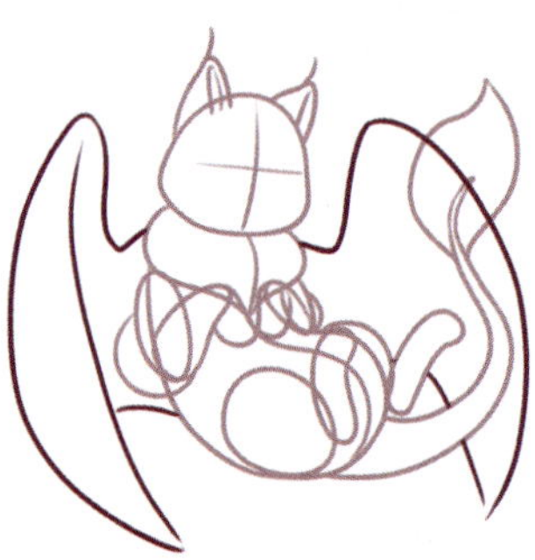

10. Sketch the wings at each shoulder with a line that goes up and arcs down to a point. Add a curve to the left wing.

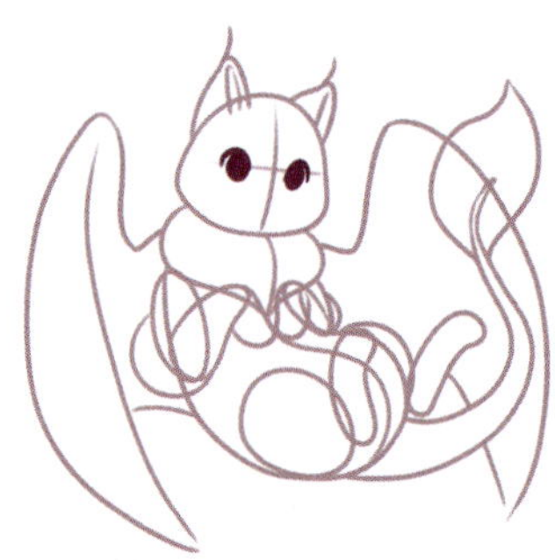

11. Draw two oval eyes with a curve around the top.

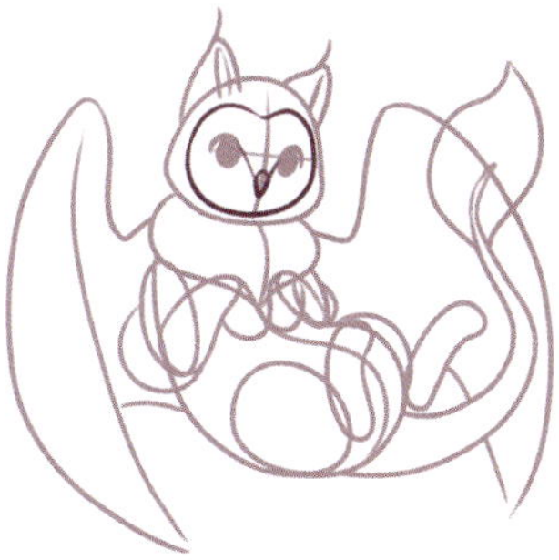

12. Draw a rounded heart shape around the face. Draw a V between the eyes with a small beak in the center.

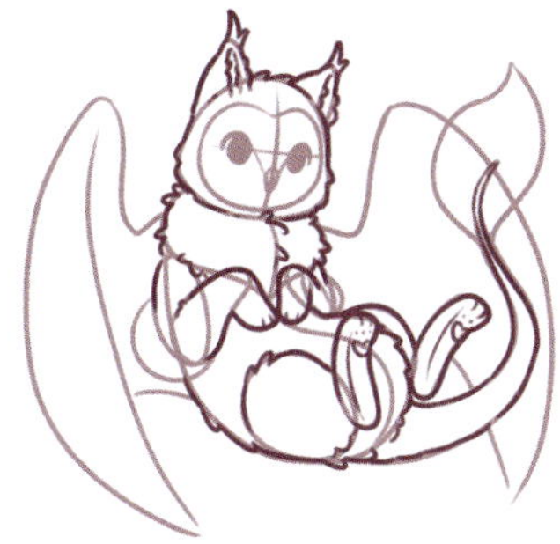

13. Lightly go over the basic sketch, adding details to the head and body. Define the fur with soft W shapes. Add the toe beans and paw pads on the feet.

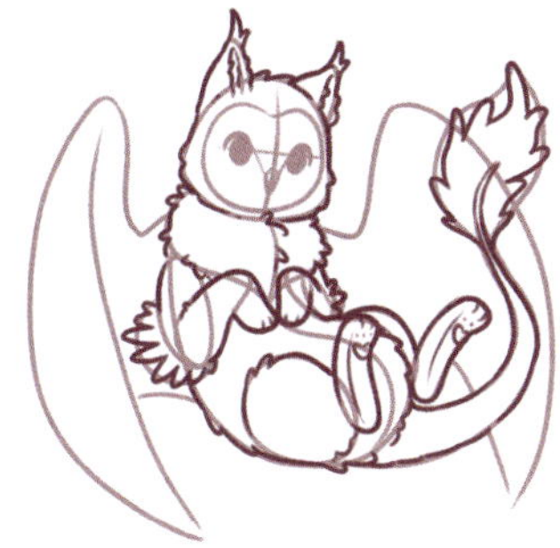

14. Sketch feathers on the elbows and the tip of the tail.

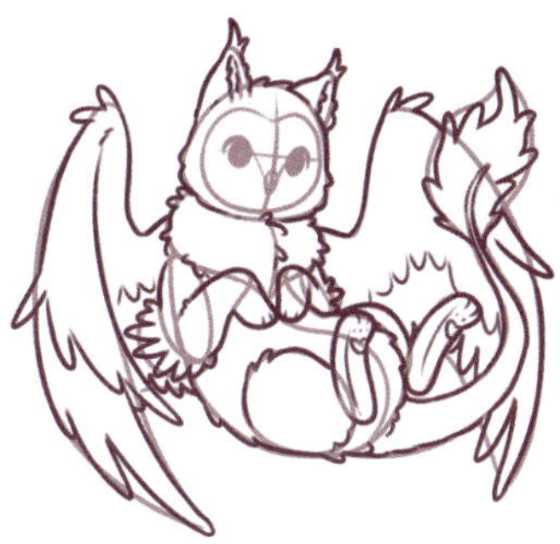

15. Sketch the wings, using long U shapes along the bottom and middle for the feathers.

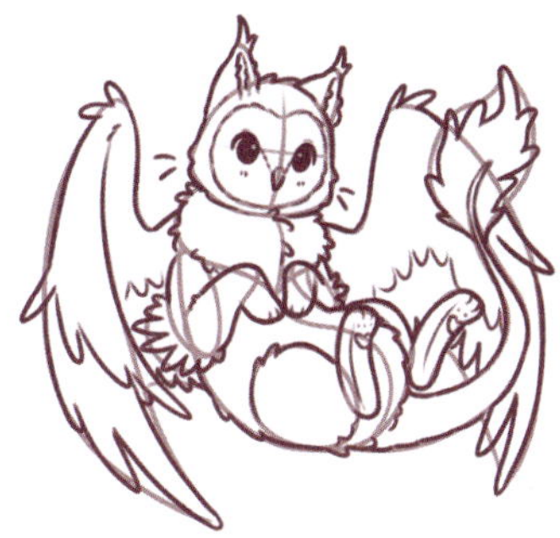

16. Sketch the face detail, adding highlights in the eyes and dashes on the cheeks.

17. Neatly draw the line art over the sketch. Add some sparkles if you'd like! Then erase the sketch underneath.

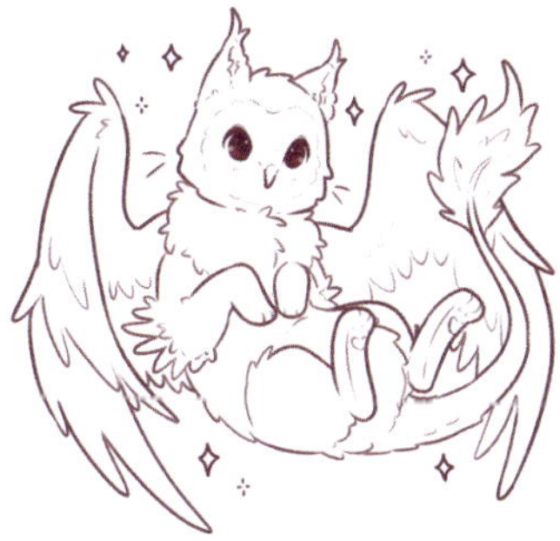

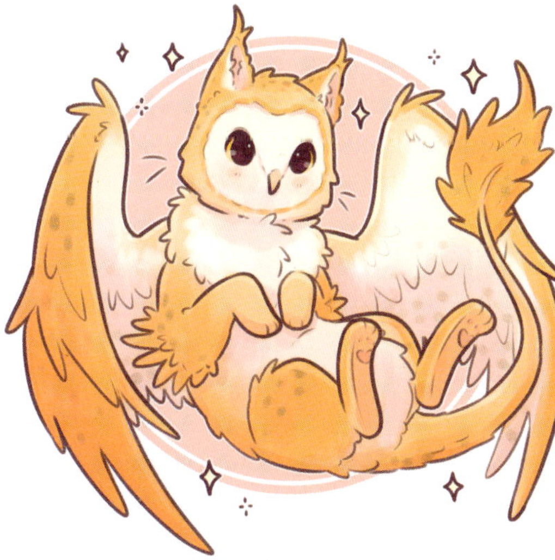

18. Finishing up, I used a traditional barn owl coloring, with gold for the body and white on the face and stomach.

RAVEN + CAT

Here's a combination of a black cat's head, body, and legs with raven wings for a very witchy griffin.

1. Lightly sketch an oval with pointed sides. Add a plus sign guideline for the face.

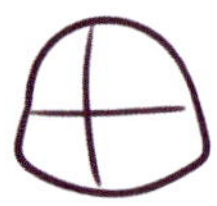

2. On top of the head, draw two triangle ears. Add little flicks on top of the ears and a smaller triangle inside the ears.

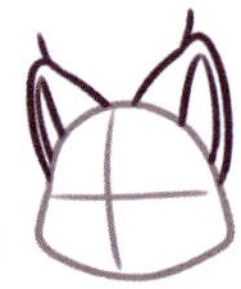

3. Draw a rounded V neck with a curved guideline down the middle.

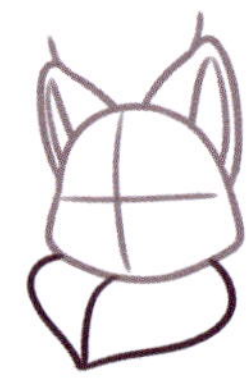

4. Add a bean-shaped body. Continue the guideline down the left side.

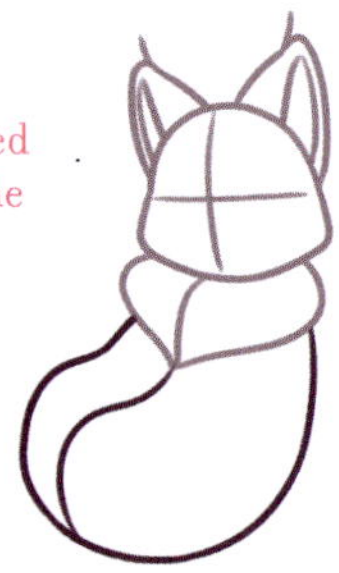

5. Draw two oval arms pointed toward the head. Draw a curve to join the right arm to the body.

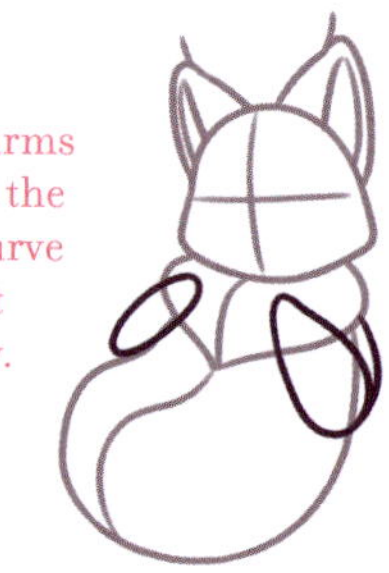

6. Draw little U-shaped paws at the ends of the ovals, pointed down. Add small "thumbs" on the inner sides.

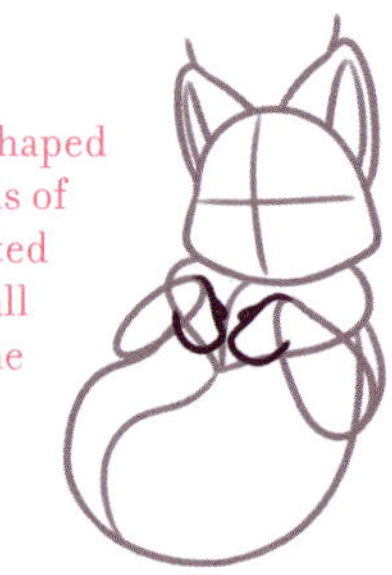

7. At the bottom-right of the body, draw a circle for the back leg. Draw a curve on the other side of the body for the left leg. At the ends of the legs, draw curved oval feet.

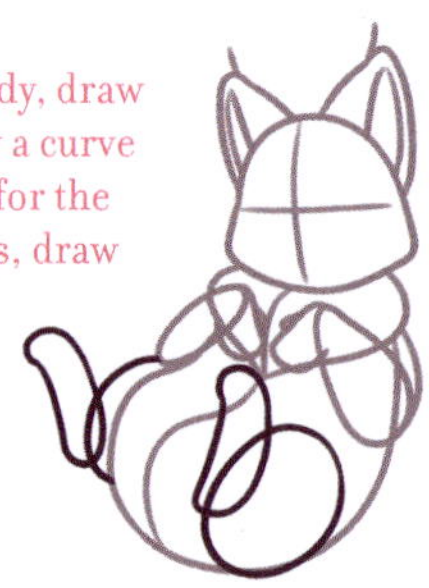

8. Sketch the tail curling out from the end of the body with two curved lines narrowing into a teardrop tip.

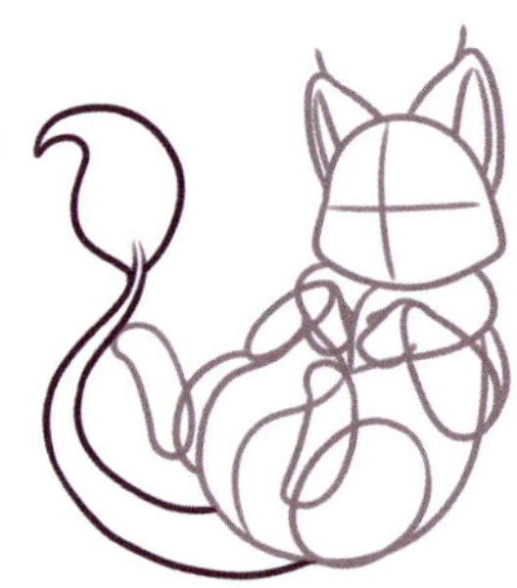

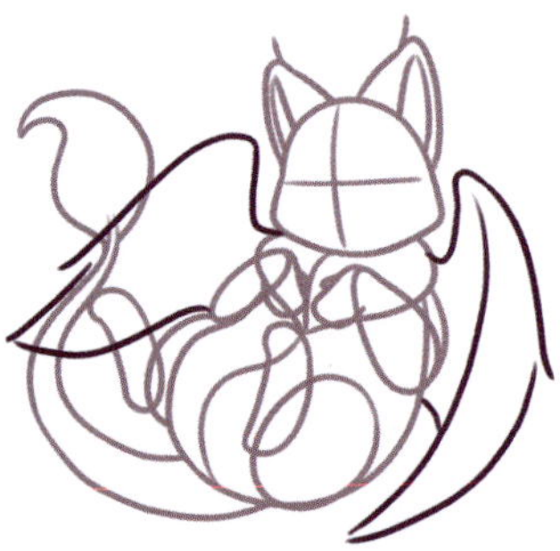

9. Sketch the wings at the shoulders with arcing lines.

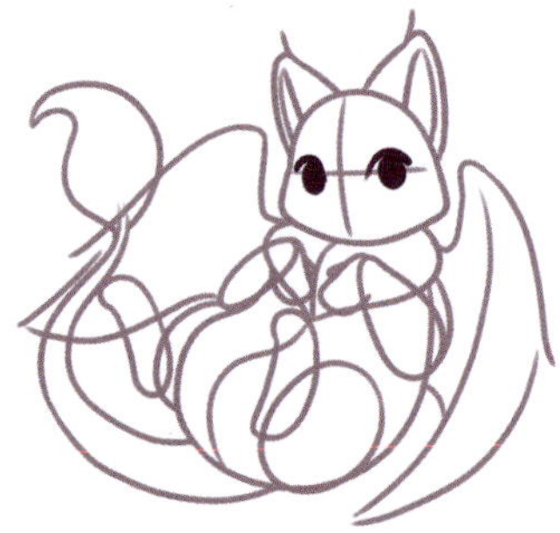

10. Draw two oval eyes with a curve around the top.

11. In the middle of the face, draw a small, triangle nose and a small W mouth. Add a U under the mouth for the tongue sticking out.

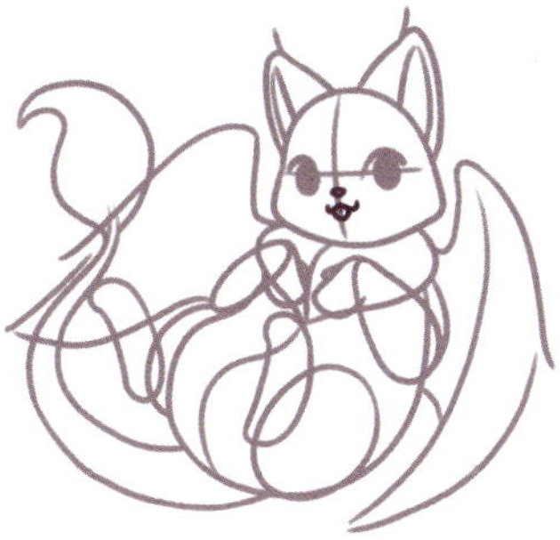

12. Lightly go over the basic sketch, adding details of the head and body. Define the fur with soft W shapes. Add the toe beans and paw pads to the feet. Keep the top paws smooth as these will be bird feet.

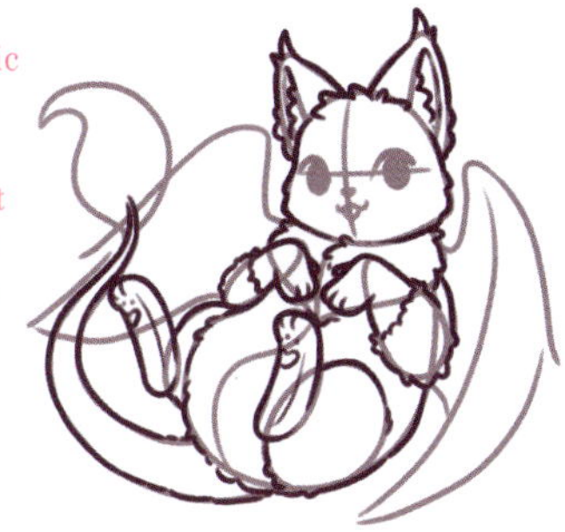

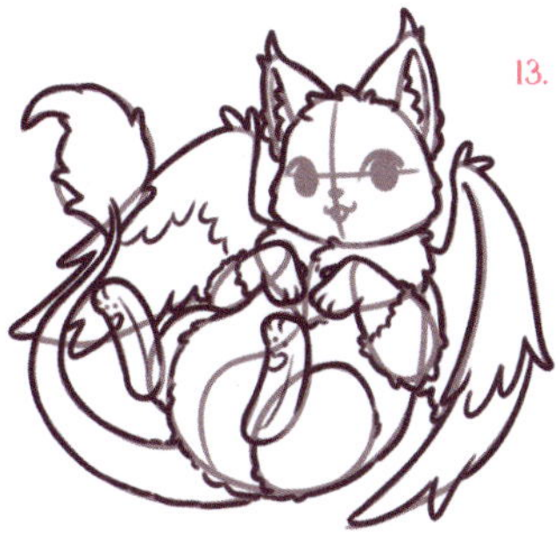

13. Sketch the wings and tail tuft, using long U shapes for the feathers.

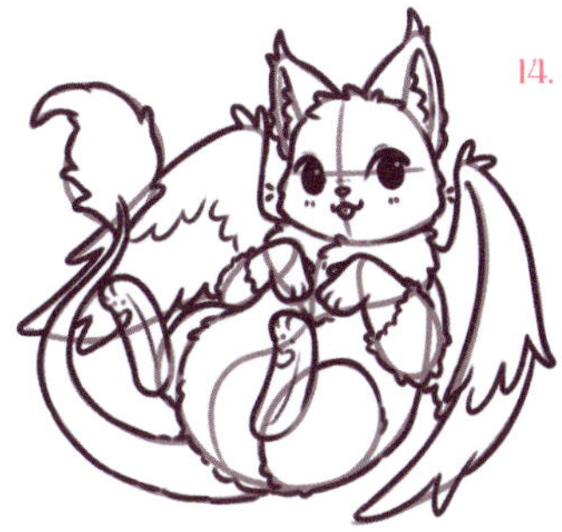

14. Sketch the face detail. Add highlights in the eyes and dashes on the cheeks for blush and on the sides of the head for whiskers.

15. Neatly draw the line art over the sketch. Add some sparkles if you'd like! Then erase the sketch underneath.

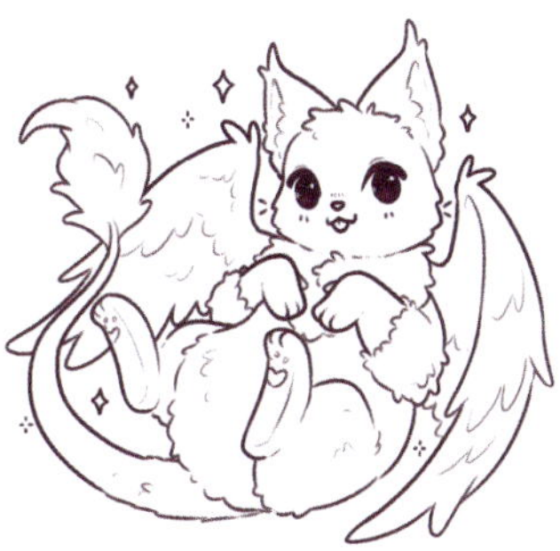

16. When coloring, use black for the fur, light blue for the eyes, and gray for the front bird's feet.

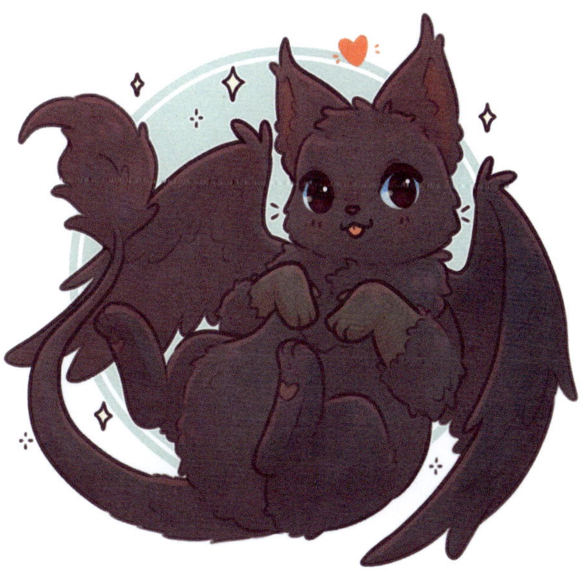

SHARK + DOG

The similar coloring of the husky and the great white shark inspired this combo! It has the head and body of a dog, with the tail and fins of a shark.

1. Lightly sketch an oval with pointed sides. At the bottom, add a hexagonal snout. Add a plus sign guideline for the face.

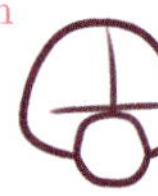

2. Add two triangle ears on top of the head, with two smaller triangles inside.

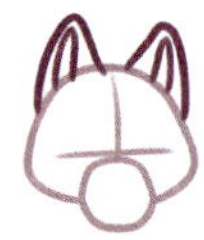

3. On the left of the head, draw the left leg with an oval and two Us coming down, one under the other.

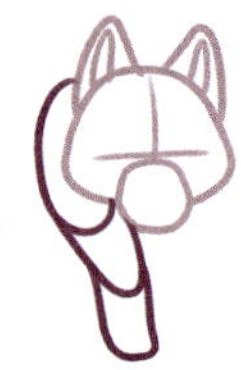

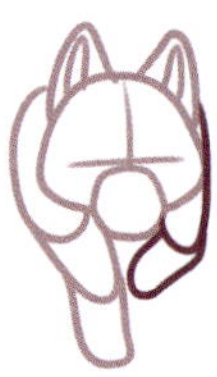

4. On the right side of the head, draw the right leg with two Us connected to each other but pointed to the left.

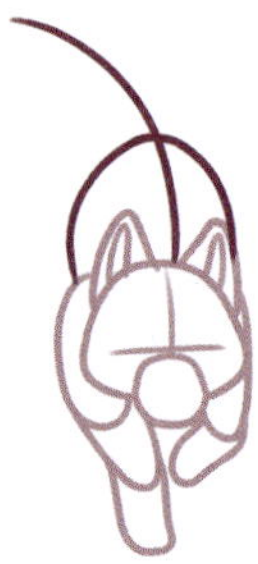

5. Draw a large U on top of the head for the upper body and a guideline curving through the middle for the spine.

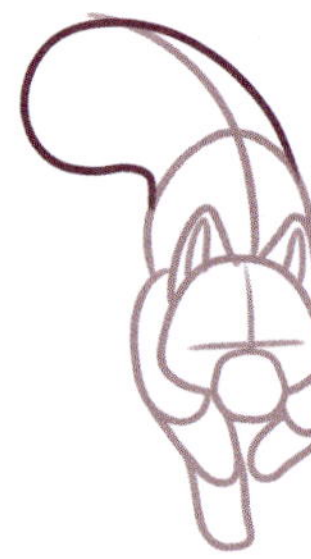

6. Behind the upper body, draw a bean-shaped lower body.

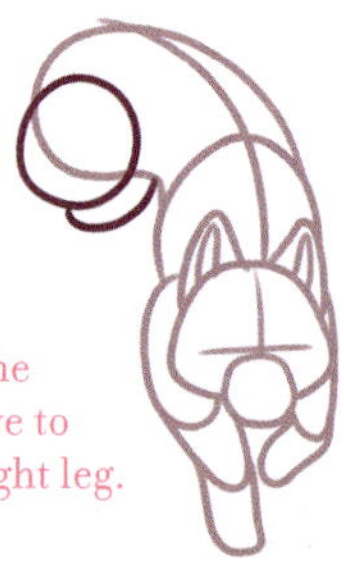

7. Draw a circle for the back leg and a curve to the right for the right leg.

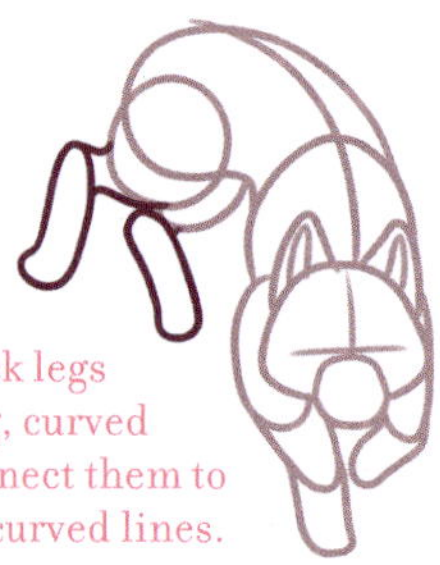

8. Under the back legs draw two long, curved oval feet. Connect them to the legs with curved lines.

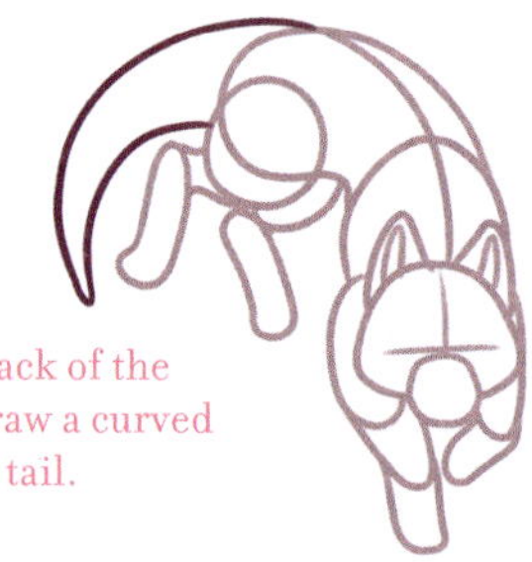

9. At the back of the body, draw a curved pointed tail.

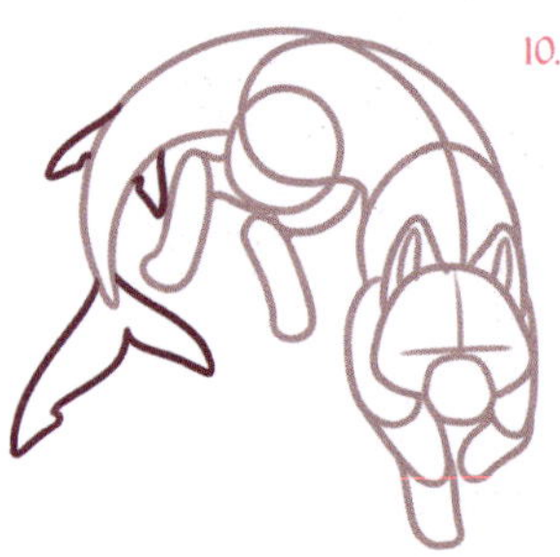

10. Add a shark fin to the tip of the tail in a V shape and two fins on the sides.

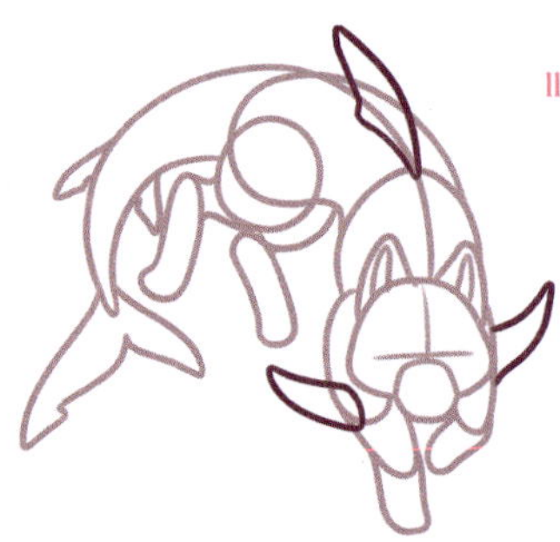

11. Add a triangle along the back for the dorsal fin and two triangles on the side of the front legs for pectoral fins.

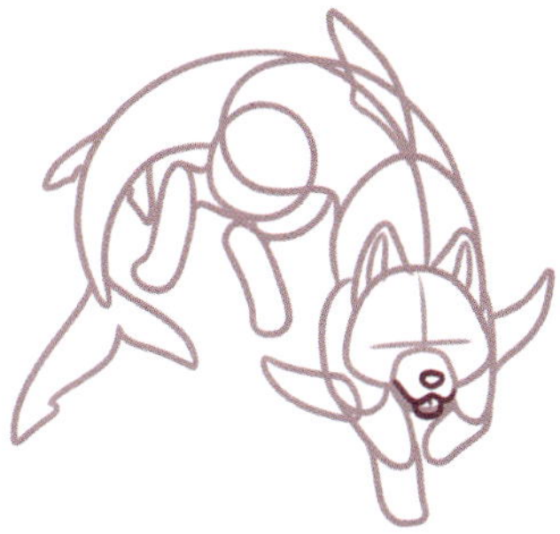

12. On the snout, draw a rounded triangle nose and a W mouth. Draw a small U below the mouth for the tongue sticking out.

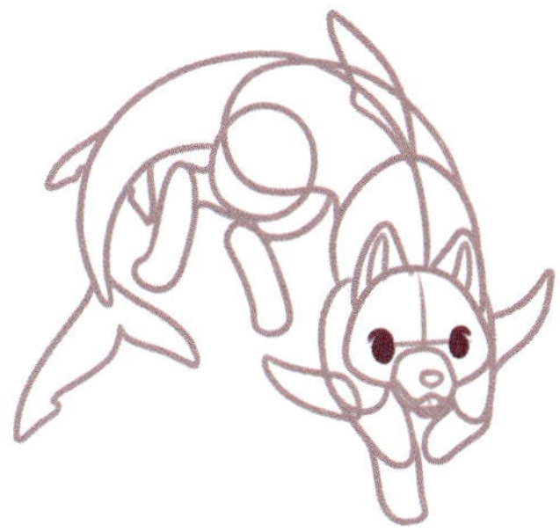

13. Draw two oval eyes with a curve around the top.

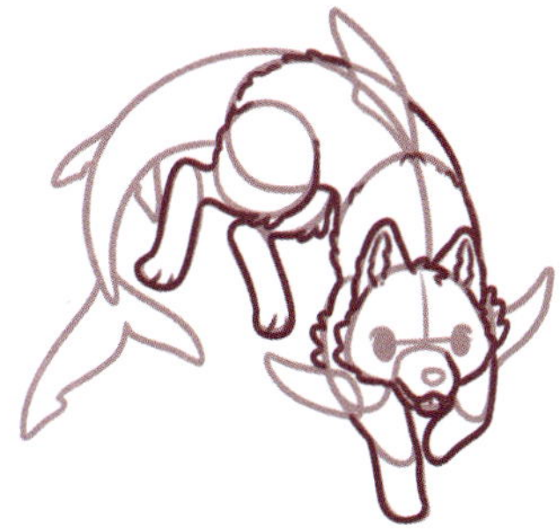

14. Lightly go over the basic sketch, adding details of the head and body. Define the fur with soft W shapes.

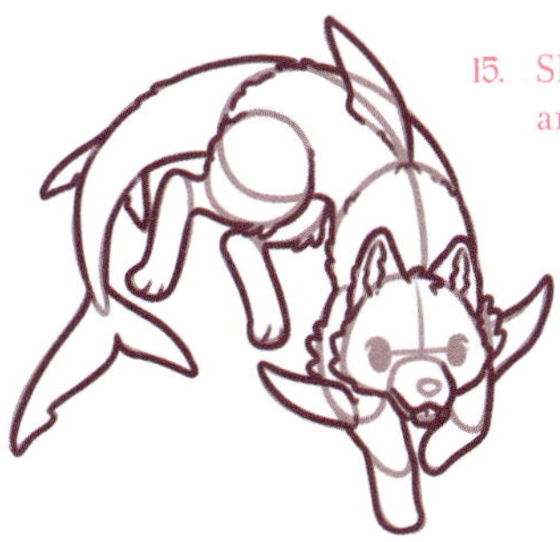

15. Sketch the fins and the tail.

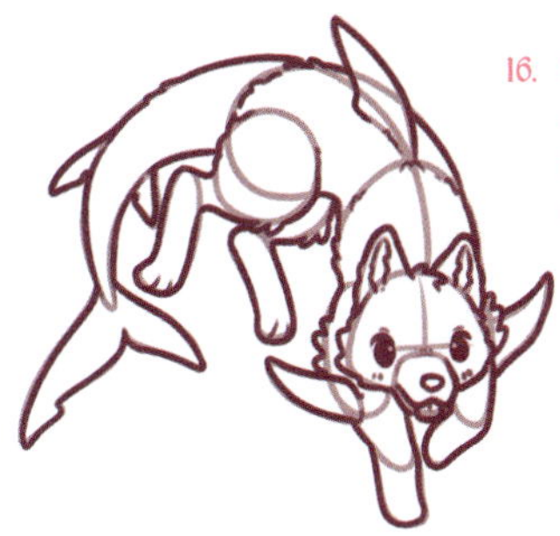

16. Sketch the face detail, adding highlights in the eyes and dashes on the cheeks.

17. Neatly draw the line art over the sketch. Add some sparkles if you'd like! Then erase the sketch underneath.

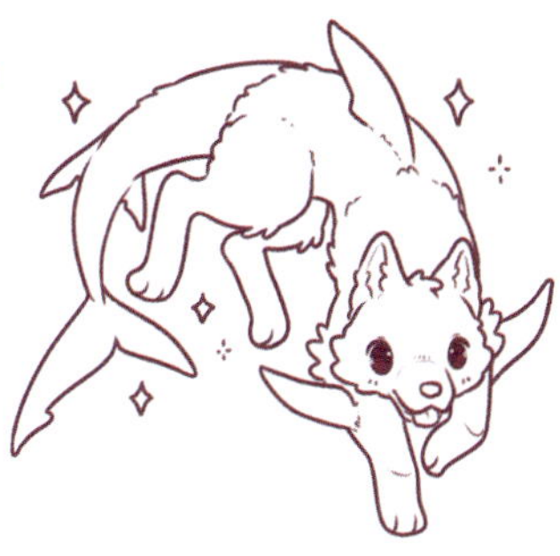

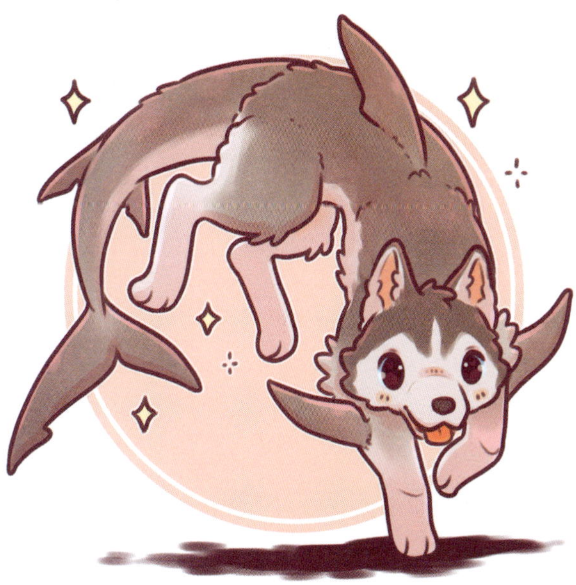

18. Finally, add color! I think gray along the top of the body and fins, and white on the face, paws, and belly works best with this combination.

FOX + KOI

Here's a combo of a fennec fox and a koi fish, with the body and giant ears of the fox and the flowing fins and the whiskers (barbels) of the koi.

1. Lightly sketch an oval with pointed sides. Leave a space in the bottom-middle for the snout. Add a plus sign guideline for the face.

2. At the space, draw a rounded rectangle snout with a dip along the bottom. Add two wavy whiskers coming out the sides of the snout.

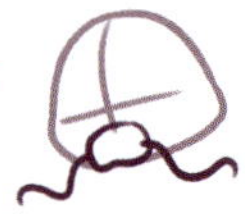

3. Add two large triangle ears on top of the head, each with a smaller triangle inside.

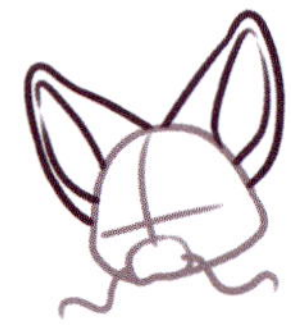

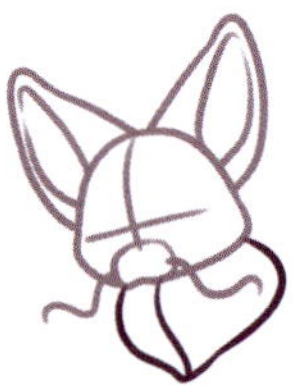

4. Draw a rounded V neck with a curved guideline down the middle.

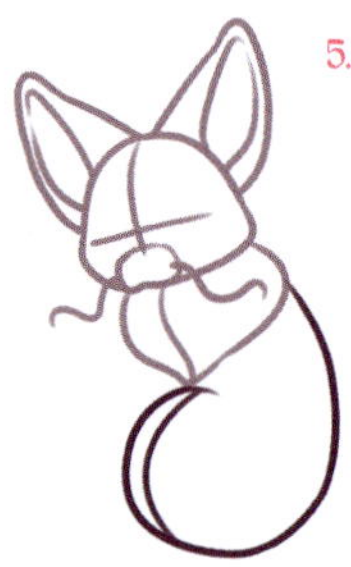

5. Add a bean-shaped body and continue the guideline down the left.

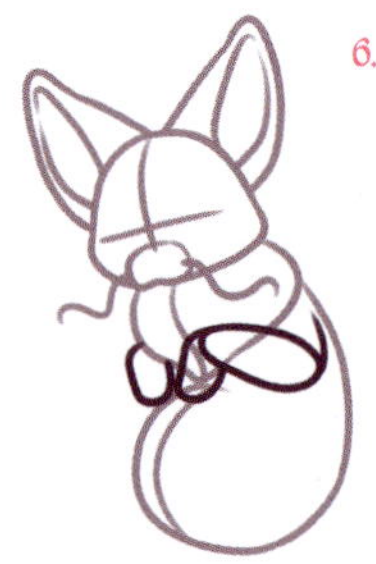

6. Draw an oval for the right front leg under the neck. Connect a U-shaped paw and another paw to the left.

7. At the bottom-right of the body, draw a circle haunch with a curved oval foot at the bottom. For the left leg, draw a curve and another foot.

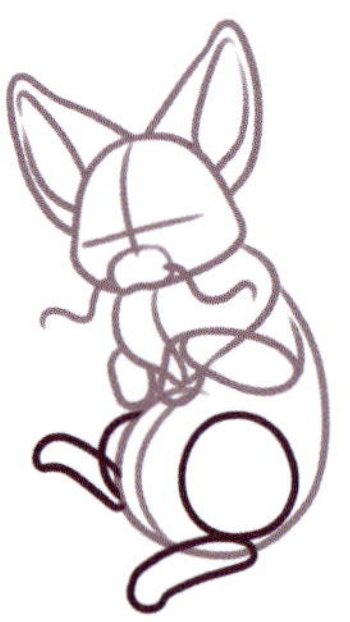

8. Between the feet, draw a large flowing tail that moves up.

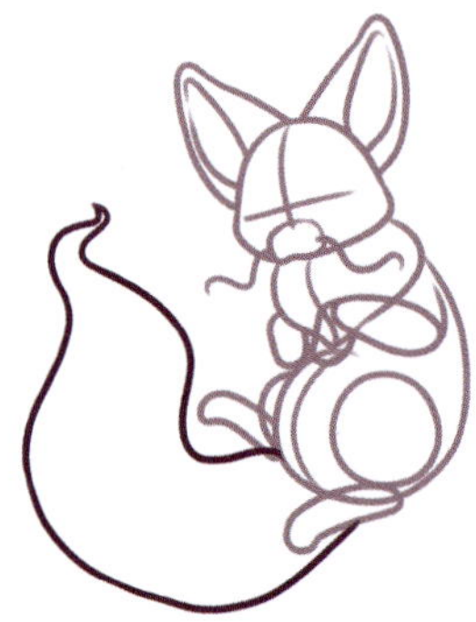

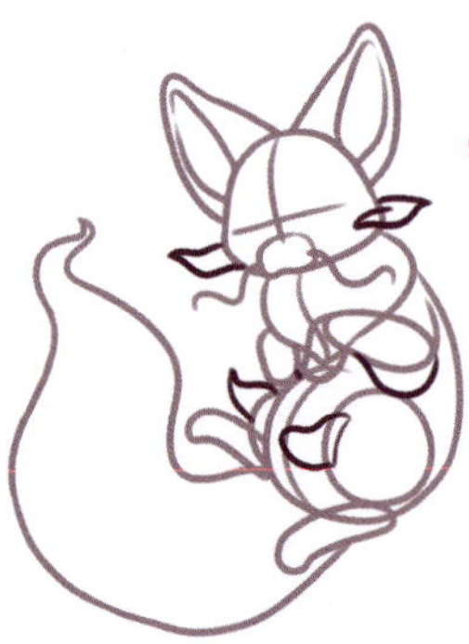

9. Draw small, triangle fins on the sides of the face, under the elbows, and on top of the knees.

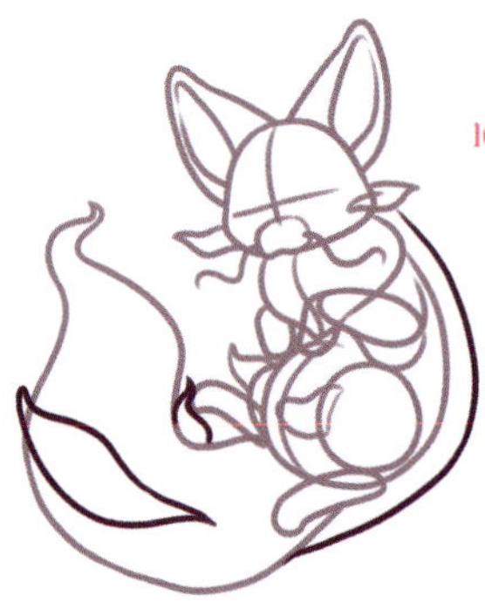

10. Draw a long, curved fin along the back. Then add two fins on the sides of the tail.

11. Draw two oval eyes with a small curve around the top. At the middle of the snout, draw a small, triangle nose.

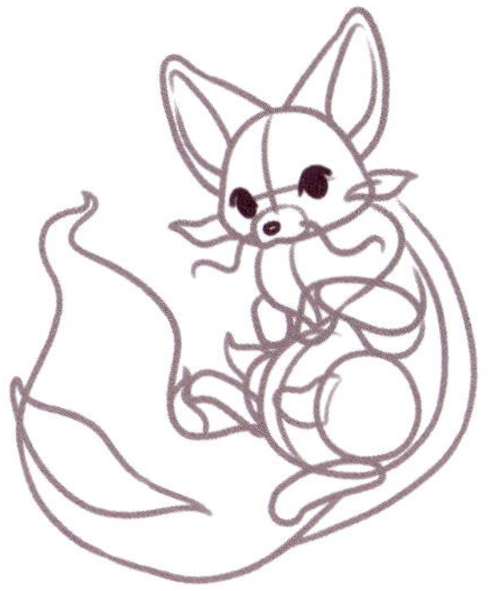

12. Lightly go over the basic sketch, adding details to the head and body. Define the fur with soft W shapes. Add the fish whiskers.

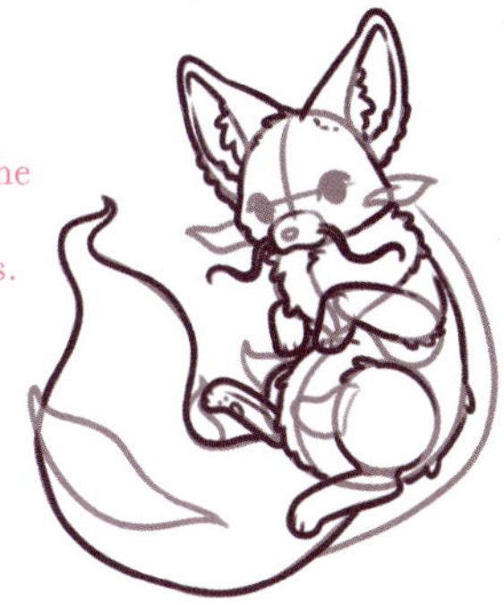

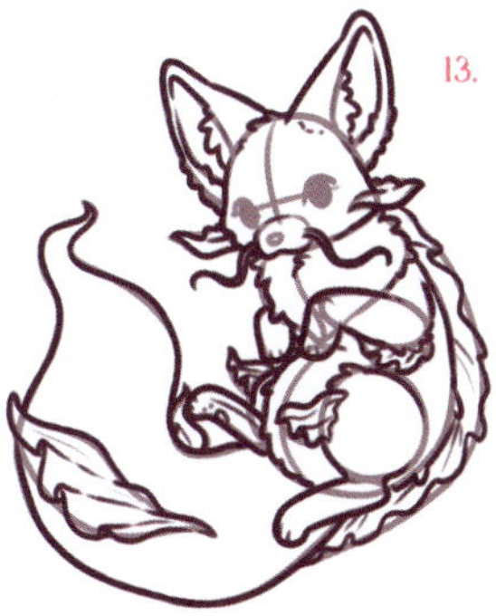

13. Draw details on the fins with short lines.

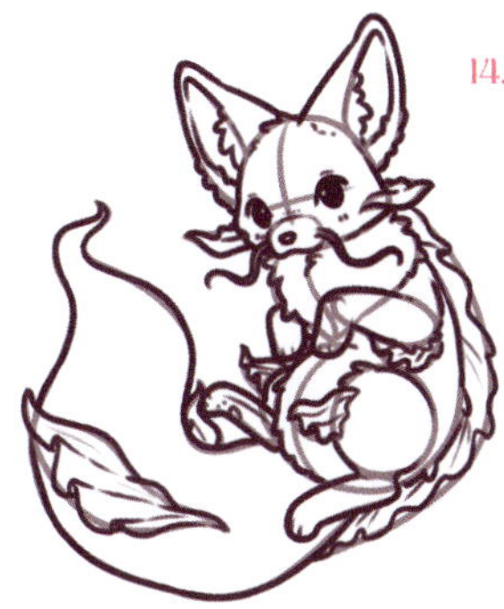

14. Sketch the face detail, adding highlights in the eyes and dashes on the cheeks.

15. Neatly draw the line art over the sketch. Add some bubbles if you'd like! Then erase the sketch underneath.

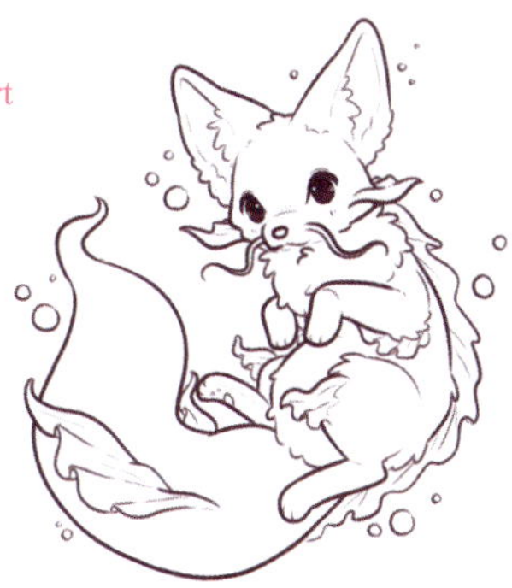

16. Time for color! I went with a traditional koi fish color scheme with orange along the back and white along the stomach, and brown patches on the top of the head and along the body.

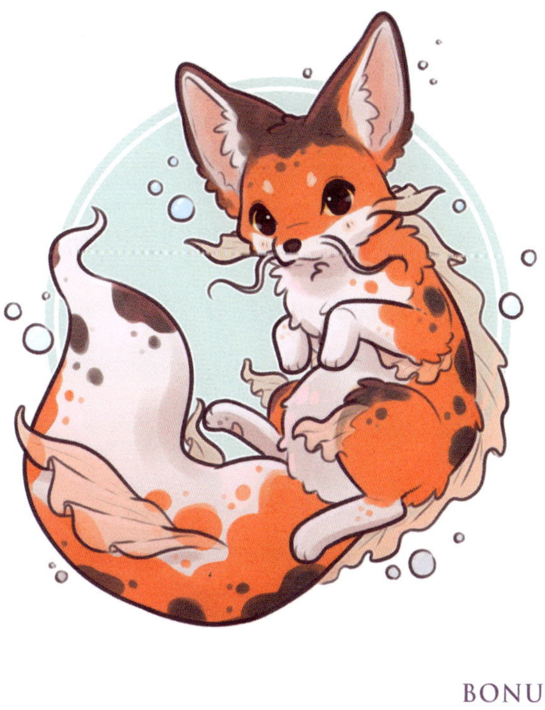

OTTER + FISH

I couldn't resist the chance to create an otter creature, so here's an otter–fish hybrid with the body of an otter and the fins of a fish.

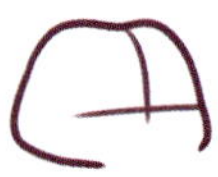

1. Lightly sketch a rectangle head. Leave a space along the bottom-middle for the snout and draw a dip on the top of the head. Add a plus sign guideline for the face.

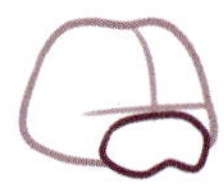

2. At the space, draw a rounded rectangle snout with a dip along the bottom.

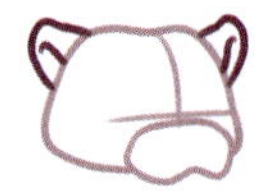

3. On the sides of the head, draw semicircle ears with a curved line inside.

4. Draw a large U neck and a rounded V chest underneath. Add a guideline curving through the middle and to the right.

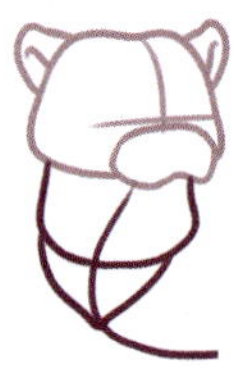

5. At the end of the guideline, draw an oval arm. Attach a small U-shaped paw. Draw a partial left paw.

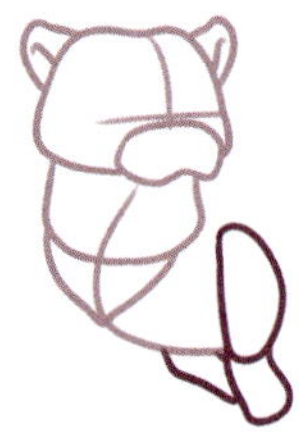

6. Draw two curving lines for the back of the body with a tail that curves under the body and tapers to a point.

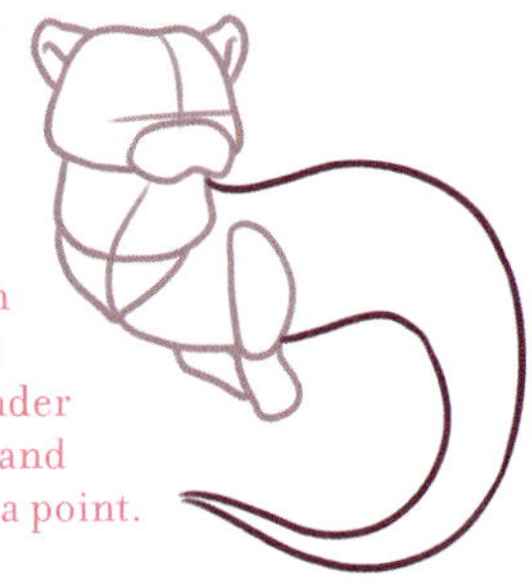

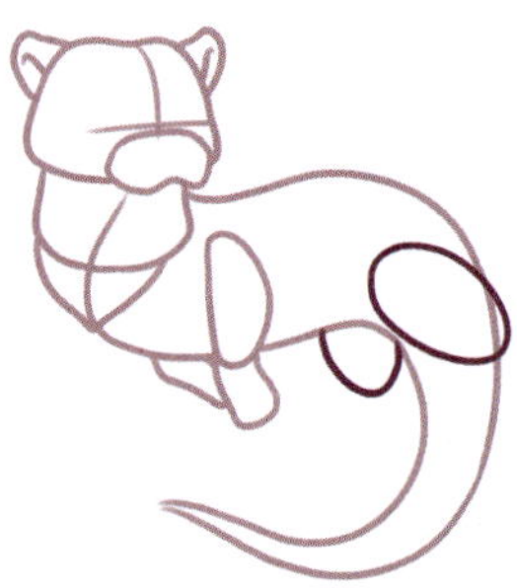

7. Where the tail begins to curve, draw an oval leg. To the left, draw a semicircle for the other back leg.

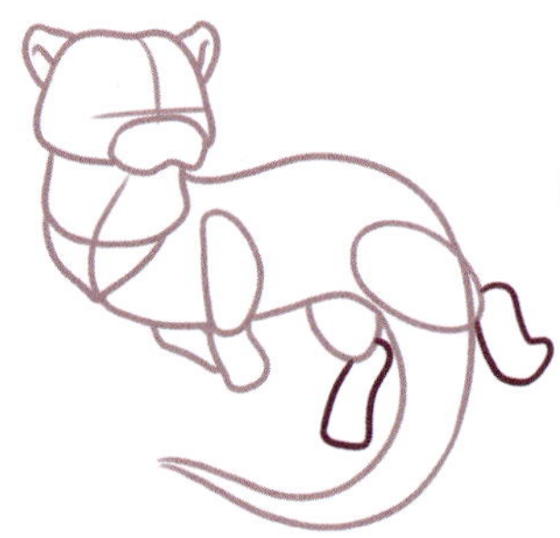

8. At the end of the back legs, draw two curved, rectangle feet.

9. Add small, pointed fins on the sides of the face, behind the arm, and on the sides of the tail.

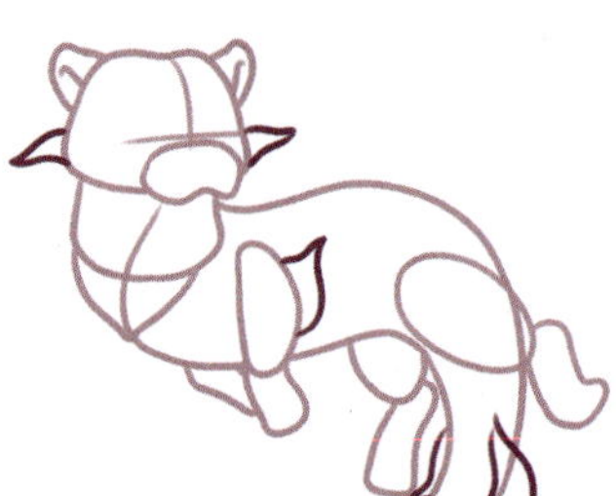

10. Draw a rounded fish tail with forked ends. Then add a fin along the spine from the top of the head to the small fins on the tail.

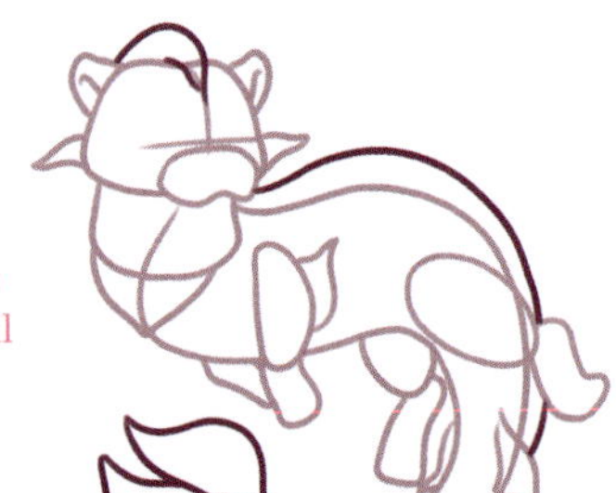

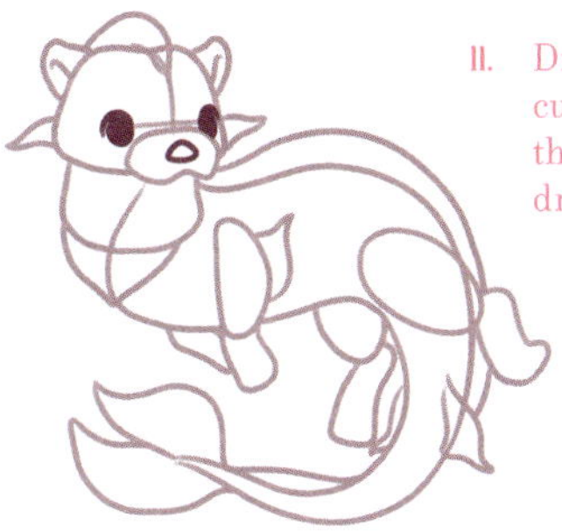

11. Draw two oval eyes with a curve around the top. At the middle of the snout, draw a triangle nose.

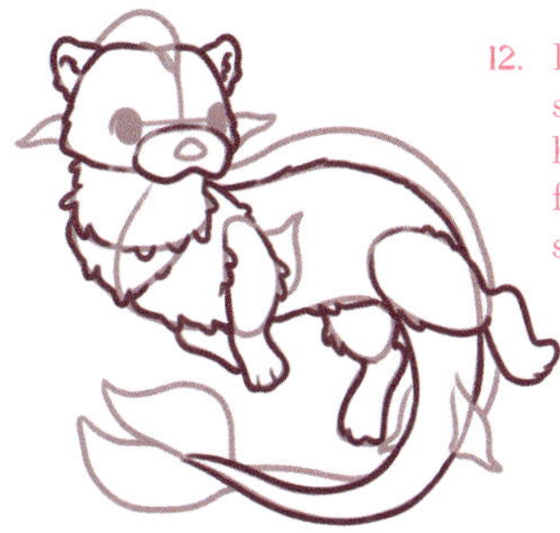

12. Lightly go over the basic sketch, adding details to the head and body. Define the fur with soft W shapes. Add short toe lines to the paws.

13. Draw details on the fins with slanted lines.

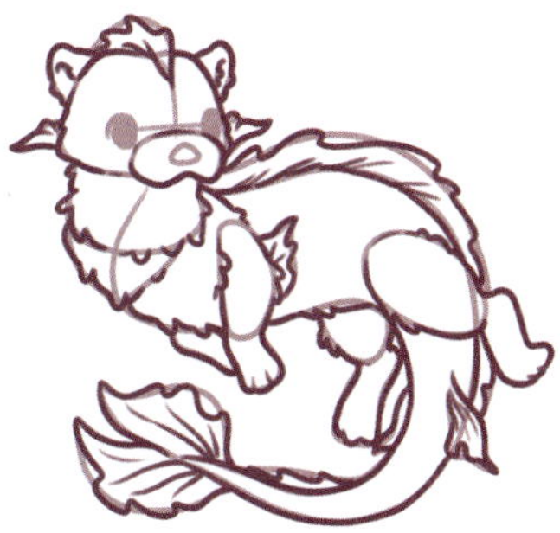

14. Sketch the face detail. Add highlights in the eyes, and dashes on the cheeks for blush as well as large whiskers around the sides of the head.

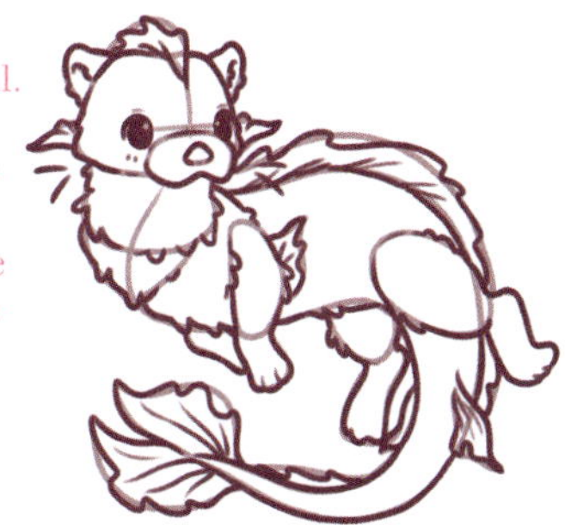

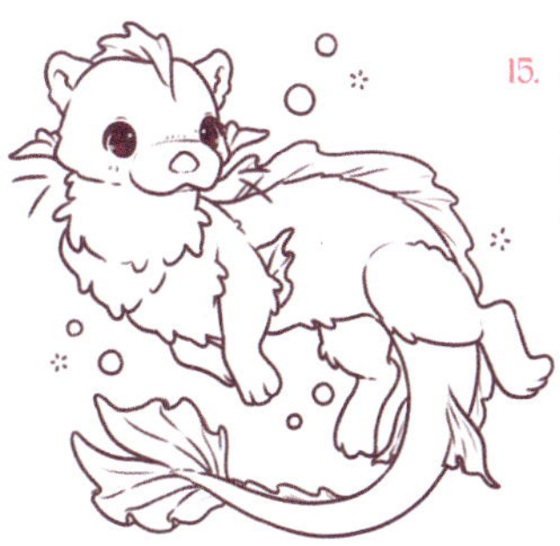

15. Neatly draw the line art over the sketch. Add some bubbles if you'd like! Then erase the sketch underneath.

16. Finish up with color! I chose the traditional river otter color scheme with a brown body and pale brown on the chest. I used blue for the fins.

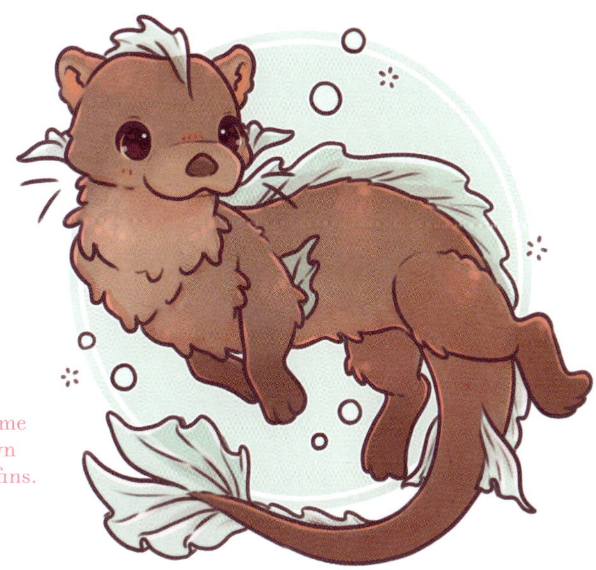

FERRET + EAGLE

A surpisingly cute combo is the winged ferret, with the long body of the ferret and multiple sets of eagle wings along the back and tail.

1. Lightly sketch an oval with pointed sides. Leave a space along the bottom-middle for the snout. Add a plus sign guideline for the face.

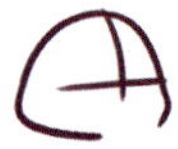

2. At the space, draw a rounded rectangle snout with a dip along the bottom. Draw a line under the dip for a lip.

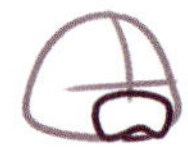

3. On the sides of the head, draw two semicircle ears. Add a line in the ears and little flicks on the tips.

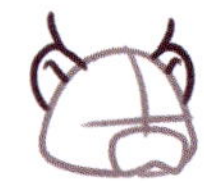

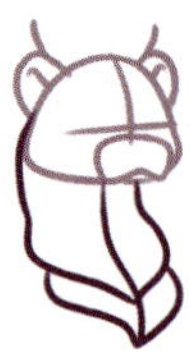

4. Draw a long, curved V neck with a smaller V chest underneath. Add a guideline down the middle.

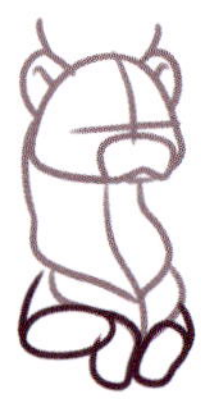

5. Under the chest, draw an oval for the left arm. Connect a U-shaped paw pointed down with the right paw next to it and a small curve for the arm.

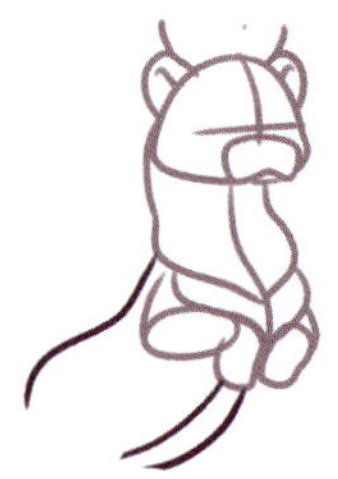

6. Draw an incomplete bean-shaped body. Continue the guideline down the right.

7. Draw an oval for the left leg and a semicircle to the right for a partial right leg.

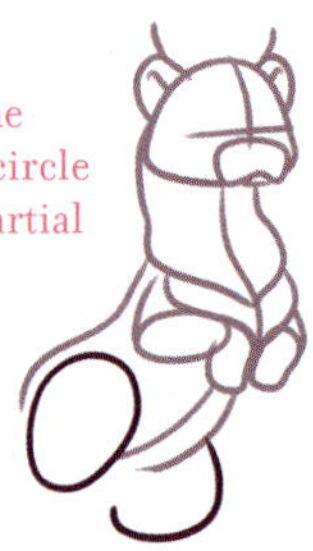

8. At the end of the back legs, draw curved oval feet with the left pointed to the right and the right pointed down.

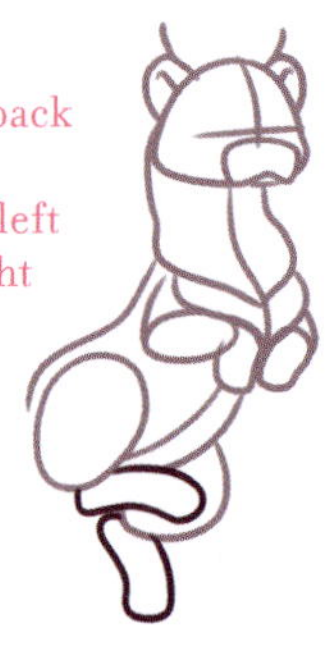

9. Complete the body with a tail curling up and around the body and a teardrop-shaped tip.

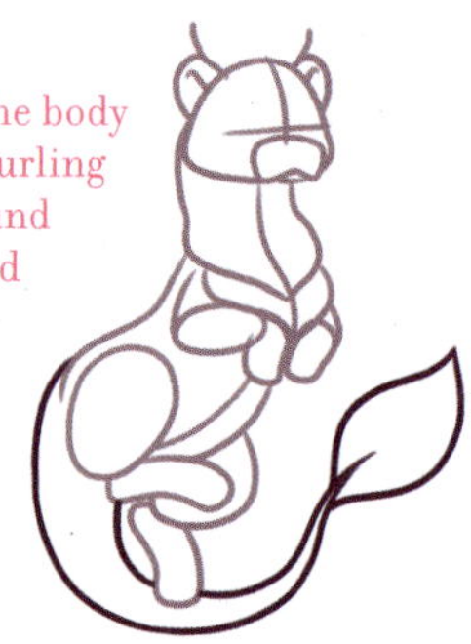

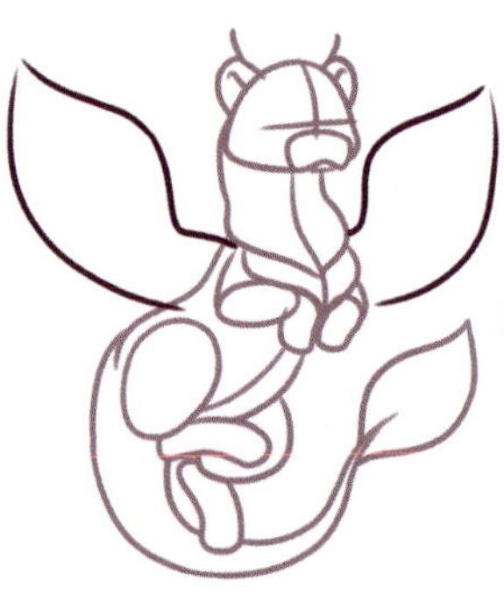

10. On the sides of the shoulders, sketch the wings with arcing teardrop shapes.

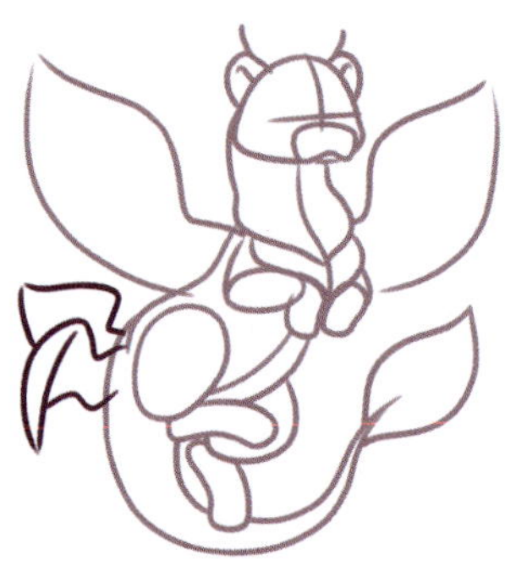

11. Below the left wing, sketch two smaller triangle wings.

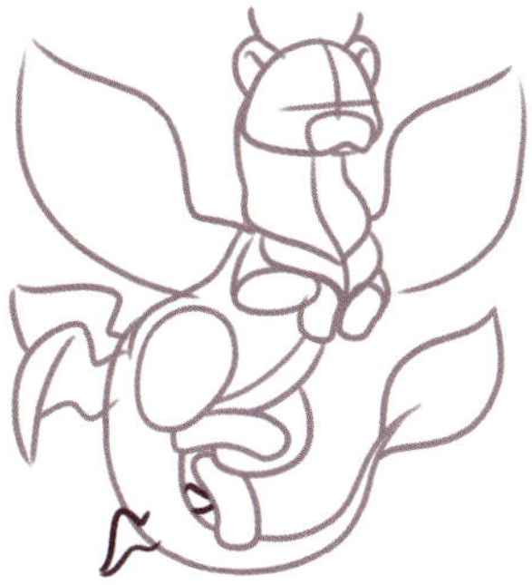

12. Along the tail, by the right foot, sketch two very small wings.

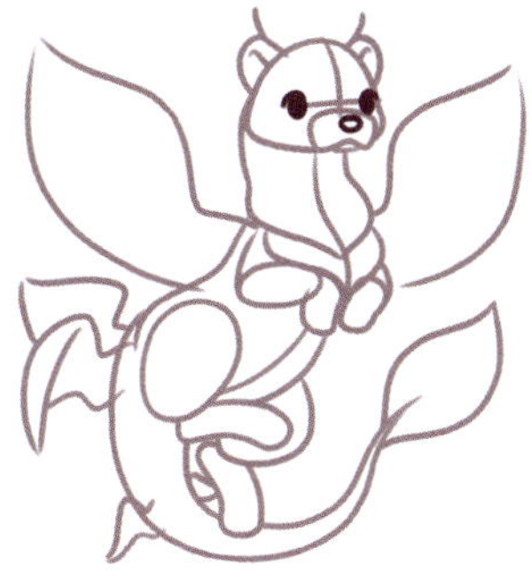

13. Draw two oval eyes with a curve around the top. At the top of the snout, draw an oval nose.

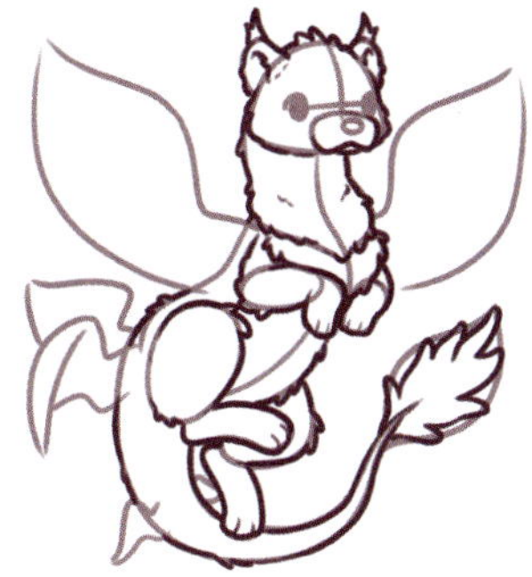

14. Lightly go over the basic sketch, adding details of the head and body. Define the fur with soft W shapes. Add toe lines on the paws and add feathers on the tail tuft.

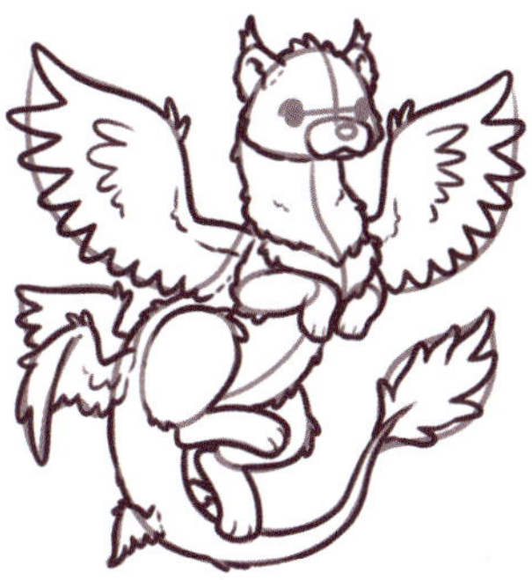

15. Sketch the wings, using U shapes along the bottom and across the middle.

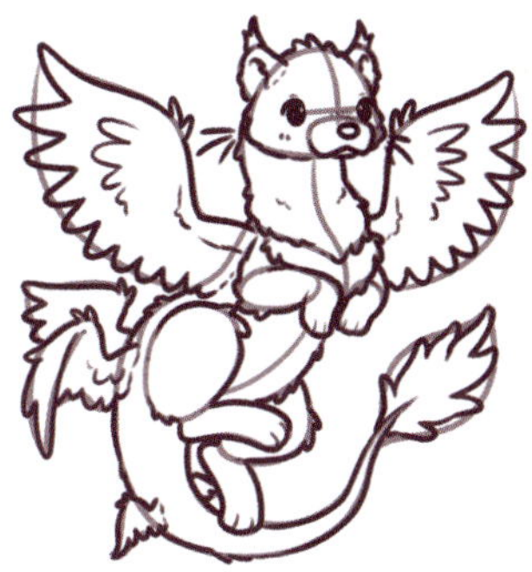

16. Sketch the face detail. Add highlights in the eyes and dashes on the cheeks for blush as well as around the sides of the head for whiskers.

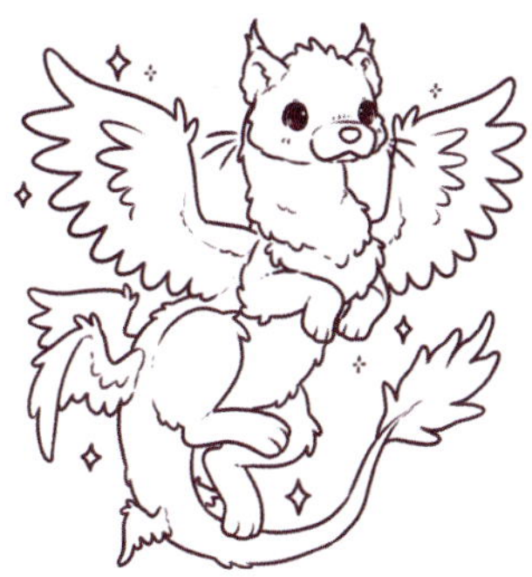

17. Neatly draw the line art over the sketch. Add some sparkles if you'd like! Then erase the sketch underneath.

18. Lastly, add color! I used a pale gold color scheme with dark gold for the little mask marking around the eyes and on the ends of the feet and tail.

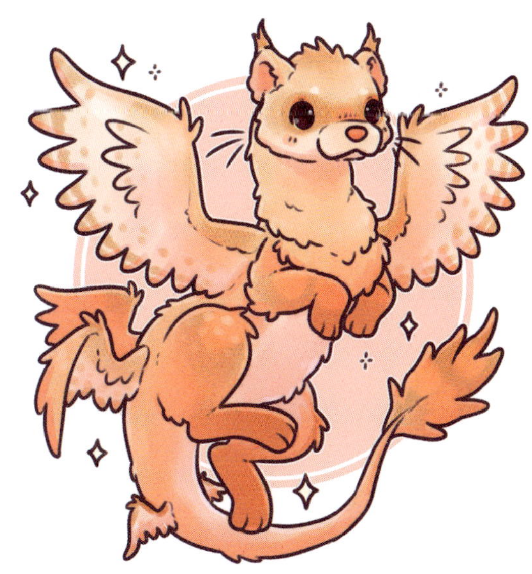

SNOWY OWL + SNOW LEOPARD

For a fluffy snow-themed griffin, I fused the snowy owl with a snow leopard, using the head and wings of the owl and the body of the leopard.

1. Lightly sketch an oval with pointed sides. Add a plus sign guideline for the face.

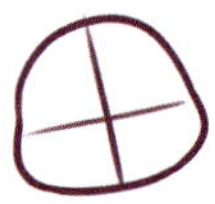

2. On the sides of the head, draw semicircle ears. Add a line inside the ears and little flicks on the tips.

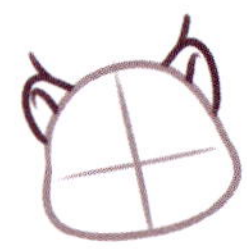

3. Draw an incomplete oval for the chest with a guideline down the middle.

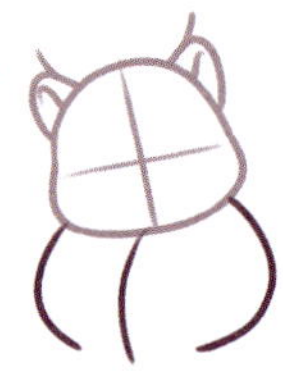

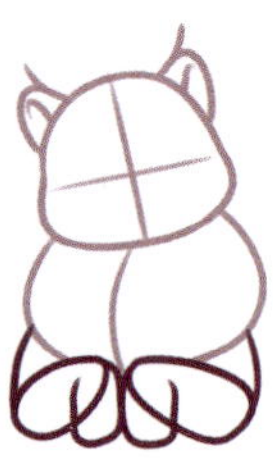

4. Add two oval arms that point up and meet in the middle. At the middle, draw two U-shaped paws pointed down. Connect the arms to the body with curved lines.

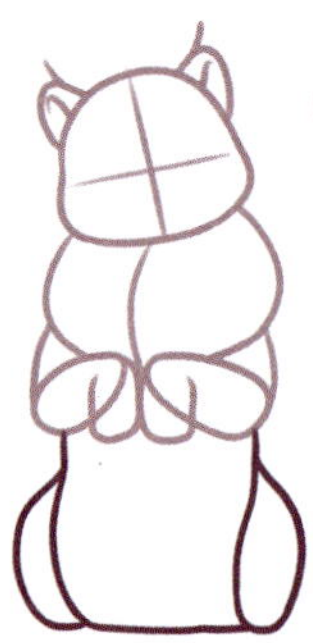

5. Draw a rectangle with curvy sides for the lower body. On the bottom sides, draw two curved lines for the lower legs.

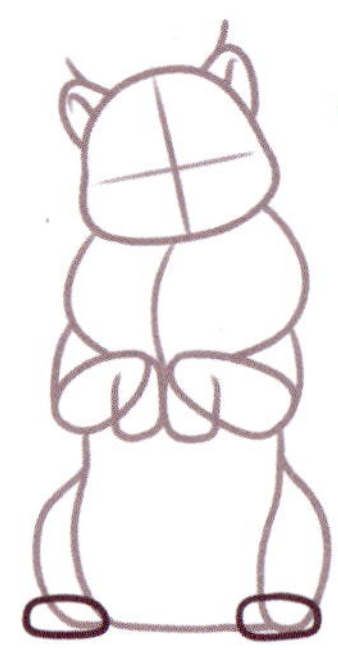

6. At the bottom of the legs, draw two rounded rectangle paws.

7. Draw a curve next to the right leg. Continue the tail on the left, curling up into a rounded triangle tip.

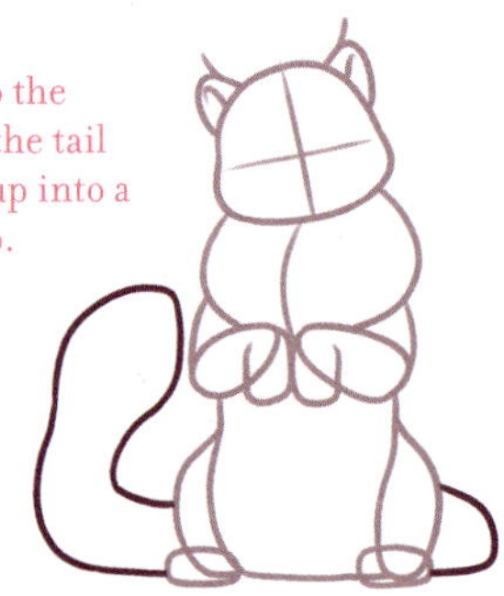

8. Sketch the wings on the sides of the body with an arched top and arcing lines.

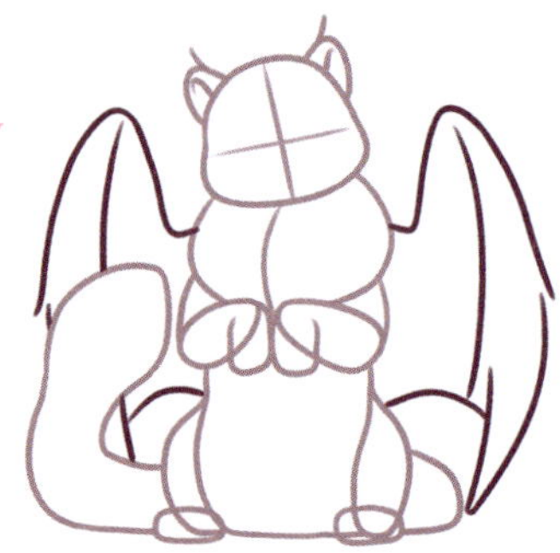

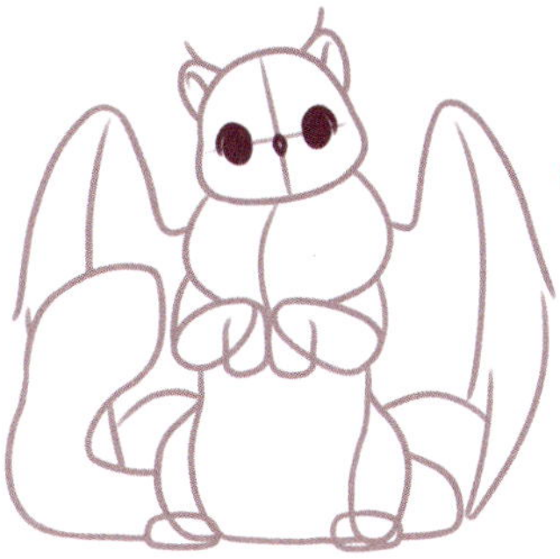

9. Draw two oval eyes with a curve around the top. At the middle of the face, draw a small, diamond-shaped beak.

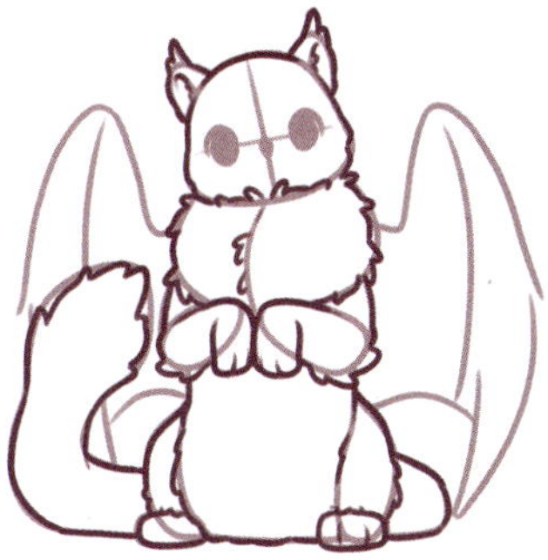

10. Lightly go over the basic sketch, adding details to the head and body. Define the fur with soft W shapes. Add toe lines on the paws.

11. Sketch the wings using long U shapes along the bottom and across the middle for the feathers.

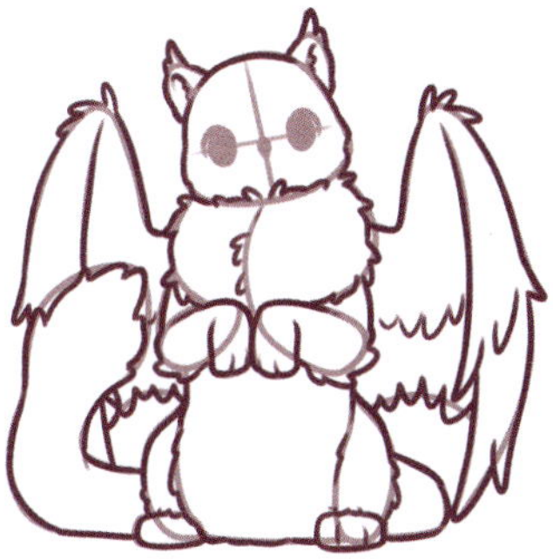

12. Sketch the face detail. Add highlights in the eyes and dashes on the cheeks for blush and around the sides of the head for whiskers. Make a heart-shaped outline around the facial features.

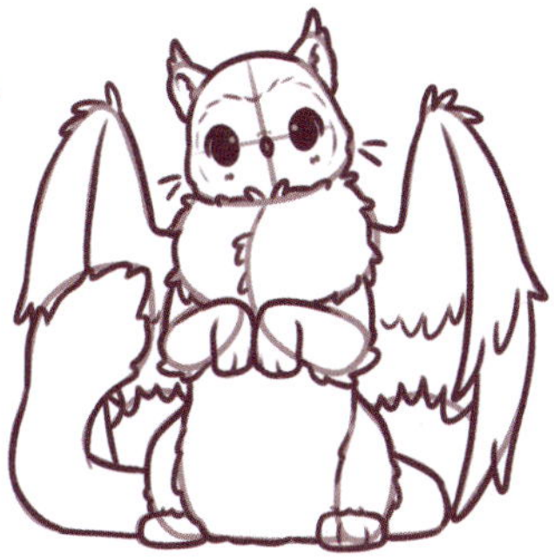

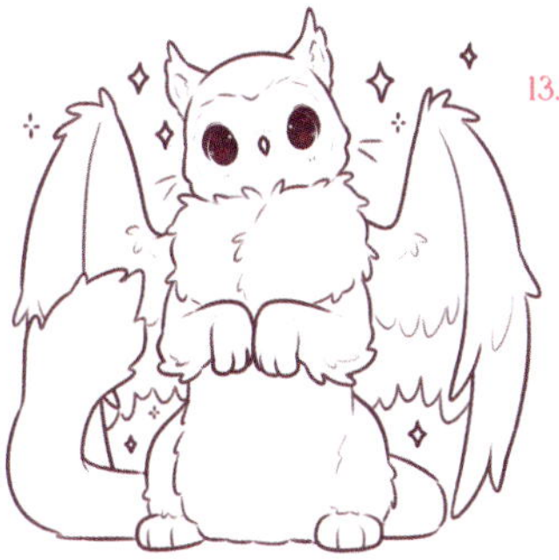

13. Neatly draw the line art over the sketch. Add some sparkles if you'd like! Then erase the sketch underneath.

14. Finally, add the color! On a white body, add some black or gray spots and dashes of the snowy owl, and some larger C-shaped spots of the snow leopard. Make the eyes a bright yellow.

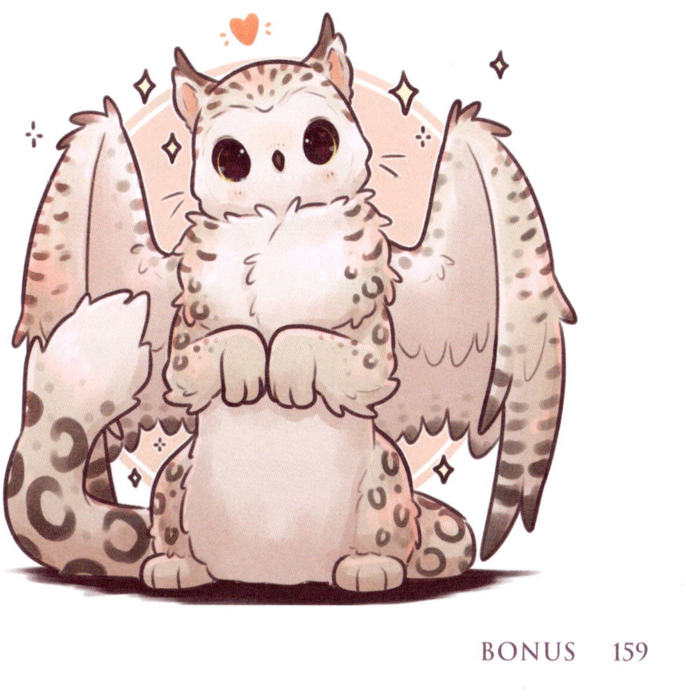

First published in 2024 by Rock Point, an imprint of The Quarto Group,
142 West 36th Street, 4th Floor, New York, NY 10018, USA
T (212) 779-4972 F (212) 779-6058 www.Quarto.com

10 9 8 7 6 5 4 3 2 1

ISBN: 978-1-63106-977-2

Digital edition published in 2024
eISBN: 978-0-76038-574-6

Library of Congress Cataloging-in-Publication Data

Names: Lord, Naomi, author.
Title: Cute creature art class : learn to draw over 50 magical monsters / Naomi Lord.
Description: New York, NY : Rock Point, [2024] | Summary: "Refine your drawing skills with step-by-step tutorials to create 57 fantasy creatures with Cute Creature Art Class"-- Provided by publisher.
Identifiers: LCCN 2023033466 (print) | LCCN 2023033467 (ebook) | ISBN 9781631069772 (paperback) | ISBN 9780760385746 (ebook)
Subjects: LCSH: Comic books, strips, etc.--Japan--Technique. | Cartoon characters--Japan. | Animals, Mythical, in art.
Classification: LCC NC1764.5.J3 L67 2024 (print) | LCC NC1764.5.J3 (ebook) | DDC 743/.6--dc23/eng/20230809
LC record available at https://lccn.loc.gov/2023033466
LC ebook record available at https://lccn.loc.gov/2023033467

Group Publisher: Rage Kindelsperger
Editorial Director: Erin Canning
Creative Director: Laura Drew
Managing Editor: Cara Donaldson
Editor: Katelynn Abraham
Cover Design: Beth Middleworth
Interior Design: Kim Winscher

Printed in China